D0302918

EFFECTIVE PRACTICES
FOR CHILDREN WITH AUTISM

EFFECTIVE PRACTICES FOR CHILDREN WITH AUTISM

EDUCATIONAL AND BEHAVIORAL SUPPORT INTERVENTIONS THAT WORK

EDITED BY

JAMES K. LUISELLI, DENNIS C. RUSSO,
WALTER P. CHRISTIAN, AND SUSAN M. WILCZYNSKI

OXFORD
UNIVERSITY PRESS

2008

OXFORD
UNIVERSITY PRESS

Oxford University Press, Inc., publishes works that further
Oxford University's objective of excellence
in research, scholarship, and education.

Oxford   New York
Auckland   Cape Town   Dar es Salaam   Hong Kong   Karachi
Kuala Lumpur   Madrid   Melbourne   Mexico City   Nairobi
New Delhi   Shanghai   Taipei   Toronto

With offices in
Argentina   Austria   Brazil   Chile   Czech Republic   France   Greece
Guatemala   Hungary   Italy   Japan   Poland   Portugal   Singapore
South Korea   Switzerland   Thailand   Turkey   Ukraine   Vietnam

Published by Oxford University Press, Inc.
198 Madison Avenue, New York, New York 10016

www.oup.com

Library of Congress Cataloging-in-Publication Data
Effective practices for children with autism : educational and behavioral support
interventions that work / edited by James K. Luiselli . . . [et al.].
p. ; cm.
Includes bibliographical references and index.
ISBN 978-0-19-531704-6
1. Autistic children—Rehabilitation—Standards.   2. Autistic children—Education—Standards.
3. Evidence-based psychiatry.   4. Evidence-based pediatrics. I. Luiselli, James K.
[DNLM: 1. Autistic Disorder—therapy.   2. Behavior Therapy—methods.   3. Child.
4. Education, Special—methods.   5. Evidence-Based Medicine. WM 203.5 E265 2008]
RJ506.A9E39 2008
618.92'85882—dc22   2007037223

9

Printed in the United States of America
on acid-free paper

Contents

SECTION 4—BEHAVIOR SUPPORT AND INTERVENTION

Preface

James K. Luiselli, Dennis C. Russo, Walter P. Christian, and
Susan M. Wilczynski

Children who have autism require comprehensive educational and treatment services. But given the myriad of therapeutic approaches that are recommended to professionals, parents, and the lay public, what are the most effective approaches for teaching skills, overcoming behavior challenges, and improving quality of life? This question speaks to the issues of evidence-based and empirically supported practices. Put succinctly, research must inform practitioners through scientifically controlled evaluations of methods that can be extended to "real world" settings where children with autism live, go to school, socialize, and recreate. However, identifying and validating effective practices is a complex and multifaceted process that is currently lacking consensus within the professional community and is in need of detailed explication. This book brings together multiple contemporary perspectives on intervention effectiveness in the area of autism education and behavior support.

We had several objectives in publishing the book. First, much has been written about evidence-based practices and empirically supported treatments but without a unifying conceptual basis. We wanted to clarify this situation, trace the development of practice standards within the autism field, and comment about present status and future directions. Another objective was to write about topics that would resonate with a large readership interested in empirically derived practices. Accordingly, we selected authors who represent a variety of disciplines and orientations but have in common a commitment toward efficacy evaluation, procedural effectiveness, and research-to-practice dissemination. We believe that each chapter in the book consolidates important knowledge from this vantage point in what is a "state-of-the-art" summary.

Section 1 of the book addresses theoretical and evidentiary aspects of practice standards. The lead chapter, by Detrich, reviews the origins and evolution of evidence-based and empirically supported practices within medicine and psychology. The next two chapters give an historical account of the development of practice guidelines within autism services (Romanczyk and Gillis) and a description of a consensus panel approach for identifying best practices (Wilczynski and Christian). The section concludes with a chapter by Wacker, Berg, and Harding on the unique contributions of single-case research methodology toward outcome evaluation.

In *Section 2*, we present chapters that delineate practice standards for large-scale program development. Frea and McNerney discuss early intensive behavior analysis, clarify sometimes conflicting research findings, and highlight future directions. In a similar vein, Dunlap, Iovannone, and Kincaid advise about the types of procedures that should constitute an effective educational program. The chapter by Ghezzi considers the critical topic of generalized behavior change and how it can be promoted in young learners. We also thought it beneficial to examine best practices for "training the trainers," the topic considered by Sturmey in the final chapter of this section.

The next two sections of the book are about specific evidence-supported instructional and intervention methods. *Section 3* concerns procedures for increasing skills. It begins with four chapters dealing with defined methodologies, namely discrete trial training (Tarbox and Najdowski), direct instruction (Weiss), naturalistic teaching (Allen and Cowan), and video-assisted learning (Darden-Brunson, Green, and Goldstein). The remaining chapters look at procedures within three developmental domains: social skills (Machalicek, Davis, O'Reilly, Beretvas, Sigafoos, Lancioni, Green, and Edrisinha), play (Lifter), and communication (Schlosser and Wendt). *Section 4* is devoted to behavior support. Three of the chapters isolate distinct approaches toward behavior change through antecedent intervention (Luiselli), positive reinforcement (Kern and Kokina), and consequence (behavior-contingent) manipulation (Lerman). The last chapter, by Symon and Boettcher, covers behavior intervention from a parent and family systems perspective.

Our hope is that the book stimulates further discourse about effective practices, leading to optimal services that improve the lives of children with autism. We are grateful to Oxford University Press for publishing the book and to the many staff who assisted along the way. Our sincerest appreciation goes to the authors for contributing their expertise and writing such informative chapters. Many of our colleagues offered guidance during formative stages of the book, and we thank them for the advice. Finally, authors and editors cannot publish books without support, encouragement, and counsel from their families, which is what we received throughout this project.

CONTRIBUTORS

Keith D. Allen, Ph.D.
Professor of Pediatrics and
    Psychology
Muntor-Meyer Institute for
    Genetics and Rehabilitation
University of Nebraska Medical Center

Wendy K. Berg, M.A.
Research Psychologist
Center for Disabilities and
    Development
The University of Iowa

Michele R. Bishop
Behavior Analysis Program
Department of Psychology
University of Nevada
Reno, NV

Mendy A. Boettcher, Ph.D.
Clinical Instructor
Lucille Packard Children's Hospital
Child and Adolescent Psychiatry
Stanford University

Lauren Christian
Research Assistant
National Autism Center
Randolph, MA

Richard Cowan, Ph.D.
Assistant Professor
Department of Educational
    Foundations and Special Services
Kent State University

Felicia Darden-Brunson, Ph.D.,
    CCC-SLP
Professor
Department of Communication
Georgia State University

Tonya Davis, M.Ed.
Graduate Student
Department of Special Education
The University of Texas at Austin

Ronnie Detrich, Ph.D.
Senior Fellow
Wing Institute
Oakland, CA

Glen Dunlap, Ph.D.
Professor
University of South Florida

Chaturi Edrisinha, Ph.D.
Assistant Professor
Department of Community Psychology
St. Cloud State University

William D. Frea, Ph.D.
Director
Autism Spectrum Therapies
Culver City, CA

Patrick M. Ghezzi, Ph.D., BCBA
Director
Behavior Analysis Program and
UNR Early Childhood Autism
    Program
Department of Psychology
University of Nevada, Reno

Jennifer Gillis, Ph.D.
Assistant Professor
Department of Psychology
Auburn University

Howard Goldstein, PhD
Donald M. Baer Professor
Department of Communication
    Disorders
Florida State University

Anna Green, M.S., CFY-SLP
Department of Communication
    Disorders
Florida State University

Vanessa Green, Ph.D.
Lecturer
College of Education
University of Tasmania

Jay W. Harding, Ed.S.
Project Coordinator
Center for Disabilities and
    Development
The University of Iowa

Rose Iovannone Ph.D.
Assistant Professor
Department of Child and Family
    Studies
Florida Mental Health Institute
University of South Florida

Lee Kern, Ph.D.
Professor
College of Education
Lehigh University

Donald Kincaid, Ph.D.
Associate Professor
Department of Child and Family
    Studies
Florida Mental Health Institute
University of South Florida

Anastasia Kokina, M.A.
Graduate Student
College of Education
Lehigh University

Giulio Lancioni, Ph.D.
Professor and Chair
Department of Psychology
University of Bari

Dorothea C. Lerman, Ph.D., BCBA
Professor
Department of Psychology
University of Houston,
    Clear Lake

Karin Lifter, Ph.D.
Professor
Department of Counseling
    and Applied Educational
    Psychology
Northeastern University

James K. Luiselli, Ed.D., ABPP, BCBA
Senior Vice President-Applied
    Research, Clinical Training, and
    Peer Review
May Institute
Randolph, MA

Wendy Machalicek, M.Ed., BCBA
Graduate Student
Department of Special Education
The University of Texas at Austin

Erin K. McNerney
Director of Clinical Services
Autism Spectrum Therapies
Culver City, CA

Adel C. Najdowski, Ph.D., BCBA
Research and Development
    Manager
The Center for Autism and Related
    Disorders
Tarzana, CA

Mark O'Reilly, Ph.D., BCBA
Professor
Department of Special Education
The University of Texas at Austin

Raymond G. Romanczyk, Ph.D.
Director
Institute for Child Development
Binghamton University

Ralf W. Schlosser, Ph.D.
Professor and Chair
Speech-Language Pathology and
    Audiology
Northeastern University

Jeff Sigafoos, Ph.D.
Professor
College of Education
University of Tasmania

Peter Sturmey, Ph.D.
Professor
Department of Psychology
Queens College-City University of
    New York

Jennifer B. G. Symon, Ph.D.
Assistant Professor
College of Charter School of
    Education
California State University

Rachel S. F. Tarbox, Ph.D., BCBA
Director, Specialized Outpatient
    Services
Co-Director, Research &
    Development
The Center for Autism and Related
    Disorders
Tarzana, CA

David P. Wacker, Ph.D.
Professor
Center for Disabilities and
    Development
The University of Iowa

Mary Jane Weiss, Ph.D., BCBA
Assistant Research Professor
Douglass Developmental Disabilities
    Center
Rutgers University

Oliver Wendt, Ph.D.
Professor
Department of Educational Studies, and
Department of Speech, Language
    and Hearing Sciences
Purdue University

Susan M. Wilczynski, Ph.D., BCBA
Executive Director
National Autism Center
Randolph, MA

SECTION 1

STANDARDS OF PRACTICE IN AUTISM EDUCATION AND INTERVENTION

1. Evidence-Based, Empirically Supported, or Best Practice? A Guide for the Scientist-Practitioner

Ronnie Detrich

Practitioners working with individuals with autism must make decisions about interventions every day. Over the last decade, the basis for those decisions has become a controversial topic. The terms *evidence-based interventions, evidence-based practices, empirically supported treatments*, and *best practices* have become ubiquitous in education and other human services disciplines. As is often the case when a new expression arrives on the scene, these terms are not well understood and are often applied inappropriately. Concurrently, the number of interventions claimed to be effective with children with autism has increased dramatically, leaving the practitioner in the difficult role of judging the veracity of the competing claims about effectiveness. The purpose of this chapter is to provide a framework for thinking about the various terms, to review the implications for the scientist-practitioner, and ultimately, to offer guidelines to practitioners as they move toward evidence-based practices. For ease of reading, the term *practitioner* is used in lieu of *scientist-practitioner*, but this does not imply a diminished status for the scientist in this discussion.

■ Definition of Evidence-Based Practice

The evidence-based practice movement had its origins in medicine (Sackett et al. 2000) and has spread to other human service disciplines over the last decade. The rapid spread to other disciplines has not been accompanied by a clear understanding of what evidence-based practice is. Sackett and colleagues defined evidence-based practice in medicine as "the integration of best research evidence with clinical expertise and patient values" (2000, p. 7). The evidence-based practice movement is an effort to ensure that scientific

FIGURE 1.1. Relationship among components of evidence-based practice.

knowledge informs the practitioner's decisions regarding interventions. It does not minimize the decision-making responsibility of the individual practitioner. Scientific knowledge functions as a filter in the selection of interventions.

Some difficulty arises from the term *evidence-based practice*. In some instances, it is synonymous with "evidence-based intervention." On other occasions, it is used to describe a more comprehensive process, as suggested by Sackett and coworkers (2000). The identification of evidence-based interventions is a necessary first step, but systematic, comprehensive, evidence-based practice requires more. Careful consideration of variables that affect implementation of interventions and evaluation of their impact are also components of evidence-based practice.

Ultimately, the evidence-based practice movement is a consumer protection effort rooted in the assumption that interventions with an empirical base are more likely to yield positive benefits for consumers than are interventions without an empirical base. Inherent in the values of evidence-based practice are the ideas that consumers should be part of the decision-making process and that information about the evidentiary status of an intervention is necessary for informed consent. From a practitioner's perspective, evidence-based practice involves the three specific steps, illustrated in Figure 1.1. The three steps of identifying, implementing, and evaluating evidence-based interventions are the framework for this chapter.

■ Context for Evidence-Based Practice

The rapid expansion in the use of the term "evidence-based" in psychology, education, and related disciplines raise questions about the sources of influence that account for this increase. The evidence-based practice movement in human services began in the 1990s with a variety of initiatives of the American Psychological Association (APA). In 1993, a task force created the

Template for Developing Guidelines: Interventions for Mental Disorders and Psychosocial Aspects of Physical Disorders (APA 1995). This was subsequently revised as the *Criteria for Evaluating Treatment Guidelines* (APA 2002, *Criteria*). These two reports established the twin criteria of efficacy and clinical utility. *Efficacy* refers to the strength of the evidence of the causal relationship between an intervention and a disorder. *Clinical utility* is the generalizability of the evidence.

In 1995, Division 12 (Clinical Psychology) of the APA created the Task Force on Promotion and Dissemination of Psychological Procedures, which published criteria for identifying "empirically validated treatments" (Chambless et al. 1996), a term that was subsequently changed to "empirically supported treatments" (Chambless and Hollon 1998). In 1998, Division 16 (School Psychology) and the Society for the Study of School Psychology established the Task Force on Evidence-Based Interventions in School Psychology (Kratochwill and Stoiber 2000). Other divisions within APA have established their own task forces to address issues of evidence-based interventions within their sub-disciplines. By 2000, issues stemming from the concepts of evidence-based, empirically supported, and empirically validated treatments were part of psychologists' vocabulary.

Federal legislation is a second, more recent source of influence on the interest in evidence-based interventions. The No Child Left Behind Act of 2001 mandates that interventions based on scientific research be used to improve educational outcomes for the nation's students. Similarly, the Individuals with Disabilities Education Improvement Act (IDEA) of 2004 places considerable emphasis on scientifically based instructional practices to improve the performance of students receiving special education services. These regulations go so far as to specify that, in the child's annual Individualized Education Program, special education services are to be based on "peer reviewed research to the extent practicable" (IDEA 2004).

A third source of influence is from the various professional organizations responsible for serving children and adolescents. Many of these organizations have embedded in their code of ethical conduct statements regarding reliance on scientific knowledge to inform practice. APA requires its members to base their work on the "established scientific and professional knowledge of the discipline." (APA 2002, *Ethical principles*). The National Association of School Psychology (NASP) has a number of standards relevant to basing practice on scientific research. The following statements are drawn from the NASP *Professional Conduct Manual* (2000):

1. Standard III F 4: School psychology faculty members and clinical or field supervisors uphold recognized standards of the profession by providing training related to high-quality, responsible, and research-based school psychology services.

2. Standard IV 4: School psychologists use assessment techniques, counseling and therapy procedures, consultation techniques, and other direct and indirect service methods that the profession considers to be responsible, research-based practice.
3. Standard IV C 1b: Decision making related to assessment and subsequent interventions is primarily data-based.
4. Standard IV 6: School psychologists develop interventions that are appropriate to the presenting problems and are consistent with the data collected. They modify or terminate the treatment plan when the data indicate the plan is not achieving the desired goals.

Finally, the Behavior Analysis Certification Board (BACB) has standards that emphasize the importance of evidence in the delivery of behavioral services. The following statements are from the BACB *Guidelines for Responsible Conduct* (2004):

1. Standard 2.09a: The behavior analyst always has the responsibility to recommend scientifically supported, most effective treatment procedures. Effective treatment procedures have been validated as having both long-term and short-term benefits to clients and society.
2. Standard 2.09b: Clients have a right to effective treatment (i.e., based on the research literature and adapted to the individual client).
3. Standard 4.04: The behavior analyst collects data or asks the client, client-surrogate, or designated other to collect data needed to assess progress within the program.
4. Standard 4.05: The behavior analyst modifies the program on the basis of data.

It is clear from the various codes that reliance on interventions with a scientific base is responsible, ethical behavior. After the implementation of an evidence-based intervention, it is also responsible conduct to evaluate the impact and make changes to the program based on data. This relationship between evidence-based practice and practice-based evidence is one of the defining features of a systematic, evidence-based practice.

Although there seems to be broad interest in evidence-based practice, it is not without controversy (Norcross, Beutler, and Levant 2006). At the heart of this controversy are issues related to the nature of evidence and the process by which interventions are validated as evidence-based.

■ Scope of the Problem

Kazdin (2000) identified more than 550 named interventions for children and adolescents. Of these, only a very small number have been empirically evaluated. The situation may be even worse for interventions focused on individuals with autism. Long (2006) reported that when the term "autism cure" was searched on the Google search engine in February, 2005, and again in February, 2006, the number of web pages had increased from 528,000 to 5,290,000. Many of the interventions promoted on these sites have not been evaluated. Science cannot work as fast as the 1-year growth rate of web pages. If the Internet is a significant source of information for practitioners and parents, then they are being overwhelmed with information about autism interventions and have no reliable means for evaluating the claims. Recent research about the quality of health care information on the Internet suggests that much of the information is inaccurate or of low quality, and often it is provided with the aim of selling a health care product (Cline and Haynes 2001). Although there is no direct evidence about the quality of information on autism interventions specifically, there is no reason to think that this information would be of a better quality. Many of the autism web pages contain testimonials and claims by experts but offer little experimental evidence.

As disturbing as the proliferation of web sites with unauthenticated claims is, there are equally disturbing concerns about the training of practitioners. There are data to suggest that evidence-based interventions are not effectively disseminated in training programs. In a survey of training directors in school psychology, a large percentage reported that they were unfamiliar with the evidence-based interventions described on the survey (Shernoff, Kratochwill, and Stoiber 2003). The consequence is that students in school psychology are not being prepared to implement evidence-based interventions.

In a similar survey of directors of clinical training in psychology (Crits-Christoph, Frank, and Chambless 1995), it was reported that, on average, these programs provided training at any level on slightly less than half of the 25 interventions that were identified as empirically validated. Perhaps of greater concern is the fact that the range for training in evidence-based interventions was from 0% to 96%. Finally, one fifth of the programs reported that they provided no training on 75% or more of the validated interventions. The results of these surveys are disappointing. It is likely that clinicians working in practice settings have not been trained in empirically validated interventions. Kazdin and colleagues (Kazdin, Siegel, and Bass 1990; Weisz and Kazdin 2003) reported that the most preferred and most common interventions in practice settings have not been evaluated; this leaves the practitioner recommending treatments that have not been evaluated to consumers who do not have easy access to credible information.

■ The Nature of Evidence

Before there can be any discussion of validated evidence-based interventions, there has to be some agreement as to what constitutes evidence. The scientific method includes various types of evidence and various methods for obtaining it. The types of evidence fall broadly into the categories of quantitative or qualitative data. *Quantitative data* reflect events that can be counted, such a words read correctly per minute, and that can be independently verified by a second person. *Qualitative data* are subjective measures of an event that cannot be independently verified by a second observer. A rating scale concerning treatment acceptability provides an example of qualitative data, even though a numerical rating is assigned to each level of acceptability. The rating has no independent status apart from the subjective experience of the rater.

The methods for obtaining evidence can be placed in the categories of experimental or descriptive research. *Experimental research* systematically changes one variable at a time and measures the impact of that change. An example of experimental research is varying the level of difficulty of a reading passage and measuring the effect of this intervention on words read correctly per minute. *Descriptive research* does not manipulate variables but rather describes "naturally" occurring relationships between two or more variables. Measures of a child's disruptive behavior in 30-minute intervals across the day is an example of descriptive research. In this instance, nothing is systematically changed to evaluate impact; rather, a specific behavior is measured across the day as it occurs.

Each type of evidence and research method answers particular types of questions. No single method can answer all questions. In discussing evidence-based interventions, we are ultimately concerned with quantitative, experimental evidence. This type of evidence directly answers questions about the impact an intervention has on a class of social or academic behaviors. If a causal ("cause-effect") relationship between an intervention and a class of behaviors is not established, then discussions about qualitative aspects of the intervention and its effects are unimportant. Descriptive methods and qualitative evidence can be important in guiding researchers to evaluate particular interventions, but they cannot demonstrate the impact of the intervention on a class of behaviors. For example, if the goal of an intervention is to increase language skills for a child with autism and there is no increase in language skills, then qualitative questions such as the acceptability of the intervention are unimportant. An ineffective intervention is unacceptable, and high ratings of acceptability do not justify implementation.

For the scientist-practitioner, there are advantages to limiting the discussion of evidence-based interventions to experimental demonstrations of impact. The primary benefit is that any claims of effectiveness based on testimonials and expert opinion are filtered out and not used as a basis for selection. The lack of experimental evidence does not necessarily imply that an intervention is ineffective; it simply it may not have been evaluated. However, responsible, ethical conduct dictates that practitioners recommend interventions that have a scientific base.

Difficulties in Accessing Evidence

Limiting the discussion to experimental evidence does not solve all of the problems for the scientist-practitioner. There is a large amount of experimental evidence in the professional journals, and not all of it is consistent or of the same quality. The number of journals that publish experimental research on autism makes it very difficult for a practitioner to remain current on a given area, much less the entire body of literature on autism interventions.

It has been estimated that school psychologists spend about 1 hour per week reading professional literature (Hosp and Reschly 2002). This is not enough time to master a body of literature on any given topic. In a practice context, it is not surprising that professional reading occurs infrequently. Not only do practitioners have many demands on their time that compete with reading, but the consequences of not reading are more remote, and perhaps less certain, than the consequences of failing to do other parts of their job (Weisz and Addis 2006). It is unlikely that the reading practices of school psychologists are very different from those of other practice-level professionals.

An additional difficulty for many practitioners is that they have not been adequately trained to evaluate the quality of the research that is published in professional journals. Research published in journals is written with other researchers as the primary audience. When making decisions about interventions, practitioners do not necessarily have the skills to discriminate among research studies whose results are contradictory.

The fact that studies are published in a wide variety of journals poses problems even for those practitioners, who are interested in reading the primary source literature. It is unlikely that practitioners will have easy access to all of the relevant journals, so they may not be aware of significant research in a given area. The response effort required to stay current, because of the widespread distribution of publications, limited training in evaluating research, and limited time available for reading, is a powerful constraint on practitioners' acquiring information on evidence-based interventions through professional journals.

■ Standards of Evidence

Given the difficulties described, an alternative is required. One recent approach to determining effective interventions is to establish standards for reviewing research and then publish ratings of the strength of the evidence for a particular intervention. There are two methods for determining strength of evidence: the threshold and the hierarchy of evidence methods.

The *threshold method* requires a specific quantity of research of a specific quality to validate an intervention as being evidence-based. If there is an insufficient quantity or quality of research concerning an intervention, then it is determined that there is no evidence about its impact. In the threshold approach, the common standard required to make claims that an intervention is evidence-based is two randomized clinical trials showing impact (Edlund et al. 2004). If this standard is not met, the intervention cannot be considered evidence-based even if there is a large body of research on the topic that is not of the type that meets the standard. The concern with the threshold approach is that effective interventions will not be validated as evidence-based because there is insufficient research that meets the threshold criteria.

The *hierarchy of evidence method* places the strength of evidence along a continuum. In this approach, more research can be considered in the review. Usually, there are four or five points on the continuum, each with a different threshold, ranging from "Well Established" to "No Supporting Evidence." For example, the Task Force on Evidence-Based Interventions in School Psychology (2003) set up four levels in their classification system ("Strong Evidence," "Promising Evidence," "Marginal/Weak Evidence," and "No Evidence"). The limitation with a hierarchy of evidence approach is that an intervention may be determined to be effective when, in fact, it is not. With either type of approach, there are inherent risks. One approach may be too restrictive, and the other may be too inclusive.

Given the relative infancy of the evidence-based practice movement in education, perhaps it is better to err on the side of being too inclusive. Practitioners must make decisions about interventions every day, and it is better that those decisions be based on credible, if not perfect, evidence, rather than relying solely on other sources of information. Waiting for research that meets the more rigorous evidentiary standards of a threshold approach will leave the practitioner with little evidence-based guidance when selecting an intervention. Relying on the best available evidence gives the practitioner a basis for making decisions. The bias in this chapter is that some evidence is better than no evidence for the purposes of guiding decisions. The caveat is that it is necessary to understand the strength of evidence associated with a particular intervention, to know the standards for establishing the strength of evidence, and to be willing to revise intervention options as better evidence emerges.

Approaches to Standards of Evidence

In the last few years, a number of organizations have developed standards for evaluating the strength of evidence. A representative list of these organiza-

TABLE 1.1

Organizations with Standards for Validating Interventions

Organization	Focus
What Works Clearinghouse	Academic and social interventions for school-aged children
National Autism Center	Educational and behavioral interventions for individuals with autism
Task Force on Evidence-Based Interventions in School Psychology (jointly sponsored by Division 16 of the American Psychological Association and the Society for the Study of School Psychology)	Academic and social interventions in schools
Task Force on Psychological Interventions Guidelines (sponsored by Division 12 of the American Psychology Association)	Psychological interventions for children, adolescents, and adults
Evidence-Based Treatments for Children and Adolescents (sponsored by Division 53 of the American Psychology Association and Network on Youth Mental Health)	Psychological interventions for children and adolescents
Society for Prevention Research	Prevention programs
American Academy of Neurology	Neurological interventions
Campbell Collaboration	Interventions in crime and justice, education, and social welfare

tions is presented in Table 1.1, along with the focus of their interventions. The details of each of these standards are beyond the scope of this chapter; however, even a brief review will show that there are considerable differences in the way in which each organization establishes the strength of evidence for an intervention. It is possible for an intervention to be validated as effective by one set of standards but fail to meet the criteria of a second set of standards. This is especially likely when the two sets of standards employ different approaches to validating interventions (i.e., threshold versus hierarchy of evidence).

As an example, the What Works Clearinghouse (part of the U.S. Institute of Education Sciences) uses a threshold approach that requires studies based on group designs, and randomized clinical trials are necessary to validate an intervention as "Meeting Evidence Standards." Currently, because there is no place for single-participant research designs in the What Works Clearinghouse evidence standards (2006), any intervention evaluated with single-participant designs will necessarily be classified as "Does Not Meet Evidence Screens." On the other hand, the same intervention reviewed with the standards promulgated by the National Autism Center's National Standards Project (Wilczynski 2006) may well meet evidentiary criteria. It is the responsibility of the practitioner to determine which standards were used to evaluate an intervention. When looking for information about effective interventions, the practitioner should consider the primary goals of each of the organizations that have developed standards. For instance, the What Works Clearinghouse is primarily reviewing interventions for general education, so it is not a relevant source for information about autism interventions. Consulting this web site would leave the practitioner with the impression that there are no interventions for individuals with autism that have an evidence base. If a practitioner is seeking information about autism interventions, the most relevant source is the National Autism Center (Wilczynski 2006).

Most of the published standards are in agreement about criteria for evaluating research based on group designs. In general, randomized clinical trials are considered the "gold standard" (Mosteller and Boruch 2002; Shalverson and Towne 2002; Towne, Wise, and Winters 2005). Well-designed quasi-experimental studies are acceptable but are considered weaker evidence. The status of single-participant methods is much less clear. Some standards have no established criteria for this method (e.g., What Works Clearinghouse), and those that do have standards differ as to what constitutes sufficient evidence (e.g., Division 53 of APA, National Autism Center) (Wilczynski 2006). The lack of clarity regarding single-participant methods presents particular challenges for evaluating autism research, because much of the work in this area has used this research methodology (Odom et al. 2003).

Limitations of Standards

The recent interest in evidence-based interventions in education and mental health has provided an excellent start, but there is much work to do. At this time, there is relatively little information about which interventions are evidence-based, because, once standards are developed, it is necessary to apply them to the body of knowledge of an intervention or problem area. Until these reviews are completed by the various organizations with standards, there can be no statements about the evidentiary status of interventions. These reviews are ongoing, but it will take some time before a significant number of interventions have been evaluated with a set of standards.

Another limitation is that the mechanisms for disseminating information to practitioners about evidence-based interventions are just emerging. One of the primary means for dissemination is via web sites such as the What Works Clearinghouse, which posts reviews of interventions as they are completed. Similarly, Division 53 of the APA and the Network on Youth Mental Health (NYMH) jointly host a web site (APA and NYMH n.d.) that provides information about evidence-based interventions in the categories of anxiety disorders, depression, attention-deficit hyperactivity disorder, and conduct/oppositional problems. The difficulty for the practitioner working with individuals with autism is that there is currently no comparable source of information for interventions in autism. The National Autism Center's National Standards Project (Wilczynski 2006) will ultimately be a source of information regarding evidence-based interventions for individuals with autism.

■ Empirically Supported Interventions

The federal mandates and ethical requirements to use interventions that have a scientific basis place a burden on the practitioner. The paucity of information about which interventions have been validated creates a dilemma. Without easy access to reliable and relevant information, the practitioner is in the position of relying on other sources of information to select interventions. Reliance on sources such as expert opinion is contrary to an evidence-based practice approach, because such alternatives have many sources of potential bias (Gambrill 2005).

Until more interventions are validated, an alternative is to construct interventions that contain only elements that are based on established scientific principles of behavior. For example, if we are interested in increasing the language skills of young children with autism, there is a very large body of evidence to support the use of positive reinforcement procedures. Demonstrations of the effects of positive reinforcement on a wide variety of behaviors, including language, are readily available (Cooper, Heron, and Heward 1987). More specifically, there are many examples of the use of positive reinforcement to increase language skills of individuals with autism (Koegel and Koegel 1995). Among the variety of procedures described, there are at least two commonalities: high rates of opportunities to respond and high rates of positive reinforcement for correct responding. It follows that an intervention based on these principles is more likely to be effective than an intervention not based on these principles. This approach to developing interventions has been described as *formative* (Layng, Stikeleather, and Twyman 2006). The greater the correspondence between the principles of behavior and the elements of an intervention, the more empirically supported the intervention is.

Modifying Evidence-Based Interventions

In the discussion of evidence-based practice, much has been made of the tension between implementing the intervention as it was validated and modifying the intervention to reflect local circumstances (Chorpita 2003; Hoagwood, Burns, and Weisz 2002; Elliott and Mihalic 2004). The problem arises when the modifications to the intervention change it in ways that have not been evaluated, raising questions about the effectiveness of the new intervention and its evidentiary status. Modifying an intervention in ways that are consistent with principles of behavior is less likely to negate the impact of the intervention.

The formative approach of basing the modifications on established principles of behavior maintains the scientific integrity of the intervention and is consistent with the definition of evidence-based practice (Sackett et al. 2000). It starts with the best available scientific evidence and then requires the practitioner to make judgments about how to arrange an intervention so that it is the best match for the individual. Relying on a formative approach also recognizes the realities of working with individuals with autism. The unique characteristics of each individual with autism and the living and educational settings in which they are served almost always necessitate modifications to existing evidence-based protocols.

This formative approach offers at least two advantages for the practitioner. First, it allows the practitioner to develop interventions informed by science-based knowledge when no interventions have been validated as evidence-based. Second, it allows the practitioner to modify an evidence-based intervention to reflect contextual variables that exist for a particular individual or family. Although the formative approach has great value to the practitioner, it will ultimately be necessary to evaluate the modified intervention to make any definitive claims that it is evidence-based. The term "evidence-based" should be reserved for interventions that have been evaluated against a set of standards; the term "empirically supported" should be applied to those interventions that are developed through a formative process.

■ Best Practice Guidelines

Best practice guidelines are another approach that has guided the selection of effective interventions. These guidelines are developed through a very different process than evidence-based standards. The usual method for constructing best practice guidelines is to assemble noted experts in a field and gain agreement from these experts about what constitutes best practice. Although the individuals of a best practice work group are well established within their field, this does not mean that their perspectives are without bias. Gambrill (2005) described the types of biases that may influence the decision making of experts. Among these biases are conflicts of interest, theoretical perspectives, selective reading of the literature, and personal experiences that inform judgments.

Relying on consensus to develop best practice guidelines results in inclusion of only those practices that have universal support among the committee members. New, effective interventions will not necessarily be included in a best practice guideline. This is especially likely if there are theoretical differences between the intervention and the perspectives of the committee members. Best practice guidelines reflect a type of social validation for an intervention (Wolf 1978). Such guidelines reflect the current values of a professional group and may change over time as research emerges supporting new, alternative, or less intrusive interventions.

The proper role of best practice guidelines is that, once a set of evidence-based interventions have been identified, the guidelines can inform the selection of an effective, socially valid intervention. For example, the use of intense punishment, such as electric shock, to suppress the frequency of self-injury has an established evidence base (Lerman and Vorndarn 2002), but the use of punishment procedures is not without controversy (Repp and Singh 1990). Other evidence-based approaches to treating self-injury, such as functional communication training, are consistent with contemporary best practice guidelines (Carr and Durand 1985; DeLeon, Rodriquez-Catter, and Cataldo 2002).

■ Implementing the Intervention

Identifying an evidence-based intervention does not ensure that it will be effective in a practice setting. There are many characteristics of research that make generalization from a research setting to a practice setting tenuous. A primary function of intervention research is to establish a causal relationship between an intervention and a class of behaviors (Johnston and Pennypacker 1993). In order to obtain unambiguous results, researchers often impose strict subject selection criteria and carefully arrange the research environment. Participants with co-morbid conditions along with autism are usually excluded from such studies, because these other conditions may moderate the impact of an intervention that is designed to remediate some aspect of autism. Similarly, those responsible for implementing the intervention may have a higher level of training, may be supervised more closely to ensure high treatment integrity, and may have a greater investment in the outcome than their counterparts in the typical practice setting. Finally, the research setting may have many more financial and other resources available than typical practice settings do. The constraints on subject characteristics, and the research setting itself, are very different from typical practice conditions. Often, these differences make it difficult to directly translate efficacious research-based interventions to practice settings. Because of these differences, practitioners may view research as irrelevant, impractical, and impossible to apply clinically (Hoagwood et al. 2001; Kazdin 2004; Schoenwald and Hoagwood 2001; Shriver and Watson 2005).

Much of the published research is *efficacy research*. Its specific function is to identify important variables that contribute to intervention effectiveness (Chorpita 2003; Kazdin 2004; Schoenwald and Hoagwood 2001; Shriver and Watson 2005). For example, the impact of early intensive behavior interventions for young children with autism might be examined in a university laboratory school. *Effectiveness research* evaluates the impact of an intervention under more typical conditions (Chorpita 2003; Kazdin 2004; Schoenwald and Hoagwood 2001; Shriver and Watson 2005). Examining the impact of early intensive behavioral interventions as they are implemented by public school teachers under typical conditions is an example of effectiveness research.

The challenge for the practitioner is to select interventions that have evidentiary support under conditions similar to those in which the practitioner is working. To make the determination about which intervention is most appropriate, the practitioner must compare the characteristics of the research subjects, those responsible for implementation, and the research setting in which the intervention was studied against these same characteristics for the client being served and the setting in which the practitioner is working. A list of relevant features for comparison is presented in Table 1.2. By making these comparisons, the practitioner can establish a degree of confidence in the intervention as it moves from the research setting to the practice setting.

Considerations When Selecting an Intervention

A lower evidence rating does not imply that an intervention is less effective, but rather that the strength of the evidence does not meet higher evidentiary standards. Although it may seem obvious that practitioners would select interventions with the strongest evidence rating, there are contextual variables that may result in selection of an intervention with a weaker evidence base (Albin et al. 1996; Ringeisen, Henderson, and Hoagwood 2003). For example, Lovaas (1996) suggested that teachers implementing discrete trial procedures should wear protective clothing, such as bathing caps and heavy covers over the arms and legs, to prevent injury from physical assault. Although there is a growing evidence base for discrete trial methods (McEachin, Smith, and Lovaas 1993; Eikeseth, Smith, Jahr, and Eldevik 2002), in many public

TABLE 1.2

Characteristics for Comparison between Research and Practice

Individual
  Age
  Functioning level
      IQ
      Language skills
      Social interaction skills
  Co-morbid conditions
  Gender
Service Setting
  Home
    Characteristics of family
      Socioeconomic status (SES)
      Number of parents
      Educational level of parents
      Siblings
  School
    Type of placement
      General education classroom
      Mixed-category special day class versus autism-specific
      Opportunity to interact with typically developing peers
  Residential setting (e.g., group home)
Characteristics of Implementation
  Implementers
    Level of education
    Relationship to individual
    Level of training
  Characteristics of supervision
    Level of training of supervisor
    Frequency of supervision
    Duration of supervision
Characteristics of Organization Providing Service
  Type of organization

school settings these precautions are so different from the existing culture that it is unlikely that teaching staff would wear the recommended protective clothing. Without the protective clothing, the risk of injury increases. This may result in teachers' being unwilling to implement those elements that occasion aggressive behavior. Selectively implementation of the discrete trial procedures may lower treatment integrity to such an extent that the child with autism will not benefit from the intervention.

An alternative is to choose an intervention that has a lower evidence rating but has greater acceptability, such as incidental teaching (Hart and Risley 1975; Koegel and Koegel 1995). This method take advantage of the child's motivation and interest. This may result in a lower frequency of aggression, which reduces the need for protective clothing, and may increase treatment integrity. Implementing the intervention with greater integrity may result in greater benefit for the child, even though incidental teaching methods may have lower evidence ratings than discrete trial procedures. The need to wear protective clothing and to manage aggressive behavior increase the response effort associated with discrete trial procedures. Incidental teaching interventions may be easier for teachers, and they are more contextually consistent with public school cultures. Response effort for the teacher has been linked to higher ratings of treatment acceptability (Elliott et al. 1984; Witt, Martens, and Elliott 1984) and, indirectly, to treatment integrity (Albin et al. 1996; Detrich 1999).

Issues of Implementation

Once an intervention is selected, issues of training and treatment integrity become primary concerns. An evidence-based intervention is more likely to be effective if it is implemented well. There is no reason to assume that those responsible for implementation will be skilled in all of the procedural details of an intervention. It may be necessary for the practitioner to train those responsible for implementation and then to routinely assess treatment integrity to ensure that there has been no drift from the intervention protocol. There is evidence that direct training in the elements of an intervention can increase treatment integrity (Sterling-Turner, Watson, and Moore 2002). In addition, it has been well documented that implementation of an intervention without routine follow-up assessments of treatment integrity results in declines in the accuracy of implementation (Mortensen and Witt 1998; Noell et al. 1997; Witt et al. 1997). Therefore, an evidence-based practice approach requires systematic assessment of treatment integrity. Witt and colleagues (2004) suggested that practitioners should systematically evaluate treatment integrity across the four domains of problem definition and monitoring, classroom instruction and behavior management, intervention integrity, and intervention design.

■ Evaluating the Intervention: Progress Monitoring

Evidence-based interventions only increase the probability of success. It is necessary to assess the impact of an intervention to ensure that the benefits were actually achieved. In a comprehensive evidence-based practice approach, progress monitoring is the third fundamental component, as described in Figure 1.1. The basic principle of progress monitoring is frequent and systematic sampling of performance to determine whether progress is occurring and at what rate (Bushell and Baer 1994; Cooper, Heron, and Heward 1987). Curriculum-based measurement procedures exemplify well-developed progress monitoring (Shinn 1989). Practice-based evidence allows the practitioner, those responsible for implementation, and consumers (parents and children with autism) to have the same information when making programming decisions about continuing, adjusting, or discontinuing an intervention.

Infrequent measures are not useful for the purposes of progress monitoring. For example, measuring a child's language skills annually does not provide immediate information so that decisions can be made about interventions designed to improve language skills. Allowing a year to pass before making decisions about an intervention increases the risk of wasting a year of the child's life with an ineffective intervention. As described in the codes of ethical conduct for NASP and BACB, progress monitoring is responsible, ethical behavior (BACB 2004; NASP 2000).

The quality of decisions about the effect of an intervention is directly related to the quality of the data informing that decision. The methods used to assess progress must meet the standards of reliability and validity. *Reliability* refers to the consistency of the assessment method. For example, two individuals using the same method for assessing a child's reading fluency should obtain similar results. To the extent that this is true, there is greater confidence in the obtained data. A *valid* instrument is one that measures what it purports to measure. For example, a valid measure of reading comprehension must start by having the child read a passage and then answer questions about the passage. A measure of reading comprehension that is based on having someone else read to a child is not valid, because it actually measures listening comprehension. In an evidence-based practice approach, the quality of the data is of equal concern whether selecting an intervention or evaluating its impact.

■ Summary

Comprehensive evidence-based practice offers the potential of great benefit for the practitioner serving children with autism; however, it is not a simple or straightforward process. It is necessary to have knowledge about the nature of the evidence used to evaluate an intervention and the standards used to validate the intervention as being evidence-based. Once an evidence-based intervention has been identified, it is necessary for the practitioner to generalize from the research base to a specific practice setting. The reliance on evidence is not complete once an intervention has been selected. It is then necessary for the practitioner to assess the integrity of the implementation and its impact on individual consumers.

Much of the burden for the success of the evidence-based practice movement is placed on the practitioner, but the tools available to assist the evidence-based practitioner are just emerging. In an attempt to assist the practitioner until there is a well-established technology infrastructure, guidelines have been embedded in each of the sections of this chapter and are briefly summarized here. It is hoped that guidelines such as these can help bridge the gap between research and practice and that our clients will reap the benefits of the evidence-based practice movement.

Guidelines for Practitioners

1. Claims of evidence base should be restricted to quantitative, experimental evidence that demonstrates a causal relationship between an intervention and a class of social or academic behaviors.
2. Decisions about interventions should be based on the best available experimental evidence.
3. The practitioner should understand the rating structure associated with various professional organizations' strength of evidence standards.
4. The practitioner should use the specific professional organization's standards that are most relevant to an individual case.
5. In the absence of clear evidence-based guidance from standards, interventions should be developed using a formative approach that builds interventions from the established body of scientific principles of behavior. This allows interventions to be empirically supported.
6. When the practitioner is modifying an intervention to meet local circumstances, the modifications should be based on established principles of behavior, so that the scientific integrity of the intervention is maintained.
7. The term "evidence-based" is restricted to those interventions that have been evaluated against a set of standards and have met the evidence criteria of those standards; the term "empirically supported" should be reserved for those interventions based on scientific knowledge.
8. Best practice guidelines are social validation statements about interventions. They should be used to select an intervention from a field of evidence-based and empirically supported interventions. They should not be used as an alternative to evidentiary standards.

9. To the greatest extent possible, there should be evidence that the selected intervention has impact in situations similar to those that apply to a particular client. Broadly, the dimensions to consider are the characteristics of the research participants, those implementing the intervention, and the setting.
10. The practitioner should directly train those responsible for implementation.
11. The practitioner should routinely assess for treatment integrity.
12. To establish impact of an intervention, the practitioner should frequently and systematically monitor progress.

■ References

Albin, R.W., Lucyshyn, J.M., Horner, R.H., and Flannery, K.B. (1996). Contextual fit for behavioral support plans: A model for "goodness of fit." In *Positive behavioral support: Including people with difficult behavior in the community* (eds. L.K. Koegel, R.L. Koegel, and G. Dunlap), pp. 81–98. Baltimore: P.H. Brookes.

American Psychological Association. (1995). *Template for developing guidelines: Interventions for mental disorders and psychosocial aspects of physical disorders.* Washington, D.C.: APA.

American Psychological Association. (2002). Criteria for evaluating treatment guidelines. *American Psychologist, 57,* 1052–1059.

American Psychological Association. (2002). *Ethical principles of psychologists and code of conduct.* Available at http://www.apa.org/ethics/ (accessed October 24, 2007).

American Psychological Association (Division 53, Society of Clinical Child and Adolescent Psychology) and the Network on Youth Mental Health. (n.d.). *Evidence-based treatment for children and adolescents.* Available at http://www.wjh.harvard.edu/%7Enock/Div53/EST/index.htm (accessed October 24, 2007).

Behavior Analysis Certification Board. (2004). *BACB guidelines for responsible conduct for behavior analysts.* Available at http://www.bacb.com/consum_frame.html (accessed October 24, 2007).

Bushell, D., and Baer, D.M. (1994). Measurably superior instruction means close, continual contact with the relevant outcome data: Revolutionary. In *Behavior analysis in education: Focus on measurably superior instruction* (ed. R. Gardner), pp. 3–10. Pacific Grove, Calif.: Brooks/Cole.

Carr, E.G., and Durand, V.M. (1985). Reducing behavior problems through functional communication training. *Journal of Applied Behavior Analysis, 18* (2), 111–126.

Chambless, D.L., Sanderson, W.C., Shoham, V., Johnson, S.B., Pope, K.S., Crits-Christoph, P., Baker, M., Johnson, B., Woody, S.R., Sue, S., Beutler, L.,

Williams, D.A., and McCurry, S. (1996). An update on empirically-validated therapies. *The Clinical Psychologist,* 49 (2), 5–18.

Chambless, D.L., and Hollon, S.D. (1998). Defining empirically supported therapies. *Journal of Consulting and Clinical Psychology,* 66 (1), 7–18.

Chorpita, B.F. (2003). The frontier of evidence-based practice. In *Evidence-based psychotherapies for children and adolescents* (eds. A.E. Kazdin and J.R. Weisz), pp. 42–59. New York: Guilford Press.

Cline, R.J.W., and Haynes, K.M. (2001). Consumer health information seeking on the Internet: The state of the art. *Health Education Research,* 16 (6), 671–692.

Cooper, J.O., Heron, T.E., and Heward, W.L. (1987). *Applied behavior analysis.* Columbus, Ohio: Merrill.

Crits-Christoph, P., Frank, E., Chambless, D.L., Brody, C., and Karp, J.F. (1995). Training in empirically validated treatments: What are clinical psychology students learning? *Professional Psychology: Research and Practice,* 26 (5), 514–522.

DeLeon, I.G., Rodriquez-Catter, V., and Cataldo, M.F. (2002). Treatment: Current standards of care and their research implications. In *Self-injurious behavior: Gene-brain-behavior relationships* (eds. S.R. Schroeder, M.L. Oster-Granite, and T. Thompson), pp. 81–92. Washington, D.C.: American Psychological Association.

Detrich, R. (1999). Increasing treatment fidelity by matching interventions to contextual variables within the educational setting. *School Psychology Review,* 28 (4), 608–620.

Eikeseth, S., Smith, T. Jahr, E., and Eldevik, S. (2002). Intensive behavioral treatment at school for 4–7 year old children with autism: A 1-year comparison controlled study. *Behavior Modification,* 26 (1), 49–68.

Edlund, W., Gronseth, G., So, Y., and Franklin, G. (2004). *Clinical practice guideline process manual.* St. Paul, Minn.: American Academy of Neurology.

Elliott, D.S., and Mihalic, S. (2004). Issues in disseminating and replicating effective prevention programs. *Prevention Science,* 5 (1), 47–53.

Elliott, S., Witt, J., Galvin, G., and Peterson, R. (1984). Acceptability of positive and reductive behavioral interventions: Factors that influence teachers' decisions. *Journal of School Psychology,* 22 (4), 353–360.

Gambrill, E.D. (2005). *Critical thinking in clinical practice: Improving the quality of judgments and decisions* (2nd ed). Hoboken, N.J.: Wiley.

Hart, B. and Risley, T.R. (1975). Incidental teaching of language in the preschool. *Journal of Applied Behavior Analysis,* 8 (4), 411–420.

Hoagwood, K., Burns, B.J., Kiser, L., Ringeisen, H., and Schoenwald, S.K. (2001). Evidence-based practice in child and adolescent mental health services. *Psychiatric Services,* 52 (9), 1179–1189.

Hoagwood, K., Burns, B.J., and Weisz, J.R. (2002). A profitable conjunction: From science to service in children's mental health. In *Community treatment for youth: Evidence-based interventions for severe emotional and behavioral disorders* (eds. B.J. Burns and K. Hoagwood), pp. 327–338. New York: Oxford University Press.

Hosp, J.L., and Reschly, D.J. (2002). Regional differences in school psychology practice. *School Psychology Review,* 31 (1), 11–29.

Individuals with Disabilities Education Improvement Act of 2004. Public Law 108–446 (118 STAT. 2647).

Johnston, J.M., and Pennypacker, H.S. (1993). *Strategies and tactics of behavioral research* (2nd ed). Hillsdale, N.J.: L. Erlbaum Associates.

Kazdin, A.E. (2000). *Psychotherapy for children and adolescents: directions for research and practice.* New York: Oxford University Press.

Kazdin, A.E. (2004). Evidence-based treatments: Challenges and priorities for practice and research. *Child and Adolescent Psychiatric Clinics of North America,* 13 (4), 923–940, vii.

Kazdin, A.E., Siegel, T.C., and Bass, D. (1990). Drawing on clinical practice to inform research on child and adolescent psychotherapy: Survey of practitioners. *Professional Psychology: Research and Practice,* 21 (3), 189–198.

Koegel, R.L., and Koegel, L.K. (1995). *Teaching children with autism: Strategies for initiating positive interactions and improving learning opportunities.* Baltimore: P.H. Brookes.

Kratochwill, T.R., and Stoiber, K.C. (2000). Empirically supported interventions and school psychology: Conceptual and practical issues. Part II. *School Psychology Quarterly,* 15, 233–253.

Layng, T.V.J., Stikeleather, G., and Twyman, J.S. (2006). Scientific formative evaluation: The role of individual learners in generating and predicting successful educational outcomes. In *The scientific basis of educational productivity* (eds. R.F. Subotnik and H.J. Walberg), pp. 29–44. Greenwich, Conn.: Information Age Publishing.

Lerman, D., and Vorndran, C.M. (2002). On the status of knowledge for using punishment implications for treating behavior disorders. *Journal of Applied Behavior Analysis,* 35 (4), 431–464.

Long, E.S. (2006). *The National Standards Project: Promoting evidence-based education and treatment practices for autism.* Paper presented to the California Association for Behavior Analysis, Burlingame, Calif., February 2006.

Lovaas, O.I. (1996). The UCLA young autism of service delivery. In *Behavioral intervention for young children with autism: A manual for parents and professionals* (ed. C. Maurice, G. Green, and S.C. Luce), pp. 241–250. Austin, Tex: Pro-Ed.

McEachin, J.J., Smith, T., and Lovaas, O.I. (1993). Long-term outcome for children with autism who received early intensive behavioral treatment. *American Journal of Mental Retardation,* 97, 359–372.

Mortensen, B.P., and Witt, J.C. (1998). The use of weekly performance feedback to increase teacher implementation of a prereferral academic intervention. *School Psychology Review,* 27 (4), 613–627.

Mosteller, F., and Boruch, R.F. (2002). *Evidence matters: Randomized trials in education research.* Washington, D.C: Brookings Institution Press.

National Association of School Psychology. (2000). *Professional conduct manual.* Available at http://www.nasponline.org/standards/ProfessionalCond.pdf (accessed October 24, 2007).

No Child Left Behind Act of 2001. Public Law 107–110 (115 STAT. 1425).

Noell, G.H., Witt, J.C., Gilbertson, D.N., Ranier, D.D., and Freeland, J.T. (1997). Increasing teacher intervention implementation in general education settings through consultation and performance feedback. *School Psychology Quarterly,* 12 (1), 77–88.

Norcross, J.C., Beutler, L.E., and Levant, R.F. (2006). *Evidence-based practices in mental health: Debate and dialogue on the fundamental questions.* Washington, D.C.: American Psychological Association.

Odom, S.L., Brown, W.H., Frey, T., Karasu, N., Smith-Canter, L.L., and Strain, P.S. (2003). Evidence-based practices for young children with autism: Contributions from single-subject design research. *Focus on Autism and Other Developmental Studies,* 18 (3), 166–175.

Repp, A.C., and Singh, N.N., eds. *Perspectives on the use of nonaversive and aversive interventions for children with developmental disabilities.* Pacific Grove, Calif.: Brooks Cole Publishing.

Ringeisen, H., Henderson, K., and Hoagwood, K. (2003). Context matters: Schools and the "research to practice gap" in children's mental health. *School Psychology Review,* 32 (2), 153–169.

Sackett, D.L., Straus, S.E., Richardson, W.S., Rosenberg, W., and Haynes, R.B., eds. (2000). *Evidence-based medicine: How to teach and practice EBM.* Edinburgh, U.K.: Churchill Livingstone.

Shalverson, R.J., and Towne, L., eds. *Scientific research in education.* Washington, D.C.: National Academy Press.

Schoenwald, S.K., and Hoagwood, K. (2001). Effectiveness, transportability, and dissemination of interventions: What matters when? *Psychiatric Services,* 52 (9), 1190–1197.

Shernoff, E.S., Kratochwill, T.R., and Stoiber, K.C. (2003). Training in evidence-based interventions (EBIs): What are school psychology programs teaching? *Journal of School Psychology,* 41 (6), 467–483.

Shinn, M.R., ed. (1989). *Curriculum-based measurement: Assessing special children.* New York: Guilford Press.

Shriver, M.D., and Watson, T.S. (2005). Bridging the great divide: Linking research to practice in scholarly publications. *Journal of Evidence-Based Practices for Schools,* 6, 5–18.

Sterling-Turner, H., Watson, T.S., and Moore, J.W. (2002). The effects of direct training and treatment integrity on treatment outcomes in school consultation. *School Psychology Quarterly,* 17 (1), 47–77.

Task Force on Evidence-based Interventions in School Psychology. (2003). Procedural and coding manual for review of evidence-based interventions.

Available at http://sp-ebi.org/documents/_workingfiles/EBImanual.pdf (accessed November 18, 2006).

Towne, L., Wise, L.L., and Winters, T.M., eds. (2005). *Advancing scientific research in education.* Washington, D.C.: National Academies Press.

Weisz, J.R., and Addis, M.E. (2006). The research-practice tango and other choreographic challenges: Using and testing evidence-based psychotherapies in clinical care settings. In *Evidence-based psychotherapy: Where practice and research meet* (eds. C.D. Goodheart, A.E. Kazdin, and R.J. Sternberg). Washington, D.C.: American Psychological Association.

Weisz, J.R., and Kazdin, A.E. (2003). Concluding thoughts: Present and future of evidence-based psychotherapies for children and adolescents. In *Evidence-based psychotherapies for children and adolescents* (eds. A.E. Kazdin and J.R. Weisz), pp. 439–451. New York: Guilford Press.

What Works Clearinghouse. (2006). *Evidence standards for reviewing studies.* Institute of Education Sciences, U.S. Department of Education. Available at http://ies.ed.gov/ncee/wwc/pdf/study_standards_final.pdf (accessed October 24, 2007).

Wilczynski, S. (2006). *National Standards Project: Conceptual model for reviewing the ASD literature.* Unpublished manuscript.

Witt, J.C., Martens, B.K., and Elliott, S.N. (1984). Factors affecting teachers' judgments of the acceptability of behavioral interventions: Time involvement, behavior problem severity, and type of intervention. *Behavior Therapy,* 15, 204–209.

Witt, J.C., Noell, G.H., LaFleur, L.H., and Mortensen, B.P. (1997). Teacher use of interventions in general education settings: Measurement and analysis of the independent variable. *Journal of Applied Behavior Analysis,* 30 (4), 693–696.

Witt, J.C., VanDerHeyden, A.M., and Gilbertson, D. (2004). Troubleshooting behavioral interventions: A systematic process for finding and eliminating problems. *School Psychology Review,* 33 (3), 363–383.

Wolf, M.M. (1978). Social validity: The case for subjective measurement or how applied behavior analysis is finding its heart. *Journal of Applied Behavior Analysis,* 11, 203–214.

2. Practice Guidelines for Autism Education and Intervention: Historical Perspective and Recent Developments

Raymond G. Romanczyk and Jennifer M. Gillis

■ What are Practice Guidelines?

In many ways, practice guidelines are the logical extension of the evidence-based approach to intervention. Guidelines for clinical practice come from many sources: educators, researchers, clinicians, government regulators, insurance companies, and, of course, consumers. But evidence-based practice guidelines are relatively new. The Agency for Health Care Policy and Research (AHCPR) was established in 1997. Now called the Agency for Healthcare Research and Quality (AHRQ), it is part of the U.S. Public Health Service and is the primary federal agency involved with health services research. To promote evidence-based practice, this Agency has established Evidence-Based Practice Centers (EPCs), which "develop evidence reports and technology assessments on topics relevant to clinical, social science/behavioral, economic, and other health care organization and delivery issues—specifically those that are common, expensive, and/or significant" (Anonymous 2007)

The AHCPR clinical practice guideline methodology uses principles for developing practice guidelines recommended by the U.S. Institute of Medicine (1992). This methodology is considered to be the standard for developing evidence-based clinical practice guidelines (Eddy and Hasselblad 1994; Holland 1995; Schriger 1995; Woolf 1991, 1995).

In 1995, essentially in parallel to the AHCPR efforts, a Division 12 (Clinical Psychology) Task Force of the American Psychological Association (APA) developed criteria for "empirically supported therapies" (EST), to provide guidelines for researchers, practitioners, and consumers evaluating psychological treatments or interventions. They established three categories to describe degrees of evidence: well-established, probably efficacious, and experimental. Chambless and Ollendick (2001) reviewed eight other groups that subsequently developed criteria and guidelines for evaluating psychological treatments. Specific criteria for each category were mostly similar to those of the APA Task Force, but there was more variability across groups when defining criteria for experimental treatments. Table 2.1 displays the Task Force's criteria for ESTs.

■ Best Practice Guidelines

Best practice guidelines are intended to inform consumers and service providers about the current status of optimal care guidelines as compared to generally accepted practice parameters for specific conditions or disorders. Such guidelines do not require service providers to follow the content. Instead, guidelines are intended to set a higher standard for care. There are many position papers and advocacy statements that purport to be best practice guidelines but in fact are not. Rather, there is an accepted methodology for evaluating treatments in order to produce best practice guidelines (Holland et al. 2005).

This methodology has only recently been applied to autism spectrum disorders (ASD). The New York State Department of Health (NYSDOH) Early Intervention Program (EIP) was the first to use this methodology to develop a series of evidence-based clinical practice guidelines. In 1996, the EIP began a multiyear project to develop evidence-based clinical practice guidelines focused on identification, assessment, and intervention for young children with developmental problems likely to require early intervention services. The clinical practice guidelines project was intended to improve the quality and consistency of care by providing families, service providers, and public officials with recommendations about best practices. The four specific objectives were (*a*) to improve knowledge by providing families, professionals, and government officials with accurate background information and evidence-based recommendations regarding assessment and intervention; (*b*) to enhance communication among all individuals involved with early intervention services to promote improved decision making regarding assessment, intervention approaches, and progress measurement; (*c*) to facilitate program evaluation and quality improvement efforts by defining appropriate outcomes measures and quality criteria for early intervention services; and (*d*) to promote research by identifying limitations in current practice.

Six separate multidisciplinary panels of clinicians and parents, assisted by a research methodologist and an information retrieval staff, were convened to develop separate clinical practice guidelines for infants and young children with the following developmental problems: autism/pervasive developmental disorders (PDD), communication disorders, Down syndrome, hearing

TABLE 2.1

American Psychological Association Criteria for Empirically
Supported Treatments

Category I: Well-Established Treatments

1. At least two good between-group design experiments must demonstrate efficacy in one or more of the following ways:

   a. Superiority to pill or psychotherapy placebo or to other treatments

   b. Equivalence to already established treatment with adequate sample sizes

OR

2. A large series of single-case design experiments must demonstrate efficacy with both of the following:

   a. Use of good experimental design

   b. Comparison of intervention to another treatment

PLUS

3. Experiments must be conducted with treatment manuals or equivalent clear description of treatment.

4. Characteristics of samples must be specified.

5. Effects must be demonstrated by at least two different investigators or teams.

Category II: Probably Efficacious Treatments

1. Two experiments must show that the treatment is superior to a waiting-list control group.

OR

2. One or more experiments must meet criteria Ia or Ib, III, and IV for well-established treatments (Category I), but criterion V is not met.

OR

3. A small series of single-case design experiments must meet criteria II, III, and IV for well-established treatments.

Category III: Experimental Treatments

1. Treatment not yet tested in trials meeting task force criteria for methodology.

From Chambless and Ollendick (2001).

impairment, motor disorders, and vision impairment. These independent panels developed the clinical practice guidelines. Using AHCPR methodology, information retrieval specialists completed a comprehensive review of the literature specific to each disorder. The resulting published articles were subjected to analysis of methodological integrity, and articles meeting minimum standards were then rated as to strength of results.

Information gathered from these research studies was evaluated by the panels to draw conclusions and produce the guidelines. Specifically, for the autism/PDD guidelines, more than 8000 research reports were reviewed and evaluated, using objective criteria for sound research methodology. It is important to underscore the methodology used by these panels. Unlike consensus panels, which are typically composed of a selected group of professionals who provide their expert opinion, these panels were formed from a cross section of professionals and consumers, both with and without specific expertise in the particular disorder. The panels relied on an evidence-based methodology rather than personal opinion. For a more detailed explanation of the NYSDOH process, the interested reader is referred to the review by Noyes and colleagues (2005).

All six clinical practice guidelines have now been completed. The guidelines on autism/PDD and on communication disorders were published in 1999 and have been widely disseminated to public early intervention officials, service providers, parents, and others. The guidelines for Down syndrome were published in 2006. The remaining three clinical practice guidelines are currently in press. These six clinical practice guidelines provide evidence-based recommendations on best practices for the majority of serious developmental problems seen in children from birth to 3 years of age.

As discussed earlier, one goal of the NYSDOH committee was to use scientific evidence to inform the clinical decision-making process for assessment and treatment. Therefore, the quality of research studies used to provide such scientific evidence needed to meet rigorous criteria. However, when providing best practice guidelines to the field, which includes a diverse group of consumers, researchers, practitioners, and public officials, it is important to provide such information in a palatable format. A good example of this was the strategy of the NYSDOH to publish three versions of the guidelines. The *Quick Reference Guide* provides summaries of both the recommendations and background information. This is useful to many, because it is straightforward and easy to read, providing the reader with focused information. The second text, the *Report of the Recommendations,* provides all of the recommendations, with background information and a summary of the supporting evidence. This text adds a more elaborate description of the recommendations and supporting evidence. The third text, *The Guideline Technical Report,* is more dense and includes all of the information in the *Report of the Recommendations* as well as a full report of the research process used and the scientific evidence that was reviewed. In this manner, from any vantage point, the NYSDOH has made information readily available to diverse consumers, for uses ranging from a parent's bringing the *Quick Reference Guide* to an IEP meeting to a psychologist's reviewing specific information about assessments from the *Guideline Technical Report.* As an example, in the *Autism/PDD Guideline Technical Report,* the section on assessment provides evaluators with guidelines for appropriate, developmentally sensitive, assessment. Recommendations are provided with regard to carrying out the assessment, considerations when choosing assessments for the purpose of developmental surveillance, and how the findings from a developmental assessment should be used to benefit the child with autism/PDD.

Beyond rigorous methodology and cross checks, another critical element of good scientific methodology is replicability. That is, it is critical in science that someone, other than the original researcher, be able to follow the published procedures and obtain the same results. In other words, it is necessary for the results to be reproducible by other, independent, researchers. The same applies to the process of establishing guidelines. If the process is objective and well specified, then another group should be able to duplicate the findings, because they are not based on mere opinion but rather on an analytical process that has specific rules.

Several other noteworthy, objective treatment reviews have been published recently. One is *Educating Children with Autism,* authored by the Committee on Educational Interventions for Children with Autism, Division of Behavioral and Social Sciences and Education, of the National Research Council (NRC) and published by the National Academies Press (NRC 2001). The Committee was composed of some of the most prominent figures in autism research in the nation. The report was commissioned by the U.S. Department of Education's Office of Special Education Programs to "consider the state of the scientific evidence of the effects and features of early educational intervention on young children with autism spectrum disorders" (NRC 2001, 2). The Committee took a traditional research approach and cited the NYSDOH process. They stated that, "To achieve a systematic and rigorous assessment of research studies, the committee established guidelines for evaluating areas of strength, limitations, and the overall quality of the research" (14). This report does not offer specific treatment recommendations, as does the NYSDOH guidelines, but provides evaluative statements. For example, in the context of sensory integration therapy, the report states, "These interventions have also not yet been supported by empirical studies" (99). The report also states that, "By far, the bulk of autistic spectrum disorders intervention research has been conducted from the perspective of applied behavior analysis" (148).

Another important example of replication comes from the Report of the Surgeon General concerning mental health in the United States (U.S. Department of Health and Human Services 1999). Although the report was written within the context of the published research base, it did not rely on a specific methodology such as that of the AHCPR. It was quite specific, however, in its conclusions. In the section on children, specific reference to autism was made. The report stated (U.S. Department of Health and Human Services 1999 Chapter 3):

Because autism is a severe, chronic developmental disorder, which results in significant lifelong disability, the goal of treatment is to promote the child's social and language development and minimize behaviors that interfere with the child's functioning and learning. Intensive, sustained special education programs and behavior therapy early in life can increase the ability of the child with autism to acquire language and ability to learn. Special education programs in highly structured environments appear to help the child acquire self-care, social, and job skills. Only in the past decade have studies shown positive outcomes for very young children with autism. Given the severity of the impairment, high intensity of service needs, and costs (both human and financial), there has been an ongoing search for effective treatment.

Thirty years of research demonstrated the efficacy of applied behavioral methods in reducing inappropriate behavior and in increasing communication, learning, and appropriate social behavior.

It is important to point out that these two examples were not true replications of the process used in the NYSDOH guidelines. The same is true for other formal reviews, such as those of Simpson (2005 Odom and colleagues (2003), and the MADSEC Autism Task Force (2000). Given the impressive resources expended by the NYSDOH to complete their guidelines using the AHCPR methodology, the lack of a true replication is understandable. For this reason, the current effort of the National Autism Center to produce a comprehensive, evidence-based review is of particular interest and importance.

Only 10 years after coining of the term, "evidence based medicine," the publication of the Division 12 Task Force's report on ESTs, and the establishment of the AHCPR guidelines, the federal No Child Left Behind Act (NCLB) was enacted into law in 2002. NCLB was enacted in part to require standards for effective educational interventions through the use of evidence-based education (EBE). EBE must utilize "research that applies rigorous, systematic and objective procedures to obtain relevant knowledge" (NCLB, 20 USC 1208(6)). NCLB is likely to provide a great impetus for continuing research on effective intervention as well as a clamor for objective reviews of the research literature.

However, the AHCPR methodology, the EST guidelines and criteria, and the NCLB have not had an overly positive impact for the field of ASD. There has been no great consumer rejection of the myriad of nonvalidated intervention packages. This is perhaps a function of the long history of parental choice in treatment options and the unbridled acceptance of "innovation" as a good quality in autism treatment approaches. Also, new funding streams have not emerged for research on programmatic intervention, and no comprehensive treatment programs for ASD currently meet the criteria for an EST, which requires random group assignment (Simpson, 2005). For a variety of sensible reasons, outcome studies of comprehensive programs for children with ASD have not included random group assignment. However, given significant resources, the necessary random-assignment research studies, with long-term outcome, can be conducted.

Research in treatment outcome for ASD also needs to address many factors that may be associated with outcome, such as age at start of intervention, intensity of intervention, procedural integrity, type of intervention, and comorbid symptoms or disorders. The challenge to the field of ASD is to develop ethical research designs and methods to examine these variables with as much scientific rigor as possible.

Perhaps the most important factor for explaining the lack of progress is that there is no consensus that evidenced-based treatment is the correct path. Many argue that research is not relevant and that providers should use their "best judgment"; they decry the infringement of objective research on clinical practice. In contrast, Szatmari (2004) exemplified the values that we, like many, hold: Research is the tool we use to make ethical treatment decisions, even if the choice the research leads us to is not necessarily our personal preferred approach. This perhaps defines the role of a professional—to offer what is best for the individual receiving services and not what is best or most comfortable for the provider. Szatmari stated (97):

> I would ask then, on what basis do I make a clinical decision? If I see a young child with autism, I have a choice: I can refer him to behaviour therapy or not. I would prefer to make my clinical decision on the basis of the best available evidence. What is the alternative to using evidence as a guide? I could do nothing, but that would be clinical paralysis and that surely is unethical. I could make a decision at random by simply flipping a coin, but that does not feel like an ethical thing to do if there is existing evidence (although randomisation in an N of 1 trial may be the best solution if there is inadequate evidence). I could make my decision on the basis on how I was trained. But as I was trained many years ago, that information is now quite out of date. I could instead make my decision based on what I know about the pathophysiology of autism (just like many physicians make clinical decisions about prescribing medication for depression on the basis of their knowledge of neurotransmitters in mood disorders). But as what we know about pathophysiology of autism is so limited (and, I would argue, is equally limited for all psychiatric disorders), I think it is very difficult, if not impossible, to make clinical decisions about treatment based on our very incomplete knowledge of aetiology. Finally, I could make my clinical decision based on my values. What values do I hold about the most appropriate, the most humane, the most empowering form of treatment? In fact, I personally do not find

applied behavioural analysis (ABA) very humane. The use of massed dis-
creet trials to teach simple tasks such as matching often looks intrusive
and critical. I would much prefer a more developmental sociocognitive
approach and indeed such treatments are available but they do not yet
have the evidence to support them. But if I were to choose a treatment
based on my values over the evidence, I would have to do so by the rules
of informed consent. To be ethical, I would have to make that preference
known to the parents of this child with autism and they would also have
to choose (or not to choose) my values over the evidence. I wonder what
a reasonable adult would do in such a circumstance? I bet they would
choose treatment that is supported by the evidence over and above my
own values and so would choose behaviour therapy.

■ Conclusion

It is an interesting commentary on society that we have come so far in advocating for consumers in general but have made so little progress in determining
specific, agreed-upon guidelines for best practice in ASD. Although government regulation now restrains the type of blatant, false claims for purported
treatment made at the turn of the last century, objective quality control standards are undermined by sophisticated marketing. Consumers are bombarded
daily with cleverly written advertisements for all sorts of helpful products that
are "not intended to diagnose or treat specific medical conditions." Within the
field of autism treatment, marketing has also had great influence. As the terms
"evidenced-based practice" and "empirically supported" have become more
widely discussed in professional and policy circles and held out to the public as important consumer characteristics, various self-promoters and service
programs have learned to simply co-opt the terms, knowing that the typical
consumer is not aware of the complexity of the issue. Therefore, it is not unusual to see such terms used in promotional brochures for programs utilizing
treatment approaches that actually have no research support.

As the number of new claims of "breakthroughs" in treatment grows
seemingly daily, the words popularized by Carl Sagan, in referring to the per-
vasiveness of pseudo-science in society, are of continuing value: "Extraordinary claims require extraordinary proof." However, the marketing ploys of
appealing to "common sense" and risk aversion must also be addressed—for
example, the statement that a treatment approach is an "important addition
to standard treatments." The "How could it hurt?" justification is based on the
common assumption that more is better, which is clearly not the case with the
treatment of autism (Romanczyk, Gillis, White, DiGennaro, in press). Fortunately, there remain significant numbers of parents, professionals, government
officials, and agencies concerned with accurate information about treatment
options for autism. A well-established methodology exists for evaluating

claims of efficacy. The continuing task is not only to use this methodology but also to distribute the resulting information with the same dedication as the marketers of unsubstantiated interventions.

■ References

Anonymous. (2006). Harvey W. Wiley: Pioneer consumer activist. *FDA Consumer.* Available at http://www.fda.gov/fdac/features/2006/106_wiley.html (accessed October 26, 2007).

Anonymous. (2007). *Evidence-Based Practice Centers overview.* Rockville, Md.: Agency for Healthcare Research and Quality. Available at http://www.ahrq. gov/clinic/epc (accessed October 26, 2007).

Chambless, D.L., and Ollendick, T.H. (2001). Empirically supported psychological interventions: controversies and evidence. *Annual Review of Psychology,* 52, 685–716.

Eddy, D.M., and Hasselblad, V. (1994). Analyzing evidence by the confidence and profile method. In *Clinical practice guideline development: Methodology perspectives* (eds. K.A. McCormick, S.R. Moore, and R.A. Siegel). (AHCPR Publication No. 95–0009). Rockville, Md.: Agency for Health Care Policy and Research, Public Health Service, U.S. Department of Health and Human Services.

Holland, J.P. (1995). Development of a clinical practice guideline for acute low back pain. *Current Opinion in Orthopedics,* 6, 63–69.

MADSEK Autism Task Force (Report of). (2000). *Maine Administrators of Services for Children with Disabilities.* Manchester, ME.

Matson, J.L., Benavidez, D.A., Compton, L.S., Paclawskyj, T., and Baglio, C. (1996). Behavioral treatment of autistic persons: A review of research from 1980 to the present. *Research in Developmental Disabilities,* 17 (6), 433–465.

National Research Council. (2001). *Educating children with autism.* Committee on Educational Interventions for Children with Autism, Division of Behavioral and Social Sciences and Education. Washington, D.C.: National Academy Press.

New York State Department of Health. (1999). *New York State Department of Health clinical practice guideline: The guideline technical report. Autism/ pervasive developmental disorders: Assessment and intervention for young children (age 0–3 years).* (Publication No. 4217.) Albany, NY: New York State Department of Health Early Intervention Program.

New York State Department of Health Early Intervention Program. (1999). *Clinical practice guideline: Quick reference guide. Autism/pervasive developmental disorders: Assessment and intervention for young children (age 0–3 years).* (1999 Publication No. 4216). Albany, NY: New York State Department of Health Early Intervention Program.

New York State Department of Health Early Intervention Program. (1999). *Clinical practice guideline: Report of the recommendations. Autism/pervasive developmental disorders: Assessment and intervention for young children (age 0–3 years).* (1999 Publication No. 4215). Albany, NY: New York State Department of Health Early Intervention Program.

No Child Left Behind Act of 2001. Public Law 107–110 (115 STAT. 1425).

Noyes-Grosser, D.M., Holland, J.P., Lyons, D., Holland, C.L., Romanczyk, R.G., and Gillis, J.M. (2005). New York State clinical practice guidelines: I. Rationale and methodology for developing guidelines for early intervention services for young children with developmental disabilities. *Infants and Young Children,* 18 (2), 119–135.

Odom, S.L., Brown, W.H., Frey, T., Karasu, N., Smith-Canter, L.L., and Strain, P.S. (2003). Evidence-based practices for young children with autism: Contributions for single-subject design research. *Focus on Autism and Other Developmental Disabilities,* 18 (3), 166–175.

Romanczyk, R.G., Gillis, J.M., White, S., and DiGennaro, F. (In press). Comprehensive treatment packages for ASD: Perceived vs. proven effectiveness. In *Autism Spectrum Disorder* (ed. J. Matson). Cambridge, MA: Elsevier.

Schriger, D.L. (1995). Training panels in methodology. In *Clinical practice guideline development: Methodology perspectives* (eds. K.A. McCormick, S.R. Moore, and R.A. Siegel). (AHCPR Publication No. 95–0009). Rockville, Md.: Agency for Health Care Policy and Research, Public Health Service, U.S. Department of Health and Human Services.

Simpson, R.L. (2005). Evidence-based practices and students with autism spectrum disorders. *Focus on Autism and Other Developmental Disabilities,* 20, 140–149.

Szatmari, P. (2004). Response to Dr. Gupta. *Evidence-Based Mental Health,* 7 (4), 97–98.

U.S. Department of Health and Human Services. (1999). *Mental health: A report of the Surgeon General—Executive summary.* Rockville, Md.: U.S. Department of Health and Human Services, Substance Abuse and Mental Health Services Administration, Center for Mental Health Services, National Institutes of Health, National Institute of Mental Health.

U.S. Institute of Medicine. (1992). *Committee on Clinical Practice Guidelines for Clinical Practice: From Development to Use* (eds. M.J. Field and K.N. Lohr). Washington, DC: National Academy Press.

Woolf, S.H. (1991). *AHCPR interim manual for clinical practice guideline development.* (AHCPR Publication No. 91–0018). Rockville, Md.: Agency for Health Care Policy and Research, Public Health Service, U.S. Department of Health and Human Services.

Woolf, S.H. (1995). An organized analytic framework for practice guideline development: Using the analytic logic as a guide for reviewing evidence, developing recommendations, and explaining the rationale. In *Clinical practice guideline development: Methodology perspectives* (eds. K.A. McCormick, S.R. Moore, and R.A. Siegel). (AHCPR Publication No. 95–0009). Rockville, Md.: Agency for Health Care Policy and Research, Public Health Service, U.S. Department of Health and Human Services.

3. The National Standards Project: Promoting Evidence-Based Practice in Autism Spectrum Disorders

Susan M. Wilczynski, Lauren Christian,
and the National Autism Center

Children are being diagnosed with autism spectrum disorders (ASD) at an alarming rate. Based on estimates by the Centers for Disease Control and Prevention (CDC) (2001), approximately 24,000 children are born each year who will eventually be given a diagnosis on the autism spectrum. Autism spectrum disorder is now more common than Down syndrome, pediatric AIDS, and diabetes combined (CDC 2001). The diagnosis serves only as the starting point for patient care. Once the child receives a diagnosis, parents and professionals need to make decisions about treatment and educational services.

Just as the number of ASD cases has increased, so too have the number of "treatments" proliferated. Like most people in this technologically advanced age, parents often turn first to the Internet as a source of information about how to proceed. However, the Internet offers no help in identifying which of the interventions touted as "cures" or "helpful hints" actually have support in the empirical literature. Information and misinformation abound in newspaper and magazine articles, leaving families inundated with sometimes conflicting recommendations about treatment approaches. Further confusing the issue, many intervention approaches are marketed by individuals who wrap themselves in the cloak of science (Green, 1999). Spectacular statistical claims are offered by promoters of these treatments, even though no peer-reviewed studies have been published to support their use. Families' desperation for a cure, paired with their lack of scientific training, often makes them vulnerable to both charlatans and good-hearted individuals who do not understand the scientific process but truly believe they have the answer. This era of pseudoscience would make P.T. Barnum proud, but it leaves many professionals asking, "Which way to the great egress?" Action is necessary to clear away the confusion and to support families in their decision making about autism treatment.

Families are not the only ones looking for answers. Teachers are often motivated to incorporate each new and novel treatment approach into educational programming. They are often encouraged to "leave no stone unturned," and this may result in a strategy in which interventions are introduced and exited from educational programming based on popularity rather than data-based decision-making. Principals and special education directors often invest the meager dollars available to them in teacher training workshops on the treatment du jour instead of the intervention with the highest level of research support.

Even individuals who have received training in scientific methodology can fall prey to this problem. Keeping abreast of the latest research on the treatment of ASD can be daunting. More and more studies are being published on treatment of the core deficits of communication, social interaction, and restricted, repetitive, nonfunctional behaviors (American Psychological Association [APA] 2005), as well as interventions addressing collateral features (e.g., aggression, self-injury, disruptive behaviors, inattention, hyperactivity, sleep problems, motivation). This is critical for the identification of treatments that work. Yet, so many studies are being published in the area that only professionals who can afford to dedicate their training almost exclusively to ASD are able to become familiar with the entire literature base.

Other fields of study have faced the same problem in the past. Evidenced-based medicine emerged as a response to physicians' failure to use the best-supported treatments in medical management (Sackett 2000). Physicians led the way in patient care by systematically evaluating the research evidence supporting various treatment options and conveying this information to relevant consumers (e.g., physicians, nurses). Physicians now have ready access to clear, concise information about the best-supported treatment options for their patients. Because evidenced-based practice emerged at a time when information technology was flourishing, this information has also become readily available to consumers.

Physicians were not the only professionals who banned together to provide compelling guides for patient care. Psychologists, educators, speech language pathologists, and a broad range of allied health professional have all recognized the importance and value of evidence-based practice (APA 2005). In fact, efforts to provide consumers information about treatments for ASD have been made in the past. The New York State Department of Health Early Intervention Clinical Practice Guidelines (1999) outlined the strength of evidence supporting a variety of early intervention treatment options for children with ASD. The Maine Administrators of Services for Children with Disabilities Autism Task Force (2000) published their review of eight treatment options for school-aged children with ASD. Most recently, the Committee on

Educational Interventions for Children with Autism of the National Research Council (2001) published a report providing recommendations to families regarding a broad range of issues related to ASD, focusing on treatment in young children.

Although each of these clinical guidelines can be used to forward evidence-based practice in ASD, the utility of these reports is currently somewhat limited. First, scholars involved in these projects examined studies conducted before 1999. Therefore, these documents no longer reflect the most up-to-date empirical evidence on the treatment of ASD. Second, the process used by each of these task forces to identify effective treatments and make recommendations was not transparent (i.e., detailed explanations were not made available to the general public). Making determinations about treatment efficacy behind closed doors yields questions at best, and skepticism at worst, about the conclusions drawn by these groups. Finally, these reports were not sufficiently comprehensive regarding educational and behavioral treatment options for all children and adolescents served in schools and behavioral treatment programs. Increasingly, parents, educators, and service providers need information about research-supported treatments for older children and young adults with ASD. For these reasons, it is clear that a transparent process for evaluating the most recent research literature and providing information about the strength of evidence supporting treatment options for both children and adolescents is necessary.

An evidence-based practice guideline dedicated to treatments for individuals younger than 22 years of age (e.g., years during which those with ASD are likely to be served by school systems) is necessary. Yet, evidence-based practice guidelines have historically been restricted, to ensure that an adequate review of the literature is completed by qualified experts in a given domain. Given the necessity of expanding the scope of evidence-based guidelines to a broader age range than has been completed in the past, different restrictions are required. Specifically, the focus of the National Standards Project, as described in this chapter, is limited to interventions that can reasonably be implemented with integrity in most school or behavioral treatment programs. A review of the biomedical literature for ASD will be left to another body of qualified professionals.

Additional exclusion criteria for the National Standards Project apply to studies with the following foci: medications or nutritional supplements, complementary/alternative medical interventions (with the exception of curative diets), participants identified with psychosis or axis II diagnosis outside of mental retardation, individuals other than those with ASD, and predictors of outcomes. In addition, studies that could not reasonably be performed in most school settings are not included. Finally, articles that used only qualitative analyses, were literature reviews or opinion statements, did not allow for the separate analysis of ASD if more than one population was studied, or were published in non–peer-reviewed journals are excluded from consideration. Therefore, the National Standards Project represents an unprecedented effort to use a transparent process to examine empirical evidence supporting interventions that can be provided in educational and behavioral treatment settings for individuals younger than 22 years of age.

The National Autism Center is a nonprofit organization dedicated to supporting effective, evidence-based treatment approaches for individuals with ASD and to providing direction to families, practitioners, organizations, and policy-makers. The National Standards Project is one of the primary national activities of the National Autism Center. The National Standards Project began with two plenary sessions in which the conceptual model for evaluating the literature was developed by leaders in research and treatment of ASD. The conceptual model was then reviewed by each of these leaders and by a second team of experts, representing diverse fields of study and theoretical orientation, in order to improve the model and to ensure that it reflects the broad research interests of professionals working in this area. The conceptual model for reviewing the literature is discussed in the remainder of this chapter.

■ Process for Evaluating Empirical Evidence

Overview

Decisions about educational and treatment programming are sometimes made on the basis of a single professional reading a single article describing an intervention. Although we can generally have more confidence in professional recommendations that are based on a single study rather than on no studies at all, science dictates that a series of sequential studies affords far greater confidence in the probability that a treatment will, indeed, be effective. Therefore, the process for evaluating empirical evidence must involve an examination of the number of peer-reviewed studies supporting a given treatment. First, however, a thorough evaluation of the experimental rigor of each published study should occur, because not all studies are created equally, and the conclusions that can be drawn from individual studies should vary in relation to the scientific merit of the experiments described. Once all studies have been reviewed for scientific merit, the strength of evidence supporting a given treatment can be described in terms of both the number and the quality of studies supporting it.

The general procedure used in the National Standards Project begins with a comprehensive examination of the literature that meets the inclusion criteria. Once the literature search has been completed, articles are disseminated among scholars who *(a)* have expertise in ASD, *(b)* represent diverse fields of study contributing to this literature base, and *(c)* establish a high degree of inter-rater reliability using the coding manual for evaluating research articles. Many of these individuals were involved in the development of the National Standards Project by guiding its initial development or by providing critical feedback to improve the conceptual model for evaluating the literature.

The remainder of this chapter is dedicated to the methodology used to establish the National Standards Project. It is important to categorize the literature in multiple ways (e.g., comprehensive programs versus focused interventions, interventions designed to increase appropriate behavior versus treatments intended to decrease problem behaviors) so that families, educators, and service providers can interpret the results of the National Standards Project in a way that is meaningful to them. Second, the Scientific Merit Rating Scale (SMRS), the assessment system for examining individual articles, is discussed in the next section, followed by a description of the process for aggregating results across articles for a given treatment. The organization and segmentation of the ASD literature is described in the final section.

Scientific Merit Rating Scale

The SMRS is a scoring system designed to evaluate the quality and usefulness of articles in drawing firm conclusions about the effectiveness of an intervention (Table 3.1). Five key dimensions of experimental rigor and potency for determining effectiveness of interventions are rated: *(a)* research design, *(b)* measurement of the dependent variable, *(c)* measurement of the independent variable or procedural fidelity, *(d)* participant ascertainment, and *(e)* generalization of treatment effects. *Research design* refers to the extent to which experimental control was demonstrated. *Measurement of dependent variable* is defined as the extent to which accurate and reliable data were collected to capture the most direct and comprehensive sample possible. *Measurement of independent variable* reflects the extent to which procedural integrity was adequately verified to have occurred with a high degree of accuracy. *Participant ascertainment* refers to the extent to which independent, blind evaluators used well-established diagnostic procedures when determining eligibility for inclusion into the study. *Generalization of treatment effects* is defined as the degree to which treatment effects were objectively established to generalize across time, settings, stimuli, and persons. Each dimension is given a score ranging from 0 to 5, and scores are combined to yield a total score.

In addition to the SMRS score, each article is coded to indicate treatment effects: *(a)* beneficial treatment effects reported, *(b)* no treatment effects reported, or *(c)* adverse treatment effects reported. For group-design studies, beneficial treatment effects are reported if statistically significant effects are

TABLE 3.1

Scientific Merit Rating Scale

Rating	Design		Measurement of Dependent Variable		Measurement of Independent Variable (Procedural Integrity or Treatment Fidelity)	Participant Ascertainment	Generalization of Tx Effect(s)
	Group	Single-Case*	Test, Scale, or Checklist	Direct Behavioral Observation			
5	Number of groups: 2 or more Design: random assignment and/or no significant differences pre-Tx Participants: $n \geq 10$ per group or sufficient power for lower number of participants Data loss: none	A minimum of 3 comparisons of control and treatment conditions Number of data points per condition: ≥ 5 Number of participants: ≥ 3 Data loss: no data loss possible	Type of measurement: observation-based Protocol: standardized Psychometric properties solid instrument Evaluators: blind and independent	Type of measurement: continuous or discontinuous with calibration data showing low levels of error Reliability: IOA $\geq 90\%$ or kappa ≥ 0.75 Percentage of sessions: reliability collected in $\geq 25\%$ Type of conditions in which data were collected: all sessions	*For focused interventions:* Control and experimental (Tx) procedures are extensively operationally defined Implementation accuracy measured at $\geq 80\%$ Implementation accuracy measured in 25% of total sessions IOA for treatment fidelity $\geq 90\%$ *For comprehensive programs:* Written manual or detailed curriculum that includes replicable intervention strategies for 100% of strategies Formal or standardized treatment fidelity measure exists with 1 form of validity (including face validity) Formal or standardized treatment fidelity measure exists with 1 form of reliability established at 0.90 or higher Repeated measurement of treatment fidelity with multiple staff members reported	Diagnosed by a qualified professional Diagnosis confirmed by independent and blind evaluators for research purposes using at least 1 psychometrically solid instrument DSM or ICD criteria reported to be met	*Focused interventions:* Objective data Tx effects sustained for at least 2 mo Tx effects generalized across at least 2 of the following: setting, stimuli, persons *Comprehensive programs:* Objective data Tx effects sustained for at least 12 mo Tx effects sustained with ≥ 3 dependent variables

4	Number of groups: 2 or more Design: matched groups; no significant differences pre-Tx Participants: $n \geq 10$ per group or sufficient power for lower number of participants Data loss: some data loss possible	A minimum of 3 comparisons of control and treatment conditions Number of data points per condition: ≥5 Number of participants: ≥3 Data loss: some data loss possible	Type of measurement: observation-based Protocol: standardized Psychometric properties sufficient Evaluators: blind but not independent	Type of measurement: continuous or discontinuous with no calibration data Reliability: IOA ≥80% or kappa ≥0.75 Percentage of sessions: reliability collected in ≥20% Type of conditions in which data were collected: all sessions	*Focused interventions:* Control condition is operationally defined at a rudimentary level Experimental (Tx) procedures are extensively operationally defined Implementation accuracy measured at ≥80% Implementation accuracy measured in 20% of total sessions IOA for treatment fidelity ≥80% *Comprehensive programs:* Written manual or detailed curriculum that includes replicable intervention strategies for 75% of strategies Formal or standardized treatment fidelity measure exists with 1 form of validity (including face validity) Formal or standardized treatment fidelity measure exists with 1 form of reliability established at 0.80 or higher Repeated measurement without reference to number of staff involved	Diagnosis provided/confirmed by independent and blind evaluators for research purposes using at least 1 psychometrically sufficient instrument	*Focused interventions:* Objective data Tx effects sustained for at least 1 mo Tx effects generalized across at least 2 of the following: setting, stimuli, persons *Comprehensive programs:* Objective data Tx effects sustained for at least 6 mo Tx effects sustained with ≥2 dependent variables

TABLE 3.1 *(continued)*

Rating	Design — Group	Design — Single-Case*	Measurement of Dependent Variable — Test, Scale, or Checklist	Measurement of Dependent Variable — Direct Behavioral Observation	Measurement of Independent Variable (Procedural Integrity or Treatment Fidelity)	Participant Ascertainment	Generalization of Tx Effect(s)
3	Number of groups: 2 or more Design: pretreatment differences controlled statistically Data loss: some data loss possible	A minimum of 2 comparisons of control and treatment conditions Number of data points per condition: ≥3 Number of participants: ≥2 Data loss: some data loss possible	Type of measurement: observation-based measurement Protocol: nonstandardized or standardized Psychometric properties adequate Evaluators: blind OR independent	Type of measurement: continuous or discontinuous with no calibration data Reliability: IOA ≥80% or kappa ≥0.4 Percentage of sessions: reliability collected in ≥25% Type of conditions in which data were collected: experimental sessions only	*Focused interventions:* Control condition is operationally defined at a rudimentary level Experimental (Tx) procedures are extensively operationally defined Implementation accuracy measured at ≥80% Implementation accuracy measured in 20% of total sessions IOA for treatment fidelity: not reported *Comprehensive programs:* Written manual or detailed curriculum that includes replicable intervention strategies for 50% of strategies Formal or standardized treatment fidelity measure exists (e.g., checklists outlining model components) in a form that would allow the model implementer or other outside observer to evaluate implementation of essential model components, but no psychometric data have been collected on instrument	Diagnosis provided/confirmed by independent OR blind evaluators for research purposes using at least 1 psychometrically adequate instrument	*Focused interventions:* Objective data Tx effects sustained for at least 2 wk Tx effects generalized across at least 1 of the following: setting; stimuli; persons *Comprehensive programs:* Objective data Tx effects sustained for at least 3 mo Tx effects sustained with ≥2 dependent variables

2	Number of groups and design: if 2 groups, pre-Tx difference not controlled OR a 1-group repeated measures pre-test/post-test design Data loss: significant data loss possible	A minimum of 2 comparisons of control and treatment conditions Number of data points per condition: ≥3 Number of participants: ≥1 Data loss: significant data loss possible	Type of measurement: observation-based or subjective Protocol: nonstandardized or standardized Psychometric properties modest Evaluators: neither blind nor independent required	Type of measurement: continuous or discontinuous with no calibration data Reliability: IOA ≥80% or kappa ≥0.4 Percentage of sessions: not reported Type of conditions in which data were collected: not reported	*Focused interventions:* Control condition is operationally defined at an inadequate level or better Experimental (Tx) procedures are operationally defined at a rudimentary level or better Implementation accuracy measured at ≥80% Implementation accuracy regarding percentage of total sessions: not reported IOA for treatment fidelity: not reported *Comprehensive programs:* Written manual or detailed curriculum that includes replicable intervention strategies for <50% of strategies Only informal procedures used to document treatment fidelity or more formal measure exists for some but not all essential model components Single measurement without reference to number of staff involved	Diagnosis confirmed by researcher who was neither blind nor independent using at least 1 psychometrically modest instrument	*Focused interventions:* Objective data Tx effects sustained for at least 1 wk OR Tx effects generalized across at least 1 of the following: setting, stimuli, persons *Comprehensive programs:* Objective data Tx effects sustained for at least 2 mo Tx effects sustained with ≥1 dependent variable

TABLE 3.1 *(continued)*

Rating	Design		Measurement of Dependent Variable		Measurement of Independent Variable (Procedural Integrity or Treatment Fidelity)	Participant Ascertainment	Generalization of Tx Effect(s)
	Group	Single-Case*	Test, Scale, or Checklist	Direct Behavioral Observation			
1	Number of groups and design: 2-group, post-test only OR retrospective comparison of 1 or more matched groups Data loss: significant data loss possible	A minimum of 1 comparison of control and treatment conditions Number of data points per condition: ≥3 Number of participants: ≥1 Data loss: significant data loss possible	Type of measurement: observation-based or subjective Protocol: nonstandardized or standardized Psychometric properties weak Evaluators: neither blind nor independent required	Type of measurement: continuous or discontinuous with no calibration data Reliability: IOA <80% or kappa ≥0.4 or kappa <0.4 Percentage of sessions: not reported Type of conditions in which data were collected: not reported	*Focused interventions:* Control condition is operationally defined at an inadequate level or better Experimental (Tx) procedures are operationally defined at a rudimentary level or better IOA and procedural fidelity: data are unreported *Comprehensive programs:* Written manual or detailed curriculum that includes replicable intervention strategies for <50% of strategies Statements published regarding treatment fidelity without formal or informal data offered Single measurement without reference to number of staff involved	Diagnosis provided by review of records or psychometric support for the instrument is weak	*Focused interventions:* Informal or subjective data Tx effects sustained for at least 1 wk OR Tx effects generalized across at least 1 of the following: setting, stimuli, persons *Comprehensive programs:* Objective data Tx effects sustained for at least 1 mo Tx effects sustained with ≥1 dependent variable

*For all designs except alternating treatments design (ATD). For an ATD, the following criteria apply:

5 = Functional relation demonstrated between at least 1 independent variable and the dependent variable via comparisons of baseline and treatment condition(s), strong separation between data series for at least 2 independent variables, ≥5 data points per condition, follow-up data supporting treatment effectiveness, carryover effects minimized through counterbalancing of key variables (e.g., time of day), and condition discriminability; $n \geq 3$.

4 = Functional relation demonstrated between at least 1 independent variable and the dependent variable via comparisons of baseline and treatment condition(s), strong separation between data series for at least 2 independent variables, ≥5 data points per condition, carryover effects minimized through counterbalancing of key variables (e.g., time of day), and condition discriminability; $n \geq 3$.

3 = Strong separation between data series for at least 2 independent variables, ≥5 data points per condition, carryover effects minimized through counterbalancing of key variables OR condition discriminability; $n \geq 2$.

2 = Moderate separation between data series for at least 2 independent variables, ≥5 data points per condition; $n \geq 2$.

1 = Moderate separation between data series for at least 2 independent variables, ≥5 data points per condition; $n \geq 1$.

0 = Does not meet criteria for a rating of 1.

DSM, *Diagnostic and Statistical Manual of Mental Disorders (4th ed, text revision)*; ICD, *International Classification of Diseases and Related Health Problems (10th revision)*; IOA, interobserver agreement; Tx, treatment.

Source: National Autism Center. *National Standards Report: Evidence-Based Practice and Autism Spectrum Disorders*. Randolph, MA: Author.

found in favor of a treatment. For single-case design studies, beneficial treatment effects are broken into three categories (strong, moderate, and weak), based on the extent to which (a) a functional relation has been established and is replicated, (b) a point of comparison across conditions exists (e.g., there is a steady state, the data in the control condition allow for a sufficient comparison to the experimental condition), (c) the magnitude of change is consistent, and (d) the percentage of nonoverlapping data points is impressive.

Strength of Evidence Classification System

Individual articles are coded so they can help identify the degree of scientific support for a given intervention. The Strength of Evidence Classification System (SECS) states the criteria required to meet each of the six levels of scientific support against which any treatment may be compared. These levels of scientific support reflect the extent to which scientific evidence is currently available when the composite scores of the SMRS are aggregated. The SECS developed and used for the National Standards Project builds on systems proposed by other scholars promoting evidence-based practice. This classification system is based on extensive work in evidence-based medicine, particularly the work of the Agency for Healthcare Research and Quality (AHRQ) (West et al. 2002). In addition, the SECS merges recommendations from the APA's Presidential Task Force on Evidence-Based Practice (APA 2005)and the Task Force on Evidence-Based Interventions in School Psychology (APA 2003) for the construction of evidence-based practice guidelines and the work of psychologists in defining empirically supported interventions (Chambless et al. 1998). In addition, the scholarly work of Horner and colleagues (2005) carefully considered the use of single-case design methodology when identifying evidence-based practice. Collectively, these resources set the stage for the development of the SECS.

The six levels of scientific support reflect a four-point continuum (strongest support, strong support, moderate support, and emerging treatment) along with two additional categories (unestablished treatment and discredited treatment). The scores on the SMRS map directly on the four-point continuum of the SECS (Table 3.2), and beneficial treatment effects must be reported. This reflects the idea that not only are more studies required of treatments enjoying the highest levels of research support, but these studies should employ more rigorous controls and allow readers to draw firm conclusions about study outcomes. Another question that arises in determining the strength of evidence supporting treatments is, "How do we address treatments with conflicting published outcomes?" On the one hand, a conflicting report could be the result of chance or poor experimental control. On the other hand, serious concern should be raised about treatments with multiple conflicting reports. The decision to minimize the impact of poorly controlled studies on the classifica-

← ← ← Increasing Confidence in Efficacy

Strongest Support	Strong Support	Modest Support	Emerging Treatment
Multiple* published, peer-reviewed studies using experimental research designs with a score of 5 on the SMRS demonstrating strong beneficial treatment effects. These may be supplemented by studies with lower scores on the SMRS demonstrating beneficial treatment effects.	Multiple* published, peer-reviewed studies using experimental research designs with a score of 4 on the SMRS demonstrating moderate or strong beneficial treatment effects. These may be supplemented by studies with higher or lower scores on the SMRS demonstrating strong beneficial treatment effects when a higher classification criterion has not been met.	Limited* published, peer-reviewed studies using experimental research designs with a score of 3 on the SMRS demonstrating moderate or strong beneficial treatment effects. These may be supplemented by studies with higher or lower scores on the SMRS demonstrating beneficial treatment effects when a higher classification criterion has not been met.	Few* published, peer-reviewed studies using quasi-experimental research designs with a score of 2 on the SMRS demonstrating weak to strong beneficial treatment effects. These may be supplemented by studies with higher or lower scores on the SMRS demonstrating beneficial treatment effects when a higher classification criterion has not been met.

*Multiple is defined as 2-group design or 6 single-case design studies with no conflicting results OR at least 3-group design or 9 single-case design studies with no more than 1 study with conflicting results. Limited is defined as 1-group design or 3 single-case design studies with no conflicting results OR at least 2-group design or 6 single-case design studies with no more than 1 study with conflicting results. Few is defined as 2 single-case design or group design studies with no conflicting results. Conflicting results are reported when a better or equally controlled study that is assigned a score of at least 3 reports either (a) no beneficial treatment effects or (b) adverse treatment effects.

Unestablished Treatment

Claims of treatment efficacy based solely on very poorly controlled studies (scores of 0 or 1 on the SMRS), testimonials, narrative accounts, unverified clinical observations, opinions, speculations; or a treatment does not reach the criterion for any of the other classifications.

Discredited Treatment

Multiple published, peer-reviewed studies using experimental research designs with scores of 3 or higher on the SMRS demonstrating no beneficial treatment effects and/or adverse treatment effects AND no studies with scores of 3 or higher on the SMRS demonstrating moderate or strong beneficial treatment effects.

SMRS, Scientific Merit Rating Scale.

Source: National Autism Center. National Standards Report: Evidence-Based Practice and Autism Spectrum Disorders. Randolph, MA: Author.

tion rendered to a given treatment, while simultaneously limiting the SECS classification describing a treatment that has more than one well-controlled study suggesting that it is ineffective, takes into consideration each of these concerns.

The "unestablished treatment" category reflects the fact that, for some treatments, reports in the literature are based exclusively on testimonials, or on very poorly controlled research from which no strong conclusions can be drawn irrespective of the reported outcomes, or conflicting evidence has been published. The "discredited treatment" category serves as a warning to consumers that well-controlled studies have demonstrated that an intervention is not effective in helping individuals with ASD in the way in which it is intended or that adverse treatment effects have been reported. This may be the case even if poorly controlled studies originally suggested the treatment held promise.

■ Organization

Comprehensive Programs versus Focused Interventions

Children receive services in a broad number of contexts, with a variety of different treatment targets resulting from their unique and individualized needs. Some children require comprehensive programming to address all of the core deficits of ASD, whereas others are served in less restricted environments but need focused interventions to either improve a skill deficit or decrease or eliminate a behavioral excess. Families, educators, and service providers need to be able look up the scientific evidence to support each of these types of treatments.

Comprehensive Programs

At a minimum, comprehensive programs address the core impairments associated with ASD. Although they may also address associated features such as behavior problems or motivation, in order to be considered a comprehensive program, an educational or treatment program must tackle problems with communication, social interaction, and restricted, repetitive, nonfunctional patterns of behavior, interest, or activity. In addition, procedural guides, manuals, or curricula must be published in a refereed journal article, book chapter, or book. The remaining criteria for comprehensive programs are that (a) a clear theoretical or conceptual framework must be delineated and (b) treatment must occur with a high degree of intensity (e.g., 25 hours or more per week, treatment extending across at least 9 months). Examples of comprehensive programs include the Young Autism Project and replication sites, the London Early Autism Project (LEAP), the Walden Early Childhood

Program, Treatment and Education of Autistic and related Communication handicapped CHildren (TEACCH), and the Developmental, Individual-Difference, Relationship-Based (DIDRB) model.

Focused Interventions

Parents, educators, and service providers often request information about interventions that focus on improving life skills outside the context of a comprehensive program. These focused interventions often address specific behaviors that are necessary to either increase developmentally appropriate skills or decrease severe behaviors problems. In the discussion that follows, focused interventions are broken down into these two areas of interest: Focused Interventions I addresses developmentally appropriate behaviors that need to be increased, and Focused Interventions II addresses interventions designed to decrease severe behavior problems. All definitions that follow were drawn from the National Standards Report (unpublished).

■ Focused Interventions I: Developmentally Appropriate Skills to be Increased

There are a large number of ways in which the literature addressing developmentally appropriate skills that need to be increased can be segmented and coded. The literature examining skill domains could result in hundreds of categories if the finest distinctions were made. However, this would yield an unwieldy document of limited usefulness to parents, educators, and service providers. In the National Standards Project, the decision was made to divide Focused Interventions I into eight categories based on feedback from the expert panelists who first developed the conceptual model for evaluating the literature and on extensive feedback from conceptual reviewers with expertise in ASD who were not involved in the original development of the conceptual model. Each of the categories described includes primary dependent measures, examples of which are given in the following discussion. For all of the categories, these measures may be broken down further to allow more refined and sensitive assessment.

Academic Skills

The category of academic skills represents tasks that are precursors to or are required in order to succeed with school activities. Dependent measures associated with these tasks include preschool activities (e.g., sequencing; identification of colors or letters), fluency, latency, reading, writing, mathematics, science, history, and skills required to study or to perform well on examinations.

Higher Cognitive Functions

Higher cognitive function tasks require complex problem-solving skills outside the social domain. Dependent measures associated with these tasks include critical thinking, IQ, problem-solving, working memory, executive functions, organizational skills, and theory of mind tasks.

Communication Skills

The communication tasks involve verbal or nonverbal signaling to a social partner regarding content of sharing of experiences, emotions, or information, or affecting the partner's behavior, and behaviors that involve understanding a partner's intentional signals for the same purposes. This systematic means of communication involves the use of sounds or symbols. Dependent measures associated with these tasks include requesting, labeling, receptive skills, conversation, greetings, nonverbal skills, expressive skills, syntax, speech, articulation, discourse, vocabulary, and pragmatics.

Personal Responsibility

The category of personal responsibility targets tasks that involve activities which are embedded in everyday routines. Dependent measures associated with these tasks include feeding, sleeping, dressing, toileting, motor skills, cleaning, family and/or community activities, health and fitness, phone skills, time and money management, and self-advocacy.

Interpersonal Skills

The interpersonal tasks that make up this category require social interaction with one or more individuals. Dependent measures associated with these tasks include joint attention, perspective-taking, friendship, social and pretend play, social skills, social engagement, social problem-solving, and appropriate participation in group activities. The area of pragmatics is not included in this list, because it is addressed in the communication section.

Learning Readiness

Learning readiness tasks serve as the foundation for successful mastery of complex skills in other domains. Dependent measures associated with these tasks include imitation, following instructions, sitting skills, attending to environmental sounds, and attention to tasks (which may also be described as "on-task" or "off-task" with the goal of decreasing off-task behavior).

Independent Play and Leisure

The play tasks involve nonacademic and non–work related activities that do not involve self-stimulatory behavior or require interaction with other persons. Dependent measures associated with these tasks include functional independent play (i.e., manipulation of toys to determine how they "work" or appropriate use of toys that do not involve pretense) and use of media (e.g., television, computer, radio, games).

Vocational Skills

The vocational tasks are those required to execute semi-independent or independent work. Dependent measures associated with these tasks include using a timecard, computer skills, monitoring work quality, accepting feedback, safety in the workplace, securing assistance or requesting a break in the workplace (coded as a vocational rather than a communication skill), and adhering to dress code.

■ Focused Intervention I: Individual or Stimuli Required for Intervention Implementation

Controversy within the field of autism is no more evident than when the requisite interventionist involved or the materials required to produce meaningful change are debated. For this reason, the literature involving Focused Interventions I is also described in terms of the individual or the stimuli required for intervention implementation. Specifically, interventions identified in the category Focused Intervention I are parsed into four categories: (a) adult-directed, (b) child-directed, (c) peer-assisted, and (d) technology-assisted.

Adult-Directed Treatments

Adult-directed treatments involve teaching interactions that are initiated by an adult with a predetermined target identified before the interaction begins. Adult-directed interactions do not rely on the involvement of peers and do not require specific external implements for the execution of the intervention. Examples include discrete trial training and precision teaching.

Child-Directed Treatments

Child-directed treatments involve teaching interactions in which the adult waits until an event is initiated by the child with ASD and peers are not involved. The adult may create an environment in which a child is more likely to initiate the interaction, but the adult does not provide the teaching interaction until the child has initiated the event. The teaching interaction may involve either spontaneous targets or predetermined targets reflecting an array of skills deemed to be appropriate for the child's developmental level. Examples include incidental teaching, floor-time, and natural language paradigm.

Peer-Assisted Treatments

Peer-assisted treatments concern teaching interactions that involve peer facilitation. The peer may be highly or loosely directed by adults. Examples include peer tutoring and structured peer play.

Technology-Assisted Treatments

Technology-assisted treatments involve a teaching opportunity that cannot be facilitated without the use of specific external implements, such as computers, videos, musical instruments, pre-identified sensory stimuli, communication boards, the Picture Exchange Communication System (PECS), visual activity schedules, written texts, social stories, scripting, visual supports, and self-monitoring interventions using these stimuli.

Combined Treatments

Finally, combined treatments are coded only if the authors explicitly stated that they had combined two or more of the previous categories (e.g., discrete trial with incidental teaching).

■ Focused Interventions II: Target Behaviors Addressed

Parents, educators, and service providers often find themselves interested in decreasing inappropriate behaviors that interfere with successful acquisition of life skills. Knowing the exact number and quality of studies that have been conducted for a given treatment to decrease these severe problem behaviors may improve the likelihood that an effective intervention will be employed. For this reason, Focused Interventions II (interventions designed to decrease severe problem behaviors) is divided into three general categories: (a) problem behaviors; (b) restricted, repetitive, nonfunctional patterns of behavior, interest, or activity; and (c) sensory and emotional regulation—with several subcategories falling within each general category. By parsing the literature into these components, the National Standards Project allows consumers to more quickly identify the intervention to consider first.

Problem Behaviors

Problem behaviors are those that can harm the individual with ASD or others, result in damage to objects, or interfere with the expected routines in the community. Problem behaviors also may be associated with difficulties with emotional or sensory regulation. They include the following:

- Self-injury—behaviors that directly cause physical harm to one's own body. Examples include head-banging, eye-poking, scratching, and biting.
- Aggression—behaviors that cause physical harm to someone else's body. Examples include scratching, biting, kicking, and hitting.
- Disruptive behaviors—behaviors that interrupt expected school, household, or community routines by distracting others from the present activity. Examples include yelling, throwing oneself on ground, and excessive crying or whining.
- Destruction of property—behaviors that cause harm to material goods. Examples include throwing and kicking objects.
- Hazardous behaviors—behaviors that involve ignoring rules of safety and could indirectly result in harm to oneself. Examples include touching electrical sockets or sources of fire or heat, crossing the street without looking both ways, and climbing onto objects of considerable height, such as a roof.
- Sexually inappropriate behavior—behaviors that fail to comply with laws governing sexual behavior. Examples include public masturbation, exposure of sexual parts to a member of the community, touching the sexual parts of another person without their consent, and public disrobing.

Restricted, Repetitive, Nonfunctional Patterns
of Behavior, Interest, or Activity

This category is reserved for limited, frequently repeated, maladaptive patterns of motor activity, speech, and thought. Symptoms of anxiety (see "Sensory and Emotional Regulation") should be coded in lieu of in this category if persistent thoughts or repetitive acts are clearly established to be causing marked distress to the individual. The following is a list of representative behaviors:

- Stereotypic and compulsive behaviors—restricted, repetitive, maladaptive patterns of behavior or activity with the exclusion of echolalia. Examples include rocking, twirling, toe-walking, finger-flicking, preoccupation with parts of objects, opening and closing doors, turning lights on and off, insistence on sameness or routines, and difficulty with transitions.

- Echolalia—immediate or delayed repetition of an utterance made by another person or source (e.g., movie, television show). Many professionals believe that echolalia should be encouraged to promote functional communication, so this code should be given only when professionals have set decreasing this behavior as a goal.
- Restricted interest—extremely limited interest in topics of conversation or study, as evidenced by *(a)* repeated, socially inappropriate attempts to steer a conversation to a single topic; *(b)* failure to change topic in the presence of clear signs that the listener is not engaged; or *(c)* independent study consistently restricted to one or two domains of interest.

Sensory and Emotional Regulation

Sensory and emotional regulation involves the extent to which an individual can flexibly modify his or her level of arousal or response in order to function effectively in the environment. Problem behaviors may be associated with difficulties with emotional or sensory regulation, but they should be coded only in the problem behaviors section.

- Stimulus refusal—avoidance or refusal to come in contact with specific stimuli (e.g., based on texture, taste, sights, sounds, or odors). Stimulus refusal may or may not be associated with the term "tactile defensive." When a behavior associated with stimulus refusal or the term "tactile defensive" fits one of the preceding categories (i.e., self-injury, aggression, tantrum, destruction of property, stereotypy, echolalia, restricted interest, anxiety, depression, or sexually inappropriate behavior), the article should not be coded as stimulus refusal; rather, it should be coded in the alternative category that matches the behavior of interest.
- Sleep disturbance—impairment in the ability to initiate or maintain sleep that does not meet the definition for depressive symptoms.
- Anxiety—The intense presence of undesirable physiological symptoms (e.g., palpitations, sweating, trembling or shaking; sensations of shortness of breath or smothering, choking, nausea, or abdominal distress; feeling dizzy, unsteady, lightheaded, or faint; paresthesias [numbness or tingling sensations]; chills or hot flashes) or excessive fear or worrying (e.g., fears of losing control, dying, having an agoraphobic attack, being unable to escape, being in contact with a specific stimulus, social situations) consistent with symptoms associated with an anxiety disorder. Examples of disorders associated with anxiety include generalized anxiety disorder, separation anxiety disorder, social phobia, social anxiety disorder, specific phobia, panic disorders with or without agoraphobia, selective mutism, post-traumatic stress disorder, acute stress disorder, anxiety disorder due to a medical

condition or substance use, and anxiety disorder not otherwise specified. Symptoms of obsessive-compulsive disorder should be coded in
this category only if persistent thoughts or repetitive acts are clearly
established to be causing marked distress to the individual; otherwise,
these behaviors should be coded in the "Restricted, Repetitive, Nonfunctional Patterns of Behavior, Interest, or Activity" section.

• Depressive symptoms—Significant symptoms of depression or depressive episode, including depressed mood, diminished interest or pleasure
in everyday activities, weight change unassociated with diet, psychomo-
tor agitation or retardation, fatigue, feelings of worthlessness or excessive
or inappropriate guilt, diminished ability to concentrate or take decisive
action, recurrent thoughts of dying, suicidal ideation or suicidal attempt,
and sleep disturbance (which, if it occurs in isolation, should be coded as
sleep disturbance).

■ Additional Segmentations of the Literature

Treatment Name

Parents, educators, and service providers often hear the name of a new treatment and would like to know more about it. The National Standards Project
allows interested parties to look up the strength of evidence supporting treatment based on the name of the treatment as it was published in the literature.

Age

The literature is also segmented based on the age of the child, using school-age
classification for organization. Specifically, studies are identified in the categories of *(a)* infant/toddler (ages 0–2 years), *(b)* preschool (3–5), *(c)* elementary
school (6–9), *(d)* middle school (10–14), *(e)* high school (15–18), *(f)* early
adult (19–21), or *(g)* mixed age group (i.e., any combination of *a-f*). Under
each of these divisions, the strength of evidence supporting a treatment is
identified based on treatment name.

Diagnosis

Increasingly, parents, educators, and service providers want to learn more
about the best-supported treatments related to a specific disorder on the
autism spectrum. Therefore, the literature is also categorized according to
diagnosis rendered. Specifically, studies are identified as addressing *(a)* autism or autistic disorder, *(b)* Asperger's syndrome, *(c)* pervasive developmental disorder, or *(d)* mixed population. Under each of these diagnostic

classifications, the strength of evidence supporting a treatment is identified based on treatment name.

■ Conclusions

The results of the National Standards Project are expected to be available in the spring of 2008. By organizing the information in a way that reflects the questions and concerns raised by parents, educators, and service providers, it should help promote evidence-based practices. Like its predecessors, the National Standards Project will not escape criticism of the methodology used to evaluate individual articles and the accumulated evidence supporting comprehensive programs or focused interventions. Nevertheless, the effort made to secure input from experts and scholars from across the country, representing diverse fields of study and theoretical orientations, could produce strategies for examining the literature that will prove most useful at this point in time. Necessarily, the results of the National Standards Project will need to be updated to remain of the highest utility to consumers.

Evidence-based practice requires the integration of research-supported treatments with data-based clinical judgment and decision making, as well as family values concerning treatment (Sackett et al. 2000). The results of the National Standards Project should be interpreted within this context. Those interventions that hold strongest or strong levels of research support after completion of the National Standards Project should be given greatest consideration when selecting treatments. There may be times when a convincing rationale for using interventions that do not have this level of research support is made. For example, interventions with the highest level of research support may not be sustainable in the treatment environment, and urgent action may be necessary while staff build capacity to provide the most effective treatments. In such situations, professionals face some tough decisions. Some service providers may be ethically bound to remove themselves from the case if, for example, a discredited intervention is selected. In addition, service providers may need to educate staff about the importance of collecting frequent data so that decisions about whether to "stay the course" can be made rapidly. Finally, many providers will need to systematically build capacity for provision of the best-supported interventions through training of staff and administrators.

Although the National Standards Project provides identification of treatments that have the highest levels of research support, service providers must find ways of incorporating family values about treatment into decision making as well. Family values should always be solicited. If multiple treatment options are equally effective for the target behaviors, it stands to reason that the intervention most consistent with the family's values should be selected. In some cases, service providers may need to educate families about various treatment options, because family values about treatments may be influenced by marketing or "word of mouth" and would change in the face of informed data. Not surprisingly, the three tenets of evidence-based practice (research, clinical judgment, and family values) can come into conflict with each other, and service providers must give careful consideration to each tenet as they promote evidence-based practice.

■ References

American Psychological Association. (2003). *Report of the Task Force on Evidence-Based Interventions in School Psychology.* Available at http://www.sp-ebi.org/documents/_workingfiles/EBImanual1.pdf (accessed October 26, 2007).

American Psychological Association. (2005). *Report of the 2005 Presidential Task Force on Evidence-Based Practice.* Available at http://www.apa.org/practice/ebpreport.pdf (accessed October 26, 2007).

American Psychiatric Association. (2005). *Diagnostic and statistical manual of mental disorders* (4th ed, text revision). Washington, D.C.: American Psychiatric Association.

Centers for Disease Control and Prevention. (2001). *Autism Information Center, Division of the Department of Health and Human Services.* Available at http://www.cdc.gov/ncbddd/autism/ (accessed October 26, 2007).

Chambless, D.L., Baker, M.J., Baucom, D.H., Beutler, L., Calhoun, K.S., Crits-Christoph, P., Daiuto, A., DeRubeis, R., Detweiler, J., Haaga, D.A.F., Bennett Johnson, S., McCurry, S., Mueser, K.T., Pope, K.S., Sanderson, W.C., Shoham, V., Strickle, T., Williams, D.A., and Woody, S.R. (1998). Update on empirically validated therapies: II. *The Clinical Psychologist,* 51 (1), 3–16.

Green, G. (1999). Science and ethics in early intervention for autism. In *Autism: Behavior analytic perspectives* (eds. P.M. Ghezzi, W.L. Williams, and J.E. Carr), pp. 11–28). Reno, Nev.: Context Press.

Horner, R.H., Carr, E.G., Halle, J., McGee, G., Odom, N., and Wolery, M. (2005). The use of single-subject research to identify evidence-based practice in special education. *Exceptional Children,* 71, 165–179.

Maine Administrators of Services for Children with Disabilities. (2000). *Report of the MADSEC Autism Task Force.* Available at http://www.madsec.org/docs/ATFReport.doc (accessed October 26, 2007).

National Research Council. (2001). *Educating children with autism.* Committee on Educational Interventions for Children with Autism, Division of Behavioral and Social Sciences and Education. Washington, D.C.: National Academy Press.

New York State Department of Health Early Intervention Program. (1999). *Clinical practice guideline: Report of the recommendations. Autism/pervasive developmental disorders: Assessment and intervention for young children (age 0–3 years*). Albany, NY: New York State Department of Health Early Intervention Program.

Sackett, D.L., Straus, S.E., Richardson, W.S., Rosenberg, W., and Haynes, R.B. (2000). *Evidence-based medicine: How to practice and teach EBM* (2nd ed). New York: Churchill Livingstone.

West, S., King, V., Carey, T.S., Lohr, K.N., McKoy, N., Sutton, S.F., and Lux, L. (2002). *Systems to rate the strength of scientific evidence.* Evidence Report/Technology Assessment No. 47. Prepared by the Research Triangle Institute–University of North Carolina Evidence-Based Practice Center under Contract No. 290–97–0011. (AHRQ Publication No. 02-E016.) Rockville, Md.: Agency for Healthcare Research and Quality.

World Health Organization. (1990). *The ICD-10 classification of diseases and related health problems* (10th revision). Geneva: WHO.

4. SINGLE-CASE RESEARCH METHODOLOGY TO INFORM EVIDENCE-BASED PRACTICE

David P. Wacker, Wendy K. Berg, and Jay W. Harding

Applied behavior analysts have established a long history of developing and evaluating successful interventions for persons who have autism (Ferster and Demeyer 1961). In large part, this success is based on a two-part rule: "Do good and take data" (Risley 2001, 267). As discussed by Baer and colleagues (1968), there are two critical dimensions of the procedures used by applied behavior analysts: they should be effective, and they should be analytical. By "effective," they meant that the procedures should lead to a socially meaningful change in behavior. By "analytical," they meant that the procedures should show why behavior changed. Single-case designs provide a methodology for establishing this evidence by demonstrating the effects of independent variables (IVs) that are responsible for changes in the target behavior or dependent variable (DV). Through the process of establishing evidence, effective technologies are developed for changing behavior in socially meaningful ways.

This chapter first presents a brief overview of single-case designs and then describes the use of representative designs with persons diagnosed with developmental disabilities. For each design, we provide case examples from both our existing research programs (Berg et al. 2003; Wacker et al. 2004) and the extant literature. The intent is to show how lawful relations between IVs and DVs can be evaluated to inform evidence-based practice.

■ Overview of Single-Case Designs

This summary of single-case designs can highlight only their fundamental characteristics. Numerous reference materials are available for more in-depth investigation, including a monograph, *Methodological and Conceptual Issues in Applied Behavior Analysis* (Iwata et al. 2000), published by the *Journal of Applied Behavior Analysis*. Further descriptions and applications of these designs have been published by Pierce and Epling (1995) and Kennedy (2005), and the conceptual basis of the designs was discussed by Johnston and Pennypacker (1993).

Experimental designs are used to show validity. As Baer (2001) discussed, experimental designs increase our understanding of why changes in behavior occur by testing a specific explanation or hypothesis. Validity is established by showing that the IVs hypothesized to alter behavior are, in fact, responsible for changes that occur in behavior. If we can show that specified IVs reliably produce changes in target behavior, we have demonstrated experimental control. In applied behavior analysis, experimental control is referred to as *functional control,* because we are showing a functional relation between IVs in the environment (e.g., specific classes or applications of reinforcement) and changes in a response (e.g., self-injury, manding).

Single-case designs are used to demonstrate experimental control with each individual who is evaluated. As Kennedy (2005) discussed, the goal is to provide evidence that the IV (e.g., the intervention) produced a change in behavior for the individual, not to show how a group, in general, responded to the IV. Therefore, internal validity (Campbell and Stanley, 1966) is a critical component that distinguishes single-case designs from case studies.

Internal Validity

Internal validity refers to the ability to attribute changes in behavior to the IV and not to extraneous variables. Case studies often show substantial behavioral change, but the results may be correlational. For example, a student's behavior may be shown to improve with intervention by observing how the student performed before the intervention (condition A) and then during the intervention (condition B). This demonstration of behavioral change from A to B may be substantial and may be valid, but validity cannot be established because of the correlational features of this type of assessment. Behavior change was *correlated* with a change of conditions from A to B, but this constitutes only a necessary, not a sufficient, demonstration of a functional relation. That is, we cannot say with certainty that the intervention was responsible for the student's behavior change.

Replication

To demonstrate a functional relation, behavior change must be replicated. Replication can take many forms, but the critical component is that the change in behavior observed from condition A to condition B is replicated at least once. Replication shows that the variability in behavior was orderly or lawful and can be attributed to the specified IV rather than to extraneous variables such as practice, time in assessment, or changes in the environment unrelated to the IV. Replication of the A and B conditions provides a better demonstration of control over behavior and functions, similar to the use of a control group or placebo condition in group designs.

All single-case designs involve evaluations of how behavior changes when A is changed to B (and perhaps to C, to D, and so on, with each letter representing a change or alteration in the hypothesized IV). Given that replicated changes in behavior between the A and B conditions provide the basis for validity, it is critical to carefully consider both conditions. The A condition represents a control condition for B and is composed of two essential features. First, A represents how behavior would persist in the absence of intervention (i.e., baseline) or during the current procedures. To prove that the change in the behavior is attributable to B, the behavior must show stability in terms of its level, trend, or variability. If stability is not achieved with A (e.g., if improvement in behavior occurs during A), then changes in behavior that occur with B may not be attributable to the specified IV. Second, the IV hypothesized to control behavior—the variable changed during B—must be carefully observed and recorded during A. Observation of both the target response and the variables functioning as IVs should be recorded and analyzed as precisely during A as during B.

When A changes to B, all variables except the hypothesized IV should be held constant. If all other variables are held constant, changes in behavior can be attributed to the change in IV. This may be a change in a single variable (e.g., attention is provided), alteration of an existing IV (e.g., the schedule of attention is varied), or changes in a package of variables (e.g., the addition of prompts to request attention, a denser schedule of attention, and a time-out procedure).

In most cases, replication is achieved in one of three ways. First, following changes in behavior from A to B, the A condition is repeated, as in a reversal design. If behavior returns to its previous level, trend, or variability, replication has been achieved and experimental control is demonstrated. In applied contexts, a second B phase is then also conducted if improvement in behavior occurred during the initial B condition.

Second, changes from A to B can be replicated concurrently, as in a multielement design. Changes from A to B occur rapidly (e.g., with each session), and each time B is conducted, behavior changes. This is the tactic used by most researchers who conduct functional analyses of problem behavior (Iwata et al. 1982/1994). Rather than attempting to achieve steady-state responding in A, then in B, and so on, in a sequential manner, the multielement design shows stable changes in behavior each time the IV is altered, either randomly or in a counterbalanced manner, with one or more other conditions. If changes in behavior occur reliably each time B is provided, then a relative difference in behavior has been shown to occur between A and B.

A third form of replication occurs when the change in behavior between A and B can be demonstrated across stimulus contexts, such as across different persons (e.g., teachers) or settings (e.g., classrooms), as in a multiple baseline design. In this case, the change from A to B in each context is conducted sequentially (e.g., three sessions in the first context, eight sessions in the next context, and so on) to show that changes in behavior occur only with changes in IVs. For example, if behavior improves with increased attention (B) in one classroom but remains stable in a second classroom, then the B condition can be conducted in the second classroom to determine whether the changes observed in the first classroom will be replicated.

■ Single-Case Design Options

Multiple versions of single-case designs permit us to match the design to the question we are attempting to answer about behavior. Each version of these designs provides replication and demonstration of experimental control; the selection of one design option over another in applied contexts in often more a matter of preference than of validity. In other situations, practical issues or hypotheses about the behavior provide direction for selecting a design. For example, some changes in behavior should not be reversed (e.g., aggression toward peers) or are not hypothesized to be reversible (e.g., learning a new skill). In other situations, the B condition may be similar to the A condition (e.g., changes in schedules of attention), and it is hypothesized that the participant may not discriminate the changes from A to B if these conditions change in a rapid fashion. To determine which option to select for any given evaluation, consider the effects that are hypothesized, and then choose a design option that both answers the questions and is practical given the situation and the expected outcomes.

The following sections describe several types of single-case designs: reversal, multiple baseline, multielement, and concurrent schedules designs. Exemplars of each type were selected from our current research to show the variety of design options available and the reasons why a specific option might be selected.

Reversal Designs

Reversal designs are the most direct method for evaluating the effects of an IV on a DV. In its simplest form, a reversal design involves measuring the DV while systematically introducing and removing the IV. The first phase of a reversal design is usually a baseline condition, which continues until stable responding for the DV is observed across sessions. Conducting repeated observations of the DV when the IV is absent provides a sample of what the DV might look like if the IV were not implemented. The IV is implemented in the next phase of the design (B), and repeated observations are conducted to determine whether the DV changed in comparison to the measures taken during baseline (A). After a consistent pattern of responding is achieved, the IV is removed, and additional baseline sessions are conducted. If the changes in behavior observed from A to B are a result of the effects of the IV rather than other extraneous factors, the DV should return to levels similar to those observed in the initial baseline condition. Although an A-B-A design is often acceptable for demonstrating that an IV affected behavior, repeating the B phase of the design (i.e., re-introducing the IV) is done in applied situations to end the evaluation with effective treatment.

Shabani and colleagues (2002) used a reversal design (A-B-A-B) to evaluate the effects of using a vibrating pager to prompt three children with autism to initiate verbal interactions with same-age peers in the context of play. During the initial baseline sessions, observers recorded the occurrence of verbal initiations and verbal responses for each participant during 10-minute sessions in which the participants and same-age peers were in the same play area with a variety of toys. No prompts to initiate verbal exchanges were provided to participants during the baseline phase. After completion of the baseline observations, a vibrating pager was placed in each participant's pocket, and the participants were taught to initiate verbal exchanges with a therapist each time the pager vibrated. After each participant demonstrated independent initiations of a verbal exchange when the pager vibrated, training was discontinued, and the participants wore the vibrating pager in the play area with same-age peers. This tactile prompt phase was conducted in the same manner as the baseline phase, except that the vibrating pagers were present and set to vibrate at least once every 25 seconds. No additional prompts or programmed consequences were provided during this phase of the evaluation.

The results of the study of Shabani and colleagues (2002) for one participant, Mike, are shown in Figure 4.1. During the initial baseline conditions, Mike engaged in verbal initiations (closed data points) in fewer than 20% of the intervals for each session. With the introduction of the IV (vibrating pager, labeled "tactile prompt" in Figure 4.1), Mike's engagement in verbal initiations increased to an average of 75% of the intervals. To determine whether the increase in verbal initiations was caused by the presence of the vibrating pager or by the training session that occurred before that condition, the vibrating pagers were removed and the baseline condition was repeated. As shown in Figure 4.1, Mike's engagement in verbal initiations decreased to fewer than 20% of the session intervals. When the vibrating pagers were returned, Mike's engagement in verbal initiations increased to the level observed in the first tactile prompt phase.

Shabani and colleagues (2002) also recorded the occurrences of the participants' verbal responses (open data points in Figure 4.1) to verbal initiations from their peers. For Mike, the introduction of the vibrating pager in the first tactile prompt phase resulted in an increase in verbal responses from the

EFFECTS OF A TACTILE PROMPT

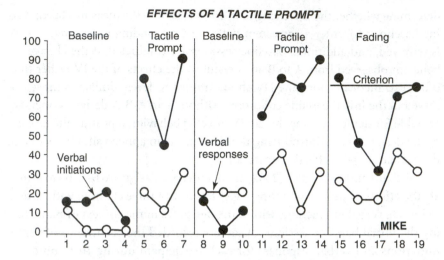

FIGURE 4.1. Example of reversal design. This study evaluated the effects of vibrating pagers on verbal interactions. (See text for details.) From Shabani, D.B., Katz, R.C., Wilder, D.A., Beauchamp, K., Taylor, C.R., and Fischer, K.J. (2002). Increasing social initiations in children with autism: Effects of a tactile prompt. *Journal of Applied Behavior Analysis, 35,* 79–83.

baseline condition. However, when the vibrating pager was removed, Mike continued to engage in verbal responses at a level similar to the level observed during the tactile prompt phase. In this case, the DV of verbal responses did not increase and decrease reliably with the introduction and removal of the vibrating pager. As a result, a functional relation between the presence of the vibrating pager and the occurrence of verbal responses was not shown for Mike. In a final phase of the investigation, the experimenters reduced the frequency of the pager's vibrations to prompt Mike to engage in verbal initiations at a level similar to levels of verbal exchanges observed for same-age peers.

The results of the A-B-A-B design for Mike showed that, after training, the vibrating pager reliably increased the occurrence of Mike's verbal initiations in comparison to the verbal initiations observed during the two baseline conditions when the pager was absent. In other words, the design showed a functional relation between the presence of the vibrating pager and the occurrence of verbal initiations. Mike's engagement in verbal responses also increased with the introduction of the vibrating pager after the completion of training. However, the occurrence of verbal responses did not decrease when the pager was removed for the second phase of baseline observation. These results suggest that factors other than the presence of the vibrating pager influenced the occurrence of verbal responses from Mike. Two potential factors are *(a)* an increase in Mike's skills during the training sessions that occurred between the end of the first baseline phase and the introduction of the tactile prompt phase, and *(b)* the naturally occurring reinforcement that may have occurred as Mike's verbal responses extended his social exchanges with same-age peers. These two potential factors highlight one of the limitations of the reversal design. The introduction of the IV may produce durable changes in the DV that are not reversible (e.g., if the IV is associated with skill acquisition). Such results are usually desirable from a clinical standpoint but limit the utility of the reversal design in determining the effects of the IV on the DV.

Case Example with Lucy: Use of a Microswitch

A reversal design (A-B-C-B-C-B-C) was used by Harding and associates (2005) to evaluate the effects of child positioning on the independent use of a microswitch and the occurrence of self-injury during functional communication training (FCT). Lucy, aged 3 years 5 months, was diagnosed with severe developmental delays and visual impairment; she engaged in self-injury (hand-biting, eye-pressing). Although an initial functional analysis was inconclusive (i.e., self-injury was elevated across all test conditions), a subsequent choice assessment indicated that Lucy consistently chose to activate a musical toy. An FCT program was conducted by Lucy's mother at home to teach her to request music by touching a microswitch. In this program, Lucy was placed in a prone position on the floor and was given physical assistance to touch a microswitch. Attempts to engage in self-injury were blocked and resulted in the termination of music.

The tangible condition (condition A) from Lucy's functional analysis was used as a baseline. During condition B (FCT: prone position), Lucy initially displayed a reduction in self-injury but required frequent physical assistance to activate the microswitch. The investigators probed a second treatment condition, condition C (FCT: supported), in which Lucy was placed in a seated position between her mother's legs. Self-injury remained low, but Lucy's independent use of the microswitch increased. A reversal to condition B resulted in a decrease in Lucy's independent use of the microswitch. The investigators conducted additional replications of this reversal to demonstrate experimental control. The results indicated that self-injury was reduced from baseline levels across both conditions, but Lucy's independent use of the microswitch remained highest in condition C.

Case Example with Jacob: Reducing Self-Injury and Stereotypy

Jacob, a 5-year old boy with autism and mental retardation, engaged in self-injurious and stereotypical behaviors to the exclusion of engaging in adaptive activities, such as playing with toys. We conducted a series of baseline sessions in which Jacob had access to preferred toys and attention with no contingencies for problem behavior (noncontingent reinforcement, or NCR). After steady responding was achieved in the baseline condition, we introduced a differential reinforcement (DR) treatment in which Jacob gained access to preferred toys and attention contingent on completing a small work task without engaging in problem behavior. Jacob was allowed to maintain access to the toys and attention as long as problem behavior did not occur. Problem behavior resulted in the re-introduction of the work task. The introduction of the DR treatment resulted in a consistent reduction in problem behavior for Jacob. To determine whether the reduction in behavior was caused by the DR contingency or by extraneous variables, we removed the contingency and repeated the NCR baseline condition. The NCR condition resulted in an increase in problem behavior. The DR contingency was re-introduced, and Jacob's behavior decreased to levels observed during the original DR treatment phase.

Multiple Baseline Designs

The multiple baseline design provides an alternative method to evaluate the effects of an IV on behavior when the effects of the IV may not be reversible or a reversal to baseline levels of behavior is not acceptable. The multiple baseline design begins with a baseline phase in which the IV is absent. The baseline phase is conducted across two or three situations in which the DV is of interest. For example, if a child engages in problem behavior across settings (e.g., home, classroom, playground), the problem behavior can be measured across the different settings. The baseline condition is continued within each situation until stable responding is observed within at least one of the settings. The IV is introduced in that setting while baseline conditions continue in the remaining settings. Sessions with the IV are continued until a stable pattern of behavior emerges, and the IV is then introduced in the next setting. After stable responding is observed in the second setting, the IV is introduced in the third setting.

A functional relation between the IV and DV is demonstrated to the degree that (a) occurrences of the DV remain steady within each baseline setting until the IV is introduced and (b) the DV changes reliably with the introduction of the IV in that setting. One advantage of the multiple baseline design is that the intervention does not need to be removed to demonstrate a functional relation. Two disadvantages of the design are that the baseline condition is extended before the IV is introduced in each situation, and the introduction of the IV in one situation may affect the DV in another situation. For example, if the IV is introduced in a classroom setting while baseline conditions continue on the playground, the changes observed in the DV in the classroom may generalize to the playground.

Marckel, Neef, and Ferreri (2006) used a multiple baseline design to evaluate the effects of teaching two children with autism to use multiple descriptor symbols to request items when a Picture Exchange Communication System (PECS) symbol for the specific item was not available. Before the beginning of the baseline condition, a group of preferred items was identified for each child, and the PECS symbol for each preferred item was removed from the child's PECS book. During baseline sessions, one preferred item was placed on a table in front of the child, and the child was instructed to request the item using the remaining pictures from his PECS book. Baseline sessions were conducted across three sets of descriptor symbols: pictures showing functions (e.g., eat, drink, read); colors; and shapes. Selection of the PECS descriptor symbols was the DV. The purpose of the baseline condition was to determine whether the child would select a descriptor symbol that matched the object on the table (e.g., a symbol for the function "eat" to request a sandwich).

The top panel of Figure 4.2 shows the number of function descriptors selected independently by one participant, Khan, during baseline (BL, left side of panel) and during training (right side of panel). Khan's baseline and training results for the remaining two descriptor symbols (colors and shapes) are shown in the middle and bottom panels of Figure 4.2, respectively. Khan's selection of descriptors ranged from 0 to 5 during baseline. Training for selecting a symbol that matched the function of the preferred item was initiated for Khan while baseline conditions continued for the remaining two sets of descriptor symbols. Khan's selection of function symbols increased steadily with the introduction of training, but his selection of color and shape symbols remained unchanged. Training was then introduced for selecting the color symbol that corresponded with the item on the table. Khan's selection of color symbols increased dramatically with the introduction of training, but his selection of shape symbols remained at or near zero occurrences. Training was then initiated with the shape symbols, and Khan's selection of these symbols increased with the first session of training. Khan's results show that *(a)* he did not independently select alternative descriptors to request items before training and *(b)* training was effective in increasing his selection of alternative descriptor symbols.

Case Example with Al: Evaluation of Functional
Communication Training Across Behavioral Functions

A multiple baseline design combined with a multielement design was used by Lee and associates (2003) to evaluate treatment effects across multiple topographies of problem behavior. Al, aged 3 years 10 months, had been diagnosed with mental retardation, and he displayed property destruction, self-injury, and noncompliance. An initial functional analysis conducted in Al's home was inconclusive; problem behavior was elevated across all conditions. A multiple baseline design was used during FCT to further evaluate whether behavior was responsive to social reinforcement.

Extended baseline sessions were conducted across functional analysis escape, tangible, and attention conditions; in this way, each tier of the multiple baseline design evaluated a different behavioral function. An initial

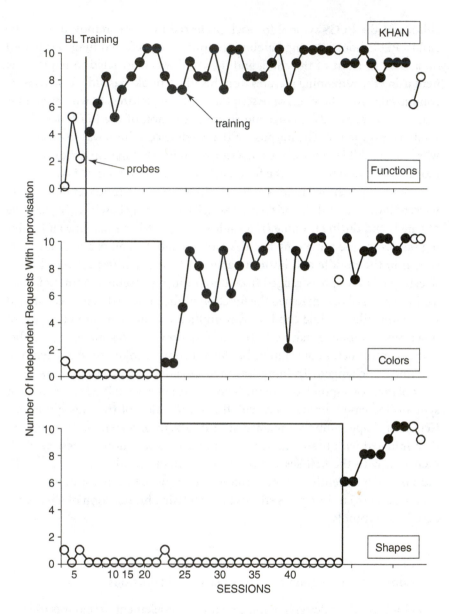

FIGURE 4.2. Example of multiple baseline design. This study evaluated the use of descriptor symbols to request items. (See text for details.) From Marckel, J.M., Neef, N.A., and Ferreri, S.J. (2006). A preliminary analysis of teaching improvisation with the picture exchange communication system to children with autism. *Journal of Applied Behavior Analysis*, 39, 109–115.

FCT program for escape was implemented by Al's mother, to teach him to follow directions and request a break, while baseline sessions in the tangible and attention conditions were continued. Following a reduction in disruptive behavior during the first FCT program, a second FCT program was conducted to teach Al to request tangibles (preferred toys) while baseline sessions in attention were continued. After a reduction in disruptive behavior during FCT for tangibles was demonstrated, a third program was initiated to teach Al to request his mother's attention. The multiple baseline design demonstrated that *(a)* disruptive behavior was maintained by escape and tangible reinforcement, whereas destructive behavior was maintained by parent attention; and *(b)* the systematic introduction of FCT for each behavioral function resulted in a reduction across problem behaviors.

Case Example with Sean: Effects of Two Versions of Treatment

Sean, a 20-year-old man who was blind and had mental retardation, engaged in two forms of self-injury that were both maintained by automatic reinforcement. A multiple baseline design was used to compare the effects of two potential treatments on Sean's engagement in self-injury. The first treatment, noncontingent access to a preferred leisure item (NCR), was implemented across three different sets of leisure items (a ball, a ribbon, and a group of items including the ball and ribbon). A DR treatment plan, in which access to the leisure item was contingent on the absence of self-injury, was introduced for the ball while NCR baseline conditions continued for the ribbon and the group of items. After a reduction in self-injury was observed with the ball, the DR contingencies were introduced for the second leisure item (ribbon). The introduction of the DR contingency resulted in a substantial reduction in one form of self-injury but did not reduce the occurrence of the remaining behavior. When the DR contingencies were introduced for the set of leisure items, both forms of self-injury decreased to zero. The multiple baseline provided a method for evaluating the effects of the DR contingencies across different leisure items. The results showed that the DR contingency was effective when the ball was available, either in isolation or as part of a group of leisure items. However, the contingencies were effective in reducing only one form of self-injury with the ribbon.

Multielement Designs

In a multielement design, two or more conditions are alternated to demonstrate experimental control (Kennedy 2005). The purpose of the design is to evaluate whether a response occurs differentially across conditions, in order to identify a functional relation. In its simplest form, the investigator alternates between conditions A and B across multiple sessions. If the response occurred at different levels during the two conditions (i.e., responding was differentiated), then functional control was demonstrated.

The multielement design is particularly useful in comparing multiple experimental conditions. Peyton, Lindauer, and Richman (2005) conducted a three-phase study to evaluate the variables that controlled a young girl's noncompliant vocal behavior (NVB). Figure 4.3 shows the multielement designs that were used in this investigation. Suzie, aged 10, was diagnosed with autism and developmental delays and engaged in NVB. During phase 1, a functional analysis (Iwata et al. 1982/1994) was conducted within a multielement design to identify the maintaining conditions for her NVB. In this analysis, Suzie's NVB was compared across escape, attention, alone, and free-play conditions. During phase 2, the researchers compared two conditions: (a) demands without removal of task materials and (b) demands with removal of task materials. In phase 3, they assessed the effects of nondirective and directive prompts.

The results of phase 1 of the study by Peyton and colleagues (2005) are shown in the top panel of Figure 4.3 and demonstrate a functional relation between Suzie's NVBs per minute and the escape condition. That is, Suzie's NVB occurred at higher levels during the escape condition in comparison to the free play or other test conditions. During phase 2, the authors analyzed both NVBs per minute and percent compliance across the task removal and no task removal conditions. Results showed that rates of NVB were similar during the conditions (i.e., the behavior was not differentiated), and rates of compliance were relatively high across conditions. Phase 3 showed that NVB occurred at high rates in the directive prompts condition compared with near-zero rates in the nondirective prompts condition (i.e., the behavior was differentiated), although rates of compliance remained similar.

Case Example with Susan 1: A Functional Analysis Showing a Social Function

A functional analysis conducted by Harding and coworkers (1999) used a multielement design to identify the maintaining conditions for problem behavior. The participant, Susan, was 4 years 3 months old. Susan was diagnosed with autism and developmental delays and engaged in aggressive behavior, self-injury, and tantrums. All procedures were conducted in Susan's home, using her mother as the therapist. During the functional analysis, the investigator compared escape, attention, and free play conditions. The results showed that Susan engaged in high levels of problem behavior to escape from nonpreferred tasks. In contrast, problem behavior occurred at relatively low levels during the free play and attention conditions. Thus, the multielement design demonstrated a social function for Susan's problem behavior: negative reinforcement.

Case Example with Madison: Evaluation of an Automatic Function

Madison, an 11-year-old girl with severe mental retardation, engaged in self-injury when she was left alone in a room but not during times in which she was engaged in activities with her family. We hypothesized that Madison engaged in self-injury while she was alone for one of two possible reasons: (a) the only time that she could engage in the behavior without interruption was when

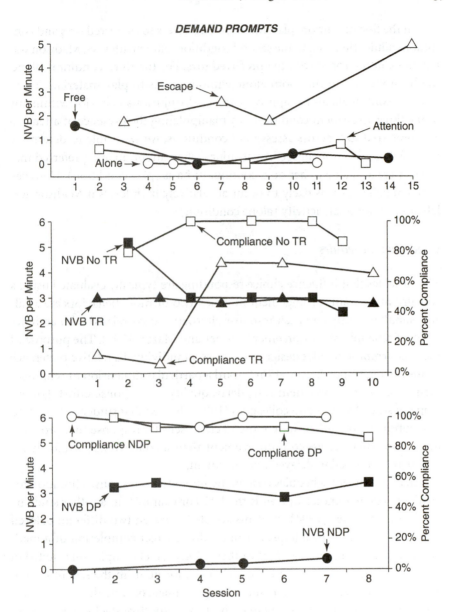

FIGURE 4.3. Example of multielement design. This study evaluated noncompliant verbal behavior. (See text for details.) From Peyton, R.T., Lindauer, S.E., and Richman, D.M. (2005). The effects of directive and nondirective prompts on noncompliant vocal behavior exhibited by a child with autism. *Journal of Applied Behavior Analysis*, 38, 251–255.

she was alone or *(b)* other, more-preferred activities were not immediately available to her when she was alone. We conducted three assessment conditions that varied according to the presence of attention and access to preferred activities within a multielement design to evaluate the effects of attention and preferred toys on Madison's behavior.

In the first condition, play, Madison had access to preferred toys and continuous adult attention. In the second condition, alone with toys, Madison was left alone in the room with the preferred toys. For the third condition, alone, Madison was left in the room alone without access to play materials. There were no contingencies for appropriate or self-injurious behavior within any of the three assessment conditions. By manipulating the presence of attention and preferred toys across assessment conditions, we were able to determine that Madison did not engage in self-injury when attention and preferred materials were available to her on a continuous basis (play condition). However, problem behavior was likely to occur at relatively high levels if Madison was left alone without an activity (alone condition).

Concurrent Schedules

The variables that influence choice responding are typically evaluated using a concurrent-operants arrangement in which two or more behaviors are available simultaneously and each response alternative is correlated with an independent schedule of reinforcement (Fisher and Mazur, 1997). The purpose of the concurrent schedules design is to assess an individual's relative preference by measuring response allocation toward a particular dimension of reinforcement, such as reinforcement rate, delay, quality, or response effort. For example, a study by Neef and colleagues (1993) showed that students diagnosed as emotionally disturbed were more likely to select a response that provided more immediate access to reinforcement than a concurrently available response that resulted in delayed reinforcement.

In a concurrent schedules design, the individual's response allocation toward a particular choice option is the DV. For example, in another study by Neef and associates (1994), students selected between two different colored stacks of arithmetic problems. For one color, correct completion of a math problem resulted in money; for the other color, correct completion resulted in "program money," which could be exchanged for items in the school's token economy. The investigators measured the percentage of time during each session that each student allocated to each of the respective stacks. Results were displayed to show the individuals' choice responding and, thus, their relative preference between the two reinforcers (i.e., actual money or token money). A higher allocation toward one option over the other would demonstrate that their responding was controlled by a particular outcome.

Concurrent operants arrangements have been used to evaluate an individual's relative preference between concurrently available items or activities (e.g., Fisher et al. 1992). This approach has also demonstrated that this relative preference for items or activities can be used to predict the reinforcement value of those same stimuli (Piazza et al. 1996). That is, a highly preferred item is more likely to be an effective reinforcer for target behavior than a less preferred item.

Although concurrent operants procedures may indicate a relative preference for specific reinforcer dimensions across available alternatives, they are most often used in combination with another single-case design to demonstrate a functional relation. A number of investigations have used a concurrent operants paradigm in combination with a reversal design to demonstrate how manipulating dimensions of reinforcement can used to reduce problem behavior that is maintained by negative reinforcement (Harding et al. 1999; Hoch et al. 2002; Horner and Day 1991; Peck et al. 1996).

Hoch's group (2002) evaluated the effects of concurrent schedules of reinforcement with three children diagnosed with autism who displayed problem behavior maintained by negative reinforcement. Figure 4.4 shows a combination of concurrent operants, A-B-A-B reversal design, and maintenance probes with one participant. Mickey, aged 9, was diagnosed with autism and engaged in aggressive behavior. In condition A (no reinforcement), Mickey was presented with a worksheet. A blank sheet of paper covered all except one problem. If he completed a problem on the worksheet, the next problem was revealed. No programmed contingencies (i.e., no positive or negative reinforcements) were provided for task completion. Concurrently, if Mickey engaged in aggression, the task was removed and Mickey received a 60-second time-out (negative reinforcement). In condition B (negative reinforcement/preferred activities), completing one problem resulted in a 60-second break from his work and access to preferred activities. Aggressive behavior again resulted in removal of the task and a 60-second time-out.

Figure 4.4 shows the responses per minute of aggression and percentage of tasks completed. During the first, no reinforcement (NO SR) condition, Mickey engaged in high rates of aggressive behavior and did not complete any tasks. During the negative reinforcement/preferred activities (SR−/PA) condition, aggressive behavior dropped to zero or near-zero rates, and Mickey completed almost all of his tasks. During a reversal to the NO SR condition, aggression and task completion were variable. In the return to the SR−/PA condition, aggression decreased and task completion increased. In a final phase (maintenance), response requirements were gradually increased, and Mickey was provided with a leaner schedule of reinforcement. He continued to display reduced levels of aggression and high levels of task completion. Notably, escape extinction was not in place during any of these conditions; Mickey could "escape" from his work by either engaging in aggression or completing his work task.

Case Example with Susan: Assessing the Role of Attention in Escape-Maintained Problem Behavior

An investigation by Harding and colleagues (1999) demonstrated how positive and negative reinforcement influenced time allocation between two

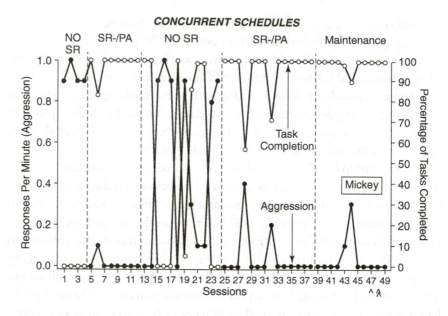

FIGURE 4.4. Example of concurrent schedules design combined with a reversal design. This study evaluated task completion under contrasting reinforcement schedules. (See text for details.) From Hoch, H., McComas, J.J., Thompson, A.L., and Paone, D. (2002). Concurrent reinforcement schedules: Behavior change and maintenance without extinction. *Journal of Applied Behavior Analysis*, 35, 155–169.

concurrently available choice options. Susan, who was described in the previous section, engaged in problem behavior that was maintained by negative reinforcement. In condition A, Susan could move freely between two choice areas. In one area, she played alone with a less preferred toy (Alone/LP); in the other area, she received task instructions from her mother with a highly preferred toy (I/HP). In condition B, Susan could play alone with a highly preferred toy (Alone/HP) or receive instructions with a less preferred toy (I/LP).

The results showed that when parent instructions were paired with a highly preferred toy (condition A), Susan was likely to allocate her time to this choice option. In contrast, during condition B, Susan was more likely to avoid instructions with a less preferred toy and allocated her time to playing alone with a highly preferred toy. Moreover, Susan was more likely to complete tasks with a highly preferred toy, and her problem behavior gradually decreased across both of the choice conditions. In this example, the concurrent schedules design showed the variables that controlled Susan's time allocation and task completion. This information was used to develop a treatment program that was successful in reducing Susan's problem behavior and increasing her compliance to parent requests with less preferred activities.

Case Example with Ned: Assessing Preferred Stimuli

Ned was a 9-year old boy with Down syndrome and autism who played with string to the exclusion of engaging in other, more appropriate activities. The results of a functional analysis indicated that playing with string was reinforcing in itself and was not maintained by social consequences, such as gaining attention or escaping nonpreferred activities. An additional phase of assessment, concurrent schedules, was conducted in an attempt to identify stimuli that would be of relatively greater value (more highly preferred) to Ned than maintaining access to the string. If we could identify an item that was more preferred than string, then we could use that item to reinforce the absence of string play with Ned.

The observation room was divided into two areas, an alone side and an alternative stimuli side. The alone side contained a few pieces of string but no other leisure or work materials. The stimuli contained on the alternative side of the room varied across concurrent operant conditions. In one condition, the alternative side of the room contained Ned's mother and play materials. In other conditions, the alternative side contained leisure items without an adult present, Ned's mother (attention) without leisure items, or Ned's mother and work materials. If Ned entered the side of the room with the alternative stimuli, the stimuli were provided to him on a noncontingent basis. If Ned entered the alone side of the room, he was allowed to play with the string without interruption, but access to attention and leisure or work materials was withheld as long as he remained on that side of the room. Ned chose the side of the room that contained attention and access to toys for 9 out of 10 sessions, and he chose the side of the room that contained only toys for 6 of 8 sessions. These results showed that gaining access to attention and toys was more preferred for Ned than gaining access to string.

■ Summary

In this chapter, we provided case examples from the literature and from our ongoing research representing four single-case designs: reversal, multiple baseline, multielement, and concurrent schedules. These examples showed how the designs could be used to answer various questions. Sometimes these questions were addressed with a single design and sometimes with a combination of designs (e.g., Susan).

We provided an overview of rules that are used in constructing the designs, but we also hoped to show that the designs can be dynamic. For example, with Susan, when a negative reinforcement function was identified within a multielement design, we further evaluated the role of attention during demands within a concurrent schedules design. Single-case designs can be combined or constructed in a sequential manner to address questions that may arise during an initial evaluation. Ongoing treatment represents an ongoing phase of evaluation. Even when treatment is shown to be effective initially, the role of evaluation continues as we seek to show not only the effectiveness of treatment but also why the treatment was effective.

■ References

Baer, D.M. (2001). A small matter of proof. In *A history of the behavioral therapies* (eds. W. Donohue, D. Henderson, S. Hayes, J. Fisher, and L. Hayes), pp. 252–265. Reno, Nev.: Context Press.

Baer, D.M., Wolf, M.M., and Risley, T.R. (1968). Some current dimensions of applied behavior analysis. *Journal of Applied Behavior Analysis*, 1, 91–97.

Berg, W.K., Wacker, D.P., Ringdahl, J.E., and Bosch, J. (2003). *Competing stimuli and automatic reinforcement.* Rockville, Md.: Department of Health and Human Services, National Institute of Child Health and Human Development.

Campbell, D.T., and Stanley, J.C. (1966). *Experimental and quasi-experimental designs for research.* Chicago: Rand McNally.

Ferster, C.B., and Demeyer, M.K. (1961). The development of performances in autistic children in an automatically controlled environment. *Journal of Chronic Diseases*, 13, 312–345.

Fisher, W.W., and Mazur, J.E. (1997). Basic and applied research on choice responding. *Journal of Applied Behavior Analysis*, 30, 387–410.

Fisher, W., Piazza, C.C., Bowman, L.G., Hagopian, L.P., Owens, J.C., and Slevin, I. (1992). A comparison of two approaches for identifying reinforcers for persons with severe and profound disabilities. *Journal of Applied Behavior Analysis*, 25, 491–498.

Harding, J.W., Wacker, D.P., Berg, W.K., Cooper, L.J., Asmus, J., Mlela, K., et al. (1999). An analysis of choice making in the assessment of young children with severe behavior problems. *Journal of Applied Behavior Analysis*, 32, 63–82.

Harding, J.W., Wacker, D.P., Berg, W.K., Lee, J.F., and Ibrahimovic, M. (2005). *Analysis of child positioning during functional communication training.* Poster presented at the annual conference of the Association for Behavior Analysis, Chicago, May 2005.

Hoch, H., McComas, J.J., Thompson, A.L., and Paone, D. (2002). Concurrent reinforcement schedules: Behavior change and maintenance without extinction. *Journal of Applied Behavior Analysis*, 35, 155–169.

Horner, R.H., and Day, H.M. (1991). The effects of response efficiency on functionally equivalent competing behaviors. *Journal of Applied Behavior Analysis*, 24, 719–732.

Iwata, B.A., Dorsey, M.F., Slifer, K.J., Bauman, K.E., Richman, G.S. (1994). Toward a functional analysis of self-injury. *Journal of Applied Behavior Analysis*, 27, 197–209. (Reprinted from *Analysis and Intervention in Developmental Disabilities*, 2, 3–20, 1982.)

Iwata, B.I., Neef, N.A., Wacker, D.P., Mace, F.C., and Vollmer, T.R., eds. (2000). *Methodological and conceptual issues in applied behavior analysis* (2nd ed, Reprint Series, Vol. 4). Lawrence, Kan.: Society for the Experimental Analysis of Behavior.

Johnston, J.M., and Pennypacker, H.S. (1993). *Strategies and tactics of behavioral research* (2nd ed). Hillsdale, N.J.: Lawrence Erlbaum Associates.

Kennedy, C.H. (2005). *Single-case designs for educational research.* Boston: Allyn & Bacon.

Lee, J.F., Harding, J.W., Wacker, D.W., and Berg, W.K. (2003). *Analysis of multiple functional problem behavior during functional communication training.* Poster presented at the annual conference of the Association for Behavior Analysis, San Francisco, May 2003.

Marckel, J.M., Neef, N.A., and Ferreri, S.J. (2006). A preliminary analysis of teaching improvisation with the picture exchange communication system to children with autism. *Journal of Applied Behavior Analysis, 39,* 109–115.

Neef, N.A., Mace, F.C., and Shade, D. (1993). Impulsivity in students with serious emotional disturbance: The interactive effects of reinforcer rate, delay, and quality. *Journal of Applied Behavior Analysis, 26,* 37–52.

Neef, N.A., Shade, D., and Miller, J.S. (1994). Assessing influential dimensions of reinforcers on choice in students with serious emotional disturbance. *Journal of Applied Behavior Analysis, 27,* 575–583.

Peck, S.M., Wacker, D.P., Cooper, L.J., McComas, J.J., and Richman, D. (1996). Choice-making treatment of young children's severe behavior problems. *Journal of Applied Behavior Analysis, 29,* 263–290.

Peyton, R.T., Lindauer, S.E., and Richman, D.M. (2005). The effects of directive and nondirective prompts on noncompliant vocal behavior exhibited by a child with autism. *Journal of Applied Behavior Analysis, 38,* 251–255.

Piazza, C.C., Fisher, W.W., Hagopian, L.P., Bowman, L.G., and Toole, L. (1996). Using a choice assessment to predict reinforcer effectiveness. *Journal of Applied Behavior Analysis, 29,* 1–9.

Pierce, W.D., and Epling, W.F. (1995). The applied importance of research on the matching law. *Journal of Applied Behavior Analysis, 28,* 237–241.

Risley, T. (2001). Do good, take data. In *A history of the behavioral therapies* (eds. W. Donohue, D. Henderson, S. Hayes, J. Fisher, and L. Hayes), pp. 267–287. Reno, Nev.: Context Press.

Shabani, D.B., Katz, R.C., Wilder, D.A., Beauchamp, K., Taylor, C.R., and Fischer, K.J. (2002). Increasing social initiations in children with autism: Effects of a tactile prompt. *Journal of Applied Behavior Analysis, 35,* 79–83.

Wacker, D.P., Berg, W.K., and Harding, J.W. (2004). *Maintenance effects of functional communication training.* Rockville, Md.: Department of Health and Human Services, National Institute of Child Health and Human Development.

SECTION 2

PROGRAM PRACTICE GUIDELINES

5. EARLY INTENSIVE APPLIED BEHAVIOR ANALYSIS INTERVENTION FOR AUTISM

William D. Frea and Erin K. McNerney

T his is an exciting time in the history of early intervention for children with autism. Researchers in the field of applied behavior analysis (ABA), which dominates the empirical literature of this area, continue to challenge themselves to better define how to develop programs that are both structured enough to ensure rapid acquisition of skills and naturalistic enough to allow for generalized and functional use of those skills. The alarming increase in the prevalence of autism spectrum disorders (ASD) has resulted in more organized efforts to understand how to assess, treat, and research these populations (Lord et al. 2005). One of the most debated topics is how to better define the parameters of an intensive early intervention. The field is far from reaching a consensus on this issue, but there is some general agreement that such interventions include ABA methodology, significant parent and family involvement, and competent clinicians overseeing the program (National Research Council 2001).

It is a confusing and difficult road for families first learning of a diagnosis of autism. This is the first step toward their role as researcher, therapist, advocate, and a host of other future responsibilities. The rise in awareness of autism, along with the increasing incidence of the disorder, has resulted in a plethora of alternative interventions and the typical pseudoscience to promote them (Green 1996; Schreibman 2005). It is also true that the field of behavior analysis has not always made parents' paths easier. The various descriptions and terminologies used by ABA programs often have dizzying results. Terms such as "discrete trial training," "pivotal response training," "verbal behavior," "Lovaas method," "incidental teaching," "milieu teaching," and a long list of others make each family's research a difficult process. Compounding this dilemma is the fact that within each behavioral camp there exists serious debate as to which methods are most important within each approach. For example, discrete trial training, by far the most popular approach, is conducted differently by different agencies and researchers across the country.

We will continue to see behavior analysts address the same goals using different programs, descriptions, and terms. This is a reality in any science that grows in popularity at the rate that ABA has. Recently, however, the parameters of intensive early intervention have become clearer. There is healthy debate about the number of hours that are expected, the methodology of the program, and the curricular targets.

■ What Is an Intensive Program?

Intensive early intervention programs provide daily one-on-one treatment. For young children, this usually takes place in the home and has a strong parent education component. Often the child is 2 years old when treatment begins, although it is becoming more common to see children in early intervention before their second birthday. The program often grows in the number of weekly hours as the young child better tolerates instruction. Behavior analysts use a range of methodologies to individualize the child's program, evaluate progress, and promote rapid program modification as the child improves. Parents are expected to learn ABA methods, basic data collection and analysis, and an ever-expanding curriculum.

There is a growing debate as to what makes a good intensive early intervention program. In the fields of developmental disabilities and education, the debate over the parameters of early intervention has been occurring for many years. There is general consensus that the intensity, or number of hours, in a child's program has a significant impact on developmental outcomes (Eldevik et al. 2006; Ramey et al. 1992). Most professionals would also agree that the extent of parent participation is equally as critical as the number of professional hours (Koegel and Koegel 2006; Laski, Charlop, and Schreibman 1988; Sallows and Graupner 2005; Schreibman 2000).

One factor that overrides the level of intensity is methodology. Applied behavior analysis currently represents the primary intensive early intervention approach, and it has demonstrated the level of empirical validation to warrant funding of daily sessions for young children (Anderson et al. 1987; Birnbrauer and Leach 1993; Fenske et al. 1985; Harris et al. 1991; Koegel, O'Dell, and Koegel 1987; Lovaas 1987; McEachin, Smith, and Lovaas 1993; Sherer and Schreibman 2005; Smith 1999; Taylor and Harris 1995; Weiss 1999). However, there are a number of alternative methodologies that are also being promoted for intensive, daily delivery. This chapter discusses intensive early interventions synonymously with ABA methodology, because this is the only evidence-based approach to intensive early intervention for children with autism at this time.

The research on early treatments for autism is vast and provides a number of successful approaches. Until more research is performed that compares the various ABA approaches, it is much too early to discuss what may be the best ABA program for any individual child (Sherer and Schreibman 2005). Parents should expect to learn multiple ABA methods within their child's program. For example, an ABA program can include both teaching language while the child is playing with a motivating toy and prompting specific language targets using a highly structured teaching method while seated at a table. An individual child may benefit more from a particular ABA approach, or may need to move between one approach and another, depending on the goals of the program at a given time. The decisions as to which approaches to use will be based more on what is working for the child than what has been determined in the present literature. An approach to selecting the best treatment components for a specific child has yet to be empirically validated.

Making the debate over intensive early intervention more urgent is the disagreement about intensity. There is much confusion today concerning what it takes for an autism intervention to be called an intensive ABA program. The professionals that provide such services are not always in agreement about what intensive programs should look like, although most believe that it is necessary for these programs to adhere to ABA principles and methods throughout each session.

The number of hours of direct instruction provided per week is the major issue of the current intensity debate. The National Research Council (2001) developed a consensus of 25 hours per week of instruction but stopped short of saying how much of that instruction should be applied behavior analytical. Some behaviorists consider 25 hours to be an appropriate goal for the number of direct ABA hours provided per week for an intensive program (e.g., Anderson et al. 1987; Howard et al. 2005).

■ History of Early Intervention for Children with Autism

The work of Dr. Ivar Lovaas in the 1970s brought the reality of successful treatment of individuals with autism to the forefront of the clinical literature. He developed the quintessential discrete trial model that is still in use at many clinics, laboratories, and agencies around the world. The basic structure of Lovaas' program has been presented primarily in clinical descriptions (Lovaas 1981, 2002) and in an historical outcome study (Lovaas 1987). Lovaas' program at the University of California, Los Angeles (UCLA) targeted children younger than 4 years of age and included a curriculum of 40 hours per week, year-round, for 3 years. The curriculum heavily emphasized speech and language. It initially targeted imitation skills and the reduction of interfering behaviors and then expanded to include receptive and expressive language and more complex interactional and pre-academic skills. Basic skills were presented in massed trials and continued until mastery was achieved. After basic skills were mastered, new sets of drills involving more complex skills were introduced. Subsequent maintenance checks were incorporated to ensure that learned skills were not forgotten.

Lovaas and his colleagues have published two major outcome studies reporting on a group of 19 children who received intensive services (an average of 40 hours per week) for a period of 2 or more years (Lovaas 1987; McEachin, Smith, and Lovaas 1993). The children were younger than 41 months of age at the start of their treatment. These children were compared with a control group of children with autism who were enrolled in various special education programs and minimal weekly behavior analysis services (approximately 10 hours per week). Measures were taken on the children's pre-treatment and post-treatment IQ scores and educational placement. Overall, it was reported that approximately 90% of the experimental group achieved significant improvements in IQ and educational/classroom placements, compared with minimal changes in IQ and educational placement for children in the control groups. Specifically, the authors reported that 47% of the experimental group achieved IQs in the "normal" range after treatment, compared with a pre-treatment mean IQ of 63. The 1993 follow-up study (McEachin, Smith, and Lovaas 1993) re-evaluated the children from the experimental group to determine whether gains in IQ and educational placement had been maintained since the previous evaluation. Children in the experimental group were found to have higher IQ scores, less restrictive educational placements, and more adaptive behavior than the children in the control group at follow-up, indicating that the gains from the Young Autism Project were maintained over time. In addition, the authors described several of the children from the experimental group, previously diagnosed with autism, as achieving "normal functioning."

Obviously, claims such as these have a tremendous impact on researchers, practitioners, educators, and particularly parents of children with autism. In many school districts around the country, parents who are unhappy with their children's lack of progress in school and believe that a critical window for early intervention is closing have successfully sued their public school system, forcing it to provide intensive, discrete trial programs ("Alternatives to Lovaas therapy" 1996; Gresham and MacMillan 1998). Not everyone, however, has been supportive of this approach. There have been several responses to the UCLA project's findings (Gresham and MacMillan 1998; Schopler, Short, and Mesibov 1989; Schreibman 2005). Although most who have commented on the Young Autism Project agree that the results are important and promising, there has been a widespread call to view the outcomes as preliminary until the results have been independently replicated (Foxx 1993; Kazdin 1993; Schreibman 2005).

Of concern are several methodological issues that threaten the validity of these studies, such as (*a*) nonrandom assignment of children to experimental and control groups, *(b)* use of different measures of intelligence for different children, and *(c)* different measures of intelligence for pre-test and post-test. Others have criticized the use of the term "normal functioning." Mundy (1993) suggested that the outcome measures used in the 1987 study were not sensitive to the complex pragmatic and relational problems that can co-occur with a normal IQ but which still result in significant impairment for children with autism. Additionally, there is some concern that the children selected for UCLA's experimental group were of higher intellectual functioning than might be evidenced in a random, representative sample of children with autism (Schopler, Short, and Mesibov 1989; Schreibman 2005). This suggests a need to acknowledge that the promising results reported in the 1987 and 1993 papers may apply only to a select group of children. The most serious reservation lies in the inability of others to replicate the study. Because no one who has not been directly associated with Lovaas has been able to replicate his results, the field has been cautious about his conclusions.

Most agree that future research on intensive interventions should attempt to incorporate children with heterogeneous features in an attempt to delineate whether certain children benefit less than others, as well as the characteristics of the children who benefit most. Also, clinical outcomes need to be assessed. Most agree that Lovaas' measures of IQ and educational placement did not address the core characteristics of autism.

Although it is important to evaluate Lovaas' claims closely, no one can deny the impact that his work has had on the lives of individuals with autism. It is commonly accepted now that young children with autism can make enormous gains within ABA programs. The work of Ivar Lovaas was pivotal in demonstrating to the world that children with autism could learn.

■ Selecting Intervention Components

As described earlier, intensive intervention for children with autism remains synonymous with ABA approaches to treating the disorder. Behavior analytic programs typically incorporate a number of empirically validated techniques (e.g., discrete trials, visual schedules, incidental teaching methods, picture exchange, errorless learning, token systems, video modeling). As with any good behavior analytical program, intensive early intervention does not apply to a single methodology or approach to programming. The field of ABA is still a long way from identifying a systematic approach to selecting intervention components that best fit an individual child (Sherer and Schreibman 2005).

Compounding the problem of selecting appropriate intervention methods is the disagreement about diagnosing autism and, more importantly, categorizing subsets of autism. There is strong debate regarding the best approaches to diagnosing children on the autism spectrum (Charman and Baird

2002; Javaloyes 2006; Lecavalier 2005; Sigman, Spence, and Wang 2006; Tryon et al. 2006; Volkmar et al. 2004; Volkmar and Klin 2005; Williams and Brayne 2006). It is assumed that the ASDs most likely denote numerous genetic derangements yet to be identified. Because ASD is currently diagnosed through behavior observation, treatment providers must rely on assessment of the individual child's needs. The issue of how to best categorize the many subsets of autism makes researching treatment selection approaches very difficult. The broad diagnosis of autistic disorder or the label of ASD provides little in describing the characteristics of the individual participants in a given study. There are many "autisms," and the ability to articulate a treatment selection process will require a better method for categorizing the subtypes of ASD.

Currently, the field is still in its infancy in terms of what is needed to identify the basic questions of program design. Intervention comparisons of intensive versus nonintensive, or intensive versus eclectic, approaches are currently being debated in the field of ABA. Where to begin to tease apart the complex variables of individual intensive programs has not adequately been addressed. This is understandable, given the variability of approaches to treatment development across universities and clinical programs.

■ Examples of Recent Research in Applied Behavior Analysis

Replicating the UCLA Results

Although a total of 15 replication sites have been put into place since the 1987 UCLA study was reported, only a handful of outcome studies have been published. Smith (2007) described the difficult process of managing the replication efforts. Three of the sites closed with no useful data produced, and the data from the other 12 sites have been difficult to pull together. There has been a very low dropout rate across all sites, indicating that attrition is not a problem. The problems have been more with the need to change research designs and methods and the difficulty of managing the quantity of data produced (Smith 2007). IQ remains the primary outcome measure, and overall the results have been significant. Classroom placement also remains an outcome of interest; however, there is some debate as to how the presence of an instructional assistant in a regular education classroom should be interpreted. Whereas IQ differences have been very impressive between participants in the intensive groups versus the various control groups, the results for receptive and expressive language have been less impressive.

Sallows and Graupner (2005) assigned 24 children with autism into either a clinic-directed program or a parent-directed program through matched random process. The clinic-directed group received an average of 38 hours per week of direct intervention. The children in the parent-directed programs averaged 31.5 hours per week, with the exception of one child who received 14 hours per week. Although the parent-directed programs had dramatically less supervision and fewer direct intervention hours, the outcomes were similar to those of the clinic-directed programs. The authors speculated that this unexpected outcome might be due to parents' "taking on the senior therapist role, filling cancelled shifts themselves, actively targeting generalization, and pursuing teachers and neighbors to find peers for daily play dates with their children." The authors reported that improvements in IQ, language, adaptive, social, and academic measures were similar for both groups. These findings are particularly noteworthy, because this study was performed at an official Lovaas replication site. The authors not only conformed to a rigorous protocol set by the National Institute of Mental Health (NIMH), but they conducted their research in collaboration with Dr. Lovaas.

Smith, Groen, and Wynn (2000) compared an intensive treatment group, averaging 24.5 hours per week of individual treatment, with a parent training–only group. This was the first randomized clinical trial to attempt to replicate the Lovaas' 1987 study. The children in the parent training group did not receive an intensive level of hours, in contrast to the "parent-directed group" in the Sallows and Graupner's (2005) replication study. The parent training participants received only 3 to 9 months of parent training. This consisted of 10 to 15 hours per week of special education classes and 5 hours per week of parent training. The intensive treatment group outperformed the parent training group on intellectual, visual-spatial, and academic measures. The outcomes for language were not significant. The overall gains reported were substantially smaller than those reported by Lovaas (1987). It is noteworthy that the number of treatment hours per week in the intensive treatment group gradually decreased over 1 to 2 years.

Cohen, Amerine-Dickens, and Smith (2006) published their results on the Central Valley Autism Project, which is also a replication site for Lovaas' UCLA model. They compared 21 children in an intensive (35 to 40 hours per week) program with 21 age- and IQ-matched children in special education classrooms. The program was 20 to 30 hours per week for children younger than 3 years of age, and 35 to 40 hours per week for those over 3 years. Generalization activities and community outings were included in those 35 to 40 hours; the average number of hours per week spent in discrete trial instruction is unclear. The children in the intensive ABA program fared much better than those in special education classes. The intensive treatment group saw a mean 25-point increase in IQ (from 62 to 87) at year 3, whereas the special education group saw an average 14-point IQ gain (from 59 to 73). Significant gains were reported for language comprehension, but there was not a significant result for expressive language. As with the Lovaas (1987) study, education placement was included as a dependent measure. Six (29%) of the 21 children in the intensive ABA group were fully included in regular education classrooms without assistance in year 3 of the study. Another 11 were included with assistance, which is not a clear indicator of their ability. Most noteworthy is the fact that these results were achieved in a community rather than a research setting, and they demonstrated that the rigorous standards of the Lovaas' UCLA treatment model could be met by a community agency.

Eldevik and colleagues (2006) reported data from the replication site in Oslo, Norway. They compared an ABA program with an eclectic special education program. Children received an average of 12 hours per week in either a behavioral program or an eclectic program. The children in the behavioral program made larger gains in intellectual functioning, receptive and expressive language, and communication skills. The authors noted that the 12 hours of behavior therapy represented a low-intensity program and speculated that the gains they observed might be modest compared with those of more intensive programs.

The Norwegian site researchers also published a study on outcomes for children who began their intensive behavioral treatment between the ages of 4 and 7 years (Eikeseth et al. 2002, 2007). They compared an ABA treatment group to an eclectic treatment group, with both receiving their interventions at school. Children in the eclectic group received one-on-one therapy with a combination of methods such as ABA, Treatment and Education of Autistic and related Communication handicapped CHildren (TEACCH), sensory-motor and so on. Both groups had an average of 28 to 29 hours of therapy per week. Significantly greater gains were seen in the ABA group for IQ, language comprehension, expressive language, communication, and overall adaptive behavior. The researchers found a mean increase of 17 IQ points for the ABA group and 4 IQ points for the eclectic group after 1 year of treatment, and 25 and 7 points, respectively, at follow-up (approximately 31 months from baseline). Of particular interest is the subset of children in the ABA group who scored in the average IQ range at follow-up. Seven (54%) of the 13 participants in the ABA group saw their mean scores go from 70 to 104 (verbal mean, 105; performance mean, 103). Only 2 of the 12 students in the eclectic group had IQ scores that rose to average levels. The IQ and communication gains in this study were statistically significant only in the first year, so it is possible that most of the gains in intellectual functioning and communication for this population take place during the first 12 months of treatment.

There have been some other impressive findings from the various replication attempts. First, it appears that the present-day modifications in the UCLA protocol have not had a negative effect on outcome. For example, strong results are still achieved without the use of punishment. Also, giving more control of the program to parents does not appear to result in a less impressive outcome. The play focus of the programs is possibly the most major shift from the methods of the 1970s and 1980s. Sallows, Graupner, and Sherman (2007) reported that the most critical factor for them was ensuring that the children were having fun. The play-focus of their Wisconsin Early Autism Project represents the current standard of intensive ABA interventions. The motivation and happiness they looked for in their participants played a key role in how their methods were structured.

More Common Interpretations of "Intensive"

The number of hours necessary to achieve a strong therapeutic effect appears to be less than the 40 per week first targeted by Lovaas. Anderson and colleagues (1987), in a study often referenced as a replication of Lovaas' results, demonstrated impressive results with a home-based program that provided 15 to 25 hours of behavioral therapy per week. Sheinkopf and Siegel (1998) found great improvement in children who received 12 to 27 (average of 19) hours per week. Luiselli and colleagues (2000) saw significant results in a program in which most of the children received 15 hours of therapy per week. Birnbrauer and Leach (1993), in a partial replication, provided an average of 19 hours of instruction and had very positive results. It needs to be understood that, unlike the program that Lovaas was delivering 25 years ago, parent training is a standard and significant part of all programs today. This adds dramatically to the number of total hours of teaching provided to the children (Koegel and Koegel, 2006).

The positive effect of a program is more reliant on its behavioral emphasis than on the total number of hours. "Eclectic" programs that include multiple methodologies and philosophies do not appear to provide the same results as programs that are entirely applied behavior analytic. Howard. and coworkers (2005) compared the effects of three treatment approaches: 25 to 40 hours per week of intensive ABA, 30 hours per week of an eclectic classroom-based program that included either 1:1 or 1:2 instruction ratio, and 15 hours per week of public preschool. All 61 participants were young children with ASD. As in the later study by Cohen, Amerine-Dickens, and Smith (2006), they found that the children in the intensive group had far better outcomes. There was no difference in outcomes between the 30-hour eclectic classroom and the 15-hour traditional preschool. They did find accelerated rates of skill acquisition for the intensive ABA group. Children in the intensive group met or exceeded normal rates of development for the year they were in treatment.

Luiselli and colleagues (2000) examined 16 children who received between 6 and 20 hours per week of behavioral intervention, some beginning before and some after 3 years of age. There was no significant difference between the two age groups; both had good results across six developmental domains. Eleven of the 16 participants had programs of 15 hours per week. The program was described as "comprehensive" and included discrete trial instruction and incidental teaching opportunities.

The studies described here demonstrate many of the critical questions being raised in this field today. Although it is important to rely on proven ABA methodologies when designing intensive early intervention programs, many variables need to be considered in addition to the teaching approach. Number of hours, type of preschool program, level of professional involvement, amount of supervision, age of the child, and types of measurement are all examples of variables that require extensive future research.

■ A Range of ABA Methodologies

Traditionally, ABA programs have involved collecting data on many specific behaviors, prompting the child to demonstrate those behaviors numerous times within a session, and shaping more advanced forms of those behaviors over time. Recently, a growing number of professionals have been incorporating ABA principles into what are considered more developmentally appropriate intervention contexts. Terms such as "play-based" ABA and "naturalistic" interventions are used to promote such programs. The field acknowledges both the traditional discrete trial methods and naturalistic methods as being valid ABA approaches with many empirically based studies to back them up. Consumers are thus faced with the challenge of how to evaluate an ABA program and how to weigh the importance of structure (play-based versus discrete trial) when planning a child's overall program.

Use of more natural, play-based ABA strategies appears to complement the more structured, traditional ABA methods (Bernard-Opitz, Ing, and Kong 2004; Del Prato 2001). Standard practice is to adhere to evidence-based behavioral methods while attending to developmental sequences and strategies to ensure functional growth.

In a 2002 meeting sponsored by the National Institutes of Health, 23 experts and stakeholders commented on the challenges of identifying evidenced-based treatments. Lord and colleagues (2005, 699) stated:

> Because almost all studies of ASD treatments used behavioral techniques (Lovaas 1987) with some attention to developmental sequences and communicative intent . . ., the content of the interventions and the fidelity and intensity with which they were carried out often varied more than the methods used.

The group concurred that "the most effective ways to integrate developmental and other approaches with behavioral methods have not yet been tested systematically" (Lord et al. 2005). So it is assumed that great caution needs to be taken to avoid straying too far from the evidence-based behavioral methods until controlled research provides proper guidance.

■ Prognostic Indicators

Understanding the prognostic indicators for children with autism is quite difficult (Howlin et al. 2004; Ruble and Dalrymple 1996). Currently, there is a risk that treatment providers will neglect to consider the child-related variables that mediate the success of the program. Researchers have identified positive prognostic indicators such as early language, joint attention, imitation, flexibility, and cognitive shifting (Howlin, Mawhood, and Rutter, 2000; Nordin and Gillberg 1998; Szatmari et al. 2003). Cognitive ability (i.e., baseline IQ), for example, has often been viewed as a predictor for the level of success achievable by an intensive early intervention program (Lovaas 1987; Nordin and Gillberg 1998; Rogers 1996; Sherer and Schreibman 2005). However, Smith, Groen, and Wynn (2000) found that there was not a correlation between intake IQ and outcome. The only possible predictors of the "best-outcome children" they found were mastery of verbal imitation and mastery of expressive labels after the first 3 months of treatment.

Significant behavior problems that are not successfully reduced early in treatment have a negative effect on outcome. In particular, the amount of self-stimulatory behavior displayed may impede the progress of intervention (Koegel and Covert 1972; Varni et al. 1979).

As the early indicators of positive outcome become better understood, it may be possible to target these behaviors at the beginning of the early intervention curriculum. It is common for the very early stages of the program to address joint attention, imitation, and compliance. There is no agreed-upon curriculum in the field at this time.

■ Initial Programming

Regardless of the amount of play-based instruction that a child's program may have, it is typical for ABA-based programs to introduce intervention in a more structured format. For example, after rapport has been established and a variety of reinforcers have been identified, therapy may begin in its most structured, discrete trial form. This is particularly critical for children who are most delayed and need rapid acquisition early on.

There exist as many curricula for early intervention programs as the programs themselves. A curriculum can be understood as the particular design of the environment, materials, and teaching interactions within an intervention program (National Research Council 2001). Ideally, a good curriculum is one that is developmentally appropriate, well defined, and easily replicated.

When designing an early intervention program, it is important to tailor the curriculum based on the child's needs; however, one must first ensure that prerequisite skills for future learning are in place and fluent in the child. Highly structured, or discrete trial–based, methodologies are useful when teaching new behaviors and provide an efficient and data-based way to teach and monitor a child's progress toward learning such skills.

Autism Spectrum Therapies is a nonpublic agency in Southern California that provides early intervention, classroom support, and behavioral services to children with autism. The children in our early intervention programs receive between 10 and 40 hours per week of ABA therapy. We base their hours on the progress being made as well as the individual program components required for a specific child. For example, a child may require many fewer hours with our therapist as their program becomes more play-based and the parent component increases. Initially, however, we address the prerequisite skills for learning.

Autism Spectrum Therapies has developed a Learning-to-Learn curriculum that children pass through before play-based strategies are introduced. This allows us to gauge the rate of skill acquisition that can be achieved with a specific child and ensures that we have established compliance, attending/orienting to instructional materials, choice making, and simple imitation skills early in the intervention process. These prerequisite learning-to-learn skills are systematically targeted in a more structured, discrete trial–based approach before moving on to teach skills in broader areas such as social communication, symbolic play, and peer interaction. The amount of time spent in the Learning-to-Learn curriculum is often quite brief, but this depends on the child's individual progress. It is common to ensure a foundation of learning before expecting the child to initiate learning opportunities, which is a component in some ABA programs (Hart 1985; Koegel and Koegel 2006; Kaiser, Yoder, and Keetz 1992).

Compliance

In terms of intensive early intervention for young children with autism, compliance with treatment is necessary for the child to learn the skills being taught. Behaviors that interfere with learning, such as severe aggression, self-injurious behavior, or elopement, should be addressed before commencing a skill-based curriculum. Compliance in this context refers to skills such as the ability to sit and attend for at least a few minutes at a time (long enough for several trials or opportunities to practice a skill to be presented), the ability to tolerate transitions from breaks back to therapy and brief separations from parents or caregivers, and receptive understanding and general compliance with simple instructions.

Attending/Orienting to Social Stimuli

Children with autism typically demonstrate impairment in attending or orienting to social stimuli in their environment (e.g., responding when their name is called, responding positively to praise) (Dawson et al. 1988). This skill emerges in the first months of life in typically developing children (Morales, Mundy, and Rojas 1998; Rochat and Striano 1999). Impairment in attending to or orienting to social stimuli has been suggested to be one of the most basic deficits in autism and a factor in later impairments in social communication (Dawson et al. 1988; Mundy and Neal 2001). Dawson and colleagues (2004) found that children with autism were more likely to fail to orient to social stimuli such as humming, calling the child's name, snapping fingers, and patting hands on thighs. Attending to another person (i.e., the therapist) and orienting to social stimuli such as the behaviors mentioned are critical initial skills for children with autism to learn in order to continue to make progress as intervention continues and skills become more complex.

Related to orienting to social stimuli, joint attention has become a much researched topic in recent years. Joint attention is described as the ability to "coordinate attention between interactive social partners with respect to objects or events in order to share an awareness of the objects or events" (Mundy et al. 1986). Joint attention encompasses specific behaviors such as sharing attention with alternating eye gaze, following another person's eye gaze or point, and directing the attention of another through eye gaze, gesture, or point. Development of joint attention skills, which can often be seen in typically developing infants before 12 months of age, is fundamental for later development of communicative competence (Carpenter, Nagell, and Tomasello 1998). Impairment in joint attention may be a critical factor in the later deficits seen in language, play, and social development for children with autism (Mundy 1995). In order to target the more complex skills involved in joint attention, it is critical that a child be able to attend to another person and to orient to social stimuli.

Few studies have addressed changes in joint attention after behavioral intervention, and even fewer have looked at teaching children with autism joint attention skills. Pierce and Schreibman (1995) found increases in supported joint attention (another individual changes the child's interaction with an object) and coordinated joint attention (child's gaze shifts between an object and another person during interaction) after peer-implemented naturalistic behavioral intervention. Kasari and colleagues (2001) demonstrated that a child with autism could be taught pointing and showing, using a milieu (behavioral and developmental) teaching approach.

Because responding to joint attention bids emerges before joint attention initiations in typical children (Dunham and Moore 1995), it follows that teaching children with autism to respond to others' bids should be taught before teaching them joint attention initiations. Whalen and Schreibman (2003) conducted training in joint attention skills for children with autism. These children did not respond to joint attention bids made by an adult, nor did they initiate joint attention with others. Training consisted of two phases: response training, in which the child was taught to respond to joint attention bids made by an adult, and initiation training, in which the child was taught to initiate joint attention by using coordinated gaze shifting and protodeclarative pointing. All five of the participants learned to respond to joint attention bids after training, and four of them learned to initiate joint attention with the examiner after training. The researchers found that the improvements in joint attention initiation generalized to other settings as well as to the child's primary caregiver. The individual skills that coordinate into what we define as joint attention are clearly critical to many areas of development. Although the findings are preliminary, it appears that these skills can be taught to young children with autism. It remains to be seen what long-term effects will emerge from such training, but, thus far, results are promising.

Choice Making

The positive effects of using choice as an antecedent behavioral condition for children with autism have been well documented in the literature. Providing choice can improve responsiveness and engagement, increase adaptive behaviors, and decrease challenging behaviors (Dunlap et al. 1994; Dyer, Dunlap, and Winterling 1990; Kern et al. 1998; Kern et al. 2001; Koegel, Dyer, and Bell 1987). To effectively use choice as an intervention component, the child must first demonstrate the ability to make a choice or indicate preference. Therefore, choice making is a prerequisite to any naturalistic or play-based approach. If the child cannot indicate a preference or choice, intervention will continue to be adult-directed. Targeting choice making at the onset of intervention is likely to accelerate the later programming of incidental/natural teaching opportunities.

Imitation

Another skill essential to future learning is imitation. Imitation can include a simple task such as copying one action, or more complex skills such as vocal imitation and learning entire social routines. The ability to imitate others is critical in the development of social relationships (Meltzoff and Moore 1992). Such social learning is a way for children to learn new skills and engage in nonverbal social interaction. Studies have shown that children as young as 6 months of age are able to engage in some imitation (Abravanel and Gingold 1985; Meltzoff and Moore 1989; Nielsen 2006). Children with autism often have significant impairment in the ability to imitate (Rogers and Pennington 1991; Smith and Bryson 1994). Once a child demonstrates the ability to engage in simple imitation, the stage is set for teaching more complex skills.

How quickly a child moves through a learning-to-learn curriculum varies widely depending on factors such as the child's baseline skill level and the intensity of treatment (both number of hours per week as well as method of instruction). Data should be collected daily and monitored at least weekly so that program modifications can be made in a timely manner.

■ Play-Based and Naturalistic Approaches

Possibly the biggest contribution to the ABA literature on early intervention in recent years has been the study of play-based approaches (e.g., Koegel and Koegel 2006). The literature on incidental teaching has developed into methods that are expected in any early intervention program. Researchers in this area have responded to the concern that the tight structure of discrete trials, although critical to rapid acquisition, comes at a cost of poor generalization and prompt-dependency.

Many clinicians, teachers, parents, and researchers question the appropriateness of using primarily artificial and highly structured conditions to teach language and communication. Language must become functional across settings. When language is taught under maximum stimulus control, prompt-dependency is often the result, with little or no use of spontaneous language occurring in other environments (Schreibman and Ingersoll 2005). As principles of generalization would dictate, removal of language development from its natural social context results in limits to its functional use in nontreatment environments (Stokes and Osnes 1988). Additionally, in a review of discrete trial and "normalized" behavioral interventions targeting language skills, Del Prato (2001) found that interventions providing normalized language training (defined as interventions that were more loosely structured and incorporated indirect teaching during typical activities, child initiation, natural reinforcers, and reinforcement of attempts) were more effective than discrete trial training for young children with autism.

Play-based teaching strategies address issues of generalization and spontaneous speech production. If discrete trial methodologies represent therapist-guided, highly structured learning environments for language, then play-based methodologies represent the philosophical opposite. Learning that occurs in more natural contexts (e.g., play and social routines in classroom or home), uses reinforcement that would occur naturally in social contexts, and is guided by the child's choices or preferences is more likely to become part of the child's ongoing and functional communication (Koegel and Koegel 2006).

Hart and Risley (1968, 1975) first outlined an incidental teaching approach that included teaching strategies such as modeling, manding and modeling, time delay, and incidental teaching within the classroom setting. Researchers have examined these strategies and further developed milieu teaching strategies to assist caregivers in supporting language development across functional routines in the home and school (e.g., Cavallaro and Bambara 1982; Halle, Marshall, and Spradlin 1979; Warren and Kaiser 1986; Warren, McQuarters, and Rogers-Warren 1984).

Examples of such strategies include teaching the parent to "bait" the environment with items that are highly desirable to the child (e.g., favorite toys, activities, snacks). Ideally, these objects are placed within sight but out of reach, creating a "need" for the child to communicate to the adult in order to gain access or assistance obtaining the item. The parent prompts a request by asking, "What do you want?" If the child does not respond, the request is modeled, "I want phone." The child's imitation of the verbal model is reinforced through access to the preferred item.

This methodology provides a modeling procedure that begins with establishing attention and a model to the child. If the child does not respond correctly, he or she is given a corrective model or feedback. Once the child acquires words, generalization is programmed through the mand-model procedure (Rogers-Warren and Warren 1980). This requires the child to respond to questions such as, "What do you want?" Opportunities for initiation are provided through the use of a time-delay procedure (Halle, Baer, and Spradlin 1981). With this procedure, situations are present or arranged where the child will need assistance. A delay is used as a prompt for the child to request assistance.

Building on the incidental teaching model of Hart and Risley, the methods included in pivotal response training (Koegel and Koegel 2006; Koegel, O'Dell, and Koegel 1987) represent a similar set of procedures that provide for the manipulation of variables within natural language teaching conditions. Critical variables include the use of frequent child choice of stimuli, reinforcement of child attempts, reinforcers that are natural to the interactions, and variation of stimulus materials. Grounded in the philosophy of earlier incidental teaching approaches, this paradigm is intended to be taught to parents and to be conducted in the child's natural environments from the beginning of the intervention (Laski, Charlop, and Schreibman 1988). In this way, generalization and maintenance of language gains are immediately promoted.

Play-based ABA methods are designed to enhance the motivation to respond to social and environmental stimuli, so that the child begins to self-initiate interactions, thereby increasing learning opportunities throughout the day (Koegel, Koegel, and McNerney 2001). Child-choice is possibly the most important variable of these methods. This refers to incorporating stimulus items (e.g., toys, activities) chosen or preferred by the child into teaching opportunities. The clinician follows the child's lead but maintains a structured environment and retains the child's attention. Studies have demonstrated that providing opportunities for children to take part in choosing some stimulus materials leads to increased engagement and decreased challenging behaviors during teaching activities (Dyer, Dunlap, and Winterling 1990; Kern et al. 1998; Koegel, Koegel, and Surratt 1992; Sigafoos 1998).

In contrast to more structured methods, play-based ABA approaches vary stimulus materials frequently throughout the session. Variation in target stimuli refers to presenting tasks in slightly different ways (as opposed to always presenting a task in exactly the same manner and sequence), as well as interspersing new (acquisition) and previously learned (maintenance) tasks. Such variation has been shown to decrease challenging behaviors and increase responsivity (Dunlap 1984; Winterling, Dunlap, and O'Neill 1987). Ideally, the environment is arranged so that clear prompts, or opportunities to respond and use skills, are provided to the child by the caregiver or clinician. These opportunities can take the form of verbal prompts (e.g., labeling a desired item, asking "What do you want?"), gesture prompts (e.g., showing or pointing to an item), time delay, or other environmental arrangements (e.g., placing a desired item in sight but out of the child's reach and looking expectantly at the child, breaking up an item into smaller pieces) (Koegel 1995). Teaching is embedded within play-based interaction. Emphasis is on reciprocal interaction, turn-taking, and shared control of stimulus items. Both the child and the partner are considered active participants, in contrast to the child being a passive participant and the clinician being in control of the learning opportunity (Koegel and Mentis 1985).

Increasing the child's motivation is a powerful aspect of play-based strategies. When provided many choices and a variety of stimuli, the child demonstrates greater interest in the session. This is observed in terms of increased approaches to stimulus materials, independent responding to natural cues in the play sequence, and the ability to tolerate longer session time. One factor that defines a natural or play-based intervention is the reinforcement of the child's attempts to respond correctly. Reinforcement of a child's attempts refers to a broadening of the shaping criteria used when teaching a behavior; it can increase the child's acquisition of language and academic-based tasks (Koegel, Carter, and Koegel 1998; Koegel and Egel 1979; Koegel, O'Dell, and Dunlap 1988). Reinforcers that are naturally and directly related to the interaction can teach the child the direct relationship between a response and reinforcement (Koegel and Koegel 1995), which in turn leads to more functional learning, particularly as the child encounters natural contingencies in his or her everyday environment.

■ Choosing an Appropriate Level of Structure

Once a child demonstrates the ability to engage in prerequisite learning-to-learn skills, the structure of therapy sessions can be adapted to match the child's learning style. Some skills may be taught in highly structured, discrete trial format, whereas others may be taught in more naturalistic, play-based formats such as those described earlier. Data collected on what skills the child has learned, and how quickly, serve to guide the clinician in programming each session. More than one ABA approach may be effective for a child with autism. Discrete trial approaches are clearly effective for teaching new behaviors and discriminations to children with autism; however, children also need play-based, naturalistic approaches to make initiations and generalize the learned skills, as well as to reduce dependence on an adult to provide cues and prompts (Smith 2001).

A child who has made rapid gains in a discrete trial format may continue to make rapid gains when the structure is modified to a more naturalistic, play-based approach. On the other hand, if the data reflect that the child does not continue to make rapid gains when intervention becomes less structured, more structure can be re-introduced and data can be monitored weekly to assess the child's rate of skill acquisition. This flexibility in programming reflects a focus on responding to the child's performance and individual needs, as opposed to strictly following a standard discrete trial or play-based methodology only. As children continue to make developmental gains and respond to reinforcement in the natural environment, intervention may shift to a predominantly play-based approach.

Autism Spectrum Therapies' model for programming in play-based methods incorporates an emphasis on weekly review of the child's progress to evaluate the rate of skill acquisition. If a child's rate of acquisition decreases significantly when the program shifts (whether to more or to less structure), the program can be adjusted to the approach that provides the maximum rate of skill acquisition. Program modification occurs frequently, and the ABA approaches used within the program can be adapted before the child is allowed to continue in a program that is not well-suited to his or her needs.

■ Transition to School

Transition to a structured preschool program is the best result for a successful intensive early intervention. In successful cases, the child is prepared for group learning and socialization as the program expands to peers and siblings. There is much debate as to whether a home-based ABA program should continue in parallel with the preschool program. In general, this depends on the child's ability to learn in a group setting and the school's ability to provide ABA methods effectively.

Outstanding examples of preschool programs that are based on the principles of ABA have been reported (Handleman and Harris 2001). Consistent with the diversity of the field of ABA, these range from highly structured programs that use a high proportion of discrete trials (McClannahan and Krantz 2001; Meyer et al. 2001) to more loosely structured programs using incidental teaching methods (McGee et al. 1992; McGee, Morrier, and Daly 2001). All have rigorous staff training procedures and data collection procedures for evaluating the consistency of the methods used and their effectiveness on individual child development.

It is critical for the professionals overseeing the early intervention program to be involved in the process of transition to preschool. This may include training school staff, maintaining some form of an in-home program, and possibly providing ongoing consultation and/or supervision in the classroom. Alternatively, if a school district has employed qualified behavior analysts to oversee the education of students with autism, the transition can be simplified. It may involve the observation of the home program by school personnel before transition and a series of collaborative team meetings to ensure effective continuation of services.

■ Earliest Intervention

How early is early intervention? Certain characteristics have been identified that appear to distinguish typical development from development in children later diagnosed with autism. A study involving retrospective analysis of videotape records determined that the best predictor of a later diagnosis of autism in a child 12 months of age was the child's frequency and duration of looking at other people (Osterling and Dawson 1994). A follow-up study of first-birthday videotapes found that the amount of time spent looking at others discriminated children with autism from typically developing peers as well as from children with other developmental delays (Osterling et al. 2002). Other distinguishing characteristics that have been identified by 12 months of age include orienting/attending to nonsocial novel visual stimuli, poor response to name, mouthing of objects, and social touch aversions (Baranek 1999). In a longitudinal study of at-risk infants who had a sibling with autism, Zwaigenbaum and colleagues (2005) found that, by 12 months of age, siblings later diagnosed with autism were distinguishable from infants identified as "low risk" by the following behavioral characteristics: atypicalities in eye contact; visual tracking differences; disengagement of visual attention; less frequent orienting to name, imitation, social smiling, and reactivity; lower social interest and affect; and sensory-oriented behaviors. Screening assessments have also identified characteristics of autism in infants 18 months of age (Baird et al. 2000).

Although many ABA programs provide therapy to toddlers and preschoolers, currently there are few reports in the literature regarding intensive intervention with infants (6 months and older) who are identified as being at risk for autism. To address the needs of this population, Autism Spectrum Therapies developed an intervention model designed to provide infants with intervention and parents with education and ABA-based strategies to stimulate their child's development. This Parent Education Program for Stimulating Infants targets core areas associated with autism within the natural daily routines of the family. Children aged 6 to 16 months have participated in the program, with the majority being between 12 and 14 months. Sessions are typically conducted on 3 or 4 days each week and follow a general time-limited curriculum, beginning with providing basic education to parents about developmental milestones and their child's skill levels, followed by lesson plans targeting specific skills and strategies. Each session includes checking in with the parent, a structured teaching segment, an unstructured play segment, debriefing with the parent, and a weekly homework assignment to practice a technique during typical family routines. The clinician reviews the homework assignment with the parent the following week. Handouts are provided each week on topics such as how to choose developmentally appropriate toys, how to create learning opportunities, and descriptions and examples of specific ABA strategies; these are explained and modeled by the clinician.

Areas such as joint attention, symbol use and gestures, and reciprocal interactions are targeted within the infant program, and parents are taught ABA techniques to elicit specific skill development within each domain (e.g., how to elicit eye contact, how to teach use of a gesture such as pointing). Sessions are conducted within the family's home, during regularly occurring routines (e.g., mealtime, bathtime, playtime). The clinician collects data on the child's progress toward identified goals and milestones while the child is interacting with the parent. The clinician also collects data on the parent's fidelity of implementation of the ABA strategies taught thus far.

Preliminary data collected on this parent education program for infants at risk for autism indicate that parents usually can learn to independently implement the ABA strategies taught during specific routines and, to some extent, can generalize those strategies to other routines as well. The children who have participated in the program have demonstrated gains in all developmental areas, although most continue to receive intensive early intervention after completion of the infant program.

This earliest of intensive ABA intervention models shows promise. It utilizes ABA methodology, incorporates family members, is conducted in the natural environment, provides education regarding typical development, and includes data collection on both parent and child performance. Long-term outcome data of infants participating in this type of program will need to be collected to evaluate its impact as the initial stage of intensive early intervention.

■ Conclusion

Early intensive ABA programs remain varied in their approaches to treating autism. Although they all adhere to evidence-based methods, the interpretation of what defines an intensive program is not clear. Applied behavior analysis is a field with an enormous empirical literature of interventions for autism. How to bring together those methodologies into treatment options that fit different profiles of autism is perhaps the most important research question to be answered. Certainly, great things are being done today to help children with autism approach typical developmental functioning. Children with autism are being included in regular education classrooms at rates never imagined even 20 years ago. This is largely due to early intervention and the integration of ABA strategies within classrooms.

The current challenge of our field is collaboration. The types of studies necessary to define comprehensive programs that blend ABA methodologies require the collaboration of well-respected researchers with strong credibility in each area. Clinicians are relying on varied approaches to data collection to inform the programs of individual children. This chapter described one approach that looks at acquisition rates to discern the level of structure a given child requires in his or her program. Certainly, there are many other variables that can be evaluated.

The current situation provides excellent possibilities for further advancement in the existing knowledge base and state-of-the-art treatments for children with autism. There are multiple approaches to choose from, all with impressive research to back them up. The field is advancing the understanding of autism treatments and better defining the need for well-rounded programs that address functional and generalized outcomes. It is anticipated that soon an evidence-based approach to the selection of treatment variables will come together to address the needs of the varied profiles that make up autism.

■ References

Abravanel, E., and Gingold, H. (1985). Learning via observation during the second year of life. *Developmental Psychology*, 21, 614–623.

Alternatives to Lovaas therapy. (1996, October). *Early Childhood Reports–Bonus Report*, LRP Publications, 10, 1–5.

Anderson, S.R., Avery, D.L., DiPietro, E.K., Edwards, G.L., and Christian, W.P. (1987). Intensive home-based early intervention with autistic children. *Education and Treatment of Children*, 10, 352–366.

Baird, G., Charman, T., Baron-Cohen, S., Cox, A., Swettenham, J., Wheelwright, S., and Drew, A. (2000). A screening instrument for autism at 18 months of age: A 6-year follow-up study. *Journal of the American Academy of Child and Adolescent Psychiatry*, 39, 694–702.

Baranek, G.T. (1999). Autism during infancy: A retrospective video analysis of sensory-motor and social behaviors at 9–12 months of age. *Journal of Autism and Developmental Disorders*, 29, 213–224.

Bernard-Opitz, V., Ing, S., and Kong, T.Y. (2004). Comparison of behavioural and natural play interventions for young children with autism. *Autism*, 8 (3), 319–333.

Birnbrauer, J.S., and Leach, D.J. (1993). The Murdoch early intervention program after 2 years. *Behaviour Change*, 10, 63–74.

Carpenter, M., Nagell, K., and Tomasello, M. (1998). Social cognition, joint attention, and communicative competence from 9 to 15 months of age. *Monographs of the Society for Research in Child Development*, 63 (4, Serial No. 255), 1–143.

Cavallaro, C.C., and Bambara, L. (1982). Two strategies for teaching language during free play. *Journal of the Association for Persons with Severe Handicaps*, 7, 80–93.

Charman, T., and Baird, G. (2002). Practitioner review: Diagnosis of autism spectrum disorder in 2- and 3-year-old children. *Journal of Child Psychology and Psychiatry*, 43 (3), 289–305.

Cohen, H., Amerine-Dickens, M., and Smith, T. (2006). Early intensive behavioral treatment: Replication of the UCLA model in a community setting. *Developmental and Behavioral Pediatrics*, 27, 145–155.

Dawson, G., Meltzoff, A., Osterling, J., Rinaldi, J., and Brown, E. (1988). Children with autism fail to orient to naturally occurring social stimuli. *Journal of Autism and Developmental Disorders*, 28, 479–485.

Dawson, G., Toth, K., Abbott, R., Osterling, J., Munson, J., Estes, A., and Liaw, J. (2004). Early social attention impairments in autism: Social orienting, joint attention, and attention to distress. *Developmental Psychology*, 40, 271–283.

Delprato, D.J. (2001). Comparison of discrete-trial and normalized behavioural language intervention for young children with autism. *Journal of Autism and Developmental Disorders*, 31, 315–327.

Dunham, P., and Moore, C. (1995). Current themes in research on joint attention. In *Joint attention: Its origins and role in development* (eds. C. Moore and P. Dunham), pp. 15–28. Hillsdale, N.J.: Erlbaum.

Dunlap, G. (1984). The influence of task variation and maintenance tasks on the learning and affect of autistic children. *Journal of Experimental Child Psychology*, 37, 41–64.

Dunlap, G., dePerczel, M., Clarke, S., Wilson, D., Wright, S., and Gomez, A. (1994). Choice making to promote adaptive behavior for students with emotional and behavioral challenges. *Journal of Applied Behavior Analysis*, 27, 505–518.

Dyer, K., Dunlap, G., and Winterling, V. (1990). Effects of choice-making on the serious problem behaviors of students with severe handicaps. *Journal of Applied Behavior Analysis*, 23, 515–524.

Eikeseth, S., Smith, T., Jahr, E., and Eldevik, S. (2002). Intensive behavioral treatment at school for 4- to 7-year old children with autism: A 1-year comparison controlled study. *Behavior Modification*, 26, 49–68.

Eikeseth, S., Smith, T., Jahr, E., and Eldevik, S. (2007). Outcome for children with autism who began intensive behavioral treatment between ages 4 and 7. *Behavior Modification*, 31, 264–278.

Eldevik, S., Eikeseth, S., Jahr, E., and Smith, T. (2006). Effects of low-intensity behavioral treatment for children with autism and mental retardation. *Journal of Autism and Developmental Disorders*, 36, 211–224.

Fenske, E.C., Salenski, S., Krantz, P.J., and McClannahan, L.E. (1985). Age at intervention and treatment outcomes for autistic children in a comprehensive intervention program. *Analysis and Intervention in Developmental Disabilities*, 5, 49–58.

Foxx, R.M. (1993). Rapid effects awaiting independent replication. *American Journal on Mental Retardation*, 97, 375–376.

Green, G. (1996). Evaluating claims about treatments for autism. In *Behavioral intervention for young children with autism* (eds. C. Maurice, G. Green, and S.C. Luce), pp.15–28. Austin, Tex.: PRO-ED.

Gresham, F.M., and MacMillan, D.L. (1998). Early intervention project: Can its claims be substantiated and its effects replicated? *Journal of Autism and Developmental Disorders*, 28, 5–13.

Halle, J.W., Baer, D.M., and Spradlin, J.E. (1981). Teachers' generalized use of delay as a stimulus control procedure to increase language use in handicapped children. *Journal of Applied Behavior Analysis*, 14, 387–400.

Halle, J.W., Marshall, A.M., and Spradlin, J.E. (1979). Time delay: A technique to increase language use and facilitate generalization in retarded children. *Journal of Applied Behavior Analysis*, 12, 431–440.

Handleman, J.S., and Harris, S.L. (2001). *Preschool education for programs for children with autism*. Austin, Tex.: PRO-ED.

Harris, S.L., Handleman, J.S., Gordon, R., Kristoff, B., and Fuentes, F. (1991). Changes in cognitive and language functioning of preschool children with autism. *Journal of Autism and Developmental Disorders*, 21, 281–290.

Hart, B. (1985). Naturalistic language training techniques. In *Teaching functional language: Generalization and maintenance of language skills* (eds. S. Warren and A.K. Rogers-Warren), pp. 63–88. Baltimore: University Park Press.

Hart, B., and Risley, T.R. (1968). Establishing the use of descriptive adjectives in the spontaneous speech of disadvantaged preschool children. *Journal of Applied Behavior Analysis*, 1, 109–120.

Hart, B., and Risley, T.R. (1975). Incidental teaching of language in the preschool. *Journal of Applied Behavior Analysis*, 8, 411–420.

Howard, J.S., Sparkman, C.R., Cohen, H., Green, G., and Stanislaw, H. (2005). A comparison of intensive behavior analytic and eclectic treatments for young children with autism. *Research in Developmental Disabilities*, 26, 359–383.

Howlin, P., Goode, S., Hutton, J., and Rutter, M. (2004). Adult outcome for children with Autism. *Journal of Child Psychology and Psychiatry*, 45, 212–229.

Howlin, P., Mawhood, L., and Rutter, M. (2000). Autism and developmental receptive disorder: A follow-up comparison in early adult life. II: Social, behavioural, and psychiatric outcomes. *Journal of Child Psychology and Psychiatry,* 41, 561–578.

Javaloyes, M.A. (2006). The need for reviewing international diagnostic categories in pervasive developmental disorders. *Autism,* 10, 525.

Kaiser, A.P., Yoder, P.J., and Keetz, A. (1992) Evaluating milieu teaching. In *Communication and language intervention series. Vol. 1: Causes and effects in communication and language intervention* (eds. S.F. Warren and J. Reichle), pp. 9–47. Baltimore: Paul H. Brookes.

Kasari, C., Freeman, S., and Papprella, T. (2001). Early intervention in autism: Joint attention and symbolic play. In *International review of research on mental retardation* (ed. L.M. Glidden). New York: Academic Press.

Kazdin, A.E. (1993). Replication and extension of behavioral treatment of autistic disorder. *American Journal on Mental Retardation,* 97, 377–379.

Kern, L., Mantegna, M.E. , Vorndran, C.M., Bailin, D., and Hilt, A. (2001). Choice of task sequence to reduce problem behaviors. *Journal of Positive Behavior Interventions,* 3, 3–10.

Kern, L., Vorndran, C.M., Hilt, A., Ringdahl, J.E., Adelman, B.E., and Dunlap, G. (1998). Choice as an intervention to improve behavior: A review of the literature. *Journal of Behavioral Education,* 8, 151–169.

Koegel, L.K. (1995). Communication and language intervention. In *Teaching children with autism* (eds. R.L. Koegel and L.K. Koegel). Baltimore: Paul H. Brookes.

Koegel, L.K., and Koegel, R.L. (1995). Motivating communication in children with autism. In *Learning and cognition in autism* (eds. E. Schopler and G. Mesibov), pp. 73–87. New York: Plenum.

Koegel, R.L., Carter, C.M., and Koegel, L.K. (1998). Setting events to improve parent-teacher coordination and motivation for children with autism. In *Antecedent control: Innovative approaches to behavioral support* (eds. J. Luiselli and M. Cameron), pp. 167–186). Baltimore: Paul H. Brookes.

Koegel, R.L., and Covert, A. (1972). The relationship of self-stimulation to learning in autistic children. *Journal of Applied Behavior Analysis,* 5, 381–388.

Koegel, R.L., Dyer, K., and Bell, L. (1987). The influence of child-preferred activities on autistic children's social behavior. *Journal of Applied Behavior Analysis,* 20, 243–252.

Koegel, R.L., and Egel, A.L. (1979). Motivating autistic children. *Journal of Abnormal Psychology,* 88, 418–426.

Koegel, R.L., and Koegel, L.K. (2006). *Pivotal response treatments for autism: Communication, social, and academic development.* Baltimore: Paul H. Brookes.

Koegel, R.L., Koegel, L.K., and McNerney, E.K. (2001). Pivotal areas in intervention for autism. *Journal of Clinical Child Psychology,* 30, 19–32.

Koegel, R.L., Koegel, L.K., and Surratt, A.V. (1992). Language intervention and disruptive behavior in preschool children with autism. *Journal of Autism and Developmental Disorders,* 22, 141–153.

Koegel, R.L., and Mentis, M. (1985). Motivation in children with autism: Can they or won't they? *Journal of Child Psychology and Psychiatry,* 26, 185–191.

Koegel, R.L., O'Dell, M.C., and Dunlap, G. (1988). Producing speech use in non-verbal autistic children by reinforcing attempts. *Journal of Autism and Developmental Disorders,* 18, 525–538.

Koegel, R.L., O'Dell, M.C., and Koegel, L.K. (1987). A natural language paradigm for teaching non-verbal autistic children. *Journal of Autism and Developmental Disorders,* 17, 187–199.

Laski, K.E., Charlop, M.H., and Schreibman, L. (1988). Training parents to use the Natural Language Paradigm to increase their autistic children's speech. *Journal of Applied Behavior Analysis,* 21, 391–400.

Lecavalier, L. (2005). An evaluation of the Gilliam Autism Rating Scale. *Journal of Autism and Developmental Disorders,* 35, 795–805.

Lord, C., Wagner, A., Rogers, S., Szatmari, P., Aman, M., Charman, T., Dawson, G., Durand, V.M., Grossman, L., Guthrie, D., Harris, S., Kasari, C., Marcus, L, Murphy, S., Odom, S., Pickles, A., Scahill, L., Shaw, E., Siegel, B., Sigman, M., Stone, W., Smith, T., and Yoder, P. (2005). Challenges in evaluating psychosocial interventions for autistic spectrum disorders. *Journal of Autism and Developmental Disorders,* 35, 695–708.

Lovaas, O.I. (1981). *Teaching Developmentally Disabled Children: The ME book.* Baltimore: University Park Press.

Lovaas, O.I. (1987). Behavioral treatment and normal educational and intellectual functioning in young autistic children. *Journal of Consulting and Clinical Psychology,* 55, 3–9.

Lovaas, O.I (2002). *Teaching individuals with developmental delays: Basic intervention techniques.* Austin, Tex.: PRO-ED.

Luiselli, J.K., Cannon, B.O., Ellis, J.T., and Sisson, R.W. (2000). Home-based behavioral intervention for young children with autism/pervasive developmental disorder. *Autism,* 4, 426–438.

McClannahan, L.E., and Krantz, P.J. (2001). Behavior analysis and intervention for preschoolers and the Princeton Child Development Institute. In *Preschool education programs for children with autism* (eds. J.S. Handleman and S.L. Harris). Austin Tex.: PRO-ED.

McEachin, J.J., Smith, T., and Lovaas, O.I. (1993). Long-term outcome for children with autism who received early intensive behavioral treatment. *American Journal on Mental Retardation,* 97, 359–372.

McGee, G.G., Almeida, M.C., Sulzer-Azaroff, B., and Feldman, R. (1992). Promoting reciprocal interactions via peer incidental teaching. *Journal of Applied Behavior Analysis,* 25, 117–126.

McGee, G.G., Morrier, M.J., and Daly, T. (2001). The Walden Early Childhood Programs. In *Preschool education for programs for children with autism* (eds. J.S. Handleman and S.L. Harris). Austin, Tex.: PRO-ED.

Meltzoff, A.N., and Moore, M.K. (1989). Imitation in newborn infants: Exploring the range of gestures imitated and the underlying mechanisms. *Developmental Psychology,* 25, 954–962.

Meltzoff, A.N., and Moore, M.K. (1992). Early imitation within a functional framework: The importance of person identity, movement and development. *Infant Behavior and Development*, 15, 479–505.

Meyer, L.S., Taylor, B.A., Levin, L.L., and Fisher, J.R. (2001). Alpine Learning Group. In *Preschool education for programs for children with autism* (eds. J.S. Handleman and S.L. Harris). Austin Tex.: PRO-ED.

Morales, M., Mundy, P., and Rojas, J. (1998). Brief report: Following the direction of gaze and language development in 6-month-olds. *Infant Behavior and Development*, 21, 373–377.

Mundy, P. (1993). Normal versus high-functioning status in children with autism. *American Journal on Mental Retardation*, 97, 381–384.

Mundy, P. (1995). Joint attention and social-emotional approach behavior in children with autism. *Development and Psychopathology*, 7 (1), 63–82.

Mundy, P., and Neal, R. (2001). Neural plasticity, joint attention and a transactional social-orienting model of autism. In *International Review of research in mental retardation. Vol 23: Autism* (ed. L. Glidden), pp. 139–168. New York: Academic Press.

Mundy, P., Sigman, M., Ungerer, J., and Sherman, T. (1986.) Defining the social deficits of autism: The contribution of non-verbal communication measures. *Journal of Child Psychology and Psychiatry*, 27, 657–669.

National Research Council. (2001). *Educating children with autism*. Washington, D.C.: National Academy Press.

Nielsen, M. (2006). Copying actions and copying outcomes: Social learning through the second year. *Developmental Psychology*, 42, 555–565.

Nordin, V., and Gillberg, C. (1998). The long-term course of autistic disorders: Update on follow-up studies. *Acta Psychiatrica Scandanavica*, 97, 99–108.

Osterling, J., and Dawson, G. (1994). Early recognition of children with autism: A study of first birthday home video tapes. *Journal of Autism and Developmental Disorders*, 24, 247–257.

Osterling, J.A., Dawson, G., and Munson, J.A. (2002). Early recognition of 1-year-old infants with autism spectrum disorder versus mental retardation. *Developmental Psychopathology*, 14, 239–251.

Pierce, K., and Schreibman, L. (1995). Increasing complex social behaviors in children with autism: Effects of peer-implemented pivotal response training. *Journal of Applied Behavior Analysis*, 28, 285–295.

Ramey, C.T., Bryant, D.M., Wasick, B.H., Sparling, J.J., Fendt, K.H., and LaVange, L.M. (1992). The infant health and development program for low birthweight, premature infants: Program elements, family participation, and child intelligence. *Pediatrics*, 89, 454–465.

Rochat, P., and Striano, T. (1999). Social-cognitive development in the first year. In *Early social cognition: Understanding others in the first months of life* (ed. P. Rochat), pp. 3–34). Mawhah, N.J.: Erlbaum.

Rogers, S.J. (1996). Brief report: Early intervention in autism. *Journal of Autism and Developmental Disorders*, 26, 243–246.

Rogers, S.J., and Pennington, B.F. (1991). Executive function deficits in high-functioning autistic individuals: Relationship to theory of mind. *Journal of Child Psychology and Psychiatry*, 32, 1081–1105.

Rogers-Warren, A.K., and Warren, S.F. (1980). Mand for verbalization: Facilitating the display of newly-taught language. *Behavior Modification*, 4, 361–382.

Ruble, L.A., and Dalrymple, N.J. (1996). An alternative view of outcome in autism. *Focus on Autism and Other Developmental Disabilities*, 11, 3–14.

Sallows, G.O., and Graupner, T.D. (2005). Intensive behavioral treatment for children with autism: Four-year outcome and predictors. *American Journal on Mental Retardation*, 110, 417–438.

Sallows, G.O., Graupner, T.D., and Sherman, M. (2007). *Treatment strategies for increasing the number of children with autism who reach normalcy.* Workshop presented at the 33rd Annual Association for Behavior Analysis International Convention, San Diego, Calif., May 2007.

Schopler, E., Short, A., and Mesibov, G. (1989). Relation of behavior treatment to "normal functioning": Comment on Lovaas. *Journal of Consulting and Clinical Psychology*, 57, 162–164.

Schreibman, L. (2000). Intensive behavioral/psychoeducational treatments for autism: Research needs and future directions. *Journal of Autism and Developmental Disorders*, 30, 373–378.

Schreibman, L. (2005). *The science and fiction of autism.* Cambridge, Mass.: Harvard University Press.

Schreibman, L., and Ingersoll, B. (2005). Behavioral interventions to promote learning in individuals with autism. In *Handbook of autism and pervasive developmental disorders* (Vol. 2) (eds. F.R. Volkmar, R. Paul, A. Klin, and D. Cohen), pp. 882–896. Hoboken, N.J.: John Wiley and Sons.

Sheinkopf, S., and Siegel, B. (1998) Effects of very early intensive behavior intervention for autistic children. *Journal of Autism and Developmental Disorders*, 28, 15–23.

Sherer, M.R., and Schreibman, L. (2005). Individual behavior profiles and predictors of treatment effectiveness for children with autism. *Journal of Consulting and Clinical Psychology*, 73, 525–538.

Sigafoos, J. (1998). Choice making and personal selection strategies. In *Antecedent control: Innovative approaches to behavioral support* (eds. J. Luiselli and M. Cameron), pp. 187–221. Baltimore: Paul H. Brookes.

Sigman, M., Spence, S.J., and Wang, A.T. (2006). Autism from developmental and neuropsychological perspectives. *Annual Review of Clinical Psychology*, 2, 327–355.

Smith, T. (1999). Outcome of early intervention for children with autism. *Clinical Psychology: Research and Practice*, 6, 33–49.

Smith, T. (2001). Discrete trial training in the treatment of autism. *Focus on Autism and Other Developmental Disabilities*, 16, 86–92.

Smith, T. (2007). *Overall results from the multisite Young Autism Project.* Paper presented at the 33rd Annual Association for Behavior Analysis International Convention, San Diego, Calif., May 2007.

Smith, T., Groen, A.D., and Wynn, J.W. (2000). Randomized trial of intensive early intervention for children with pervasive developmental disorder. *American Journal on Mental Retardation,* 105, 269–285.

Smith, I.M., and Bryson, S.E. (1994). Imitation and action in autism: A critical review. *Psychology Bulletin* 116, 259–273.

Stokes, T.F., and Osnes, P.G. (1988). The developing applied technology of generalization and maintenacne. In *Generalization and maintenance: Life-style changes in applied settings* (eds. R.H. Horner, G. Dunlap, and R.L. Koegel), pp. 5–20. Baltimore: Paul H. Brookes.

Szatmari, P., Bryson, S.E., Boyle, M.H., Streiner, D.L., and Duku, E. (2003). Predictors of outcome among high functioning children with autism and Asperger syndrome. *Journal of Child Psychology and Psychiatry,* 44, 520–528.

Taylor, B.A., and Harris, S.L. (1995). Teaching children with autism to seek information: Acquisition of novel information and generalization of responding. *Journal of Applied Behavior Analysis,* 28, 3–14.

Tryon, A.P., Mayes, S.D., Rhodes, R.L., and Waldo, M. (2006). Can Asperger's Disorder be differentiated from autism using DSM-IV criteria? *Focus on Autism and Other Developmental Disabilities,* 21, 2–6.

Varni, J.W., Lovaas, O.I., Koegel, R.L., and Everret, N.L. (1979). An analysis of observational learning in autistic and normal children. *Journal of Abnormal Child Psychology,* 7, 31–43.

Volkmar, F.R., and Klin, A. (2005). Issues in the classification of autism and related conditions. In *Handbook of autism and pervasive developmental disorders* (eds. F.R. Volkmar, R. Paul, A. Klin, and D. Cohen), pp. 5–41. Hoboken, N.J.: John Wiley and Sons.

Volkmar, F.R., Lord, C., Bailey, A., Schultz, R.T., and Klin, A. (2004). Autism and pervasive developmental disorders. *Journal of Child Psychology and Psychiatry,* 45, 135–170.

Warren, S.F., and Kaiser, A.P. (1986). Incidental language teaching: A critical review. *Journal of Speech and Hearing Disorders,* 51, 291–299.

Warren, S.F., McQuarters, R.J., and Rogers-Warren, A.K. (1984). The effects of mands and models on the speech of unresponsive language-delayed preschool children. *Journal of Speech and Hearing Disorders,* 49, 43–52.

Weiss, M.J. (1999). Differential rates of skill acquisition and outcomes of early intensive behavioral intervention for autism. *Behavioral Interventions,* 14, 3–22.

Whalen, C., and Schreibman, L. (2003). Joint attention training for children with autism using behavior modification procedures. *Journal of Child Psychology and Psychiatry,* 44, 456–468.

Williams, J., and Brayne, C. (2006). Screening for autism spectrum disorders: What is the evidence? *Autism* 10, 11–35.

Winterling, V., Dunlap, G., and O'Neill, R.E. (1987). The influence of task variation on the aberrant behaviors of autistic students. *Education and Treatment of Children,* 10, 105–119.

Zwaigenbaum, L., Bryson, S., Rogers, T., Roberts, W., Brian, J., and Szatmari, P. (2005). Behavioral manifestations of autism in the first year of life. *International Journal of Developmental Neuroscience,* 23, 143–152.

6. Essential Components for Effective Autism Educational Programs

Glen Dunlap, Rose Iovannone, and Donald Kincaid

■ Essential Components for Educational Programs

Students with autism present educators with perhaps the greatest challenge of any student population. This is the case for many reasons, including the heterogeneity of the students' characteristics and needs, the idiosyncratic and occasionally severe nature of the students' behavioral challenges, the dramatic increase in the prevalence of autism spectrum disorder (ASD) (Centers for Disease Control and Prevention 2000; Huff 2006), the strongly held and diverse opinions regarding appropriate intervention, and the litigious atmosphere engendered by these opinions (Baird 1999; Yell and Drasgow 2000). These factors have combined to oblige school officials in districts across the country to implement processes for formulating appropriate and effective programs for serving the educational needs of students across the full range of the autism spectrum.

This challenge facing educational professionals is formidable because there is no well-established consensus regarding appropriate educational practice for students with autism. Although the literature regarding interventions for ASD is extensive, it is also extraordinarily diverse and confusing. To a greater extent than with any other population, the literature comprises a perplexing amalgamation of experimental and quasi-experimental research, case studies, theoretical positions and speculations, and compelling anecdotes (e.g., Olley 1999). Exacerbating the situation is the ongoing influx of new and unproven recommendations in the popular media and on the Internet. As many authors have noted (e.g., Dunlap 1999; Heflin and Simpson 1998; Olley 1999), professionals and parents can have great difficulties attempting to distinguish legitimate, well-documented approaches from strategies that have no conceptual or empirical justification.

In response to this state of muddle, a number of efforts have been implemented to identify elements of effective intervention programs for young children with autism. These initiatives have been conducted by states and provinces (e.g., New York Department of Health 1999; Perry and Condillac 2003), by specialized task forces and councils (e.g., Hurth et al. 1999; National Research Council [NRC] 2001), and by a number of individual authors (Dawson and Osterling 1997; Dunlap and Robbins 1991; Powers 1992). The results of these efforts vary in their degrees of specificity, but they tend to identify a number of common features supported by combinations of data and professional agreement. Among the features that have been identified are supportive learning environments, family involvement, behavior-oriented instruction, focused and specialized curricula, and the importance of beginning intervention at an early point in the child's development. Indeed, a common feature is that all of these efforts to distill effective program practices have addressed the needs of young (e.g., preschool) children with autism. Similar attention to features of effective educational programs for older children, adolescents, or adults has not been reported.

The need for clear guidelines for school programs for students with autism continues to be an issue confronting educators nationwide. One attempt to address this need was offered by Iovannone and colleagues (2003). They considered the work conducted in relation to young children with autism and extracted six core elements of effective educational practice that they argued were empirically supported and should be included in sound, comprehensive programs for all students with autism.

This chapter provides a description of these six core elements in the context of school programs for students with autism. The first sections of the chapter describe some issues that should be considered in developing educational programs and how they can be situated in the context of larger school systems of discipline and educational support. The bulk of the chapter is then devoted to discussions of the six core elements: *(a)* systematic instruction, *(b)* individualization, *(c)* structured and comprehensible learning environments, *(d)* specialized curricular features, *(e)* functional approach to problem behaviors, and *(f)* family involvement.

■ Some Issues in Educational Programming for Students with Autism

Before discussing the core elements of effective educational programs, it is important to review some issues that should always be considered in the development of programs for individual students with ASD. One of the issues influencing the identification of effective practices for children with ASD is the *heterogeneity of the disorder* (Heflin and Simpson 1998). By definition, children with ASD exhibit a variety of deficits in domains such as social, communicative, behavioral, and cognitive functioning (American Psychiatric Association

1994; NRC 2001). However, each child affected by autism may exhibit delays or disorders in some of these areas but not others, and to varying degrees from mild to severe. The challenge of matching a child's needs to effective educational services is further complicated by a large variety of environmental factors that affect the child's functioning and development. Each child carries a unique set of social, familial, community, and school experiences that must be considered if an optimally beneficial intervention is to be provided. That is, it is not only the diversity of a child's developmental characteristics but also the diversity of life contexts that affects the determination of effective educational practices (Albin et al. 1996; Harris, Handleman, and Jennett 2005). The heterogeneity of the ASD population indicates that schools must plan for a full range of curricular and placement options if the individualized needs of all students are to be accommodated.

A second issue pertains to the concept of *evidence-based practice* and, more generally, *data-based accountability.* On one hand, it is important to select educational interventions that have an empirical foundation. That is, educators (and parents and other care providers) should ask whether a proposed intervention has data suggesting its effectiveness in addressing the instructional objectives identified for the student (Simpson 2005; Odom et al. 2003). Such evidence is most reliable when it comes from peer-reviewed journals and has been replicated many times in different settings and by different researchers (Horner et al. 2005 *The use of single subject research*).

However, although it may indicate a likelihood of educational benefit, the presence of empirical justification does not guarantee that a given intervention will be effective with a specific child in a specific circumstance. Therefore, it is essential that interventions be accompanied by the collection of objective data that allow parents and practitioners to determine whether the intervention is producing desired outcomes. For instructional objectives that are judged to be priorities by the educational team, data-based accountability is accomplished by following a well-established process. First, the behaviors that determine the success or failure of the intervention must be defined in clear and objective terms (O'Neill et al. 1997). Second, the intervention should be described in operational terms so that all team members understand what is to be done and what is being evaluated. Such evaluation is expedited when only one intervention is implemented at a time, so that it is apparent which intervention was responsible for changes in behavior. Still, in some cases, it is desirable to implement an intervention "package" that comprises several components or intervention strategies. With such an approach, the evaluation is of the package and not of the separate elements that are included in the multicomponent strategy. Finally, it is important to collect data on the identified targeted behaviors before and after intervention to determine whether change occurred. The data collection procedures should be as simple as possible while still ensuring the provision of valid indices of the instructional objective, and the evaluation process should include data collection (and summation) at frequent enough intervals to permit rapid detection of inadequacies and modification of instructional strategies, as appropriate.

The third major issue related to educational programming for students with ASD pertains to the overall *school environment*. The school environment is a set of critical context variables that affects the selection and application of effective educational and behavioral supports. The school environment is shaped by policies and practices at the federal, state, district, school, and classroom levels that combine to provide students with very different educational experiences. For instance, federal, state, and district policies concerning whether students with ASD will be educated in regular education classrooms, special education classrooms, or specialized schools directly affect the educational experiences of these students. Philosophies and practices at the school level may include *(a)* the administrative support provided to teachers, *(b)* the staff's philosophies on educating students with disabilities and inclusion, and *(c)* the development of a positive school climate that ensures a high quality of instruction for all students.

The development of a positive school climate is a critical outcome that is being addressed by the School-Wide Positive Behavior Support (SWPBS) movement and similar systems-change efforts. SWPBS is the application of evidence-based strategies and systems to assist schools to increase academic performance, increase safety, decrease problem behavior, and establish positive school cultures (Sugai et al. 2000, 2005). SWPBS is a three-tiered preventive approach that includes primary (universal systems for all students), secondary (interventions for classrooms and targeted groups of at-risk students), and tertiary (interventions for students with severe behavior problems) levels of support. At the level of the entire school, for targeted groups of students, or for individual students, SWPBS advocates a preventive teaching and re-inforcement approach for addressing behavior problems (Horner et al. 2005 *Schoolwide positive behavior support*). The philosophy, process, and practice of SWPBS affect all students within a school, including students with ASD. For instance, at the entire school level, teaching and reinforcing of appropriate expectations and rules for all students can have a significant impact on students with ASD, regardless of whether they are in a special school, in a segregated classroom, or partially or fully included in a regular classroom (Freeman et al. 2006). These philosophies and effective teaching strategies for student behavior change can extend to students with ASD. In addition, the implementation of effective school-wide behavior support practices can also decrease the amount of school resources (e.g., time, funds, personnel) that have been ineffectively applied to the entire student population. As a result, fewer students may require intensive behavior supports, and there may be more adequate resources at the school level to address their curricular, instructional, and behavior needs. Because it is likely that students with ASD will require and benefit from individualized curricular, instructional, and behavioral supports, a school that is effectively implementing SWPBS approaches should also be able to implement more effective supports with those students who face the most complex challenges.

In addition to a school-wide behavior support system, the quality of the instruction for all students also has a significant impact on students with ASD. Westling and Fox (2004) identified 12 effective educational practices that should be present in the curriculum and instruction of all students:

1. A careful plan of instruction
2. Efficient management of instructional time
3. Effective management of student behavior
4. Design of instructional groups to meet learning needs
5. Careful presentation of instructional stimuli and procedures
6. Establishment of smooth, efficient classroom routines
7. Provision of frequent feedback to the student
8. Monitoring of students' performance
9. Review and reteaching of material as necessary
10. Integration of workplace readiness skills into instruction (e.g., problem-solving skills)
11. Appropriately high expectations for students
12. Interaction with students in a positive, caring way

The extent to which these features are present in the school and classroom context has a great deal to do with the effectiveness of educational practices for all students, including students with ASD.

■ Essential Components of Effective Instruction
   for Students with Autism Spectrum Disorders

Whereas inclusion of all 12 of the effective instructional principles is essential for any educational program, a continual challenge facing both educators and parents of children with ASD is providing strategies that are evidence-based, specific to the unique behaviors of the disorder, and acceptable to all relevant persons. The core challenges in the social and communication areas for students with ASD require a more specialized focus on strategies that have been proven to ameliorate deficits and enhance acquisition and maintenance of core skills (NRC 2001).

As previously mentioned, it seems reasonable to assume that the core elements of early intervention programs would be equally effective if present in programs for school-aged students (i.e., 8 to 21 years), keeping in mind that each component would be adjusted for the chronological age, varying abilities, and changing needs of the student throughout the educational life-span. The six core components identified by Iovannone and colleagues (2003) are described here: systematic instruction, individualized supports, structured learning environments, specialized curriculum focus, functional approach to problem behaviors, and family involvement.

Systematic Instruction

One critical element that researchers agree must be present in all comprehensive and effective programs is the provision of systematic instruction. Systematic instruction is the identification of meaningful goals and the explicit planning for specific, direct instruction that allows the student to successfully achieve the goals. Planning activities include identifying and defining socially valid educational teaching goals, specifying and implementing direct instructional procedures for teaching, evaluating and monitoring the effectiveness of instruction, and making appropriate adjustments based on data (Hurth et al. 1999; Westling and Fox 2004). The use of systematic instruction increases the likelihood of increased student achievement of skills (Heflin and Alberto 2001; Simpson 2001), provides a structured plan for generalizing and maintaining learned abilities, and enhances the probability of attaining high levels of engagement.

Of key importance in the thoughtful planning for instruction is the identification of socially valid goals—or *what* to teach—and the consideration of how this instruction is to be embedded within the curriculum, including the general education curriculum. Too often, teaching objectives for students with ASD focus on discrete, isolated skills. It is not uncommon to see an Individual Education Plan that includes short-term goals that address tying shoes, zippering clothing, making eye contact, pointing to a color, putting a puzzle piece into a four-piece inlaid puzzle, and so forth. Kleinert and Kearns (2001) suggested that these types of behaviors are actually activities rather than skills, and they proposed that educators focus on the broad, critical skills necessary to perform the actions. Examples of critical skills necessary to complete independent or self-help domain activities include communicating the need for materials, requesting help when necessary, making choices, and initiating comments to others involved in the activity. With such targeting of broader behaviors or skills that can be repeated in the context of multiple meaningful activities throughout the day, teaching moments exponentially increase. For example, the opportunity to tie one's shoes may occur naturally only once or twice a day. In contrast, the critical skills of asking for help can occur in every activity and context throughout the student's day.

An important component of systematic instruction is the ongoing data collection process. Having a systematic method for collecting data on instructional goals has consistently been identified as a major factor in school districts' winning or losing due process cases related to methodology disagreement (Etscheidt 2003; Yell and Drasgrow 2000). The consistent collection of data allows a teacher to determine whether the student is progressing at the desired rate and whether the instructional methods used are appropriate. Data collection methods do not have to be complicated or time-consuming to inform educators about the effectiveness of instruction. For instance, simple methods such as weekly probes on instructional programs and daily administration of five-point behavior rating scales have been used by teachers to gauge the progress of their students.

Research conducted over several decades has shown that the use of strategies based on applied behavior analysis (ABA) principles has been effective in systematically teaching students with ASD. It is important to understand that ABA is not a specific program, procedure, or technique; rather, it involves methods and principles that are applied to socially valid behaviors in varied ways (Dunlap 1999). Principles and procedures such as reinforcement, shaping, prompting and fading, and stimulus change are provided at the necessary level and intensity that fit the context and the individual characteristics of the student. Common interventions based on ABA principles range from intensive, directed approaches (e.g., discrete trial training) to more naturalistic approaches (e.g., incidental teaching, pivotal response training). Hundreds of studies have used ABA-based strategies to increase the acquisition, maintenance, and generalization of skills of students with ASD from kindergarten through 12th grade. For instance, studies have been conducted to improve language (Eikeseth et al. 2002), teach orthographic symbols (Hetzroni and Shalem 2005), teach grocery shopping (Morse and Schuster 2000), increase independent academic behavior (Callahan and Rademacher 1999), and reduce inappropriate vocalizations while increasing time on task (Mancina et al. 2000). Generally, ABA-based approaches represent the standard of a systematic orientation to instruction.

Individualized Supports and Services

Although the orientation of ABA has been demonstrated to be effective, it is generally agreed that there is no evidence for recommending one specific approach or one program as being superior for all individuals with ASD (Heflin and Simpson 1998). The best approach is one that integrates strategies based on evidential standards that can support and meet the needs of students displaying heterogeneous behaviors and characteristics, as well as the needs of the families and professionals with whom they are associated (Simpson 2005). Schools are mandated by the Individuals with Disabilities Education Improvement Act of 2004 (IDEA) to provide students with a continuum of supports, services, and placements ranging from inclusion in general education to instruction in specialized settings. The optimal level of supports and services required for a student with ASD to receive an appropriate education is individually determined; some students may be placed in general education settings with minimal or moderate modifications, whereas others may require major adaptations and a curriculum emphasizing functional skills of daily living. The most effective practice is to provide flexible placement and support options that will effectively meet each student's individualized goals (Dunlap and Robbins 1991).

Although no one specific strategy is effective for all students with ASD, it is clear that some strategies have more efficacy than others. An essential key toward providing appropriate individualized supports is to match specific strategies, supports, and services to each student's unique profile and the family's characteristics (Dunlap 1999). Schools should consider the following when providing supports: *(a)* incorporating family preferences when determining the goals to be taught and the instructional delivery method; *(b)* fitting the student's preferences and interests into the instructional content and strategies (Hurth et al. 1999); and *(c)* focusing on the student's strengths and challenges to determine the most appropriate level of intensity and instruction that will meet the individual goals (NRC 2001).

When planning for individualized supports, it is important to implement strategies that are designed to produce high rates of student academic engaged time. Engagement, the amount of time that the student is attending to and actively interacting with his or her social environments (Dunlap 1999; Hurth et al. 1999), has been cited as one of the strongest predictors of positive student outcomes (Logan, Bakeman, and Keefe 1997; Rogers 1999). When a student is engaged, connections and interactions with the environment are occurring, leading to availability for learning (Hurth et al. 1999). Although students with ASD are diverse in their presentation of behaviors, difficulties in motivating them to respond to their environments have been well documented (Dunlap 1999; Dunlap and Robbins 1991; Koegel and Mentis 1985; Olley and Reeve 1997; Simpson and Myles 1998). Engagement is unlikely to occur unless educators deliberately design individualized strategies intended to motivate the student, including changes to the physical environment, incorporation of preferred activities and materials, and capitalization on spontaneous interests and initiations (Hurth et al. 1999).

One strategy, pivotal response training (PRT), has been generating increased attention as a method to promote motivation in students with ASD (Koegel, Harrower, and Koegel 1999; Koegel and Koegel 2006; Koegel, Koegel, and Carter 1999; Pierce and Schreibman 1997). Pivotal response training, a comprehensive developmental approach based on ABA principles, concentrates on targeting pivotal behaviors (e.g., motivation, self-initiation, responding to multiple cues) that result in widespread collateral changes in other, nontargeted behaviors (Koegel et al. 1999). Strategies used in the PRT approach include following the child's lead, using preferred items or activities, providing

clear instructions, teaching within natural contexts, providing choices, reinforcing all attempts, varying and interspersing tasks, and using naturally occurring reinforcers. Impressive documentation of the efficacy of PRT strategies
for increasing engagement and motivation has been recorded (Koegel and Egel
1979; Koegel et al. 1999).

In addition to PRT, a variety of specific strategies, based on the student's
individualized characteristics, behaviors, and preferences, have been shown to
increase engagement. Approaches include, but are not limited to, the following:
using preferred objects and natural reinforcers to increase self-initiation and
spontaneous questions (Koegel et al. 1998), interspersing easy and difficult tasks
to increase participation in and response to instructional activities (Dunlap
1984; Heckaman et al. 1998), incorporating idiosyncratic or perseverative interests into instructional tasks to increase social interactions (Baker, Koegel, and
Koegel 1999), and using picture activity schedules to increase on-task behaviors
(Bryan and Gast 2000; MacDuff, Krantz, and McClannahan 1993).

Comprehensible and Structured Learning Environments

The recommendation to provide students with ASD with "structure," and a
"structured environment," is almost universal; however, the term "structured"
is not uniformly defined. A structured program is one in which the curriculum
and behavioral expectations are clear and fully comprehensible to both the
students and the educational staff in the classroom (Olley and Reeve 1997). A
litmus test for determining the comprehensibility of a classroom is to observe
the students for 10 minutes and attempt to identify what each one is supposed
to be doing. If the observer is unable to do so, it is understandable that the students (and the staff) may be uncertain as well. A comprehensible environment
is one that is arranged to facilitate, elicit, enhance, and support the acquisition of critical skills, including language, behavior, social interactions, and
academics. When an environment is comprehensible, a student with ASD can
(a) know what is currently happening within the learning process, (b) predict
what will happen next, (c) anticipate the requirements of specific settings, and
(d) learn and generalize various skills (Earles, Carlson, and Bock 1998; Hurth
et al. 1999; Gresham et al. 1999; Volmer 1997).

Examples of strategies that assist in facilitating the comprehensibility of
the environment include providing visual cues or environmental supports
that organize the instructional setting (Heflin and Alberto 2001), providing
a schedule of activities (Rogers 1999; Simpson and Myles 1998), promoting
choice making (Dalrymple 1995), giving behavioral support (Earles, Carlson,
and Bock 1998), defining boundaries of different areas in the classroom and
school (Heflin and Alberto 2001; Volmer 1997), providing time relations
(Earles, Carlson, and Bock 1998; Heflin and Alberto 2001), and facilitating
transitions, flexibility, and change (Simpson and Myles 1998). It is important

to appreciate that supports such as these, which serve to heighten the comprehensibility and predictability of a student's environment, can be provided in any setting. That is, "structure" is not a function of being placed in a particular (e.g., self-contained) setting.

Although environmental supports that facilitate the comprehensibility of classroom and school settings appear to be widely used with students who have ASD, research exploring their efficacy is just now emerging. Representative studies pertaining to environmental support strategies for school-aged students with ASD include examinations of visual schedules to facilitate transitions (Dettmer et al. 2000) and video priming to reduce disruptive transition behavior (Schreibman, Whalen, and Stahmer 2002).

Specialized Curriculum Focus

Core challenges for students with ASD are in the areas of language and social interaction. Specifically, students with ASD have difficulties in social situations that require social reciprocity and expressive or receptive communication. In addition, deficits in functional and spontaneous communication and pretend play exacerbate the problems students with autism have when socially interacting with peers and adults. Therefore, curricula provided for students with ASD should emphasize and focus on improving these areas. In particular, critical social skills such as engaging in social situations, initiating and responding to social bids, participating in appropriate recreational or leisure skills, and increasing social language comprehension and communication should be targeted, and instructional activities that provide opportunities for practicing these skills should be embedded within daily routines (Olley 1999).

For teachers and other educators, an important consideration is the method of communication that will be taught. Although verbal language is always the desired mode of communicating, it may not initially be the most efficient or most effective means of communication for some students with ASD. Communication is a core functional skill; if the student does not learn an efficient and effective means of communicating, another person will always need to be present to assist the student in situations that require communication exchanges. Therefore, all students going through our educational system should be taught an effective method of communication, whether it be conventional verbal language or communication with assistance or augmentation (Olley and Rosenthal 1985).

The literature is rife with empirical studies exploring the efficacy of interventions specifically applied to social and/or communicative behaviors of school-aged students with ASD. The strategies most commonly used to increase communication abilities are those based on ABA principles, including the use of discrete trials to increase gesture use with verbal language (Buffington et al. 1998), multiple exemplars to answer *Wh-* questions and to generalize (Jahr

2001), and fading procedures with embedded textual cues to increase the number of conversational exchanges (Sarokoff, Taylor, and Poulson 2001).

The use of augmentative and alternative communication (AAC) has an emerging literature base and shows evidence of being a viable strategy, particularly for those students who do not acquire functional speech or have difficulty comprehending spoken language (NRC 2001). However, many unanswered questions remain, including the characteristics of students for whom AAC approaches would be most effective and the characteristics of those for whom AAC might not be recommended. Still, the overriding urgency is to provide students with at least some means with which to communicate, and for many students the immediate expedient is AAC.

The Picture Exchange Communication System, or PECS (Frost and Bondy, 1994), has widespread acceptance as an AAC strategy for students with ASD. Several research studies have shown evidence that PECS is effective for some students. The PECS, using ABA principles, focuses on increasing spontaneous communication by teaching students in the initial phases to exchange picture symbols to request and comment on items. Subsequent phases target sentence formation, reciprocal interactions, and verbal language acquisition. In recent years, an increasing number of researchers have studied the use of PECS to increase communication skills in school-aged students with ASD. Studies using PECS include those that increased mands (Ganz and Simpson 2004), compared mand acquisition with sign language (Anderson 2002; Tincani 2004), explored effects on manding and verbal language development (Tincani, Crozier, and Alazetta 2006), increased spontaneous speech (Jones 2005; Kravits et al. 2002), investigated the impact of PECS on vocal imitation and visual matching (Cummings and Williams 2000), examined increasing student abilities to use PECS (Magiati and Howlin 2003), and investigated collateral improvements in social-communicative behavior and problem behavior (Charlop-Christy et al. 2002).

Although PECS is probably the most commonly used AAC approach, other pictorial strategies have been tested and found effective for students with ASD. These strategies include combining picture and text cues to increase social communication skills (Thiemann and Goldstein 2001), using video recordings to increase responses to questions (Scherer et al. 2001), utilizing vocal switches to increase spontaneous communication (Dyches 1998), and combining voice-output aids and line-drawing graphics to mand and comment (Schepis et al. 1998).

Teaching social skills to students with ASD remains a vexing challenge for educators. Social skills, by their nature, are difficult to break down into task analytical components or discrete skills that might facilitate instruction. Furthermore, social interactions require a person to be motivated to engage with another person in the environment, and, as previously noted, students with ASD are not usually motivated to engage in typical social situations. In addition, students with ASD have challenges in observing other people's behaviors and using them as social models, a key way in which social behaviors are learned (Bandura 1977). As a result, numerous approaches have been tried in the quest to increase reciprocal social interaction skills so that they are generalized across multiple social situations and with multiple people. Techniques include naturalistic methods based on ABA principles (e.g., incidental teaching, PRT), visual methods (social stories, visual supports, and video instruction), and peer supports. Peer supports, and in particular peer mediation, have shown evidence of being effective for increasing social interaction skills of students with ASD, and particularly for generalizing the skills across settings and people. Peer-mediated strategies involve teaching typical peers, preferably the same age as the student with ASD, to initiate social behaviors such as sharing, helping, showing affection, and reinforcing (Strain et al. 1977). Through the use of these play organizers, the social interaction behaviors of students with ASD are increased, with concurrent improvements in generalization and maintenance (Hoyson et al. 1984; Strain et al. 1977; Goldstein et al. 1992). In recent years, peer-mediated methods have become increasingly sophisticated, with some studies training typical peers to use PRT (Pierce and Schreibman 1997), incidental teaching (McGee et al. 1992), monitoring strategies (Kamps et al. 1992; Morrison et al. 2001) and peer tutoring (Kamps et al. 2002; Laushey and Heflin 2000).

The use of visual supports, including video-based instruction, to help students with ASD understand and predict social behaviors has been a recent focus of research. Investigators theorize that by increasing the opportunities for students with ASD to observe social models, a parallel increase will occur in the acquisition of social skills and their eventual generalization (Ayres and Langone 2005). In addition, video-based instruction serves as a priming strategy by allowing the student to preview potentially difficult situations before becoming engaged in the activity and by providing scripts and/or behaviors to perform that will smooth over the interaction. Use of video as a teaching procedure has been demonstrated to be successful in teaching an assortment of social skills to student with ASD, including pretend play (MacDonald et al. 2005), increasing social bids (Kimball et al. 2004), extending conversation (Ogletree, Fischer, and Sprouse 1995; Sherer et al. 2001; Thiemann and Goldstein 2001), and reducing problem behaviors that interfere with social interactions (Schreibman, Whalen, and Stahmer 2000).

Functional Approach to Problem Behaviors

Problem behaviors are a frequent concern for educators and families of students with ASD. Limited communication abilities and challenges in social behaviors are cited as major factors contributing to the problem behaviors commonly seen in these students (Borthwick-Duffy 1996; Koegel, Koegel, and Surratt 1992). Behavioral topographies are varied and include physical aggression, self-injury, pica, tantrums, disruptions, noncompliance, property destruction, anger outburst, and stereotypy (Horner, Diemer, and Brazeau 1992; Reichle 1990). Exhibitions of problem behaviors serve as strong barriers to students' being included in inclusive educational and community environments and often prevent them from receiving and benefiting from meaningful educational instruction (Sprague and Rian 1993).

A general consensus has emerged that proactive and positive interventions based on functional assessments have a higher likelihood of being effective for students with ASD (NRC 2001). Over the past few decades, behavioral approaches have been moving from a heavy reliance on contingency management to more comprehensive approaches that emphasize environmental adjustments to prevent the occurrence of problem behavior, teaching of new appropriate skills to replace the problem behaviors, and reinforcement of the new skills (Carr et al. 2002). This evolving approach has come to be known as positive behavior support (PBS). Positive behavior support grew from the conceptual and procedural roots of ABA and maintains a close affiliation with ABA (Dunlap 2006).

The foundation of the PBS intervention plan is the functional behavior assessment (FBA), in which an understanding emerges of the contextual situations in which problem behaviors do and do not occur and the consequences that maintain the occurrence of the behaviors. From functional assessments, along with broader goal-setting and team-building processes (Kincaid and Fox 2002), individualized behavior support plans are developed. The primary goal of PBS plans is to enhance the student's quality of life by expanding behavior repertoires and by adjusting learning environments so that they become identified as pleasant places in which to spend time. The secondary goal is to reduce problem behaviors by making them ineffective, inefficient, and irrelevant (Carr et al. 2002). A corpus of published research over the last 20 years has consistently shown evidence of the effectiveness of individualized PBS procedures for addressing problem behaviors of students with ASD (Bambara, Dunlap, and Schwartz 2004; Carr et al. 1999; Dunlap and Carr 2006; Horner et al. 1990; Koegel, Koegel, and Dunlap 1996; NRC 2001).

As previously discussed, the recent evolving literature addressing positive behavior supports has expanded in its focus from individualized PBS interventions (tertiary level) to applying PBS principles at three levels: universal or primary, targeted group or secondary, and individualized or tertiary (Horner et al. 2005). An assumption of the three-tiered model is that all intervention levels need to be implemented in order to address the behavioral needs of 100% of the students on a school campus. The increased focus and appeal of school-wide or universal applications of PBS has generated empirical questions, including, "Does school-wide PBS meet the needs of students with ASD and problem behaviors?" and "How do schools implement with fidelity a three-tiered model of intervention that addresses the behavioral needs of all students, including those with the most significant disabilities?" One suggestion is to have support teams in place for each level of intervention or, at a minimum, two teams. One team focuses on implementing universal interventions while the other team focuses on secondary and tertiary supports for students whose needs are not being met by universal interventions (Freeman et al. 2006). With this infrastructure in place, students with ASD and problem behaviors have access to the individualized PBS process, which has a long history of documented effectiveness.

Family Involvement

Although no educator denies the importance of family involvement, promoting active family participation in the development of educational supports for students with ASD is a constant challenge for school district personnel. Although IDEA stressed the inclusion of families in educational planning for their children, there is considerable variation in the degree of family involvement that is actually implemented (Spann, Kohler, and Soenksen 2003; Stoner and Angell 2006). Schools do a good job of attempting to meet the minimum requirements mandated by IDEA by making sure that families have adequate notice for meetings and ensuring that meetings occur at mutually agreeable times. But they do not do as good a job of engaging in collaborative relationships that help build the capacity of parents in making decisions about their child's education (Turnbull and Turnbull 2001). Various reasons have been suggested for this less than desirable state of relations between families of students with ASD and schools, but the most prevalent one is that schools often perceive parents as being inconsistent, adversarial, and unpleasant (Stoner et al. 2005). Frequently, parents are viewed as being secondary members of a school team, with the educational professionals holding the primary decision-making roles (Hardman, Drew, and Egan 1995; Turnbull and Turnbull 2001).

Part of the problem with promoting family/school relationships may be in the lack of agreement on the definition of family involvement. It has been suggested that the broader term "family engagement" should be substituted for "family involvement," to allow a shift in the way we view and understand family/school relationships (Barton et al. 2004). By adapting the definition supplied for "engagement" earlier in the chapter, "family engagement" can be described as the quality and amount of activities that the family is doing to actively interact with educational environments to enhance their child's programming. Indicators of engaged families, then, could include the positive impacts their activities have on their child's program, highlighting the benefits of shared control with the school professionals.

When families are involved, they can have a powerful impact on their child's education and on relationships with schools. Family involvement has been credited with higher student learning outcomes (Eccles and Harold 1993), increased generalization of learned behaviors (Koegel, Koegel, and Schreibman 1991), and higher acceptance of school programs by the family (Stancin et al. 1984).

Recent research has focused on factors that inhibit or enhance family and school relationships and family involvement. There is evidence of a positive correlation between the level of the family's trust in school professionals and the family's level of involvement. Through a qualitative study of eight families of students with autism, Stoner and Angell (2006) found that families who had high levels of trust in the school's professionals became engaged at multiple levels. They exhibited support for the teacher and for the child's classroom, including providing materials to teachers, volunteering in the classroom, and going to administrators to obtain specific actions that would benefit the classroom and the child. Stoner and Angell also found that family support for the teacher became stronger as the trust became deeper.

Research has supported the effectiveness of strategies to enhance the family partnership with the school. Collaborative processes designed to strengthen family and school partnerships have been shown to build the competence of families (Ruble and Dalrymple 2002). Positive effects of active inclusion of families have been demonstrated through the use of various strategies, including teaching families to implement interventions and matching supports to their preferences and characteristics (Frea and Hepburn 1999), providing training to improve their interactions during unstructured home activities (Koegel, Bimbela, and Schreibman 1996), and facilitating them through PBS to prevent problem behaviors in home settings (Boettcher et al. 2003; Lorimer et al. 2002).

Although there is a wealth of research providing methods of including families and evidence of its benefits, there continues to be evidence suggesting that interactions between families and schools are less than ideal, as indicated by the number of due process hearings lost for failing to include family participation in meaningful ways (Yell and Shriner 1997). Given that each family is affected differently by various risk factors, including stress related to lack of resources (financial and time), lack of appropriate services, and inadequate support systems, it comes as no surprise that educational personnel struggle with knowing how to best include families in the educational planning process.

Families are of vital importance in the education of students with ASD, because they are the most influential and stable people in the student's life (Dunlap 1999). Therefore, it is imperative that schools continue to strive toward meaningful inclusion of families in educational planning. Family inclusion is especially essential considering the difficulty students with ASD have in generalizing behaviors learned in one setting or with one person or one exemplar to others. If schools actively involve the families and provide the supports necessary for consistent service delivery between school and home, generalization of skills can be greatly enhanced. Collaborative partnerships with families and schools can improve the effectiveness of interventions, especially if similar strategies are used across environments.

■ Summary

Although the popular and professional literatures in autism continue to be inundated with diverse and often unfounded recommendations, it is encouraging that there are also strenuous efforts to describe and define appropriate and validated practice. The continuation of these efforts should lead to an increasing consensus regarding the critical features of effective practice and, in time, to a diminution of fringe and baseless interventions.

In this chapter, we have described six core features that characterize effective educational services for students with ASD. Each of these features is endowed with empirical support (see Iovannone et al. 2003 for additional detail on the research foundations of each feature) and a history of supportive experience accumulated by successful educational programs. The manner in which these features are incorporated into educational programs must be flexible because of the heterogeneity of the disability and the idiosyncratic nature of the educational, familial, and environmental characteristics associated with each student. Still, a concerted focus on these features, along with competence in identifying and implementing specific interventions, should go a long way toward ensuring the delivery of effective services for students with ASD.

■ Acknowledgments

Preparation of this chapter was supported in part by Grant No. H324P040003–05 from the Institute of Education Sciences and by Cooperative Agreements No. H326S030002 and H325G020003 from the Office of Special Education Programs, U.S. Department of Education. Opinions expressed herein do not necessarily reflect the position of the funders, and such endorsements should not be inferred.

■ References

Albin, R.W., Lucyshyn, J.M., Horner, R.H., and Flannery, K.B. (1996). Contextual fit for behavioral support plans: A model for "goodness of fit." In *Positive behavioral support: Including people with difficult behavior in the community* (eds. L.K. Koegel, R.K. Koegel, and G. Dunlap), pp. 81–98. Baltimore: Paul H. Brookes.

American Psychiatric Association. (1994). *Diagnostic and statistical manual of mental disorders* (4th ed., text revision). Washington, D.C.: Author.

Anderson, A.E. (2002). Augmentative communication and autism: A comparison of sign language and the Picture Exchange Communication System. Dissertation Abstracts International: Section B. The Sciences and Engineering, 62(9-B), April 2002, p. 4269.

Ayres, K.M., and Langone, J. (2005). Intervention and instruction with video for students with autism: A review of the literature. *Education and Training in Developmental Disabilities,* 40, 183–196.

Baird, M.M. (1999). Legal issues in autism. *Proceedings of the 20th National Institute on Legal Issues of Educating Individuals with Disabilities.* Alexandria, Va.: LRP Publications, Conference Division.

Baker, M.J., Koegel, R.L., and Koegel, L.K. (1999). Increasing the social behavior of young children with autism using their obsessive behaviors. *The Journal of the Association for Persons with Severe Handicaps,* 23, 300–308.

Bambara, L.M., Dunlap, G., and Schwartz, I.S., eds. (2004). *Positive behavior support: Critical articles on improving practice for individuals with severe disabilities.* Austin, Tex.: PRO-ED.

Bandura, A. (1977). *Social learning theory.* Upper Saddle River, N.J.: Prentice-Hall.

Barton, A.C., Drake, C., Perez, J.G., St. Louis, K., and George, M. (2004). Ecologies of parental engagement in urban education. *Educational Researcher,* 33 (4), 3–12.

Boettcher, M., Koegel, R.L., McNerney, E.K., and Koegel, L.K. (2003). A family-centered prevention approach to PBS in time of crisis. *Journal of Positive Behavior Interventions,* 5, 55–59.

Borthwick-Duffy, S.A. (1996). Evaluation and measurement of quality of life: Special considerations for persons with mental retardation. In *Quality of life. Vol. 1: Conceptualization and measurement* (eds. R.L. Schalock and G.N. Siperstein). Washington, D.C.: American Association on Mental Retardation.

Bryan, L.C., and Gast, D.L. (2000). Teaching on-task and on-schedule behaviors to high-functioning children with autism via picture activity schedules. *Journal of Autism and Developmental Disorders,* 30, 553–567.

Buffington, D.M., Drantz, P.J., McClannahan, L.E., and Poulson, C.L. (1998). Procedures for teaching appropriate gestural communication skills to children with autism. *Journal of Autism and Developmental Disorders,* 28, 535–545.

Callahan, K., and Rademacher, J.A. (1999). Using self-management strategies to increase the on-task behavior of a student with autism. *Journal of Positive Behavior Interventions,* 1, 117–122.

Carr, E.G., Dunlap, G., Horner, R.H., Koegel, R.L., Turnbull, A.P., Sailor, W., Anderson, J., Albin, R.W., Koegel, L.K., and Fox, L. (2002). Positive behavior support: Evolution of an applied science. *Journal of Positive Behavior Interventions,* 4, 4–16, 20.

Carr, E.G., Horner, R.H., Turnbull, A.P., Marquis, J., Magito-Mclaughlin, D., McAtee, M.L., Smith, C.E., Anderson-Ryan, K., Ruef, M.B., and Doolabh, A. (1999).

Positive behavior support for people with developmental disabilities: A research synthesis. Washington, D.C.: American Association on Mental Retardation.

Centers for Disease Control and Prevention. (2000). *Prevalence of autism in Brick Township, New Jersey, 1998: Community Report.* Atlanta, Ga.: Author.

Charlop-Christy, M.H., Carpenter, M., Le, L., LeBlanc, L.A., and Kellet, K. (2002). Using the Picture Exchange Communication System (PECS) with children with autism: Assessment of PECS acquisition, speech, social-communicative behavior, and problem behavior. *Journal of Applied Behavior Analysis,* 35, 213–231.

Cummings, A.R., and Williams, W.L. (2000). Visual identity matching and vocal imitation training with children with autism: A surprising finding. *Journal on Developmental Disabilities,* 7, 109–122.

Dalrymple, N.J. (1995). Environmental supports to develop flexibility and independence. In *Teaching children with autism* (ed. K. Quill), pp. 243–264. New York: Delmar.

Dawson, G., and Osterling, J. (1997). Early intervention in autism. In *The effectiveness of early intervention* (ed. M. Guralnick), pp. 307–326. Baltimore: Paul H. Brookes.

Dettmer, S., Simpson, R.L., Myles, B.S., and Ganz, J.B. (2000). The use of visual supports to facilitate transitions of students with autism. *Focus on Autism and Other Developmental Disabilities,* 15, 163–169.

Dunlap, G. (1984). The influence of task variation and maintenance tasks on the learning and affect of autistic children. *Journal of Experimental Child Psychology,* 37, 41–64.

Dunlap, G. (1999). Consensus, engagement, and family involvement for young children with autism. *The Journal of the Association for Persons with Severe Handicaps,* 24, 222–225.

Dunlap, G. (2006). The applied behavior analytic heritage of PBS: A dynamic model of action-oriented research. *Journal of Positive Behavior Interventions,* 8, 58–60.

Dunlap, G., and Carr, E.G. (2006). Positive behavior support and developmental disabilities: A summary and analysis of research. In *Handbook of developmental disabilities* (eds. S.L. Odom, R.H. Horner, M. Snell, and J. Blacher). New York: Guilford.

Dunlap, G., and Robbins, F.R. (1991). Current perspectives in service delivery for young children with autism. *Comprehensive Mental Health Care,* 1, 177–194.

Dyches, T.T. (1998). Effects of switch training on the communication of children with autism and severe disabilities. *Focus on Autism and Other Developmental Disabilities,* 13, 151–162.

Earles, T.L., Carlson, J.K., and Bock, S.J. (1998). Instructional strategies to facilitate successful learning outcomes for students with autism. In *Educating children and youth with autism: Strategies for effective practice* (eds. R.L. Simpson and B.S. Myles), pp. 55–111. Austin: PRO-ED.

Eccles, J.S., and Harold, R.D. (1993). Parent-school involvement during the early adolescent years. *Teachers' College Record,* 94, 568–587.

Eikeseth, S., Smith, T., Jahr, E., and Eldevik, S. (2002). Intensive behavioral treatment at school for 4- to 7-year-old children with autism: A 1-year comparison controlled study. *Behavior Modification*, 26, 49–68.

Etscheidt, S. (2003). An analysis of legal hearings and cases related to individualized education programs for children with autism. *Research and Practice for Persons with Severe Disabilities*, 28, 51–69.

Frea, W.D., and Hepburn, S.L. (1999). Teaching parents of children with autism to perform functional assessments to plan interventions for extremely disruptive behaviors. *Journal of Positive Behavior Interventions*, 1, 113–116.

Freeman, R., Eber, L., Anderson, C., Irvin, L., Horner, R., Bounds, M., and Dunlap, G. (2006). Building inclusive school cultures using school-wide positive behavior support: Designing effective individual support systems for students with significant disabilities. *Research and Practice for Persons with Severe Disabilities*, 31, 4–17.

Frost, L., and Bondy, A. (1994). *The Picture Exchange Communication System training manual.* Cherry Hill, N.J.: PECS.

Ganz, J.B., and Simpson, R.L. (2004). Effects on communicative requesting and speech development of the Picture Exchange Communication System in children with characteristics of Autism. *Journal of Autism and Developmental Disorders*, 34, 395–409.

Goldstein, H., Kaczmarek, L., Pennington, R., and Shafer, K. (1992). Peer-mediated intervention: Attending to, commenting on, and acknowledging the behavior of preschoolers with autism. *Journal of Applied Behavior Analysis*, 25, 289–305.

Gresham, F.M., Beebe-Frankenberger, M.E., and MacMillan, D.L. (1999). A selective review of treatments for children with autism: Description and methodological considerations. *School Psychology Review*, 28 (4), 559–575.

Hardman, M.L., Drew, C.J., and Egan, M.W. (1995). *Human exceptionality: Society, school, and family.* Needham Heights, Mass.: Allyn and Bacon.

Harris, S., Handleman, J. and Jennett, H. (2005). Models of educational intervention for students with autism: Home, center, and school-based programming. In *Handbook of autism and developmental disorders* (Vol. 2) (eds. P. Volkmer, R. Paul, A. Klin, and D. Cohen), pp. 1043–1054.

Heckaman, K.A., Alber, S., Hooper, S., and Heward, W.L. (1998). A comparison of least-to-most prompts and progressive time delay on the disruptive behavior of students with autism. *Journal of Behavioral Education*, 8, 171–201.

Heflin, L.J., and Alberto, P.A. (2001). Establishing a behavioral contract for learning for students with autism. *Focus on Autism and Other Developmental Disabilities*, 13, 194–211.

Heflin, L.J., and Simpson, R.L. (1998). Interventions for children and youth with autism: Prudent choices in a world of exaggerated claims and empty promises. Part 1: Intervention and treatment option review. *Focus on Autism and Other Developmental Disabilities*, 13, 194–211.

Hetzroni, O.E., and Shalem, U. (2005). From logos to orthographic symbols: A multilevel fading computer program for teaching nonverbal children with autism. *Focus on Autism and Other Developmental Disabilities,* 20, 201–212.

Horner, R.H., Carr, E.G., Halle, J., McGee, G., Odom, S., and Wolery, M. (2005). The use of single subject research to identify evidence-based practice in special education. *Exceptional Children,* 71, 165–179.

Horner, R.H., Diemer, S.M., and Brazeau, K.C. (1992). Educational support for students with severe problem behaviors in Oregon: A descriptive analysis from the 1987–1988 school year. *Journal of the Association for Persons with Severe Handicaps,* 17, 154–169.

Horner, R.H., Dunlap, G., Koegel, R.L., Carr, E.G., Sailor, W., Anderson, J., Albin, R.W., and O'Neill, R.E. (1990). Toward a technology of "nonaversive" behavioral support. *Journal of the Association for Persons with Severe Handicaps,* 15, 125–132.

Horner, R.H., Sugai, G., Todd, A.W., and Lewis-Palmer, T. (2005). Schoolwide positive behavior support. In *Individualized supports for students with problem behaviors* (eds. L.M. Bambara and L. Kern), pp. 359–390. New York: Guildford Press.

Hoyson, M., Jamieson, B., and Strain, P. (1984). Individualized group instruction of normally developing and autistic-like children: The LEAP curriculum model. *Journal of the Division of Early Childhood,* 8, 157–172.

Huff, R. (2006). *Evidence-based practice in autism.* Panel presented at the 3rd International Conference on Positive Behavior Support (APBS), Reno, Nev., March 2006.

Hurth, J., Shaw, E., Izeman, S.G., Whaley, K., and Rogers, S.J. (1999). Areas of agreement about effective practices among programs serving young children with autism spectrum disorders. *Infants and Young Children,* 12, 17–26.

Iovannone, R., Dunlap, G., Huber, H., and Kincaid, D. (2003). Effective educational practices for students with autism spectrum disorders. *Focus on Autism and Other Developmental Disabilities,* 18, 150–165.

Jahr, E. (2001). Teaching children with autism to answer novel wh- questions by utilizing a multiple exemplar strategy. *Research in Developmental Disabilities,* 22, 407–423.

Jones, C.M. (2005). Using the picture exchange communication system and time delay to enhance the spontaneous speech of children with autism. *Dissertation Abstracts International,* 65 8B (UMI No. AA13142250).

Kamps, D.M., Leonard, B.R., Vernon, S., Dugan, E.P., and Delquadri, J.C. (1992). Teaching social skills to students with autism to increase peer interactions in an integrated first-grade classroom. *Journal of Applied Behavior Analysis,* 25, 281–288.

Kamps, D., Royer, J., Dugan, E., Kravits, T., Gonzalez-Lopez, A., Garcia, J., Carnazzo, K., Morrison, L., and Kane, L. (2002). Peer training to facilitate social interactions for elementary students with autism and their peers. *Exceptional Children,* 68, 173–187.

Kimball, J.W., Kinney, E.M., Taylor, B.A., and Stromer, R. (2004). Video enhanced activity schedules for children with autism: A promising package for teaching social skills. *Education and Treatment of Children,* 27, 280–298.

Kincaid, D., and Fox, L. (2002). Person-centered planning and positive behavior support. In *Person-centered planning: Research, practice, and future directions* (eds. S. Holburn and P.M. Vietze), pp. 29–50. Baltimore: Paul H. Brookes.

Kleinert, H.L., and Kearns, J.F. (2001). *Measuring outcomes and supports for students with disabilities.* Baltimore: Paul H. Brookes.

Koegel, L.K., Camarata, S.M., Valdez-Menchaca, M., and Koegel, R.L. (1998). Setting generalization of question-asking by children with autism. *American Journal on Mental Retardation,* 102, 346–357.

Koegel, L.K., Harrower, J., and Koegel, R.L. (1999). Support for children with developmental disabilities participating in full-inclusion classrooms through self-management. *Journal of Positive Behavior Interventions,* 1, 26–34.

Koegel, L.K., Koegel, R.L., and Dunlap, G., eds. (1996). *Positive behavioral support: Including people with difficult behavior in the community.* Baltimore: Paul H. Brookes.

Koegel, L.K., Koegel, R.L., Harrower, J.K., and Carter, C.M. (1999). Pivotal response intervention I: Overview of approach. *Journal of the Association for Persons with Severe Handicaps,* 24, 174–185.

Koegel, L.K., Koegel, R.L., and Surratt, A. (1992). Language intervention and disruptive behavior in preschool children with autism. *Journal of Autism and Developmental Disorders,* 22, 141–153.

Koegel, R.L., Bimbela, A., and Schreibman, L. (1996). Collateral effects of parent training on family interactions. *Journal of Autism and Developmental Disorders,* 26, 347–359.

Koegel, R.L., and Egel, A.L. (1979). Motivating autistic children. *Journal of Abnormal Psychology,* 88, 418–426.

Koegel, R.L., and Koegel, L.K. (2006). *Pivotal response treatments for autism: Communication, social, and academic development.* Baltimore: Paul H. Brookes.

Koegel, R.L., Koegel, L.K., and Carter, C.M. (1999). Pivotal teaching interactions for children with autism. *School Psychology Review,* 28 (4), 576–594.

Koegel, R.L., Koegel, L.K., and Schreibman, L. (1991). Assessing and training parents in teaching pivotal behaviors. In *Advances in behavioral assessments of children and families: A research annual* (Vol. 5) (eds. R.J. Prinz) pp. 65–82. London: Jessica Kingsley.

Koegel, R.L., and Mentis, M. (1985). Motivation in childhood autism: Can they or won't they? *The Journal of Child Psychology and Psychiatry and Allied Disciplines,* 26, 185–191.

Kravits, T.R., Kamps, D.M., Kemmerer, K., and Potucck, J. (2002). Brief report: Increasing communication skills for an elementary-aged student with autism using the Picture Exchange Communication System. *Journal of Autism and Developmental Disorders,* 32, 225–230.

Laushey, K.M., and Heflin, L.J. (2000). Enhancing social skills of kindergarten children with autism through the training of multiple peers as tutors. *Journal of Autism and Developmental Disorders*, 30, 183–193.

Logan, K.R., Bakeman, R., and Keefe, E.G. (1997). Effects of instructional variables of engaged behavior of students with disabilities in general education classrooms. *Exceptional Children*, 63, 481–497.

Lorimer, P.A., Simpson, R.L., Myles, R.L., and Ganz, J.B. (2002). The use of social stories as a preventative behavioral intervention in a home setting with a child with autism. *Journal of Positive Behavior Interventions*, 4, 53–60.

MacDonald, R., Clark, M., Garrigan, E., and Vangala, M. (2005). Using video modeling to teach pretend play to children with autism. *Behavioral Interventions*, 20, 225–238.

MacDuff, G.S., Krantz, P.J., and McClannahan, L.E. (1993). Teaching children with autism to use photographic activity schedules: Maintenance and generalization of complex response chains. *Journal of Applied Behavior Analysis*, 26, 89–97.

Magiati, I., and Howlin, P. (2003). A pilot evaluation study of the Picture Exchange Communication System (PECS) for children with autistic spectrum disorders. *Autism*, 7, 297–320.

Mancina, C., Tankersley, M., Kamps, D., Kravits, T., and Parrett, J. (2000). Brief report: Reduction of inappropriate vocalizations for a child with autism using a self-management treatment program. *Journal of Autism and Developmental Disorders*, 30, 599–606.

McGee, G.G., Almeida, M.C., Sulzer-Azaroff, B., and Feldman, R.S. (1992). Promoting reciprocal interactions via peer incidental teaching. *Journal of Applied Behavior Analysis*, 25, 117–126.

Morrison, L., Kamps, D., Garcia, J., and Parker, D. (2001). Peer mediation and monitoring strategies to improve initiations and social skills for students with autism. *Journal of Positive Behavior Interventions*, 3, 237–250.

Morse, T.E., and Schuster, J.W. (2000). Teaching elementary students with moderate intellectual disabilities: How to shop for groceries. *Exceptional Children*, 66, 273–288.

National Research Council. (2001). *Educating children with autism.* Committee on Educational Interventions for Children with Autism, Division of Behavioral and Social Sciences and Autism. Washington, D.C.: National Academy Press.

New York Department of Health. (1999). *Clinical practice guideline: Report of the recommendations. Autism/pervasive developmental disorders: Assessment and intervention for young children (age 0–3 years).* Albany, N.Y.: New York Department of Health.

Odom, S., Brown, W., Frey, T., Karasu, N., Smith-Canter, L. and Strain, P. (2003). Evidence-based practices for young children with autism: Contributions from single-subject design research. *Focus on Autism and Other Developmental Disabilities*, 18, 166–175.

Ogletree, B.T., Fischer, M.A., and Sprouse, J. (1995). An innovative language treatment for a child with high-functioning autism. *Focus on Autistic Behavior*, 10 (3), 1–10.

Olley, J.G. (1999). Curriculum for students with autism. *School Psychology Review,* 28 (4), 595–606.

Olley, J.G., and Reeve, C.E. (1997). Issues of curriculum and classroom structure. In *Handbook of autism and pervasive developmental disorders* (2nd ed.) (eds. D.J. Cohen and F.R. Volkmar), pp. 484–508. New York: Wiley.

Olley, J.G., and Rosenthal, S.L. (1985). Current issues in school services for students with autism. *School Psychology Review,* 14, 166–170.

O'Neill, R., Horner, R., Albin, R., Sprague, J., Storey, K. and Newton, S. (1997). *Functional assessment and program development for problem behavior.* Pacific Grove, Calif.: Brookes-Cole.

Perry, A., and Condillac, R.A. (2003). *Evidence-based practices for children and adolescents with autism spectrum disorders: Review of the literature and practice guide.* Toronto, Ont.: Children's Mental Health Ontario.

Pierce, K.L., and Schreibman, L. (1997). Multiple peer use of pivotal response training to increase social behaviors of classmates with autism: Results from trained and untrained peers. *Journal of Applied Behavior Analysis,* 30, 157–160.

Powers, M.D. (1992). Early intervention for children with autism. In *Autism: Identification, education and treatment* (ed. D.E. Berkell), pp. 225–252. Hillsdale, N.J.: Erlbaum.

Reichle, J. (1990). *National Working Conference on Positive Approaches to the Management of Excess Behavior: Final Report and Recommendations.* Minneapolis, Minn.: Institute on Community Integration, University of Minnesota.

Rogers, S.J. (1999). Intervention for young children with autism: From research to practice. *Infants and Young Children,* 12 (2), 1–16.

Ruble, L.A., and Dalrymple, N.J. (2002). COMPASS: A parent-teacher collaborative model for students with autism. *Focus on Autism and Other Developmental Disabilities,* 17, 76–83.

Sarokoff, R.A., Taylor, B.A., and Poulson, C.L. (2001). Teaching children with autism to engage in conversational exchanges: Script fading with embedded textual stimuli. *Journal of Applied Behavior Analysis,* 34, 81–84.

Schepis, M.M., Reid, D.H., Behrmann, M.M., and Sutton, K.A. (1998). Increasing communicative interactions of young children with autism using a voice output communication aid and naturalistic aid and naturalistic teaching. *Journal of Applied Behavior Analysis,* 31, 561–578.

Scherer, M., Pierce, K.L., Paredes, S., Kisacky, K.L., Ingersoll, B., and Schreibman, L. (2001). Enhancing conversation skills in children with autism via video technology: Which is better, "self" or "other" as a model? *Behavior Modification,* 25, 140–158.

Schreibman, L., Whalen, C., and Stahmer, A.C. (2000). The use of video priming to reduce disruptive transition behavior in children with autism. *Journal of Positive Behavior Interventions,* 2, 3–11.

Simpson, R.L. (2001). ABA and students with autism spectrum disorders: Issues and considerations for effective practice. *Focus on Autism and Other Developmental Disabilities,* 16, 68–71.

Simpson, R.L. (2005). Evidence-based practices and students with autism spectrum disorder. *Focus on Autism and Other Developmental Disabilities,* 20, 140–149.

Simpson, R.L., and Myles, B.S. (1998). Understanding and responding to the needs of students with autism. In *Educating children and youth with autism: Strategies for effective practice* (eds. R.L. Simpson and B.S. Myles), pp. 1–23. Austin: PRO-ED.

Spann, S.J., Kohler, F.W., and Soenksen, D. (2003). Examining parents' involvement in and perceptions of special education services: An interview with families in a parent support group. *Focus on Autism and Other Developmental Disabilities,* 18, 228–237.

Sprague, J.R., and Rian, V. (1993). Support systems for students with severe problems in Indiana: A descriptive analysis of school structure and student demographics. Unpublished manuscript. Bloomington, Ind.: Indiana University Institute for the Study of Developmental Disabilities.

Stancin, T., Reuter, J., Dunn, V., and Bickett, L. (1984). Validity of caregiver information on the development status of severely brain-damaged young children. *American Journal of Mental Deficiency,* 88, 388–395.

Stoner, J.B., and Angell, M.E. (2006). Parent perspectives on role engagement: An investigation of parents of children with ASD and their self-reported roles with educational professionals. *Focus on Autism and Other Developmental Disabilities,* 21, 177–189.

Stoner, J.B., Bock, S.J., Thompson, J.R., Angell, M.E., Heyl, B.S., and Crowley, E.P. (2005). Welcome to our world: Parent perceptions of interactions between parents of young children with ASD and educational professionals. *Focus on Autism and Other Developmental Disabilities,* 20, 39–51.

Strain, P.S., Shores, R.E., and Timm, M.A. (1977). Effects of peer social initiations on the behavior of withdrawn preschool children. *Journal of Applied Behavior Analysis,* 10, 289–298.

Sugai, G., Horner, R.H., Dunlap, G., Hieneman, M., Lewis, T.J., Nelson, C.M., Scott, T., Liaupsin, C., Sailor, W., Turnbull, A.P., Turnbull, H.R. III, Wickham, D., Ruef, M., and Wilcox, B. (2000). Applying positive behavior support and functional behavioral assessment in schools, *Journal of Positive Behavior Interventions,* 2, 131–143.

Sugai, G., Horner, R., Sailor, W., Dunlap, G., Eber, L., Lewis, T., et al. (2005). *School-wide positive behavior support: Implementers' blueprint and self-assessment.* Technical Assistance Center on Positive Behavioral Interventions and Supports. Available at http://www.pbis.org (accessed November 2, 2007).

Thiemann, K.S., and Goldstein, H. (2001). Social stories, written text cues, and video feedback: Effects on social communication of children with autism. *Journal of Applied Behavior Analysis,* 34, 425–446.

Tincani, M. (2004). Comparing the Picture Exchange Communication System and sign language training for children with autism. *Focus on Autism and Other Developmental Disabilities,* 19, 152–163.

Tincani, M., Crozier, S., and Alazetta, L. (2006). The Picture Exchange Communication System: Effects on manding and speech development for
  school-aged children with autism. *Education and Training in Developmental
  Disabilities,* 41, 177–184.

Turnbull, A.P., and Turnbull, H.R. (2001). *Families, professionals, and exceptionality: Collaborating for empowerment,* 4th ed. Columbus, Ohio: Merrill/
  Prentice-Hall.

Volmer, L. (1997). Best practices in working with students with autism. In *Best
  practices in school psychology III* (eds. A. Thomas and J. Grimes), pp. 1031–
  1038. Washington, D.C.: The National Association of School Psychologists.

Westling, D.L., and Fox, L. (2004). *Teaching persons with severe disabilities,* 3rd ed.
  Columbus, Ohio: Merrill/Prentice-Hall.

Yell, M.L., and Drasgow, E. (2000). Litigating a free appropriate public education: The Lovaas hearings and cases. *The Journal of Special Education,* 33,
  205–214.

Yell, M.L., and Shriner, J.G. (1997). Inclusive education: Legal and policy implications. *Preventing School Failure,* 40, 100–108.

7. GENERALIZED BEHAVIOR CHANGE IN YOUNG CHILDREN WITH AUTISM

Patrick M. Ghezzi and Michele R. Bishop

This chapter is written for workers in the field of applied behavior analysis. Those who train teachers, students, paraprofessionals, or parents about generalized behavior change will find plenty of useful information to share with their audience regarding the meaning of generalization from a behavior analytic point of view. Those who implement and assess instructional strategies for individual children will benefit when the discussion turns to a list of *guidelines* for how to achieve generalized behavior change.

We emphasize *guidelines* to make the point that there is no one, sure-fire way to achieve generalized behavior change. Understanding this fundamental principle should discourage the practice of following a manualized or "cookbook" approach in favor of tailoring a program to suit a child's unique skills, abilities, interests, and circumstances of living.

■ The Meaning of Generalization

The meaning of generalization centers on the fact that a response is strengthened or weakened by its consequences. Consequences that strengthen a response—in the sense of increasing the likelihood that it occurs again in the future—are termed reinforcing, and the process by which this comes about is called reinforcement. The process is at work, for instance, when a student is praised by his or her teacher for correctly answering a question and when that same answer is given to the same question under the same circumstances at a later date.

Consequences that weaken a response—in the sense of decreasing the likelihood that it occurs again in the future—are termed punishing, and the process by which this comes about is called punishment. A student who is reprimanded by his or her teacher for giving an incorrect answer to a question and never again gives that same answer to the same question under the same circumstances illustrates the process.

One outcome of reinforcing or punishing a response is to strengthen or weaken other responses that share a physical likeness to it. This is called *response generalization*. A second outcome of strengthening or weakening a response is to increase the capacity of certain features (what behavior analysts call "stimuli') in the reinforcing or punishing environment to influence (behavior analysts say "control") the same response to similar features when they are present in a nonreinforcing or nonpunishing environment. This is called *stimulus generalization*. A third outcome of reinforcing or punishing a response is to increase the chance that it will occur or cease to occur with the passage of time. This is called *temporal generalization* or *maintenance*.

We elaborate on the meaning of stimulus generalization, response generalization, and temporal generalization (maintenance) and present examples of each in the following sections. Because the meaning and importance of the three aspects of generalization is best conveyed in the case of strengthening a response, what follows focuses on the reinforcement process.

Stimulus Generalization

Whenever a response to a given feature (stimulus) in the environment is reinforced, the capacity for other features to influence (control) the same response is increased. The effect is selective, however, in that only features that are similar in appearance to those in the presence of which the response is reinforced will gain an influence.

What is meant by environments that are "similar in appearance" requires some elaboration. We can think of the physical environment as containing an endless variety of things such as trees, buildings, and crayons. These things have certain features that help a person to distinguish between a building and a tree, between one tree and another tree, and between one crayon and another crayon. In behavior analytical terms, a person makes a *discrimination* by responding in one way, for instance, to a crayon ("It's a crayon") and in a different way to a building ("It's a building").

A child seldom mistakes a crayon for a building but may at times mistake a red crayon for a maroon one. It is easy to see that the similarity in the color of the two crayons is one source of the child's error; after all, red and maroon look alike, and looks can indeed be deceiving. Behavior analysts recognize this when they speak of a "stimulus dimension" along which a feature may generalize. In the case of red and maroon crayons, it is the color dimension.

When a child is reinforced for saying "red" in the presence of a red crayon, the stage is set for stimulus generalization to occur—that is, for variations in the color red to influence the child's response. When this leads to errors, as when a child says "red" when asked to name a maroon crayon or says "maroon" when asked to name a red crayon, parents and teachers ordinarily step in to correct the mistake by reinforcing the child for saying red in the presence of a red crayon and maroon in the presence of a maroon crayon. *Differential reinforcement* is therefore applied, meaning that some responses are reinforced (saying red or maroon in the presence a red or maroon crayon, respectively) and other responses are not reinforced (saying red in the presence of a maroon crayon and maroon in the presence of a red crayon). When differential reinforcement is either not applied or is applied inconsistently or haphazardly, the child is likely to continue making the same mistake and may also mistake other things that resemble each other on the color dimension, such as red and maroon hats, cars, and vegetables.

We could say that the child fails to discriminate between the two reddish crayons, yet by saying this we run the risk of locating the failure in the child. It is far better to say instead that the problem lies in the environment—first, as a matter of stimulus generalization along the color dimension, and foremost as a failure to supply the differential reinforcements that are necessary for the child to make the correct discrimination. The practical advantage of this perspective is that once a dimension along which a feature generalizes is identified, steps can be taken to remediate errors by reinforcing a response to the desired dimension.

We can also describe the social environment in terms of its unique features and corresponding dimensions. The social environment is composed of people who differ from one another in age, height, shape, clothing, hairstyle, facial appearance and a host of other features. The differential reinforcements given for making appropriate discriminations with respect to these features enable a child to distinguish parents from strangers, one parent from another parent, young people from old people, and one young person from another young person.

The features that distinguish a grandparent from a preschooler are dissimilar along a number of dimensions, which is one reason why a young child seldom mistakes a playmate for his or her grandparent. Conversely, the features that distinguish a child's father from the postman may be similar along several dimensions, which is one reason why a child might mistake his or her father for the postman. The social environment is no different from the physical environment in these respects, nor are there any fundamental differences between the two in terms of how a child learns to make an appropriate discrimination or how to remediate errors when they occur.

Thus far we have cast stimulus generalization in a negative light, as a process that contributes to a poor discrimination (e.g., between a red and maroon crayon, between a father and the postman). Stimulus generalization can just as easily be seen in a positive light as a process that enables a child to respond appropriately to an endless number and variety of features in the physical and social environment. Indeed, it has long been considered a milestone in the early development of a child when he or she responds correctly to a feature in the environment and then responds in more or less the same way to a similar feature at a later time without the benefit of a parent's or teacher's deliberate reinforcements.

Imitation

One aspect of stimulus generalization that is particularly important to a young child's social development is when he or she does or says what another child or adult did or said. The phenomenon is called *imitation,* and it is defined as "behavior that duplicates some properties [features] of the behavior of a model" (Catania 1998, 392). How a child plays with a doll, for example, provides a model for a watchful second child, who may then repeat all or some features of the first child's playful responses. If only some feature or features of the model's response is imitated, the child is showing *selective imitation.* The child who watches a playmate dress a doll may imitate only that feature of the model's response that pertains to what shoes to put on the doll.

A child may imitate all or only selected features of a model's response, immediately or after a period of time elapses. The latter effect is called *delayed imitation.* The child who sees what shoes a playmate puts on a doll may put the same shoes on the doll minutes, hours, or even days later.

The pinnacle of imitation is *generalized imitation.* This is seen when a child watches and listens closely to what other children and adults say and do and then imitates some or all features of what they said or did, immediately or later, without the explicit parental reinforcements that have followed responses of this sort in the past. The child who sees a playmate put shoes on a doll may later select similar shoes for a different doll while playing alone at home. The reinforcements for interacting with the doll in this way occur naturally for the child, adding further to the tendency to play with dolls, toys, and other objects in the present as he or she has seen other children playing with them in the past.

For children who are less proficient at imitating a model's response—notably young children with autism—steps can be taken to resolve the problem by making reinforcements contingent on responses that duplicate or closely resemble all or a selected feature of what someone said or did, either with or without delay.

Rule-Following

Another aspect of stimulus generalization that is vital to a child's early social development is rule-following. Parents routinely tell their young child what to do, when to do it, and what will happen when he or she does it. After the child enters school, teachers issue rules that tell the child how to behave in the classroom, in the cafeteria, on the playground, and so on. Parents and teachers alike ordinarily provide reinforcements to the child for following their rules, and they may also withhold reinforcements if the child ignores or breaks them.

Rules and the responses they influence are regarded as *rule-governed behavior*, which contrasts with *contingency-shaped behavior*. The difference between the two is seen, for instance, when a child burns a finger on a hot stove or is bitten on the leg by an unfamiliar dog and learns as a direct result of these painful consequences to avoid hot stoves and unfamiliar dogs. The same result can be achieved indirectly with a rule, as when a mother tells her child not to touch a hot stove or not to approach an unfamiliar dog. Despite having never been burned or bitten, the child is likely to follow these rules whenever he or she is in the vicinity of hot stoves and strange dogs. By following rules of this sort, a child develops a generalized tendency to follow rules given by parents, teachers, and other authorities.

If the process of stimulus generalization unfolds in the ways we have just described, a child is poised to acquire a wealth of responses to countless things, objects, events, and people in the physical and social environment. If the process does not unfold in these ways, a child may spend most of his or her time and effort learning the same few responses to the same few features in the physical and social environment. The result is a very limited repertoire of verbal and nonverbal behavior.

Stimulus Overselectivity

At an early age, a typically developing child responds to a feature in the physical and social environment and later makes the same response to a more or less similar feature with remarkable ease and swiftness. In contrast, a young child with autism may have a difficult time achieving this milestone in his or her early development. The difficulty arises from an unusual tendency for certain features in the child's environment to exert undue influence over the child's response to them.

Lovaas (1981, 34) gave a dramatic example of what he and his colleagues (Lovaas, Schreibman, Koegel, and Rehm 1971; Lovaas, Koegel, and Schreibman 1979) termed *stimulus overselectivity*. A young boy was taught to say "girl" when shown a picture of a girl and "boy" when shown a picture of a boy. The two pictures were then altered by showing the same two children not wearing any shoes. When the boy was shown these pictures and was asked to identify the boy and the girl, his discrimination deteriorated, meaning that he no longer distinguished the girl from the boy. What happened? Evidently, the shoes had an overly selective influence on his response, overshadowing features such as physique, clothing, and facial appearance that ordinarily form the basis for differentiating boys from girls.

Schreibman (1997) described two startling cases of stimulus overselectivity. One involved a young boy and his father. The father wore glasses, and when he removed his glasses, the son "responded to him as just another object in the environment" (204). The second case centered on a young girl whose tutor had worked with her for 6 days a week over an entire summer. The tutor changed her hairstyle at the end of the summer, arrived one day to work with the girl, and found that she no longer recognized her.

When reinforcements are given for responses in such a way as to bring them under the influence of features such as a child's shoes, a father's eyeglasses, or a tutor's hairstyle, the stage is set for stimulus overselectivity. This can happen when a teacher or parent inadvertently provides reinforcements that bear little or no relation to a child's response to a given feature in the environment. From the parent or teacher's perspective, it may be hard to tell exactly what features are influencing the child's response and the reinforcements they provide for it. From the child's perspective, however, things such as shoes, glasses, or hairstyles are, in fact, the very features in the presence of which his or her response is consistently reinforced. It is in this sense that the child is responding to, or is overly influenced by, an irrelevant feature in the environment.

The effects of stimulus overselectivity on stimulus generalization can be profound. Consider the first of Schreibman's two cases. Had the mother worn the father's glasses, the boy might have recognized his mother as his father. In the second case, if a new tutor arrived wearing a hairstyle that resembled the summer tutor's hairstyle before she changed it, the girl might have recognized the new tutor as her summer tutor. The trouble in both cases is twofold: the influence on the child's response exerted by an irrelevant feature, and the potential for stimulus generalization to occur with respect to that feature.

Various teaching techniques and instructional materials are available that center on preventing or overcoming stimulus overselectivity. In combination with the proper reinforcements, the process includes identifying the feature or features that are influencing the child's response and then slowly altering or changing that feature until it gains the desired influence (see Bickel, Stella, and Etzel 1984; Etzel 1997; Rincover and Ducharme 1987; Rosenblatt, Bloom, and Koegel 1995; Schreibman 1997). A detailed description of this process would take us too far afield, so we must be content to urge teachers and parents, first, to be alert to the possibility that a child in their care is responding to an irrelevant feature in the environment, and second, to become adept at using the methods of applied behavior analysis to combat the untoward effects of stimulus overselectivity.

Response Generalization

The meaning of response generalization is based on the fact that reinforcement directly strengthens one response and indirectly strengthens other responses that resemble the form of the directly reinforced response. It is the indirect effects of such reinforcing consequences on other responses that give response generalization its meaning.

Suppose that a young child, Andy, uses his fingers instead of a spoon to eat breakfast cereal. Andy's parents agree that it is important for their son to eat cereal with a spoon and are certain that he is capable of learning this skill. Watching her son at the breakfast table one morning, Andy's mother sees him touching the spoon in between bites of his cereal. Taking advantage of this observation and his fondness for her affection, she decides to smile and pat Andy's head the next time he touches the spoon. Moments later, he touches the spoon, and she smiles and pats his head. This first cycle of responses (touching the spoon) and reinforcing consequences (smiles and pats) continues until Andy has touched the spoon several times.

She next decides to withhold her affection until a different response appears, one that is an improvement over its predecessor. Andy shows a small improvement, grasping the spoon, which earns him another smile and a pat on the head. A second cycle of responses (grasping the spoon) and reinforcing consequences (smiles and pats) begins and continues until Andy has grasped the spoon several times. She then decides to withhold her affection until yet another improved response appears. Andy lifts the spoon, thereby starting a third response-reinforcer cycle. Over the next several mornings, she continues to reinforce new and improved responses as they emerge from older ones, until the final response appears in full form: taking a bite of breakfast cereal with a spoon.

This example illustrates a method of instruction called *response shaping*. Offered frequently as the prototype for response generalization, the method relies on a steady flow of new and improved forms to which reinforcements are applied. Of those responses, some are closer in form to the response to be shaped than are others. Differential reinforcement is therefore necessary, meaning that some forms are reinforced and others are not, including the ones that were reinforced in the earlier stages of shaping.

In our previous discussion of imitation, a model's response was regarded as a feature in the social environment that provides the impetus for a child to duplicate all or a portion of what the model said or did, either immediately or after a delay. The child's imitative response is rarely, if ever, an exact duplicate of what the model said or did, however. The significance of this is that new and improved forms occur naturally during the course of imitation, forms to which reinforcements may be applied.

Suppose that Beth is instructed by her tutor to look at a picture of a dog and then imitate the tutor's model: "It's a dog." As she imitates her tutor's model, Beth may show a small variation in emphasis, for example, by saying, "It's a DOG!" In this and countless other examples, imitation is supplying novel forms and creating additional opportunities to reinforce these forms in response to the same or similar features in the environment.

Earlier we discussed rules in the context of stimulus generalization, noting that a rule tells a child what to do, when to do it, and what will happen when he or she does it. A child may respond with a form that differs from what the rule says to do and yet may still be in compliance with it. For example, a parent may insist that the child shut the front door softly when he or she leaves and enters the home, and may even model how to do this by grasping the knob with the right hand and gently pulling it until the door closes. The child may follow this rule but deviate slightly from it, for instance, by grasping the door instead of the knob, or by using the left hand instead of the right, or by bumping the door with his or her behind. These generalized forms are all acceptable variations on that feature of the parent's rule that pertains to how to close a door softly.

Fluency

How a child grips a spoon or closes a door are just two of a countless number of instances in which the look or appearance of a response is the most apparent feature. The meaning of response form extends beyond appearances, however, to include the rate at which the response occurs. A prominent example is *behavioral fluency* (or *fluency* for short), which is defined as "the fluid combination of accuracy plus speed [of responding] that characterizes competent performance" (Binder 1996, 164). A response such as reciting the alphabet or matching printed words to their corresponding objects may show variation in how rapidly it is performed. This rapidity qualifies as a formal property of a response, no different in principle from how a child grips a spoon or closes a door. And as with any form, reinforcements can be made contingent on the speed or pace at which a response occurs.

Temporal Generalization (Maintenance)

We refer to temporal generalization parenthetically as "maintenance." A common meaning of maintenance is given by the dictionary definition of the verb, *to maintain*: "to keep or keep up; continue in or with; carry on" (Webster's New World Dictionary 1984). By this definition, a reinforced response is maintained in the sense that it persists or endures in the future. The dimension that gives temporal generalization its meaning, then, is time, which is commonly understood in behavior analysis as having the same ontological status as space and matter (see Baum 1997).

A less common meaning of maintenance refers to the "continuation of the conditions that generate a performance" (Catania 1998, 396). On this definition, it is not the passage of time per se that determines whether a response persists or decays but rather the relative stability of events in the environment from one moment to the next. It is not enough to say that a response "is maintained" in the future without alluding to the conditions that prevail in the present.

Suppose that Andy now uses a spoon to eat different foods served in different places with different people at different times of the day and night, and that, with the proper reinforcements, the child who once mistook a red for a maroon crayon will make the correct discrimination for the rest of his or her life. The response in each case persists in the future, but only so long as the conditions in the future are similar to the conditions in the present. It may be hard to imagine an environment devoid of utensils or colored crayons; yet, without them, it is easy to see that the responses they sustain would quickly diminish.

Another major determinant of whether a response persists over time is how reinforcements for it are scheduled. A schedule is *continuous* when each and every instance of a given response produces a reinforcer; it is *intermittent* when a reinforcer follows the same response only every now and then.

A response that is reinforced intermittently is also one that encounters nonreinforcement intermittently. This brings to mind *extinction*, which refers to "discontinuing the reinforcement of responding (or the reduction in responding that it produces)" (Catania 1998, 389). *Resistance to extinction* refers to a response that is more or less resilient to the effects of nonreinforcement (extinction). As a rule, a continuously reinforced response recurs less often when reinforcement is not forthcoming (i.e., it is *less* resistant to extinction), whereas an intermittently reinforced response occurs more often (it is *more* resistant to extinction).

A response to the physical and especially the natural social environment is seldom continuously reinforced but is instead reinforced intermittently. The child in class who raises a hand to answer a question posed by the teacher is not always called on, yet hand-raising persists. The child on the playground is not always successful at getting his or her peers to jump rope or ride a seesaw, yet the child's attempt to solicit the cooperation of playmates endures. The longevity of the response in each case is due to intermittent reinforcement and the resistance to extinction that it produces.

Summary

We have seen that the effects of reinforcement on a response extend beyond increasing the likelihood that the response will occur again in the future. Prominent among these added effects are stimulus generalization, response generalization, and temporal generalization (maintenance). These three aspects of generalization have been described in considerable detail, and common examples of each have been given in order to foster a basic understanding of their meaning.

We turn next to presenting numerous *guidelines* for achieving generalized behavior change. To reiterate what was said at the start of this chapter, *guidelines* are used because there is no single way to achieve generalized behavior change that will be universally effective.

■ Guidelines for Promoting Generalized Behavior Change

Nine guidelines for promoting generalized behavior change in children with autism are described in the remainder of this chapter and are listed in Table 7.1. These guidelines have many sources (e.g., Baer 1982, 1999; Cooper, Heron, and Heward 2007; Cuvo 2003; Drabman, Hammer, and Rosenbaum 1979; Horner, Dunlap, and Koegel 1988; Kirby and Bickel 1988; Stokes and Baer 1977; Stokes and Osnes 1986, 1989). Interested readers are encouraged to study these references for the light they shed on the theory and research that underlies the guidelines.

Before we begin, a comment is in order regarding what Stokes and Baer (1977) termed the "train and hope" approach to achieving generalized behavior change. This refers to the practice of reinforcing desirable responses without regard to planning for generalization to other responses, features, or time frames. Training and then hoping for generalization is not a guideline per se and was not offered as such by Stokes and Baer. Nevertheless, it is important to understand that generalization is no different from any naturally occurring process in that it often "just happens" without a plan in place for achieving it. Isolating the factors responsible for unwitting instances of generalization constitutes a lively area for research. Indeed, many of the guidelines presented here are rooted in studies that were designed to closely examine nescient instances of generalization.

TABLE 7.1
Guidelines for Promoting Generalized Behavior Change

Stimulus Generalization

1. Reinforce the desired response to a variety of features.

2. Vary the teaching materials and instructions.

3. Include features in the teaching environment that are common to the nonteaching environment.

4. Teach rule-governed behavior.

5. Allow features in the natural environment to influence desirable responses.

Response Generalization

6. Reinforce a variety of desirable response forms.

7. Relax the requirement for reinforcement.

8. Establish fluent responding.

Temporal Generalization (Maintenance)

9. Use intermittent reinforcement for desirable responses.

The value of the train and hope approach is that it leads to *probing* for generalization. What this means is that a child is placed in an environment where the chances are good that generalization will occur. For example, suppose that Teddy's mother regularly encourages her son to look at, smile, and say "Hi" to his tutor whenever she arrives at his home for a teaching session. The mother and tutor routinely reinforce this response to the point where it occurs whenever the tutor arrives. Now suppose that Teddy and his mother are at the grocery store and see Teddy's tutor there shopping. Without encouragement from his mother, Teddy looks at his tutor, smiles, and says "Hi." This fortuitous instance of stimulus generalization (from home to the grocery store) can be contrasted with a more deliberate approach. Teddy's mother and tutor could have devised a plan to "accidentally on purpose" meet each other at the grocery store, to see whether Teddy would smile and say "Hi" to his tutor. Whether deliberate or accidental, it is always good practice to probe for generalization first and then decide whether to spend the time and energy it takes to develop and implement a program for promoting what has already been achieved.

Stimulus Generalization

Guideline 1: Reinforce the Desired Response to a Variety of Features

Reinforcing a response to a given feature in the environment may also be reinforced when it occurs in relation to the same feature in another place and at another time. For example, a parent who reinforces the spoken response "bear" when a child is asked to name a picture of a bear in a magazine can also reinforce the same response when it is made in the presence of a bear on the television, on a cereal box, or on a kiosk at Yellowstone Park. It takes a good deal of time and energy to reinforce a desirable response to each and every feature, however, and from a technical standpoint, the practice does not qualify as teaching for stimulus generalization per se.

The practical and technically correct alternative is to reinforce a response to selected features in the environment and to then probe for stimulus generalization to more or less similar features without reinforcement. If the response occurs incompletely or inconsistently, then additional reinforcements for improved responses to those features are necessary. A complete and consistently performed response, on the other hand, is evidence that stimulus generalization has occurred. In this case the child's instruction continues, with reinforcements provided for a desirable response to a new collection of carefully selected features and with ongoing probes for stimulus generalization.

There are several keys to selecting features in the environment, but the main one is that they should be those that the child encounters in his or her everyday environment. For example, normally developing young children routinely ask each other all sorts of what, why, and how questions throughout the day. With that in mind, Secan, Egel, and Tilley (1989) selected a small number of questions pertaining to what ("What is in your lunch?"), why ("Why is she crying?"), and how ("How do you move the ball?") and then reinforced each of four young children with autism for answering them correctly. A new set of what, why, and how questions were then presented to each child as probes to see whether the old set of questions influenced their answers to the new set. Each child in the study was moderately successful at giving appropriate answers to the new set of what, why, and how questions. We say "moderately successful" because the probes revealed that additional reinforcements were needed for some children in order for them to answer the new questions correctly. By probing for responses to new questions, Secan and her colleagues were in a position to determine whether training on the old set was sufficient to produce stimulus generalization to the new set or whether additional reinforcements for responding correctly to the new questions was necessary.

Guideline 2: Vary the Teaching Materials and Instructions

Stokes and Baer (1977, 358) recommended using "looser, more variable" instructions and teaching materials instead of, or in addition to, "a precisely repetitive handful of [instructions and materials]." A good example of this is seen when a child is first learning to comply with an instruction to "come here" and "sit down." The instruction may be repeated to the child in a precise manner until he or she regularly complies with it, at which point the instruction may be varied in a way that eventually approximates a more colloquial request, for instance, "C'mon over anhavaseat."

Charlop-Christy and Kelso (1996) maintained that variations in instructions and teaching materials, or both, can be incorporated into every task and activity that the child with autism encounters. This is sound advice and may help prevent the development of stimulus overselectivity by exposing the child to a variety of features and then reinforcing responses to only those that are relevant to the task at hand. In teaching a child about occupations, for instance, he or she may be shown a picture of a gray-haired, middle-aged Caucasian man with glasses who is wearing a white laboratory coat and has a stethoscope around his neck. What is relevant to the correct response ("It's a doctor") is the white coat and stethoscope; age, race, gender, hairstyle, and eyewear are irrelevant. Presentation of variations in those irrelevant features, in combination with differential reinforcement, enables the child to say "It's a doctor" whenever he or she sees someone wearing a laboratory coat and a stethoscope.

Guideline 3: Include Features in the Teaching Environment
That Are Common to the Nonteaching Environment

The advantages of incorporating common features across teaching and nonteaching (or probe) environments were illustrated in a study by Charlop, Schreibman, and Thibodeau (1985). Seven young boys with autism were reinforced for imitating two responses, "I want cookie" and "I want apple," in the presence of these snacks, which the teacher always gave to the child immediately after he or she gave a correct imitative response. Once the two "I want" responses occurred at an acceptable level without the teacher's having to model them, each child was placed at different times in three nonteaching environments: (a) an unfamiliar room (a room different from the one where each child first learned to imitate), in which the teacher gave the snacks to the child when he or she asked for them; (b) a second unfamiliar room, in which an unfamiliar adult (a person other than the teacher) gave the snacks to the child when he or she asked for them; and (c) a familiar room (the room in which each child first learned to imitate), in which the teacher presented two new snacks (pretzels and French fries) and gave them to the child when he or she asked for them properly.

Charlop and her colleagues (1985) found that each child asked correctly for snacks in each of the three nonteaching environments. The key to this result was the features common to the teaching and nonteaching environments, which prominently included the reinforcement contingency between asking for and receiving a snack. Although this is inconsistent with the technical requirement that a test for stimulus generalization be conducted without reinforcement, the results obtained by Charlop's group nonetheless indicate that stimulus generalization can be achieved when a contingency is maintained while other features in the environment are changing.

Maintaining a contingency of reinforcement across environments is especially helpful when teaching a child how to ask properly for an item or activity. After Skinner (1957), behavior analysts designate asking as *manding*. In recent years, mand training has received a great deal of attention as a way to teach verbal responses to young children with autism (e.g., Sundberg and Partington 1998).

Several requirements must be met to maintain a contingency between a mand (e.g., "I want juice") and its reinforcement (the child receives juice). One requirement is that the child's request be granted immediately. This means that the activity or item must be readily and conveniently available. If a child is learning to mand for apple juice, for instance, then apple juice should be available at home, in the car, at the park, and in all the other environments in which the child might ask for apple juice.

There are practical limits to what can reasonably be given to a child. For instance, "I want a pony" is a mand that may be impossible to grant. The best practice in such a case is to ignore the unreasonable request in favor of one that is more sensible and that can be granted immediately or within a period of time sufficient to maintain the contingency between asking for and receiving the item or activity that the child requests.

Another requirement is that that the item or activity requested be available only when the child asks appropriately for it. This may be difficult for parents who are accustomed to letting their child have free or unrestricted access to preferred snacks, toys, and activities. Parents may object to restricting access to what their child requests on the grounds that it is harsh or mean-spirited. To the contrary, if a child is able to ask properly for something, then providing the child with numerous opportunities to practice "using words" (or some other response form, such as gesture, sign, or picture) teaches the child that it is far easier and more enjoyable to ask someone for something than to go without it or to whine, fuss, or throw a tantrum for it.

Guideline 4: Teach Rule-Governed Behavior

According to Stokes and Osnes (1989, 349), the manner by which a rule is used to influence a response boils down to how it is "transported by the client as part of the treatment." A child may literally carry a rule, for example, by using a notebook containing step-by-step written or pictorial instructions on how to perform a given task. Alternatively, a child may be taught to follow a rule without the aide of materials or devices. In this case, the obedient child may figuratively carry the rule wherever he or she goes as a relatively permanent member of a repertoire of rule-following behavior.

Suppose that a young child with autism is learning to wash his or her hands at home. A first goal might be to provide reinforcements for following a sequence of pictorial instructions posted next to the bathroom sink. As hand washing comes under the influence of the pictures, a second goal might be to gradually fade these supports to the point where the child is washing his or her hands without them. Taught in this way, the child's hand washing becomes a permanent response that is made in the neighbor's bathroom, the school washroom, the restaurant lavatory, or in any other location where soiled hands can be cleaned.

Guideline 5: Allow Features in the Natural Environment to Influence Desirable Responses

Baer (1999) drew attention to what he called "natural communities of reinforcement" to make the point that the hallmark of an effective intervention is one that binds the child's responses to their reinforcements in his or her everyday environment. These communities are usually abundant and readily available at home, in school, and around the neighborhood, and they prominently include the people with whom a child interacts throughout the day, the places where he or she commonly goes, and the events that transpire in those places.

The environment can be a harsh place, however, and nowhere is this more apparent than in the natural social environment. For a young child with autism who is unaccustomed to interacting with unfamiliar people or is unresponsive to them, there may be few, if any, reinforcements available to support desirable social behavior.

The well-known work of Strain and his colleagues (e.g., Strain and Kohler 1999) on peer-mediated social skills training for young children with autism is particularly relevant to this guideline. They argue that one reason the young child with autism tends to interact infrequently with a typical peer is because the typical peer is inclined to ignore the child, especially after one or two failed attempts at engaging the child, for instance, in a playful activity. As Strain and Kohler (1999) put it, "The isolate behavior of these children must be viewed, in part, as a function of the developmentally homogeneous, socially unresponsive environments in which they are most often taught" (193).

The typical child's inclination to ignore or give up in response to an unsuccessful attempt at engaging a young child with autism can be overcome. In general, the strategy involves (a) teaching the typical peer a variety of playful responses that are likely to gain and sustain the attention of the child with autism, (b) instructing the typical child to persist in attempts to engage the child whenever he or she is socially unresponsive, and (c) allowing the two children to play together on a regular basis (i.e., to probe), with reinforcements provided as needed by a teacher or parent to the typical child for carrying out his or her role.

The effects of peer-mediated social skills training appear for the most part to be quite robust, often producing immediate and substantial increases in the number of prosocial interactions between the typical child and the child with autism. Moreover, the training tends to enhance the interactions between the child with autism and typical peers who do not participate in peer-mediated training (Chandler, Lubeck, and Fowler 1992). This latter effect is a prime example of stimulus generalization at work.

The peer-mediated approach relies heavily on a child's ability to imitate the social behavior and interactions of other children. This ability is difficult for many young children with autism, which is the main reason why behavior analysts who work intensively with these children spend so much of their time and energy modeling responses and providing reinforcements for imitating them. This practice is a means to an end, as the ultimate goal is for a child to show generalized imitation.

Response Generalization

Guideline 6: Reinforce a Variety of Desirable Response Forms

As mentioned earlier, one way to promote stimulus generalization is to reinforce a desirable response to a variety of carefully selected features in the environment (Guideline 1). A variation on this guideline is to reinforce a variety of carefully selected responses to the same or a similar feature in the environment. In other words, just as the same response can be reinforced in the presence of different features in the environment, so, too, can different responses be reinforced in the presence of the same feature in the environment.

Reinforcing each and every desirable response to the same feature or features in the environment takes a great deal of patience and time. The alternative is to carefully select a few responses that are correct or appropriate to a given feature, and then, once those responses are occurring reliably, to probe the child's response to see whether new or improved forms appear. If the child shows the desired form consistently, then it is reasonable to assume that the responses that were initially reinforced were sufficient in number and type to achieve response generalization. On the other hand, if the child shows the desired form sporadically or inconsistently, then additional reinforcements for improved responding are necessary.

Shaping relies on response generalization to supply new and improved forms to which reinforcements are applied; this is the prototype for response generalization. However, there are additional processes that affect the form of a response. One is imitation, in which new and improved forms arise from the imperfect match between a model's response and the observer's reaction to it. A second is rule-following, which typically leads to variations in response forms during the course of complying with a given rule. The point here is that there are several sources for desirable response forms. When parents and teachers are alert to these sources and take full advantage of them, they create a wealth of opportunities for the child to acquire desirable responses to the same or similar features in the physical and social environment.

Guideline 7: Relax the Requirement for Reinforcement

It follows from the previous section (Guideline 6) that the requirement for what constitutes a reinforced response should be relaxed to include all forms that are correct or appropriate to a given feature in the environment, regardless of their source. Restricting reinforcement to one or a few clearly delineated responses may be good practice in the beginning stages of instruction, but eventually those restrictions must be relaxed in favor of allowing a response to vary around a standard for what constitutes an acceptable form.

A good example of this guideline is seen in an early study on response generalization by Goetz and Baer (1973). Three young girls with deficient block-building play skills were each reinforced for showing any appropriate response that deviated from a previous response. This practice led to an increase in the number of new and improved forms.

Nonverbal responses of the sort that occur while a child is playing with blocks, toys, and other objects are not the only candidates for applying this guideline. Verbal responses also may differ in their form while still being appropriate to the occasion. There are many acceptable ways that a child greets his or her mother, such as embracing her, saying "Hi Mom," or saying "Hello Mommy." Greeting a playmate with "high fives" or "Hey dude, how's it goin'?" is an acceptable form as well.

These and countless other examples of variations in the formal properties of a response arise naturally during the course of a child's everyday interactions with his or her environment. For some children—notably children with autism—desirable new forms may not arise as naturally. In this case, it is necessary to reinforce new and improved response forms whenever and wherever they arise, with occasional probes to see whether response generalization has occurred.

Promoting stimulus generalization by allowing features in a child's everyday environment to influence his or her desirable responses to them was described in Guideline 5. A variation on that guideline is to capitalize on the opportunities present in the child's everyday environment to develop new and improved response forms to a given feature. Baer's (1999) concept of "natural communities of reinforcement" is relevant here as well, in that the reinforcements for new and improved forms of responding are ordinarily abundant in the child's home, school, neighborhood, and community.

Guideline 8: Establish Fluent Responding

Fluency-based instruction has a long and venerable history in behavior analysis (Lindsley 1996). The approach has recently gained the attention of practitioners who work with young children with autism as a way of improving the ease and efficiency of their responses (Zambolin, Fabrizio, and Isley 2004; King, Moors, and Fabrizio 2003).

The method is ordinarily reserved for responses that already occur reliably and with a high degree of accuracy. Consider the young boy who promptly and accurately imitates the actions of his tutor whenever he is given the instruction, "Do this." The aim for this child would be to increase the rate or speed at which he imitates his tutor's actions. Time would be set aside to practice imitating at a faster pace, with reinforcements provided, for instance, for performing three actions (e.g., raise arms, touch nose, and clap hands) in 5 seconds without an error. Once the child achieves this intermediate rate, more actions would be added on subsequent days until the child achieves the desired rate (or *frequency aim*) of, for example, six imitations in 5 seconds with no errors.

Proponents of fluency-based instruction emphasize the benefits of the method by pointing to an array of positive outcomes for the learner. According to Johnston and Layng (1996), once learners achieve a given frequency aim for a particular skill, they will *(a) remember* and perform the skill, at the frequency aim, after a significant period of no practice (1 month or longer); *(b)* show performance *endurance*—that is, perform the skill at the frequency aim for periods of time that are longer than the timing period used during practice; *(c)* perform the skill with *stability*—that is, without being easily distracted; *(d)* easily *apply* the skill as a prerequisite or component of a more complex performance to be learned; and *(e)* demonstrate increasing capacity to learn skills instantly, and on their own, as they move through a subject matter (286–287).

Because the method is still new in its application to young children with autism, it is too early to say whether all or some of these benefits will accrue to them. However, the evidence from roughly 60 years of research and practice with other children with disabilities, typical children, adolescents, and adults seems sufficient to recommend its use as way of enhancing not only response generalization but also stimulus and temporal generalization.

Temporal Generalization (Maintenance)

Guideline 9: Use Intermittent Reinforcement for Desirable Responses

How reinforcements are scheduled for a particular response plays a significant role in determining whether the response will persist or diminish over time. A study by Koegel and Rincover (1977, Experiment 2) showed how responses maintained on an intermittent schedule resist the effects of extinction. Six children with autism were each taught various imitative responses (e.g., raise arms, clap hands, touch nose) that were either reinforced continuously or on a fixed ratio (FR) schedule that for some children required two correct responses (FR 2) or five correct responses (FR 5). Once responding had stabilized, each child was put in a nonteaching (probe) environment with an unfamiliar model to see whether their imitative responses would persist when reinforcement was no longer provided. Responses that were reinforced continuously in the teaching environment extinguished quickly in the nonteaching environment, whereas responses on the FR 2 and especially the FR 5 schedule persisted.

There are several easy-to-use methods available to make the transition from a continuous to an intermittent schedule of reinforcement of a response. One method is to arrange an unpredictable or variable ratio of responses to reinforcers, for instance, by requiring an average of four desirable responses for each reinforcer. A second method is to reinforce the next response after an unpredictable or variable period of time, such as after every 15 seconds, on the average. Care must taken, however, to change gradually from continuous to intermittent reinforcement, and also to gradually increase the response or time requirements for reinforcement. This practice, called *schedule thinning,* helps prevent extinction of desirable responses that may occur if the increment in the number of responses or length of time is too large.

Intermittent schedules have the added advantage of making it difficult for a child to tell when reinforcement is available. The rationale for this is that, if reinforcements are unpredictable or indiscriminable, the child will continue responding without regard to whether a reinforcer will follow his or her next response. Indeed, it may be beneficial to occasionally deliver a reinforcer independent of the child's response, to further loosen a predictable response-reinforcer relation. Care must be taken, however, not to reinforce an undesirable response that may be occurring the moment a reinforcer is given.

Another way to make it less obvious where and when reinforcement for desirable behavior is possible is to delay the timing of reinforcement. Fowler and Baer (1981) found that reinforcements given to preschoolers in the afternoon for desirable peer-related social responses sustained the same responses the next morning for almost 3 months (temporal generalization) in both a teaching and a nonteaching (probe) environment. A practical note on delaying reinforcement is to set aside a given reinforcer for a short period of time initially, working gradually up to a point at which the delay is occupied either by the natural reinforcements that follow the child's response in his or her everyday environment or by the child's waiting patiently for the reinforcer.

The crucial role that a child's everyday environment plays in promoting stimulus generalization was discussed in Guideline 5, and a variation on it was presented with regard to achieving response generalization in Guideline 6. That it once again appears here, in the context of temporal generalization (maintenance), underscores how universally important it is to bind a child's responses to the natural reinforcements available in his or her everyday environment.

Maintaining desirable responses in a child's everyday environment requires a good deal of knowledge about the child's circumstances of living. This knowledge ranges from knowing about the reinforcements inherent in a family's enduring traditions, customs, and values to knowing how, when, and where reinforcements are arranged for a child's desirable, day-to-day responses. Parents, siblings, relatives, and teachers clearly are in the best position to reinforce responses naturally. Other adults and children with whom the child regularly interacts (e.g., neighbors and their children) can be enlisted as natural reinforcing agents, and still others in the community who are less involved in the child's daily life (e.g., grocery clerks, postal workers) can be encouraged to accept a child's more or less incipient responses as small steps along the way to achieving enduring behavior change.

■ Summary and Conclusions

We have listed, described, and given examples for nine guidelines that promote stimulus, response, and temporal generalization. Transcending these guidelines are three matters that bear repeating. First, no single approach to promoting generalized behavior change is right for every child. Children with autism are unique individuals, each with their own skills, abilities, interests, and lifestyles; like all children, they grow and mature at different rates. Respecting these individual differences encourages the practice of tailoring a program for achieving generalized behavior change to suit a child's circumstances of living. Second, teachers and parents should probe often for generalization. This practice ensures that valuable resources are not spent on promoting generalization when it has already been achieved, and it also pinpoints where generalization has not been achieved and what might be done to promote it. Finally, the everyday environment should be allowed to influence desirable responses and to supply the natural reinforcements for them. A child's everyday environment endures long after his or her formal instruction ends, so it is imperative that responses established in the instructional environment be supported by the people and places that form the child's daily life.

It is sometimes the case that following any one guideline for promoting one aspect of generalization promotes another aspect of generalization. Suppose that a young child with autism, Tommy, is being taught how to play with his typically developing peer, Brian, and that probes for the effects of this instruction take place with another typically developing peer, Cliff, who is not directly involved in Tommy's instruction. To the extent that Tommy and Brian play well together, the chances are good, although by no means guaranteed, that (a) Tommy will also play well with Cliff (stimulus generalization), (b) the form of Tommy's playful responses with Cliff will differ in appearance from those that were taught to him directly (response generalization); and (c) all or parts of Tommy's playful responses will persist over time (temporal generalization or maintenance).

There is a saying among people who work in real estate that the three most important features of a property are location, location, and location. Behavior analysts who specialize in the education and treatment of young children with autism might portray their work in the same light: The three most important features of an intervention are generalization, generalization, and generalization.

■ Acknowledgments

The authors thank Richard Foxx, Sid Bijou, and Larry Williams for their helpful comments on an earlier version of this paper.

■ References

Baer, D.M. (1982). The role of current pragmatics in the future analysis of generalization technology. In *Adherence, compliance, and generalization in behavioral medicine* (ed. R.B. Stuart), pp. 192–212. New York: Bruner/Mazel.

Baer, D.M. (1999). *How to plan for generalization,* 2nd ed. Austin, Tex.: PRO-ED.

Baum, W.M. (1997). The trouble with time. In *Investigations in behavioral episte-mology* (eds. L.J. Hayes and P.M. Ghezzi), pp. 47–59. Reno, Nev.: Context Press.

Bickel, W.K., Stella, E., and Etzel, B.C. (1984). A reevaluation of stimulus over-selectivity: Restricted stimulus control or stimulus control hierarchies. *Journal of Autism and Developmental Disorders,* 14, 137–157.

Binder, C. (1996). Behavioral fluency: Evolution of a new paradigm. *The Behavior Analyst,* 19 (2), 163–197.

Catania, A.C. (1998). *Learning,* 4th ed. Upper Saddle River, N.J.: Prentice-Hall.

Chandler, L.K., Lubeck, R.C., and Fowler, S.A. (192). Generalization and maintenance of preschool children's social skills: A critical review and analysis. *Journal of Applied Behavior Analysis,* 25, 415–428.

Charlop-Christy, M.H., and Kelso, S.E. (1996). *How to treat the child with autism: A guide to treatment at the Claremont Autism Center.* Claremont, Calif.: Claremont McKenna College, Department of Psychology.

Charlop, M., Schreibman, L., and Thibodeau, M.G. (1985). Increasing spontaneous verbal responding in autistic children using a time delay procedure. *Journal of Applied Behavior Analysis,* 18, 155–166.

Cooper, J.O., Heron, T.E., and Heward, W.L. (2007). *Applied behavior analysis,* 2nd ed. Upper Saddle River, N,J,: Pearson Education.

Drabman, R.S., Hammer, D., and Rosenbaum, M.S. (1979). Assessing generalization in behavior modification with children: The generalization map. *Behavioral Assessment,* 1, 203–219.

Cuvo, A.J. (2003). On stimulus generalization and stimulus classes. *Journal of Behavioral Education,* 12, 77–83.

Etzel, B.C. (1997). Environmental approaches to the development of conceptual behavior. In *Environment and behavior* (eds. D.M. Baer and E.M. Pinkston), pp. 52–79. Boulder, Colo.: Westview Press.

Fowler, S.A., and Baer, D.M. (1981). "Do I have to work all day?" The timing of delayed reinforcement as a factor in generalization. *Journal of Applied Behavior Analysis,* 14, 13–24.

Goetz, E.M., and Baer, D.M. (1973). Social control of form diversity and the emergence of new forms in children's blockbuilding. *Journal of Applied Behavior Analysis,* 6, 209–217.

Horner, R.H., Dunlap, G., and Koegel, R.L., eds. (1988). *Generalization and maintenance: Life style changes in applied settings.* Baltimore: Paul H. Brookes.

Johnson, K.R., and Layng, T.V.J. (1996). On terms and procedures: Fluency. *The Behavior Analyst,* 19 (2), 281–288.

King, A., Moors, A.L., and Fabrizio, M.A. (2003). Concurrently teaching multiple verbal operants related to preposition use to a child with autism. *Journal of Precision Teaching,* 19 (1), 38–40.

Kirby, K.C., and Bickel, W.K. (1988). Toward an explicit analysis of generalization: A stimulus control interpretation. *The Behavior Analyst,* 11 (2), 115–129.

Koegel, L.K., and Rincover, A. (1977). Research on the difference between generalization and maintenance in extra-therapy responding. *Journal of Applied Behavior Analysis,* 10, 1–12.

Lindsley, O.R. (1996). The four operant freedoms. *The Behavior Analyst,* 19 (2), 199–210.

Lovaas, O.I. (1981). *Teaching developmentally disabled children: The ME book.* Baltimore: University Park Press.

Lovaas, O.I., Koegel, R.L., and Schreibman, L. (1979). Stimulus overselectivity in autism: A review of research. *Psychological Bulletin,* 86, 1236–1254.

Lovaas, O.I., Schreibman, L., Koegel, R.L., and Rehm, R. (1971). Selective responding by autistic children in a two stimulus situation. *Journal of Abnormal Psychology,* 77, 211–222.

Rincover, A., and Ducharme, J.M. (1987). Variables influencing stimulus overselectivity and tunnel vision in developmentally delayed children. *American Journal of Mental Deficiency,* 91, 422–430.

Rosenblatt, J., Bloom, P., and Koegel, R.L. (1995). Overselective responding: Description, implications, and intervention. In *Teaching children with autism: Strategies for initiating positive interactions and improving learning opportunities* (eds. R.L. Koegel and L.K. Koegel), pp. 33–42). Baltimore: Paul H. Brookes.

Schreibman, L. (1997). The study of stimulus control in autism. In *Environment and behavior* (eds. D.M. Baer and E.M. Pinkston), pp. 203–209. Boulder, Colo.: Westview Press.

Secan, K.E., Egel, A.L., and Tilly, C.S. (1989). Acquisition, generalization, and maintenance of question-answering skills in autistic children. *Journal of Applied Behavior Analysis,* 22, 181–196.

Skinner, B.F. (1957). *Verbal behavior.* New York: Appleton-Century-Crofts.

Stokes, T.F., and Baer, D.M. (1977). An implicit technology of generalization. *Journal of Applied Behavior Analysis,* 10, 349–367.

Stokes, T.F., and Osnes, P.G. (1986). Programming the generalization of children's social behavior. In *Children's social behavior: Development, assessment, and modification* (eds. P.S. Strain, M.J. Guralnick, and H.M. Walker), pp. 407–443. Orlando, Fla.: Academic Press.

Stokes, T.F., and Osnes, P.G. (1989). An operant pursuit of generalization. *Behavior Therapy,* 20, 337–355.

Strain, P.S., and Kohler, F. (1999). Peer-mediated interventions for young children with autism: A 20 year retrospective. In *Autism: Behavior analytic perspectives* (eds. P.M. Ghezzi, W.L. Williams, and J.E. Carr), pp. 189–211. Reno, Nev.: Context Press.

Sundberg, M.L., and Partington, J.W. (1998). *Teaching language to children with autism or other developmental disabilities.* Pleasant Hill, Calif.: Behavior Analysts, Inc.

Zambolin, K., Fabrizio, M.A., and Isley, S. (2004). Teaching a child with autism informational questions using precision teaching. *Journal of Precision Teaching,* 20 (1), 22–25.

8. BEST PRACTICE METHODS IN STAFF TRAINING

Peter Sturmey

The success of applied behavior analysis (ABA) is completely dependent on modifying the behavior of mediators, such as staff, peers, and parents. Typical ABA interventions depend on analysis of the behavior of other people and its relationship to the student behavior of interest. Once that relationship is known, an intervention is designed based on that information that modifies the behavior of the intermediaries in order to change the behavior of the student. Even interventions that appear to be primarily delivered through mechanical devices or modification of the physical environment require people to turn the devices on and off, to maintain and not disable the devices, and to not alter the physical environment such that treatment cannot be delivered. The importance of staff training was known early, when the basic researchers left the laboratory and immediately recognized the importance—and difficulty—of training staff to deliver ABA interventions (Bensberg and Barnett 1968). Since that time, considerable attention has been paid by applied researchers to determine staff training needs, the limitations of typical current staff training practices, and how these important skills should be taught.

■ Staff Training Needs

There are large numbers of personnel working in services for children with autism spectrum disorders (ASD). These include early interventions and pre-school staff, such as those working directly with young children, as well as staff that supervise them and/or train parents and administrators. In addition, many people work in special education, including special education teachers, teacher assistants, speech pathologists, physical therapists, behavior analysts, psychologists, psychiatrists, pediatricians, nurses, program supervisors and administrators, and other consultants. There are also a considerable number of staff who work with families in after-school programs, weekend programs, extended-year services, summer camps, and family respite services. Finally, there are a variety of educational staff personnel in mainstream education

159

who work with children with ASD in various integrated and semi-integrated arrangements. Staff workers, in sum, play a variety of different roles, have a wide range of tasks to fulfill, and are extremely varied in training, education, and the degree of preparation to enable them to work in ASD services.

To illustrate this point, let us contrast the training needs of several different staff members. Consider a newly hired classroom assistant, Henry, who has no previous experience in ABA and a high school education. Henry may have to deliver approximately 100 different individual behavioral skills intervention programs to eight children in one classroom. He will interact directly with students individually and in groups, implement and document specific interventions, and work with student in formal structured situations, such as discrete trial teaching (DTT), and less structured situations, such as incidental teaching and leisure time. Occasionally, Henry may undertake additional duties, such as being assigned to a specific student with behavioral challenges, serving as a substitute for other classroom assistants, or interacting with the teacher, program supervisor, family members, and consultants on a child's progress, functional assessment, and child health and safety.

This classroom assistant may receive 2 or 3 days of training before the beginning of the school year on policies, procures, child safety, and a variety of administrative matters. Henry may receive some general information presented in written or spoken format and perhaps a 10-minute videotape of one or two teaching methods. During this training, he will have no direct experience of working with children with ASD and, indeed, may not even be too sure what such a child is like. After this training, the program administrator tells the classroom assistants and their teacher that they will receive on-the-job training in the classroom, and a couple of weeks later a program administrator ensures that a checklist of experiences has been signed off.

Consider a second staff person, Helen, who is a licensed special education teacher with a masters degree in special education. Helen has received training in many aspects of special education, but ASD was only small part of that education, and the program she was in evaluated progress by requiring written papers and lesson plans. (A professor who came out to review the student teachers' progress in the classroom spent only 20 minutes observing them in the classroom and 1 hour in a meeting reviewing a lesson plan). Although Helen completed a several weeks of class practicum, her mentor had little knowledge or skill in ABA and perhaps was opposed to it.

Now this licensed teacher must review and evaluate existing Individual Education Plans (IEPs), assess new students, select teaching objectives, prioritize curricular areas for children and write IEPs, and conduct functional behavior assessments (FBAs). Additionally, she will be responsible for training and supervising the new cadre of classroom assistants, including Henry, and communicating effectively with a variety of other professional staff. Helen must also supervise her classroom assistants and deal with tardiness, abuse of sick time, and interactional problems that occasionally occur between staff members.

Finally, let us consider the training needs of a consulting licensed professional, Frank, who recently began working in an early intervention service for children with ASD and previously worked in a mainstream setting with typical children. Frank has a good working knowledge of educational practices and of typical child development and assessment, but he has little knowledge or skill relating to teaching children with ASD, training staff and family members, or dealing with more complex and intransigent challenging behavior. Although Frank graduated from an accredited doctoral program 10 years ago and attends conferences annually, he has had little direct training experiences to prepare him for his current role.

These three staff members have differing degrees and quantities of preparation and training for their job, but all are in need of very different kinds of staff training.

The number of staff working with students with ASD has increased. This reflects a number of factors. First, the number of children identified with ASD has greatly increased (Chakrabati and Fombonne 2005; Fombonne 1999), and this has led to a substantial expansion of services for children with ASD (U.S. Department of Education 2005). Second, children with ASD are more likely to be identified at an earlier age than previously. This has led to an expansion of early intervention services for children with ASD aged 3 years and younger. Finally, there has been a greater focus on the less severe forms of ASD, such as pervasive developmental disorders and Asperger's syndrome. In 1996, Pickett (cited in National Research Council 2001, 187) estimated that there were approximately 280,000 paraprofessionals in special education settings but did not identify how many of them worked with students with ASD; in any case, the figure is far greater today.

There have been relatively few empirical studies of staff training needs. (See Thousand, Burchard, and Hasazi, 1986, for a model of how to use multiple methods to assess staff training needs). However, various expert panels have made recommendations. For example, the New York Department of Health (1999) recommended that ABA early intervention educational programs focus on identification of child skills, structured individual and group interactions, programming of generalization, and reinforcer assessment. It advocated reduction of challenging behaviors though functional analysis and teaching of appropriate and incompatible behaviors through differential reinforcement. They recommended teaching communication skills, including functional use of language, nonverbal communication, and nonverbal forms of communication for children who do not yet talk. Finally, they also proposed that early intervention programs teach social behavior, including appropriate social responses, reciprocal interactions, and the use of peer modeling. The National Research Council's (2001, 184) review of educating children with autism identified very similar areas of competence for special education teachers and added competency in the use of inclusion, adaption of the environment, assistive technology, and effective use of data collection systems.

The training needs of staff working with students with ASD are extremely varied. Many staff at all levels of education and training are inadequately trained, and there are large and growing numbers of staff to be trained. However, there is some consensus from expert review panels that staff should be trained in certain basic behavioral methods that address the social, language, academic, and behavioral needs of students with ASD. Therefore, best practice in staff training would require that staff training (a) assess the needs of staff members, (b) tailor staff training to individual staff needs, and (c) address the priority areas identified by consensus panels.

■ Desirable Features of Staff Training

Reid and Parsons (1995) asserted that staff training should be efficient, effective, and acceptable. "Efficient" means that training is delivered quickly, with the minimal resources necessary to produce the change in staff behavior desired. Further, services should be able to deliver staff training on the scale required by the organization's size, rate of staff turnover, resources available for staff training, and the priorities of the organization. For example, courses that take days or weeks, can be delivered only by a few experts, are held at a distance from the workplace, and are expensive are unlikely to be efficient. However, staff training methods that can be delivered by current staff in the workplace in a timely fashion, within the context of a typical workday, are much more likely to be implemented and to be efficient.

Effectiveness is a more elusive concept than it appears to be at first. Some might consider a staff training procedure to be effective if it produces the desired change in staff behavior. However, this begs the question of judging the desired level of staff performance. The reason for training staff is to produce student outcomes, and this should be the criterion by which the effectiveness of staff training is judged. For example, a staff training procedure that teaches a staff member to correctly take data on a teaching program would not be said to be effective unless the child learned the skill. This example illustrates the necessity of identifying and teaching functional staff skills that result in child learning.

Staff training procedures should also be acceptable to the participants, their supervisors, and the organization. If a staff training procedure is too effortful or embarrassing to participants or interferes with their important goals at work, then services are unlikely to adopt it.

In addition to Reid and Parson's three criteria, staff training should address relevant needs and promote generalization of durable skills. Too often, staff training is provided because the trainer is interested in the training, because a training package is available, or because regulations require the training. Without careful analysis of staff training needs, the training may be irrelevant. The expert panels mentioned previously have identified some of the training needs of staff members working with students with ASD.

Staff training should also address generalization of staff skills (Ducharme and Feldman 1992). Although generalization of student behavior is a primary focus, work on staff training has largely ignored the generalization of staff behavior. Both stimulus and response generalization of staff behavior are relevant here. Consider, for example, a staff member who has been successfully trained to accurately teach a child with ASD a color discrimination program. We expect that staff member to be able to conduct similar programs accurately with other stimulus materials, with other children, and with the same child when the child shows, none, some, or a great deal of challenging behavior and in other settings. We may hope that he or she could also teach other, untrained discrimination programs, such as size or shape. In some circumstances, we expect considerable response generalization of staff performance. For example, if staff members have been taught to conduct incidental teaching during lunch time in response to student approaches to food and drink items, we might also expect them to accurately perform incidental teaching in other situations, such as when a student approaches objects or people. In natural language paradigm, staff members should teach with considerable flexibility, producing many novel teaching behaviors as a student emits novel responses to novel stimuli. Finally, staff training should produce durable changes in staff behavior, so that staff can continue to teach students effectively over long periods of time without costly monitoring and retraining.

Best practice requires that staff training be effective enough to produce the desired change in student behavior, be acceptable to staff and administrators, be efficient enough to address the very large numbers of staff who need training, and produce generalization of change in staff behavior.

■ Typical Approaches to Staff Training

Most approaches to staff training emphasize verbal and written instructions without rehearsal and acquisition of the actual skills needed when working in the classroom with students. This problem is ubiquitous. Services may be motivated to cut corners, and oversight of public services emphasizes paperwork to document that some form of staff training occurred—but not necessarily effective staff training producing a meaningful child outcome. A quick, verbal in-service training that requires a staff member to be physically present but to emit no behavior, suffices for these purposes. Professional training for teachers and other special education professionals continues to emphasize writing and talking. Skills acquisition is too often left to practicum sites of dubious quality. Future professionals are required to spend a certain number of hours on site, perhaps produce a written report, and maybe ask an onsite supervisor to provide ratings on ill-defined criteria. On-line training and degrees also have the same problems. In too many cases, higher education produces many teachers and professionals who can "talk the talk," but few who can "walk the walk." In short, typical practice bears little resemblance to best practice.

■ Behavioral Skills Training

Applied behavior analysis approaches to staff training are quite different from traditional methods. Staff training is seen as one specific example of a broader approach to teaching skills to people. Therefore, staff training is fundamentally no different from other skills training problems, such as teaching industrial workers to assemble shoes, teaching social skills to someone with schizophrenia, or doing an accurate maintenance check on a vehicle. Applied behavior analysis uses a set of procedures, collectively termed behavioral skills training (BST), to teach skills (Miltenberger 2003). Behavioral skills training typically consists of four components: instructions, modeling, rehearsal, and feedback to mastery.

Instructions

In contrast to traditional methods, BST keeps the verbal part of training to a minimum. Instructions given at the beginning of training can be as little as 2 to 5 minutes long. Instructions might consist of a statement from the trainer describing why the skill being taught is important, presenting a written copy and describing the steps of a task analysis of the specific skill, and asking and answering any questions briefly. It is important that the trainer present the verbal and written information in language that staff can easily understand. Difficult language can inhibit understanding (McGaw and Sturmey 1989) and has other undesirable effects, such as reduced staff acceptability.

Modeling

Behavioral skills training then moves quickly on to presenting a model of the skill being taught. A model may be presented live, by the trainer showing the staff what to do, either with a student or through role play, or with the use of videotape. Each of these methods of modeling has pros and cons. Working live with a student might have some unexpected surprises for the trainer, and the presence of an audience might change the student's behavior. More subtly, when using a live model, the trainer may not be able to present all the relevant aspects of the teaching procedure. For example, if the student makes no correct responses, then the trainer cannot model reinforcement. One possibility is to use a trained confederate student who can present the opportunity of all possible scenarios to the trainer to model for the staff.

Role play is also another possible way to provide models. Again, the person role playing the role of the child may require careful coaching before the training to ensure that his or her behavior is conducive to training. Another potentially efficient way of providing models for correct performance is to use videotape. Tapes can be edited to provide models of all possible scenarios and to provide multiple models with different kinds of staff, programs, and students. It is possible, as in other work on modeling, that model similarity between the material on the videotape and the audience may be important to learning. Therefore, it may be preferable to have other staff members similar to the audience as models, rather than professionals or other people. Making and editing videotaped models can be time-consuming and requires parental consent for use of the videotape.

Rehearsal

Rehearsal involves the trainee's practicing the skills being taught. This may be done live with a student, in role play, or by a combination of these methods. In typical BST staff training studies, rehearsal consists of multiple brief sessions lasting perhaps 2 to 5 minutes or 3 to 20 trials. These sessions are interspersed with some form of feedback. Sometimes, the trainer also models steps that were performed incorrectly in previous sessions. There are many procedural variations of this component of BST.

Feedback

The fourth component of BST is feedback, and again there are many procedural variations. Feedback can be given verbally, in the form of comments from the trainer. To make the verbal feedback component acceptable, Reid and Parsons (1995) recommended beginning and ending with positive comments, providing corrective feedback that emphasizes what the trainee should do in the middle, and avoiding negative, sarcastic, or derisory comments. For example, a trainer might say, "Thanks for letting me watch you doing incidental teaching with Josephina. You did a good job of using juice, which she wants, and waiting for her to reach for her juice without any prompting. You also got three approaches in 2 minutes, which was good. Maybe next time, try giving her only a quarter of a cup instead of a whole cup of juice. That way, you will be able to have more teaching trials, and juice will be a powerful reward for a longer time. If you keep teaching like this, she will learn to say 'j' consistently every time. Thank you." Feedback can also be written, may include scores, and may include various forms of graphical feedback, such as graphs of staff and student performance or other staff behavior. Feedback may be either immediate or delayed. Immediate feedback is probably preferred by many staff members and is perhaps more likely to be effective than delayed feedback. However, delayed feedback may be necessary, for example, if scoring videotapes or audiotapes must be scored and is also effective (Reid and Parsons 1997).

The ABC Model of Behavior Change

The BST package can be analyzed in terms of the antecedents, behaviors, and consequences (ABC) model of behavior change that runs throughout ABA. The trainer provides several kinds of antecedents, including general instructions, written prompts in the form of the written task analysis, and specific instructions to engage in the teaching task. The staff behavior includes correct and incorrect teaching behaviors. The consequences for staff behavior may include feedback from the trainer and changes in student behavior.

My own observations of staff training in this area suggest that there is often an immediate improvement in staff performance compared to baseline after instructions are given; staff emit easy steps that they previously had not. This suggests that some of the antecedents may be important in inducing staff to emit the easy responses that are already in their repertoire. This is often followed by a gradual improvement in performance as they acquire the remaining steps, suggestive of the effects of feedback to shape and differentially reinforce more difficult or new staff responses and to bring the staff performance under the appropriate stimulus control of the child's behavior. For example, it may take several brief sessions to teach a staff member slightly more complex skills such as consistently using the exact instruction written in a program without repetition or any other verbalization or consistently prompting "hands down" when a students' hands begins to move from their lap before engaging in stereotypy.

So far, researchers have not conducted many studies as to the effective components and procedural variations in BST of staff teaching. However, it is noteworthy that many of the studies discussed in the next section included active baseline conditions in which staff received instructions and/or written analyses of tasks, and yet this intervention, which is not unlike many typical staff training practices, did not produce any changes in staff behavior. This suggests that verbal and written instructions are probably not the active component of BST; perhaps modeling, rehearsal, and feedback are the effective components.

Best practice for teaching skills to staff involves identification of priority skills, task analysis of those skills, and the use of BST as the method to teach those skills.

■ Applications of Behavioral Skills Training

Researchers and practitioners have used BST to teach a wide variety of educational staff many different and important teaching skills. These include DTT, stimulus preference assessment (SPA), mand training, incidental teaching, implementation of functional analyses and interventions for challenging behaviors, and increasing student engagement. The following sections describe some illustrative studies; however, an exhaustive review is beyond the scope of this chapter.

Discrete Trial Teaching

Discrete trial teaching is a teaching the method that is most commonly used and most extensively researched with students with ASD (Duker, Didden, and Sigafoos 2004; Smith 2001). It is an important component of the beginning of education for many children with ASD as teachers gain initial instructional control of the student by teaching them to sit down, stay in place, attend when their name is called, and acquire imitation, receptive language, and matching skills (Anderson, Taras and O'Malley Cannon 1996; Lovaas 1981; Taylor and McDonough 1996). It is also a component of intensive early intervention programs that may produce large developmental gains for some children with ASD (Lovaas 1987; Sallows and Graupner 2005). Although there are other important ABA intervention methods and the status of DTT is not unchallenged (Del Prato 2001; Mirenda-Linne and Melin 1992), it remains the one that is most commonly used.

Sarakoff and Sturmey (2004) analyzed the task of DTT into 10 steps (Table 8.1). Similar task analyses can be found in the work of Anderson and colleagues (1996); Codding and colleagues (2005); Koegel, Russo, and Rincover (1977); Leblanc, Ricciardi, and Luiselli (2005); and Ryan and Hemmes (2005, Appendix B). In more recent research, a modification to this task analysis has been made to require that teachers vary the intertrial interval, to make it more likely that the student's correct responding comes under the stimulus control of the teacher's instruction rather than the passage of time.

In addition to these staff behaviors, one may commonly observe various idiosyncratic problems with staff implementation of DTT that training should address. For example, Breines and Sturmey (in press) extended this task analysis to identify idiosyncratic staff performance problems. We compared the behavior of members of the teaching staff who were consistently associated with a high versus low proportion of intervals of student stereotypy. We identified specific staff behaviors, such as leaving dividers open and talking to other staff, placing reinforcers behind the staff member such that reinforcers were delivered late and perhaps contingent on stereotypy (!), and providing music reinforcer for 5 minutes instead of 30 seconds, thereby releasing the staff member for social interaction with peers. In contrast, staff

TABLE 8.1

Ten-Step Task Analysis of Discrete Trial Teaching

Step	Staff Response
Step 1	Eye contact
Step 2	Readiness response
Step 3	Delivers instructions once
Step 4	Verbal instructions
Step 5	Correction procedure
Step 6	Appropriate reinforcement
Step 7	Specific praise
Step 8	Immediacy of reinforcement
Step 9	Data collection
Step 10	Intertrial interval

From Sarakoff, R.A., and Sturmey, P. (2004). The effects of behavioral skills training on staff implementation of discrete-trial teaching. *Journal of Applied Behavior Analysis, 37,* 535–538.

members who were associated with a low proportion of intervals of student stereotypy kept dividers in place and did not talk to other staff members, had reinforcers on the desk and delivered them within 2 seconds, and delivered the music reinforcer for only 30 seconds, as specified in the program.

There are other potential staff performance problems that training in DTT should address. It is not uncommon to observe staff members during receptive language programming inadvertently provide inappropriate antecedents to students, such as gestures, eye pointing, and body posture. Context cues such as pulling a chair away from the student at the beginning of every trial of "stand up" and following this immediately by a trial of "sit down" may also be problematic in that they provide antecedents other than the instruction that are reliably predictive of the behavior and reinforcement. Likewise, one may observe staff members permitting a student to make multiple incorrect responses before the correct response, while the child carefully observes the staff member for social cues as to the correct response. The staff member may then record this as a correct trial. In this situation, the staff member may be inadvertently teaching chains of incorrect responses and bringing the child's correct response under the stimulus control of social sues from the teacher rather than the instruction itself.

A final component of DTT that staff training should address is generalization from the teaching situation. This is an essential component of DTT. It may include procedures such as using multiple exemplars of stimulus material during DTT (e.g., many red, yellow, and blue objects during color discrimination), probing for generalization during imitation training by providing unre-inforced trials on novel models, probing for generalization in novel situations and with novel people who are trainers, and so on. Some generalization procedures involve quite delicate fading and shaping procedures that require good teaching skills and are difficult to perform.

Koegel and colleagues conducted an early study to train 11 teachers to teach 12 children with autism using 27 different individual programs, including self-help skills, academic, language, and imitation skills. The teacher training procedure included (a) reading a training manual, (b) observing videotapes of correct and incorrect teaching, and (c) rehearsing teaching a child with autism using the methods illustrated on the videotape. A trainer provided brief verbal feedback every 5 minutes regarding steps conducted correctly and incorrectly and modeled correct performance of steps conducted incorrectly. These steps were conduced until the trainer was "subjectively satisfied with the teacher's performance" (Koegel et al. 1977, 199). Training took place over a period of 5 days at 5 hours per day or 10 days at 2.5 hours per day. All teachers completed training within 25 hours of training. During baseline observation, 10 of the 11 teachers completed fewer than 58% of the steps of DTT correctly, and 2 performed none of the steps correctly. Moreover, the children failed to learn their programs or even decreased their rates of correct responding, indicating that teacher performance was ineffective (or even harmful) in baseline. After training was completed, all 11 teachers performed 90% to 100% of the steps of DTT correctly in 26 teaching sessions. Importantly, during post-training, all 26 sessions of child data showed improved responding. In graphs of four representative children, Koegel and coworkers showed that the children who failed to acquire tasks during baseline consistently and rapidly acquired all assigned programs, including the introduction of fading procedures, after staff training. None of the teachers reported that this training method was excessively demanding. This early study is important because it demonstrated that qualified special education teachers may teach so ineffectively that children with ASD actually *lose* skills during teaching. However, these teachers can acquire effective DTT skills, with the result that the same students learn rapidly.

Ryan and Hemmes (2005) used a broadly similar approach to teach three special education instructors of children with autism aged 2 to 3 years who received approximately 20 hours per week of intensive early intervention behavioral services. Ryan provided lectures on 20 topics, including autism, ABA, DTT, peer interaction, and trouble-shooting. Training continued until trainees passed 20 written and oral quizzes with 100% accuracy. This took 25 to 35 sessions of 1 to 2 hours each. Ryan also videotaped instructors teaching children three different kinds of educational programs. This recording was used for verbal feedback on the correct use of DTT. The trainer also asked for acknowledgement of any teaching problems and used role play or in vivo practice. After training, the three instructors demonstrated correct DTT responses on

95%, 92%, and 89% of opportunities. Two of the teachers demonstrated lower performance of contingent reinforcement. The performance of trained staff was notably higher than that of four untrained teachers, who had a correct score on only 49% to 71% of the steps All staff trainees rated all items on an anonymous treatment acceptability questionnaire as "very satisfied."

These two studies, and similar ones (e.g., Crocket et al. in press), demonstrate that staff can be trained effectively and acceptably. However, they are limited in that the time taken to train participants—approximately 25 hours per staff member in each case—may not be efficient. Therefore, more recent studies have gone on to evaluate briefer methods of staff training in DTT.

Sarakoff and Sturmey (2004) used instruction, modeling, rehearsal, and feedback to teach three special education teachers who were working with one child receiving home-based early intervention services. All had a masters degree in special education and 5 to 24 months of experience using DTT. They were videotaped while teaching the child at home. During baseline, the experimenter gave each teacher a copy of the task analysis of DTT, and at the beginning of each session the teacher was told to perform DTT to the best of their abilities. During training, the experimenter reviewed each component of DTT with the teacher and provided a copy of the skill task analysis, a graph of the teacher's baseline performance of DTT, and a chart of the data from the previous teaching session broken down into the 10 steps of the task analysis. The experimenter than gave the teacher feedback on his or her performance. The teacher practiced three trials of DTT with the student and received immediate verbal feedback on performance. This pattern of feedback, rehearsal, and modeling was continued for a total of 10 minutes per session. At the end of each 10-minute session, the teacher was asked to conduct 10 trials of DTT with the student. Teachers were said to be trained if they made at least 90% correct responses on three consecutive training sessions. During baseline, the three teachers had correct scores on 43%, 49%, and 43% of the steps of teaching, and two of them showed a gradual worsening of teaching skills. After training, they scored 97%, 98%, and 99% and taught consistently. This study showed that DTT can be taught much more efficiently than in previous studies.

Breines and Sturmey (in press) replicated and extended the study of Sarakoff and Sturmey (2004). They identified staff members who were associated with a high proportion of intervals of student stereotypy. As noted earlier, they also identified individual problematic behaviors of staff during teaching. Three boys with autism, aged 9 to 12 years, whom staff had identified as having high rates of stereotypy with certain staff members, participated in the study. They attended a special school that provided ABA education. Three staff members who were identified as having the highest proportion of intervals of student stereotypy participated. Training in DTT was delivered using the same method as was used by Sarakoff and Sturmey (2004). During baseline, the three staff members almost no correct DTT responses. After BST, all three emitted correct DTT responses in almost 100% of opportunities. Importantly, data on student stereotypy also showed a systematic decrease for all three students (from 55%, 20%, and 65% during baseline to 7%, 5%, and 10% after training, respectively). This study replicated that of Sarakoff and Sturmey (2004) in that it showed that staff could be trained to conduct DTT very rapidly. Indeed, Leblanc (2005) and Lerman (2004) and their colleagues have also reported similar rapid acquisition of DTT with trainee teachers, teachers, and classroom assistants. Further, as in the study by Koegel and associates (1977), this approach was validated in that the changes in staff use of DTT were consistently associated with reduction in stereotypy in students with autism for whom this had been identified as a significant problem.

Summary of Discrete Trial Teaching

Educational staff and teachers can be taught to use DTT. Koegel and colleagues (1977) and Breines and Sturmey (in press) showed that incorrect implementation of DTT (during baseline) may be associated with students' not learning and exhibiting stereotypy. When staff are taught effectively, students who previously did not learn and exhibited stereotypy then learned and showed lower levels of stereotypy. These changes in student behavior validate the staff training. Although earlier studies (Koegel et al. 1977; Ryan and Hemmes 2005) were effective and acceptable, they were not efficient. Their methods of staff training required more hours than is typically available in many programs if large numbers of staff are to be trained. More recently, abbreviated forms of BST have been employed that rely little on instruction and knowledge of principles but focus on modeling, rehearsal, and feedback.

   In preparing this chapter, I was unable to find any staff training studies addressing the issue of generalization of staff teaching from specific training programs and children to other training programs. Further, studies have not yet addressed other aspects of staff use of DTT, such as avoiding inadvertent cuing of student performance, avoiding context-inappropriate cues, and programming generalization of student performance from one-on-one DTT teaching situations, people, and materials to untrained situations, people, and materials. Future research should address these important issues.

Other Applications of Behavioral Skills Training

Behavioral skills training has been applied to a very wide range of staff teaching skills. Lavie and Sturmey (2002) taught three assistant teachers to conduct SPAs with eight children with ASD. Roscoe, Fisher, Glover, and Volkert (2006) also taught staff to conduct SPAs. Schepis, Reid, Ownbey, and Parsons (2001) taught support staff to embed teaching within natural routines of young children with disabilities, including a child with autism, in an inclusive preschool setting. Lerman and associates (2004) taught a variety of behavioral skills to staff, including DTT, SPAs, and other behavioral skills.

Researchers have also applied BST to address the assessment and treatment of challenging behavior (Iwata et al. 2000; Moore et al. 2002). Wallace and coworkers (2004) taught three staff members, including a special educator, how to conduct analog baselines. Other studies have reported similar efforts with other groups of staff (e.g., Shore et al. 1995). Although no articles on training staff to correctly implement behavioral intervention procedures specifically with students with ASD were located for this chapter, several articles addressing other populations and other settings support the application of BST to teach staff to implement behavioral interventions for challenging behaviors (Codding et al. 2005; Shore et al. 1995).

■ Dissemination

If ABA methods of teaching students with ASD are to be widely disseminated in routine services, dissemination cannot depend on a few specialist professional, regional or national consultants or even on staff training specialists who remain in their offices, away from classrooms and students. Rather, team supervisors in early education programs, special education teachers, local supervisors, school psychologists, and staff trainers must be able to teach their own staff within the available resource restrictions.

To address this need, pyramidal methods of skills training have been developed in which supervisors are taught the target skill, how to teach that skill, and how to take data on other staff members' performance using BST (Neef 1995). This approach has been used widely in institutional settings (Page, Iwata, and Reid 1982; Shore et al. 1995) and in mainstream educational settings (Noell et al. 2000; Witt et al. 1997). Most impressively, pyramidal training has also been used to disseminate positive behavior support (PBS) intervention skills statewide in North Carolina (Reid et al. 2003; Rotholtz and Ford 2003).

Reid and colleagues (2003) developed a PBS training curriculum in collaboration with local service providers that included modules such as choice making and FBAs. Training took place both in the classroom and on the job. The training format was performance based in that staff trainees had to participate in role play and complete quizzes in the class. For example, in the choice-making modules, trainees had to describe the skill of making a choice, write a task analysis of the skill, demonstrate the skill, and observe and give feedback to another person demonstrating the skill until the mastery criterion was met. To pass the course, staff had to pass multiple quizzes, in-class role-play demonstrations, and on-the-job demonstrations of skills learned. Observational data showed that few supervisors met the mastery criterion in baseline, but almost all did so after training. Further, of 386 supervisors who attended training over a 22-month period, 328 (85%) met the criterion. Social validation data showed that 95% of these staff found the training "extremely useful" or "useful," and 97% recommended it to other staff. So far, I am unaware of similar large-scale applications in educational services for students with autism. This needs to be addressed in future research.

Best practice in the area of dissemination skills requires that those skills be disseminated via local supervisors and trainers. They should learn both the skills of interest and training skills using BST.

■ Future Directions

Behavioral skills training has been used to teach a very wide range of teaching skills to staff working with students with ASD, including both basic teaching methods such as DTT and other teaching skills. Trainees have included both professional and paraprofessional staff, suggesting that BST may be broadly applicable to many staff members working in services.

Some of the skills addressed in the literature are simpler than others. For example, DTT is a relatively simple chain of staff responses which are emitted in a somewhat invariant sequence. Although staff do have to emit some different responses in response to different student behaviors, the basics of DTT remain relatively easy to teach. Similar comments might be made concerning teaching of SPA skills. In contrast, some staff performances are quite complex. For example, procedures such as shaping and lag-schedules require staff to continuously monitor the student's performance and change their own behavior in response to the child's progress or lack thereof.

Consider the examples of natural language paradigm (NLP) and incidental teaching. In NLP, educational staff are required to emit highly flexible and variable teaching responses. These include reinforcing all communicative attempts, switching teaching materials frequently, maintaining high rates of child mands, taking turns with the materials among other responses, and so on (Koegel, O'Dell, and Koegel 1987). Therefore, these staff performances may be more varied and under more complex stimulus control than DTT. Laski, Charlop, and Schreibman (1988) taught nine parents to use NLP with their eight children with autism using only five to nine 150-minute teaching sessions, so perhaps teaching staff to conduct NLP may also be amenable to relatively rapid BST. In the second example, incidental teaching, staff must emit a relatively simple response chain after a student approaches a stimulus (i.e., block the approach, prompt a language response or a more elaborate language response, and reinforce a correct response). However, staff performance in incidental teaching contains several subtleties. For example, if the child does not approach an object after a given period of time, the staff member should exchange it for a different object. Likewise, before beginning the incidental teaching session, the staff member should have identified reinforcers and should use these in the teaching session. Hence, incidental teaching, like NLP, does not consist of a simple invariant chain of staff response but involves several skills that are under more complex stimulus control than DTT. Both of these examples involve staff performance that is variable and flexible. Future research could investigate the use of procedures to increase variability in staff performance (e.g., Lee, Sturmey, and Fields 2007).

Most of the studies reported here included data on social validity and consumer satisfaction. Most reported data from simple Likert rating scales. Future research could be strengthened if consumer satisfaction and social validity data were also collected from trainers. Additionally, polling of trainees and trainers for suggestions about training might be a valuable source of information to guide future training.

Most of the papers reported here taught isolated skills. This may be legitimate in the early stages of research to simplify the problem studies. However, in so simplifying the problem, a mismatch between research and practice can result. For example, although some studies effectively teach a skill, such as SPA (e.g., Lavie and Sturmey 2002), the practical usefulness of this approach may be more limited than it first appears to be. For example, this procedure is practical, and indeed efficient, if a supervisor or consultant is available to tell the staff *when* to conduct the SPA and *how* to use the results of the SPA. However, suppose that in a classroom or treatment team no one has the skills to evaluate teaching programs and identify why the programs are not working or how to apply the results of an SPA to a currently ineffective teaching program. In this situation, merely training staff to conduct an SPA will not result in student learning. Instead, staff need training on the wider array of teaching skills that will permit the student with ASD to learn. Therefore, future research should focus on teaching functional clusters of teaching skills that result in meaningful student progress.

A second area to which research has paid little attention is the generalization of staff performance (see Ducharme and Feldman, 1992, for an exception). Future staff training studies should systematically evaluate whether generalization of staff behavior occurs and what mechanisms, such as multiple exemplar training, loose training, and general case training, can be used to promote generalization of staff performance.

A third area for future research is identifying the components of BST that are effective. As noted earlier, it seems unlikely that instructions alone are an important component, whereas modeling, rehearsal, and feedback may be. An interesting study that relates to this issue comes from Roscoe and colleagues (2006), who manipulated the discriminative versus reinforcing functions of feedback used during BST. In one condition, feedback emphasized instructions rather than monetary consequences of performance; in a second condition, feedback emphasized monetary consequences over instructions.

The researchers found that the discriminative function condition resulted in the greater acquisition of staff use of SPA.

A final area for future research is the organization of these disparate studies into a staff training curriculum that both addresses important staff skills and uses BST as the vehicle to train staff. At this time, studies are scattered throughout various academic journals and are not readily available to staff and supervisors for use in routine settings, although the skills taught by Lerman and colleagues (2004) approximate such a package.

■ References

Anderson, S.R., Taras, M., and O'Malley Cannon, B. (1996). Teaching new skills to young children with autism. In *Behavioral intervention for young children with autism* (ed. C. Maurice), pp. 181–217. Austin, Tex.: PRO-ED.

Bensberg, G.J., and Barnett, C.D. (1968). *Attendant training in southern residential facilities for the mentally retarded.* Atlanta: Southern Regional Education Board.

Chakrabati, S., and Fombonne, E. (2005). Pervasive developmental disorders in preschool children: Confirmation of high prevalence. *American Journal of Psychiatry,* 162, 1133–1141.

Codding, R.S., Feinberg, A.B., Dunn, E.K., and Pace, G.M. (2005). Effects of immediate performance feedback on implementation of behavior support plans. *Journal of Applied Behavior Analysis,* 38, 205–219.

Crockett, J.L., Fleming, R.K., Doepke, K.J., and Stevens, J.S. (2007). Parent training: Acquisition and generalization of discrete trials teaching skills with parents of children with autism. *Research in Developmental Disabilities,* 28, 23–36.

Delprato, D.J. (2001). Comparisons of discrete-trial and normalized behavioral language intervention for young children with autism. *Journal of Autism and Developmental Disabilities,* 31, 315–325.

Dib, N., and Sturmey, P. (2007). Reducing student stereotypy by improving teachers' implementation of discrete-trial teaching. *Journal of Applied Behavior Analysis,* 40, 339–343.

Ducharme, J.M., and Feldman, M.A. (1992). Comparison of staff training strategies to promote generalized teaching skills. *Journal of Applied Behavior Analysis,* 25, 165–179.

Duker, P., Didden, R., and Sigafoos, J. (2004). One-to-one training: Instructional procedures for learners with developmental disabilities. Austin, Tex.: PRO-ED.

Fombonne, E. (1999). The epidemiology of autism. *Psychological Medicine,* 29, 769–786.

Iwata, B.A. Wallace, M.D., Kahng, S. Lindberg, J.S., Roscoe, E.M., Conners, J., Hanley, G.P., Thompson, R.H., and Worsdell, A.S. (2000). Skill acquisition in the implementation of functional analysis methodology. *Journal of Applied Behavior Analysis,* 33, 181–194.

Koegel, R.L., O'Dell, M.C., and Koegel, L.K. (1987). A natural language teaching paradigm for nonverbal autistic children. *Journal of Autism and Developmental Disabilities,* 17, 187–200.

Koegel, R.L., Russo, D.C., and Rincover, A. (1977). Assessing and training teachers in the generalized use of behavior modification with autistic children. *Journal of Applied Behavior Analysis,* 10, 197–206.

Laski, K.E., Charlop, M.H., and Schreibman, L. (1988). Training parents to use the natural language paradigm to increase their autistic children's speech. *Journal of Applied Behavior Analysis,* 21, 391–400.

Lavie, T., and Sturmey, P. (2002). Training staff to conduct a paired-stimulus preference assessment. *Journal of Applied Behavior Analysis,* 35, 209–211.

LeBlanc, M-P., Ricciardi, J.N., and Luiselli, J.K. (2005). Improving discrete trial instruction by paraprofessional staff through an abbreviated performance feedback intervention. *Education and Treatment of Children,* 28, 76–82.

Lee, R., Sturmey, P., and Fields, L. (2007). Schedule-induced and operant mechanisms that influence response variability: A review and implications for future research. *The Psychological Record* 57 (4).

Lerman, D.C., Vorndran, C.M., Addison, L., and Kuhn, S.C. (2004). Preparing teachers in evidence-based practices for young children with autism. *School Psychology Review,* 33 (4), 510–526.

Lovaas, O.I. (1981). *Teaching developmentally disabled children: The me book.* Austin, Tex.: PRO-ED.

Lovaas, O.I. (1987). Behavioral treatment and normal educational and intellectual functioning in young autistic children. *Journal of Consulting and Clinical Psychology,* 55, 3–9.

McGaw, S., and Sturmey, P. (1989). The effects of text readability and summary exercises on parent knowledge of behaviour therapy: The Portage parent readings. *Educational Psychology,* 9, 127–132.

Miltenberger, R. (2003). *Behavior modification: Principles and procedures,* 3rd ed. Belmont, Calif.: Thompson.

Mirenda-Linne, F., and Melin, L. (1992). Acquisition, generalization and spontaneous use of color adjectives: A comparison of incidental teaching and traditional discrete trial procedures for children with autism. *Research in Developmental Disabilities,* 13, 191–210.

Moore, J.W., Edwards, R.P., Sterling-Turner, H.E., Riley, J., DuBard, M., and McGeorge, A. (2002). Teacher acquisition of functional analysis methodology. *Journal of Applied Behavior Analysis,* 35, 73–77.

National Research Council. (2001). *Educating children with autism.* Washington, D.C.: National Academy Press.

Neef, N.A. (1995). Research on training trainers in program implementation: An introduction and future directions. *Journal of Applied Behavior Analysis,* 28, 297–299.

New York State Department of Health Early Intervention Program. (1999). *Clinical practice guideline: Quick reference guide. Autism/pervasive developmental*

disorders: Assessment and intervention for young children (age 0–3 years).
(1999 Publication No. 4216). Albany: New York State Department of Health
Early Intervention Program.

Noell, G.H., Witt, J.C., LaFleur, L.H., Mortenson, B.P., Ranier, D.D., and LeVelle,
J. (2000). Increasing intervention implementation in general education fol-
lowing consultation: A comparison of two follow-up strategies. *Journal of
Applied Behavior Analysis,* 33, 271–284.

Page, T.J., Iwata, B.A., and Reid, D.H. (1982). Pyramidal training: A large-scale
application with institutional staff. *Journal of Applied Behavior Analysis,* 15,
335–351.

Reid, D.H., and Parsons, M.B. (1995). *Motivating human service staff: Supervisory
strategies for maximizing work effort and work enjoyment.* Morganton, N.C.:
Habilitative Management Consultants, Inc.

Reid, D.H., and Parsons, M.B. (1997). A comparison of staff acceptability of immediate versus delayed verbal feedback in staff training. *Journal of Organizational Behavior Management,* 16, 35–47.

Reid, D.H., Rotholtz, D.A., Parsons, M.B., Morris, L., Braswell, B.A., Green, C.W.,
and Schell, R.M. (2003). Training human service supervisors in aspects of
PBS: Evaluation of a statewide, performance based program. *Journal of Positive Behavior Intervention,* 5, 35–46.

Rotholtz, D.A., and Ford, M.E. (2003). Statewide system change in positive behavior support. *Mental Retardation,* 41, 354–364.

Roscoe, E.M., Fisher, W.W., Glover, A.C., and Volkert, V.M. (2006). Evaluating
the relative effects of feedback and contingent money for staff training of
stimulus preference assessments. *Journal of Applied Behavior Analysis,* 39,
63–77.

Ryan, C.S., and Hemmes, N.S. (2005). Post-training discrete-trial teaching performance by instructors of young children with autism in early intensive
behavioral intervention. *The Behavior Analyst Today,* 6 (1), 1–12.

Sallows, G.O., and Graupner, T.D. (2005). Intensive behavioral treatment for children with autism: Four-year outcome and predictors. *American Journal on
Mental Retardation,* 110, 417–438.

Sarakoff, R.A., and Sturmey, P. (2004). The effects of behavioral skills training on
staff implementation of discrete-trial teaching. *Journal of Applied Behavior
Analysis,* 37, 535–538.

Schepis, M.M., Reid, D.H., Ownbey, J., and Parsons, M.B. (2001). Training support staff to embed teaching within natural routines of young children with
disabilities in an inclusive preschool. *Journal of Applied Behavior Analysis,* 34,
313–327.

Shore, B.A., Iwata, B.A., Vollmer, T.R., Lerman, D.C., and Zarcone, J.R. (1995).
Pyramidal staff training in the extension of treatment for severe behavior
disorders. *Journal of Applied Behavior Analysis,* 28, 323–332.

Smith, T. (2001). Discrete trial training in the treatment of autism. *Focus on Autism and Other Developmental Disabilities,* 16, 86–92.

Taylor, B.A., and McDonough, K.A. (1996). Selecting teaching programs. In *Behavioral intervention for young children with autism* (ed. C. Maurice), pp. 63–177. Austin, Tex.: PRO-ED.

Thousand, J.S., Burchard, S.N., and Hasazi, J.E. (1986). Field-based generation and social validation of managers and staff competencies for small community residences. *Applied Research in Developmental Disabilities, 7*, 263–283.

U.S. Department of Education. (2005). *Digest of education statistics: 2005. Table 51. Percentage distribution of disabld students 6 to 21 years old receiving education services for the disabled, by educational environment and type of disability: Fall 1989 through fall 2004.* Available at http://nces.ed.gov/programs/digest/d05/tables/dt05_051.asp (accessed November 2, 2007).

Wallace, M.D., Doney, J.K., Mintz-Resudek, C.M., and Tarbox, R.S.F. (2004). Training educators to implement functional analyses. *Journal of Applied Behavior Analysis, 37*, 89–92.

Witt, J.C., Noell, G.H., LaFleur, L.H., and Mortenson, B.P. (1997). Teacher use of interventions in general education settings: Measurement and analysis of the independent variable. *Journal of Applied Behavior Analysis, 30*, 693–696.

SECTION 3

PROCEDURES FOR INCREASING SKILLS

9. DISCRETE TRIAL TRAINING AS A TEACHING PARADIGM

Rachel S. F. Tarbox and Adel C. Najdowski

Discrete trial training, or DTT, is one of the best-known and best-researched behavior analytical techniques for teaching skills to children with autism (Smith 2001; Stahmer, Ingersoll, and Carter 2003). Discrete trial training involves breaking complex skills down into subskills and teaching them through repeated practice; each unit of instruction is called a *trial* (Leaf and McEachin 1999). The origin of the discrete trial is in the methods that were used in laboratory research conducted by Thorndike, Watson, Pavlov, and Hull starting in the late 1920s. For example, the law of effect, which states that the strength of a behavior depends on the consequences the behavior has had in the past, was first described by Thorndike in 1911, after he demonstrated this behavior-consequence relationship using the discrete trial in his now famous experiments conducted with cats in a "puzzle box." When the cats performed the response required to escape the box and gain access to food, Thorndike returned the cats to the box for another trial. This was the first documented demonstration of the defining feature of the discrete trial: the behavior of the participant ends the trial.

The discrete trial was not applied to teaching young children until the late 1950s (Lindsley 1996). Wolf, Risley and Mees (1964) provided one of the earliest demonstrations of the discrete trial in an applied setting when they used the procedure to teach a young boy with autism vocal-verbal behavior. Although the use of the discrete trial dates back more than 80 years, it was popularized as a teaching tool for young children with autism through the groundbreaking work of Lovaas and colleagues (1971, 1981, 1987). It remains the preferred method of intervention during the initial stages of early intensive applied behavior analytic treatment for this population (Smith, Donahoe, and Davis, 2000).

This chapter describes the five parts of a discrete trial and DTT more generally, including the advantages and disadvantages of DTT as a teaching paradigm. We explain how DTT has been applied to teaching skills to children with autism and describe the outcome data coming from research using DTT. Finally, we link this research to recommendations for practitioners and speculate about future areas of research and practice related to DTT.

■ Description of Discrete Trial Training

Parts of a Discrete Trial

Discrete trials are called "discrete" because every instructional trial has a definite beginning and end (Leaf and McEachin 1999). Based on the three-term contingency in applied behavior analysis (ABA), discrete trials are instructional units composed of an antecedent, a response, and a consequence. Including the three-term contingency, there are five parts to a discrete trial: *(a)* an antecedent stimulus, which becomes a discriminative stimulus (S^D), *(b)* a prompt, *(c)* a response, *(d)* a consequence, and *(e)* an intertrial interval (Smith 2001).

The antecedent stimulus is anything in the environment that is meant to evoke a response. This could be a vocal stimulus (e.g., "What do you want?") or a nonvocal stimulus such as the presence of a desired object (e.g., cookie) that is meant to evoke the response, "cookie." When the child responds correctly to the antecedent stimulus and receives a reinforcer as a consequence for doing so, the antecedent stimulus then becomes a discriminative stimulus or S^D, which signals reinforcement for a correct response.

A prompt is a supplementary stimulus delivered either simultaneously with the antecedent stimulus or immediately after the antecedent stimulus; it is meant to assist the child in responding correctly to the antecedent stimulus. For example, the child's teacher may provide a full vocal model to assist the child in responding to the question "What do you want" by saying "cookie." As the child begins to echo the full vocal prompt, it may be faded by giving only partial vocal prompts (e.g., prompts may be faded from "cook," to "coo," to "c," to mouthing the sound "c," and to finally saying nothing). The goal is to transfer stimulus control from the prompt to the S^D so that the child is responding appropriately to the S^D in the absence of a prompt.

The response is anything the child says or does and is usually categorized as either a correct response, an incorrect response, or a failure to respond. For example, if the child responds "cookie" to the antecedent stimulus, "What do you want," the response is correct. If the child says "cook," the response is incorrect. If the child says nothing, there is no response. The child is usually given 3 to 5 seconds to respond to the S^D before a consequence is given (Leaf and McEachin 1999).

The consequence depends on the child's response. If the child responds correctly, the consequence is immediate praise, pats, edibles, leisure items, or other items preferred by the child. If the child responds incorrectly or fails to respond, the consequence is either vocal feedback (e.g., "no," "try again," "uh uh") or the absence of reinforcement of any kind, including attention (e.g., looking away and failing to provide reinforcers) (Smith 2001).

The intertrial interval occurs after the consequence is provided and lasts for a couple of seconds before the next discrete trial begins. If the child is given a tangible reinforcer for correct responding, the intertrial interval lasts just long enough for the child to consume the reinforcer. If the child is not given a tangible reinforcer, the intertrial interval is just long enough for the teacher to record data regarding the child's response and to remove and rotate the positioning of any tangible antecedent stimuli necessary for the next trial.

Discrete Trial Training as a Teaching Paradigm

Virtually every operant response is acquired via exposure to the three-term contingency or through discrete trials. That is, a response to an antecedent stimulus is learned when it is followed by a reinforcer. If we agree that this is the way in which organisms learn, then we should also agree that behaviors learned using other teaching paradigms in ABA—including incidental teaching (Hart and Risley 1975); modified incidental teaching sessions (Charlop-Christy and Carpenter 2000); natural language paradigm (Koegel, O'Dell, and Koegel 1987), also called natural environment training (NET) (Sundberg and Partington 1999); mand-model (Rogers-Warren and Warren 1980); pivotal response training (Pierce and Schreibman 1995) and milieu language teaching (Alpert and Kaiser 1992)—are acquired via exposure to discrete trials.

What makes DTT unique from these other teaching procedures is the high degree of structure that is inherent in the procedure. For example, DTT involves strict teaching phases through which each new response must pass in order to be considered mastered. Specifically, an unknown response, chosen by a teacher, is targeted and introduced using massed trials. Massed trials involve presenting the same antecedent stimulus (or stimuli) across a number of trials (e.g., 5 to 10), wherein correct responses and successive approximations are reinforced. Targets usually continue in the massed trial phase until a criterion is met (e.g., 80% to 100% correct responding across a predetermined number of trials, trial blocks, or sessions). Then the target is randomly replaced with other, previously mastered targets across a number of trials (e.g., 5 to 10) until the same or a similar criterion is met. In this way, presentation of the target antecedent stimulus is randomly rotated with the presentation of two or more antecedent stimuli to which the child can respond with reliable accuracy. Once the child is able to respond in accordance with a preset criterion in this phase, the skill is considered known and mastered, and new targets are introduced.

Advantages and Disadvantages of Discrete Trial Training

There are many potential advantages and disadvantages associated with DTT procedures (see Sundberg and Partington 1999, for a more extensive list). One advantage is that DTT allows for a high number of teaching trials to take place during each teaching session. This is important so that the child can practice skills until proficiency is demonstrated. Teachers can be trained to implement

DTT fairly straightforwardly. Specifically, teachers can follow a predetermined curriculum, making it possible for nonvocal antecedent stimuli to be chosen in advance and for vocal antecedent stimuli to be scripted. Because of the structure of DTT, it is relatively easy to collect data on a child's responses, and this makes it easy to evaluate the child's progress. All verbal operants (e.g., mands, echoics, tacts, and intraverbals) are given attention during DTT instruction. Because DTT programs do not necessarily focus on teaching manding repertoires, reinforcers do not necessarily have to be natural reinforcers. Therefore, reinforcers can be prepared rather easily and can be made available throughout teaching sessions.

Whereas the structure of DTT provides many advantages, it can also lead to some poential disadvantages. For example, the structure of the teaching arrangement may lead to rote responding, and the child may need special programming for generalization. Along these same lines, it may be difficult for the child to move from this structured teaching arrangement to the natural environment, where prompting and fading strategies and continuous and immediate reinforcement are not always provided. Therefore, it will probably be necessary to plan to thin the reinforcement schedule and to program for more natural contingencies during DTT. The structure may also inhibit the teacher's ability to interact naturally with the child. Therefore, teachers will need more extensive training in how to interact naturally with children when using DTT. Finally, when the teacher chooses to work on verbal operants other than manding, the child's motivation may be reduced and problem behavior may increase. Therefore, teachers need to be able to find potent reinforcers that will compete with the child's motivation or creative ways to work on targets that are related to the child's motivation.

■ Applications of Discrete Trial Training to Children with Autism

Several investigations have been published that document the effectiveness of DTT. Studies have been conducted that suggest how to select responses to target for acquisition and how to prompt and reinforce those responses (e.g., Newsom 1998; Smith 1993). A number of large-scale investigations have demonstrated the benefits of incorporating DTT as part of an intensive, comprehensive ABA-based program (for a review, see Smith 1999). In addition, numerous investigators have shown that DTT can help children diagnosed with autism gain a variety of particular skills across a number of domains, including communication, social interaction, and self-care skills (Newsom 1998). Finally, DTT has been shown to aid in the management of problem behaviors such as escape or avoidance. Specifically, many programs that have been designed to decrease problem behavior have included DTT as a means to increase alternative adaptive behavior when the function of a particular problem behavior has been identified. A summary of the major studies across these areas is described in the following paragraphs.

Among the studies published on the effectiveness of early intensive behavioral treatment (IBT), the best outcomes (i.e., achievement of normal or near-normal functioning in all skill domains) were documented for children who received this kind of intervention consisting of some DTT for at least 30 hours per week for 2 to 3 years, beginning before 6 years of age. In the longest and best documented study, Lovaas (1987) found that 47% of the children receiving intensive early intervention using ABA and incorporating DTT were able to function independently and successfully in regular classrooms. Another 40% or so made substantial improvements but continued to need some specialized intervention; and about 10% made minimal gains and continued to need intensive intervention. Across several studies that have been conducted since the initial Lovaas investigation, children achieved average increases of approximately 20 points on standardized tests of intelligence, as well as similar increases on standardized tests of language and adaptive behavior (e.g., Anderson et al. 1987; Birnbrauer and Leach 1993; Fenske et al. 1985; Harris et al. 1991; Sheinkopf and Seigel 1998; Smith, Groen, and Wynne 2000; Weiss 1999).

Most recently, Howard and colleagues (2005) conducted a comparison of IBT and "eclectic" treatments (services provided by local public school districts) for young children with autism and demonstrated that children who received IBT incorporating DTT had higher mean standard scores in all skill domains, compared with children in the eclectic comparison groups. Most often, the descriptions of programs implemented in all of the large-scale outcome studies have specified that DTT is best used as a tool to teach the basic beginning skills and that other teaching methods may be employed to teach more advanced skills. Additionally, most programs specify that, once a skill is acquired, other teaching methods are used to contribute to maintenance and generalization of the acquired skills.

In addition to the numerous investigations that have documented the effects of using DTT as part of a comprehensive IBT program for children with autism, several empirical investigations have evaluated the effects of DTT on the acquisition of particular target behaviors. The skills most commonly addressed have been language and play skills, which also mark two of the primary deficits displayed by individuals diagnosed with autism.

Discrete trial training has been used to establish a variety of language skills, including receptive language (e.g., Lovaas 1977), expressive language (e.g., Howlin 1981), and conversation skills (e.g., Krantz and McClanahan 1981). Of the several studies that have investigated DTT methodology for teaching language skills, the areas that have typically been targeted are language comprehension and production of various language content and forms.

Across several studies, children have made significant gains using a variety of DTT formats. Children have acquired gestural communication (Buffington et al. 1998), basic phonological skills (e.g., Koegel, O'Dell, and Dunlap 1998), responses to *Wh-* questions (Handleman 1979), and complex sentence structures (e.g., Krantz et al. 1981; Risley, Hart, and Doke 1972). They also have learned several other basic and complex language skills, such as plurals (Baer, Guess, and Sherman 1972), adjectives (Risley, Hart, and Doke 1972), and opposites, prepositions, and pronouns (Lovaas 1977). Discrete trial training has been demonstrated to aid in the acquisition of sign language (Carr, Kolinsky, and Leff-Simon 1987). Although the specific DTT procedures have varied across these investigations (e.g., differential reinforcement, correction, prompt fading), the basic structure of the discrete trial has remained consistent, and, as such, these investigations have further supported the robust effects of this teaching methodology.

Several investigations have also documented the effectiveness of using DTT methodology to teach children with autism play skills. For example, Greer and colleagues (1985) investigated the relationship between toys as conditioned reinforcers and stereotypy. During toy play conditioning procedures, DTT was employed and the trials were scored in terms of whether the child *(a)* self-initiated, *(b)* required a partial physical prompt, or *(c)* required full physical guidance to play with the toy. Training techniques consisted of imitation of appropriate play on the part of the therapist; the vocal instruction, "You do it"; and reinforcement for independent play. Several other investigations have used DTT to teach children to imitate basic play skills and then have also used this methodology to further develop these skills. For example, once a simple discrimination is established, DTT may be used to sequence two consecutive play skills, then three, and so on (e.g., Lovaas et al. 1981).

Discrete trial training has been demonstrated to be an integral part of interventions that are designed to decrease problem behavior. Functional analysis methodology (Iwata et al. 1994) has gained increased support as the preferred method of identifying what, if any, environmental variables maintain a particular problem behavior. Once the function of a problem behavior is identified via a functional behavior assessment, a function-based treatment can be designed to decrease the problem behavior and to increase a functionally equivalent, more appropriate replacement behavior. Often, this is referred to as functional communication training (FCT), and numerous investigation have used DTT as a method to teach the FCT response (Carr and Durand 1985). For example, if the results of a functional behavior assessment suggest that a particular problem behavior (e.g., aggression) is maintained by escape from difficult demands, an FCT response may be to ask an adult for assistance with the task. In this case, DTT may be used to teach the child to say "help" when presented with the difficult demand. Similarly, DTT may be used to teach the child to comply with more difficult demands in the future

by structuring the teaching sessions, providing reinforcement for correct responses, and no longer providing escape contingent on the problem behavior
(Piazza, Moes, and Fisher 1996). These are just a few examples of the ways in
which DTT may be incorporated into treatments for problem behaviors.

In summary, the effectiveness of DTT has been documented across several
investigations. In addition to the large-scale studies that have demonstrated
the benefits of incorporating DTT as part of an intensive, comprehensive
ABA-based program, DTT has proved beneficial for both increasing skill deficits in areas such as communication and social interactions and increasing
behaviors that are functionally equivalent to problematic behaviors targeted
for reduction. In addition to being familiar with the strong empirical evidence
for DTT, it is also important for practitioners to consider several recommendations for those who use DTT. Some primary recommendations are outlined
in the next section.

■ Recommendations for Practitioners

From the review of empirical evidence presented earlier on the documented
effectiveness of DTT for skill acquisition, it is clear that this teaching technology is a scientifically sound empirical approach that can be used across
a variety of domains. Although there is a plethora of support for DTT, the
practitioner must also be aware of a number of considerations regarding its
implementation. These include the skill level of the practitioner, the amount
of DTT that may be appropriate in a comprehensive program for a particular child, the curriculum that should be used, and the extent to which DTT
should be combined with other ABA-based teaching methodologies.

It is important to clarify the level of proficiency required to provide DTT.
At one level, a professional may be qualified to assess skill deficits and design
curricula to teach the required skills to a child with autism. This individual
should have an advanced degree, specific training in behavior analysis, and
a strong history of having worked with and designed programs for children
with autism. At a second level, an individual may have the experience necessary to implement the teaching techniques but may not be qualified to design
programs nor manipulate programs when problems arise. This individual requires ongoing supervision from the more advanced practitioner, but, with
supervision, he or she can work directly with a child and provide DTT. It is the
responsibility of the caregiver to ensure that the practitioners working with
their children have the experience and training necessary to protect against
inappropriate instruction and to ensure success.

Directly related to the skill level of the child is the amount of intervention the child receives. There has been much debate regarding how many
hours of IBT should be provided to a child with autism, and a consensus

has not been met. However, it is difficult to argue against the idea that the amount hours should vary depending on a child's incoming skills and deficits. Further, it has not been delineated, within a given IBT program, how much time should be allocated to DTT. It has, however, been established that DTT is the preferred methodology for establishing basic discriminations on which to build with the use of other teaching techniques. The successful outcome studies mentioned in the previous section typically specified that the majority of the programming time early in the IBT program should be dedicated to DTT. However, a child's individual learning style and incoming skill level should influence decisions about time allocated to DTT. Although further research is needed in this area, some professionals (e.g., Green 1996) have suggested that, for children who begin treatment before 4 years of age, 40 hours per week of DTT is beneficial. Again, it should be noted that there is still controversy regarding this recommendation (e.g., Feinberg and Beyer 1998); more importantly, all professionals do agree that the amount of time dedicated to DTT should decrease as a child progresses in his or her individual program.

Thus far, the merits of DTT have been clearly outlined. A few recommendations for practitioners have been provided regarding the parameters of implementation of DTT, but a more important consideration is the point at which it may be necessary to combine DTT with other ABA-based teaching methodologies. Although DTT is the only instructional method shown by empirical research to be effective for teaching new skills to individuals with autism, numerous experts have emphasized that DTT should be only one component of an ABA-based IBT program for children with autism. This is an especially important distinction, given that there is a continued misconception that DTT is synonymous with ABA (Baer 2005). Not only is this now popularized mischaracterization of ABA false, but there have been numerous published examples in which it was more appropriate to incorporate other ABA-based teaching techniques in an IBT program for a child with autism.

Typically, in an IBT program for a child with autism, various ABA methods are used to build functional skills and to promote generalization of those skills (Green, Brennan, and Fein 2002). Often, DTT is described as the most useful method for teaching initial basic discriminations, but then other procedures, such as incidental teaching, may be used to help children independently initiate those skills that they have learned (for a review, see Matson et al. 1996). Within the incidental teaching approach, the therapist responds to the child's actions, so that generalization of the acquired skills may be strengthened (Fenske, Krantz, and McClannahan 2001).

Other teaching techniques, such as NET, may also prove useful for generalization of skills acquired via DTT. With NET, skills are taught in a more natural environment and in a more "playful" manner. Also, the reinforcers used to increase appropriate responding are always directly related to the task;

for example, a child is taught to say the word for a preferred item, such as "car," and, contingent on making the correct response, is given access to the toy car. Within the framework of Skinner's (1957) analysis of verbal behavior, NET is primarily based on mand training (by incorporating establishing operations and the delivery of specific reinforcement), is in contrast to DTT, which within this framework can be conceptualized as tact training (by using nonverbal and verbal stimuli and nonspecific reinforcement). For further discussion of these points, see Sundberg and Partington (1998). The incorporation of NET into an IBT program may address some of the weaknesses of DTT—specifically, that DTT is teacher initiated, that typically the reinforcers used to increase appropriate behavior are unrelated to the target response, and that rote responding can often occur.

Additional teaching techniques that are well grounded in the principles of behavior analysis but are beyond the scope of this chapter include pivotal response teaching (e.g., Koegel and Koegel 2006) and precision teaching (e.g., Binder 1996). These techniques have been repeatedly demonstrated to be effective in isolation and in combination with DTT, and they should always be taken into consideration by practitioners who primarily use DTT.

Now that some basic recommendations for practitioners have been outlined, it is important to clarify that both the recommendations and the description of DTT provided have been very broad. The information offered thus far has been derived from a number of sources, including sources that are not particular to DTT but rather assist in general education with respect to ABA teaching methodologies. Practitioners are encouraged to refer to manuals that have been designed for individuals interested in applying ABA-based methodologies to the education of children with autism (e.g., Lovaas 2003), as well as textbooks on the basic principles of behavior analysis (e.g., Cooper, Heward, and Heron 2006). Additionally, although several sources are available for learning more about how to use ABA-based methodology to remediate skill deficits demonstrated by individuals with autism, these sources do not necessarily provide a practitioner with information regarding *what* to teach. Fortunately, there are also several books that outline curricula for this population (e.g., Leaf and McEachin 1999; Lovaas 1971, 1981, 2003; Maurice, Green, and Foxx 2001; Sundberg and Partington 1998).

In summary, there are a number of issues that a practitioner should consider when designing and implementing DTT programs for individuals with autism. Although the areas that have been covered are by no means exhaustive, each point addressed requires consideration. Practitioners are responsible for ensuring that they have the appropriate skill level, that the amount of DTT provided for a particular child has been well considered, that established curricula have been referenced for selection of target skills, and that the potential benefit of incorporating other ABA-based teaching methodologies has been addressed.

■ Summary and Future Research

This chapter described the five parts of a discrete trial and DTT more generally, including the advantages and disadvantages of DTT as a teaching paradigm. This was followed by a description of how DTT has been applied to teaching skills to children with autism and a review of outcome data coming from research using DTT. Finally, several recommendations for practitioners were provided. Each of these topics suggests areas for further empirical investigation.

In addition to DTT applications, research on other issues related to DTT methodology would be beneficial. As mentioned earlier, there are a number of disadvantages to DTT that have been highlighted by professionals and researchers in the published literature. Disadvantages such as the notion that DTT may lead to more rote responding on the part of the learner, or that acquiring a skill via DTT may hinder generalization of those skills, have been repeatedly acknowledged. Both of these potential disadvantages are, in fact, empirical questions that require further investigation. They could be more closely evaluated and compared to other teaching strategies with the use of within-subject research methodology across skills that are almost identical in level of difficulty for a particular learner (i.e., that require the same prerequisite skills and relatively equal amounts of response effort). For example, more empirical research could be specifically gathered on the extent to which skills acquired via DTT, as opposed to other ABA-based teaching methodologies, are more readily generalized across settings and people. The benefit of conducting these types of investigations would not necessarily be to demonstrate which is the superior teaching strategy, but rather to identify the conditions under which skills are most readily acquired and generalized and how best to combine aspects of established teaching methodologies to create new and improved methods.

Beyond issues related to future research with respect to DTT methodology and applications is a larger and arguably more important avenue: the global effects of intensive ABA-based intervention and the role that DTT plays in them. As noted earlier, there is a plethora of empirical support for intensive ABA-based intervention. Beyond the documented successful large-scale outcome studies, ABA-based intervention has been supported by several consensus panels and expert opinions (New York Department of Health 1999 *Quick reference guide,* 1999 *Report of the recommendations,* 1999 *The guideline technical report;* Rush and Frances 2000; Committee on Educational Interventions for Children with Autism 2001). There is no doubt that DTT plays an important role in intensive ABA-based treatment programs. However, there is still controversy regarding how many hours should be dedicated to DTT and whether DTT is useful beyond a certain skill level. These issues require further empirical evaluation, and the results of such studies need to be disseminated.

Not only does dissemination help to inform practice, but continued documentation of the fact that DTT is only one aspect of ABA will help to dismantle the popularized mischaracterization that DTT is synonymous with ABA (Baer 2005).

■ References

Alpert, C.L., Kaiser, A.P. (1992). Training parents as milieu language teachers. *Journal of Early Intervention,* 16, 31–52.

Anderson, S.R., Avery, D.L., Pietro, E.K., Edwards, G.L., and Christian, W.P. (1987). Intensive home-based early intervention with autistic children. *Education and Treatment of Children,* 10, 352–366.

Baer, D.M. (2005). Letters to a lawyer. In *Focus on behavior analysis in education: Achievement, challenges and opportunities* (eds. L. Heward, T.E. Heron, N.A. Neef, S.M. Peterson, D.M. Sainato, G. Carteldge, R. Gardner, L.D. Peterson, S.B. Hersh, and J.C. Dardiq), pp. 5–30. Upper Saddle River, N.J.: Pearson Prentice-Hall.

Baer, D.M., Guess, D., and Sherman, J. (1972). Adventures in simplistic grammar. In *Language of the mentally* retarded (ed. R.L. Shiefelbusch), pp. 93–105. Baltimore: University Park Press.

Binder, C. (1996). Behavioral fluency: Evolution of a new paradigm. *The Behavior Analyst,* 19, 163–197.

Birnbrauer, J.S., and Leach, D.J. (1993). The Murdoch Early Intervention Program after two years. *Behavior Change,* 10, 63–74.

Buffington, D.M., Krantz, P.J., McClannahan, L.E., and Poulson, C.L. (1998). Procedures for teaching appropriate gestural communication skills to children with autism. *Journal of Autism and Developmental Disorders,* 28, 535–545.

Carr, E.G., and Durand, V.M. (1985). Reducing behavior problems through functional communication training. *Journal of Applied Behavior Analysis,* 18, 111–126.

Carr, E.G., Kologinsky, E., and Leff-Simon, S. (1987). Acquisition of sign language by autistic children: III. Generalized descriptive phrases. *Journal of Autism and Developmental Disorders,* 17, 217–229.

Charlop-Christy, M.H., Carpenter, M.H. (2000). Modified incidental teaching sessions: A procedure for parents to increase spontaneous speech in their children with autism. *Journal of Positive Behavior Interventions,* 2, 98–112.

Committee on Educational Interventions for Children with Autism. (2001). *Educating children with autism.* Washington, D.C.: National Academy Press.

Cooper, J.O., Heron, T.E., and Heward, W.L. (2006). *Applied behavior analysis.* Upper Saddle River, N.J.: Pearson Prentice-Hall.

Feinberg, E., and Beyer, J. (1998). Creating public policy in a climate of clinical indeterminacy: Lovaas as the case example du jour. *Infants and Young Children,* 10, 54–66.

Fenske, E.C., Krantz, P.J., and McClannahan, L.E. (2001). Incidental teaching: A not discrete-trial teaching procedure. In *Making a difference: Behavioral intervention for autism* (eds. C. Maurice, G. Green, and R. Foxx), pp. 75–82. Austin, Tex.: PRO-ED.

Fenske, E.C., Zalenski, S., Krantz, P.J., McClannahan, L.E. (1985). Age at intervention and treatment outcomes for autistic children in a comprehensive intervention program. *Analysis & Intervention in Developmental Disabilities*, 5, 49–58.

Green, G. (1996). Early behavioral intervention for autism: What does the research tell us? In *Making a difference: Behavioral intervention for autism* (eds. C. Maurice, G. Green, and R. Foxx), pp. 29–44. Austin, Tex.: PRO-ED.

Green, G., Brennan, L.C., and Fein, D. (2002). Intensive behavioral treatment for a toddler at high risk for autism. *Behavior Modification*, 26, 69–102.

Greer, R.D., Becker, B.J., Saxe, C.D., Mirabella, R.G. (1985). Conditioning histories and setting stimuli controlling engagement in stereotypy or toy play. *Analysis & Intervention in Developmental Disabilities*, 5, 269–284.

Handleman, J.S. (1979). Generalization by autistic-type children of verbal responses cross-settings. *Journal of Applied Behavior Analysis*, 12, 283–294.

Harris, S.L., Handleman, J.S., Gordon, R., Kristoff, B., Fuentes, F. (1991). Changes in cognitive and language functioning of preschool children with autism. *Journal of Autism and Developmental Disorders*, 21, 281–290.

Hart, B., and Risley, T.R. (1975). Incidental teaching of language in the preschool. *Journal of Applied Behavior Analysis*, 8, 411–420.

Howard, J.S., Sparkman, C.R., Cohen, H.G., Green, G., Stanislaw, H. (2005). A comparison of intensive behavior analytic and eclectic treatments for young children with autism. *Research in Developmental Disabilities*, 26, 359–383.

Howlin, P.A. (1981). The effectiveness of operant language training with autistic children. *Journal of Autism and Developmental Disorders*, 21, 281–290.

Iwata, B.A., Dorsey, M.F., Slifer, K.J., Bauman, K.E., Richman, G.S. (1994). Toward a functional analysis of self-injury. *Journal of Applied Behavior Analysis*, 27, 197–209.

Koegel, R.L., and Keogel, L.K. (2006). *Pivotal response treatments for autism: Communication, social and academic development.* Baltimore, Md: Paul H. Brookes.

Koegel, R.L., O'Dell, M.C., and Koegel, L.K. (1987). A natural language teaching paradigm for nonverbal autistic children. *Journal of Autism and Developmental Disorders*, 17, 187–200.

Koegel, R.L., O'Dell, M., Dunlap, G. (1988). Producing speech use in nonverbal autistic children by reinforcing attempts. *Journal of Autism and Developmental Disorders*, 18, 525–538.

Krantz, P.J., Zalewski, S., Hall, L., Fenski, E., and McClannahan, L.E. (1981). Teaching complex language to autistic children. *Analysis and Intervention in Developmental Disabilities*, 1, 259–297.

Leaf, R., and McEachin, J. (1999). *A work in progress: Behavior management strategies and curriculum for intensive behavioral treatment of autism.* New York: DRL Books.

Lindsley, O.R. (1996). The four operant freedoms. *The Behavior Analyst,* 19, 199–210.

Lovaas, O.I. (1981). *Teaching developmentally disabled children: The ME book.* Austin, Tex: PRO-ED.

Lovaas, O.I., (1987). Behavioral treatment and normal educational and intellectual functioning in young autistic children. *Journal of Consulting and Clinical Psychology,* 55, 3–9.

Lovaas, O.I. (1977). *The autistic child: Language training through behavior modification.* New York: Irvington.

Lovaas, O.I. (2003). *Teaching individuals with developmental delays: Basic intervention techniques.* Austin, Tex: PRO-ED.

Lovaas, O.I., Ackerman, A.B., Alexander, D., Firestone, P., Perkins, J., and Young, D. (1981). *Teaching developmentally disabled children: The ME book.* Austin, Tex: PRO-ED.

Maurice, C., Green, G., and Foxx, R. (2001). *Making a difference: Behavioral intervention for autism.* Austin, Tex: PRO-ED.

Matson, J.L., Benavidez, D.A., Compton, L.S., Paclawskjy, T., and Baglio, C. (1996). Behavioral treatment of autistic persons: A review of research from 1980 to the present. *Research in Developmental Disabilities,* 17, 433–465.

Newsom, C.B. (1998). Autistic disorder. In *Treatment of childhood disorders* (2nd ed) (eds. E.J. Mash and R.A. Barkley), pp. 416–467. New York: Guilford.

New York State Department of Health (1999). *Clinical practice guidelines: Quick reference guide. Autism/pervasive developmental disorders. Assessment and intervention for young children (age 0–3 years).* (Publication No. 4216.) Albany: New York State Department of Health Early Intervention Program.

New York State Department of Health. (1999). *Clinical practice guidelines: Report of the recommendations. Autism/pervasive developmental disorders: Assessment and intervention for young children (age 0–3 years).* (Publication No. 4215.) Albany: New York State Department of Health Early Intervention Program.

New York State Department of Health. (1999). *Clinical practice guidelines: The guideline technical report. Autism/pervasive developmental disorders: Assessment and intervention for young children (age 0–3 years).* (Publication No. 4217.) Albany: New York State Department of Health Early Intervention Program.

Piazza, C.C., Moes, D.R., and Fisher, W.W. (1996). Differential reinforcement of alternative behavior and demand fading in the treatment of escape-maintained disruptive behavior. *Journal of Applied Behavior Analysis,* 29, 569–572.

Pierce, K., Schreibman, L. (1995). Increasing complex social behaviors in children with autism: Effects of peer-implemented pivotal response training. *Journal of Applied Behavior Analysis,* 28, 285–295.

Risley, T., Hart, B., and Doke, L. (1972). Operant language development: The outline of a therapeutic technology. In *Language of the mentally retarded* (ed. R.L. Shiefelbusch), pp. 107–123. Baltimore: University Park Press.

Rogers-Warren, A., Warren, S.F. (1980). Mands for verbalization: Facilitating the display of newly trained language in children. Behavior Modification, 4, 361–382.

Rush, A.J., and Frances, A., eds. (2000) The expert consensus series: Treatment of psychiatric and behavioral problems in mental retardation. *American Journal on Mental Retardation,* 105, 159–228.

Sheinkopf, F.J., and Siegel, B. (1998). Home-based behavioral treatment of young autistic children. *Journal of Autism and Developmental Disorders,* 28, 15–23.

Skinner, B.F. (1957). *Verbal Learning.* New York: Appleton-Century-Crofts.

Smith, T. (1993). *Autism.* In Effective Psychotherapies (ed. T.R. Giles), pp. 107–113. New York: Plenum.

Smith, T., (1999). Outcome of early intervention for children with autism. *Clinical Psychology: Research and Practices,* 6, 33–49.

Smith, T. (2001). Discrete trial training in the treatment of autism. *Focus on Autism and Other Developmental Disabilities,* 16, 86–92.

Smith, T., Donahoe, P.A., and Davis, B.J. (2000). The UCLA treatment model. In *Preschool education programs for child with autism* (2nd ed) (eds. S.L. Harris and J.S. Handleman), pp. 23–39). Austin, Tex: PRO-ED.

Smith, T., Groen, A., and Wynn, J.W. (2000). Outcome of intensive, early behavior intervention for children with mild to moderate mental retardation. *American Journal on Mental Retardation,* 105, 269–285.

Stahmer, A.C., Ingersoll, B., Carter, C. (2003). Behavioral approaches to promoting play. *Autism,* 7, 401–413.

Sundberg, M.L., and Partington, J.W. (1998). *Teaching language to children with autism or other developmental disabilities.* Pleasant Hill, Calif.: Behavior Analysts, Inc.

Sundberg, M.L., and Partington, J.W. (1999). The need for both discrete trial and natural environment training for children with autism. In *Autism: Behavior analytic perspectives* (eds. P.M. Ghezzi, W.L. Williams, and J.E. Carr), pp. 139–156. Reno, Nev.: Context Press.

Weiss, M.J. (1999). Differential rates of skill acquisition and outcomes of early intensive behavioral intervention for autism. *Behavioral Interventions,* 14, 3–22.

Wolf, M.M., Risley, T.R., and Mees, H.L. (1964). Application of operant conditioning procedures to the behavior problems of an autistic child. *Behavior Research and Therapy,* 1, 305–312.

10. Skill Acquisition, Direct Instruction, and Educational Curricula

Mary Jane Weiss

There are many different and effective ways to build skills in learners with autism. Historically, a variety of applied behavior analysis (ABA) instructional methods have been used to teach a wide range of skills efficiently and effectively to learners on the autism spectrum. There is massive documentation concerning the effectiveness of ABA strategies to teach a wide variety of skills across curricular domains. Strategies employed include discrete trial instruction (DTI, also called discrete trial teaching or DTT), incidental teaching, pivotal response training, shaping, and chaining. All of these methods have distinct advantages and unique applications. A comprehensive ABA program typically uses various teaching methods for specific goals and in different contexts.

In recent years, the utility of some other instructional approaches has been discussed. Specifically, the potential relevance of rate-building for fluency has been raised as a possibility for learners on the autism spectrum. Historically, ABA intervention has not focused on speed of response as an important aspect of behavior. Incorporating this focus into programming makes responses more functionally available in natural environments.

Another instructional approach that has been discussed as potentially relevant for learners on the autism spectrum is direct instruction. The focus of direct instruction is on specific behavioral targets, scripted teaching formats, and data-based decision making, so it fits well with other ABA approaches to teach skills to this population of learners. In addition, several commercially available curricula that use elements of this approach may improve how learners with autism are taught basic skills.

This chapter reviews the ways in which skills have been taught historically and how rate-building and direct instruction procedures might be incorporated into programming for children with autism spectrum disorders (ASD's).

■ Skill Acquisition: Discrete Trial Instruction

Discrete trial instruction has been the primary instructional method used to teach a wide variety of skills. Discrete trial instruction uses sequenced instruction and repeated opportunities to build core skills in a wide variety of areas (Lovaas 1981; Lovaas et al. 1973; Smith 1993). Whereas it was once common for clinicians to teach in blocks of isolated trials (e.g., doing "touch head" 10 times in a row), it is now much more common to practice the skill over the course of the day and to mix in newer skills with mastered material (i.e., task variation and interspersal procedures). Task variation and interspersal procedures have been shown to increase correct responses with new material, to promote attention to the teacher, and to reduce student frustration (Dunlap 1984; Mace et al. 1988; Winterling, Dunlap, and O'Neill 1987; Zarcone et al. 1993). Other changes that have occurred in the context of DTI include the use of errorless teaching procedures to prevent repeated errors (e.g., Etzel and LeBlanc 1979; Lancioni and Smeets 1986; Terrace 1963; Touchette and Howard 1984), a focus on rapid pacing to increase learning opportunities, and teaching skills in the context of functional daily routines.

Within DTI, the assessment of skill acquisition has historically focused on the student's attaining a set mastery criterion. In general, clinicians have focused on percentage of correct responses as an indicator of mastery, expecting 80% or 90% correct performance to establish mastery (e.g., Anderson, Taras, and O'Malley Cannon 1996; Leaf and McEachin 1999). Typically, some consistency in the demonstration of the skill has also been required, such as achieving the target percentage correct across several different sessions, days, or clinicians.

In recent years, several naturalistic forms of ABA instruction have become popular. These approaches have many advantages and applications. It is still true, however, that many skills are best taught within a discrete trial context (e.g., Sundberg and Partington 1999). This is especially true for skills that require a great deal of repetition, skills that are not intrinsically motivating, and skills in certain curricular areas, such as matching, preacademic skills, tacting (labeling for the purpose of vocabulary development), and receptive language tasks. Discrete trial instruction is efficient, effective, and appropriate for teaching many skills.

Over time, clinicians using DTI procedures have also highlighted the importance of generalization. Skills that generalize across settings, instructors, instructions, and materials are much more likely to be available to the learner when they are needed. Generalization of skills is considered essential to mastery.

■ Skill Acquisition: Naturalistic Instruction

Some forms of instruction seem to generalize more easily and effectively than others. Skills taught more naturalistically clearly generalize much more readily and with far less effort than those taught through discrete trials (e.g., Fenske, Krantz, and McClannahan 2001; McGee, Krantz, and McClannahan 1985). Naturalistic approaches that are used within ABA include incidental teaching, natural language paradigm, pivotal response training, and natural environment training (NET). Although it is still the case that the clinician teaching in a naturalistic format must attend to stimulus generalization issues and plan for stimulus control from the onset of instruction, it is usually not necessary to plan for generalization as methodically if the initial teaching protocol is a naturalistic approach. In other words, naturalistic formats often provide *some* generalization for free. In part because of this advantage, more emphasis has been placed recently on naturalistic methods to build skills in learners with autism.

Other advantages of the more naturalistic approaches include an increased emphasis on building the response class of initiations and better preparation for natural settings (e.g., Fenske, Krantz, and McClannahan 2001; Sundberg and Partington 1998). Although DTI is extremely effective in increasing responsivity, it generally does not lead to increased initiations. Furthermore, the diversity of targets, methods, and settings that characterizes the more naturalistic ABA approaches helps to prepare learners for the diversity of experiences they are likely to encounter in natural environments.

Skills taught within more naturalistic approaches include language and communication skills. Incidental teaching has been highly successful in building a wide range of language and conversational skills and emphasizes requiring the elaboration of a response from the learner. The teacher prompts for an elaborated response after the learner has initiated interest in an item or a conversation (Hart and Risley 1982). Incidental teaching ensures that teaching is happening in an intrinsically motivating situation and that the learner gains natural reinforcement (e.g., access to the preferred item) by providing more elaborate responses.

Emphasis on learner interests is part of many other naturalistic approaches as well, including natural language paradigm and pivotal response training (Koegel and Koegel 2005; Koegel, Koegel, and Surrat 1992; Koegel, O'Dell, and Koegel 1987; Laski, Charlop, and Schreibman 1988). In these approaches, the child's interests are used to guide instruction. This is in stark contrast to DTI, in which the teacher determines all elements of teaching, including instructional targets, materials, and topics. Furthermore, there is an attempt to teach in natural contexts, such as in play, and with materials that are of high interest to the learner.

Natural environment training (Sundberg and Partington 1998) resembles these other naturalistic approaches and similarly emphasizes following the child's lead, using interesting materials and activities, and embedding instruction into the natural experience of the child. In addition, NET uses the verbal behavior language classification system developed by Skinner (1957) to identify functional expressive language skills to teach. The use of this taxonomy ensures thorough and comprehensive attention to varied expressive language functions. Partington and Sundberg (1998) augmented this system with an emphasis on other core skills in all curricular domains.

It is probably the case that naturalistic procedures are a better means of teaching requesting and conversational skills. It is also true that skills taught naturalistically generalize more easily. Perhaps most importantly, naturalistic approaches easily build initiation skills and offer a balance to the responsivity-based training of DTI.

■ Skill Acquisition: Achieving Fluency

In recent years, individuals interested in ASD's have become focused on fluency as an outcome of instruction. Although the criterion for mastery used in autism intervention programs has historically been percentage of correct responses, many clinicians have also begun to consider the student's rate of response as an important aspect of behavioral performance, because rate of response seems most likely to predict fluency. *Fluency* has been defined as the combination of accuracy plus speed that characterizes competent performance (Binder 1996). Fluent skills are demonstrated easily and quickly, with a quality of automaticity and an absence of hesitation (Binder 1996; Dougherty and Johnston 1996). Fluency has been a goal of precision teaching, a form of instructional measurement that has existed for many years and that graphs student progress in rate on a special graph called the Standard Celeration Chart (SCC). As a measurement system and the teaching procedures that flow from it, this approach has been successful with a wide array of learners (e.g., Lindsley 1992).

Applied behavior analysts have been slow to adopt and incorporate the methods of precision teaching and its emphasis on rate of response. Cooper (2005) suggested that this reluctance or hesitation may be due to somewhat differing orientations and goals. Within ABA, clinicians generally seek steady states of responding in each phase or condition of intervention. In precision teaching, transition or dynamic states of responding are sought. These types of dynamic response patterns characterize acquisition and celeration (change in rate across time—or, student learning). Certainly, the procedures and emphases are compatible and complementary, and each field has something to offer to the other (Cooper 2005).

The concept of fluency may be especially relevant to the population of individuals with ASD's, who often achieve percent correct targets but who may have great difficulty with the component skills required to perform the task expertly. Their performance may look effortful, difficult, and slow. They may also demonstrate long latencies before responding, leading to missed social opportunities (Weiss 2001, 2005). For example, many students can achieve

90% accuracy with a variety of tasks but still remain dysfluent. The dysfluency may eventually impede the child's ability to keep up with the group, to perform at an acceptable rate, or to combine skills in necessary ways. A student may be able to match two dimensional pictures accurately but may have trouble doing it quickly. In fact, it may be difficult for the student to grasp, place, and release the cards. Such deficits in component skills will later affect the performance of many tasks, even if accuracy goals are met. A student who has difficulty in grasping, placing, and releasing may later have trouble keeping pace with classmates as they do a variety of activities involving manipulation of materials. Similarly, a child who has achieved mastery with 100% accuracy but who is very slow at receptively labeling objects may not be able to follow a teacher's instructions given at a rate that other students can comprehend.

Rate-building procedures usually involve having the learner practice skills until he or she can engage the skill at a target rate. Initially, there is a baseline assessment of speed, and this baseline is compared to the aim, or goal rate. Short timings (often initially as brief as 10 seconds) are performed with the learner, and incremental daily improvement goals are set. It is customary to involve the learner in setting and reviewing the daily goal. It is also typical to coach the student along during the timing, to facilitate best performance. Students usually complete as many timings as they need on a particular day to reach their daily improvement goals. As skills strengthen and daily goals are met, timing length increases. The learner must then meet the new daily goal while practicing for a longer duration, building endurance in skill demonstration.

One area of curricular focus for clinicians using precision teaching involves basic motor skills that are essential to performing many of the tasks associated with daily, independent self-help skills. In these situations, rate-building approaches often focus on the fluency of core component motor skills, commonly referred to as 6 + 6 skills (Binder 1996; Haughton and Kovacs 1977; Kovacs and Haughton 1978). These 12 core motor skills (e.g., reach, point, grasp, place, release, twist) are embedded into a multitude of daily tasks, and dysfluency in them can impede acquisition of more complex academic, daily living, and vocational skills. It can be difficult for newcomers to this approach to understand how component skills affect composite skills. Tooth brushing, for example, involves many core motor component skills. One must twist off the toothpaste cap, grasp the toothbrush, squeeze out the toothpaste, pull and push the toothbrush across teeth, and so on. Problems in any of these motor components will impede success in the larger goal.

In recent years, many clinicians serving individuals with autism have become interested in the concept of fluency and in using instructional procedures that focus on achieving fluency as an outcome (e.g., Fabrizio and Moors 2003). Clinicians often value selecting instructional arrangements that promote the development of fluent responding in students because of the outcomes associated with fluency. It is widely noted that skills taught to fluency are associated with outcomes such as *(a)* stability (persistence despite distraction), *(b)* endurance (increased capacity for sustained attention and duration), *(c)* application (generalization and use of skills in novel ways), and *(d)* retention (maintenance) (Johnson and Layng 1992; Haughton 1980). These are all important and challenging aspects of skill demonstration and maintenance for learners on the autism spectrum.

There are several ways in which rate-building is being applied to learners on the autism spectrum. In one common application, clinicians focus on deficits in core component motor skills (6 + 6). The rationale for focusing on these deficits includes dysfluencies that are apparent in the component skills themselves and difficulties in the demonstration of composite skills that rely on the component skills. For example, a learner who is deficient in grasping and releasing may have difficulty in matching and sorting programs, as well as in daily living skills such as dressing and eating appropriately. A student who has difficulty in touching materials at a fluent rate may demonstrate ineffective skills in receptive labeling tasks.

Another common application is to use rate-building as a phase of instruction after acquisition. In other words, the student may first learn a skill (through a variety of potential instructional strategies including DTI) and then be asked to demonstrate the skill at a rapid rate through rate-building. After acquisition, the student would begin timed practice, with a daily improvement goal. Whereas some clinicians use aims available from a broader population, others use aims specific to the autism population (Fabrizio and Moors 2003). (It is also possible to sample fluent performers and identify an aim in that way.) Daily goals may be derived from an aim line on a SCC, as is typical in precision teaching. Alternatively, a daily goal may be based solely on an individual learner's performance (e.g., Moors and Fabrizio 2002). The assessment of the outcomes of fluency—stability, endurance, and application—can be done at various junctures in teaching. The attainment of such outcomes defines fluent performance.

Rate-building procedures have also been used to address social skill deficits specific to autism. Many clinicians have been interested in the impact of attention to frequency and latency of responses in the functional demonstration of social skills, including social responsiveness. Many individuals with autism exhibit long latencies to respond. In school settings, long latencies to respond have significant social consequences. Delayed responses to greetings, social initiations, and invitations to play often result in lost social opportunities. Peers do not usually wait 7 to 10 seconds for replies, especially at young ages. As a result, the peer does not get reinforced for his or her effort. Very often, their social overtures diminish over time. Even teachers often find such delays in responses excessive in group situations. A teacher may need to move on to other students and topics when faced with a long latency to respond, to ensure the continued momentum of the lesson and attention of the group.

Focusing on reducing latencies to respond and on rate-building for social responses leads to responses that are more functional and more likely to be re-inforced. This has great potential utility for individuals with ASD's. In addition, the use of the SCC has been demonstrated to have relevance in the assessment of socially relevant skills, such as joint attention. As an example, Fabrizio and colleagues (2003) demonstrated the use of the SCC to assess the impact of preference and degree of manipulativeness of toys on shifting attention. Social skills remain the most elusive and most difficult to remediate, so these proce-dures to assess and treat such deficits are encouraging and exciting.

Many clinicians have been using the concepts and procedures of preci-sion teaching and using the SCC to track progress in target behaviors. Oth-ers do not use the SCC per se, but track rates to evaluate progress and assess for the outcomes of fluency in determining mastery. In any case, clinicians typically set a daily improvement goal. Attainment of the daily improvement goal is usually associated with the receipt of a special reward and with ceasing of practice for that day (Fabrizio and Schirmer 2002). Attainment of goals for many days without errors may also lead to reductions in demands in fu-ture sessions, thereby maximizing motivation for each practice session (e.g., Fabrizio, Schirmer, and Ferris 2002).

Advantages of incorporating such procedures into educational interven-tions for people with ASD's include achievement of the outcomes of fluency, the addition of rate data to progress evaluations, and the ability to track and target errors as well as correct responses (Weiss 2005). Perhaps most impor-tantly, responses potentially become much more readily available to learners in natural contexts and natural environments.

There has been some discussion in the field about whether rate-building per se is responsible for all of the positive effects seen with the achievement of fluency (e.g., Doughty, Chase, and O'Shields 2004). It may be that practice, in and of itself, facilitates learning and mastery (e.g., Ericsson, Krampe, and Tesch-Romer 1993; Samuels 2002). It could also be that reinforcement is the primary mechanism for improved performance. Ultimately, it is not entirely clear whether such outcomes could be achieved without the full implementa-tion of a rate-building protocol, but with more attention to fluency-building procedures and to tracking certain aspects of behavior such as latency. How-ever, it is much harder to count latency in clinical settings than frequency, especially as latencies begin to reduce. Accuracy and reliability are likely to be higher with frequency tracking.

■ Skill Acquisition: Direct Instruction

The interest in rate-building has occurred along with exploration of the utility of direct instruction (DI) for individuals with ASD's. Direct instruction has a long history of meeting the needs of learners with many and differing complex learning issues. Historically, learners exposed to DI procedures have been those who have failed in other kinds of teaching interactions, have made many errors, have failed to understand corrective sequences, and have generally fallen further behind each academic year (Engelmann 2004).

There has been widespread concern over poor educational outcomes for many years. Increasingly, there has been a focus on poor basic skills as the root cause of problems in educational achievement (e.g., Snow et al. 1998). The educationally disadvantaged do include groups such as children with learning disabilities, impoverished students, and members of minority groups. However, many others also fit this description (Hempenstall 2004).

Educators have failed to embrace the practices outlined and demonstrated to be most effective for students who are not making sufficient educational progress (Heward 2005). Effective instruction has been demonstrated to include clear goals, sufficient and continuous instructional opportunities, extensive coverage of content, monitoring of student progress, appropriate pacing and selection of materials, and immediate feedback (Rosenshine and Berliner 1978; Hempenstall 2004). Effective instruction also emphasizes active engagement, self-regulation, strategic instruction, and explicit instructional techniques (Ellis, Worthington, and Larkin 1994). There is significant support for the components of effective instruction. In particular, a model that incorporates demonstration, practice, and feedback has been shown to be the most helpful approach to academic achievement (Hempenstall 2004).

Direct instruction integrates all of these elements of instruction in published sets of instructional programs. Direct instruction incorporates a specific process of instructional design, an organization of instruction to ensure that each student's needs are met, and scripted student–teacher interaction patterns that ensure engagement and skill acquisition (Watkins and Slocum 2004). It has been shown to be applicable and appropriate with a wide array of learners, including those with special needs. One of the hallmark characteristics of a DI approach is the emphasis on the development of learning strategies, as opposed to rote learning. Direct instruction approaches identify generalizable strategies that will efficiently teach a student a skill much faster than a rote learning approach. Skills are also sequenced very carefully, with a focus on moving from easier to harder tasks, separating similar types of content to increase discriminability for the learner, and continually assessing learner skills.

Curricula are scripted to ensure adherence to protocol and maximum numbers of learning opportunities for students (Watkins and Slocum 2004). To ensure a high rate of teacher–student interaction that promotes learning, teachers use a variety of strategies including active student participation, choral (group) responding, signaling, pacing, teaching to mastery, correction procedures, and motivation (Watkins and Slocum 2004). Many of these procedures go together and are related. For example, a teacher uses a signal to ensure that unison choral responding happens simultaneously. In this way, the teacher can hear errors more readily and can be sure that weaker students are not simply echoing their peers' responses. Brisk pacing is also an essential component of DI and has been demonstrated to be associated with better performance (e.g., Engelmann and Becker 1978; Brophy and Good 1986).

■ Curricular Content and Direct Instruction

Direct instruction has been applied to a variety of curricular areas, including language, reading, mathematics, and writing. Although the intervention and research done in these areas exists outside the realm of ASD's, many clinicians see a utility for these procedures with learners on the autism spectrum. In fact, these are curricular areas that are often difficult for teachers of individuals with autism to effectively address. Many of the curricula that exist for children with autism do not adequately or completely emphasize academic skills. When these skills are included, they are often treated in an incomplete or elementary way. Therefore, many learners on the spectrum who can master more complex skills in this area are not taught the skills in the most efficient or methodical manner. Direct instruction approaches may meet the needs of these learners in effective ways, and the scripted available curricula may provide methodical manuals for teachers of learners with autism to follow. It may also be necessary to modify several elements of the DI curricula approaches for this group of learners.

Language

In language, the focus has been primarily on oral language (Waldron-Soler and Osborn 2004). Children with poor oral language skills have been shown to have difficulty in reading and in academic achievement in general (Rescorla 2002). Language for Learning, Language for Thinking, and Language for Writing (formerly DISTAR Language I, II, and III, respectively) is a curricular series designed to assist learners in developing competent oral language skills. Prerequisites include verbal imitation of words and phrases, answering simple questions, answering concrete yes/no questions, pointing to and labeling common objects, and following simple receptive commands (Osborn and Becker 1980; Waldron-Soler and Osborn 2004). Content areas include items such as sentence structure, prepositions, opposites, and if/then reasoning. Initially, there is a great deal of teacher–student interaction, which then fades into independent work. Fast pacing and choral responding are used to maximize engagement and ensure universal comprehension. There has been substantial research on the efficacy of the earlier DISTAR versions of this approach. The newer versions of the curricular series have also been found to be effective in remediating deficits (e.g. Waldron-Soler et al. 2002; Benner et al. 2002).

Reading

Reading is another area that has been successfully targeted through DI techniques. Difficulty in reading may be the best predictor of lack of success in school (e.g., Slavin et al. 1994). The Report of the National Reading Panel (2000) and Put Reading First (Armbruster, Lehr, and Osborn 2001) identified five areas that are critical to reading success: phonemic awareness, phonics, fluency, vocabulary, and text comprehension. Critical elements of phonemic awareness training include the identification and manipulation of sounds in spoken words, whereas phonics addresses these skills in written words. Fluency-building activities might include practicing passages repeatedly until fluent rates of oral reading are achieved. Reading aloud, whether with adults, with partners, or in choral responding activities, is important to developing fluency as a reader (Stein and Kinder 2004). Vocabulary skills can be built through a variety of oral language activities as well as through explicit instruction and instruction in the use of vocabulary-building resources (e.g., dictionaries). Text comprehension is critical for continued developmental progress in reading.

Direct instruction programs that teach reading include Reading Mastery (formerly DISTAR Reading), Horizons, and Corrective Reading. Reading Mastery and Horizons are designed for elementary students, and Corrective Reading helps readers in grades 3 through 12. The effectiveness of DI reading programs is impressive. Adams and Engelmann (1996) found a 0.69 effect size for studies using DI reading programs, which is roughly equivalent to a 10-point increase in IQ. Reading Mastery, Horizons, Corrective Reading, and other DI approaches have been found to be effective, especially with struggling readers, in comparison to other approaches (e.g., Ligas 2002; Schieffer et al. 2002; Tobin 2003).

Mathematics

Mathematical skills have been shown to be very related to success in school and are necessary for almost every vocational environment (Snider and Crawford 2004). Perhaps even more importantly, math skills are essential in everyday life activities such as cooking and managing personal finances. In the population of individuals with autism, independence is partly determined by competency in math skills.

Several different curricula exist to target mathematics from a DI approach. DISTAR Arithmetic was developed for kindergarteners and for students in need of remediation. The emphasis is on comprehension before memorization. Corrective mathematics targets remedial need students in grades 3 to 12. Addition, subtraction, multiplication, and division are the core foci. Connecting Math Concepts is a developmental approach for average youngsters, and the emphasis is on the development of problem-solving skills.

Research on the effectiveness of DI for math skills has been impressive, with very large effect sizes (Adams and Engelmann 1996; Snider and Crawford 2004). These findings have extended to individuals with disabilities.

Writing

Handwriting requires attention to both composition (i.e., idea development) and mechanics such as punctuation (Isaacson and Gleason 1997). Direct instruction approaches to both of these elements of effective writing exist (e.g., Expressive Writing I and II, the Reasoning and Writing series) and have been shown to be successful (Frederick and Steventon 2004). Although the research is more limited for learners with special needs, it is encouraging (e.g., Anderson and Keel 2002).

■ Direct Instruction and Applied Behavior Analysis: Evidence of a Good Fit

There are several characteristics of DI that are easily incorporated into an ABA program for students with autism. The ability to train and supervise teachers in the implementation of DI may be the most important variable in the success of instruction (Marchand-Martella, Blakely, and Schaefer 2004). Although this is an enormous challenge in most educational environmental environments, it is less daunting in specialized programs for children with autism, which are typically richer in training and supervisory resources than their general education counterparts. (Personnel may lack specific DI experience, however.) Training requires workshops and in-service training as well as in-class coaching. The coaching should include modeling, direct observation, and direct feedback regarding implementation, and such coaching should continue until teacher trainees demonstrate that they can effectively implement DI across several different lessons and groups of learners. These types of staff training supports, although not usually focused on DI, are commonly found in specialized programs for students with autism. Some of the content for students with autism would need to be specifically targeted in training supervisors and teachers (e.g., group organization, following scripts, use of signals), but other elements are simply variations of procedures used in ABA instruction on a daily basis (e.g., error correction procedures, pacing, reinforcement).

The DI approach is also characterized by careful and thorough assessment, individual program planning, and continuous assessment of progress. Behavior analytic teachers, unlike many other educators, are very familiar with data collection, assessment of progress, and data-driven decision making. Whereas this is a formidable challenge in many educational environments, it is a relatively easy addition for educators of children with autism. The focus of DI on engagement and student success is also very familiar to behavior analysts working with children with autism. Procedures developed for recording DI engagement can easily be incorporated into other observational recording procedures (e.g., Fabrizio, Schirmer, and Ferris 2002).

■ Possible Direct Instruction Modifications for Individuals with Autism

One challenge in using the DI approach for students with ASD's is its emphasis on homogeneous grouping (Marchand-Martella, Blakely, and Schaefer 2004). Given the diversity of student needs and characteristics in this population of learners and the smaller numbers of students served in such programs, it may be difficult to establish groups with similar levels and needs. If a program for students with autism exists within a larger environment (e.g., a public school), it might be possible to have the child with autism join other classrooms for DI experiences. In a specialized program for children with autism, it may require some flexibility in classroom assignments for certain core learning activities to ensure that homogeneous grouping is achieved.

Another potential challenge in fitting a DI approach into an ABA program for students with autism is the focus on group behavior in evaluation tools. In many of these observations, the foci are both individual and group behavior (e.g., Did every student respond?, Did all students answer on signal?, Did all students answer correctly?) It may be useful to focus extra attention on individual performance for learners on the autism spectrum, or for some students in this population of learners.

Additionally, whereas some learners with autism may be able to follow the scripted curricula without significant accommodations, others may need some revisions in the usual approach. Choral responding, in particular, may not be easily achieved with a group of individuals with ASD's. This particular strategy may be better suited to inclusive environments in which one or a few individuals with autism are learning alongside peers with different issues. Learners with autism may also need additional practice in translating the hand signals used by instructors, to ensure their comprehension. Finally, because issues of latency to respond are so prominent in this population of learners, it may be helpful to address latency issues before exposure to a specific educational curriculum.

■ Summary and Conclusions

Individuals with ASD's present a challenge for educators. They have difficulty learning material, generalizing knowledge, and demonstrating skills in functionally relevant ways and at appropriate rates. Historically, DTI has been used to build core skills, with an increased emphasis in recent years on the use of task interspersal procedures, errorless learning procedures, embedded generalization strategies, and high rates of instruction. Discrete trial instruction is effective in building responsivity and in establishing a wide variety of core skills, and it is best used in combination with other ABA procedures that target different deficits.

Naturalistic ABA teaching procedures facilitate generalization and build the response class of initiation. Rate-building procedures help to address problems in speed of response and in latency to response, which are critically important to ensure the functional availability of responses in the natural environment. The use of all of these procedures provides a comprehensive approach to address the multiplicity of issues posed by a learner with autism.

TABLE 10.1

Resources for Direct Instruction (DI) Programs

Sample DI Programs for Language Skills

Language for Learning (Engelmann and Osborn, 1999, SRA/McGraw-Hill)

Language for Thinking (Engelmann and Osborn, 2002, SRA/McGraw-Hill)

Language for Writing (Engelmann and Osborn, 2003, SRA/McGraw-Hill)

Sample DI Programs for Reading Skills

Corrective Reading series (Engelmann et al., 1999, SRA)

Horizons series (Engelmann et al., 1998, SRA/McGraw-Hill)

Journeys series (Engelmann et al., 2000, SRA/McGraw Hill)

Language through Literature series (Dodds et al., 2002, SRA/McGraw-Hill)

Reading Mastery series (Engelmann et al., 2003, SRA/McGraw-Hill)

Sample DI Programs for Writing Skills

Basic Writing Skills series (Gleason and Stults, 1983, SRS/McGraw-Hill)

Readers and Writers (Dodds and Goodfellow, 1993, SRA/McGraw-Hill)

Reasoning and Writing (Engelmann et al., 2001, SRA/McGraw-Hill)

Sample DI Programs for Math Skills

Connecting Math Concepts (Engelmann et al., 2003, SRA/McGraw-Hill)

Corrective Mathematics series (Engelmann et al., 1981, SRA/McGraw-Hill)

DISTAR Arithmetic (Engelmann and Carnine, 1975, SRA/McGraw-Hill).

Direct instruction focuses on effective instructional design, individual assessment of progress, scripted curricula, and core skills essential for school success, and it is potentially a relevant and needed resource for educators of children with autism. In particular, DI resources in teaching language, reading, mathematics, and writing (Table 10.1) may be highly useful for the population of students with ASD's who have the capacity to make significant progress in those areas. DI approaches may need some modifications as they are extended to individuals with ASD's.

■ Acknowledgments

Sincere thanks to Michael Fabrizio for his comments and suggestions on this chapter.

■ References

Adams, G.L., and Engelmann, S. (1996). *Research on direct instruction: 25 Years beyond DISTAR.* Seattle: Educational Achievement Systems.

Anderson, D.M., and Keel, M.C. (2002). Using *Reasoning and Writing* to teach writing skills to students with learning disabilities and behavior disorders. *Journal of Direct Instruction,* 2 (1), 49–55.

Anderson, S., Taras, M., and O'Malley Cannon, B. (1996). Teaching new skills to children with autism. In *Behavioral intervention for young children with autism: A manual for parents and professionals* (eds. C. Maurice, G. Green, and S.C. Luce), pp. 181–194. Austin, Tex.: PRO-ED.

Armbruster, B.B., Lehr, F., and Osborn, J. (2001). *Put reading first: The research building blocks for teaching children to read.* Jessup, Md.: National Institute for Literacy.

Benner, G.J., Trout, A., Nordess, P.D., Nelson, J.R., Epstein, M.H., Knobel, M., Epstein, A., Maguire, K., and Birdsell, R. (2002). The effects of *Language for Learning* program on the receptive skills of kindergarten children. *Journal of Direct Instruction,* 2 (2), 67–74.

Binder, C. (1996). Behavioral fluency: Evolution of a new paradigm. *The Behavior Analyst,* 19 (2), 163–197.

Brophy, J., and Good, T. (1986). Teacher behavior and student achievement. In *Third handbook of research on teaching* (3rd ed) (ed. M.C. Wittrock), pp. 328–375. New York: Macmillan.

Cooper, J.O. (2005). Applied research: The separation of Applied Behavior Analysis and Precision Teaching. In *Focus on behavior analysis in education* (eds. W.L. Heward, T.E. Neef, D.F. Bicard, S. Endo, D.L. Coury, and M.G. Aman), pp. 295–303. Upper Saddle River, N.J.: Pearson.

Dougherty, K.M., and Johnston, J.M. (1996). Overlearning, fluency, and automaticity. *The Behavior Analyst,* 19 (2), 289–292.

Doughty, S.S., Chase, P.N., and O'Shields, E.M. (2004). Effects of rate building on fluent performance: A review and commentary. *The Behavior Analyst*, 27 (1), 7–23.

Dunlap, G. (1984). The influence of task variation and maintenance tasks on the learning of autistic children. *Journal of Experimental Child Psychology*, 37, 41–64.

Ellis, E.S., Worthington, L.A., and Larkin, M.J. (1994). *Executive summary of the research synthesis on effective teaching principles and the design of quality tools for educators.* (Technical Report No. 6 produced for the National Center to Improve the Tools of Educators). Eugene: University of Oregon.

Engelmann, S. (2004). Introduction. In *Introduction to Direct Instruction* (ed. Marchand-Martella, N.E., Slocum, T.A., and Martella, R.C.), pp. 1–7. Upper Saddle River, NJ: Pearson.

Engelmann, S., and Becker, W.C. (1978). System for basic instruction: Theory and applications. In *Handbook of applied behavior analysis* (eds. A.C. Catania and T.A. Brigham), pp. 325–377. New York: Irvington.

Ericsson, K.A., Krampe, R.T., and Tesch-Romer, C. (1993). The role of deliberate practice in the acquisition of expert performance. *Psychological Review*, 100, 363–406.

Etzel, B.C., and LeBlanc, J.M. (1979). The simplest treatment alternative: The law of parsimony applied to choosing appropriate instructional control and errorless learning procedures for the difficult-to-teach child. *Journal of Autism and Developmental Disorders*, 9, 361–382.

Fabrizio, M.A., and Moors, A.L. (2003). Evaluating mastery: Measuring instructional outcomes for children with autism. *European Journal of Behavior Analysis*, 4 (1), 23–36.

Fabrizio, M.A., and Schirmer, K. (2002). Teaching visual pattern imitation to a child with autism. *Journal of Precision Teaching and Celeration*, 18 (1), 80–82.

Fabrizio, M.A., Schirmer, K., and Ferris, K. (2002). Tracking curricular progress with precision. *Journal of Precision Teaching and Celeration*, 18 (2), 78–79.

Fabrizio, M.A., Schirmer, K., Vu, E., Diakite, A., and Yao, M. (2003). Analog analysis of two variables related to the joint attention of a toddler with autism. *Journal of Precision Teaching and Celeration*, 19 (1), 41–44.

Fenske, E.C., Krantz, P.J., and McClannahan, L.E. (2001). Incidental teaching: A not-so-discrete-trial teaching procedure. In *Making a difference: Behavioral intervention for autism* (eds. C. Maurice, G. Green, and R.M. Foxx), Austin, Tex.: PRO-ED.

Frederick, L.D. and Steventon, C. (2004). Writing. In *Introduction to direct instruction* (eds. N.E. Marchand-Martella, T.A. Slocum, and R.C. Martella), pp. 140–177. Upper Saddle River, N.J.: Pearson.

Hart, B.M., and Risley, T.R. (1982). *How to use incidental teaching for elaborating language.* Austin, Tex.: PRO-ED.

Haughton, E.C. (1980). Practicing practices: Learning by activity. *Journal of Precision Teaching*, 1, 3–20.

Haughton, E.C., and Kovacs, M. (1977). *Curriculum snapshot—271 pinpoints: Cross-age performance standards.* Grimbsy, Ont.: Kovacs and Associates.

Hempenstall, K. (2004). The importance of effective instruction. In *Introduction to direct instruction* (eds. N.E. Marchand-Martella, T.A. Slocum, and R.C. Martella), pp. 1–27. Upper Saddle River, N.J.: Pearson.

Heward, W.L. (2005) Reasons applied behavior analysis is good for education and why those reasons have been insufficient. In *Focus on behavior analysis in education* (eds. W.L. Heward, T.E. Neef, D.F. Bicard, S. Endo, D.L. Coury, and M.G. Aman), pp. 316–348. Upper Saddle River, N.J.: Pearson.

Isaacson, S.L., and Gleason, M.M. (1997). Mechanical obstacles to writing: What can teachers do to help students with learning problems? *Learning Disabilities Research and Practice,* 12 (3), 188–194.

Johnson, K., and Layng, T.V.J. (1996). On terms and procedures: Fluency. *The Behavior Analyst,* 19 (2), 281–288.

Koegel, R.L., and Koegel, L.K. (2005). *Pivotal response treatments for autism: Communication, social, and academic development.* Baltimore, Md.: Paul H. Brookes.

Koegel, R.L., Koegel, L.K., and Surrat, A. (1992). Language intervention and disruptive behavior in preschool children with autism. *Journal of Autism and Developmental Disorders,* 22, 141–153.

Koegel, R.L., O'Dell, M.C., and Koegel, L.K. (1987). A natural language teaching paradigm for nonverbal autistic children. *Journal of Autism and Developmental Disorders,* 17, 187–200.

Kovacs, M., and Haughton, E.C. (1978). *Body control guidelines.* Grimsby, Ont.: Kovacs and Associates.

Laski, K.E., Charlop, M.H., and Schreibman, L. (1988). Training parents to use the natural language paradigm to increase their children's speech. *Journal of Applied Behavior Analysis,* 21, 391–400.

Lancioni, G.E., and Smeets, P.M. (1986). Procedures and parameters of errorless discrimination training with developmentally impaired individuals. In *International review of research in mental retardation,* Vol. 14 (eds. N.R. Ellis and N.W. Bray), pp. 135–164. Orlando, Fla.: Academic Press.

Leaf, R., and McEachin, J., eds. *A work in progress: Behavior management strategies and a curriculum for intensive behavioral treatment of autism.* New York: DRL Books.

Ligas, M.R. (2002). Evaluation of Broward County Alliance of Quality Schools project. *Journal of Education for Students Placed at Risk,* 7 (2), 117–139.

Lindsley, O.R. (1992). Precision teaching: Discoveries and effects. *Journal of Applied Behavior Analysis,* 25, 51–57.

Lovaas, O.I. (1981). *Teaching developmentally disabled children: The ME book.* Baltimore: University Park Press.

Lovaas, O.I., Koegel, R.L., Simmons, J.Q., and Long, J. (1973). Some generalization and follow-up measures on autistic children in behavior therapy. *Journal of Applied Behavior Analysis,* 6, 131–166.

Mace, F.C., Hock, M.L., Lalli, J.S., West, B.J., Belfiore, P., Pinter, E., and Brown, D.F. (1988). Behavioral momentum in the treatment of noncompliance. *Journal of Applied Behavior Analysis,* 21, 123–141.

Marchand-Martella, N., Blakely, M., and Schaefer, E. (2004). Aspects of school-wide implementations. In *Introduction to direct instruction* (eds. N.E. Marchand-Martella, T.A. Slocum, and R.C. Martella), pp. 304–334. Upper Saddle River, N.J.: Pearson.

Maurice, C., Green, G., and Luce, S.C., eds. (1996). *Behavioral intervention for young children with autism: A manual for parents and professionals.* Austin, Tex.: PRO-ED.

McGee, G.G., Krantz, P.J., and McClannahan, L.E. (1985). The facilitative effects of incidental teaching on preposition use by autistic children. *Journal of Applied Behavior Analysis,* 18, 17–31.

Moors, A., and Fabrizio, M. (2002). Using tool skill rates to predict composite skill frequency aims. *Journal of Precision Teaching and Celeration,* 18 (2), 28–29.

National Reading Panel (Report of). (2000). *Report of the National Reading Panel. Teaching children to read: An evidence based assessment of the scientific research literature on reading and its implications for reading instruction.* Jessup, MD: National Institute for Literacy.

Osborn, J., and Becker, W.C. (1980). Direct instruction language. *New Directions for Exceptional Children,* 2, 79–92.

Partington, J., and Sundberg, M. (1998). *The assessment of basic language and learning skills.* Pleasant Hill, Calif.: Behavior Analysts, Inc

Rescorla, L. (2002). Language and reading outcomes to age 9 in late-talking toddlers. *Journal of Speech, Language, and Hearing Research,* 45, 360–371.

Rosenshine, B.V., and Berliner, D.C. (1978). Academic engaged time. *British Journal of Teacher Education,* 4, 3–16.

Samuels, S.J. (2002). Reading fluency: Its development and assessment. In *What research has to say about reading instruction* (eds. A.E. Farstrup and S.J. Samuels), pp. 166–183. Newark, Del.: International Reading Association.

Schieffer, C., Marchand-Martella, N.E. , Martella, R.C., Simonsen, F.L., and Waldron-Soler, K.M. (2002). An analysis of the Reading Mastery program: Effective components and research review. *Journal of Direct Instruction,* 2 (2), 87–119.

Slavin, R.E., Karweit, N.L., Wasik, B.A., Madden, N.A., and Dolan, L.J. (1994). Success for all: A comprehensive approach to prevention and early intervention. In *Preventing early school failure* (eds. R.E. Slavin, N.L. Karweit, and B.A. Wasik), Boston: Allyn and Bacon.

Skinner, B.F. (1957). *Verbal behavior.* New York: Appleton-Century-Crofts.

Smith, T. (1993). Autism. In *Effective psychotherapies* (ed. T.R. Giles), pp. 107–113. New York: Plenum.

Snider, V.E., and Crawford, D. (2004). Mathematics. In *Introduction to direct instruction* (eds. N.E. Marchand-Martella, T.A. Slocum, and R.C. Martella), pp. 206–245. Upper Saddle River, N.J.: Pearson.

Snow, C.E., Burns, M.S., and Griffin, P., eds. (1998). *Preventing reading difficulties in young children.* Washington, DC: National Academy Press.

Stein, M., and Kinder, D. (2004). Reading. In *Introduction to direct instruction* (eds. N.E. Marchand-Martella, T.A. Slocum, and R.C. Martella), pp. 100–139. Upper Saddle River, N.J.: Pearson.

Sundberg, M.L., and Partington, J.W. (1998). *Teaching language to children with autism or other developmental disabilities.* Pleasant Hill, Calif.: Behavior Analysts, Inc.

Sundberg, M.L., and Partington, J.W. (1999). The need for both DT and NE training for children with autism. In *Autism: Behavior analytic approaches* (eds. P.M. Ghezzi, W.L. Williams, and J.E. Carr), pp. 139–156. Reno, Nev.: Context Press.

Terrace, H. (1963). Discrimination learning with and without errors. *Journal of the Experimental Analysis of Behavior,* 6, 1–27.

Tobin, K.G. (2003). The effect of direct instruction and prior phonological awareness training in the development of reading in first grade. *Journal of Direct Instruction,* 3, 25–36.

Touchette, P.E., and Howard, J. (1984). Errorless learning: Reinforcement contingencies and stimulus control transfer in delayed prompting. *Journal of Applied Behavior Analysis,* 17, 175–181.

Waldron-Soler, K.M., Martella, R.C., Marchand-Martella, N.E., Warner, D.A., Miller, D.E., and Tso, M.E. (2002). Effects of a 15 week Language for Learning implementation with children in an integrated preschool. *Journal of Direct Instruction,* 2 (2), 75–86.

Waldron-Soler, K.M., and Osborn, J. (2004). Language. In *Introduction to direct instruction* (eds. N.E. Marchand-Martella, T.A. Slocum, and R.C. Martella), pp. 66–99. Upper Saddle River, N.J.: Pearson.

Watkins, C.L., and Slocum, T.A. (2004). The components of direct instruction. In *Introduction to direct instruction* (eds. N.E. Marchand-Martella, T.A. Slocum, and R.C. Martella), pp. 28–65. Upper Saddle River, N.J.: Pearson.

Weiss, M.J. (2001). Expanding ABA intervention in intensive programs for children with autism: The inclusion of natural environment training and fluency based instruction. *The Behavior Analyst Today,* 2 (3), 182–187.

Weiss, M.J. (2005). Comprehensive ABA programs: Integrating and evaluating the implementation of varied instructional approaches. *Behavior Analyst Today,* 6 (4), 249–256.

Winterling, V., Dunlap, G., and O'Neill, R.E. (1987). The influence of task variation on the aberrant behaviors of autistic students. *Education and Treatment of Children,* 10, 105–119.

Zarcone, J.R., Iwata, B.A., Hughes, C.E., and Vollmer, T.R. (1993). Momentum versus extinction effects in the treatment of self-injurious escape behavior. *Journal of Applied Behavior Analysis,* 26, 135–136.

11. NATURALISTIC TEACHING PROCEDURES

Keith D. Allen and Richard J. Cowan

■ History and Definition of Naturalistic Procedures

Early behavioral treatments for children with autism used principles of reinforcement and punishment to create highly effective teaching interactions. Children with autism were often taken out of the "natural" environment and taught in individualized, tightly controlled situations. In this way, distractions could be minimized, correct responding could be prompted, and consequences could be reliably delivered. Commonly labeled "discrete trial training," this teaching method made sense because basic behavioral research had clearly demonstrated that the rate of learning could be increased through immediate and frequent delivery of potent consequences. In addition, teaching these children the complex discriminations required for language and social development was thought to require careful control of teaching conditions.

Teaching done under tightly controlled conditions has also been labeled "artificial" or "analog" teaching (DelPrato 2001), in large part because the conditions are different in structure from the "natural" conditions of everyday activities and from learning at home or in the classroom. Teaching under these analog conditions resulted in impressive gains in the areas of social and language skills and reductions in disruptive and injurious repetitive behaviors (McGee, Almeida, Sulzer-Azaroff, and Feldman 1992).

However, this analog approach was not without problems. Teaching in a highly controlled situation was found to result in responding that was under the control of a few highly specific stimuli. That is, the treatment gains observed in the controlled clinic setting seldom carried over to other situations, to other people, or to other tasks. Indeed, early behavioral technology tended to rely on a "train and hope" approach, in which teachers would train in the analog setting and then hope that the skill would transfer, or generalize, to other critical settings, people, or tasks without needing to be specifically taught (Stokes and Baer 1977).

An alternative to the passive "train and hope" approach that characterizes analog discrete trial training is to systematically arrange the training so that generalization is more likely to occur. Indeed, there is widespread agreement that generalization should not be expected unless there are specific procedures implemented to facilitate its occurrence (e.g., Edelstein 1989; Kendall 1989; Stokes and Baer1977; Stokes and Osnes 1989). Although a number of tactics have been proposed for promoting generalization, they can be grouped into three general principles: use natural consequences, train diversely, and incorporate mediators (Stokes and Osnes 1989).

The use of *natural consequences* acknowledges that behaviors are more likely to generalize when teachers use reinforcers that are functionally (i.e., naturally) related to the target response (such as saying "truck" to get a truck), rather than using potent but unrelated arbitrary reinforcers (such as saying "truck" to get candy). To *train diversely,* one must allow for natural variations in the conditions of training and use a variety of different stimuli in teaching. Finally, *incorporating mediators* involves using stimuli in training that will also be present in other situations and natural conditions. Each of these principles serve to "loosen up" the tightly controlled teaching environment, making it more like conditions the learner will experience in natural everyday life. In other words, these procedures generally arrange for teaching to be more "naturalistic" and less analog.

A number of researchers (e.g., DelPrato 2001; Koegel, Koegel, and Carter 1999; LeBlanc et al. 2006) have described the distinctive qualities of such naturalistic procedures by comparing them to less naturalistic, analog strategies; their findings are highlighted in Table 11.1. For example, naturalistic procedures typically are initiated and paced by the child rather than the teacher, and they take place in a variety of locations and positions rather than in a controlled, isolated setting. Naturalistic training procedures often require that the stimulus be selected by the child; this can vary from episode to episode. In contrast, analog learning trials usually require that the learning stimulus be selected by the teacher and remain the same across multiple trials. Naturalistic conditions allow the desired object, selected by the child and used as the training stimulus, to serve as a natural reinforcer, whereas analog conditions often necessitate reinforcers that are not functionally related to the stimulus. Finally, naturalistic teaching approaches typically have no predetermined order of responses, and a variety of prompts may be used to elicit a desired response, whereas analog teaching often targets a single acceptable response for repeated training trials with the same prompt.

Although this dichotomous approach to classifying training procedures as either naturalistic or analog may be helpful to some extent, perhaps it is more beneficial to think of "natural" and "analog" interventions as falling on a continuum with respect to their ability to help children discriminate and generalize (Cowan and Allen, 2007; LeBlanc et al. 2006). "Analog" procedures have been demonstrated to be quite effective at teaching complex and conditional

TABLE 11.1

Key Elements of Analog and Naturalistic Procedures

Analog Procedures	Naturalistic Procedures
Incorporate highly structured sessions	Incorporate loosely structured sessions
Teach in "work" or academic context	Teach in context of play or everyday events
Trials initiated and paced by the teacher	Trials initiated and paced by the child
Take place in the same 1:1 setting	Take place across a variety of settings
Stimulus always selected by the teacher	Stimulus may be selected by the child
Use the same stimuli repeatedly	Use a variety of stimuli across trials
There is often a single acceptable response	No predetermined order of responses
Teacher uses the same prompt repeatedly	Teacher uses a variety of prompts
Rely on artificial reinforcers	Incorporate naturalistic reinforcers

Compiled from the following sources: DelPrato 2001; Koegel, Koegel, and Carter, 1999; Miranda-Linne and Melin, 1992; Charlop-Christy and LeBlanc 1999).

discriminations to children and thereby produce good stimulus control. This can be particularly valuable when teaching new or complex skills. However, stimulus control always comes at the expense of generalization, and vice versa. A child who calls all four-legged animals "doggie" or who confuses the letters *b*, *d*, and *p*, has demonstrated stimulus generalization, and it is clear that better discrimination training is required to produce better stimulus control. Analog training procedures can meet this need. At the same time, children who perform only in the "work" or academic environment show poor generalization but precise stimulus control, and it is clear that better generalization training under more naturalistic conditions is required. Therefore, practitioners should not interpret the continuum as a reflection of "good and bad." Instead, they should recognize that effective teaching may require selecting from a continuum of approaches, sometimes blending structured, analog (i.e., discrete trial) teaching with naturally occurring (i.e., naturalistic) teaching opportunities (Sundberg and Partington 1999). The choice will depend on the goals of the training. Practitioners must first determine the individual child's strengths and needs with regard to a skill (or set of skills) and then intentionally select and execute the teaching approach best linked to the current learning objective.

In making these choices, however, practitioners should also recognize that naturalistic teaching procedures provide other potential benefits besides the promotion of generalization. For example, naturalistic teaching procedures reflect a developmentally normalized approach to instruction (LeBlanc et al. 2006). That is, the procedures are typically employed in the context of naturally occurring events, such as snack or play, rather than in a separate "work" or academic environment (Charlop-Christy and LeBlanc 1999). Therefore, the procedures can often be easily employed in homes, day care, and integrated educational environments.

Finally, and perhaps most importantly, naturalistic teaching procedures have been demonstrated to be effective in enhancing a variety of skills in children with autism. The effectiveness of naturalistic teaching has been demonstrated most commonly in the development of early language and communication skills (e.g., L.K. Koegel et al. 1998; McGee et al. 1992). However, they have also been demonstrated to be effective in teaching social interactions (e.g., Kaiser, Hancock, and Nietfeld 2000; Kohler et al. 2001; Krantz and McClannahan 1993, 1998; Pierce and Schreibman 1995, 1997), and play skills (e.g., Stahmer 1995; Thorp, Stahmer, and Schreibman 1995).

Although all naturalistic teaching procedures share many of the positive attributes described previously, there are a variety of different approaches. Researchers and practitioners often combine naturalistic strategies to develop individualized instructional approaches or to address unique problems. However, there are several common naturalistic approaches that appear repeatedly within the professional literature and are accompanied by relatively strong empirical support. These include incidental teaching and related modifications, the natural language paradigm (NLP), script-fading, and milieu teaching.

To assist practitioners in making decisions about which naturalistic procedures may be most appropriate for inclusion in the individualized instructional approaches they are developing, each of the most common naturalistic approaches is described in the following sections. In addition, to illustrate the essential features of some of the more widely referenced naturalistic instruction approaches, diagrams of incidental teaching, the mand-model procedure, time-delay, and the NLP are included. Finally, there are brief examples demonstrating the application of each approach and a brief review of the empirical evidence that helps support these naturalistic teaching approaches as interventions that work.

■ Incidental Teaching

Incidental teaching (Hart and Risley 1968) was one of first, if not the first, naturalistic teaching procedure developed. The "incidental" aspect refers to interactions that arise naturally in an unstructured situation, such as free play. It was designed specifically to promote the development of more elaborate language in delayed and disadvantaged children. As depicted in Figure 11.1, incidental teaching typically begins with arranging the instructional environment to appeal to the interests of the child; that is, child-preferred materials and activities are strategically placed throughout the environment. Access to these materials and activities is restricted, to enhance the likelihood that the child will demonstrate a verbal response (e.g., label or describe the object) in order to access the materials. The trial begins when the child initiates an interaction with the teacher (or parent) in an effort to access a particular object or activity. This child-initiated aspect of the teaching interaction is a defining feature of incidental teaching. Once the child verbally initiates, the teacher then requests more elaborated language by prompting the child to request, for example, a specific color or size or by requesting that the child form a complete sentence. The teacher then reinforces the child with attention and access to the desired object. If the child initiates an interaction with the teacher but does not spontaneously produce a verbal response to the stimulus, the teacher may prompt a verbal response by patiently waiting, but he or she may also ask the child to name the desired object or even model an appropriate verbalization if the child does not initiate. An appropriate response at any point is reinforced with access to the desired object.

Incidental Teaching Application

Mrs. Smith has a classroom with an array of toys such as blocks, manipulative toys, sand play materials, paints and easels, dolls, work bench tools, balls, and so on. However, she has arranged things so that many of these toys are available only on request. For example, the blocks, manipulative toys, and dollhouse materials are in glass-fronted cabinets. The sand play materials, work bench tools, and balls are on the tops of cabinets, where they can be seen but are out of reach. If Joshua wants any of these materials, he must request them from Mrs. Smith or one of her assistants. An incidental teaching trial begins when

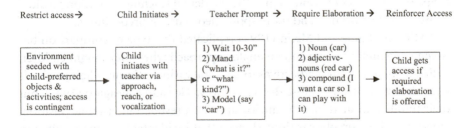

Restrict access → 　Child Initiates → 　Teacher Prompt → 　Require Elaboration → 　Reinforcer Access

| Environment seeded with child-preferred objects & activities; access is contingent | Child initiates with teacher via approach, reach, or vocalization | 1) Wait 10-30" 2) Mand ("what is it?" or "what kind?") 3) Model (say "car") | 1) Noun (car) 2) adjective-nouns (red car) 3) compound (I want a car so I can play with it) | Child gets access if required elaboration is offered |

FIGURE 11.1. Child-initiated teaching interactions in incidental teaching. Note: In incidental teaching, the rate of training is controlled by the rate of child initiations.

Joshua approaches one of the teachers and initiates an interaction by naming or requesting a toy (e.g., "want truck"). The teacher then requests that Joshua elaborate his request by naming which color truck or by saying "the whole thing" (e.g., "I want the red truck"). If Joshua indicates an interest in accessing one of the toys but does not make a request (e.g., pointing), the teacher waits to see whether Joshua will make the request without a prompt. If Joshua says nothing, the teacher may ask, "What do you want?" If Joshua merely points, the teacher prompts with, "What is that called?" Finally, if Joshua cannot name the object, the teacher may name it for Joshua. In all cases, when Joshua provides the desired response, he is praised and handed the desired object.

Incidental Teaching Research

In a series of well-controlled studies, Hart and Risely demonstrated that incidental teaching can foster the spontaneous use, elaboration, and generalization of language in preschool-aged children from disadvantaged backgrounds or with developmental delays (Hart and Risley 1968, 1974, 1982). Since then, similar procedures have proved effective in teaching children with autism a variety of tasks. For example, McGee and colleagues (1985), taught children with autism to use prepositions to describe the location of preferred items. In addition, they compared the relative efficacy of incidental teaching versus highly structured analog training procedures with regard to skill acquisition and generalization. The two approaches differed in terms of who selected the teaching stimuli, who initiated the teaching interaction, the type of reward used, and the location of instruction. In the analog condition, the stimuli and teaching were selected and initiated by the teacher. The appropriate behavior was rewarded with a desired item not associated with the task, and training took place in a 1:1 discrete trial training format, removed from the criterion setting. In contrast, in the incidental teaching condition, the child selected the stimuli and initiated the teaching interaction. The target behavior was rewarded with access to the desired stimuli, and training took place in a naturalistic, play-like setting. Although both the analog and incidental teaching conditions were effective in teaching children to appropriately use a variety of prepositions to describe the location of various items, the incidental teaching condition resulted in greater generalization and more spontaneous use of prepositions.

Miranda-Linne and Melin (1992) replicated this type of comparison between incidental teaching and an analog approach when they taught children with autism to use color adjectives to describe various stimuli. Their methods were almost identical to those described by McGee and colleagues (1985), but their results indicated that the analog approach resulted in faster acquisition. However, follow-up observations showed that incidental teaching resulted in equal retention, greater generalization, and equal to greater levels of spontaneous responses across both target and novel settings.

McGee and colleagues (1986) also used incidental teaching to teach children with autism to read the written label of a desired toy. Again, teaching began only when the child initiated interactions with child-preferred stimuli. Teaching occurred during play, and the child's responses were rewarded with access to the stimuli. The children demonstrated rapid acquisition of the reading skill and showed good generalization on probes with new stimulus materials.

Together, these studies provide evidence to support the use of the basic incidental teaching procedure to promote language development in children who are disadvantaged, developmentally delayed, or even autistic. In direct comparisons with highly structured analog teaching procedures, the incidental teaching approach has appeared to produce better generalization of learned skills in children with autism. Nevertheless, the incidental teaching approach has some practical disadvantages. The rate of learning opportunities is controlled by the child and is heavily dependent on the child's initiation of interactions with others. Many children with autism do not initiate interactions with others. As a result, modifications to the incidental teaching procedure have been developed to allow teachers to have more control over the initiation of teaching and the rate of instruction.

■ Modifications to Incidental Teaching

The Mand-Model Procedure

The mand-model procedure (Rogers-Warren and Warren 1980) was developed as a modification of incidental teaching with a specific focus on eliminating the dependence on child initiations. The original incidental teaching procedure (see Figure 11.1) included a variety of different forms of prompts that could be used if the child has already initiated an interaction but does not make a verbal response. However, the use of these prompts was still dependent on the child's first initiating an interaction. In contrast, the mand-model procedure places the mand prompt earlier in the teaching sequence. Rather than waiting for the child to approach the teacher and initiate an interaction, the teacher may initiate a teaching interaction based on a child's perceived interests or preferences. This allows the teacher to more directly control the number of opportunities for the child to engage in language instruction.

The term *mand* is derived from B.F. Skinner's (1957) work outlining the behavioral principles associated with the development of language and is defined as a request or demand for information or a response. In the mand component (Figure 11.2), a teacher approaches the child and mands (i.e., requests) that the child name or describe what he wants or what he is doing (e.g., "Tell me what you want"). Note that the mand-model approach does not require that access to all preferred materials and activities be restricted. With this procedure, a teacher may now approach a child who is already engaged with an activity and mand for information about the activity.

The model component (e.g., say "truck") is used when the child fails to offer a response to the mand or when the response is incorrect. If the child's response is a request for access, the response is naturally reinforced with access. If the response to the mand is merely descriptive of an activity in which the child is already engaged, then the response is reinforced with praise and teacher attention. Thus, the reinforcer in this procedure is not always a natural reinforcer.

Mand-Model Application

Mrs. Smith has a classroom with a variety of toys and materials with which Joshua might wish to play. A mand-model trial begins when the teacher can identify Joshua's interests. If Joshua is not yet engaged with a toy or materials but seems interested, he is approached by Mrs. Smith, who requests that Joshua name or describe the material. If Joshua responds with an appropriate verbal response, he is praised and handed the desired material. If he does not respond or provides only a partial response, the teacher provides a model of the correct response or prompts Joshua to "say the whole thing." If Joshua happens to be already engaged with some preferred materials, the teacher may still approach Joshua and initiate a mand-model trial. In this case, the teacher might say, "Tell me what you are doing" or "What is that?" If Joshua responds appropriately, he receives praise and continued attention from the

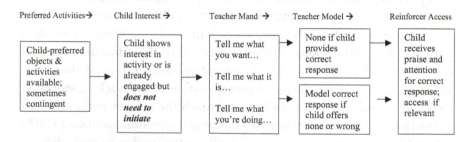

FIGURE 11.2. Teacher controlled teaching opportunities for children not initiating in the mand-model. Note: This modification to incidental teaching was developed to teach fundamental communication skills to children who were not initiating. In contrast to incidental teaching, the teacher initiates the teaching interactions and the rate of training is controlled somewhat more by the teacher. In addition, trials conducted while the child is already engaged with a preferred activity may result in social, but not necessarily natural reinforcers. As a result, this procedure is somewhat less naturalistic than incidental teaching.

teacher. If Joshua does not respond appropriately, the teacher models the correct response.

Mand-Model Research

Initial investigations of the mand-model procedure showed that verbalizations more than doubled and that vocabulary and complexity of utterances increased in children with severe language delays (Rogers-Warren and Warren 1980). In addition, the procedure did not produce a dependence on teacher prompts as the child began to initiate more often (Warren, McQuarter, and Rogers-Warren 1984). Subsequent studies also confirmed that the mand-model procedure can be an effective naturalistic means of teaching children to request items (e.g., Mobayed et al. 2000). However, to date there have been no direct evaluations of the mand-model procedure alone as a means of improving language in children with autism. Instead, the mand-model procedure is commonly combined with other naturalistic procedures as a form of "milieu" teaching.

Time-Delay Procedure

The time-delay procedure is a nonverbal cuing approach that was developed in response to concerns that the incidental teaching and mand-model modification could result in children who were too dependent on verbal prompts (Halle, Marshall, Spradlin 1979). Indeed, the original incidental teaching included mands and models as verbal prompts for children who did not verbally initiate, and the mand-model modification simply moved the verbal prompt earlier in the teaching sequence to give the teacher more control. Prompt dependency was a reasonable concern. It is important to note that the original incidental teaching procedure did include a time-delay element before the mands and models were introduced (see Figure 11.1), but the incidental teaching approach was still dependent on child-initiated teaching, and the utility of the time-delay element was unclear. As a result, Halle and colleagues (1979) modified the incidental teaching procedure by moving the time-delay element earlier in the sequence, allowing the teacher to have more control over the initiation of teaching interactions while still encouraging children to initiate a response without requiring a mand or a model.

When using the time-delay approach (see Figure 11.3), as with incidental teaching, the teacher inserts a time-delay before the delivery of help or delivery of a desired object. However, the teacher is not dependent on the child's initiating the teaching interaction. To initiate a teaching opportunity a teacher might approach a child on a swing, put a hand on the chain, and wait for a response. Likewise, a teacher might look for a child who is in need of help (e.g., putting on a coat), then approach the child, kneel down in front of the child, and delay a response. If the child does not offer a spontaneous response, the teacher may either mand for one or model the desired response. Time-delays can also be inserted gradually, before the model, to fade a child's dependence on the model. That is, time-delay may be incorporated before both mands and models to systematically fade the child's dependence on those prompts.

Time-Delay Application

Mrs. Smith has a classroom with a variety of toys and materials with which Joshua might wish to play. She notices Joshua trying to open a jar with marbles in it, approaches, kneels, and waits 5 to 10 seconds for him to ask for help. If he does, she praises him, opens the jar, and hands it to him. If Joshua does not respond, she can mand ("What do you want?") or model ("I need help") the correct response. If Joshua responds with an appropriate verbal response, he is praised and handed the desired material. As Joshua gets good at this, the teacher uses time-delay not only when she first approaches, before the mand, but also before delivery of the model if she has used a mand. Although the teacher may initially provide the model very quickly to help Joshua be successful, the time-delay before the model is gradually lengthened to give Joshua a chance to respond independently.

Time-Delay Research

Halle and colleagues originally tested the time-delay modification of incidental teaching with children with severe disabilities who were in line for lunch at a state institution. Food trays were withheld for 15 seconds or until a complete

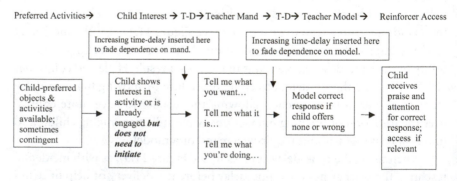

FIGURE 11.3. Time-Delay (T-D) used to minimize or fade child dependence on verbal prompts. Note: The original incidental teaching procedure includes a time-delay component to encourage children to initiate a response without requiring a mand or model by the teacher. The time-delay, however, can be inserted elsewhere as well, to fade dependence on models that have been used to help initiate responding. As a result, the time-delay procedure helps make the mand-model procedure more naturalistic.

meal request was made. If the child did not make a request, a model was provided (e.g., "tray, please."), but no mand. The time-delay alone evoked requests in half of the children, whereas models were required for the other half (Halle et al. 1979). The procedures were then extended into a preschool classroom for children with severe developmental and language delays. Teachers were taught to identify time-delay opportunities during naturally occurring free play, snack time, recess, and lunch. Teachers were asked to use a 5-second time-delay in these situations to create language opportunities and to use models if necessary. Children were reinforced with access to the desired objects or help as requested. The investigators found that the time-delay was easy to teach and use and that teachers could generalize the use of the time-delay to novel situations (Halle, Baer, Spradlin 1981).

Whereas these early studies with nonautistic children allowed a time-delay to occur before the verbal prompt, Charlop and colleagues were concerned about children with autism, who often will not initiate a response even with a nonverbal, time-delay prompt. As a result, they evaluated a procedure in which, during a structured teaching interaction, they presented a highly preferred object to the child and immediately provided a model: "I want [object label]." Correct imitation was reinforced by access to the object. After several successful requests, the teacher inserted a time-delay, gradually increasing the time between presentation of the object and delivery of the model. All of the children learned to request items spontaneously and to generalize these requests to novel situations and stimuli (Charlop, Schreibman, and Thibodeau 1985).

Note that the particular time-delay procedure used by Charlop and coworkers (1985) was not used within the context of normal play or everyday activities and was more highly structured than typical incidental teaching or the original time-delay procedures. Efforts to extend study of the time-delay procedure to social responses of children with autism required compromising other naturalistic aspects of the procedure. For example, Charlop and Walsh (1986) taught children to respond to a hug by saying "I love you," and Charlop and Trasowech (1991) had parents teach children to use social greetings. Models were initially provided immediately to help the child be successful, but then a brief time-delay before the model was gradually introduced. The time-delay was gradually increased as the child showed success or shortened if he or she gave an incorrect response or no response. In both cases, teaching occurred in the context of natural situations, but the reinforcers were arbitrary and not naturally linked to the response (i.e., food was provided for a correct response). The procedure was effective in teaching the targeted responses, and they generalized to novel outdoor and home situations.

Finally, Charlop-Christy and Carpenter (2000) compared their previously researched time-delay incidental teaching procedure with a new, modified "additional trials" incidental teaching procedure. In the modified procedure, after the child initiated a response, he or she was required to repeat the response two additional times before the terminal reinforcer. Results showed better acquisition and generalization of target phrases under the modified procedure. However, the responses targeted in time-delay incidental teaching were social greetings—responses that do not have obvious natural reinforcers. All of the responses targeted during the modified procedure were requests—responses that do have obvious natural reinforcers. This raises concerns about the validity of this particular comparison.

Altogether, these results provide consistent evidence that the time-delay modification to incidental teaching can increase language development, improve spontaneity, and enhance generalization in children with autism. Although no specific studies have investigated the implementation of a time-delay after the mand during the mand-model approach, it is easy to see how a time-delay could be applied both before the mand and before the model to reduce dependence on these types of verbal prompts.

Behavior Chain Interruption

The behavior chain interruption strategy provides an alternative approach to the time-delay modification as a means of increasing the spontaneity of a child's communicative initiations. In the original incidental teaching strategy, access to preferred materials and activities was restricted from the outset, in an effort to increase the motivation to spontaneously initiate an interaction. The behavior chain interruption strategy restricts access in the *middle* of an activity sequence. The procedure involves interrupting the flow or chain of purposeful behavior in the midst of a routine that is familiar to the child (Goetz, Gee, and Sailor 1985). Whether the number and length of each step in the chain is important is not clear. Reviews of the literature suggest that the most critical element is simply that the interruption occurs in the midst of a chain within a naturally occurring activity (Carter and Grunsell 2001).

Behavior Chain Interruption Application

Joshua's mother has been helping Joshua learn to make a sandwich for lunch each day. She supervises as Joshua gets out the bread, peanut butter, and knife and then spreads the peanut butter on the bread. Today, when Joshua looks in the cabinet where the lunch-making materials are stored, he finds that the bread and peanut butter are there, but the knife is missing. At other times, the jar on the peanut butter is too tight or the bread bag has only one slice of bread. His mother requires that Joshua request a knife, ask for help with the lid, or request more bread before the routine can continue. She may use a time-delay procedure as a nonverbal prompt for Joshua to spontaneously make the request. However, if Joshua does not make a request, she may present a mand and/or model to help Joshua. If a mand or model is required, on subsequent trials she gradually delays the delivery of the mands and models to give Joshua a chance to respond without being prompted.

Behavior Chain Interruption Research

Alwell and colleagues (1989) used a variety of strategies to interrupt behavior chains associated with three students with severe disabilities. Within the context of ongoing, student-specific routines, the instructor interrupted the ongoing activity using one of the following strategies: delaying the presentation of an item necessary to complete a routine, placing or holding an item necessary for a routine out of the child's reach, locking the drawer containing a part of a favorite toy, placing a favorite toy on top of a cabinet, or holding an item down as a child reached for it. Immediately after interrupting the behavior chain, the instructor waited 5 seconds for a response. Appropriate responses were rewarded with verbal praise and access to the item or action requested. If the child failed to respond or responded inappropriately, the adult modeled the correct response and used physical guidance to prompt the student through it. In situations in which modeling and physical prompts were incorporated, a second trial was inserted to teach the student the correct response. Alwell's group (1989) found that, in addition to learning the appropriate responses to the interruption, all three students generalized these responses to novel conditions and out-of-routine contexts.

Gee and associates (1991) taught three students with severe disabilities to use an augmentative communication device to request the continuation of an interrupted behavior chain. For example, one of the students was assisted in placing his lunch in the microwave but was not assisted in removing the food and placing it on the table so that he could eat it. The instructor interrupted the ongoing routine and waited for the child's response. If necessary, the student was physically prompted to use the device to request continuation of the routine. The physical prompt was then gradually faded, and the time-delay was systematically increased.

In a review of the research evaluating behavior chain interruption, Carter and Grunsell (2001) described considerable support for the use of these types of procedures to help establish and maintain requesting, both at the start and in the middle of routines. They noted some reservations in that response prompting was often necessary to get requesting going. In addition, whereas requesting was found to generalize to untaught routines, they expressed concern that some of the interruption strategies seemed contrived and that generalization to noncontrived routines had not been studied. Therefore, it may not be reasonable to assume that that communication would be used except in the context of an interruption. Finally, although these studies on behavior chain interruption have targeted children with severe or multiple disabilities, they have not targeted children with autism in particular. Nevertheless, preparing the environment so that language-based interactions will be more likely to occur is increasingly recognized as a valuable element of any naturalistic procedure (R.L. Koegel et al. 1998). Indeed, these types of procedures are often included as a part of the milieu teaching described later.

■ Natural Language Paradigm and Pivotal Response Training

The NLP (Koegel, O'Dell, and Koegel 1987) is a teaching approach designed to enhance the quantity and quality of language through incorporating motivation into teaching. The NLP emphasizes a child's motivation as a critical component to effective teaching. As a result, the approach identifies specific tactics to increase a child's motivation to learn. These include *(a)* use of the child's choice in stimulus selection; *(b)* use of natural reinforcers, functionally related to the task; *(c)* interspersal of mastered skills trials along with emerging skills trails; *(d)* reinforcement of communicative attempts; and *(e)* turn-taking (Koegel, O'Dell, and Koegel 1987; Koegel et al. 1999; Laski, Charlop, and Schreibman 1988). This combination of tactics is depicted in Figure 11.4. Because this model can include a variety of prompting procedures embedded within ongoing, natural interactions, it has been likened to milieu teaching, which is described later (Koegel and Koegel 2006).

One of the features that distinguishes the NLP from other naturalistic procedures is its emphasis on the incorporation of both mastered and emerging skills trials into the natural learning environment. The developers hypothesized that interspersal of trials requiring easier, mastered responses strengthens the child's motivation to continue when presented with more challenging, unmastered acquisition tasks. The NLP also places more emphasis on rewarding attempts as a means of enhancing motivation. This includes all reinforcing attempts, even if those attempts are out of sequence with the approximations predicted in a typical shaping program.

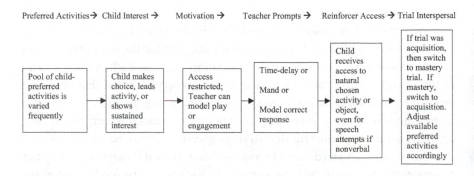

FIGURE 11.4. Natural Language Paradigm (NLP) emphasizing tactics to increase motivation. Note: Access is not restricted until the child makes a choice, leads the play or shows sustained interest. The teacher also makes a specific effort to intersperse mastery trials along with acquisition trials. Any attempts at speech are rewarded.

Koegel and colleagues have also emphasized that, although motivation is a critical element of effective teaching, there are additional "pivotal" responses that children with autism must learn to generalize behavior change (Koegel, Koegel, and Carter 1999). Pivotal response training still incorporates the essential, motivation-related features of the NLP (Gillett and LeBlanc, in press). However, it also targets behaviors that are considered to be "pivotal," in that a change in the pivotal behavior produces improvement in a number of other behaviors. In addition to motivation, three additional, distinct pivotal responses have been identified. First, because children with autism can often be very selective in their responding, it is considered pivotal for children with autism to learn to respond to multiple cues in any environment. Therefore, pivotal response training incorporates a variety of prompts and stimuli across successive trials. Second, it is considered pivotal that children with autism be able to self-initiate. This is based on the notion that once children with autism learn to self-initiate and generalize this response to novel settings, the door is opened to additional learning opportunities. Therefore, pivotal response training incorporates teaching the child with autism to query for information, a common means of both initiating social interactions and acquiring information. Finally, it is considered pivotal that children with autism learn more self-management, so pivotal response training teaches the child to identify, observe, and record their own target behavior and to self-administer consequences (Koegel et al. 1999). Together, the NLP and pivotal response training emphasize both how to teach (i.e., target motivation) and what to teach (i.e., target pivotal skills).

Natural Language Paradigm Application

Mrs. Smith and Joshua's parents have identified an array of Joshua's preferred toys, activities, foods, and materials in the classroom, at snack, at home, and even at the mall. Some are things he knows and can easily name or describe, and others he is just learning. They wait until Joshua naturally chooses an activity, such as doing a puzzle, but sometimes they present him with options such as a truck, ball, or top. Once he has chosen, they then restrict access and/or model engaging the activity. The teacher or parent initially uses time-delay to see whether Joshua will make the request or describe the activity, but they can prompt with mands and models. In all cases, if Joshua makes any attempt at all to verbally respond to the mand or model, he is praised and handed the desired object. The parent or teacher then retrieves the material or object and presents new options, being sure to give Joshua a mix of easy and more difficult tasks.

Natural Language Paradigm and Pivotal Response Training Research

In a seminal study, Koegel, O'Dell, and Koegel (1987) introduced and investigated the NLP, which was used to teach children verbal responses both in and out of the clinic setting. In addition, they compared this approach to an analog teaching condition that incorporated teacher-selected flash cards, massed trials on each approximation of the behavior, and arbitrary reinforcers. Data analyses revealed that, compared with the analog condition, the NLP approach resulted in accelerated levels of acquisition and higher levels of generalization and spontaneity.

In another comparison study, children with autism were taught to improve their speech intelligibility (R.L. Koegel et al. 1998). The analog condition again included an isolated teaching environment, stimulus items selected by clinician, arbitrary reinforcers unrelated to the task, massed trials, and shaping of approximations. In contrast, the NLP condition incorporated play-based activity, child-preferred stimuli, rewarding of any verbal attempts, and natural reinforcers. Although both conditions resulted in an increase in speech intelligibility, the functional use of the target words in conversation occurred only when naturalistic procedures were used for teaching. The results of these comparative studies are consistent with those of other studies comparing naturalistic and analog teaching methods, suggesting that naturalistic procedures may result in higher rates of maintenance, generalization, and/or spontaneous use of newly acquired skills.

Other teams of investigators have also found the NLP to be an effective approach (e.g., Smith and Camarata 1999). Laski and coworkers (1988) taught parents to use the NLP through direct instruction, modeling, and coaching. The parents were able to produce an increase in their children's spontaneous and generalized use of verbalizations across multiple stimuli and settings. These finding were replicated in a study designed to also measure the effects of NLP-based training on the appropriate play of children with autism (Gillett and LeBlanc, in press). The authors reported that children increased their use of verbalizations and increased the appropriateness of their play as a result of parent-implemented procedures. These studies provide evidence to support the effectiveness of the NLP across a variety of settings and adult trainers.

In addition to these studies on the NLP, numerous researchers have examined the effectiveness of pivotal response training. For example, in two separate studies, Pierce and Schreibman (1995, 1997) taught peer "tutors" both how and what to teach a fellow student with autism. The peers gave the student choices, varied toys regularly, modeled appropriate social behaviors, reinforced attempts, encouraged turn-taking, and taught the student to respond to multiple stimulus cues. The implementation of this intervention by the peers of children with autism in play-based settings resulted in prolonged interactions between the children with autism and their peers. In addition, the children with autism demonstrated initiation in both play and conversation and increased their engagement in language and joint attention behaviors. Taken together, these studies demonstrated that peers can act as effective peer tutors in delivering naturalistic procedures to enhance social initiation and maintenance in children with autism.

Koegel and colleagues also specifically targeted self-initiations as a pivotal response. In one study (L.K. Koegel et al. 1998), they used a variety of highly desirable stimuli, hidden in paper bags, to prompt children with autism to spontaneously question, "What's that?" In a second study (Koegel, Carter, and Koegel 2003), they trained children to self-initiate by using books with pop-up features to prompt the question, "What happened?" or "What is happening?" Prompts were used to teach question asking and were then systematically faded. Probes were used in both training and novel settings to determine whether the child would generalize the use of self-initiations and labels across settings and stimuli. In both studies, once the child initiated an interaction by asking the question, the experimenter provided the child with access to the highly desired toy or book. Results indicated an increase in self-initiations with evidence of generalization to novel conditions.

Finally, Stahmer and associates studied the effectiveness of pivotal response training on the use of symbolic and sociodramatic play in children with autism (Stahmer 1995; Thorp, Stahmer, and Schreibman 1995). Symbolic play included activities such as pushing a block across the carpet and pretending it was a car or pretending to peel a plastic banana. Sociodramatic play included adopting the role of a real or fictitious character or substituting make-believe objects for real objects. Treatment involved modeling play with a preferred toy or object. If the child responded, both approximations and exact responses were reinforced with access to the preferred object. In addition, training sessions included both mastered and emerging play skills. After treatment, the children demonstrated an increase in symbolic or sociodramatic play. In addition, the play skills generalized to new situations, and the children were more responsive to peers.

■ Script-Fading

Script-fading (Krantz and McClannahan 1993) is a procedure that incorporates the use of visual and/or auditory prompts in a variety of applied settings, to enhance the overall quality of social interactions between children with autism and their peers. It is probably the least naturalistic procedure of those presented in this chapter because of its incorporation of teacher-selected stimuli, arbitrary reinforcers, and more structured teaching interactions. However, as with pivotal response training, script-fading was developed in response to the need to teach children with autism to self-initiate across multiple settings in the context of everyday, routine events. Because it is typically embedded in routine events and takes place across a variety of settings, it has some characteristics of other naturalistic procedures and is reviewed here.

Script-fading involves first developing a variety of "scripts" that are relevant to a particular social setting, such as the lunchroom. The scripts are typically selected and developed by the trainer, who has identified routine situations in which the child needs to improve his or her social interactions. These scripts may be pictorial, written, or auditory. The child is prompted to use the script in the routine applied setting. The child's use of the scripts is typically reinforced with arbitrary reinforcers. The prompt is gradually faded as the child begins to use the phrases more consistently and with greater spontaneity. Visual prompts are faded by gradually and systematically decreasing the number of words contained in the written prompt, or by gradually cutting away parts of pictorial prompts until nothing remains. Auditory prompts are faded by gradually decreasing the number of words presented via the auditory prompting device. To enhance both the quality and quantity of social communication, this procedure is systematically introduced across a variety of social settings (e.g., lunchroom, morning recess, afternoon recess, semistructured group activities).

Script-Fading Application

Mrs. Smith and Joshua's parents have identified a number of natural situations in which they would like Joshua to initiate social interactions more often. They have created a number of written scripts that Joshua must use when he enters a group of peers at recess, in the lunchroom, and in the backyard. Joshua can keep the script in his pocket and is prompted (e.g., "Joshua, use your script") to retrieve it and read it as he approaches a group of peers (e.g., "Hi, what are you guys doing?"). Joshua is praised for using the script, and in subsequent opportunities the prompts to use the script are faded (e.g., time-delay). Most importantly, the written prompts themselves are faded (e.g., "Hi, what are you guys …"; "Hi, what are you …"; "Hi, what are …"; "Hi, what …"; "Hi …").

Script-Fading Research

Krantz and McClannahan (1993) first used written scripts as prompts to guide students with autism to initiate and maintain social communication with peers in the classroom setting. The researchers developed individualized scripts to reflect activities students had recently engaged in with other students, as well as activities students were planning in the near future. Students were trained and coached in applied settings to use the written prompt to guide them in both initiating interactions with peers and responding appropriately when approached by peers. Once the students were consistently using the scripts, they were gradually faded. The researchers found that, in addition to demonstrating an increase in "spontaneous" use of the script, the participants showed a systematic, gradual increase in the use of unscripted initiations with peers.

In a related study, Sarakoff and colleagues (2001) incorporated scripts for social communication into naturally occurring activities by attaching textual phrases to either snack packages (e.g., "Gummy Savers are my favorite!") or video-game boxes. These researchers used fading procedures very similar to those reported by Krantz and McClannahan (1993). Data analyses revealed that the children with autism increased their use of both "spontaneous" (unprompted) scripted phrases and unscripted statements across a variety of generalized conditions.

Krantz and McClannahan (1998) used visual scripts as prompts to guide students with autism to initiate and maintain social communication with adults in a preschool classroom setting. Because the scripts were pictorial prompts that did not contain words, the scripts were faded by gradually cutting away portions of the visual cue. Whereas the text scripts described earlier required a five-step fading sequence, the visual prompts in this study were faded in three steps. The authors reported that the students increased their spontaneous use of scripted phrases and that these responses generalized to novel teachers and settings.

In another variation of the script-fading procedure, Stevenson, Krantz, and McClannahan (2000) used audiotaped messages as auditory scripts to guide students in their initiations toward and responses to adults in applied settings. In this study, students were taught to use a specific auditory device to provide their cue. Auditory prompts were faded one word at a time. Analyses of outcome data revealed an increase in both scripted and unscripted interactions between the students and teachers across both the training and novel settings.

■ Milieu Teaching

Milieu teaching involves integration of a variety of these naturalistic procedures within the context of everyday activities, which can include incidental teaching, mands, models, time-delay procedures, and various aspects of the NLP (e.g., Kaiser, Hancock, and Nietfeld 2000; Hancock and Kaiser 2002). Consistent with these other naturalistic procedures, milieu teaching seeks to base teaching episodes on a child's ongoing actions and interests. In addition, although episodes may be initiated by an adult, teaching typically occurs only when a child shows an interest. More so than the other procedures alone, however, milieu teaching emphasizes combining approaches and embedding teaching episodes within the context of child's routine activities or settings (e.g., Kohler et al. 1997). Partly as a result of this emphasis, significant others (e.g., parents, siblings) are often specifically targeted to function as teachers or trainers (e.g., Alpert and Kaiser 1992). This is not to suggest that procedures such as incidental teaching, mand-model, time-delay, or NLP are not conducted within the context of routine activities or that parents and siblings cannot implement these procedures, but only that milieu teaching has typically emphasized this approach.

Milieu Teaching Application

Mrs. Smith has decided to conduct milieu teaching in the lunchroom, on the playground, and in the home environment. She arranges for teachers, parents, and siblings to be using the procedures. The environments are arranged to include many activities that Joshua enjoys, some of which are available to him only on request. For example, some of the playground toys are out of reach, his lunch must be requested, and some of his favorite toys at home are in glass-fronted cabinets. When Joshua approaches one of the teachers or a parent or sibling and spontaneously indicates an interest in accessing one of the items, he is required to elaborate his request. The adult or sibling can model an expanded version, if necessary, and then give him the item when he responds. However, the adults or siblings may also approach Joshua and present a mand or model if Joshua looks interested or is already engaged. They may also approach him and initiate turn-taking activities or interrupt routines. Whereas the teachers may initially provide mands and models very quickly to help Joshua be successful, they gradually delay the delivery of the mands and models to give Joshua a chance to respond without being prompted.

Milieu Teaching Research

In one of the first evaluations of milieu teaching, Alpert and Kaiser (1992) taught parents of preschool children to use incidental teaching, time-delays, mands, and models within the natural surroundings of everyday life to encourage language development. Although the preschool children in the study had language delays, they were not identified as autistic. Parents were trained in the clinic and then in the home via instruction, modeling (video-taped and live), and rehearsal plus feedback. Results showed that the parents learned and used the procedures across routine activities and the children increased their mean length of utterances, total words produced, and novel words produced. These results were later replicated by Kaiser's group using siblings as the trainers (Hancock and Kaiser 1996) and by other investigators targeting non–language-based goals (Fox and Hanline 1993).

Since then, Kaiser and colleagues have used milieu teaching to target the social communication of children with autism. However, they purportedly have enhanced the milieu teaching by including "responsive interaction" techniques. These techniques look very much like components of an NLP and include asking parents to respond to a child's utterance by expanding or extending it into a more complete form, to encourage turn-taking, and to allow the child to select stimulus materials. In the initial study (Kaiser, Hancock, and Nietfeld 2000), parents were taught milieu teaching during 24 individual training sessions. The researchers found that parents of children with autism learned to use the milieu teaching techniques in their home, and all of the children improved the complexity and diversity of their language production. They later demonstrated that skilled interventionists could use the same milieu teaching techniques in a structured clinic setting and produce generalized benefits in the home (e.g., Hancock and Kaiser 2002), although teaching in a structured clinic setting by a skilled interventionist seems contradictory to the very notion of milieu teaching.

Kohler and colleagues have investigated what appears to be milieu teaching, although they did not label the procedure as such. For example, they embedded numerous naturalistic techniques, including incidental teaching, NLP features, mands, and models, within a child's routine activities. They followed the child's ongoing actions and interests and used them to guide teaching decisions. They used consequences logically and naturally linked to the child's interests. However, teachers were permitted to occasion interests and actions by manipulating the environment. These procedures were combined with peer-based methods in which peers were included in teaching interactions. Results showed that teachers had good integrity and that using peers enhanced the benefits of the naturalistic procedures in terms of increasing social interactions in children with autism (Kohler et al. 1997).

Kohler and associates (2001) also used milieu teaching that included an environment structured to evoke child interest and blocked access to desired things or things placed out of reach, forgotten, or sabotaged. In addition, teachers followed the child's lead and use objects of child interest in teaching. Finally, teachers joined the child's play, encouraged turn-taking, invited the child to make choices, used incidental teaching, used comments and questions, required expanded talk, and invited interactions with peers. Teacher training required 45 minutes of didactic instruction plus handouts, followed by daily rehearsal and feedback. Results showed that the teachers had little success using the procedure with just didactic instruction and handouts. Only when practice and feedback were included did their performance improve, as did the social interactions of the target children. The teachers apparently found the children with autism to be indifferent, avoidant, or even oppositional to the naturalistic procedures and reported that they felt the procedures required a considerable amount of skill and spontaneity.

■ Naturalistic Teaching Comparisons

Each of the naturalistic teaching procedures described in this chapter incorporates a variety of the naturalistic elements presented in Table 11.1. Some of the procedures clearly incorporate more naturalistic elements than others, but each is designed to improve the transfer of skills into the natural environment. As a result, the overlap is considerable. However, there are unique differences. Table 11.2 summarizes the unique features of each of the naturalistic procedures. Notice that these features often entail modifications to accommodate the needs of children with autism. These modifications typically give the teacher more control and, as a result, often involve restricting some of the more naturalistic aspects of the procedure. This appears to be necessary to deal with the specific behavioral deficits that are characteristic of children with autism relative to other children with nonautistic speech and language disabilities. Such deficits typically include lack of social initiations, prompt dependency, and poor motivation. So, for example, mands were added to incidental teaching to allow teachers to initiate teaching interactions, time-delays were added to reduce the prompt dependency often seen in children with autism, and mastery trials were added to the NLP to assist teachers in motivating children with autism to participate in learning trials.

TABLE 11.2
Unique Elements of Naturalistic Teaching Approaches

Approach	Unique Aspects
Incidental Teaching	Learning trials initiated by child only, not teacher
Mand-Modeling	Allows teacher to initiate naturalistic teaching trials with verbal prompts
Time-Delay	Fades dependence on verbal prompts; increases sponteneity
Behavior Chain Interruption	Disrupts natural sequences to create teaching opportunities

Natural Language Paradigm	Emphasizes increasing child motivation through
	
	    Mastery trials are interspersed
	    Attempts are reinforced
	    Turn-taking is incorporated

Pivotal Response Training	Specifically targets increase in self-initiations, response to multiple cues, and self management
Script-Fading	Pictorial/written prompts used to increase social initiations in routine activities
Milieu Teaching	Combines any or all elements of naturalistic teaching procedures embedded in natural context of routine daily events

▪ Conclusions

One can conclude that the conceptual and empirical support for use of naturalistic teaching procedures with children with autism is rather extensive. All of these procedures, developed specifically to enhance the spontaneity and generalization of language, social, and play skills, have been demonstrated to be of particular benefit to children who are disadvantaged, developmentally delayed, or autistic. In addition, most of these procedures have been evaluated by multiple teams of investigators, adding to the confidence that the results have external validity. Finally, direct comparisons with highly structured analog teaching procedures have suggested that, in many cases, the naturalistic procedures produce better generalization of learned skills in children with autism.

As a result of this empirical support, practitioners can and should use naturalistic procedures with confidence as a part of a comprehensive, evidence-based approach to educating children with autism. However, there are additional reasons to consider their use. For example, one of the obstacles to an evidence-based practice is the difficulty of translating laboratory or clinic-based research into actual practice in the classroom or in the home with teachers, parents, siblings, or peers. Naturalistic procedures provide the benefit of often having been evaluated in precisely the environment in which the application is to occur. In addition, many procedures have been evaluated with teachers, parents, siblings, and peers as trainers.

Naturalistic teaching procedures are also explicitly designed to minimize the aversiveness of the instructional context by incorporating fun ways to get children to happily engage in learning (LeBlanc et al. 2006). For example, the use of child-selected materials and child-initiated activities may help increase a child's responsiveness to the teaching materials. In addition, the reinforcement of a child's attempt at responding and the use of natural reinforcers may enhance his or her motivation to participate in teaching interactions. Indeed, there is some evidence that increasing a child's willingness to participate in teaching interactions can decrease noncompliance and disruptive problem behaviors during instruction (Koegel, Koegel, and Surratt 1992).

Despite these many benefits, there remain important reasons to exercise some caution in the use of naturalistic procedures. First, comparison studies have not universally found that naturalistic procedures produce better generalization than analog procedures do (e.g., Elliott, Hall, and Soper 1991). Different outcomes may reflect, in part, individual differences in level of disability or differences in the particular naturalistic procedure used, but more research in this area is required to fully understand what variables predict good outcome and generalization.

Second, at least some teachers and parents have indicated frustration with implementing naturalistic procedures with children with autism (e.g., Kohler et al. 2001). This is not surprising, given that children with autism can be difficult to motivate and may resist leading adults to natural situations where teaching can occur. Frustrations may also be more likely to occur when several procedures are combined, as in milieu teaching, which can require as many as 24 sessions of training and experience (e.g., Kaiser, Hancock, and Nietfeld 2000). Practitioners may benefit from comparison studies evaluating the ease with which adults can be trained to implement the various naturalistic procedures.

Third, most of the studies evaluating naturalistic procedures have focused on the development of communication, and a preponderance of these have focused on requesting. These are, in fact, critical skills for children with autism and deserve emphasis. Additionally, a variety of studies have been conducted to evaluate the application of naturalistic procedures to the development of social and play skills. More extensive development of the latter area is required to guide practitioners regarding the conditions under which naturalistic procedures will be most effective in teaching these skills.

A final point warrants consideration. The development of naturalistic teaching procedures represents advances from within a number of disciplines, primarily psychology, special education, and communication sciences (Goldstein 2002). Teaching children with autism can be a difficult, painstaking endeavor, and the development and evaluation of interventions can only benefit from the attention of multiple disciplines. However, one consequence of this multidisciplinary pursuit is that those striving for an evidence-based practice must attend to research developments in each of the disciplines. Only then can a practitioner integrate the best available research evidence with his or her own clinical expertise to provide services tailored to the unique needs of an individual child and family.

■ Acknowledgments

The writing of this manuscript was supported, in part, by Project #8188 from the Maternal and Child Bureau (Title V, Social Security Act), Health Resources and Services Administration, Department of Health and Human Services and by grant 90DD0533 from the Administration on Developmental Disabilities (ADD), Administration for Children and Families, Department of Health and Human Services. Correspondence may be addressed to Keith D. Allen, Ph.D., Munroe-Meyer Institute, 985450 Nebraska Medical Center, Omaha, NE 68198 or kdallen@unmc.edu

■ References

Alpert, C., and Kaiser, A. (1992). Training parents as milieu language teachers. *Journal of Early Intervention,* 16 (1), 31–52.

Alwell, M., Hunt, P., Goetz, L., and Sailor, W. (1989). Teaching generalized communicative behaviors within interrupted behavior chain contexts. *Journal of the Association for Persons with Severe Handicaps*, 14, 91–100.

Carter, M., and Grunsell, J. (2001). The behavior chain interruption strategy: A review of research and discussion of future directions. *Journal of the Association for Persons with Severe Handicaps*, 26, 37–49.

Charlop, M.H., Schreibman, L., and Thibodeau, M.G. (1985). Increasing spontaneous verbal responding in autistic children using a time delay procedure. *Journal of Applied Behavior Analysis*, 18, 155–166.

Charlop, M.H., and Trasowech, J.E. (1991). Increasing autistic children's daily spontaneous speech. *Journal of Applied Behavior Analysis*, 24, 247–761.

Charlop, M.H., and Walsh, M. (1986). Increasing autistic children's spontaneous verbalizations of affection: An assessment of time delay and peer modeling procedures. *Journal of Applied Behavior Analysis*, 19, 307–314.

Charlop-Christy, M., and Carpenter, M. (2000). Modified incidental teaching sessions: A procedure for parents to increase spontaneous speech in their children with autism. *Journal of Positive Behavioral Interventions*, 2 (2), 98–112.

Charlop-Christy, M., LeBlanc, L.A. (1999). Naturalistic teaching strategies for acquisition, maintenance and generalization in children with autism. In *Autism: Behavior analytic perspectives* (eds. P.M. Ghezzi, W.L. Williams, and J.E. Carr), pp. 167–184. Reno, Nev.: Context Press.

Cowan, R., and Allen, K.D. (2007). Using naturalistic procedures to enhance learning in individuals with autism: A focus on generalized teaching within the school setting. *Psychology in the Schools*, 44 (7), 701–715.

DelPrato, D.J. (2001). Comparisons of discrete-trial and normalized behavioral language intervention for young children with autism. *Journal of Autism and Developmental Disorders*, 31, 315–325.

Edelstein, B.A. (1989). Generalization: Terminological, methodological and conceptual issues. *Behavior Therapy*, 20, 311–324.

Elliott, R., Hall, K., and Soper, H. (1991). Analogue language teaching versus natural language teaching: Generalization and retention of language learning for adults with autism and mental retardation. *Journal of Autism and Developmental Disabilities*, 21, 433–447.

Fox, L., and Hanline, M.F. (1993). A preliminary evaluation of learning within developmentally appropriate early childhood settings. *Topics in Early Childhood Special Education*, 13 (3), 308–328.

Gee, K, Graham, N., Goetz, L., Oshima, G., and Yoshioka, K. (1991). Teaching students to request the continuation of routine activities by using time delay and decreasing physical assistance in the context of chain interruption. *The Journal of the Association for Persons with Severe Handicaps*, 16, 154–167.

Gillett, J.N., and LeBlanc, L.A. (2007). Parent-implemented natural language paradigm to increase language and play in children with autism. *Research in Autism Spectrum Disorders*, 1(3), 247–255.

Goetz, L., Gee. K., and Sailor, W. (1985). Using a behavior chain interruptions strategy to teach communication skills to students with severe disabilities. *Journal of the Association for Persons with Severe Handicaps*, 10, 21–30.

Goldstein, H. (2002). Communication intervention for children with autism: A review of treatment efficacy. *Journal of Autism and Developmental Disorders*, 32 (5), 373–396.

Halle, J.W., Baer, D.M., and Spradlin, J.E. (1981). An analysis of caregivers' generalized use of delay in helping children: A stimulus control procedure to increase language use in handicapped children. *Journal of Applied Behavior Analysis*, 14, 389–409.

Halle, J.W., Marshall, A.M., and Spradlin, J. (1979). Time delay: A technique to increase language use and facilitate generalization in retarded children. *Journal of Applied Behavior Analysis*, 1, 109–120.

Hart, B.M., and Risley, T.R. (1968). Establishing use of descriptive adjectives in the spontaneous speech of disadvantaged preschool children. *Journal of Applied Behavior Analysis*, 1, 109–120.

Hart, B.M.., and Risley, T.R. (1974). Using preschool materials to modify the language of disadvantaged children. *Journal of Applied Behavior Analysis*, 7, 243–256.

Hart, B.M., and Risley, T.R. (1982). *How to use incidental teaching for elaborating language.* Lawrence, Kan.: H and H Enterprises.

Hancock, T., and Kaiser, A. (1996). Siblings use of milieu teaching at home. *Topics in Early Childhood Education*, 16 (2), 168–190.

Hancock, T., and Kaiser, A. (2002). The effects of trainer-implemented enhanced milieu teaching on the social communication of children with autism. *Topics in Early Childhood Education*, 22 (1), 39–54.

Kaiser, A.P., Hancock, T.B., and Nietfeld, J.P. (2000). The effects of parent-implemented enhanced milieu teaching on the social communication of children who have autism. *Journal of Early Education and Development*, 11 (4), 423–446.

Kendall, P.C. (1989). The generalization and maintenance of behavior change: Comments, considerations, and the "no cure" criticism. *Behavior Therapy*, 20, 357–364.

Koegel, L.K., Camarata, S., Valdez-Menchaca, M., and Koegel, R.L. (1998). Setting generalization of question-asking by children with autism. *American Journal on Mental Retardation*, 102, 346–357.

Koegel, L.K., Carter, C.M., and Koegel, R.L. (2003). Teaching children with autism self- initiations as a pivotal response. *Topics in Language Disorders*, 23 (2), 134–145.

Koegel, L.K., Koegel, R.L., Harrower, J.K., and Carter, C.M. (1999). Pivotal response intervention 1: Overview of approach. *The Journal of the Association for Persons with Severe Handicaps*, 24, 175–185.

Koegel, R.L., Camarata, S., Koegel, L.K., Ben-Tall, A., and Smith, A. (1998). Increasing speech intelligibility in children with autism. *Journal of Autism and Developmental Disorders*, 28, 241–251.

Koegel, R.L., and Koegel, L.K., eds. (2006). *Pivotal response treatments for autism: Communication, social, and academic development.* Baltimore, Md: Paul H. Brookes.

Koegel, R.L., Koegel, L.K., and Carter, C.M. (1999). Pivotal teaching interactions for children with autism. *School Psychology Review,* 28 (4), 576–594.

Koegel, R.L., Koegel, L.K., and Surratt A. (1992). Language intervention and disruptive behavior in preschool children with autism. *Journal of Autism and Developmental Disorders,* 22, 141–153.

Koegel, R.L., O'Dell, M.C., and Koegel, L.K. (1987). A natural language paradigm for teaching nonverbal autistic children. *Journal of Autism and Developmental Disabilities,* 17, 187–199.

Kohler, F.W., Anthony, L.J., Steighner, S.A., and Hoyson, M. (2001). Teaching social interactions in the integrated preschool: An examination of naturalistic tactics. *Topics in Early Childhood Special Education,* 21, 93–103.

Kohler, F.W., Strain, P.S., Hoyson, M., and Jamieson, B. (1997). Merging naturalistic teaching and peer-based strategies to address the IEP objectives of preschoolers with autism: An examination of structural and child behavior outcomes. *Focus on Autism and Other Developmental Disabilities,* 12, 196–206.

Krantz, P.J., and McClannahan, L.E. (1993). Teaching children with autism to initiate to peers: Effects of a script-fading procedure. *Journal of Applied Behavior Analysis,* 26, 121–132.

Krantz, P.J., and McClannahan, L.E. (1998). Social interaction skills for children with autism: A script-fading procedure for beginning readers. *Journal of Applied Behavior Analysis,* 31, 191–202.

Laski, K.E., Charlop, M.H., and Schreibman, L. (1988). Training parents to use the naturalistic language paradigm to increase their autistic children's speech. *Journal of Applied Behavior Analysis,* 21, 391–400.

LeBlanc, L., Esch, J., Firth, A., and Sidener, T. (2006). Behavioral language interventions for children with autism: Comparing applied verbal behavior and naturalistic teaching approaches. *Analysis of Verbal Behavior,* 22, 49–60.

McGee, G.G., Almeida, C., Sulzer-Azaroff, B., and Feldman, R. (1992). Promoting reciprocal interactions via peer incidental teaching. *Journal of Applied Behavior Analysis,* 25, 117–126.

McGee, G.G., Krantz, P.J., and McClannahan, L.E. (1985). The facilitative effects of incidental teaching on preposition use by autistic children. *Journal of Applied Behavior Analysis,* 18, 17–31.

McGee, G.G., Krantz, P.J., and McClannahan, L.E. (1986). An extension of incidental teaching procedures to reading instruction for autistic children. *Journal of Applied Behavior Analysis,* 19, 147–157.

Miranda-Linne, F., and Melin, L. (1992). Acquisition, generalization, and spontaneous use of color adjectives: A comparison of incidental teaching and traditional discrete-trial procedures for children with autism. *Research in Developmental Disabilities,* 13, 191–210.

Mobayed, K.L., Collins, B.C., Strangis, D., Schuster, J., and Hemmeter, M. (2000). Teaching parents to employ mand-model procedures to teach their children requesting. *Journal of Early Intervention, 23,* 165–179.

Pierce K., and Schreibman, L. (1995). Increasing complex social behaviors in children with autism: Effects of peer-implemented pivotal response training. *Journal of Applied Behavior Analysis, 28,* 285–295.

Pierce K., and Schreibman, L. (1997). Multiple peer use of pivotal response training to increase social behaviors of classmates with autism: Results from trained and untrained peers. *Journal of Applied Behavior Analysis, 30,* 285–295.

Rogers-Warren, A., and Warren, S. (1980). Facilitating the display of newly trained language in children. *Behavior Modification, 4,* 361–382.

Sarakoff, R.A., Taylor, B.A., and Poulson, C.L. (2001). Teaching children with autism to engage in conversational exchanges: Script fading with embedded textual stimuli. *Journal of Applied Behavior Analysis, 34,* 81–84.

Skinner, B.F. (1957). *Verbal behavior.* New York: Appleton-Century-Crofts.

Smith, A., and Camarata, S. (1999). Using teacher-implmented language instruction to increase language intelligibility of children with autism, *Journal of Positive Behavior Interventions, 1,* 141–151.

Stahmer, A.C. (1995). Teaching symbolic play skills to children with autism using pivotal response training. *Journal of Autism and Developmental Disorders, 25,* 123–141.

Stevenson, C.L., Krantz, P., and McClannahan, L.E. (2000). Social interaction skills for children with autism: A script-fading procedure for nonreaders. *Behavioral Interventions, 15,* 1–20.

Stokes, T.F., and Baer, D. (1977). An implicit technology of generalization. *Journal of Applied Behavior Analysis, 10,* 349–367.

Stokes, T.F., and Osnes, P.G. (1989). The operant pursuit of generalization. *Behavior Therapy, 20,* 337–355.

Sundberg, M., and Partington, J. (1999). The need for both discrete trial and natural environment language training for children with autism. In *Autism: Behavior analytic perspectives* (eds. P. Ghezzi, W. Williams, and J. Carr), pp. 139–156. Reno, Nev.: Context Press.

Thorp, D.M., Stahmer, A.C., and Schreibman, L. (1995). Effects of sociodramatic play training on children with autism. *Journal of Autism and Developmental Disorders, 25,* 265–281.

Warren, S., McQuarter, R., and Rogers-Warren, A. (1984). The effects of mands and models on the speech of unresponsive language-delayed preschool children. *Journal of Speech and Hearing Disorders, 49,* 43–52.

12. Video-Based Instruction for Children with Autism

Felicia Darden-Brunson, Anna Green, and Howard Goldstein

Video-based instruction has been used to ameliorate a variety of communication, social, and life skill challenges commonly exhibited by children with autism. The rationale for using video-based instruction extends from two premises. First, observational learning is a basic learning mechanism that has broad applicability to teaching new skills. Observational learning is such a robust phenomenon that it is difficult to imagine how children's socialization would be possible without it (Bandura 1977). Second, researchers have posited that visual supports are especially effective with children with autism, because their visual perception abilities are often seen as an area of strength (Grandin 1995; Hodgdon 1995; Quill 1997). Consequently, visual modeling, perhaps through video, might be especially effective with children with autism. This chapter discusses the potential role that observational learning, particularly video-based instruction, plays in educating children with autism. The most common uses of video-based instruction are video feedback, video modeling, and video self-modeling.

■ Observational Learning

Observational learning, or the ability to learn new responses by observing the behavior of others, has been an effective and widely used teaching strategy (Bandura 1977). Observational learning procedures typically employ forms of modeling, observation, and imitation. As a result of observing the behaviors of a model, individuals can learn a new response or refine an existing response (Browder, Schoen, and Lentz 1986). Observational learning procedures have been used to teach a variety of behaviors to children with disabilities in clinical and classroom settings, such as appropriate play (e.g., verbal and motor responses or scripts); social interaction (turn-taking, perspective taking, verbal responses, and initiations); attention to and interaction with materials, activities, and people (Werts, Caldwell, and Wolery 1996); and language skills (Goldstein and Brown 1989; Goldstein and Mousetis 1989; Hundert and Houghton 1992).

241

Social learning theory posits that learning occurs within a social context based on continuous reciprocal interaction among cognitive, behavioral, and environmental influences. According to social learning theory, observational learning reflects the use of four essential processes: attention, retention, reproduction, and motivation (Bandura 1977). *Attention* is necessary to observe the behavior of others and the outcomes of those behaviors. Factors that hinder attention (e.g., competing stimuli) reduce learning. Characteristics of the model (e.g., attractiveness, race, self-likeness) are thought to influence attention. *Retention* is needed to remember the behavior that is modeled. Imagery and language are thought to facilitate storage and retrieval of learned information. Representations that are incomplete (i.e., lacking all salient features relevant to a discrimination) could hinder observational learning. The third process is *reproduction*. Bandura (1977) made a distinction between learning through observation and the actual imitation of what has been learned, because observational learning may not necessarily be revealed in overt performance. Imitation or reproduction of the learned behavior is a true indication that the representations have been processed or learned. Finally, *motivation* to perform the observed behavior may be affected by a number of factors (e.g., ease of completing the behavior, value of the outcome, model characteristics, attachment to model). Motivation is likely to be higher if the model is similar to the observer and if the behavior is seen as having functional value.

Yando, Seitz, and Zigler (1978) pointed out the need to account for the observer's developmental level. Motor abilities and cognitive representation abilities, such as attention span, memory capacity, coding capabilities, and cognitive structures, are developmental factors that may influence what is learned observationally. They also argued that intrinsic motivators, as well as extrinsic reinforcement, are likely to influence observational learning.

Glidden and Warner (1982) sought to test these hypotheses in their review of the literature on imitation in children with disabilities. They reviewed 67 studies, 15 of which could be classified according to developmental factors and 10 according to motivation factors. Their review revealed enormous variation in the target population as well as a high degree of variation in the modeled behaviors. They found no clear relationship between developmental level and imitation. On the other hand, they concluded that there was clear evidence that motivational systems of individuals with disabilities affected their level of imitation. Operant conditioning principles clearly applied to imitation responses, but conclusions about intrinsic motivators were tenuous at best. They suggested that the consistent finding that peer models yielded more effective outcomes than older, less peer-like models may reflect motivational factors.

The age, gender, and similarity of a model to the observer have been found to be important factors in modeling (Bandura 1969). The most successful models may be individuals who possess characteristics closest to those of the learner (Bandura 1969, 1977, 1986; Hosford and Mills 1983; Piaget 1962). Overall, optimal characteristics of a model reflect similarity on multiple dimensions, including race, age, attitudes, and social background; display of problems and concerns similar to those of the subject; and exhibition of similar, but slightly higher, levels of competence. One would assume that this *principle of similarity* would facilitate observational learning regardless of whether modeling is presented via pictures, on video, or live. According to Bandura (1977), however, other characteristics may also matter. For example, energetic models who display appealing interpersonal skills tend to be preferred to models who display negative interpersonal skills.

Modes of Observational Learning

The literature has documented the benefits of video-based instruction to teach children with autism social, cognitive, language, and daily living skills (Alberto, Cihak, and Gama 2005; Apple, Billingsley, and Schwartz 2005; Branham et al. 1999; Hepting and Goldstein 1996; Mechling, Pridgen, and Cronin 2005; Nikopoulos and Keenan 2004; Shipley-Benamou, Lutzker, and Taubman 2002) and to decrease negative behaviors (Brown and Middleton 1998; Buggey 2005; Mechling, Gast, and Cronin 2006). However, this innovative approach has raised questions concerning the advantages and limitations of video-based instruction and how it compares to other forms of modeling (Alberto, Cihak, and Gama 2005; Charlop-Christy, Le, and Freeman 2000; Cihak et al. 2006; Gena, Couloura, and Kymissis 2005). Effects of video-based instruction need to be compared with those of other modes of observational learning, such as in vivo modeling and static-picture prompts. However, such comparative analyses pose a challenge because of the limited number of studies comparing video-based intervention with other modes of instruction.

Definitions and Terminology

In vivo or live modeling is an observational technique in which the child observes and imitates the targeted skill or skills performed by an adult or peer in real time. *Static-picture prompting* is an observational technique in which the child views still photographs or pictures of the targeted skills in a single picture or in a sequence of pictures. *Video modeling* (VM) involves watching an adult, peer, or sibling, engaging in target behaviors on a video. *Video self-modeling* (VSM) indicates that the target child serves as the model and views herself or himself performing the targeted behavior accurately and independently (Dowrick 1991). *Video feedback* is the procedure of recording behavior and conducting a guided- or self-evaluation while reviewing the footage; the discussion typically contrasts positive and negative examples or components of the behaviors being learned. Models are typically functioning at a slightly higher level than the target individual and may be videotaped in a role-play situation or in a natural setting. These modeling procedures employ predictable, repetitive sequences (Stahmer, Ingersoll, and Carter 2003) whereby learners are given the opportunity to attend to the model, retain modeled behavior, reproduce the behavior, and experience positive reinforcement themselves or vicariously by observing the model being reinforced (Bandura 1977). In the following sections, we discuss the similarities and differences among these modeling procedures and the apparent strengths and weaknesses of each.

■ In Vivo Modeling

Live models have been used to teach children with autism discrimination skills, language skills, and play skills (Egel, Richman, and Koegel 1981; Goldstein and Mousetis 1989; Ingersoll and Schreibman 2006; Jahr, Eldevik, and Eikeseth 2000). For example, four peers (three typically developing students and one high-functioning child with autism) modeled discrimination tasks (color, shape, preposition, and yes/no discriminations) for four students with autism (ages 2 to 7 years) in a study by Egel, Richman, and Koegel (1981). The children with autism exhibited mild to moderate cognitive deficits but demonstrated functional expressive and receptive language skills and preexisting imitation skills. The children observed behaviors such as picking the red one; picking the square; saying "on the chair" in response to "Where is the girl?"; and responding "yes/no" to "Is this a house?" All four children learned to make accurate discriminations by observing and imitating the behaviors of age-matched peers. The children demonstrated learning in 20 or fewer trials and demonstrated maintenance when tested 2 days later.

Goldstein and Mousetis (1989) had students with mental retardation (ages 7 to 15 years) serve as models to teach peers with more severe cognitive impairments (ages 6 to 9 years) to combine known and unknown words into two- or three-word utterances. Peers modeled correct answers to "What did I do?" by describing the examiners' manipulation of objects placed in different locations in a toy house with furniture. Later, target students were reinforced when they demonstrated observational learning as reflected by accurate production of utterances in response to similar stimuli, such as "penny behind the couch." Their production of utterances with novel combinations of objects, prepositions, and locations reflected widespread generative language learning as well as observational learning.

Adults have served as models to teach play skills to children with autism. Ingersoll and Schreibman (2006) used a five-phase modeling procedure that moved from adult modeling with familiar toys and actions to gradually introduced novel toys and novel actions. They found that four out of five 2-to 3-year-old children with autism learned to imitate pretend-play sequences using familiar and novel toys. The pretend-play behaviors generalized to spontaneous play and to novel settings and therapists. Moreover, the language that was modeled, but was not prompted, also resulted in improvements in imitative and/or spontaneous language during play. Jahr, Eldevik, and Eikeseth (2000) taught children with autism (ages 4 to 12 years) to initiate cooperative play by combining verbal descriptions with adult modeling. Modeling alone was not effective, but new skills emerged when the children were required to describe the modeled behavior (e.g., "You built a fence") before they were given an opportunity to imitate the model. This verbal mediation aided the observational learning process, and the new behaviors were maintained 6 to 16 months after intervention.

In summary, in vivo modeling has been effective for teaching children ranging in age from 2 to 15 years in a variety of settings and different types of behaviors (discriminations, longer sentences, pretend play, play initiations), using typically and non-typically developing children and adult models. Despite the successes of in vivo modeling, investigators have pointed out a number of potential limitations. Gena, Couloura, and Kymissis (2005) noted that in vivo modeling can require intense training for the models. Implementing in vivo modeling also can be demanding on the interventionists, and it may be difficult to implement with sufficient consistency. Consequently, investigators have explored the potential of preparing videos that can be edited to offer precise and consistent modeling and can be viewed repeatedly. Improvements in the availability, quality, and flexibility of video recording and editing equipment and software also contribute to the growing interest in VM.

Thelen and colleagues (1979) suggested that VM has several advantages over in vivo modeling. Video allows interventionists to capture typical modeling sequences that may be difficult to simulate in the clinical setting. Video editing capabilities allow interventionists to tape multiple takes and manipulate the video footage to ensure that the desired behaviors are captured. Further, VM may have the advantage of providing opportunities for observing multiple models, more efficient use of therapeutic time, and potential reuse with other clients (Charlop-Christy, Le, and Freeman 2000; Gena, Couloura, and Kymissis 2005; Thelen et al. 1979).

■ Video Modeling

Identifying efficient and effective teaching strategies to address social-communication deficits has been a challenge for those designing treatment programs. VM is an innovative approach to addressing this issue. It has been used effectively in a variety of settings, with various populations, to teach many types of behavior, including social interaction, communication, community skills, and motor skills (Branham et al. 1999; Charlop-Christy and Daneshvar

2003; Charlop-Christy, Le, and Freeman 2000; Dowrick and Raeburn 1995; LeBlanc et al. 2003). Two examples of using VM to teach perspective-taking skills are described here.

LeBlanc and colleagues (2003) used VM and reinforcement to teach children ages 7 to 13 years, who had been diagnosed with autism, perspective-taking skills in a multiple baseline design across tasks. The children viewed an adult model completing the tasks and then answered perspective-taking questions. VM was effective for teaching the target behaviors but with limited generalization. Difficulty with social-communication skills and reciprocal interactions for individuals with autism has prompted further research in the area of VM. In another study focusing on perspective-taking skills, Charlop-Christy and Daneshvar (2003) used adult models in different perspective-taking situations to teach three children. ages 6 to 9 years, appropriate responses to target questions (e.g., "Where will Barney look for the cookie?"). A multiple baseline design across children and tasks was used to assess learning and generalization across untrained stimuli. All three children were successful at answering trained and untrained perspective-taking questions, demonstrating both stimulus and response generalization.

Because of its efficiency and effectiveness, videotape has been used with adult models and peer models to teach new skills and to improve the use of skills. D'Ateno, Mangiapanello, and Taylor (2003) used adult video models to teach complex play sequences to a preschooler with autism. Rachel, a 3-year-old girl, learned to use scripted and nonscripted play sequences, both verbal (e.g., "Come on drink the tea") and motor (e.g., placing plates on the table or pouring tea) after viewing video vignettes of an adult speaking to a doll during play activities such as tea party, baking, and shopping.

Through the use of models on video, VM has revolutionized the conceptualization of observational learning. The idea of creating access to target behaviors for use at any location and at almost any moment places a new perspective on the use of modeled behaviors for teaching purposes. There is a wealth of support for the use of VM as a teaching strategy for a variety of purposes and individuals. However, questions remain concerning how to make VM as efficient as possible. One promising approach that has begun to be applied to children with autism is VSM.

■ Video Self-Modeling

Dowrick and Raeburn (1977) argued that, if one is to maximize similarity between the model and the observer, then one should consider using self-as-a-model. The process typically involves identifying a behavior that needs to be improved or replaced with an alternative behavior. The child is then videotaped, either a role-play situation or in the natural setting, and is prompted to perform the desired behavior. The tape is edited to show only the desired, appropriate behavior, with prompts and inaccurate performance edited out. If a desired behavior occurs infrequently, it may be necessary to use role play and prompting to compile an adequate sample of positive behavior (Buggey 1999).

Video self-modeling interventions can be classified into three types: positive self-review, video feed-forward, and video feedback. Investigators have proposed that selection of these three types of VSM may be guided by different purposes and by what is being learned in relation to the child's present behavioral repertoire. Dowrick (1999) suggested that VSM focus on positive models. PSR refers to individuals viewing themselves successfully engaging in a behavior or activity. PSR can be used with low-frequency behaviors (i.e., a behavior that the individual can sometimes do, but with some difficulty) or with behaviors that were once mastered but are no longer used. In the latter case, the individual is simply videotaped while engaging in the low-frequency behavior or while receiving assistance to complete the task. After editing of the tape, the positive self-review intervention involves repeatedly watching the target task being performed independently and successfully. The goal is for individuals to learn from what they did right, not from what they did wrong.

Video feed-forward interventions are typically used when individuals already possess the necessary skills in their behavioral repertoire but may not be able to put these skills together to complete an activity. For instance, a person may have the ability to get out of bed, brush her teeth, get dressed, and comb her hair but cannot perform these skills in the proper sequence. In a video feed-forward intervention, the target person is videotaped while engaging in each of these tasks, and then the segments are spliced together to form the proper sequence. The same can be done with typical social, self-help, or communication interaction sequences. For instance, the person could be videotaped demonstrating three different skills: initiating an interaction, maintaining a reciprocal interaction, and appropriately terminating the interaction. The three scenes could then be blended together to portray one successful, fluent sequence of events.

Video feedback or review differs from the other types of VSM, because it includes viewing positive and negative exemplars of behavior. In video feedback, the individual already possesses the necessary skills in his or her behavioral repertoire but may not utilize these skills consistently within or across contexts and situations. For instance, a person may have the ability to enter into a conversation and initiate a topic of conversation, but appropriate use of conversational initiations is inconsistent. In a video feedback intervention, the target person is videotaped while engaging in instances of appropriate and inappropriate conversation initiation, and then the interventionist and target person view the video and identify appropriate and inappropriate instances of conversation initiation. The videotape review is used as a feedback mechanism to increase instances of appropriate conversation initiations.

Video self-monitoring has been used effectively in a variety of settings with various populations to teach many behaviors, including social interaction, communication, community skills, and motor skills (Branham et al. 1999; Brown and Middleton 1998; Buggey 1995; Charlop-Christy, Le, and Freeman 2000; Dowrick and Raeburn 1995). Video self-monitoring also has been used in educational settings to teach alternatives to disruptive classroom behaviors (Kehle et al. 1986; Lonnecker et al. 1994), to teach academic skills (Schunk and Hanson 1989), to facilitate behavior change in classroom settings (Clark et al. 2000; Kehle et al. 1986; Lonnecker et al. 1994), and to teach task fluency of self-help skills performed in home routines (Lasater and Brady 1995).

VSM has a number of characteristics that make it especially appropriate for use in natural settings. First, the use of VSM typically does not require specialized training of parents, teachers, or staff. Second, because the child is videotaped in the natural setting, generalization of skills is more likely to occur. Third, research indicates that VSM can be used effectively to address a variety of behaviors, from academic skills to aggression. Fourth, once the videotape is produced, it does not require a lot of time or effort on the part of the parent or teacher to implement a VSM program. Finally, VSM is considered to be a positive behavioral support strategy, because inappropriate behaviors are ignored and positive behaviors are emphasized (Buggey 1999). Compared to other instructional interventions, VSM has some advantages, including immediate effects, portability, time effectiveness, and cost-efficiency (Hitchcock, Dowrick, and Prater 2003).

■ Types of Models

There are a variety of ways to implement video-based instruction. These different techniques and strategies also are confounded by the use of different types of models. Investigators such as Buggey (1995) support the use of self-as-model; however, other models (e.g., adults, siblings, peers) have been used successfully to modify, increase, decrease, and teach a diverse set of behaviors. Bandura (1977) and Dowrick (1991) represent investigators who argue that observational learning is increasingly more likely to occur as the similarity of the model to the observer increases. The observer can identify with the model. However, this does not mean that observational learning is precluded when models are dissimilar to the observer.

Adult Models

The literature indicates that video-based instruction has been successful when adults serve as models to teach adolescents and young adults community skills, such as withdrawing cash from an ATM machine, debit card purchasing, and fast food purchasing (Alberto, Cihak, and Gama 2005; Mechling, Pridgen, and Cronin 2005). In addition, adult modeling has been successful in teaching preschool and school-age children skills such as grocery shopping (Alcantara 1994), perspective-taking (Charlop-Christy and Daneshvar 2003; LeBlanc et al. 2003), play with objects and pretend play (Hine and Wolery 2006; MacDonald et al. 2005), verbal responding to questions (Mechling, Pridgen, and Cronin 2005), and task completion (Mechling, Gast, and Cronin 2006). A review of these studies revealed that children with autism are able to attain skills by watching and imitating an adult model or nondescript models (e.g., hands only).

The acquisition of these behaviors is achieved at different rates and to varying extents depending on the child's cognitive and motor abilities. For example, in the study by Mechling, Pridgen, and Cronin (2005), all students were reported as learning verbal responses required for purchasing fast food. Participants' preexisting skills appeared to be related to these acquisition rates. For example, student 1 had the highest IQ and demonstrated by far the quickest learning of purchasing skills (16 trials). In contrast, student 2, who was motor delayed and had difficulty performing the motor sequences necessary to complete the tasks, required 37 trials. Student 3 had difficulty learning the verbal responses necessary to complete the tasks and required 41 trials. In two other studies using nondescript models, Mechling, Gast, and Langone (2002) and Mechling (2004) used video instruction to teach three teenagers, two with intellectual disabilities and one with autism, to maneuver around a grocery store and shop for various items. The participants watched the videos at home and then made trips to the local grocery store. In both studies, the results indicated that VM by adults was successful in teaching generalized reading of aisle signs and the location of items.

In a study focusing on conversational speech, Charlop and Milstein (1989) used adult VM with three school-age children (6 to 7 years old) with autism. The children viewed 45-second videos of adults engaging in conversation about particular toys. The children reached criterion after 3, 6, and 20 presentations of their video. They also increased their use of unmodeled, new responses during conversation and increased appropriate question asking. This study yielded quite positive results despite the use of adult models for young children. Through nondescript and adult models, children with autism spectrum disorders (ASD) have learned multistep tasks and behaviors in changing environments with variable stimuli.

Peer Models

Peer models have been used to teach social language skills, such as compliment giving (Apple, Billingsley, and Schwartz 2005; Maione and Mirenda 2006; Simpson, Langone, and Ayres 2004), community skills (Branham et al. 1999; Haring et al. 1987), social initiations, reciprocal play, and sociodramatic play (Dauphin, Kinney, and Stromer 2004; Nikopoulos and Keenan 2004). For example, one study used peer models to teach sharing, social greetings, and compliance skills to 5- and 6-year-old children with autism (Simpson, Langone, and Ayres 2004), and another study used peer models to teach compliment-giving skills to children with high-functioning ASD.

Simpson, Langone, and Ayres (2004) employed a video stacking procedure. Stacking is a computer-based version of flashcards with embedded video of peer models. First, a still frame of the targeted behavior was presented with a description (e.g., "This is how to get along in school"). Then, a video clip with a peer model showed a child getting along in school. All four participants appeared to show improvements in their rate of unprompted social behavior, but interpretation was compromised because of high baseline performance. Dauphin, Kinney, and Stromer et al. (2004) employed a similar video procedure that displayed slides with embedded video of a child demonstrating what to do and say for sociodramatic play routines. Tim, a 3-year-old boy with autism, viewed the slides and video of play sequences involving animals completing different actions (e.g., "Dinosaur want to hop"; "Cow want to run"; "Blue want to climb"). The study involved three phases: a computer phase, a notebook schedule phase, and a combination of the two. After completing the third phase, Tim was on schedule and participating in sociodramatic play 88% of the time, an increase from 10%.

Apple, Billingsley, and Schwartz (2005) taught two 5-year-old boys with autism to give compliments in response to peers' comments, such as "Look at my shoes." Peer VM was effective in teaching the boys to express compliments, such as "Neat!" or "I like your picture." However, they did not begin initiating compliments until VM was augmented with tangible reinforcement contingent on complimenting. When VM was removed but reinforcement remained available, both students maintained their complimenting in response to peers' comments. After a return to baseline conditions, initiation of compliments extinguished, but responses continued above baseline levels. In a second experiment, Apple, Billingsley, and Schwartz (2005) replaced the reinforcement phase with a prompt fading and self-management phase (two students wore a wrist counter, and one used a checklist). During VM only, two new participants, ages 4 and 5 years, learned to respond to compliments but did not initiate compliments. During the self-management phase, all of the children initiated and responded to compliments with peers, and two of three children generalized this skill to other settings.

Sibling Models

Siblings may be particularly valuable as video models for children with autism, because siblings often attempt to engage their brother or sister in conversation, express interest in helping their sibling learn a skill, and are often readily available as a play partner (Reagon, Higbee, and Endicott 2006). Siblings have served as models to teach play-related statements and pretend-play skills, such as "You be the bad guy, I'll be the good guy" and "Let's play with the trains" (Reagon, Higbee, and Endicott. 2006; Taylor, Levin, and Jasper 1999).

Taylor, Levin, and Jasper (1999) conducted two experiments using sibling dyads. In the first experiment, a 6-year-old child with autism learned to use scripted prompts (e.g., "These hot dogs taste yummy") across three activities after viewing videotapes of his sister modeling the target behavior and practicing the scripts with an adult during intervention sessions. He quickly learned play-related statements for dinosaurs, airplanes, and picnic activities in 3, 8, and 5, trials, respectively. Mastery was quickest in the dinosaur activity, which was hypothesized to be the favorite activity. Generalization to unscripted comments was not noted. In the second experiment, a 9-year-old boy with autism learned to make scripted and unscripted comments after participating in a forward-chaining VM procedure. Forward chaining involves viewing the video in segments and requiring the participant to demonstrate mastery of the target behaviors presented in each segment as they are added sequentially. For example, after watching a video segment with four scripted comments, the child would be required to produce the comments in the probe session before proceeding to the next step; that step would involve six comments, the next one eight comments, and so on, until the video is watched in its entirety. After the forward-chaining procedure, the child in the study by Taylor's group produced an average of 8.3, 9.4, and 8.6 comments per session using batman, cars, and marine activities, respectively. Although he averaged more scripted comments during the marine activity and more unscripted comments during the cars activity, he produced scripted and unscripted comments for all activities.

Reagon, Higbee, and Endicott (2006) extended the Taylor, Levin, and Jasper (1999) study by removing a component of the procedure that required practicing with an adult after watching the video; they also included appropriate play measures and changed the setting. Their findings indicated that sibling models can be effective in teaching pretend-play skills. Moreover, VM can be effective as the sole intervention. The authors identified several potential benefits to using siblings as models, such as availability, parental support of sibling participation, and increased probability of generalization to the home setting.

■ Comparisons of Model Types and Video Modeling

In the previously discussed studies, all model types seem to offer effective means for teaching a variety of behaviors. It is difficult to compare across studies to determine whether adults, peers, siblings, or self are more effective as models, especially because learning did not always result in generalized performance without the addition of reinforcement, prompting, or self-management procedures. The studies described in this section sought to compare directly the effects of adults, peers, and self as models.

Adult versus Peer Model or Self-Model Comparisons

Few studies to date have compared the effectiveness of skill acquisition based on model type. Jones and Schwartz (2004) sought to compare the effects of sibling, peer, and adult in vivo models to teach labeling skills to children with autism. They found that preschoolers with autism learned observationally to label novel items (actions, professions, and opposites), with no consistent differences based on model type.

In a study comparing self-models to peer models, Sherer et al. (2001) taught five 3- to 11-year-olds with autism to answer conversational questions. Results varied among children, and the authors concluded that peer and self-models were equally effective when teaching children with autism to respond to questions. Two concerns raised were the cost- and time-effectiveness of using the child with autism as a model and the lack of a protocol to determine whether the children preferred themselves or others on video. The authors suggested that making videos using children with autism as models can be complicated by difficulties getting the child to perform the appropriate behavior and to attend to instruction.

Both of these studies evaluated effectiveness by determining the number of sessions required to reach criterion, which may not be a sensitive measure, especially if the behaviors learned potentially vary in difficulty. Furthermore, a preference assessment may reveal idiosyncratic differences that predict learning from different types of models.

Video Modeling versus In Vivo Modeling and Static Pictures

Three studies have compared VM to in vivo modeling (Branham et al. 1999; Charlop-Christy, Le, and Freeman2000; Gena, Couloura, and Kymissis 2005), and two studies have compared VM to static picture modeling (Alberto, Cihak, and Gama 2005; Cihak et al. 2006).

Branham and colleagues (1999) taught high school students to cash checks, to cross streets, and to mail letters. The authors' goal was to determine which of three instructional techniques combined with constant time-delay was most efficient: *(a)* video modeling (VM) + in vivo modeling (IM); *(b)* classroom simulation (CS) + IM; or *(c)* CS + VM + IM. The findings indicated that the CS + IM condition was most efficient across participants in terms of instructional time, averaging 16 minutes, compared with 29 minutes for the VM + IM condition and 43 minutes for the CS + VM + IM condition.

However, the number of instructional sessions required to reach criterion showed no large advantage across conditions (average, 12 to 16 sessions). One of the difficulties in interpreting this study is that VM and IM were not compared independently of one another, nor against the CS component alone. Although the overall effectiveness of the instructional conditions did not appear to differ greatly, the authors concluded that VM procedures were economical. This was based on a cost analysis that estimated the total cost for VM to be $5.27 (not including video equipment purchase), compared with $25 for 3 hours of IM during community-based instruction outings (including the driver's salary and gas for the school-owned minibus).

Direct comparisons of only VM and in vivo modeling are needed to provide a clearer picture of which intervention is more effective. For example, Charlop-Christy, Le, and Freeman (2000) found VM to be superior to in vivo modeling when teaching 7- to 11-year-old children with autism various tasks such as labeling expressive emotions, conversational speech, and self-help skills. Of the five participants, four reached criterion quicker and were able to generalize the targeted skills to a novel setting after VM. The one exception was a child who required only two presentations to reach the mastery criterion in both conditions. The total number of presentations needed to meet criterion was as high as 11 for the in vivo condition, compared with 4 for the VM condition. Further, a cost- and time-efficiency analysis showed that cumulative time for the in vivo condition (635 minutes) greatly exceeded the time needed in the VM condition (170 minutes); the difference was almost 8 weeks. Likewise, the cumulative cost of the in vivo condition ($127) exceeded the cost of the VM condition ($58).

Gena, Couloura, and Kymissis (2005) compared the effectiveness of in vivo modeling and reinforcement versus a combination of VM and reinforcement contingencies to teach preschoolers affective behaviors such as showing sympathy, appreciation, and disapproval. In contrast to Charlop-Christy, Le, and Freeman (2000), they found both intervention approaches to be equally effective. Moreover, the behaviors were maintained at 1month and 3 months after intervention and were generalized to new scenarios and people. Costs and time expended were not analyzed.

Alberto, Cihak, and Gama (2005) evaluated the use of static picture prompts versus VM to teach 11- to 15-year-old students with moderate mental retardation. Participants were taught two task sequences: withdrawing money from an ATM and purchasing items at a store. All students learned to perform these daily living activities successfully in both conditions. No consistent differences were found in the number of trials to criterion, number of errors, or number of instructional sessions; three of the eight students learned better using static picture prompts, two students learned better using VM, and three students demonstrated mixed effects. Cihak et al. (2006) also compared the effects of static picture prompting versus video prompting when employed in a group instructional format. Consistent with the previous study, they found both procedures to be equally effective.

Based on these comparison studies, one cannot conclude that video-based instruction is better than in vivo modeling or static picture prompts. The studies reviewed indicated that all modes are potentially effective. It is difficult to compare and contrast these studies because of limited replication, different targeted behaviors, and different combinations of treatment components. Because the independent and dependent variables differed within and across the studies, it is difficult to determine which treatment or subject characteristics might give an advantage of one mode over others. For example, the contradictory findings of Gena, Couloura, and Kymissis (2005) and Charlop-Christy, Le, and Freeman (2000) could be attributable to a number of factors. The former study used adult models in the in vivo mode and a child model in the VM mode, whereas the latter used child models in both conditions. There is no conclusive evidence that favoring one type of model over another or video instruction over live models.

Even though there is no conclusive evidence that VM or VSM is more effective than other types of modeling, it is clear that video instruction is effective for targeting a variety of behaviors (Hitchcock, Dowrick, and Prater 2003). However, if VM or VSM is the intervention of choice, it seems appropriate to address potential target skills and recommendations for the use of video instruction.

■ Identifying Target Skills for Video Instruction

What behaviors have been found to be amenable to video-based instruction? A majority of the video-based instruction studies of individuals with autism have focused on improving communication skills (Buggey 1995, 2005; Charlop-Christy, Le, and Freeman 2000; Hepting and Goldstein 1996; MacDonald et al. 2005; Maione and Mirenda 2006; Mechling, Pridgen, and Cronin 2005; Reamer, Brady, and Hawkins 1998; Simpson, Langone, and Ayres 2004; Taylor, Levin, and Jasper 1999). Perhaps this is not surprising, because 26% to 61% of children with ASD are estimated to have no means of appropriate functional communication (Weitz, Dexter, and Moore 1997). In addition to communication, video instruction holds promise for teaching skills in other domains as well. Positive outcomes suggest that VSM can be used to successfully support social skills, positive behaviors, activities of daily living, and academic performance (Hitchcock, Dowrick, and Prater 2003).

There are a number of factors that may play a role in predicting which skills are amenable to video instruction. First, skill selection may be restricted based on what behaviors can be efficiently and effectively depicted on videotape.

Certain behaviors are relatively easy to depict on video. For example, Dowrick and Raeburn (1995) taught motor skills to children with physical disabilities (i.e., cerebral palsy and spina bifida). These skills (e.g., dressing, walking, clapping) seem to be concrete, repetitive, and relatively easy to capture on video. In contrast, communication skills are more abstract and more transient, especially when the learner must attend to auditory and visual stimuli at the same time. The types of behaviors or tasks selected for video instruction should be appropriate for the client and enable the client to accomplish target goals; they should be behaviors and tasks performed in typical activities and routines; and they should not be inappropriate for video. For example, one may consider bathing a too intrusive intervention that is not suitable for VM (Lasater and Brady 1995).

The quality of the videotapes depends on the technical expertise of the videographer. A production crew with a good cinematographer, director, professional cast, and editor may be able to zoom in and accentuate the salient features of behaviors being targeted. Most interventionists lack this expertise and are limited in what they can depict successfully on video. The reality is that the interventionist is more likely to make do with a digital camcorder, using typical children or children with autism as models, with the benefit of easy-to-use video editing software. The end product should be an edited video that depicts the model performing more proficiently than the learner's current level of functioning. Gathering adequate examples of behavior (often prompted) and editing the footage requires videotaping, directing, and editing skills. Alternatively, video-based instruction may warrant collaboration between interventionists and more skilled videographers.

Second, the functioning level of the child in relation to targeted skills must be considered. Modeling scripted play routines would be inappropriate for a child who does not read, imitate verbalizations, or use language in a functional manner. More appropriate goals might focus on functional communication that involves imitating gestures, producing simple vocalizations, or using an augmentative communication system. Selection of target skills needs to be consistent with the developmental level or functioning of the child. The larger the discrepancy between the modeled behavior and the child's behavior, the less likely it is that the child will learn observationally. Even though cognitive ability plays a large role in behavior change, motivation may be increased through the use of video instruction. thereby enhancing the individual's ability to learn the target skill (Mechling, Gast, and Cronin 2006; Schreibman, Whalen, and Stahmer 2000). Investigators have examined the relationship between "current skill levels" and "target skill levels" in individuals with developmental delays (Abbeduto, Furman, and Davies 1989; Atlas and Lapidus 1988; Rast and Meltzoff 1995), as well as nonlinguistic concepts and language in typically developing children (Gopnik and Meltzoff 1986; Goldfield and Reznick 1990), and Piagetian stages in typically developing children (Lifter and Bloom 1989; McCune 1995). These investigations have demonstrated a correlation between "current skill levels" and "target skills levels" for children both with and without disabilities.

Third, differences in intervention effects are likely to relate to whether one is teaching new skills, modifying skills in the individual's repertoire, increasing skill fluency, or reducing undesirable behaviors. Certainly, it is easier if one can capitalize on an existing skill that can be shaped into a new, expanded skill. For example, if a child is using language to respond, it may be appropriate to use this skill set to help the child to initiate verbal interactions. However, if he or she has limited skills upon which to build, it may be most appropriate to target a new, pivotal behavior, such as requesting (e.g., pointing, reaching). Addressing undesirable behaviors may take priority if those behaviors are dangerous or preclude learning. Video modeling may be especially effective for teaching replacements for undesirable behaviors, especially behaviors that may interfere with learning other skills. This includes the importance of ensuring that communicative partners do not respond to old forms of communication when teaching new forms (Schlosser 2000). The following sections discuss the use of video instruction to teach new skills, to build on existing skills, and to reduce undesired behaviors.

Using Video Instruction to Teach a New Skill

As reported previously, Taylor, Levin, and Jasper (1999) taught two boys to direct appropriate play comments (e.g., "These hot dogs taste yummy") to their siblings. Through VM, one child learned to direct scripted, play-related comments to his sibling. However, this new skill did not generalize to unscripted comments in novel situations. Using VM and a forward-chaining procedure, the second child learned to direct scripted and unscripted play-related comments to his sibling.

Other investigators have needed to supplement video instruction to promote generalization of behaviors. For example, Hepting and Goldstein (1996) used VSM to teach three preschoolers with developmental disabilities to use linguistic structures such as "attribute + object" or "action + object" semantic relations. Once the intervention was initiated, all three children began expressing their new linguistic structures during viewing sessions. After VSM, one child began to produce attributes, a second child began to combine articles and attributes, and the third child began to request and use the plural -s. However, consistent use of target structures during requesting opportunities in the classroom were not demonstrated until the videotapes were viewed in the child's classroom and children were prompted to use their new language skills.

In other circumstances, researchers appear to have had little difficulty in establishing generalization of newly acquired skills. LeBlanc and colleagues

(2003) used VM and reinforcement to teach young school-age children perspective-taking skills in a multiple baseline design across tasks. The children viewed an adult model completing the tasks and then answered perspective-taking questions. The idea was to help the children understand that another person's beliefs about events may be different from reality (e.g., a person may believe that a bag labeled "cookies" contains cookies, but it may be found on examination to contain raisins). Training phases continued until the child responded correctly to three consecutive trials in the testing session. All three children progressed from a baseline of zero to meeting the mastery criterion after 7, 3, and 4 sessions, respectively. All of the children mastered the perspective-taking tasks and generalized to variations of the task that required novel vocal ("under the bowl") or motor (pointing) responses.

Kinney, Vedora, and Stromer (2003) used VM to teach generative spelling to Ana, a child with autism, in a four-phase procedure. The first phase involved watching an adult model spelling on a board; this was followed by imitating the spelling in the video and viewing a play scene with toys. In the second, third, and fourth phases, different training matrices were introduced to enhance Ana's ability to spell untrained words. Ana learned to spell 55 words during the study. Four weeks after intervention, she passed two 27-word spelling tests with an average of 94% accuracy. Further, informal observation indicated that her success with generative spelling might have had a direct influence on her literacy skills, because she was able to read 53 of the 55 words by sight. Generalized spelling of new words was successful only after the introduction of matrix training.

Dowrick and Raeburn (1995) focused on teaching gross motor skills (e.g., walking, crawling, feeding, toileting), and Darden (2006) focused on fine motor skills (giving and pointing) in response to verbal prompts. Dowrick and Raeburn (1995) compared the effects of VSM with and without editing. In the VSM condition, children observed themselves at advanced skill levels. In the comparison condition, children viewed videos of their typical behavior. Participants were 18 children, aged 5 to 13 years, who had various developmental disabilities and were taught a variety of physical and self-help skills. Each child was assigned two target behaviors, and one behavior was randomly selected for self-modeling. All of the children participated in six viewing sessions. Occupational and physical therapists, who were unaware of the behaviors that were targeted, assessed the children before and after intervention. In 14 of the 18 cases, children showed significantly better progress after viewing the altered videotapes. Only one child demonstrated better progress for a target behavior in the unaltered video condition. This elegantly designed study demonstrated the importance of editing video segments to show unprompted, competent performance. Although VSM was shown to be effective with a variety of motor behaviors, it is not clear whether skills that are more abstract, harder to picture, or require more complex discrimination or motor abilities also can be learned through VSM.

Darden (2006) used VSM to teach four preschoolers with autism to make requests by giving pictures in response to a specific verbal cue (e.g., "Let's play with the puzzle. Give me the picture of puzzle"). In the VSM-only condition, two of the children learned to give pictures; a third child learned to give pictures when VSM was augmented with matching a picture to the video prompt. However, only one of the four children learned to discriminate among the pictures accurately based on VSM alone. The other children required direct teaching to learn to discriminate among the pictures. Nevertheless, learning of the general motor responses (giving and pointing) provided evidence of VSM's effectiveness for teaching behaviors that are concrete and more easily depicted on video.

Video instruction was shown to be relatively effective in teaching a variety of new skills. However, participants demonstrated generalized use of their new skills in only a few of those studies (Kinney, Vedora, and Stromer 2003; LeBlanc et al. 2003). The number of sessions required to reach mastery criteria ranged from 6 to 33. The least number of sessions was required to learn the motor and self-help tasks (Dowrick and Raeburn 1995); more sessions were required to learn language skills (Buggey 1995; Hepting and Goldstein 1996; LeBlanc et al. 2003).

Using Video Instruction to Build on Existing Skills

Video instruction also has been used to build on existing skills, including social interaction skills, use of language during play, task completion, and parental assistance. For example, Simpson, Langone, and Ayres (2004) built on existing social skills (e.g., greeting, following directions, sharing) for four 5- and 6-year olds with autism. Rapid acquisition occurred after the children viewed video clips of classmates without disabilities engaging in the target behaviors. The children were asked to identify instances of target and nontarget behaviors in the video clips. Afterward, they were provided classroom opportunities to engage in target skills throughout the day. Baseline probes indicated that participants demonstrated these skills, but proficiency ranged from 8% to 83%. Because their baseline levels were high, these children may have required few intervention sessions to reach criterion. Children demonstrated 100% mastery (12 of 12 opportunities) after 2 to 6 sessions for one of their three target behaviors (i.e., "sharing" for two children and "greetings" for the other child). Despite significant improvements, each child had at least one behavior that did not reach this stringent mastery criterion.

Because academic and communication behaviors are perceived as critical for life success, many investigators focus on improving behaviors involving language and cognition. For example, Wert and Neisworth (2003) used VSM to teach 3- to 6-year-old children spontaneous requesting (e.g., "Give me Play-Doh" or "my turn") during play activities with Play-Doh, action figures, trains, puzzles, and board games. The children watched the videotapes at home approximately 1 hour before they came to school. Parents either videotaped or observed their child watching the video clip. The investigators did not provide information about the use of prompting during the video viewing. However, for data collection at school, teachers were informed not to use any prompting during the targeted play activities. The intervention resulted in increased spontaneous requesting in all four children.

MacDonald and associates (2005) used scripted play scenarios involving 17 verbalizations and 15 play actions; this resulted in rapid acquisition for two boys with autism who had limited repertoires of repetitive pretend play. The boys learned to engage in play sequences that included verbal narration (e.g., "bringing the treasure box") and motor actions (e.g., steering the ship) in scripted play across all play sets and behaviors. During scripted play, the boys used unscripted play actions; however, these behaviors did not generalize to novel unscripted play sequences.

In contrast, both Buggey (1995) and Maione and Mirenda (2006) reported generalized use of verbs and social language in conversational speech by their subjects. Buggey (1995) combined VSM and VM in a multiple baseline design across participants to teach three preschoolers with developmental delays to use the copula, *is* (e.g., "The dog is brown"). The videotapes illustrated correct productions of the target behavior by both an adult and a child. Although the children did not demonstrate complete mastery, they improved to between 34% and 47% usage, from baseline levels of 3% to 13%, and intervention levels typically remained above baseline levels. The children also generalized the behavior to natural conversation.

Maione and Mirenda (2006) evaluated the influence of VM and video feedback on verbal social interaction skills of a child with autism. In baseline, the child participated in parallel play and verbally interacted with peers only when prompted. In the video-alone condition, the child showed improved verbal interaction across two activities (Play-Doh and tree house). For the third activity (cars), VM, video feedback, and prompting were required to produce an effect. However, the child generalized from scripted to unscripted verbalizations and initiated interaction more frequently during the third activity after training.

It is difficult to come up with conclusive evidence about the effect of using video instruction to expand on existing skills based on three studies. The number of sessions needed to achieve behavior changes in these studies was small (i.e., 1 to 6). In one study (Simpson, Langone, and Ayres 2004), the children presented with high levels at baseline; however, this does not appear to be a general limitation in studies building on existing skills. In summary, we believe that trends suggest success for this area as well, and that less training may be required for building on existing skills with the use of video.

Using Video Instruction to Decrease Undesired Behaviors

The use of VM to focus on decreasing or replacing behaviors seems complex and intriguing. Interacting with others in a desirable manner promotes an environment conducive to learning, acquiring adaptive behaviors, and participating in social interactions. Undesirable behaviors inhibit or reduce the quality of interactions in settings with peers, teachers, and family. Therefore, it is not surprising that inappropriate behaviors have been successfully addressed through video instruction.

In particular, video feedback has been used successfully to reduce undesired behaviors and increase or maintain levels of pro-social behaviors (O'Reilly et al. 2005). Kern-Dunlap and colleagues (1992) used video feedback to reduce undesirable peer interactions (i.e., verbal insults, insulting gestures, and aggression). In a multiple baseline design across children, five school-age boys with behavior disorders viewed themselves on video interacting with classmates. The video feedback intervention required them to identify and describe examples of desirable and undesirable behaviors. The intervention resulted in decreases in undesirable behaviors for all five boys.

Graetz, Mastropieri, and Scruggs (2006) also used video feedback to reduce undesirable behaviors. A 13-year-old boy with autism viewed a tape of himself engaging in appropriate and inappropriate behaviors and then discussed the behaviors with the interventionist, his teacher, and his parents. His teachers and parents reported a decrease in his hand-wringing and arm-flailing. Interestingly, the boy initiated viewing the tapes at times when he was agitated, seemingly as a self-control strategy.

Buggey (2005) used VSM to show children alternatives to undesirable behaviors. Two students (one with autism and one with Asperger's syndrome) significantly decreased tantrum behaviors after viewing themselves performing alternative positive behaviors on video. In a second study, a student with pervasive developmental delay decreased pushing behaviors after observing himself engaging in appropriate behaviors only, such as hugging a classmate or sharing a toy. These improvements were immediate and were maintained through follow-up.

Brown and Middleton (1998) sought to compare VSM with an overcorrection procedure to reduce hand-flapping in a 6-year-old boy with autism. After the child was observed in baseline, overcorrection was introduced; after a return to baseline, VSM was introduced, then withdrawn, and then reinstated. The child participated in 6 sessions per condition. Results indicated that VSM was as effective as overcorrection. Although there appeared to be no differences in the effectiveness of the two intervention procedures, VSM provided a positive alternative to the punishment procedure.

Researchers have addressed a variety of inappropriate behaviors, including insults, tantrums, and body posturing, with the use of video instruction. In summary, VSM and video feedback have been shown to reduce the frequency of undesirable behaviors by modeling or pointing out appropriate alternative behaviors. Maintenance and generalization of such changes is likely to require some modification of the children's environments to ensure that replacement behaviors are reinforced.

Conclusions

Although the initial start-up cost can be expensive, the innovative techniques of VM offer many advantages, such as reduction in instructional time and labor and more consistency in therapeutic delivery. To implement video-based instruction, one must start with an operational definition of the target behavior; the desired behavior must be defined so that it is observable and measurable. Once the target behavior is identified, the instructional plan must be devised. This can be achieved by writing out scripts or articulating a step-by-step task analysis. One may want to observe the child to determine what, if any, parts of the target skills or behaviors are already in his or her repertoire. The next step is to devise an assessment procedure that allows one to document baseline performance, to verify that the child is not able to perform the target behavior or skill before intervention.

After assessment and target behavior identification, the video vignettes must be created (taping and editing). Taping involves capturing the target behaviors, if present, in the model's repertoire or prompting the behavior via verbal, gestural, and/or physical cues in the appropriate context. Selection of recording equipment remains tricky because a variety of digital formats are available. Nevertheless, the increasingly economical digital cameras provide for flexibility and ease of use.

Selecting the model and choosing the perspectives are other key components. One must decide what types of models are available to support intervention development. The choices include self, peer, sibling, adult, and point-of-view modeling (e.g., hands only). One's choices may vary based on the target behaviors to be modeled. A taping environment must also be selected, and, again, the choice may vary based on the target behaviors to be modeled. Natural settings may be preferable for most skills sets, to maximize the efficiency of taping and promote generalization. However, more contrived settings may offer more control over lighting, background noise, and other potential distractions. Moreover, if the background setting is not salient or is barely visible given a close-up perspective, more controlled settings may prove simpler to use. Regardless of the type of setting, video allows for the presentation of events in a manner that supports a variety of cues associated with the environment (e.g., sight, sound, movement); this is not possible with verbal description or pictorial representation (Schreibman, Whalen, and Stahmer 2000).

Most importantly, the target behavior or behaviors need to be captured on video. This can be accomplished by videotaping a behavior that is present at low frequency or by prompting the behavior. Prompting needs to be done unobtrusively, so that it is easier to edit prompts out of the video. Therefore, it is critical to use gesture and physical prompts outside the view of the camera. For example, physical prompts may be delivered at the elbow or the shoulder, and gestural prompts may be delivered across from the target individual, out of camera view.

To prepare for taping, it may be beneficial to rehearse the target behaviors on camera, with a cooperative adult actor serving as the individual to be videotaped completing the behaviors. This may help elucidate the timing and steps involved in completing the behaviors, and it allows the videographer to try out ideas about lighting, props, clothing options, and so on. If the behaviors are complex, it may be necessary to shoot the video in scenes that can be edited together to create a single episode. Once the target behaviors are captured, it is typically necessary to edit the video to remove any prompts or other undesired behaviors.

Editing allows one to depict the model completing the target behavior at an advanced skill level. Little or no editing may be required if one is depicting simple behaviors using typically functioning peer models. The video should be as brief as possible and should depict the behavior in a manner that is not too far above the target individual's functioning level. If it is necessary to edit scenes together, the scenes should flow with few, if any, differences in camera shot, angle, contrast, and model clothing.

Next, one must decide when the learner should view the video—either before entering or while in the target context. The child may also be allowed to view the video after the target context or possibly during random intervals, depending upon the nature of the behavior and the video viewing context. If the child is viewing the video during an intervention session, it may be most appropriate to allow video viewing before or during the activity. In the classroom, it may be more appropriate to view the video before the activity. At home, caregivers have many opportunities for viewing the video before, during, or after the target activity, as well as in random video viewings throughout the day. Video modeling alone may be sufficient for children to learn responses, but it does not ensure performance. The need to set the occasion for the newly learned behavior and to program for natural contingencies to reinforce the behavior should not be overlooked.

In summary, this review of the literature indicates that video-based instruction holds much promise for children with autism. Video-based instruction has been used to teach people with autism across the lifespan (preschool- and elementary school-aged children, adolescents, and young adults). Video modeling has been used by parents, teachers, therapists, and researchers in home, at school, and in community environments to teach a variety of skills and behaviors, such as self-care, daily living, academic, communication, and social skills, and even to reduce aggression, self-injury, and tantrums. Video-based instruction is often used as an observational learning component of an instructional package that may entail other empirically supported instructional principles, such as prompting and fading, applying reinforcement contingencies, and generalization programming.

■ Acknowledgments

Preparation of this chapter was partially supported by grants from the U.S. Department of Education, Office of Special Education and Rehabilitative Services (H84325D030046) and National Institute on Deafness and other Communication Disorders (5F31DC6613) awarded to Florida State University.

■ References

Abbeduto, L., Furman, L., and Davies, B. (1989). Relation between the receptive language and mental age of persons with mental retardation. *American Journal on Mental Retardation, 93*, 535–543.

Alberto, P.A., Cihak, D.F., and Gama, R.I. (2005). Use of static picture prompts versus video modeling during simulation instruction. *Research in Developmental Disabilities, 26* (4), 327–339.

Alcantara, P.R. (1994). Effects of videotape instructional package on purchasing skills of children with autism. *Exceptional Children, 61* (1), 40–55.

Apple, A.L., Billingsley, F., and Schwartz, I.S. (2005). Effects of video modeling alone and with self-management on compliment-giving behaviors of children with high-functioning ASD. *Journal of Positive Behavior Interventions, 7* (1), 33–46.

Atlas, J., and Lapidus, L. (1988). Symbolization levels in communicative behaviors of children showing pervasive developmental disorders. *Journal of Communication Disorders, 21* (1), 75–84.

Bandura, A. (1969). *Principles of behavior modification.* New York: Holt, Rinehart, and Winston.

Bandura, A. (1977). *Social learning theory.* New York: General Learning Press.

Bandura, A. (1986). *Social foundations of thought and action: A social-cognitive theory.* Englewood Cliffs, N.J.: Prentice-Hall.

Branham, R., Collins, B., Schuster, J., Kleinert, H. (1999). Teaching community skills to students with moderate disabilities: Comparing combined techniques of classroom simulation, videotape modeling, and community-based instruction. *Education and Training in Mental Retardation and Developmental Disabilities, 34* (2), 170–181.

Browder, D.M., Schoen, S.F., and Lentz, F.E. (1986). Learning to learn through observation. *Journal of Special Education, 20*, 447–461.

Brown, G., and Middleton, H. (1998). Use of self-as-model to promote general-ization and maintenance of the reduction of self-stimulation in a child with mental retardation. *Education and Training in Mental Retardation and Developmental Disabilities,* 33 (1), 76–80.

Buggey, T. (1995). An examination of the effectiveness of videotaped self-modeling in teaching specific linguistic structures to preschoolers. *Topics in Early Childhood Special Education,* 15 (4), 434–458.

Buggey, T. (1999). Videotaped self-modeling: Allowing children to be their own models. *Teaching Exceptional Children,* 4, 27–31.

Buggey, T. (2005). Video self-modeling applications with students with autism spectrum disorder in a small private school setting. *Focus on Autism and Other Developmental Disabilities,* 20 (1), 52–63.

Charlop, M.H., and Milstein, J.P. (1989). Teaching autistic children conversa-tional speech. *Journal of Applied Behavior Analysis,* 22, 275–285.

Charlop-Christy, M.H., and Daneshvar, S. (2003). Using video modeling to teach perspective taking to children with autism. *Journal of Positive Behavior Interventions,* 5 (1), 12–21.

Charlop-Christy, M.H., Le, L., and Freeman, K. (2000). A comparison of video modeling with vivo modeling for teaching children with autism. *Journal of Autism and Developmental Disorders,* 30 (6), 537–552.

Cihak, D., Alberto, P.A., Taber-Doughty, T., Gama, R.I. (2006). A comparison of static picture prompting and video prompting simulation strategies using group instructional procedures. *Focus on Autism and Other Developmental Disabilities,* 21 (2), 89–99.

Clark, S.K., Jenson, W.R., Kehle, T.S., and Bray, M.A. (2000). Self-modeling as a treatment for increasing on-task behavior. *Psychology in the Schools,* 37 (6), 517–522.

D'Ateno, P., Mangiapanello, K., and Taylor, B. (2003). Using video modeling to teach complex play sequences to a preschooler with autism. *Journal of Positive Behavior Interventions,* 5 (1), 5–11.

Darden, F.L. (2006). Video self-modeling to facilitate visual symbol learning in preschoolers with developmental delays. Unpublished doctoral dissertation, Florida State University. Available at http://etd.lib.fsu.edu/theses/available/etd-04102006–122138 (accessed December, 2007).[3]

Dauphin, M., Kinney, E.M., and Stromer, R. (2004). Using video-enhanced activ-ity schedules and matrix training to teach sociodramatic play to a child with autism. *Journal of Positive Behavior Interventions,* 6 (4), 238–250.

Dowrick, P.W. (1991). *Practical guide to using video in the behavioral sciences.* New York: Wiley.

Dowrick, P.W. (1999). A review of self-modeling and related interventions. *Applied and Preventive Psychology,* 8, 23–39.

Dowrick, P.W., and Raeburn, J.M. (1977). Video editing and medication to pro-duce a therapeutic self-model. *Journal of Consulting and Clinical Psychology,* 45, 1156–1158.

Dowrick, P.W., and Raeburn, J.M. (1995). Self-modeling: Rapid skill training for children with physical disabilities. *Journal of Developmental and Physical Disabilities,* 7 (1), 25–37.

Egel, A.L., Richman, G.S., and Koegel, R.L. (1981). Normal peer models and autistic children's learning. *Journal of Applied Behavior Analysis,* 14, 3–12.

Gena, A., Couloura, S., and Kymissis, E. (2005). Modifying the affective behavior of preschoolers with autism using *in-vivo* or video self-modeling reinforcement contingencies. *Journal of Autism and Developmental Disorders,* 35 (5), 545–556.

Glidden, L.M., and Warner, D. (1982). Research on imitation in mentally retarded persons: Theory-bound or ecological validity run amuck? *Applied Research in Mental Retardation,* 3, 383–395.

Goldfield, B., and Reznick, J. (1990). Early lexical acquisition: Rate, content, and the vocabulary spurt. *Journal of Child Language,* 17, 171–183.

Goldstein, H., and Brown, W. (1989). Observational learning of receptive and expressive language by preschool children. *Education and Treatment of Children,* 12, 5–37.

Goldstein, H., and Mousetis, L. (1989). Generalized language learning by children with severe mental retardation: Effects of peer's expressive modeling. *Journal of Applied Behavior Analysis,* 22, 245–259.

Gopnik, A., and Meltzoff, A. (1986). Relations between semantic and cognitive development in the one-word stage: The specificity hypothesis. *Child Development,* 57, 1040–1053.

Graetz, J.E., Mastropieri, M.A., and Scruggs, T.E. (2006). Show time: Using video self-modeling to decrease inappropriate behavior. *Teaching Exceptional Children,* 38 (5), 43–48.

Grandin, T. (1995). *Thinking in pictures and other reports from my life with autism.* New York: Doubleday.

Haring, T., Kennedy, C., Adams, M., and Pitts-Conway, V. (1987). Teaching generalization of purchasing skills across community settings to autistic youth using videotape modeling. *Journal of Applied Behavior Analysis,* 20 (1), 89–96.

Hepting, N., and Goldstein, H. (1996). Requesting by preschoolers with developmental disabilities: Video-taped self-modeling and learning of new linguistic structures. *Topics in Early Childhood Special Education,* 16 (3), 407–427.

Hine, J., and Wolery, M. (2006). Using point-of-view video-modeling to teach play to preschoolers with autism. *Topics in Early Childhood Special Education,* 26 (2), 83–93.

Hitchcock, C., Dowrick, P., and Prater, M. (2003). Video self-modeling intervention in school-based settings: A review. *Remedial and Special Education,* 24 (1), 36–46.

Hodgdon, L.A. (1995). *Visual strategies for improving communication: Practical supports for schools and home.* Troy, Mich.: Quirk Roberts.

Hosford, R.E., and Mills, M.E. (1983). Video in social skills training. In *Using video: Psychological and social applications* (eds. P.W. Dowrick and J. Biggs), pp. 125–140. Chichester, England: Wiley.

Hundert, J., and Houghton, A. (1992). Promoting social interaction of children with disabilities in integrated preschools: A failure to generalize. *Exceptional Children,* 58 (4), 311–320.

Ingersoll, B., and Schreibman, L. (2006). Teaching reciprocal imitation skills to young children with autism using a naturalistic behavioral approach: Effects on language, pretend play, and joint attention. *Journal of Autism and Developmental Disorders* 36 (4), 487–505.

Jahr, E., Eldevik, S., and Eikeseth, S. (2000). Teaching children with autism to initiate and sustain cooperative play. *Research in Developmental Disabilities,* 21, 151–169.

Jones, C.D., and Schwartz, I.S. (2004). Sibling, peers, and adults: Differential effects of models for children with autism. *Topics in Early Childhood Special Education,* 24 (4), 187–198.

Kehle, T.J., Clark, E., Jenson, W.R., and Wampold, B.E. (1986). Effectiveness of self-observation with behavior disordered elementary school children. *School Psychology Review,* 15, 289–295.

Kern-Dunlap, L., Dunlap, G., Clarke, S., Childs, K.E., White, R.L., and Stewart, M.P. (1992). Effects of a videotape feedback package on the peer interactions of children with serious behavioral and emotional challenges. *Journal of Applied Behavior Analysis,* 25, 355–364.

Kinney, E.M., Vedora, J., and Stromer, R. (2003). Computer-presented video models to teach generative spelling to a child with an autism spectrum disorder. *Journal of Positive Behavior Interventions,* 5, 22–29.

Lasater, M.W., and Brady, M.P. (1995). Effects of video self-modeling and feedback on task fluency: A home-based intervention. *Education and Treatment of Children,* 18 (4), 389–407.

LeBlanc, L., Coates, A., Daneshvar, S., Charlop Christy, M., Morris, C., and Lancaster, B. (2003). Using video modeling and reinforcement to teach perspective-taking skills to children with autism. *Journal of Applied Behavior Analysis,* 36, 253–257.

Lifter, K., and Bloom, L. (1989). Object knowledge and the emergence of language. *Infant Behavior and Development,* 12, 395–423.

Lonnecker, C., Brady, M.P., McPherson, R., and Hawkins, J. (1994). Video self modeling and cooperative class behavior in children with learning and behavior problems: Training and generalization effects. *Behavioral Disorders,* 20 (1), 24–34.

MacDonald, R., Clark, M., Garrigan, E., and Vangala, M. (2005). Using video modeling to teach pretend play to children with autism. *Behavioral Interventions,* 20, 225–238.

Maione, L., and Mirenda, P. (2006). Effects of video modeling and video feedback on peer-directed social language skills of a child with autism. *Journal of Positive Behavior Interventions,* 8 (2), 106–118.

McCune, L. (1995). A normative study of representational play at the transition to language. *Developmental Psychology,* 31, 198–206.

Mechling, L. (2004). Effects of multi-media, computer-based instruction on grocery shopping fluency. *Journal of Special Education Technology*, 19 (1), 23–34.

Mechling, L.C., Gast, D.L., and Cronin, B.A. (2006). The effects of presenting high-preference items, paired with choice, via computer-based video programming on task completion of students with autism. *Focus on Autism and Other Developmental Disabilities*, 21, 7–13.

Mechling, L.C., Gast, D., and Langone, J. (2002). Computer based video instruction to teach persons with moderate intellectual disabilities to read grocery aisle signs and locate items. *The Journal of Special Education*, 35 (4), 224–240.

Mechling, L.C., Pridgen, L.S., and Cronin, B.A. (2005). Computer-based video instruction to teach students with intellectual disabilities to verbally respond to questions and make purchases in fast food restaurants. *Education and Training in Developmental Disabilities*, 40 (1), 47–59.

Nikopoulos, C.K., and Keenan, M. (2004). Effects of video modeling on social initiations by children with autism. *Journal of Applied Behavior Analysis*, 37, 93–96.

O'Reilly, M., O'Halloran, M., Sigafoos, J., Lancioni, G., Greene, V., Edrisinha, C., Canella, H., and Olive, M. (2005). Evaluation of video feedback and self-management to decrease schoolyard aggression and increase pro-social behaviour in two students with behvaioural disorders. *Educational Psychology*, 25 (2–3), 199–206.

Piaget, J. (1962). The role of imitation in the formation of representation/Le role de l'imitation dans la formation de la representation. *L'Évolution Psychiatrique*, 27 (1), 141–150.

Quill, K.A. (1997). Instructional considerations for young children with autism: The rationale for visually cued instruction. *Journal of Autism and Developmental Disorders*, 27, 697–714.

Rast, M., and Meltzoff, A. (1995). Memory and representation in young children with Down syndrome: Exploring deferred imitation and object permanence. *Development and Psychopathology*, 7, 393–407.

Reagon, K., Higbaee, T., and Endicott, K. (2006). Teaching pretend play skills to a student with autism using video modeling with a sibling as model and play partner. *Education and Treatment of Children*, 29 (3), 517–528.

Reamer, R.B., Brady, M.P., and Hawkins, J. (1998). The effect of video self-modeling on parents' interactions with children with developmental disabilities. *Education and Training in Mental Retardation and Developmental Disabilities*, 33 (2), 131–143.

Schlosser, R.W. (2000). *The efficacy of augmentative and alternative communication*. San Diego: Academic Press.

Schreibman, L., Whalen, C., and Stahmer, A. (2000). The use of video priming to reduce disruptive transition behavior in children with autism. *Journal of Positive Behavioral Interventions*, 2 (1), 3–11.

Schunk, D.H., and Hanson, A.R. (1989). Self modeling and children's cognitive skill learning. *Journal of Educational Psychology,* 81, 155–163.

Sherer, M., Pierce, K.L., Paredes, S., Kisacky, K.L., Ingersoll, B., and Schreibman, L. (2001). Enhancing conversation skills in children with autism via video technology: Which is better, "self" or "other" as a model? *Behavior Modification,* 25 (1), 140–158.

Shipley-Benamou, R., Lutzker, J.R., and Taubman, M. (2002). Teaching daily living skills to children with autism through instructional video modeling. *Journal of Positive Behavior Interventions,* 4 (3), 165–175.

Simpson, A., Langone, J., and Ayres, K.M. (2004). Embedded video and computer based instruction to improve social skills for students with autism. *Education and Training in Developmental Disabilities,* 39, 240–252.

Stahmer, A.C., Ingersoll, B., and Carter, C. (2003). Behavioral approaches to promoting play. *Autism,* 7, 401–413.

Taylor, B.A., Levin, L., and Jasper, S. (1999). Increasing play related statements in children with autism toward their siblings: Effects of video modeling. *Journal of Developmental and Physical Disabilities,* 11, 253–264.

Thelen, M.H., Fry, R.A., Fehrenbach, P.A., and Frautschi, N.M. (1979). Therapeutic videotape and film modeling: A review. *Psychological Bulletin,* 86, 701–720.

Weitz, C., Dexter, M., and Moore, J. (1997). AAC and children with developmental disabilities. In *Handbook of augmentative and alternative communication* (eds. S. Glennen and D. DeCoste), pp. 395–431. San Diego: Singular.

Wert, B.Y., and Neisworth, J.T. (2003). Effects of video self-modeling on spontaneous requesting in children with autism. *Journal of Positive Behavior Interventions,* 5, 30–34.

Werts, M.G., Caldwell, N.K., and Wolery, M. (1996). Peer modeling of response chains: Observational learning by students with disabilities. *Journal of Applied Behavior Analysis,* 29, 53–66.

Yando, R., Seitz, V., and Zigler, E. (1978). *Imitation: A developmental perspective.* Oxford, England: Lawrence Erlbaum.

13. TEACHING SOCIAL SKILLS IN SCHOOL SETTINGS

Wendy Machalicek, Tonya Davis, Mark O'Reilly, Natasha Beretvas,
Jeff Sigafoos, Giulio Lancioni, Vanessa Green, and Chaturi Edrisinha

Persons with autism invariably experience difficulties with social skills (McConnell 2002). From an early age, these children seem unable to initiate and maintain social interactions. Vital social skills such as establishing eye contact or sharing joint attention may be lacking, idiosyncratic, or severely impaired. This impairment in social interaction is one of the core diagnostic features of autism (American Psychiatric Association 2000). Indeed, the original account of autism described these social difficulties (Kanner 1943).

There is an extensive literature describing interventions to treat social skills with this population (McConnell 2002; Weiss and Harris 2001). A variety of strategies, including comprehensive curricula (e.g., Lovaas 1987) and interventions targeted specifically at social skills (e.g., Sainato, Goldstein, and Strain 1992), have resulted in improvements in performance. Despite these positive findings, more research needs to be conducted to isolate the active treatment variables of comprehensive curricula and to determine the ultimate robustness of social skills training protocols in terms of producing long-term and generalized behavior change (Lord et al. 2005).

Notwithstanding the need for future research, there continues to be a need to gain an accurate picture of the types of interventions that have been examined to teach social skills to this population. This chapter provides the reader with an overview of the social skills targeted and the interventions used with children with autism in school settings.

■ Methods

Studies were included in this review based on five criteria. Each study: *(a)* included participants between 3 and 21 years of age with a diagnosis of autistic spectrum disorder (ASD); *(b)* used a single-subject design; *(c)* was published in a peer-reviewed journal between 1995 and 2006; *(d)* applied an intervention in a effort to increase a variety of social skills; and *(e)* took place within the context of a classroom. Studies that focused exclusively on the assessment of social skills were excluded from this review, as were studies that did not include two or more data points for each baseline and treatment phase. Electronic searches were completed using Ebsco with 27 relevant databases, including ERIC, PschINFO, and MEDLINE. Additionally, we examined the reference sections of included studies for possible additions to the review.

■ Overview of Targeted Social Skills

This section of the chapter provides a detailed overview of the social skills that have been addressed in the intervention literature. These can be divided into five categories: conversation skills, cooperative behaviors, nonverbal social skills, pivotal behaviors, and appropriate play. Targeted conversation skills, for example, have included giving and receiving compliments and conversing on a variety of topics. Students with autism have also learned cooperative behaviors, including following directions or rules, helping a peer with an activity, and including peers in play. Researchers have also shown that students with autism can learn such nonverbal social skills as giving and receiving affection, identifying the emotions of others, and expressing one's own emotions. Targeted pivotal behaviors have included making eye contact, imitating the actions of others, and sharing joint attention. In addition, students with autism have been taught such play skills as engaging appropriately with objects and playing games with typically developing peers. Table 13.1 provides an overview of the types of social skills that have been addressed in these intervention studies.

Conversational Skills

Communication and social skills are deeply intertwined. The act of conversing with another person beautifully illustrates this connection, because conversations require both an understanding of spoken language and unspoken social communication. This section provide an overview of conversation skills to communicate the full range of competencies needed for successful conversations. Communicative exchanges involve several layers of behavior and cognition that usually happen in a very short period of time. First, a person must be aware of the particular characteristics of a situation, compare these to previously encountered situations, and respond accordingly. Second, a person must analyze what the communicative partner has said and reply intelligibly. Analyzing what another has said sometimes requires a person to understand the other person's situation and sometimes to imagine what the other must be thinking or feeling. Interpreting what another person has said can be more difficult if, as sometimes occurs, there is a difference between the literal meaning of a spoken sentence and the intended meaning of the speaker.

TABLE 13.1.
Social Skills Targeted for Intervention

1. Conversational Skills
   - *Commenting*
   - *Conversing on a variety of topics*
   - *General interactions*
   - *Giving and receiving compliments*
   - *Giving directions*
   - *Greeting others*
   - *Initiating conversations*
   - *Joining in*
   - *Maintaining interactions*
   - *Responding to others*
   - *Using a person's name*

2. Cooperative Social Behaviors
   - *Following directions*
   - *Following rules*
   - *Helping others*
   - *Including others*

3. Nonverbal Social Skills
   - *Giving and receiving affection*
   - *Identifying emotions*
   - *Smiling*

4. Pivotal Behaviors
   - *Eye contact*
   - *Imitation*
   - *Joint attention*
   - *Perspective taking*
   - *Requesting help or attention*

5. Play Skills
   - *Object engagement*
   - *Playing games*
   - *Pretend play*
   - *Sharing*
   - *Sportsmanship*
   - *Turn-taking*

The necessity to "read between the lines" poses difficulty for children with autism, apparently regardless of their cognitive functioning (Ozonoff and Miller 1996). The space between the lines, so to speak, is governed by culturally defined rules. The study of these culturally defined rules of language is called pragmatics (Bates and MacWhinney 1979; Mey 2001). The word *pragmatics* is also used to describe the ongoing, rule-bound interpretation of the unspoken pieces of a conversation. The unspoken parts of conversation include making eye contact at contextually appropriate times, interpreting and making congruous facial expressions, standing the culturally defined amount of space away from others, politeness, and discourse rules. Discourse rules include how to start a topic, change subjects, end a topic, or rephrase something that is misunderstood.

Conversations are governed by these often subtle, socially transmitted rules. Adults in the United States usually directly prompt children to say culturally relevant social niceties such as "please," "thank you," and "you are welcome." Children are also taught to address elders and people with authority with deference. Another type of conversational skill that can pose a challenge for children with autism is those interchanges described by speech act theory. Speech act theory states that, "in saying something, we do something" (Austin 1962/1975); examples include apologies, warnings for further action, promises, requests, challenges, greetings, and insults. All of the conversational skills described here can elude children with autism until they receive direct instruction in these practical skills.

Cooperative Social Behaviors

The daily routines of children are filled with small but essential compromises between friends, peers, and adults. One type of cooperation consists of complying with the rules of classrooms, community, and home. Adults generally require children to comply with instructions at their first utterance, without further discussion. This can be difficult for children with autism, because they may not fully comprehend complicated or unfamiliar directions. In everyday parlance, cooperation involves "meeting another person halfway" or engaging in "give and take." Children with autism do not always find it easy to help other children meet goals that are different from their own. They may have obsessive interests not shared by other children and may be resistant to talking about the interests of others. They may also demand strict structures for play activities when rules are frequently changed by participants, such as in pretend play. This difficulty can lead to the exclusion of children with autism from the play of their peers and may reduce their opportunities to experience typical social situations. In any case, cooperating with other children is an essential part of making and keeping friendships, and cooperating with the requests of adults is an important social skill.

Nonverbal Social Skills

As discussed previously, a large part of our interactions with others is unspoken. Among these unspoken aspects are body language, facial expressions, the qualities of our speech, and how close we stand to others (Bonniwell Haslett and Samter 1997). We also communicate through the clothes we wear and by smell (Bonniwell Haslett and Samter 1997). A small number of these skills have been taught by researchers to children with autism and are included in this review (see Table 13.1). Nonverbal social skills targeted included giving and receiving affection, identifying emotions, and smiling.

To be a good communicator, one must be able to accurately read the body language of a communicative partner and also to express one's own intent through body language. Therefore, nonverbal social skills can be thought of as both receptive and expressive. Expressive nonverbal skills include moving or positioning one's body in a way that conveys meaning to a communicative partner. For instance, frowning can convey displeasure with what a person has just said or done. On the other hand, leaning forward slightly can demonstrate a keen interest in what someone is saying.

Receptive nonverbal social skills involve discretely recognizing, interpreting, and responding to the body movements and postures of the communicative partner. For example, if an acquaintance to whom one is talking nervously glances at her wristwatch, you can assume she has another engagement. You may then cut the conversation short and say goodbye.

Another expressive nonverbal skill is the expression of affection toward family and friends. Affectionate touch can increase positive feelings between friends and family members, but touch must be contextually appropriate, welcome, and delivered in an acceptable manner. For instance, people typically shake hands with someone they have just met but may hug good friends when they see them.

Children with autism often have considerable difficulty identifying the emotions of others and expressing their own positive and negative emotions, and may have difficulty expressing affection in culturally appropriate ways. For instance, children may hug their parents by cozying up to them without using their arms, or they may display inordinate amounts of physical affection to strangers. Children may not be able to express strong emotions in an appropriate way, and such emotions may be expressed as challenging behaviors (see Machalicek et al., 2007, for a recent review).

Pivotal Behaviors

Pivotal behaviors have been described as prerequisite behaviors that serve as "keys" to improve other behaviors that are reliant on these basic skills. These basic skills include making eye contact, imitating the actions of others, sharing joint attention with another person, understanding the perspective of others, and requesting help or attention. Acquisition of these behaviors can increase a child's overall level of reinforcement and improve the child's motivation to learn. Typically developing children usually learn such fundamental behaviors through interactions with their environment, but children with autism usually require systematic instruction to learn these behaviors. If we use building a house as a metaphor to represent the development of the necessary repertoire of social skills, these fundamental skills can be thought of as the cornerstones of the house. Without these foundational skills, any further social development can be quite difficult (see Koegel and Koegel, 2006, for an overview).

For many children with autism, increasing the amount of eye contact with adults is a first behavioral objective, because eye contact is one way we get the attention of another person. Eye gaze is thought to support language development in typically developing infants, because they can examine facial expressions and the movements of the mouth during speech (Bonniwell Haslett and Samter 1997). We also regulate our interactions with other people by averting our gaze. Older children (age 6 years or older) and adults avert their gaze when they need extra concentration (Doherty-Sneddon 2003). Interpreting what eye gaze means is a concept that relies on understanding what another person is thinking and is discussed later in this section.

Imitation is an important way in which children learn new actions and educational concepts. The act of imitation involves performing a motor movement or vocalization after watching another person do the same movement or vocalization. Some researchers have found that imitation is not particularly impaired in children with autism as opposed to other children (Beadle-Brown and Whiten 2004); at other times, researchers have found that children with autism share a symptom of delayed imitation (Williams, Whiten, and Singh 2004). Nevertheless, imitation is a focus of many behavioral programs for children with autism.

Unlike typically developing children, young children with autism do not usually demonstrate joint attention with another person or otherwise communicate with a person through eye gaze (Doherty-Sneddon 2003). Joint attention is thought to be the way children increase their vocabulary competencies and come to understand their environments through mediation with adults. Basically, joint attention means that a child shares an attentional focus with another person. For example, if you are blowing bubbles toward your child and your child is both watching the bubbles and making eye contact with you, you have joint attention. Joint attention has been shown to help young children make the link between words and the actual referent object (i.e., ball and the word "ball"). Young children have been shown to pay more attention to the specific toy an adult is looking at than to a novel label for the toy (Baldwin 1991). It is a later skill developmentally, but children also use pointing with their index finger to indicate interesting objects to an adult or another child, and this is considered a form of obtaining joint attention (Doherty-Sneddon 2003) or protodeclarative pointing.

As previously mentioned, much of social communication is unspoken, and good communication requires some predictions to be made by the listener. During social exchanges, we often predict what the other person is thinking or feeling. If we can predict a person's state of mind, we can also usually predict his or her future behavior. In the research literature, the ability to predict another person's state of mind has been called perspective-taking. There is persuasive evidence that children with autism lack the ability to theorize about the perspective of another person (Baron-Cohen 1988; Baron-Cohen, and Cross 1992). Researchers have developed a hypothesis called theory of mind (TOM) to explain why children with autism have difficulty understanding another person's perspective (Baron-Cohen 1988; Baron-Cohen and Cross 1992). TOM is a fairly complicated construct, and a full discussion is not justified here, but some illustrative examples will suggest how we predict what other people are thinking. Imagine you have just sunk into your favorite chair to eat a bowl of vanilla ice cream and along comes your 2-year-old niece, who has a definite sweet tooth. She positions herself just in front of your chair and is staring at your bowl of ice cream with wide eyes. Although the child has not said a single word or reached for the bowl, you would naturally know that the child wanted a bite of your ice cream. You could predict that she would soon reach for the bowl or say something to request the ice cream. Now consider that you have just told your coworker that you are going to brew a fresh pot of coffee for a meeting, because the coffee on the burner is old and may be bitter. But the phone rings and it is an important client. Soon, you have forgotten to brew the coffee. When you remember that you were going to brew the coffee, you rush off to stop your coworker from potentially serving the old coffee. Because you told your coworker that you would put on a fresh pot of coffee, you predict that the coworker might think the old pot was actually fresh.

The last skill described under the pivotal behaviors section in Table 13.1 is requesting help or attention. Children usually learn to communicate requests (mand) for preferred foods or toys before they comment (tact). You may have heard the word *mand* used to describe communicative requesting. Mands can be generated with a voice output communication device (VOCA) or by physical gestures, picture communication, sign language, or verbal speech. Developing an initial repertoire of requesting can open up additional communities of reinforcement for children with autism as they learn that their actions have effects on their environment and on the actions of others.

Play Skills

The final category of social skills described in Table 13.1 is play skills. Early in their development, many children with autism demonstrate idiosyncratic object engagement that does not approximate appropriate toy play, such as interacting with a toy or object in a nonfunctional manner or failing to play symbolically with toys. A common diagnostic question on screening assessment tools for detecting autism involves asking whether the child spends the majority of toy play focusing on a singular aspect of the toy, such as the wheels of a toy car, or lining up objects in an obsessive manner. Learning how to play appropriately with toys and with other children is a very important skill for children with autism. Play is one of the most important ways that typically developing children learn developmental concepts (Piaget 1962; Vygotsky 1978). Toy play allows children to explore such concepts as basic mathematics, cause and effect, functional relationships between objects, spatial concepts, and symbolic play (Wolfberg 1999). Learning how to appropriately manipulate toys is an important prerequisite skill for game play and cooperative play with other children (including sharing and turn-taking). In fact, it can be said that toys offer a creative and constructive medium for cooperative play between children. If children are lacking appropriate play skills, they can become socially isolated from peers who are interested in play and object engagement.

■ Overview of Social Skills Interventions

In this section, we provide a detailed review of the various types of intervention strategies that have been used to teach social skills to children with autism in school settings, with examples and comments on their strengths and weaknesses. Four general categories of intervention were identified in the studies reviewed antecedent interventions, peer-mediated interventions, pivotal response training (PRT), and video modeling and computer instruction. The studies are categorized according to these four intervention strategies in Table 13.2, and the social skills targeted in each individual study are presented in Table 13.2.

Antecedent Interventions

The first category of interventions described in Table 13.2 is antecedent interventions. The rationale behind antecedent interventions is that the student can be prepared in some way to exhibit the appropriate behavior in a particular situation. Antecedent interventions do this in one or both of two ways. First, the intervention may serve as a reminder or clue to the individual that a particular behavior will be rewarded. Second, an antecedent intervention may enhance the motivation of the student to perform the target behavior. Three types of antecedent intervention to foster social skills for students with autism were identified in our search of the literature: social stories, priming, and self-management.

TABLE 13.2

Interventions for Teaching Social Skills to Students with Autism

Intervention	Conversational Skills	Cooperative Behaviors	Nonverbal Social Skills	Pivotal Behaviors	Play Skills
Antecedent Interventions					
Kohler et al. (2001)		X			X
Newman, Buffington, and Hemmes (1996)	X				
Newman, Reinecke, and Meinberg (2000)	X				
Sansosti and Powell-Smith (2006)	X				X
Scattone et al. (2002)		X			
Thiemann and Goldstein (2001)	X	X		X	
Zanolli, Daggett, and Adams (1996)		X	X	X	
Zanolli and Daggett (1998)			X	X	
Peer-Mediated Interventions					
Baker, Koegel, and Koegel (1998)		X			X
(1997)	X		X		X
Gonzalez-Lopez and Kamps (1997)	X			X	X
Kamps et al. (1999)	X	X			X
Kamps et al. (1998)	X	X			X
Kamps et al. (1997)	X				X
Kohler et al. (1995)	X	X	X		X
Laushey and Heflin (2000)	X			X	X

TABLE 13.2 *(continued)*

Intervention	Conversational Skills	Cooperative Behaviors	Nonverbal Social Skills	Pivotal Behaviors	Play Skills
Loncola and Craig-Unkefer (2005)					X
Morrison et al. (2001)	X			X	X
Roeyers (1996)	X				
Strain and Danko (1995)		X		X	X
Thiemann and Goldstein (2004)	X			X	
Pivotal Response Training					
Pierce and Schreibman (1997)	X	X			X
Pierce and Schreibman (1995)	X			X	X
Thorp, Stahmer, and Schreibman (1995)					X
Video Modeling and Computer Instruction					
Apple, Billingsley and Schwartz (2005)	X				
Charlop-Christy and Daneshvar (2003)				X	
LeBlanc et al. (2003)				X	
Nikopoulos and Keenan (2003)	X				X
Simpson, Langone, and Ayres (2004)	X	X			X

Social Stories

Social stories are short, individualized stories that describe a particular situation and direct the student to perform a desired behavior in that situation (Sansosti, Powell-Smith, and Kincaid 2004). They are read before the target activity to prepare the child for the upcoming environment and/or activity so that he or she can perform the targeted social skills.

The rationale of social stories is that children with autism do not notice and comprehend natural social cues, and this leads to difficulty with performing socially appropriate behavior. Therefore, social stories are used to increase the child's awareness and understanding of the environment, those in the environment, and the social cues involved, as well as to instruct the individual as to what to do in certain situations (Sansosti, Powell-Smith, and Kincaid 2004).

Social stories were developed by Carol Gray in the 1990s. Gray (2000) stipulated that social stories should contain four types of sentences. These are *descriptive* sentences, which describe the environment in which the target behavior should occur; *perspective* sentences, which describe the feelings of others in the situation; *affirmative* statements, which describe common beliefs; and *directive* sentences, which cue the student to perform a target behavior. Gray suggested including two to five descriptive, perspective, and affirmative sentences for every directive sentence in a social story.

Social stories can be used to address a variety of target skills, most commonly conversation skills, play skills, and pivotal behaviors (see Table 13.2). Targeted conversation skills include joining in, maintaining interactions, and initiating conversation. The play skill of sportsmanship and the pivotal behavior of requesting have also been addressed.

Examples from Research
Thiemann and Goldstein (2001) implemented a social story intervention with five children with autism. Four social stories were created for the following four behaviors: securing attention, initiating comments, initiating requests, and contingent responses. In addition, three of the children's social stories contained hand-drawn pictures, whereas the other two had actual photographs.

Each child was paired with two typically developing children for two 30-minute sessions per week. During the first 10 minutes of each session, the target child read his or her social story and was then asked questions regarding the story to check for comprehension. Once comprehension was determined, cue cards were placed with the hand drawn pictures or photographs. The cue cards contained appropriate phrases matching the target social skill, such as the word "look" as an example of securing attention. The child used the cue cards and pictures to review the social story and guide role play.

After the social story was completed, the child was given 10 minutes of play time with the two typically developing children to allow the child to practice the target skills. This interactive time was videotaped, and the tapes were used immediately after play to provide feedback regarding the performance of the social skills. The five children showed an increase in appropriate social skills with the use of the social story and video feedback intervention.

Sansosti and Powell-Smith (2006) implemented social stories for three students with autism. Three different stories were written on a 6-inch by 8-inch paper. Each story was individualized to the child's particular needs; the topics were sportsmanship, maintaining conversations, and joining in play activities. The children's primary caregivers were instructed to have the child read and review the stories before coming to school each morning and after returning home each night. The children were observed three times a week to determine whether the social stories affected their performance. Two of the three children showed an increase in the use of the target behavior once social stories began, but the third child did not seemed to be influenced by the intervention.

Conclusion

Social stories are a simple, cost-efficient, and easy-to-implement option for social skills intervention. In addition, several options for social story intervention exist. For example, the story can be read once a day or several times per day. Another option is who reads the story; success has been documented with the child reading the story by herself and also with the child enlisting the help of an adult to read the story. Another option is the use of questions to determine story comprehension after reading. In addition, one can opt to provide additional prompts for the target behavior after reading the story. For example, Thiemann and Goldstein (2001) provided visual prompts by pointing to the text if the student was not performing the target behavior during the social interaction activity.

Although social stories are simple, versatile, and easy to implement, they also have some drawbacks. First, there is a limited amount of solid research regarding the topic. In addition, little research has been done to determine whether children with autism will generalize the use of the skills learned to other environments, or whether they will continue to use the skills once the social story is no longer being read before the activity.

Priming

Priming is a type of antecedent intervention in which the target behavior is practiced immediately before being performed. Priming sessions consist of verbal modeling and instruction to perform a behavior, followed by reinforcement of that behavior. Priming occurs in a situation similar to the criterion setting. The sessions are usually very short in duration. Activities and consequences used during priming sessions are selected before training, using preference assessment to ensure that they are enjoyable and reinforcing (Zanolli and Daggett 1998; Zanolli, Daggett, and Adams 1996). Priming sessions are then immediately followed by an activity session, during which the same target behaviors should be demonstrated. No prompts are given during activity sessions; however, reinforcers are used, and they may be delivered by peers or by teachers.

A variety of target skills have been addressed using priming interventions, most commonly nonverbal social skills and pivotal behaviors. Nonverbal social skills that have been facilitated with priming include eye contact, smiling, and giving and accepting affection. Targeted pivotal behaviors have included requesting attention and joint attention.

Examples from Research

Zanolli, Daggett, and Adams (1996) used priming with two preschool boys with autism. Initially, a preference assessment of toys was conducted by allowing the boys to play with several toys, moving from one toy to the next as they pleased. The duration for which each child stayed with each toy was noted, and the toys that were used longest were considered preferred toys or activities. Preference for rewards was also assessed. Eight items were placed on a tray and the child was asked to pick one. This was repeated three times, and the items selected most often were considered preferred rewards.

Once activities and rewards were identified, they were used for priming. Priming sessions were conducted before activity sessions. During priming sessions, the child and a trained peer were brought to a play area, and the teacher prompted the child to engage in several social initiation behaviors. For example, the child was told to smile, look at, and touch the peer in order to gain attention, and to use specific phrases such as "Look at me." If the child performed a target behavior, the peer provided verbal praise (e.g., "Way to go!") and a predetermined reward. Activity sessions immediately followed priming sessions. During activity sessions, the target child and peer were brought to a preferred activity, prompted to greet each other, and then left to play for 5 minutes with no teacher-delivered prompts or consequences. For both boys, when priming was introduced before activity sessions, the rate of social initiations during activity sessions increased.

Zanolli and Dagget (1998) also used priming with two young boys with autism to increase social initiations. The specific behaviors for one child were to say "look" and the teacher's name. The other child's target behaviors were to say "look," smile at the teacher, and say the teacher's name. Again, preference for rewards was determined by offering a tray of items and asking the child to select one, with the items selected most often used as rewards during priming sessions.

During priming sessions, the teacher modeled a behavior, prompted the student to perform that behavior, and then rewarded appropriate responses. Activity sessions, which were fine motor work times during class, were conducted after priming. No behaviors were prompted, but spontaneous social initiations were reinforced during activity sessions. Again, when priming sessions preceded activity sessions, the rate of social initiations increased for both boys.

Conclusion

Priming can offer an efficient way to provide social skills intervention, in that it can be implemented over short periods of time before the target activity. It can reduce the amount of prompts necessary to perform social skills appropriately during classroom activities. In addition, it can be combined with peer-mediated interventions (Zanolli, Daggett, and Adams 1996). However, no studies have determined whether or for how long the target social skills will continue to be used once priming sessions are no longer conducted. Also, no work has examined whether priming is effective in producing generalized responding across settings or persons.

Self-Management

Self-management is an intervention in which the child is taught to supervise and modify his or her own behavior (Heward 1987). There are many rationales that support the use of self-management strategies. First, the teacher cannot be with the student at all times, so many behaviors get overlooked. For example, an appropriate social skill performance may not be seen by the teacher and therefore not reinforced; it would be beneficial for the child to learn to manage that behavior without the need for the teacher to reward every occurrence. A second rationale is that if the child learns to change and modify her own behavior, it is more likely that the intervention will have an effect in several settings. Finally, by making the child responsible for supervising her own behavior, the teacher has more time to focus on teaching.

Two main types of self-management exist, self-monitoring and self-reinforcement (Heward 1987). Self-monitoring teaches a child how to observe his behavior. Specifically, the child learns to recognize when a behavior has been performed and to record that occurrence. For example, a child may place a sticker on a chart each time he uses an appropriate greeting. Self-reinforcement teaches the child not only to recognize when a behavior has been performed but also to reward himself for that behavior. For example, using self-reinforcement, a child may give himself a small piece of candy when he uses an appropriate greeting. Self-management has been used to address several social skills, such as responding to others and increasing variability in play and other activities.

Examples from Research

Newman, Buffington, and Hemmes (1996) implemented self-reinforcement with three teenage boys with autism. After the boys sat at a table and read a short story, the teacher asked if they had any questions to elicit discussion. At first, a token was given to each student by the teacher for each appropriate response in the discussion. The tokens could be exchanged for several preferred activities, such as listening to music or playing in the gym. The students were then taught to reinforce themselves, by simply telling them to take a token after every appropriate response. The students were then required to remember to take the tokens without reminders from the teacher. The percentage of appropriate conversations during self-reinforcement remained high as the intervention was systematically faded from teacher-directed to self-directed.

Newman, Reinecke, and Meinberg (2000) implemented self-reinforcement with three students with autism. Individuals with autism often have an extreme need for routine and sameness and therefore repeat activities. This was the target of the study; all three students were working on varying their behaviors and responses, but with different activities. For example, one child was playing with a robot and was instructed to vary the activities the robot engaged in; another student was told to vary the pictures she drew on her paper.

Before self-management was implemented, an instructor gave the children 10 tokens throughout the play activity, regardless of the use of variation during play. These tokens could be exchanged for items at a later time. During self-management, the students were simply reminded at the beginning of the activity not to be "boring." During the activity, they were reminded with statements such as, "Tell me something different" (Newman, Reinecke, and Meinberg 2000, 147). The children were also told to take an additional token when they showed variation. During the first six sessions, the instructor reminded the students to take the token when they demonstrated variation in play. For the remainder of the play, they were required to remember to take tokens on their own.

As a result, all three children showed more variability in their activities when they self-managed than before self-management was implemented. However, they did not consistently give themselves tokens for every appropriate behavior. In fact, no child was more than 60% accurate in giving himself a token after demonstrating a varied response. Regardless of the accuracy of self-management, the target behavior improved.

Conclusion

Only two studies were found that used self-management to enhance social skills. This is surprising, because the ability to recognize and manage one's own behavior would seem to be a central goal for students with autism (Koegel and Koegel 2006). Additionally, there is a substantial amount of empirical literature demonstrating the veracity of self-management strategies (Heward 1987). Therefore, future research should continue to examine the use of self-management strategies to foster social skills development for students with autism.

Peer-Mediated Interventions

The second category of interventions identified in Table 13.2 is peer-mediated interventions; this is the type of intervention used in most of the studies described in this chapter. Although the ability to interact with adults is an area of concern, it is also important that children with autism learn to develop, enjoy, and benefit from relationships with peers. Typically developing peers can be excellent models of appropriate social and play skills. In addition, with the current emphasis on inclusion, children with autism are being taught in classrooms with typically developing peers, creating a perfect match in the natural setting for peer-mediated intervention. In peer-mediated interventions, the child's peers facilitate the instruction of social skills. Usually, this involves teaching typically developing peers to engage in particular behaviors to support the student acquire the targeted social skills.

Peer-mediated interventions have been used to address a variety of target skills, most commonly play skills, conversation skills, pivotal behaviors, and cooperative social behaviors (see Table 13.2). Play skills that have been addressed via peer-mediated interventions include sportsmanship, sharing, turn-taking, imitating, and playing games. Targeted conversation skills have included giving directions, greeting, initiating conversation, commenting, giving compliments, and responding to others. Peer-mediated interventions have also targeted such pivotal behaviors as requesting and joint attention. Finally, cooperative social behaviors including following directions and helping others have been addressed.

The implementation of peer-mediated interventions involves several factors. The first is peer selection. Typically, peers are selected based on their ability to demonstrate the targeted social skills. Whereas teacher observation is the most commonly implemented assessment of students' social skill abilities, classmate ratings (Gonzalez-Lopez and Kamps 1997) and standardized assessments (Thiemann and Goldstein 2004) can also be used to identify students with appropriate social skills. Other important characteristics of peers that can successfully be involved in peer-mediated interventions include teacher compliance, regular school attendance, age-appropriate receptive language, age-appropriate expressive language, no previous negative experience between peer and target student, and nearness in chronological age to the target student (Garrison-Harrell, Kamps, and Kravits 1997; Kamps et al. 1999; Roeyers 1996).

The ratio of typically developing peers to target students can vary from 1:1 to as much as 5:1; however, involving more than one peer is most common.

Children with autism have difficulty generalizing skills, meaning that once they learn a skill under one set of circumstances, it is difficult for them to use that skill under different circumstances. Therefore, it may be beneficial to involve several typically developing peers to encourage generalization to many peers, not just one peer trainer.

Once peers have been selected, they must be taught the skills they will need for intervention. This teaching process will include modeling of the specific behaviors to be used with the child with autism. Students will also need the opportunity to role play in order to practice and receive teacher feedback on the use of the new skills. Other components of this teaching process could include presenting a video on autism so that peers gain a better understanding of the children they will be working with (Roeyers 1996), having the peers write cartoons depicting their roles in the peer intervention (Thiemann and Goldstein 2004), and holding a group discussion about human differences (Laushey and Heflin 2000).

Another factor is the setting of peer intervention. Peer-mediated interventions can be conducted in a variety of settings, including a regular education classroom, a segregated special education classroom, or common areas such as a cafeteria or playground (Garrison-Harrell, Kamps, and Kravitz 1997; Gonzalez-Lopez and Kamps 1997; Kamps et al. 1997).

Examples from Research

Peer-mediated interventions fall into three major categories: peers as partners, peers as trainers, and peers as tutors.

Peers as Partners

Interventions in which peers are play partners serve to create a positive social environment. Rather than teaching the peer to implement a particular social skills intervention, the peers are taught basic information about children with disabilities and/or basic interaction strategies, such as how to get the attention of a child with autism. For example, Roeyers (1996) trained a group of 48 children without disabilities to serve as playmates for 85 target children. The play partner training began with a video presentation and discussion about autism that was appropriate for the children's age and level of understanding. Next, the trainees participated in role-play in which an experimenter played with a child with autism and three peers played by themselves but were coached by the other children. The peers were taught to be persistent when interacting with children with autism, such as by staying at their eye level and trying many ways of getting their attention, but no specific techniques were taught. The peer trainees offered ideas during role play and then watched to see the result of their suggestions. After training, the typically developing peers came to the school of the children with autism for 30-minute play sessions. The peer was simply instructed to "Do your best to get him [or her] to play with you" (Roeyers 1996, 310). This treatment led to increased interaction between peers and target children. Also, the target children made and responded to more initiations after intervention.

Peers as Trainers

Peers can also serve in a more involved role as trainers. When peers serve as trainers, they implement social skill intervention strategies that are typically implemented by teachers or other adults. For example, peer trainers are taught to implement strategies such as prompting, ignoring inappropriate behaviors, asking questions to promote conversation, monitoring skills, and rewarding the target child for appropriate behaviors (Garrison-Harrell, Kamps, and Kravits 1997; Gonzalez-Lopez and Kamps 1997; Morrison et al. 2001). In some instances, peer trainers have been taught to use published social skills curricula (Garrison-Harrell, Kamps, and Kravits 1997) or to implement social stories (Kamps et al. 1999).

Gonzalez-Lopez and Kamps (1997) taught 12 typically developing peers to serve as social skills trainers to 4 children with autism. The peer trainers were taught behavior management skills such as demonstration, prompting, praise, providing assistance, and ignoring disruptive behavior. After learning the behavior management skills, peers came to a special education classroom for 20- to 25-minute sessions three to four times a week. During the first 10 minutes of the session, the teacher taught small groups, consisting of three peer trainers and one target child, specific social skills such as greetings, imitating, sharing, turn-taking, and requesting. The teacher modeled the skill, and then the children practiced the behavior with examples, while the teacher provided feedback. The last 10 to 15 minutes of the session was described as play time. During play time, the teacher did not interact with the peers. The children with autism showed longer and more frequent interactions with peers once the peers were trained in the behavior management skills.

Peers as Tutors

Peer tutoring involves pairing an academically strong and typically developing child with a target child with a disability for the purpose of tutoring the target child in an academic area. The premise is that social skills will be developed during the academic-focused tutoring sessions, because the social nature of tutoring allows for facilitation of social skills. Many variations of peer tutoring exist. For example, the child with the disability can server as both a tutor and a tutee, often with rotating roles. Also, tutoring can be done with a dyad or with groups.

Kamps and colleagues (1999) created peer networks consisting of one or two fourth-grade children with autism and five typically developing fourth-grade children who tutored first-grade students. The week before tutoring began, the peer network was given tutor training during five 10- to 15-minute sessions that consisted of modeling and role-playing tutoring skills. After training, the tutoring peer network met with six first-graders in need of academic assistance for 20-minute tutoring sessions. The session was divided into a 10-minute structured tutoring session for sight words, followed by 10 minutes of unstructured free time for both tutors and tutees. The students with autism interacted with peers during play sessions longer when the play session was preceded by tutoring than when it was not. The students with autism successfully implemented the tutoring steps that they were taught during training. Finally, the first-grader tutees made larger gains in sight word reading that than did peers not involved in the tutoring intervention.

Conclusions

Peer-mediated interventions have several strengths and weaknesses. A major goal of social skills intervention is appropriate use of social skills with peers; therefore, the intervention provides the natural setting for social skills by involving peers. The procedure is a natural fit for inclusive classrooms because it places children with disabilities with those without disabilities. Peers may benefit from the experience as well. Kamps and coworkers (1999) demonstrated that peer tutoring can have a positive academic effect on a typically developing tutee. In addition, higher acceptance and tolerance for human difference can result, because peer training often includes teaching the peer trainer about differences and disabilities (Laushey and Heflin 2000; Roeyers 1996).

Peer-mediated interventions also have limitations. Socially competent peers may not always be available or willing to participate in intervention. In addition, Scheuermann and Webber (2002) suggested that peer-mediated interventions may create a hierarchical relationship in which both the target child and the peer view the peer as superior. Last, many studies have found that the target child does not always continue to use the targeted skills at the same level after intervention is complete (Kamps et al. 1999; Morrison et al. 2001).

Pivotal Response Training

A total of three studies in our review described the interventions used as PRT strategies (Pierce and Schreibman 1995; 1997; Thorp, Stahmer, and Schreibman 1995). Earlier in this chapter we described pivotal behaviors as those social skills that serve as a foundation for the development of more complex language and social skills. These foundation skills may include such behaviors as sharing joint attention, establishing appropriate eye contact, and initiating and responding appropriately during social exchange. Once such social skills are taught, the student may possess the ability and motivation to achieve more sophisticated social goals, such as establishing relationships and friendships with peers and adults.

Pivotal response training, on the other hand, incorporates a series of intervention strategies that are designed to promote acquisition, generalization, and maintenance of targeted communication and social skills (see Koegel and Koegel, 2006, for a review). The instructional strategies used in PRT are not new nor specific to PRT. In fact, most of these strategies come with several decades of empirical research to verify their effectiveness. Techniques such as training loosely, teaching in criterion settings, teaching using multiple examples, and programming common stimuli between training and generalization settings have long been considered the hallmarks of best practice for promoting generalization of skills (see Stokes and Baer 1977 for a review). PRT offers a teaching approach in which these proven intervention strategies coalesce.

Examples from Research

Pierce and Schreibman (1995) examined the use of PRT strategies to teach social skills to two 10-year-old students who were diagnosed with autism. Both students were described by their teachers as socially unresponsive and possessing limited vocabularies. The social skills targeted for instruction included initiating conversations and play with peers and maintaining these interactions once initiated. Other behaviors, such as joint attention, engagement, and onlooking, were also measured to determine whether changes in these behaviors occurred as a result of the intervention on the targeted social skills.

Two 10-year-old peers who were described by their teachers as socially skilled were selected and taught to use a series of PRT strategies when interacting with the students with autism. During instruction trials, a child with autism and a peer were placed in an empty classroom with a number of preferred toys (e.g., balls, toy cars) and asked to play together. Examples of PRT strategies used by the peer during these play interactions to encourage social behavior are presented in Table 13.3. The results of this investigation indicated that peer PRT was effective in teaching such social skills as initiating and maintaining social interactions to these two children with autism; increases in joint attention also occurred for both children. The children generalized the social skills across toys, another classroom setting, and across untrained peers, indicating a level of robustness of the intervention. These results were replicated in a subsequent study by the same authors (Pierce and Schreibman 1997).

Conclusions

Although a limited number of PRT studies have addressed interventions to teach social skills to children with autism in school settings, the results are generally positive. Children in these studies were taught to initiate and maintain play and other social interactions. Concomitant increases in other pivotal responses, such as joint attention and appropriate engagement with toys,

TABLE 13.3

Examples of Pivotal Response Training Strategies Used by Peer Trainers to Encourage Social Skills in Students with Autism

Skill	Strategy
Paying attention	Ensure that the target child is attending before delivering a prompt or suggestion.
Child's choice	Give choices between different play activities to keep motivation high.
Model appropriate social behavior	Provide frequent and varied examples of appropriate play and social skills including verbal statements (e.g., saying "This game is fun") and complex play actions (e.g., acting out a script with dolls).
Reinforce attempts	Verbally reinforce any attempt at social interaction or functional play (e.g., while playing catch, say "great throw").
Narrate play	Provide descriptions of play actions and scripts (e.g., while playing with the oven, say "I'm going to cook the pizza").

occurred as a result of these interventions. Children also generalized these learned skills across settings, play partners, and toys. Future research should continue to evaluate the use of PRT strategies to teach social skills within school settings.

Video Modeling and Computer Instruction

The use of video as an instructional tool is as old as the technology itself, but new equipment is now widely available that allows parents and teachers to create individualized, instructional videos. Video modeling and computer instruction interventions have usually involved taping a short video sequence of the child with autism, a typically developing peer, or an adult performing the target social skills and then showing this video to the child before social opportunities (see Ayres and Langone, 2005, for a recent review). The sequence of events within the video is based on the child's communication abilities and the type of social skills being taught. Researchers have touted several useful characteristics of video modeling over in vivo peer modeling, including the convenience of demonstrating multiple learning situations and the availability of the video as many times as the child needs (Ayres and Langone 2005).

The instructional methods used in video modeling interventions are relatively straightforward, but the creation of the video modeling clip itself requires careful planning and sometimes a considerable time commitment. The development of a video modeling intervention depends first on creating the video clip. The video modeling clip can become quite technologically sophisticated, and a detailed discussion of the possible technological issues is not presented here. However, we have provided a discussion of some pertinent issues that are helpful to consider when planning a video modeling clip and intervention.

First, one must choose the models who will be used in the video. Models used in the research have included typically developing peers, the children with autism themselves, and adults. Video models have been created through capturing the natural interactions of children in social situations. Alternatively, peers and adults have role played social scripts. Video models have included the voices of the models or voiceovers added to the tape during the editing process. Others have created more sophisticated presentations by capturing video of a child who cannot independently say a complete sentence speaking the individual words (e.g., "want," "to," and "play") and then editing the video so that the child appears to have uttered the entire sentence (e.g., "Want to play?").

Second, one must decide which viewer perspective is to be shown in the modeling video. For example, one could videotape the face of a model who is initiating or responding to a social interaction. Alternatively, one could record the model engaged in an activity (e.g., playing with blocks) while simultaneously initiating ("Want to play?") or responding ("Thanks for sharing!") to a social interaction. The latter is the most common method used for social skills teaching, because there is often a need to see the model saying something within the context of a specific set of activities.

Third, one must plan for generalization of the targeted social skills. All of the research studies reviewed here have planned for generalization across activities, social skills, or settings. Some of the strategies used to promote generalization have included taping the videos in naturalistic settings and taping several different examples of the targeted social skill scenario. Creating the video in the same setting in which the intervention will take place could increase generalization from the video to natural settings (Stokes and Baer 1977).

Once the video model has been created, it must be edited to fit the child's instructional needs, and an instructional delivery strategy must be planned. Edited video models are usually short (e.g., 3 to 5 minutes) and are shown to the child using a computer monitor or television screen. Alternatively, a video model can be embedded into a computer instruction program and shown at structured times during the instructional sequence. In the overview section, we provide an example of this type of intervention.

Interventionists must consider how the video model should be presented to the child with autism. The child may watch the entire video model alone or accompanied by an adult. Adults may provide prompts or cues to the child. If the video is embedded into computer instruction, having an adult nearby may be helpful for children who encounter difficulty navigating the computer program. One of the strengths of video modeling is that the video may be stopped and restarted, as frequently as the instructor wishes, for the child to rehearse the social responses. Interventionists can utilize these pauses to ask comprehension questions. Questions can also be asked after the presentation of the video model. Alternatively, comprehension questions and cues may be built into the video modeling clip, using digital video editing software found on most personal computers.

Interventionists must also think about when to show the video model to children. Usually, this occurs immediately before the social situation in which the child experiences difficulties. This allows the child to practice the social skill immediately before the problematic situation. Additionally, researchers have usually shown the video model multiple times each day. Multiple viewings increase the child's exposure to appropriate models of the targeted social skill. Most interventions also involve replaying the video clip when the child does not correctly perform the social skill. Once the child is performing the targeted social skill in natural settings, he or she may need the video model less frequently or may need it only occasionally as a reminder. Therefore, a method for fading the intervention should be planned.

Another important consideration is how to reinforce the child for participation in the video modeling intervention. Some researchers have rewarded children with preferred edibles or other items for paying attention to the video and correctly performing the social skills. Others have included scenes within the video model that are presumed to be reinforcing. For instance, the sound of people clapping, cheering, a positive comment (e.g., "That's great!"), or a clip of a favorite cartoon can be inserted into the video after the target behavior model.

Examples from Research

Five recent studies have employed video modeling to teach social skills (Apple, Billingsley, and Schwartz 2005; Charlop-Christy and Daneshvar 2003; LeBlanc et al. 2003; Nikopoulos and Keenan 2003; Simpson, Langone, and Ayres 2004). The social skills most commonly addressed in video modeling interventions were conversation skills (Apple , Billingsley, and Schwartz 2005; Simpson, Langone, and Ayres 2004; Nikopoulos and Keenan 2003); cooperative social behaviors (Simpson, Langone, and Ayres 2004); nonverbal social skills (LeBlanc et. al. 2003); pivotal behaviors (LeBlanc et al. 2003); and play skills (Nikopoulos and Keenan 2003; Simpson, Langone, and Ayres 2004). In some cases, video instruction has addressed more than one type of social skill (LeBlanc et al. 2003; Simpson, Langone, and Ayres 2004; Nikopoulos and Keenan 2003).

Simpson and associates (2004) created a computer-based instruction package with video modeling to teach social skills to four elementary school students with autism. The target social skills in this study were sharing materials with peers during an activity, following a teacher's directions, and greeting peers. Two of the students, ages 5 and 6 years, had a diagnosis of mild autism and language delays. The other two students, also 5 and 6 years old, had a diagnosis of moderate autism and more significant communication impairments. The students were primarily educated in a special education classroom but attended some general education classes each day. Before receiving the intervention, the students either demonstrated the targeted social skills at low frequencies or could demonstrate the behaviors with prompts or teacher assistance.

This intervention was unique from others identified in the literature, because the researchers created the instructional sequences from specialized computer software called HyperStudio 3.2 (Robert Wagner Publishing, Inc. 1993–1998) and inserted video modeling clips into the computer instruction. The researchers created the video modeling clips by taping two typically developing peers engaged in the targeted social skills during various activities (e.g. arithmetic, reading, arts and crafts). Nonexamples of the target skills were also taped (i.e., a segment showing the peer students doing something other than the targeted social skill). The taping took place in the same classroom where the social skills were expected to occur in order to increase the possibility that the skills shown in the video would generalize to the classroom. The VHS-formatted video segments were edited into 4- to 6-second videos and inserted into the computerized instructional sequence. During the computer-based instruction, the students with autism sat in a study carrel in their classroom to minimize distractions. A teacher sat beside each student to assist the student in navigating through the computer program but did not provide further instruction. The students used the computer program for approximately 30 minutes each day.

The success of the intervention was variable, but all four students experienced increases in the targeted social behaviors. Three students showed dramatic and immediate improvement in unprompted social behaviors once the treatment was implemented. One student showed gradual yet positive improvements in the targeted social skills.

Conclusion

The use of video modeling seems to be an effective way to teach social skills to children with autism. This is not a surprising finding, because we know that children with and without autism can learn through observation. Although video modeling does not offer an entirely new instructional method, it does offer a new medium with some unique strengths. First, most children enjoy watching movies, and some children have more interest in learning social skills via video rather than in vivo modeling. Second, video modeling allows the interventionist to selectively narrow the range of stimuli presented. Third, many distinct scenarios can be incorporated into a video modeling intervention, which may contribute to greater generalization to natural settings. Fourth, video modeling allows the child to view the video and rehearse social skills as many times as he or she needs to learn a skill. It can be more difficult to obtain real-time peer models on a repeated basis. Fifth, video modeling is a consumer friendly intervention that can be easily incorporated into a child's daily routine. Indeed, the consumer availability and popularity of digital cameras, video recorders, and video-viewing and editing software on personal computers has increased the accessibility of video modeling. Even relatively inexpensive digital cameras are capable of creating short videos suitable for a video modeling intervention.

In reviewing the studies, there is little mention of the time required to create and edit the video modeling clips, but in our experience this process can take a considerable amount of preparation time. Of course, if a basic video model of a specific social skill is created, one might be able to the segment with other, similarly situated children. We propose that future research evaluate the effects of video modeling interventions on the social skills of a small group of children. Children with autism benefit most from one-on-one instruction, but the reality of most special education settings is that some small group instruction is necessary.

■ Overall Summary

Children with autism invariably display social skills difficulties. In fact, social skills deficits may be considered a central feature of autism (McConnell 2002). These difficulties are evident early in the developmental sequence and tend to persist if not intervened upon (Lovaas 1987). It is, therefore, essential that teachers and other clinicians be familiar with intervention strategies that can be used to successfully teach new social skills to children with autism.

In this chapter, we reviewed the single-case intervention literature targeting social skills difficulties in this population. Specifically, we focused on social skills interventions that were implemented in school settings over the last decade. We identified a variety of intervention strategies and categorized them in to four general groups: antecedent interventions, peer-mediated interventions, PRT, and video modeling and computer instruction. Antecedent interventions involve a variety of techniques such as priming, self-management, and social stories. As a group, antecedent interventions can be used to practice appropriate social behaviors to be used in subsequent social contexts. Peer-mediated interventions were the most frequently researched intervention strategy in this review. This is not surprising, because peers are readily present in classroom settings, and appropriately interacting with one's peers is a priority educational goal for students with autism. Three general types of peer-mediated intervention were described: peer tutoring, peer partners, and peer trainers. Overall, these strategies seem to produce benefits for peers as well as for the students with autism. A small number of studies have described their intervention strategies as PRT. PRT interventions involve established instructional strategies that are designed to promote acquisition, generalization, and maintenance of social skills. The PRT studies reviewed were successful in producing positive change in targeted social skills. Finally, there is a developing interest in the use of video modeling and computer instruction to teach social skills to students with autism. Video and computer instruction have also produced positive change in social skills and appear promising given the widespread availability of this technology today. These four categories of intervention strategies have been used to teach a wide variety of social skills to students with autism, including conversation skills, cooperative behaviors, pivotal behaviors, and play skills.

There are also a number of caveats concerning the literature reviewed in this chapter. For example, some of the intervention techniques, such as self-management and PRT, have received little attention, with very few papers have been published in the last decade. Researchers in the field of PRT have primarily focused on teaching communication skills to very young children, and this explains, to some degree, the limited amount of PRT research on social skills with school-aged children. Self-management techniques, on the other hand, have been demonstrated to be a very powerful instructional strategy that can be used across a wide variety of skills and types of disability. Self-management holds great promise as a social skills instructional tool, and future research should be encouraged in this area.

Other intervention strategies may need further research to firmly validate their usefulness. Social stories, for example, are a popular intervention strategy and are currently receiving much attention in the research literature. However, the results from these studies are mixed, indicating that further research and possible refinement of this intervention strategy is needed. Finally, there are very few studies reported here that rigorously assessed for maintenance and generalization of the social skills taught. One of the learning difficulties experienced by children with autism is an inability to transfer new skills to new situations, places, and persons. Additionally, long-term maintenance of the social skills taught over time was lacking in many studies. Ultimately, the effectiveness of a social skill intervention should hinge on its ability to produce durable and robust change in the skills targeted. Examining the generalization and maintenance of targeted social skills should be an absolute priority in future research in this area.

■ Acknowledgments

Preparation of this chapter was supported in part by a grant from the Institute of Education Sciences, U.S. Department of Education. However, the opinions expressed in this chapter do not express the opinions of that agency.

■ References

American Psychiatric Association. (2000). *Diagnostic and statistical manual of mental disorders* (4th ed., text revision). Washington: D.C.: Author.

Apple, A., Billingsley, F., and Schwartz, I. (2005). Effects of video modeling alone and with self-management on compliment-giving behaviors of children with high-functioning ASD. *Journal of Positive Behavior Interventions,* 7 (1), 33–46.

Austin, J.L. (1962; reprinted 1975). *How to do things with words* (eds. F.O. Urmson and M. Sbisa). Cambridge, Mass.: Harvard University Press.

Ayres, K., and Langone, J. (2005). Intervention and instruction with video for students with autism: A review of the literature. *Education and Training in Developmental Disabilities,* 40 (2), 183–196.

Baker, M., Koegel, R., and Koegel, L. (1998). Increasing the social behavior of young children with autism using their obsessive behaviors. *The Journal of the Association of Persons with Severe Handicaps,* 23 (4), 300–308.

Baldwin, D. (1991). Infants' contribution to the achievement of joint reference. *Child Development,* 62, 875–890.

Baron-Cohen, S. (1988). Social and pragmatic deficits in autism: Cognitive or affective? *Journal of Autism and Developmental Disorders,* 18, 379–402.

Baron-Cohen, S., and Cross, P. (1992). Reading the eyes: Evidence for the role of perception in the development of theory of mind. *Mind and Language,* 7, 172–186.

Bates, E., and MacWhinney, B. (1979). A functionalist approach to grammar. In *Developmental pramatics* (eds. E. Ochs and B. Schieffelin), pp. 167–211. New York: Academic Press.

Beadle-Brown, J., and Whiten, A. (2004). Elicited imitation in children and adults with autism: Is there a deficit? *Journal of Intellectual and Developmental Disability,* 29 (2), 147–163.

Bonniwell Haslett, B., and Samter, W. (1997). *Child communicating: The first 5 years.* London: Lawrence Erlbaum Associates.

Charlop-Christy, M., and Daneshvar, S. (2003). Using video modeling to teach perspective taking to children with autism. *Journal of Positive Behavior Interventions,* 5 (1), 12–21.

Doherty-Sneddon, G. (2003). *Children's unspoken language.* London: Jessica Kingsley.

Garrison-Harrell, L., Kamps, D., and Kravitz, T. (1997). The effects of peer networks on social-communicative behaviors for students with autism. *Focus on Autism and Other Developmental Disabilities*, 12, 241–254.

Gonzalez-Lopez, A., and Kamps, D.M. (1997). Social skills training to increase social interactions between children with autism and their typical peers. *Focus on Autism and Other Developmental Disabilities*, 12 (1), 2–15.

Gray, C.A. (2000). *The new social storybook.* Arlington, Tex.: Future Horizons.

Heward, W.L. (1987). Self-management. In *Applied behavior analysis* (eds. J.O. Cooper, T.E. Heron, and W.L. Heward), pp. 515–549. Columbus, Ohio: Merrill.

Kamps, D.M., Dugan, E., Potucek, J., and Collins, A. (1999). Effects of cross-age peer tutoring networks among students with autism and general education students. *Journal of Behavior Education,* 9 (2), 97–115.

Kamps, D., Kravitz, T., Gonzalez-Lopez, A., Kemmerer, K., Potucek, J., and Harrell, L. (1998). What do peers think? Social validity of peer-mediated programs. *Education and Treatment of Children,* 21, 107–134.

Kamps, D.M., Potucek, J., Lopez, A.G., Kravits, T., and Kemmerer, K. (1997). The use of peer networks across multiple settings to improve social interaction for students with autism. *Journal of Behavioral Education,* 7, 335–357.

Kanner, L. (1943). Autistic disturbances of affective contact. *Nervous Child,* 2, 217–250.

Koegel, R.L., and Keogel, L.K. (2006). *Pivotal response treatments for autism: Communication, social, and academic development.* Baltimore: Paul H. Brookes.

Kohler, F., Anthony, L., Steighner, S., and Hoyson, M. (2001). Teaching social interaction skills in the integrated preschool: An examination of naturalistic tactics. *Topics in Early Childhood Special Education,* 21 (2), 93–103.

Kohler, F., Strain, P., Hoyson, M., Davis, L., Donna, W., and Rapp, N. (1995). Using group-oriented contingency to increase social interactions between children with autism and their peers: A preliminary analysis of corollary supportive behaviors. *Behavior Modification,* 19, 10–32.

Laushey, K., and Heflin, L. (2000). Enhancing social skills of kindergarten children with autism through the training of multiple peers as tutors. *Journal of Autism and Developmental Disorders,* 30, 183–193.

LeBlanc, L., Coates, A., Daneshvar, S., Charlop-Christy, M., Morris, C., and Lancaster, B. (2003). Using video modeling and reinforcement to teach perspective-taking skills to children with autism. *Journal of Applied Behavior Analysis,* 36, 253–257.

Loncola, J., and Craig-Unkefer, L. (2005). Teaching social communication skills to young urban children with autism. *Education and Training in Developmental Disabilities,* 40 (3), 243–263.

Lord, C., Wagner, A., Rogers, S., Szatmari, P., Aman, M., Charman, T., et al. (2005). Challenges in evaluating psychosocial interventions for autistic spectrum disorders. *Journal of Autism and Developmental Disorders,* 35, 695–708.

Lovaas, I.O. (1987). Behavioral treatment and normal educational and intellectual functioning in young autistic children. *Journal of Consulting and Clinical Psychology*, 55, 3–9.

Machalicek, W., O'Reilly, M., Beretvas, N., Sigafoos, J., and Lancioni, G. (2007). A review of intervention strategies to reduce challenging behavior in school settings for students with autism spectrum disorders. *Research in Autism Spectrum Disorders*, 1, 229–246.

McConnell, S. (2002). Interventions to facilitate social interaction for young children with autism: Review of available research and recommendations for educational intervention and future research. *Journal of Autism and Developmental Disorders*, 32, 351–372.

Mey, J. (2001). *Pragmatics: An introduction* (2nd ed). Malden, Mass.: Blackwell.

Morrison, L., Kamps, D., Garcia, J., Parker, D., and Dunlap, G. (2001). Peer mediation and monitoring strategies to improve initiations and social skills for students with autism. *Journal of Positive Behavior Interventions*, 3, 237–250.

Newman, B., Buffington, D.M., and Hemmes, N.S. (1996). Self-reinforcement used to increase the appropriate conversation of autistic teenagers. *Education and Training in Mental Retardation and Developmental Disabilities*, 31, 304–309.

Newman, B., Reinecke, D., and Meinberg, D. (2000). Self-management of varied responding in three students with autism. *Behavioral Interventions*, 15, 145–151.

Nikopoulos, C., and Keenan, M. (2003). Promoting social initiation in children with autism using video modeling. *Behavioral Interventions*, 18, 87–108.

Ozonoff, S., and Miller, J. (1996). An exploration of right-hemisphere contributions to the pragmatic impairments of autism. *Brain and Language*, 52, 411–434.

Piaget, J. (1962). *Play, dreams, and imitation in childhood*. New York: Norton.

Pierce, K., and Schreibman, L. (1995). Increasing complex social behaviors in children with autism: Effects of peer-implemented pivotal response training. *Journal of Applied Behavior Analysis*, 28, 285–295.

Pierce, K., and Schreibman, L. (1997). Multiple peer use of pivotal response training to increase social behaviors of classmates with autism: Results from trained and untrained peers. *Journal of Applied Behavior Analysis*, 30, 157–160.

Roeyers, H. (1996). The influence of non-handicapped peers on the social interactions of children with a pervasive developmental disorder. *Journal of Autism and Developmental Disorders*, 26, 303–320.

Sainato, D., Goldstein, H., and Strain, P. (1992). Effects of self-evaluation on preschool children's use of social interaction strategies with their classmates with autism. *Journal of Applied Behavior Analysis*, 25, 127–141.

Sansosti, F.J., and Powell-Smith, K.A. (2006). Using social stories to improve the social behavior of children with Asperger syndrome. *Behavior Interventions*, 8 (1), 43–57.

Sansosti, F.J., Powell-Smith, K.A, and Kincaid, D. (2004). A research synthesis of social story interventions for children with autism spectrum disorders. *Focus on Autism and Other Developmental Disabilities*, 19 (4), 194–204.

Scattone, D., Wilczynski, S., Edwards, R., and Rabian, B. (2002). Decreasing disruptive behaviors of children with autism using social stories. *Journal of Autism and Developmental Disorders*, 32 (6), 535–543.

Scheuermann, B., and Webber, J. (2002). *Autism: Teaching does make a difference.* Belmont, Calif.: Wadsworth.

Simpson, A., Langone, J., and Ayres, K. (2004). Embedded video and computer based instruction to improve social skills for students with autism. *Education and Training in Developmental Disabilities*, 39, 240–252.

Stokes, T., and Baer, D. (1977). An implicit technology of generalization. *Journal of Applied Behavior Analysis*, 10, 349–367.

Strain, P., and Danko, C. (1995). Activity engagement and social interaction development in young children with autism. *Journal of Emotional and Behavioral Disorders*, 3(2), 108–134.

Thiemann, K.S., and Goldstein, H. (2001). Social stories, written text cues, and video feedback: Effects on social communication of children with autism. *Journal of Applied Behavior Analysis*, 34, 425–446.

Thiemann, K.S., and Goldstein, H. (2004). Effects of peer training and written text cueing on social communication of school-age children with pervasive developmental disorder. *Journal of Speech, Language, and Hearing Research*, 47, 126–144.

Thorp, D., Stahmer, A., and Schreibman, L. (1995). Effects of sociodramatic play training on children with autism. *Journal of Autism and Developmental Disorders*, 25, 265–282.

Vygotsky, L. (1978). *Mind in society: The development of higher psychological processes.* Cambridge, Mass.: Harvard University Press.

Weiss, M., and Harris, S. (2001). Teaching social skills to people with autism. *Behavior Modification*, 25, 785–802.

Williams, J., Whiten, A., and Singh, T. (2004). A systematic review of action imitation in autistic spectrum disorder. *Journal of Autism and Developmental Disorders*, 34 (3), 285–299.

Wolfberg, P. (1999). *Play and imagination in children with autism.* New York: Teachers College Press.

Zanolli, K., and Daggett, J. (1998). The effects of reinforcement rate on the spontaneous social initiations of socially withdrawn preschoolers. *Journal of Applied Behavior Analysis*, 31 (1), 117–125.

Zanolli, K., Daggett, J., and Adams, T. (1996). Teaching preschool age autistic children to make spontaneous initiations to peers using priming. *Journal of Autism and Related Disorders*, 26, 407–422.

14. Developmental Play Assessment and Teaching

Karin Lifter

The fact that there is a chapter on play activities in this volume attests to the importance of play in children's lives, and certainly in the lives of children with autism. Play activities are very much a part of the everyday activities of childhood. Caregivers provide children with the time and space to engage with the objects, people, and events of their cultures, probably because that is what children do; children will play with the toys, pots and pans, or sticks and stones that they have available to them. Play activities also provide a context for learning. Children acquire knowledge about the permanence of objects, the particular characteristics of objects, and the relationships between objects and people in their worlds as they move toys from place to place and begin to enact the everyday activities of their cultures. Finally, developments in play contribute to developments in language and social competence. Children talk about, and interact about, what they know about. Developments in language depend, in part, on increases in children's knowledge about objects and events (Lifter and Bloom 1989; McCune 1995). Social development for young children includes the coordination of social behavior and play activities (Ariel 1992; Eckerman, Davis, and Didow, 1989; Howes and Matheson, 1992). Farmer-Dougan and Kaszuba (1999) and Pierce-Jordan and Lifter (2005) identified relationships between complexity of play and social developmental functioning.

Children who have difficulty learning also have difficulties in learning to play, which is the case for children with autism. Researchers have described the play activities of children with autism as limited in frequency and variety, with their play characterized by the functional use of objects and restrictions in symbolic quality (Blanc et al. 2005; Brown and Whiten 2000; Charman et al., 1998; Fewell and Kaminski 1988; Libby et al. 1995; Rutherford and Rogers 2003; Sigman and Mundy, 1987; Ungerer and Sigman 1981). See Jarrold (2003), Jarrold, Boucher, and Smith (1993), Williams (2003), and Wulff (1985) for reviews of play of children with autism. These children's difficulties in learning to play also contribute to, and are reflected by, their difficulties in learning language and engaging in social interactions (e.g., Barrett, Prior, and Manjiviona 2004; Blanc et al. 2005; Brown and Whiten 2000; Lewis et al. 2000; Ungerer and Sigman

1981; and Wing et al 1977). As a result of limitations in play, many intervention studies have focused on teaching play activities to children with autism; these are described later in this chapter (also see reviews by Rogers 2005; Stahmer, Ingersoll, and Carter 2003, and van Berckelaer-Onnes 2003).

Teaching play activities includes attention to *what we teach* and *how we teach*. The purpose of this chapter is to describe the connection of developmental assessment to what we teach and how we teach in play interventions for young children with autism. An understanding of this connection requires a description of play that is based on developments in play. Such descriptions, combined with the procedures of behavioral assessment, allow for an analysis of what the child knows and is ready to learn when selecting what to teach. Such an analysis also contributes to child-focused interventions in determining how we teach, inasmuch as child-focused interventions build on a child's interest and a child's readiness to learn.

For this purpose, a brief overview of descriptions of play and their links to intervention is presented first. Then follows a rationale for considering play as a developmental domain, to set the stage for an understanding of more developmentally specific categories of play and the basis for developmental assessment of play. Evidence in support of the approach of linking developmental assessment to teaching is presented next, in terms of determining what we teach and how we teach play activities. Finally, a summary and future directions are offered.

■ Overview of Descriptions of Play
   and their Links to Intervention

This section presents a general overview of the play intervention studies to provide a context for developmental play assessment linked to teaching. Three groups of studies are presented, according to how play is regarded in selecting what to teach to children. Comprehensive reviews of the play intervention studies are available (Rogers 2005; Stahmer, Ingersoll, and Carter 2003; and van Berckelaer-Onnes 2003).

The intervention studies are related to how play is described, and considerable variation exists in the conceptualizations of play among these studies. The first group of play intervention studies is based on play as a prosocial activity. In the second group, play is described in terms of broad categories of play, with an emphasis on interventions in symbolic play, sociodramatic play, and play scripts. The third group is based on more specific developmentally based categories of play. Although all three approaches have been used successfully in play intervention studies with children with autism, it is the third approach that underlies the connection of developmental assessment to teaching play activities to young children with autism

Play as a Prosocial Activity of Childhood

The approach that views play as a prosocial activity considers play as the natural activity of childhood. It is based on what children do, and it includes attention to the toys and activities of their cultures. Many intervention studies use this approach, selecting a variety of appealing toys (i.e., toys the child is interested in) or directing the child to play in a particular play area (e.g., the kitchen area) and then directly teaching a variety of play activities with these toys or in this area (Ballard and Medland 1986; Eason, White, and Newsom 1982; Haring 1985; Moran and Whitman 1985; Morrison et al. 2002; Nikopoulos and Keenan 2004; Rogers 1988; Stahmer and Schreibman 1992; Wehman 1975). For example, Haring (1985) taught children what could be done with toys, such as "flying" an airplane. Morrison and colleagues (2002) used photographic activity schedules to foster play activities in specific play areas. In short, the objectives for intervention were determined based on what could be done with appealing toys or what was appropriate play in a particular play area. Despite the difficulties in teaching play skills to these children, the studies demonstrated the value of this approach in terms of enhancing skills in a variety of age-appropriate behaviors (e.g., Rogers 2005) and diminishing maladaptive behaviors (e.g., (Eason, White, and Newsom 1982; Stahmer and Schreibman 1992).

A related set of studies focused on teaching play scripts—play that is similar to the play of the children's peers without disabilities (D'Ateno, Mangiapanello, and Taylor 2003; Jahr, Eldevik, and Eikeseth 2000; Reagon, Higbee, and Endicott 2006; Thomas and Smith, 2004). In certain cases, the focus was more on the methods of intervention (e.g., video modeling in D'Ateno, Mangiapanello, and Taylor, 2003, and Reagon, Higbee, and Endicott, 2006).

The limitations of this approach center on teaching to the toys or teaching activities in a play center or teaching particular scripts even though the children are learning prosocial activities. According to some researchers (Libby et al. 1998), the behaviors children demonstrate are often exact replicas of what they have been taught. Moreover, generalization is limited. In considering the toys when deciding what to teach, interventionists run the risk of teaching children to perform a series of activities rather than enabling them to understand and build on their emerging knowledge, which also should enhance generalization. The assumption underlying developmental assessment is that learning and generalization are enhanced with the selection of target activities based on the child's developmental readiness to learn them.

Play Interventions Based on Broad Categorical Descriptions of Play

For a large number of intervention studies, researchers taught children activities based on broad categorical descriptions of play, including symbolic play, play scripts, and sociodramatic play. For the most part, researchers targeted play activities from these broad categories because of the difficulties and limitations in symbolic play, age-appropriate play, and play involving social components observed in young children with autism. These broad categories were meaningful in the child development literature, providing a source of descriptions of play to inform intervention studies.

In developmental terms, the broad categories of play follow the order of manipulative play in the infant/young toddler, symbolic play in the older toddler, and then sociodramatic play in the preschooler. Piaget (1962) described developments in play in terms of manipulative/sensorimotor play, symbolic play, and games with rules. The terms *manipulative play* and *symbolic play* became widely used in the play literature, especially regarding the play of young children. Based on these descriptions, the limitations in symbolic play of children with autism were easy to identify. The same occurred for descriptions of sociodramatic play, which Smilansky (1968) introduced in her account of the limited sociodramatic play observed in children from disadvantaged backgrounds. Because of the importance of symbolic play in development and its connections to developments in language, and because of the limitations in symbolic play observed in children with autism and other developmental disabilities, many intervention studies have focused on teaching symbolic play, play scripts, and/or sociodramatic play (Fox and Hanline 1993; Goldstein and Cisar 1992; Kasari, Freeman, and Paparella 2006; Kim et al. 1989; Stahmer 1995; Thorp, Stahmer, and Schreibman 1995).

Although these studies demonstrated considerable success in teaching play activities to children, there is a potential limitation to this approach. The activities within each of the broad categories of play—symbolic play and sociodramatic play—may be of very different levels of developmental complexity. The descriptive studies of children's play activities, discussed later, revealed that the broad categories of symbolic play, and the earlier-appearing category of manipulative play, can be more finely differentiated. In other words, symbolic play is not a homogeneous category but a broad category of play that covers 2 to 3 years in development and can be described in terms of several subcategories. Studies have demonstrated a sequential order to the subcategories of symbolic play, with examples presented in Table 14.1.

Play Interventions Based on Specific,
Developmentally Based Categories of Play

The third approach to interventions in play for children with autism is based on regarding play in terms of specific, developmentally sequenced categories representing developmentally ordered components of the broad categories of play. These more differentiated categories were generated from empirically based, descriptive studies of children's play activities. In certain cases, procedures of behavioral assessment were applied to the categories to develop a method for determining a child's progress in play, for the purposes of developmental assessment.

An example of a play intervention based on the identification of developmentally based categories of play was provided by Lifter and colleagues (1993), who incorporated developmental specificity (DevSp) directly into the identification of target activities. These authors used the Developmental Play Assessment (DPA) (Lifter 2000; Lifter et al. 1988) to identify DevSp activities to teach to preschoolers with autism. They identified two play categories in the DPA that would be regarded as symbolic play activities, but with different cognitive requirements. In *Child-as-Agent* activities, the child extends an object to a doll figure in a pretend gesture (e.g., child extends an empty cup to doll's mouth to give it a drink). In *Doll-as-Agent* activities, the child acts as if the doll were animate and could act for itself (e.g., child puts cup in doll's hand for doll to give itself a drink; child moves a figure to load objects into a truck).

Preschoolers who participated in the study by Lifter's group were selected based on their readiness to learn Child-as-Agent (i.e., DevSp) play activities. Prerequisite skills for the contrasting Doll-as-Agent activities were completely absent in the play of these children. The Doll-as-Agent category is considered significantly more advanced than the Child-as-Agent play category (Watson and Fischer, 1977), although it was determined to be age-appropriate for their typically developing peers. Participating children were taught activities from both categories in a sequential treatments design. Results supported faster acquisition and greater generalization for the activities from the Child-as-Agent play category, in contrast to the Doll-as-Agent play category, even though both categories would be subsumed under the broad category of symbolic play.

The usefulness of developmentally based categories of play affords the identification of more finely tuned target categories for determining what to teach in a play intervention. In the 1993 study by Lifter and associates, differentiations within symbolic play proved to be important in terms of the children's acquisition of play activities. Before the approach of developmental assessment is reviewed in greater detail, the theoretical and empirical rationale for considering play as a developmental domain is presented in the next section.

■ Play as a Developmental Domain

There are theoretical and empirical bases for developmental assessment linked to intervention. Both depend on the consideration of play as a developmental domain, which yields descriptions of play that are linked to changes in development. An understanding of play as a developmental domain allows for the assessment of play when identifying what to teach to children with autism. It also informs decisions concerning procedures of how to teach.

Theoretical Bases for Play as a Developmental Domain

Lifter and Bloom (1998) argued for a definition of play that affords an analysis of play activities both for assessment and for intervention activities. They claimed that play is not only an expression of what children know but also contributes to learning in development. They argued for combining two seemingly contradictory traditions—play for fun and play for learning.

The assumption that play contributes to expression and learning in development has a long history in the cognitive/developmental literature. Piaget (1962, 93) described children's play as a "happy display of known actions," a definition derived from his notion of play as assimilation. Axline (1947, 9) described play as "the child's natural medium of self-expression." These descriptions have pervaded our contemporary understanding of play as an activity for fun (e.g., Elkind 1990).

A less widely held view of play, but one that is essential to the assumption of play as a developmental domain, is the perspective that play also serves an interpretive function in development. This perspective is related to Montessori's (1967, 180) view of play as "the child's work" and Vygotsky's (1978) view of play "as an adaptive mechanism promoting cognitive growth during the preschool years" (see Rubin, Fein, and Vandenberg 1983, 709).

Lifter and Bloom contributed to a conceptualization of play that incorporates both perspectives. They proposed a theoretical perspective that incorporates the "work" function of play as an activity for acquiring new knowledge. In their view, "actions in play display what the child already knows . . . (i.e., play as expression) . . . but also display what the child is currently thinking about *in efforts to make sense of ongoing events for advancing knowledge*" (italics added) (Lifter and Bloom 1998, 164). They emphasized the fundamental function of play for acquiring new knowledge, in that play serves as a context for interpreting (i.e., making sense of) new events. Lifter and Bloom's (1998) definition included the wide expanse of object-related activities in which infants and young children engage and was not limited to pretense play, as in many other definitions (e.g., Rubin, Fein, and Vandenberg, 1983). Such activities are important to consider for young children with disabilities. They provide the foundation for the knowledge base that is expressed with early words (Lifter and Bloom, 1989).

Empirical Bases for Play as a Developmental Domain

The empirical bases for play as a developmental domain come from two main sources of evidence. First, the many descriptive studies of the play of children

developing with and without disabilities contributed categories of development that could be sequenced to reveal progress in development. Second,
many descriptive studies provided evidence for systematic relationships
between developments in play and developments in other domains, with particular attention to language and social development.

Play of Children without Disabilities

Developments in children's play with objects were identified, for the most part,
in longitudinal and cross-sectional descriptive studies during the 1970s, 1980s,
and 1990s (Belsky and Most 1981; Fenson et al. 1976; Fenson and Ramsay 1980;
Garvey 1977; Lowe 1975; Lifter and Bloom 1989; McCune 1995; Nicolich 1977;
Watson and Fischer 1977). These studies reported that the categories formed
a developmentally ordered sequence and resulted in the description and organization of children's play into developmental taxonomies of play. The reader
is referred to Rubin and colleagues (1983) for a review of the early descriptive
studies.

Examples of these taxonomies, for purposes of illustration, are presented
in Table 14.1. The correspondences among the various sets of categories in the
table are approximate. The authors of these studies reported evidence of the
developmental sequencing of play categories. The evidence in support of the sequences included, for example, scalogram analysis (Belsky and Most 1981) and
quantitative criteria for emergence and achievement (Lifter and Bloom, 1989).

As can be seen in Table 14.1, the descriptive studies yielded much more
detailed descriptions of play activities than the broad categories of manipulative play and symbolic play (Belsky and Most 1981; Fenson et al. 1976;
Fenson and Ramsay 1980; Garvey 1977; Lifter and Bloom 1989; Lowe 1975;
McCune 1995; Nicolich 1977). In general, they identified the following developmental course of play. Infants' early play with objects consists of in-
discriminative actions on objects, such as picking up and dropping and/or
mouthing all objects, taking configurations of objects apart in order to take
hold of the objects, or simply picking up and discarding objects (categories
such as mouthing, simple manipulation, banging, and separations of configurations). Eventually, by approximately their first birthday, infants begin
to put configurations of objects back together again, moving objects from
place to place, including in and out of containers (categories such as relational play, given constructions, and imposed generic constructions). They
begin to demonstrate knowledge of conventional characteristics of individual
objects, for example, touching a brush to their hair (enactive naming, presymbolic actions). As early toddlers, children begin to exploit the unique
physical properties of objects in the relationships they construct, such as
stacking cups and blocks (categories such as relational-accommodative and
imposed specific: inanimate constructions). They begin to relate objects

TABLE 14.1

*Sample of Developmentally Sequenced Categories of Play Activities**

Belsky and Most 1981	Fenson et al. 1976	Nicolich 1977	Watson and Fischer 1977	Lifter and Bloom 1989
Manipulative Play				
Mouthing				
Simple manipulation	Banging			Separations
Functional				Separations
Relational	Relational-simple			
Functional-relational	Relational-accommodative			Given constructions; Imposed generic constructions; Imposed specific: inanimate constructions
	Relational-grouping			
Enactive naming		Presymbolic		
Symbolic Play				
Pretend self	Symbolic acts	Autosymbolic	Self as agent	
Pretend other	Symbolic acts	Single-scheme symbolic games	Passive other agent	Imposed specific: animate surrogate
Substitution			Passive substitute agent	

Sequence pretend	Sequential acts	Combinatorial symbolic games: single-scheme combinations	
		Combinatorial symbolic games: multischeme combinations	
Sequence pretend substitution		[Planned symbolic games]	
Double substitution		[Planned symbolic games]	Active other agent

*Correspondences among sets of categories are approximate.

to themselves in a pretend manner, such as drinking from a cup (pretend self, symbolic acts, autosymbolic, self-as-agent). Eventually, they begin to extend pretend activities to dolls and caregivers (pretend other, symbolic acts, passive other agent, and imposed specific: animate surrogate constructions), and they exploit the unique conventional properties of objects and people in the relationships they construct (e.g., using a tool to fix a car). They begin to substitute one object for another (substitution, as in using a bowl for a hat). They learn to link activities into chains of events that demonstrate increasing levels of planning (sequence pretend, sequential acts, combinatorial symbolic). As preschoolers, children attribute animacy to doll figures (active other agent), and they engage in sociodramatic and fantasy play. Researchers explained these developments in terms of developments in knowledge of objects in general as well as knowledge of specific objects, increases in mental representation (Lifter and Bloom 1989), and developments in the symbolic function (Nicolich 1977).

Play of Children with Developmental Delays and Disabilities

Researchers used similar descriptions to examine the play activities of children with autism and other developmental delays and disorders. They found that, along with differences in the frequency and variety of play activities and a predominance of manipulative activities, pretend play and the typical activities of the preschool-aged child were limited and often nonexistent (Fewell and Kaminski 1988; Hill and McCune-Nicolich 1981; Libby et al. 1998; Malone, Stoneman, and Langone 1994; Odom 1981; Quinn and Rubin 1984; Rogers 1988; Sigman and Mundy 1987; Stagnitti, Unsworth, and Rodger 2000; Ungerer and Sigman 1981; Williams, Reddy, and Costall 2001; and Wing et al. 1977).

Relationships between Developments in Play and Developments in Other Domains

Empirical support for play as a developmental domain also can be derived from studies in which changes in play are compared with changes in other developmental domains. If systematic relationships exist, then it can be assumed that developmental changes are occurring in play. Relationships between play and language were identified in many studies, both for children without disabilities (e.g., Lifter and Bloom 1989; McCune 1995) and for children with autism (e.g., Blanc et al. 2005; Lewis et al. 2000; Ungerer and Sigman 1981; Wing et al. 1977).

Support for a relationship between developments in play and social interaction for preschoolers with and without autism comes from research by Pierce-Jordan and Lifter (2005). They categorized social interaction independently of descriptions in play. Such descriptions as parallel play and coordinated play, which were first used in Parten (1932) and continue to be used widely, could not be used to describe play given confounding of social interaction with quality of play. Pierce-Jordan and Lifter determined that the complexity of social interaction for preschoolers with and without autism varies as a function of the children's developmental levels of play. Additional support for a relationship between play and social development can be found in Barrett, Prior, and Manjiviona (2004) and in the review by Jordan (2003).

In summary, there is considerable empirical evidence in support of play as a developmental domain. What follows is a presentation of the connection between play as a developmental domain and procedures of developmental assessment to determine what we teach.

■ Linking Developmental Assessment
to Teaching: *What We Teach*

Developmental assessment of play requires an understanding of play as a developmental domain—a domain in which progressive change can be seen as a result of children's active engagement with the people and events of their environment. Given this understanding, progressive change can be described and evaluated for the purposes of assessing activities to determine what and how to teach. This section describes procedures for developmental assessment. It also reviews the empirical evidence for developmental assessment linked to interventions in play. For the purposes of this section, the DPA is highlighted. It is one of the few assessment instruments that have been used to link developmental assessment to teaching in play interventions for young children with autism. Procedures for developmental assessment for language interventions can be found in Casby (2003).

Procedures of Developmental Assessment

Both qualitative and quantitative procedures are required for developmental assessment. The qualitative procedures require a determination of qualitatively different categories of play. The quantitative procedures require criteria for determining progress in development. Both require procedures of behavior assessment.

Qualitative Procedures

Table 14.1 presents the categories of play, also known as taxonomies of play, that were identified in several descriptive studies of children's play. Many of these taxonomies, in turn, have formed the basis for a number of play assessment scales, such as the Developmental Scale of Infant Play, by Belsky and Most (1981), presented in Vondra and Belsky (1991); the Symbolic Play Test, by Lowe and Costello, reported in Power and Radcliffe (1991, 2000); the Symbolic Play Scale, by Westby (1980), reported in (Westby, 1991, 2000); and the Developmental Play Assessment (DPA) Instrument, reported by Lifter (Lifter

2000; Lifter et al. 1988). (See Garfinkle 2004, and Lifter, 1996, for an overview of play assessment tools).

The DPA is featured here. It is based on the assumption of developmental readiness—that a child's readiness to learn qualitatively different categories of play activities can be determined, based on a systematic assessment of the child's play activities. The assessment is based on a 30-minute sample of spontaneous play activities with four groups of toys, in the presence of a familiar adult. The child's activities are evaluated according to qualitatively different categories that follow a developmental sequence (Table 14.2). Several of these categories (Presentation Combinations, General Combinations, Specific Physical Combinations, Child-as-Agent, and Specific Conventional Combinations) represent the sequence reported in Lifter and Bloom's (1989) longitudinal study of children's play and provide the backbone of the sequence presented in Table 14.2. (The categories from Lifter and Bloom (1989) were given more transparent names for the DPA.) The remaining categories were integrated into the foregoing sequence based on reports of several other studies (Belsky and Most 1981; Fenson et al. 1976; Fenson and Ramsay 1980; Lowe 1975; McCune 1995; Nicolich 1977; Watson and Fisher 1977).

Quantitative Procedures

Quantitative procedures are used to establish criteria for assessing a child's progress in play, and different assessments use different procedures. For the DPA, progress through the sequence is determined based on the quantitative criteria applied to each category. These criteria, derived from Lifter and Bloom (1989), are based on the frequency of the activities in each category and the variety of different examples of the category that are expressed. They impose a relative degree of certainty regarding how well the child knows a category of play. *Mastery* requires a minimum frequency of 10 activities, with at least four examples of the category within the 10 activities (e.g., four examples of the category "Presentation" could be "puts drivers in truck," "nests the nesting cups," "puts pieces in puzzle," and "puts beads in bead bowl"). The criteria for *emergence* are less stringent (i.e., frequency of four or more activities, including at least two exemplars); accordingly, there is less certainty, based on quantitative analysis, that the child knows the kind of activity represented by the category. Finally, with *absence* (frequency of three or fewer activities, with two or fewer exemplars), there is even less certainty. The foregoing quantitative procedures allow for a systematic assessment of progress in the developmental sequence of play categories that can be linked directly to the selection of target intervention categories and activities in terms of what to teach.

Table 14.3 presents the play assessment results of three children with pervasive developmental disorders who participated in an intervention study (Lifter et al. 2005). What can be seen in the table is how a 30-minute sample

TABLE 14.2

Sequence and Definitions of Play Categories Used in the Developmental Play Assessment*

Level	Categories	Definitions
I	Indiscriminate Actions	All objects are treated alike
II	Discriminative Actions on Single Objects	Differentiates among objects, preserving their physical or conventional characteristics (e.g., rolls round objects, squeezes stuffed animals)
	Takes-apart Combinations†	Separates configurations of objects (e.g., takes all pieces out of puzzle)
III	Presentation Combinations	Recreates combinations of objects according to their presentation configuration (e.g., puts puzzle pieces into puzzle, nests the nesting cups)
	General Combinations	Creates combinations of objects that result in simple, nonspecific configurations such as container/contained relationships (e.g., puts beads and puzzle pieces in cup)
	Pretend Self	Relates objects to self, indicating a pretend quality to the action (e.g., brings empty cup to mouth to drink)
IV	Specific Physical (physical attributes)	Preserves unique physical characteristics of objects in configuration (e.g., stacks nesting cups, strings beads)
V	Child-as-Agent	Extends familiar actions to doll figures, with child as agent of the activity (e.g., extends cup to doll's mouth)
	Specific Conventional (conventional attributes)	Preserves the unique conventional characteristics of objects in the configuration (e.g., pours from pitcher into cup, "fixes" car with wrench
VI	Single-Scheme Sequences	Extends same familiar action to two or more figures (e.g., extends cup to doll, to stuffed bear, to interactant)
	Substitutions	Uses one object to stand for another (e.g., puts bowl on head for a hat)
VII	Doll-as-Agent	Moves doll figures as if they were capable of action (e.g., moves figure to load blocks into a truck)
	Multi-scheme Sequences	Extends different actions to same figure (e.g., feeds doll with spoon, wipes with cloth, puts it to bed)

TABLE 14.2 *(continued)*

Level	Categories	Definitions
VIII	Sociodramatic Play	Adopts various familiar roles in play theme (e.g., plays house and assigns the various roles)
	Thematic Fantasy Play	Adopts roles of fantasy characters (e.g., plays "Wonder Woman" and assigns the various roles)

*The sequence reported here is a synthesis of the categories reported in many descriptive studies of play, with the categories identified in Lifter and Bloom (1989) forming the backbone of the sequence.

†Represents a category that is not counted when high frequencies of activities from subsequent categories are apparent.

From Lifter, K. (2000). Linking assessment to intervention for children with developmental disabilities or at-risk for developmental delay: The Developmental Play Assessment (DPA) instrument. In *Play diagnosis and assessment* (2nd ed) (eds. K. Gitlin-Weiner, A. Sandgrund, and C.E. Schaefer), pp. 228–261. New York: Wiley; and Lifter, K., Edwards, G., Avery, D., Anderson, S.R., and Sulzer-Azaroff, B. (1988). The Developmental Play assessment (DPA) instrument. Unpublished manuscript.

of play activities from three preschool-aged children with autism can be analyzed qualitatively and quantitatively to determine categories of play that are "mastered," those that are "emerging," those that are "next step" categories, and those that are too difficult for a given child at the time of the assessment. Those categories that are evaluated at the emerging level are the ones that are targeted for intervention.

Empirical Evidence for Developmental Play Assessment Linked to Teaching

There is both direct and indirect evidence linking developmental assessment to determinations of what kinds of play activities to teach to children. Direct evidence comes from studies in which some kind of developmentally based evaluation of the child was included when determining what to teach. The indirect evidence comes from post hoc analyses of some of the intervention studies.

Direct Evidence for Developmental Play Assessment and Teaching

Lifter and associates provided direct evidence linking developmental assessment of play to determining what to teach in play interventions. These authors

TABLE 14.3

*Play Profiles of Three Children with Pervasive Developmental Disorders**

Level	Play Categories	Jill	Mickey	Ted
I	*Indiscriminative:* Treats all objects alike			
II	*Discriminative:* Differentiates single objects	6/17 (M)	3/22 (E)	3/6 (E)
III	*Presentation Combinations:* Reassembles presentation	6/36 (M)	5/13 (M)	3/11 (E)
	General Combinations: Assembles undifferentiated configurations	5/26 (M)	4/55 (M)	7/28 (M)
	Pretend Self: Relates objects to the self in pretend	1/1 (A)*	— (A)*	2/3 (A)*
IV	*Specific Physical Combinations:* Preserves physical features in configuration	5/32 (M)	2/23 (E)*	3/12 (E)*
V	*Child-as-Agent:* Extends familiar actions to dolls, figures	3/5 (E)*	3/11 (E)*	3/7 (E)*
	Specific Conventional Combinations: Preserves conventional features in configuration	— (A)*	— (A)	— (A)*
VI	*Single-Scheme Sequences:* Extends same action to multiple figures	— (A)	— (A)	— (A)
	Substitutions: Uses one object as substitute for another	— (A)	— (A)	— (A)
VII	*Doll-as-Agent:* Attributes actions to dolls, figures	— (A)	— (A)	— (A)
	Multischeme Sequences: Extends different actions to dolls, figures	— (A)	— (A)	— (A)
VIII	*Sociodramatic/Fantasy Play:* Role adoption in play	— (A)	— (A)	— (A)
	TOTAL CODABLE ACTIONS	117	124	67

*Indicates categories of play targeted for intervention.

A, Absent or anything less than emergence; E, emergence (2 types, 4 frequencies); M, mastery (4 types, 10 frequencies).

From Lifter, K., Ellis, J., Cannon, B., and Anderson, S.R. (2005). Developmental specificity in targeting and teaching play activities to children with pervasive developmental disorders. *Journal of Early Intervention*, 27 (4), 247–267.

(2005) used the term *developmental specificity* (DevSp) to describe target play activities that they derived from developmental assessment. In these studies, the DPA was used to determine children's progress in play and to identify target categories for intervention. The results from their 1993 study, discussed earlier, supported faster acquisition and greater generalization when the target categories were identified at the "next step" level, rather than at the age-appropriate level of symbolic play. Although age-appropriate activities were identified in the play of peers, these activities were too difficult for the children with developmental disabilities to learn. Their 2005 results supported acquisition of target play activities from categories of play at adjacent levels—"emergent" and "next step"—in the DPA sequence. The play assessment results for the three children who participated in the latter study are presented in Table 14.3. The children in both studies demonstrated acquisition of new play activities within the target categories. These findings provided support for the importance of developmental specificity when targeting and teaching play activities.

Other studies have also taken developmental considerations into account in the selection of target play activities; an example is Stahmer's 1995 study of children with autism.

Indirect Evidence for Developmental Play Assessment and Teaching

In post hoc analyses of some of the intervention studies in which broad categories of play activities were targeted, the importance of developmental considerations can be seen in the selection of what to teach. For example, the children in Haring's 1985 study were reported to have considerable developmental delays and were selected as participants because they displayed low rates of object manipulation and minimal use of language (i.e., some words). The target activities Haring chose appeared to focus on teaching children the particular properties of objects, such as "flying" an airplane. Because such activities are among the earliest object-related play activities that children learn (Belsky and Most 1981), one could argue that these target activities were developmentally relevant for teaching to young children with substantial developmental delays.

Similarly, Stahmer (1995) taught symbolic play activities to children with autism who were reported to have language levels of at least 2.5 years. Because symbolic play activities are among the play repertoires of children who are functioning above the 2.5-year developmental level, one could argue here, too, that the children were at appropriate levels of readiness for learning the symbolic play activities that were targeted. Similar results can be found in other reports, such as those of Kim and colleagues (1989); Goldstein and Cisar (1992); Murphy, Carr, and Callias (1985); and, more recently, van Berckelaer-Onnes (2003).

Taken together, these intervention studies demonstrated that children with developmental disabilities can acquire and learn play activities as a result of systematic intervention procedures. Moreover, many of the studies suggest, either directly or indirectly, that children's developmental readiness to learn different kinds of play activities may influence the success of an intervention. These studies support the approach of linking developmental assessment to what we teach in teaching play activities to children with autism.

■ Linking Developmental Assessment to Teaching: *How We Teach*

The choice of what play activities to teach and the determination of how to teach these activities are linked. Play interventions based on developmental assessment allow for the identification of play objectives that the child is ready to learn. They also allow for the teaching of play activities that are child-directed. For the purposes of linking developmental assessment to how we teach, the claim is that child-directed teaching has two meanings. The first meaning is based on the child's interests, which is the more widely used definition of child-directed teaching. A second meaning of child-directed is offered here. It is based on the child's readiness to learn, which can be derived from developmental assessment. This section presents child-directed interventions based on interest and based on readiness to learn, followed by a description of child-directed teaching methods. Comprehensive reviews of play intervention methods, in terms of how play interventions are implemented, can be found in Ingersoll and Schreibman (2006); Smith, Lovaas, and Lovaas (2002); and Stahmer (1999).

Child-Directed Interventions Based on Interest

Child-directed interventions are also known as child-focused interventions (Wolery 2000). This approach is advocated as a "recommended practice" by the Division for Early Childhood (DEC 2005), of the Council for Exceptional Children. It involves building on the child's interest—what the child attends to in terms of the toys he or she looks at and picks up for play. It is an important component in building on the child's attention. In terms of methods for teaching play skills to children, researchers have based decisions on what to teach and what toys to use on the children's interests (e.g., Koegel, Koegel, and Surratt 1992).

Child-Directed Interventions Based on Readiness to Learn

The second meaning of child-directed interventions in play, which is proposed here as an extension of the definition of child-directed interventions, is derived from developmental assessment. The claim is that an objective for intervention—namely, what to teach—is child-directed if it is based on the child's level of understanding. If a target activity is at the child's leading edge of learning, the child is more likely to be able to interpret and learn the activity than if it is too hard for the child.

Children without disabilities direct their learning, which can be seen in their play activities. As children move objects from place to place, whether alone or in the presence of caregivers and peers, they create opportunities for learning. Studies of children's attention have demonstrated that children attend more to activities that are relatively new for them, as opposed to activities that they already know (Bloom and Tinker, 2001; Ruff and Lawson, 1990). The outcomes of this learning can be seen in the longitudinal studies of children's play described earlier, showing steady progression in the qualitative nature of new categories that emerge (Nicolich 1977; Lifter and Bloom, 1989) and in the quantitative shifts from a predominance of simple to a predominance of relatively more complex activities over time (Lifter and Bloom, 1989).

Children with developmental disabilities have difficulty learning to play because they have difficulty learning. They do not drive and direct their learning in ways that children without disabilities do. The selection of what to teach children based on developmental assessment attempts to support and facilitate the child's capacity to learn. By identifying activities at the levels where understanding is emerging, a procedure is fostered to increase the child's chances of actively engaging in learning. This procedure complements attention to the child's interests and provides direction for the interventionist in guiding the child's attention to activities at the leading edge of learning. Both aspects of child-directed learning—building on the child's interests and building on what the child is ready to learn—should increase children's capacity to learn in an intervention and provide necessary supports to help them direct, and drive, their learning.

Child-Directed Teaching Methods

Child-directed teaching methods, accordingly, should include attention to both interest and readiness to learn. An example of this method was provided by Lifter and colleagues (2005). In all cases, the target activities were determined to be at the "emerging" or "next step" level, based on developmental assessment with the DPA (Lifter 2000). Teaching opportunities occurred when the child was looking at or touching a target object, to build on the child's attention and interest in an object. Teachers attended to the child and described what the child was doing. If the child attended to the target objects and attempted a target activity, teachers followed the least-to-most prompt hierarchy (i.e., verbal, gestural, model, and physical prompts), as specified in

Sulzer-Azaroff and Mayer (1991), to support completion of the attempted target activity. If the child remained unengaged or played inappropriately, teachers initiated the prompting sequence by first calling attention to a target object in an attempt to capture the child's attention to an object; they waited for a few seconds to maintain attention and then initiated the prompting sequence.

These procedures incorporated guidelines for child-initiated instruction (Wolery 2000). Teaching opportunities were identified based on the child's attention and interest in the toys. These procedures also incorporated the second meaning of child-directed instruction, in that teachers built on the child's attention and interest in shaping the activity into one that the child was ready to learn, given the results of developmental assessment. Such procedures not only build on the child's interests but also provide information to teachers and other caregivers on how to shape the activity in which the child is interested, based on the results of developmental assessment. The claim here is that such procedures maximize opportunities for learning.

■ Summary and Future Directions

Summary

The descriptions of play offered in this chapter provide a framework for understanding the developmental progressions in play, which have been identified in longitudinal and cross-sectional studies. These studies provide evidence for play as a developmental domain. They also provide a system for describing play in qualitative and quantitative terms, to evaluate a child's progress in play. The evaluation of progress in play constitutes the basis for developmental assessment of play, which is used to identify what to teach and how to teach. Developmental assessment of play yields specifications for target play activities to be used in play interventions that are more specific than the broad categories of manipulative, symbolic, and sociodramatic play. This chapter presented evidence in support of the approach of linking developmental assessment to teaching and described teaching methods that build on developmental assessment. For these teaching methods, a second meaning of child-directed learning was offered to complement its basic meaning of capitalizing on the child's interests: learning is also child-directed when the child is helped to learn activities that are at his or her leading edge of development. Developmental assessment provides a means of identifying activities at the leading edge of learning, which can be linked directly to teaching. The DPA Instrument (Lifter 2000; Lifter et al. 1988) was highlighted in describing developmental play assessment and teaching.

Future Directions

For play to be a viable means of intervention, several suggestions are offered here. They center on practical recommendations and directions for future research. First, it is important to advocate for play as a developmental domain. Such advocacy elevates play to its own place on a child's Individualized Education Program (IEP). Goals and objectives in play are important for children who have delays in play. It is not enough to use play in the service of other developmental domains, given the value of play as a natural activity. Play needs to be targeted, just as goals and objectives are targeted in other domains, to help children with developmental delays and disabilities to learn and develop.

A second recommendation concerns the involvement of parents and other caregivers. The approach of linking developmental assessment to teaching is important for working with young children with autism and their families. Play activities are very much a part of the everyday activities of childhood. Caregivers provide children with the time and space to engage with the objects, people, and events of their cultures. However, it is often difficult for parents to know what to do when their children with autism are engaging in very simple or stereotypical activities. Information about the developmental progression in play and how parents and caregivers can foster activities at the leading edge of their child's learning should be of benefit to the parents as well as the children. Play activities are important for learning. They also provide important contexts for hearing the language mapped onto what the children are attending to and for engaging with caregivers and peers.

Research must continue on play interventions for children with developmental delays and disabilities. Certainly, it is important to investigate the impact of learning to play, as a result of intervention studies, on developments in other domains. Such research should validate the claim of play as a developmental domain. Recent studies in this direction include Ingersoll and Schreibman (2006) and Kasari, Freeman, and Paparella (2006). Rogers (2005), in her recent review of play intervention studies, advocated for a developmental approach to play interventions. Future studies should also included attention to interventions in which parents and other caregivers are the implementers of the intervention.

■ Acknowledgments

The author is deeply grateful to the children, families, and staff of the May Center for Early Education for their enthusiastic support for the play studies. The author sincerely appreciates the colleagueship of Stephen R. Anderson, James T. Ellis, and Barbara O'Malley Cannon. Finally, the author extends thanks to the many students who helped with this chapter: Elizabeth Bissinger, Tawny McManus, Maureen Piana, and Christine Tortolani.

■ References

Ariel, S. (1992). Semiotic analysis of children's play: A method for investigating social development. *Merrill-Palmer Quarterly,* 38 (1), 119–138.

Axline, V.M. (1947). *Play therapy.* Cambridge, Mass.: Riverside Press.

Ballard, K.D., and Medland, J.L. (1986). Collateral effects from teaching attention, imitation and toy interaction behaviors to a developmentally handicapped child. *Child and Family Behavior Therapy,* 7 (4), 47–60.

Barrett, S., Prior, M., and Manjiviona, J. (2004). Children on the borderlands of autism: Differential characteristics in social, imaginative, communicative and repetitive behaviour domains. *Autism,* 8 (1), 61–87.

Belsky, J., and Most, R. (1981). From exploration to play: A cross-sectional study of infant free play behavior. *Developmental Psychology,* 17, 630–639.

Blanc, R., Adrien, J.-L., Roux, S., and Barthélémy, C. (2005). Dysregulation of pretend play and communication development in children with autism. *Autism,* 9 (3), 229–245.

Bloom, L., and Tinker, E. (2001). The intentionality model and language acquisition: Engagement, effort, and the essential tension in development. *Monographs of the Society for Research in Child Development,* 66 (4, Serial No. 267).

Brown, J., and Whiten, A. (2000). Imitation, theory of mind and related activities in autism. *Autism,* 4 (2), 185–204.

Casby, M.W. (2003). Developmental assessment of play: A model for early intervention. *Communication Disorders Quarterly,* 24 (2), 175–183.

Charman, T., Swettenham, J., Baron-Cohen, S., Cox, A., Baird, G., and Drew, A. (1998). An experimental investigation of social-cognitive abilities in infants with autism: Clinical implications. *Infant Mental Health Journal,* 19 (2), 260–275.

D'Ateno, P., Mangiapanello, K., and Taylor, B.A. (2003). Using video modeling to teach complex play sequences to a preschooler with autism. *Journal of Positive Behavior Interventions,* 5 (1), 5–11.

DEC recommended practices in early intervention/early childhood special education (2005). (eds. S. Sandall, M. McLean, and B. Smith). Longmont, CO: Sopris West.

Eason, L.J., White, M.J., and Newsom, C.D. (1982). Generalized reduction of self-stimulating behavior: An effect of teaching appropriate play to autistic children. *Analysis and Intervention in Developmental Disabilities,* 2, 157–169.

Eckerman, C., Davis, C., and Didow, S. (1989). Toddlers' emerging ways of achieving cooperative social coordinations with a peer. *Child Development,* 60, 440–453.

Elkind, D. (1990). Academic pressures—Too much, too soon: The demise of play. In *Children's play and learning: Perspectives and policy implications* (eds. E. Klugman and S. Smilansky), pp. 3–17. New York: Teachers College Press.

Farmer-Dougan, V., and Kaszuba, T. (1999). Reliability and validity of play-based observations: Relationship between the PLAY behavior observation system and standardized measures of cognitive and social skills. *Educational Psychology,* 19 (4), 429–440.

Fenson, L., Kagan, J., Kearsley, R., and Zelazo, P. (1976). The developmental progression of manipulative play in the first two years. *Child Development,* 47, 232–236.

Fenson, L., and Ramsay, D. (1980). Decentralization and integration of the child's play in the second year. *Child Development,* 51, 171–178.

Fewell, R., and Kaminski, R. (1988). Play skills development and instruction for young children with handicaps. In *Early intervention for infants and children with handicaps: An empirical base* (eds. S. Odom and M. Karnes), pp. 145–158. Baltimore: Paul H. Brookes.

Fox, L., and Hanline, M.F. (1993). A preliminary evaluation of learning within developmentally appropriate early childhood settings. *Topics in Early Childhood Special Education,* 13 (3), 308–327.

Garfinkle, A.N. (2004). Assessing play skills. In *Assessing infants and preschoolers with special needs* (eds. M. McLean, D.B. Bailey, Jr., and M. Wolery), pp. 451–486. Englewood, NJ: Merrill/Prentice Hall.

Garvey, C. (1977). *Play.* Cambridge, Mass.: Harvard University Press.

Goldstein, H., and Cisar, C.L. (1992). Promoting interaction during sociodramatic play: Teaching scripts to typical preschoolers and classmates with disabilities. *Journal of Applied Behavior Analysis,* 25, 265–280.

Haring, T.G. (1985). Teaching between-class generalization of toy play behavior to handicapped children. *Journal of Applied Behavior Analysis,* 18, 127–139.

Hill, P.M., and McCune-Nicolich, L. (1981). Pretend play and patterns of cognition in Down's syndrome children. *Child Development,* 52, 611–617.

Howes, C., and Matheson, C. (1992). Sequences in the development of competent play with peers: Social and social pretend play. *Developmental Psychology,* 28 (5), 961–974.

Ingersoll, B., and Schreibman, L. (2006). Teaching reciprocal imitation skills to young children with autism using a naturalistic behavioral approach: Effects on language, pretend play, and joint attention. *Journal of Autism and Developmental Disorders,* 36 (4), 487–505.

Jahr, E., Eldevik, S., and Eikeseth, S. (2000). Teaching children with autism to initiate and sustain cooperative play. *Research in Developmental Disabilities,* 21 (2), 151–169.

Jarrold, C. (2003). A review of research into pretend play in autism. *Autism,* 7(4), 379–390.

Jarrold, C., Boucher, J., and Smith, P. (1993). Symbolic play in autism: A review. *Journal of Autism and Developmental Disorders,* 23, 281–307.

Jordan, R. (2003). Social play and autistic spectrum disorders: A perspective on theory, implications and educational approaches. *Autism*, 7 (4), 347–360.

Kasari, C., Freeman, S., and Paparella, T. (2006). Joint attention and symbolic play in young children with autism: A randomized controlled intervention study. *Journal of Child Psychology and Psychiatry*, 47 (6), 611–620.

Kim, Y.T., Lombardino, L.J., Rothman, H., and Vinson, B. (1989). Effects of symbolic play intervention with children who have mental retardation. *Mental Retardation*, 27 (3), 159–165.

Koegel, R.L., Koegel, L.K., and Surratt, A. (1992). Language intervention and disruptive behavior in preschool children with autism. *Journal of Autism and Developmental Disorders*, 22 (2), 141–153.

Lewis, V., Boucher, J., Lupton, L., & Watson, S. (2000). Relationships between symbolic play, functional play, verbal and non-verbal ability in young children. *International Journal of Language and Communication Disorders*, 35 (1), 117–127.

Libby, S., Powell, S., Messer, D., and Jordan, R. (1998). Spontaneous play in children with autism: A reappraisal. *Journal of Autism and Developmental Disorders*, 28 (6), 487–497.

Lifter, K. (1996). Assessing play skills. In *Assessing infants and preschoolers with special needs* (2nd) (eds. M. McLean, D. Bailey Jr., and M. Wolery), pp. 435–461. Englewood Cliffs, N.J.: Merrill.

Lifter, K. (2000). Linking assessment to intervention for children with developmental disabilities or at-risk for developmental delay: The Developmental Play Assessment (DPA) instrument. In *Play diagnosis and assessment* (2nd ed) (eds. K. Gitlin-Weiner, A. Sandgrund, and C.E. Schaefer), pp. 228–261. New York: Wiley.

Lifter, K., and Bloom, L. (1989). Object knowledge and the emergence of language. *Infant Behavior and Development*, 12, 395–423.

Lifter, K., and Bloom, L. (1998). Intentionality and the role of play in the transition to language. In *Transitions in prelinguistic communication: Preintentional and presymbolic to symbolic* (eds. A.M. Wetherby, S.F. Warren, and J. Reichle), pp. 161–195. Baltimore: Paul H. Brookes.

Lifter, K., Edwards, G., Avery, D., Anderson, S.R., and Sulzer-Azaroff, B. (1988). The Developmental Play assessment (DPA) instrument. Unpublished manuscript.

Lifter, K., Ellis, J., Cannon, B., and Anderson, S.R. (2005). Developmental specificity in targeting and teaching play activities to children with pervasive developmental disorders. *Journal of Early Intervention*, 27 (4), 247–267.

Lifter, K., Sulzer-Azaroff, B., Anderson, S.R., and Cowdery, G.E. (1993). Teaching play activities to preschoolers with developmental disabilities: The importance of developmental considerations. *Journal of Early Intervention*, 17, 139–159.

Lowe, M. (1975). Trends in the development of representational play in infants from one to three years: An observational study. *Journal of Child Psychology and Psychiatry*, 16, 33–47.

Malone, D.M., Stoneman, Z., and Langone, J. (1994). Contextual variation of correspondences among measures of play and development level of pre-school children. *Journal of Early Intervention,* 18 (2), 199–215.

McCune, L. (1995). A normative study of representational play at the transition to language. *Developmental Psychology,* 31 (2), 198–206.

Montessori, M. (1967). *The absorbent mind.* New York: Holt, Rinehart and Winston.

Moran, D., and Whitman, T. (1985). The multiple effects of a play-oriented parent training program for mothers of developmentally delayed children. *Analysis and Intervention in Developmental Disabilities,* 5 (1–2), 73–96.

Morrison, R.S., Sainato, D.M., Benchaaban, D., and Endo, S. (2002). Increasing play skills of children with autism using activity schedules and correspondence training. *Journal of Early Intervention,* 25 (1), 58–72.

Murphy, G., Carr, J., and Callias, M. (1985). Increasing simple toy play in profoundly mentally handicapped children: II. Designing special toys. *Journal of Autism and Developmental Disorders,* 15 (4), 375–388.

Nicolich, L. (1977). Beyond sensorimotor intelligence: Assessment of symbolic maturity and pretend play. *Merrill-Palmer Quarterly,* 23, 89–99.

Nikopoulos, C.K., and Keenan, M. (2004). Effects of modeling on social initiations by children with autism. *Journal of Applied Behavior Analysis,* 37 (1), 93–96.

Odom, S. (1981). The relationship of play to developmental level in mentally retarded preschool children. *Education and Training in Mental Retardation and Developmental Disabilities,* 16, 136–141.

Parten, M. (1932). Social participation among preschool children. *Journal of Abnormal and Social Psychology,* 27, 243–269.

Piaget, J. (1962). *Play, dreams, and imitation in childhood.* New York: Norton.

Pierce-Jordan, S., and Lifter, K. (2005). Interaction of social and play behaviors in preschoolers with and without pervasive developmental disorders. *Topics in Early Childhood Special Education,* 25 (1), 34–47.

Power, T.J., and Radcliffe, J. (1991). Cognitive assessment of preschool play using the Symboic Play Test. In *Play diagnosis and assessment* (eds. C.E. Schaefer, K. Gitlin, and A. Sandgrund), pp. 87–113. New York: Wiley.

Power, T.J., and Radcliffe, J. (2000). Assessing the cognitive ability of infants and toddlers through play: The Symbolic Play Test. In *Play diagnosis and assessment* (2nd ed) (eds. K. Gitlin, A. Sandgrund, and C.E. Schaefer), pp. 58–79. Hoboken, N.J.: Wiley.

Quinn, J., and Rubin, K.H. (1984). The play of handicapped children. In *Child's play: Developmental and applied* (eds. T.D. Yawkey and A.D. Pellegrini), pp. 63–80. Hillsdale, N.J.: Erlbaum.

Reagon, K.A., Higbee, T.S., and Endicott, K. (2006). Teaching pretend play skills to a student with autism using video modeling with a sibling as model and play partner. *Education and Treatment of Children,* 29 (3), 517–528.

Rogers, S. (1988). Cognitive characteristics of handicapped children's play: A review. *Journal of the Division for Early Childhood,* 12, 161–168.

Rogers, S.J. (2005). Play interventions for young children with autism spectrum disorders. In *Empirically based play interventions for children* (eds. L.A. Reddy, T.M. Files-Hall, and C.E. Schaefer), pp. 215–239. Washington, D.C.: American Psychological Association.

Rubin, K., Fein, G., and Vandenberg, B. (1983). Play. In *Handbook of child psychology: Socialization, personality, social development* (Vol. 4) (ed. E.M. Hetherington), pp. 694–759. New York: Wiley.

Ruff, H.A., and Lawson, K.R. (1990). Development of sustained, focused attention in young children during free play. *Developmental Psychology,* 26 (1), 85–93.

Rutherford, M.D., and Rogers, S.J. (2003). Cognitive underpinnings of pretend play in autism. *Journal of Autism and Developmental Disorders,* 33 (3), 289–302.

Sigman, M., and Mundy, P. (1987). Symbolic processes in young autistic children. *New Directions for Child Development,* 36, 31–46.

Smilansky, S. (1968). *The effects of sociodramatic play on disadvantaged preschool children.* New York: Wiley.

Smith, T., Lovaas, N.W., and Lovaas, O.I. (2002). Behaviors of children with high-functioning autism when paired with typically developing versus delayed peers: A preliminary study. *Behavioral Interventions,* 17, 129–143.

Stagnitti, K., Unsworth, C., and Rodger, S. (2000). Development of an assessment to identify play behaviours that discriminate between the play of typical preschoolers and preschoolers with pre-academic problems. *Occupational Therapy,* 67 (5), 291–303.

Stahmer, A.C. (1995). Teaching symbolic play skills to children with autism using pivotal response training. *Journal of Autism and Developmental Disorders,* 25, 123–141.

Stahmer, A.C. (1999). Using pivotal response training to facilitate appropriate play in children with autistic spectrum disorders. *Child Language Teaching and Therapy,* 15 (1), 29–40.

Stahmer, A.C., Ingersoll, B., and Carter, C. (2003). Behavioral approaches to promoting play. *Autism,* 7 (4), 401–413.

Stahmer, A.C., and Schreibman, L. (1992). Teaching children with autism appropriate play in unsupervised environments using a self-management treatment package. *Journal of Applied Behavior Analysis,* 25 (2), 447–459.

Sulzer-Azaroff, B., and Mayer, G.R. (1991). *Behavior analysis for lasting change.* Fort Worth, Tex.: Holt, Rinehart and Winston.

Thomas, N., and Smith, C. (2004). Developing play skills in children with autistic spectrum disorders. *Educational Psychology in Practice,* 20 (3), 195–206.

Thorp, D.M., Stahmer, A.C., and Schreibman, L. (1995). Effects of sociodramatic play training on children with autism. *Journal of Autism and Developmental Disorders,* 25 (3), 265–282.

Ungerer, J., and Sigman, M. (1981). Symbolic play and language comprehension in autistic children. *Journal of the American Academy of Child Psychiatry,* 20, 318–337.

Van Berckelaer-Onnes, I.A. (2003). Promoting early play. *Autism,* 7 (4), 415–423.

Vondra, J., and Belsky, J. (1991). Infant play as a window on competence and motivation. In *Play diagnosis and assessment* (eds. C.E. Schaefer, K. Gitlin, and
A. Sandgrund), pp. 13–38. New York: Wiley.

Vygotsky, L.S. (1978). *Mind in society: The development of higher psychological
processes.* Cambridge, Mass.: Harvard University Press.

Watson, M.W., and Fischer, K.W. (1977). A developmental sequence of agent use
in late infancy. *Child Development,* 48, 828–836.

Wehman, P.H. (1975). Establishing play behaviors in mentally retarded youth.
Rehabilitation Literature, 36 (8), 238–246.

Westby, C. (1991). A scale for assessing children's play. In *Play diagnosis and assessment* (eds. C.E. Schaefer, K. Gitlin, and A. Sandgrund), pp. 131–161. New
York: Wiley.

Westby, C. (2000). A scale for assessing children's play. In *Play diagnosis and
assessment* (2nd ed) (eds. K. Gitlin, A. Sandgrund. and C.E. Schaefer),
pp. 15–57). Hoboken, N.J.: Wiley.

Williams, E. (2003). A comparative review of early forms of object-directed play
and parent-infant play in typical infants and young children with autism.
Autism, 7 (4), 361–377.

Williams, E., Reddy, V., and Costall, A. (2001). Taking a closer look at functional
play in children with autism. *Journal of Autism and Developmental Disorders,*
31 (1), 67–77.

Wing, L., Gould, J., Yeates, S.R., and Brierly, L.M. (1977). Symbolic play in severely mentally retarded and in autistic children. *Journal of Child Psychology
and Psychiatry,* 18, 167–178.

Wolery, M.W. (2000). Child focused interventions. In *DEC recommended practices in early intervention/early childhood special education* (eds. S. Sandall,
M. McLean, and B. Smith), pp. 29–37. Longmont, Colo.: Sopris West.

Wulff, S. (1985). The symbolic and object play of children with autism: A review.
Journal of Autism and Developmental Disorders, 15 (2), 139–148.

15. AUGMENTATIVE AND ALTERNATIVE COMMUNICATION INTERVENTION FOR CHILDREN WITH AUTISM

Ralf W. Schlosser and Oliver Wendt

A considerable percentage of children with autism have severe communication impairments (i.e., little or no functional speech), to the extent that they may benefit from augmentative and alternative communication (AAC) intervention. Depending on the source consulted, up to 50% of this population fail to develop functional speech skills (Peeters and Gillberg 1999). *Augmentative and alternative communication* refers to an area of educational and clinical practice that aims to supplement or replace an individual's natural speech and/or handwriting through unaided approaches such as manual signing and gestures or through aided approaches such as graphic symbols, communication boards, and speech-generating devices (Lloyd, Fuller, and Arvidson 1997).

Systematic research into the use of AAC for children with autism dates back to the 1970s, when the use of manual signs became frequent, even though it was not called "AAC" at the time (see, for example, Carr et al. 1978). Since then, AAC intervention research with this population has increased steadily, and its scope has broadened to include other AAC modes. Early on, scholars emphasized that AAC might work with children with autism because their characteristics are a good match to the skills needed for using AAC (Mirenda and Schuler 1988). That is, children with autism were considered to be visual learners and therefore good candidates for using AAC. At that time, because there was a need to justify using AAC, rather than continuing with traditional speech therapy, for some of the children with severe communication impairments, these arguments were timely and useful. Once practitioners, families, and funding bodies began to see the value of using AAC with this population, these techniques began to be applied to many children with autism. In 1990, the Facilitated Communication technique began to be used widely with children with autism, but it was later refuted and was proven to be an invalid technique (for systematic reviews, see Biermann 1999; Nußbeck 1999; Probst 2005).

Subsequently, the earlier arguments about the characteristics of children with autism in relation to communication modes made a comeback (Mirenda 2001, 2003; Mirenda and Erickson 2000). This debate about effective modes occurred at a time when clinical psychology was popularizing the notion of "empirically supported treatments" (Lonigan, Elber, and Johnson 1998), and various allied health and education fields began to adopt the principles of an evidence-based practice (Sackett et al. 2000; Schlosser 2003). Evidence-based practice involves the integration of the best and current research evidence with clinical/educational expertise and stakeholder perspectives during clinical or educational decision making (Schlosser and Raghavendra 2004). To accomplish this, the practitioner *(a)* asks a well-built question concerning a child with autism, *(b)* searches for research evidence, *(c)* appraises the evidence, *(d)* applies the evidence by integrating it with his or her clinical/educational expertise and relevant stakeholder perspectives to arrive at a decision, and *(e)* evaluates whether the decision was successful.

The main purpose of this chapter is to offer practitioners and other stakeholders an appraisal of the evidence for AAC interventions with children with autism. To give an overview of the currently existing research base on AAC for children with autism, we extracted studies from the literature research that met the inclusion criteria for several recently conducted systematic reviews related to the topic (see later discussion). The references were accumulated and categorized based on AAC approach, including *(a)* manual signs, *(b)* the Picture Exchange Communication System (PECS) and other exchange-based approaches, *(c)* graphic symbols (selection-based), and *(d)* speech-generating devices. In addition, we reviewed the evidence on the effects of AAC interventions on speech production. This continues to be a major concern of many families and other stakeholders who are contemplating the use of AAC. Although AAC modes have been used extensively in studies of the effects of functional communication training on management of problem behaviors, we did not review these in this chapter. The reader is referred to several recently completed reviews (e.g., Bopp, Brown, and Mirenda 2004; Mancil 2006).

For the readers of this chapter, all of the reviewed studies can be considered prefiltered evidence: they met the inclusion criteria of the respective systematic reviews, they represent data-based experimental studies, and they were included in our appraisal. The availability of prefiltered evidence saves the practitioner time and resources (Schlosser and Sigafoos, 2007), which are documented barriers to the implementation of evidence-based practice (Zipoli and Kennedy 2005). It is hoped that this prefiltered evidence will greatly enhance the capacity of practitioners and other stakeholders to utilize evidence to inform their decision making. For this reason, each section offers implications for practice in light of the evidence. A secondary purpose for this chapter is to arrive at plausible directions for future research—research that is aimed at further enhancing the implementation of evidence-based practice for children with autism.

■ Methods

Inclusion and Appraisal of Studies

Whenever possible, we relied on previously conducted systematic reviews and meta-analyses as a basis for selecting and, if appropriate, appraising individual studies. Over the last several years, the number of systematic reviews has increased (e.g., Millar, Light, and Schlosser 2006; Schlosser and Wendt 2007 *Effects of AAC;* Schlosser and Wendt 2007 *Effects of the PECS;* Wendt 2006). Provided that they are well-conducted, systematic reviews rank highly on hierarchies of evidence, because they systematically utilize procedures to minimize bias while locating, appraising, and synthesizing evidence (Petticrew and Roberts 2006). For example, systematic reviews rely on a documented and comprehensive search strategy, minimizing the danger of subjective inclusion or exclusion of evidence.

If systematic reviews were not available for certain AAC interventions, we drew from narrative reviews of the literature (Mirenda 2003; Mirenda and Erickson 2000; Schlosser and Blischak 2001; Schlosser and Sigafoos 2002, 2006), supplementing them with our review of original studies. Each included study was assessed in terms of the certainty framework originally proposed by Simeonsson and Bailey (1991) which has been adapted and used by several authors (Granlund and Olsson 1999; Millar, Light, and Schlosser 2006; Schlosser and Sigafoos 2002, 2006).

This framework classifies the certainty of evidence into four groupings, from conclusive to preponderant and from suggestive to inconclusive, based on three dimensions: *(a)* design, *(b)* interobserver agreement (IOA) of the dependent variable, and *(c)* treatment integrity (TI). *Conclusive evidence* establishes that the outcomes are undoubtedly the result of the intervention, based on a sound design and adequate or better IOA and TI. *Preponderant evidence* ascertains that the outcomes not only are plausible but also are more likely to have occurred than not and represents studies with minor design flaws but adequate or better IOA and TI. *Suggestive evidence* establishes that the outcomes are plausible and within the realm of possibility because of a strong design or only minor design flaws, but IOA and/or TI is inadequate. *Inconclusive evidence* ascertains that the outcomes are not plausible due to fatal flaws in design.

The studies reviewed here are grouped according to these categories and presented in Tables 15.1 through 15.5. Within each table, the studies are sequenced from those with the best available evidence to those with less convincing evidence (e.g., suggestive evidence). Within each level of evidence, studies are sequenced alphabetically by author. Only evidence that is suggestive or better is discussed in terms of implications for practice. Studies that were deemed inconclusive are not appropriate for informing practice; they may be discussed only in terms of directions for future research.

Determining Effect Size

Based on the research design of the study, different effect size measures were applied to aggregate study outcomes to determine the effectiveness of treatment variables quantitatively. These data are presented in each table in a separate column.

Group Design Effect Size Indices and Their Interpretation

For the majority of group designs, two different effect size indices were chosen: Cohen's d and Hedges' g. Both are based on the standard mean difference. Cohen's d was derived by calculating the difference between the two group means (the control group and the experimental group) divided by the standard deviation for those means (Cohen 1988). For group studies with small samples sizes ($N < 20$), Hedges' g was used instead of Cohen's d to avoid small sample bias (Lipsey and Wilson 2001). Hedges' g is a simple correction of d based on the pooled standard deviation. It is computed by using the square root of the mean square error from the analysis of variance testing for differences between the two groups. For one particular group design that was based on multiple regression procedures (Yoder and Stone 2006 *Randomized comparison*), the difference in variances accounted for by the predictor variables (i.e., ΔR^2) served as effect size index.

Standard mean difference effect sizes such d and g can range from -3.00 to $+3.00$. Cohen (1977, 1988) established a widely used convention to interpret the magnitude of the effect size (ES): an ES lower than 0.20 is considered a small effect, an ES of 0.20 to 0.50 is a medium effect, an ES of 0.50 to 0.80 is important, and an ES greater than 0.80 is considered a large effect. No specific conventions exist for the interpretation of squared multiple correlation effect size. The magnitude of the difference in the variance accounted for by predictor variables gives an impression of how much stronger one predictor is over another.

Single-Subject Experimental Design Effect Size Indices and Their Interpretation

Single-subject experimental designs (SSED) aim at studying either increases or decreases in the target behavior. Based on this intended direction of the observed behavior, different nonparametric effect size estimators were chosen to aggregate outcomes of SSEDs and to determine the magnitude of the effect.

For studies aimed at increasing target behavior, the percentage of non-overlapping data (PND) was applied (Scruggs, Mastropieri, and Casto 1987). The PND method requires the calculation of nonoverlap between baseline and successive intervention (or generalization or maintenance) phases by identifying the highest data point in baseline and determining the percentage of data points during intervention that exceed this level.

For studies intending to decrease behavior, the percentage of zero data (Scotti et al. 1991) was used. The PZD is computed by finding the first data point in the treatment phase that equals zero and calculating the percentage of data points obtained in the treatment phase, including the first zero, that stay at zero (Scotti et al. 1991). The PZD was used because it has been proposed as a more stringent indicator of treatment efficacy that indicates more clearly the degree of behavior suppression (Campbell 2003; Scotti et al. 1991).

PND scores can range from 0% to 100% and can be interpreted using the conventions set by Scruggs, Mastropieri, Cook, and Escobar (1986): A PND greater than 90% is considered highly effective, a PND between 70% and 90% is fairly effective, a PND between 50% and 70% is of questionable effectiveness, and a PND lower than 50% reflects an unreliable or ineffective treatment. When PND scores were summarized across participants or outcome variables, the median PND score (rather than the mean) was taken as a measure of overall effectiveness, because PND scores are usually not distributed normally, and the median is less affected by outliers than the mean (Scruggs et al. 1986).

PZD scores fall in the range of 0% to 100%. PZD scores can be interpreted using the criteria established by Scotti and colleagues (1991): A PZD greater than 80% is considered highly effective, a PZD between 55% to 80% is fairly effective, a PZD between 18% and 54% indicates questionable effects, and a PZD smaller than 18% reflects an ineffective treatment.

■ Findings and Implications

The Picture Exchange Communication System

The Picture Exchange Communication System has gained widespread use and popularity in children with autism during the last 15 years (Bondy and Frost 1994). PECS is a manualized treatment for beginning communicators that involves six phases: In *Phase I: Physical Exchange,* children are taught to exchange a graphic symbol for a desired object. In *Phase II: Expanding Spontaneity,* children are taught to exchange a symbol with a communication partner who is not in the immediate vicinity. In *Phase III: Picture Discrimination,* the child learns to discriminate among symbols for requesting. In *Phase IV: Sentence Structure,* the learner is taught to apply an "I want" symbol to a blank sentence strip, along with the symbol for a desired object, and to exchange the sentence strip with a partner. In *Phase V: Responding to "What do you want,"* the learner is taught to respond to a direct question. Finally, *Phase VI: Responsive and Spontaneous Commenting* builds on acquired skills to encourage a response to additional questions (i.e., "What do you see?") and spontaneous commenting (Frost and Bondy 2004). A systematic review of the effects of PECS in individuals with autism is currently underway (Schlosser and Wendt 2007 *Effects of the PECS*), and the material presented in this chapter draws from that effort.

Inclusion of PECS Studies

We considered a PECS study only if it involved participants who were children with autism; PECS studies with adults were excluded even if they involved the teaching of PECS or similar exchange-based procedures (Bird et al. 1989; Horner and Day 1991). Similarly, studies involving individuals with intellectual disabilities were excluded even if PECS was studied (e.g., Chambers and Rehfeldt 2003). Also, the study had to use quasi-experimental group designs or SSEDs. Studies using pre-experimental designs or pre-experimental program evaluations were excluded (e.g., Carr and Felce 2006 *Brief report;* Liddle 2001; Magiati and Howlin 2003; Schwartz, Garfinkle, and Bauer 1998). Table 15.1 summarizes the 17 studies that met the criteria for inclusion. Conclusive evidence is presented first, followed by preponderant evidence, and then suggestive evidence. The seven inconclusive studies are listed on the bottom. Three of the studies used group designs, and 14 relied on SSEDs. The results for the SSEDs are presented first.

Results from Single-Subject Experimental Designs

The studies varied in terms of the phases of PECS instruction investigated. Some studies focused only on the first phase of teaching the exchange, whereas others examined several phases. Only one study examined all six phases (Travis 2006).

Among the suggestive or better studies, three examined whether PECS instruction was effective in and of itself (Charlop-Christy et al. 2002; Kravits et al. 2002; Tincani, Crozier, and Alazetta 2006). Kravits and colleagues (2002) found fairly effective results in terms of requesting, commenting, and expansions in one elementary school-aged child. PECS was highly effective in terms of requesting (Tincani, Crozier, and Alazetta 2006) and ranged from fairly ef-

TABLE 15.1 *Studies on the Effects of the Picture Exchange Communication System (PECS) and Other Exchange-Based Interventions: Summary and Appraisal*

Study	Purpose	Participants (n, CA, and IVI)	PECS Phases	Protocol Modifications	Design	Outcomes (DVs)	PND or ES	Appraisal
Anderson (2001)	To compare the effects of PECS versus manual signing in terms of requesting, vocalizations, eye contact, problem behaviors, and preference	Six children: Alex (2-7) = 0%; Cory (2-3) = 0%; John (2-11) = 10%; Maya (2-10) = 15%; Ryan (4-11) = 100%; Sara (1-11) = 0%	I–III in both conditions	Followed PECS with some exceptions (i.e., structured versus naturalistic; abbreviated vocal response to child's communication)	AATD and MPD	Requesting—acquisition, requesting—generalization, vocalizations, eye contact, problem behavior, preference	*Requesting-acquisition:* Alex = PECS 88, Sign 0; Cory = PECS 29, Sign 0; John = PECS 33, Sign 0; Maya = PECS 100, Sign 0; Ryan = PECS 100, Sign 0; Sara = PECS 50, Sign 0 *Preference:* John, Alex, and Sara preferred PECS and the others preferred signing; PNDs could not be calculated for other DVs (no time-series data)	*Conclusive—Requesting:* Strong design that allowed control of maturation, history, order and sequence effects; sets were equated in terms of preference; a teaching criterion was used; TI and IOA were strong. *Conclusive—Problem behavior:* Strong design, TI, and IOA, but the reporting as phase means precludes PND calculations. *Inconclusive—Vocalizations and eye contact:* Vocalizations and eye contact were measured only during correct responding; there was no comparable baseline.

TABLE 15.1 (*continued*)

Study	Purpose	Participants (n, CA, and IVI)	PECS Phases	Protocol Modifications	Design	Outcomes (DVs)	PND or ES	Appraisal
Yoder and Stone (2006 *A randomized comparison*)	To compare the effects of PECS with RPMT in terms of speech production	36 preschool children (mean CA, 33.6 mo)	PECS (I–IV if within the 6 mo) versus RPMT	Followed protocol, but taught additional skills after phase IV acquisition	RCT	Speech production	PECS was more successful than RPMT in terms of nonimitative spoken communicative acts (Time 2: Hedges' $g = 0.61$, $p = .03$; Time 3: Hedges' $g = 0.03$, $p = .96$) and number of different nonimitative words (Time 2: Hedges' $g = 0.49$, $p = .04$; Time 3: Hedges' $g = 0.08$, $p = .93$).	*Conclusive:* Strong design. IOA and TI were strong as well.
Yoder and Stone (2006 *Randomized comparison*)	To compare the effects of PECS with RPMT in terms of generalized turn-taking and generalized joint attention initiation	36 preschool children (mean CA, 33.6 mo)	PECS (I–IV if within the 6 mo) versus RPMT	Followed protocol, but taught additional skills after phase IV acquisition	RCT	Generalized turn-taking; generalized joint attention initiation	For children who had some pretraining joint attention skills, RPMT facilitated generalized turn-taking and generalized joint attention initiation more than PECS did (ES $\Delta R^2 = 0.24$, $p = .003$).* For children with very little pretraining joint attention, PECS facilitated generalized requests more than RPMT did (Time 2: Hedges' $g = 0.94$,	*Conclusive:* Strong design. IOA and TI were strong as well.

Study	Purpose	Participants (n, CA, and IVI)	PECS Phases	Protocol Modifications	Design	Outcomes (DVs)	PND or ES	Appraisal
Tincani et al. (2006)— Study 2	To evaluate the effects of PECS, with and without reinforcement for vocalizations, on speech production	One child: Carl (9-2)	IV	Followed protocol in A phases, reinforced vocalizations in B phases	A-B-A-B	Speech production	*Speech production:* word vocalizations = 0, word approximations = 100; no requesting data reported	*Conclusive:* Strong design. IOA and TI were strong as well.
Tincani (2004)	To compare the effects of PECS and manual signing in terms of requesting and speech production	Two children (6&7)	Carl = I Jennifer = I in comparison with sign and II as best treatment	Reinforcement for exchange was delayed up to 4 sec until a word was vocalized (Jennifer)	AATD; generalization design not reported; post-treatment only social validation design	Requesting; speech production†	*Requesting:* Carl = Signing 82, PECS 73; Jennifer = Signing 78, PECS 100 Pretreatment hand motor skills appeared to relate to success with manual signing or PECS	*Preponderant:* The natural speech design and the intervention design involved noncontinuous data collection. IOA and TI were strong. *Inconclusive—Generalization:* Data were not supplied in time-series graphic format, and the design was unclear.

TABLE 15.1 *(continued)*

Study	Purpose	Participants (n, CA, and IVI)	PECS Phases	Protocol Modifications	Design	Outcomes (DVs)	PND or ES	Appraisal
Carr and Felce (2006 *Brief report*)	To evaluate the effects of PECS instruction on initiations and dyadic interactions with teachers	24 children in the experimental group (mean CA, 5-5); 17 children in the control group (mean CA, 5-9)	I–III	I–II: followed manual III: randomly assigned half of the children to follow the manual and the other half to follow a modified procedure	Between-group design; assigned by territory (within and outside a 50-mile radius)	1. Child-to-adult total initiations 2. Child-to-adult linguistic initiations 3. Child-to-adult initiations divided by % of adult responses 4. Adult-to-child initiations with opportunities for child response 5. % of child responses in adult-to-child initiations with opportunities for child response 6. Adult-to-child initiations with no error	1. Frequency significantly higher for PECS group (Time 2: $z = 5.30$, $p < .00003$)[‡] 2. Frequency significantly higher for PECS (Time 2: $z = 6.93$, $p < .00003$) 3. Percentage significantly higher for PECS (Time 2: $z = 2.80$, $p < .0026$) 4. Frequency for PECS not different from control group (Time 2) 5. Percentage was higher for PECS (Time 2: $z = 2.3$, $p < .0107$) 6. Frequency was significantly lower for PECS (Time 2: $z = -1.65$, $p < .0495$)	*Suggestive:* Participants were not assigned at random to the two groups but by territory; therefore, it is unclear whether the groups were similar in terms of unknown characteristics. In terms of the characteristics that the children brought to the task, very little is known (e.g., How did they communicate before training? Were they able to imitate motor behavior and sounds?)

Study	Purpose	Participants (n, CA, and IVI)	PECS Phases	Protocol Modifications	Design	Outcomes (DVs)	PND or ES	Appraisal
Charlop-Christy et al. (2002)	To evaluate the effects of PECS on requesting, social-communicative behavior, speech, and problem behavior	Three children: Alex (3); Jake (5); Kyle (12) Although not formally assessed, all children were able to imitate.	I–VI	Followed protocol	MBD across subjects	PECS acquisition; social-communicative behavior (cooperative play, joint attention, requesting, initiation, eye contact); problem behavior (tantrums, grabbing, out of seat, disruptions); speech production[†] (elicited vocalizations, MLU, imitation)	*Intervals with tantrums and out of seat behavior (PZD-T/PZD-PT):* Jake Working: 66/80; Jake Playing: 66/66; Kyle Working: 66/100; Kyle Playing: 89/100 *Frequency of disruptions and grabbing (PZD-T/ PZD-PT):* Jake Working: 0/0; Jake Playing: 75/100; Kyle Working: 100/50; Kyle Playing: 88/80	*Suggestive:* Strong design and IOA, but TI was lacking. Additional shortcomings: PECS acquisition not provided in (graphic) time-series format, so neither PND nor visual analysis could be done; several outcome variables were combined, making it difficult to determine effectiveness for specific outcomes; although generalization to novel partners, settings, and materials was posited, no separate generalization data were provided; the problem behaviorintervention was not grounded in a functional assessment.

335

TABLE 15.1 *(continued)*

Study	Purpose	Participants (n, CA, and IVI)	PECS Phases	Protocol Modifications	Design	Outcomes (DVs)	PND or ES	Appraisal
Marckel et al. (2006)	To evaluate the effectiveness of using descriptors to request desired items for which no symbol is available	Two children: Ike (5) Khan (4)	IV	The use of modifiers represents an adaptation to typical protocol	MBD across descriptors, plus a CCD (successive increase in number of descriptors)	(Improvised) requesting	*Generalization* (untrained items): 100	*Suggestive:* Minor design flaws because acquisition data were not provided (only training data). Generalization probes seem to be the only ones with comparable probes in baseline. However, there were very few data points (three in tier 1, two in tier 2, and one in tier 3). IOA and TI were good.
Sidener et al. (2005)	To compare two methods (multiple schedules versus signaled delay-to-reinforcement) for maintaining practical levels of exchange-based	Four children: Evan (5-0) Abby (5-0) Amber (5-0) Rose (7-0)	I (occurred before comparison; Rose did not learn the exchange)	Adhered to protocol, except for the two conditions	A-B-A-C-A / A-C-A-B-A	Requesting	PNDs were not applied because the authors instituted a threshold of the lowest frequency of requesting—once reached, the condition was terminated.	*Suggestive:* Minor design flaws due to the attempted control of sequence effects across rather than within participants. IOA and TI were strong.

Study	Purpose	Participants (n, CA, and IVI)	PECS Phases	Protocol Modifica-tions	Design	Outcomes (DVs)	PND or ES	Appraisal
Spillane (1999)	To compare the effects of discrete trial versus incidental teaching on requesting	One child: John (10), with autism + severe mental retardation + nonspeaking	I	No men-tion of protocol	AATD combined with MBD	Requesting	*Discrete trial:* John (18) *Incidental teaching:* John (30)	*Suggestive:* AATD was appropriate, but the sets were not equated for rela-tive degree of preference (all were preferred); IOA was excellent, TI was not reported.
Tincani et al. (2006)— Study 1	To evaluate the effects of PECS on requesting and speech production	Two children: Damian (10-2) Bob (11-9)	Damian: I–IV Bob: I–II	Followed protocol	MBD across subjects plus CCD	Requesting; speech production	*Requesting:* Damian = 100; Bob = 100 *Speech production—Word vocalizations:* Damian = 0; Bob = 0 *Speech production—Ap-proximations:* Damian = 11 (I–III: 0; IV: 100); Bob = 0	*Suggestive—Behavior change:* The MBD was across only two students, and teaching and testing were confounded. IOA and TI were very good. *Inconclusive—General-ization:* The design was post-treatment only (i.e., no generalization baseline).

TABLE 15.1 (continued)

Study	Purpose	Participants (n, CA, and IVI)	PECS Phases	Protocol Modifications	Design	Outcomes (DVs)	PND or ES	Appraisal
Beck et al. (in press)	To evaluate the relative effects of PECS versus SGDs in terms of requesting and speech production	Three children: Mitchell, Brad, and Derek (CA not specified beyond "preschoolers"); IVI not reported	Mitchell: PECS I and SGD Brad: PECS I and SGD Derek: PECS I–III, SGD	Followed PECS protocol (not in SGD condition)	ATD	Picture exchange (i.e., PECS requesting) or grasping the handle and producing digitized speech in exchange for desired item (SGD requesting); verbalizations (number of utterances, % intelligible, nonimitative intelligible, number of different intelligible words per session)	PNDs were not calculated because the study was inconclusive. It would have been impossible to calculate a PND because there was no requesting baseline, verbalization data were not in time-series format, and generalization data were not depicted graphically.	*Inconclusive:* An ATD does not rule out carryover effects between conditions, because the same instructional set of graphic symbols and referents was used across conditions. In addition, only training data were made available (no testing data). IOA and TI were strong.

Study	Purpose	Participants (n, CA, and IVI)	PECS Phases	Protocol Modifications	Design	Outcomes (DVs)	PND or ES	Appraisal
Buckley and Newchok (2005)	To evaluate the effects of response effort with picture exchange during FCT, functional communication training in terms of problem behavior and requesting	One child (7)	I (exchange only)	PECS protocol was not referenced	A-B'-A-B'-B''-B'-B''	Requesting (picture exchange) and aggression in low-effort (LE) and high-effort (HE) conditions	PNDs were not calculated because the study was inconclusive (no requesting baseline); it would have been possible to calculate PND for aggression, but the findings are inconclusive.	*Inconclusive:* Fatal design flaw because the picture cards were not available during baseline, and, therefore, there is no requesting baseline. In addition, the absence of the cards did not minimize novelty effects. Moreover, sequence effects were not controlled. IOA was strong, but TI was lacking.
Frea, Arnold, and Wittinberga (2001)	To evaluate the effect of PECS on requesting and problem behavior	One child: Tim (4-0)	I–III	Adhered to PECS protocol	MBD across settings	Requesting (i.e., picture exchange); problem behavior (i.e., aggression)	Not calculated because the study was inconclusive.	*Inconclusive:* The intervention was not staggered but took place at the same time in both settings; only the testing was staggered. In addition, the discriminative stimulus "What do you want" was used during intervention testing but not during baseline. TI was not reported.

339

TABLE 15.1 *(continued)*

Study	Purpose	Participants (n, CA, and IVI)	PECS Phases	Protocol Modifications	Design	Outcomes (DVs)	PND or ES	Appraisal
Ganz and Simpson (2004)	To evaluate the effects of PECS on word vocalizations, complexity and length of productions, and non-word vocalizations	Three children: Abigail (5-8) Ramon (7-2) Ben (3-9)	I–IV	Adhered to PECS protocol	CCD	PECS acquisition; speech production (number of intelligible words, non-word vocalizations, complexity and length)	Not possible to calculate because of the absence of a baseline	*Inconclusive:* Major design flaws (no baseline and the CCD was not combined with an MBD, making it impossible to rule out history and maturation) as well as lack of TI.
Son et al. (2006)	To compare the effectiveness of PECS versus SGD on requesting and on preference for conditions	Three children: Kim (5-5) Lucy (3-8) Bruce (3)	Exchange only (analog to I)	Not reported (did not claim to have followed the protocol)	ATD	Requesting; preference	PNDs were not calculated because the study was inconclusive.	*Inconclusive:* An ATD does not rule out carryover effects between conditions, because the same instructional set of graphic symbols and referents was used across conditions. In addition, the only data made available during the intervention were data obtained during the training session (no probe data available). IOA was strong, but TI

Study	Purpose	Participants (n, CA, and IVI)	PECS Phases	Protocol Modifications	Design	Outcomes (DVs)	PND or ES	Appraisal
Travis (2006)	To evaluate the effects of the PECS in terms of requesting, commenting, and speech production	Two children: M.M. (9-10) N.N. (9-6)	I–VI	Followed protocol	MBD across subjects	Requesting; speech production	PNDs were not calculated because the study was inconclusive.	*Inconclusive:* MBD with only one replication (minor design flaw). For N.N., data in unstructured activities showed increasing baseline trends in the treated and untreated baselines (fatal flaw). There are no TI data available. IOA is at adequate levels but is based on only 10% of sessions; also, the data are not separated for each of the dependent measures. Because of the acknowledged co-intervention in the classroom and at home during nontreatment times, the source of the obtained results is difficult to interpret (fatal design flaw).

TABLE 15.1 *(continued)*

Study	Purpose	Participants (n, CA, and IVI)	PECS Phases	Protocol Modifications	Design	Outcomes (DVs)	PND or ES	Appraisal
Yokoyama, Naoi, and Yokomoto (2006)	To evaluate the effects of PECS on requesting, correspondence, speech production, and generalization (time delay, novel partner, and distance)	Three children: A (5); B (5-11); C (7-11)	I	Exchange was broken down into four steps, and tapping of "mora rhythm" was used for speech facilitation	MBD plus CCD	1. Percent correct responding: reaching, discriminating, picking it up, exchanging it, and approaching from a distance 2. Vocalizations (word approximations, babbling, vowel sounds) 3. Tapping imitations	PND data were not analyzed because of inconclusive evidence.	*Inconclusive—Correct responding:* An increasing baseline (up to ceiling) in the third child did not permit ruling out extraneous variables. *Inconclusive—Vocalizations:* Because it is unclear whether the intervention caused changes in responding, the vocalization data were also inconclusive. *Inconclusive—Correspondence and generalization:* There were no baselines under these conditions.

342

*Multiple regression effect size index is the squared multiple correlation, which explains the variance accounted for by the predictor variable, in this case pretreatment joint attention skills.

†The outcomes on speech production are available in Table 15.5 and are not repeated here.
  Effect size indices for nonparametric Mann-Whitney U test and conventions not available at this point; p values are reported instead.
  AATD, adapted alternating treatments design; ATD, alternating treatments design; CA, chronological age (yr or yr-mo); CCD, changing criterion design; DV, dependent variable; ES, effect size; FCT, functional communication training; FU, follow-up; IOA, interobserver agreement; IVI, initial vocal imitation (%); MBD, multiple baseline design; MLU, mean length of utterance; MPD, multiple probe design; P, probes; PND, percentage of nonoverlapping data; PZD-T, percent zero data for training; PZD-PT, percent zero data for post-training (maintenance); RCT, randomized controlled trial; RPMT, responsive education prelinguistic milieu teaching; SGD, speech-generating device; T, training;

fective to highly effective in enhancing eye contact, joint attention, or play, as well as requests and initiations, in three children with autism (Charlop-Christy et al. 2002). In the same study, PECS was found to be fairly to highly effective in improving imitative speech production for one of the three participants but was of unreliable effectiveness for the others. In addition, PECS was unreliable in improving mean length of utterance (MLU) and elicited speech productions across all three participants.

Charlop-Christy and colleagues (2002) also assessed the effects of PECS for reducing two types of problem behavior, tantrums/out-of-seat behavior and disruptions/grabbing. The frequency of these problem behaviors was monitored separately for play and work settings involving two participants, Jake and Kyle. Inappropriate baseline data (i.e., "floor effects") precluded PZD calculation for the playing condition. In the working condition, inappropriate baseline trends were found again, so the data for tantrum/out-of-seat behavior had to be excluded from further analysis. Subsequently, MBR and PZD scores were computed only for disruptions/grabbing in the working condition, comparing the baseline phase with the final treatment phase ("post-training"). Based on the PZD scores, the impact of PECS on reducing the frequency of disruption/grabbing can be considered to be highly effective, but it did not seem to result in complete suppression of the behavior, as indicated by the poor PZD scores. These effects, however, were obtained without a prior assessment of the functions that maintained the problem behavior—a crucial precursor to intervention development and selection (Reichle and Wacker 1993). Therefore, it is unclear whether the appropriate communicative behaviors taught were functionally equivalent to the functions served by the problem behaviors.

Two suggestive or better studies compared PECS with manual signing (Anderson 2001; Tincani 2004). Anderson (2001) showed that PECS was more effective than manual signing in terms of requesting with six learners. Tincani (2004) found that one learner was requesting more effectively with PECS and the other with signing; our PND calculations, however, show a slight advantage for PECS, even with the second learner who reportedly did better with manual signing. The PND outcome scores from both studies were combined for each intervention variable, and overall mean and median scores were computed for a further statistical comparison of PECS versus manual signs. For the acquisition of PECS, the median PND score was 85.5% (mean = 72.9%; standard deviation[SD] = 30.7), compared with a median PND score of 0% (mean = 18.8; SD = 34.8) for the acquisition of manual signs. A Mann-Whitney U test revealed that these overall PND scores were significantly different from each other ($z = -2.812, p < .01$), indicating PECS to be much more effective than manual signs. Based on these results, the PECS intervention can be interpreted as "fairly effective" for teaching requesting skills, whereas the manual signs intervention would be rated as ineffective.

Both of these studies also monitored speech productions as a result of AAC intervention. However, only Tincani's study lent itself to PND calculations. Both participants achieved gains in speech production with manual signing and with PECS that were highly effective, with a PND of 100. Based on visual inspection alone, Tincani (2004) argued that manual signing led to better speech production than PECS. We concur with this assessment and note that the PND metric is incapable of discerning a differential magnitude of the nonoverlap once both treatments are fully nonoverlapping with baseline (i.e., PND = 100%).

Four studies explored the effectiveness of various innovations to the PECS protocol (Angermeier et al. 2006; Marckel, Neef, and Ferreri 2006; Sidener et al. 2005; Tincani, Crozier, and Alazetta 2006). For instance, Tincani, Crozier, and Alazetta (2006) studied the effects of reinforcement of vocalizations during phase IV instruction, a strategy that is not written into the PECS manual. It was found that reinforcing vocalizations resulted in improvement in word approximations but not word vocalizations. These data were obtained with only one participant and therefore are subject to further investigation. In another study on innovations to the PECS protocol, Marckel and colleagues (2006) studied the effectiveness of using descriptors for requesting items for which no graphic symbol is available. This is a practical and not unusual problem faced by many individuals using AAC. Their procedure yielded highly effective (improvised) requesting in both participants, yet the small number of data points and absence of acquisition data render these findings suggestive only.

Sidener and associates (2005) examined two strategies for dealing with the problem of keeping the frequency of newly acquired requesting skills through exchanges at practical levels. Often, the high-frequency requests preclude the teaching of anything else. The authors concluded that the use of multiple schedules was an effective strategy, whereas delay-to-reinforcement was ineffective. We were unable to apply the PND, because the authors instituted thresholds of low-frequency requesting that resulted in the termination of a condition. These thresholds may have artificially curtailed variation, which would have resulted in an inaccurate PND. Finally, Angermeier and coworkers (2006) studied the effects of iconicity on requesting during the early phases of the PECS protocol. Typically, the PECS protocol suggests the use of Picture Communication Symbols (PCS), a highly iconic set of graphic symbols. The study involved four children with autism and found no differences between symbols high in iconicity and those low in iconicity (Blissymbols) in terms of requesting effectiveness and efficiency during phases I and II. This suggests that iconicity may not be a factor in facilitating requesting acquisition early in the PECS protocol.

Results from Group Studies

Two group studies from Yoder and Stone yielded suggestive or better evidence. These authors compared PECS with Responsive Education and Prelinguistic Milieu Teaching (RPMT) in 36 children with autism spectrum disorders. The first study (Yoder and Stone 2006 *A randomized comparison*) produced conclusive evidence in terms of its main analysis and focused solely on speech production. The PECS was more successful than the RPMT in terms of non-imitative spoken communicative acts and number of different nonimitative words. An additional exploratory analysis showed that the rate of growth in number of different nonimitative words was faster with PECS than with RPMT for children who began treatment with relatively high object exploration. On the other hand, the RPMT did better than the PECS for children who began treatment with relatively low object exploration. In a parallel study that involved the same participants (Yoder and Stone 2006 *Randomized comparison*) and rendered conclusive evidence, the RPMT facilitated the frequency of generalized turn-taking and generalized initiation of joint attention more than did the PECS. However, this finding applied only to children with some preexisting joint attention skills. Children with very little preexisting joint attention skills did better with PECS than with RPMT.

Implications for Practice

There is considerable empirical support for using PECS as a beginning communication strategy in children with autism. Practitioners are often contemplating multiple treatment approaches. Several of the appraised studies have compared PECS with other treatments and may be informative for the practitioner in making treatment choices. Manual signing is one of these other choices. The aggregated evidence suggests that PECS is more effective/efficient than manual signing in terms of requesting. Because this evidence was appraised at a preponderant and conclusive level, practitioners can place confidence in these findings. When the treatment goal is speech production, however, the appraised evidence to date has not yet reached a sufficient threshold to inform practice in favor of either manual signing or PECS.

Another potential choice is the use of RPMT relative to PECS. Here, the 2006 companion studies by Yoder and Stone offer conclusive evidence that informs decision making. PECS seems to be a more effective choice than RPMT in terms of speech production, whereas RPMT seems to be the better choice in terms of generalized turn-taking and initiating joint attention. Therefore, depending on the treatment goals for a particular child, the treatment choices may differ. If both communicative interaction and speech production are goals for the same child, the practitioner is presented with oppositional treatment indications. In this situation, it is best to try to prioritize the goals. The studies by Yoder and Stone also revealed the importance of preexisting object exploration skills and/or joint attention skills. These data, however, are pre-liminary in nature, because those skills were not actively manipulated in these two studies as independent variables.

Implications for Future Research

Although great strides have been made in studying the effectiveness of PECS since its development, there is clearly more to be examined, and we have sev-eral suggestions. First, the field would benefit from additional prospective studies to identify predictors of successful PECS use, both by itself and in rela-tion to other treatment choices. Second, investigations into innovations to the PECS protocol represent a laudable direction for research and should be con-tinued using rigorous methodologies. Third, the role of PECS for managing problem behavior is still in its infancy and seems a fruitful avenue for future research. In terms of methodological considerations, future research should adhere to rigorous designs (e.g., random allocation to experimental and con-trol groups rather than by geographic region—see Carr and Felce 2006 *The effects of PECS*), should incorporate treatment integrity assessments, should estimate the reliability of its measures, and should avoid using measures that collapse multiple behaviors together without any way of discerning specific effects (e.g., Charlop-Christy et al. 2002).

Speech Generating Devices

Speech-generating devices (SGDs) represent another potential option for chil-dren with autism who have little or no functional speech. SGDs provide digitized and/or synthetic speech on activation. Given the newness of the technological advances leading to the development of SGDs, it is not surprising that research into the effects of SGDs for children with autism has been undertaken only recently. However, there has been a spurt of research activity in this area. For this chapter, we updated the review of intervention studies published by Wendt (2006) that evaluated either the effects of SGDs as part of a treatment package or speech output as an independent variable. All identified studies used SSEDs.

Results on SGDs as Part of a Treatment Package

Studies in which SGDs were introduced as part of a larger treatment pack-age, such as naturalistic environmental teaching, are reported here. Table 15.2 provides a summary of six studies in this category (Dyches 1998; Olive et al. 2006; Schepis et al. 1998; Sigafoos et al. 2004; Sigafoos, Didden, and O'Reilly 2003 [acquisition data only]; Son et al. 2006). Only studies that yielded sug-gestive or better results are discussed here.

Schepis and colleagues (1998) offered suggestive evidence that the use of naturalistic teaching strategies combined with SGD use was highly effective

TABLE 15.2

Studies on the Effects of Speech-Generating Devices: Summary and Appraisal

Study	Purpose	Participants (n, CA)	Design	SGD (Type of Speech)	Outcomes	PND or ES	Appraisal
Schlosser and Blischak (2004)	To evaluate the effects of speech output and orthographic feedback on spelling performance (replication)	Four children: Scott (8) Fred (12) Justin (9) Carl (12)	AATD	Light-WRITER SL35 (synthetic speech)	Words spelled correctly with speech feedback	Scott (83) Fred (93) Justin (91) Carl (77)	*Conclusive:* Sound design; IOA and TI were solid.
					Words spelled correctly with speech + print feedback	Scott (83) Fred (93) Justin (86) Carl (68)	
					Words spelled correctly with print feedback	Scott (100) Fred (93) Justin (91) Carl (63)	
Schlosser et al. (1998)	To evaluate the effects of speech output and orthographic feedback on spelling performance	One child: Martin (10)	AATD	Light-WRITER SL35 (synthetic speech)	Words spelled correctly with speech feedback	Michael (100)	*Conclusive:* Sound design; IOA and TI were solid.

TABLE 15.2 *(continued)*

Study	Purpose	Participants (*n*, CA)	Design	SGD (Type of Speech)	Outcomes	PND or ES	Appraisal
					Words spelled correctly with speech + print feedback	Michael (84)	
					Words spelled correctly with print feedback	Michael (84)	
Schlosser et al. (2007)	To evaluate the effects of speech output (speech on versus speech off) on requesting and elicited vocalizations	Five children: Avery (9) Greg (8) Matthew (10) Michael (8) Zachary (10)	AATD	Vantage (synthetic speech)	Requesting with speech on	Avery (65) Greg (32) Matthew (31) Michael (33) Zachary (45)	*Preponderant:* Strong design, strong IOA and TI; however, training was not continued until the learning criterion was reached.
					Requesting with speech off	Avery (2) Greg (30) Matthew (3) Michael (76) Zachary (80)	
					Elicited vocalizations with speech on	Avery (0) Greg (0) Matthew (0) Michael (19) Zachary (0)	

Study	Purpose	Participants	Design	SGD	Dependent variables	Data	Certainty of evidence
Olive et al. (2006)	To study the effects of enhanced milieu teaching to introduce an SGD on elicited vocalizations	Three children: Mickey (4) Rocky (4) Terrence (5-6)	MPD across subjects	CheapTalk 4—Inline Direct (digitized speech)	Elicited vocalizations with speech off	Avery (0) Greg (0) Matthew (0) Michael (5) Zachary (0)	Suggestive: Minor design flaws because only intervention data and no probe data were collected; however, the responses were independent and self-initiated; TI and IOA were strong.
					Elicited vocalizations	Mickey (0) Rocky (0) Terrence (83)	
					Independent SGD use	Mickey (88) Rocky (100) Terrence (92)	
					Independent gestures and SGD use	Mickey (100) Rocky (92) Terrence (83)	
Parsons and La Sorte (1993)	To compare the number of spontaneous utterances using computer-assisted instruction with versus without synthesized speech	Six children: Subject 1 (4-8) Subject 2 (5-1) Subject 3 (5-8) Subject 4 (6-2) Subject 5 (6-7) Subject 6 (6-8)	A-B-BC-B-BC / A-BC-B-BC (additive and reductive)	Apple II GS + software (synthetic speech)	Frequency of spontaneous utterances with speech on	Subject 1 (83) Subject 2 (75) Subject 3 (100) Subject 4 (100) Subject 5 (50) Subject 6 (92)	Suggestive: The speech design was mapped onto the intervention design. Order effects were controlled across subjects with an n of only 3 (between-group n requirements not satisfied); no TI data.

TABLE 15.2 (*continued*)

Study	Purpose	Participants (n, CA)	Design	SGD (Type of Speech)	Outcomes	PND or ES	Appraisal
					Frequency of spontaneous utterances with speech off	Subject 1 (0) Subject 2 (0) Subject 3 (9) Subject 4 (0) Subject 5 (0) Subject 6 (0)	
Schepis et al. (1998)	To evaluate the effects of naturalistic teaching strategies and SGD use on communicative interactions	Four children: Ben (5) Cory (5) Lynn (3) Ian (3)	MPD	Cheap Talk; (digitized speech) Ben also used Black Hawk (digitized speech)	Number of communicative interactions	Ben (100) Cory (100) Lynn (100) Ian (100)	*Suggestive:* Sound design, good IOA, but TI was missing.
Sigafoos et al. (2004)	To evaluate the transfer of SGD use from a clinical setting to home and to evaluate a strategy for repairing communication breakdowns	Two children: Jason (16) Megan (20)	MBD	BIGMack (digitized speech)	Requesting SGD use repair*	Jason (28) Megan (45) Jason (100) Megan (100)	Suggestive: Minor design flaw (only two replications); IOA was strong, but TI was missing.

Author (Year)	Purpose	Participants	Design	Device	Dependent Variable	PND	Conclusion
Dyches (1998)	To evaluate the effects of switch training on communicative interactions and speech production	Two children: Alan (11-2) Nathan (10-4)	A-B-A-B	Big Red/Jelly Bean switch (digitized speech)	Number of communicative interactions†	Not calculated—inconclusive	*Inconclusive:* Design does not rule out order effects, compares "apples" in baseline with "oranges" in intervention (switch was not present in baseline); number of obligatory contexts not equated across sessions; no TI.
					Number of spontaneous communicative interactions	Not calculated—inconclusive	
					Number of verbalizations	Not calculated—inconclusive	
Sigafoos, Didden, and O'Reilly (2003)	To compare the rate of request acquisition and the maintenance of vocalizations using SGDs with and without digitized speech output	Two children: Michael (13) Jason (4)	MBD; & ATD during maintenance	BIGMack (digitized speech)	Requesting with speech on	PNDs not calculated due to inconclusive evidence	*Inconclusive—Requesting and Vocalizations:* ATD does not rule out carryover effects (using the same symbols/referents across conditions); IOA was strong, but TI was missing.
					Requesting with speech off	PNDs not calculated	
					Vocalizations with speech on and off	PNDs not calculated	

TABLE 15.2 (*continued*)

Study	Purpose	Participants (*n*, CA)	Design	SGD (Type of Speech)	Outcomes	PND or ES	Appraisal
Son et al. (2006)	To compare acquisition of requesting behavior using picture-exchange versus an SGD and to evaluate the effectiveness of allowing an individual to choose his or her AAC device	Two children: Participant 1 (5-5) Participant 2 (3-8)	ATD	TechTalk (digitized speech)	SGD use for requesting	PNDs not calculated due to inconclusive evidence	*Inconclusive:* An ATD does not rule out carryover effects (same symbols and referents were used across conditions).

*The use of a VOCA (SGD) was taught for repairing communication breakdowns.

†"Communicative interactions" in this experiment were defined as "communicating the desire to obtain a drink." "Spontaneous communication interactions" were described as "indicating the same desire without being questioned or prompted by others."

AAC, augmentative and alternative communication; AATD, adapted alternating treatments design; ATD, alternating treatments design; CA, chronological age (yr or yr-mo); ES, effect size; IOA, interobserver agreement; MBD, multiple baseline design; MPD, multiple probe design; PND, percentage of nonoverlapping data; SGD, speech-generating device; TI, treatment integrity.

(consistent PNDs of 100% for all participants) in increasing the number of communicative interactions by four children with autism. Similarly, the study by Olive and coworkers (2006) rendered suggestive evidence that enhanced milieu teaching for introducing an SGD resulted in fairly to highly effective SGD use and overall communication (including SGD use and gestures) for three children with autism. The intervention, however, was unreliable in improving vocalizations in two children; only Terrance improved his speech production. Finally, a study by Sigafoos and associates (2004) yielded suggestive evidence that SGD use could be taught successfully (PND = 100) to two youngsters with autism as a repair strategy when prelinguistic requests did not seem to be "heard" by the communication partner. Treatment involved planned ignoring of prelinguistic behaviors and least-to-most prompting in SGD use. It was also noted that once the youngsters had acquired the repair strategy, they began using the SGD to initiate requests, rather than continuing to rely on prelinguistic behaviors. However, the overall effect, taking into account all data points including the ones before the repair strategy was acquired, was unreliable or questionable. In sum, based on the evidence, it is plausible that treatment packages involving SGDs improve a variety of communicative functions and behaviors in children with autism.

Results from SGD Studies that Isolated the Effects of Speech Output

Several studies have attempted to pinpoint the specific effect of providing access to speech output in comparison to not having speech output during intervention. The targeted outcome variables included spelling (Schlosser et al. 1998; Schlosser and Blischak 2004), speech production (Parsons and La Sorte 1993; Schlosser et al. 2007), and requesting (Schlosser et al. 2007; Sigafoos, Didden, and O'Reilly 2003). Again, only studies that yielded suggestive or better evidence are presented in Table 15.2.

The two studies examining the effects of three feedback conditions (with speech, with print from the liquid crystal display, and with both speech and print) on spelling provided conclusive evidence that the copy-cover-compare method was similarly effective across these feedback conditions in that all participants reached criterion (Schlosser et al. 1998; Schlosser and Blischak 2004). The PND data calculated here offer a perhaps more nuanced point of view regarding effectiveness: Scott appeared to do better with print feedback alone, Carl and Michael did best with speech feedback alone, and Fred and Justin did equally well across all three conditions. Based on the differential number of trials to criterion used as an efficiency measure, the authors asserted that there appeared to be two distinct profiles of feedback efficiency. Some learners, who exemplify the primarily *visual profile,* spell words most efficiently when feedback involves print. Other learners, who exemplify the primarily *auditory profile,* spell words most efficiently when feedback involves speech.

One study examined the effects of teaching requesting of preferred objects with an SGD under two conditions (speech on, speech off) with five children with autism (Schlosser et al. 2007). The authors concluded that children requested more often as a result of intervention, but there was no discernable consistent pattern of either condition's being more effective than the other. Our PND calculations here suggest that the treatment was more effective for two children with speech output on, and for two children it was more effective with speech output off; the fifth child did equally well in both conditions. That being said, the PND levels of the more successful conditions were not in the highly effective range. In fact, two PND values were considered only fairly effective (70% to 90%), one was of questionable effectiveness (50% to 70%), and one was deemed unreliable (less than 50%). The intervention may not have been carried out long enough or with a dense enough schedule to yield higher acquisition levels. This made it difficult to show differences across conditions.

Two studies examined the effects of speech output on speech production. In the first study (Parsons and La Sorte 1993), which yielded suggestive evidence, six learners with autism produced more spontaneous vocalizations when working with software that provided speech (PNDs of 50% to 100%) compared with no speech (PNDs of 0% for five learners and 9% for one learner). In the second study (Schlosser et al. 2007), which rendered preponderant evidence, five children were taught to request preferred objects with an SGD under two conditions (speech on and speech off, as described earlier), and the effects on elicited vocalizations were monitored. Four of the children remained at 0% even after intervention. The only child who made minimal or unreliable gains was Michael, who was also the only child with preexisting vocal imitation skills. These two studies seem to present very contradictory findings. However, a closer look suggests that a number of methodological differences, in addition to the level of certainty, could account for these discrepant results. For example, Parsons and La Sorte (1993) counted any speech productions, whereas in the second study (Schlosser and colleagues 2007), the vocalizations had to be addressing the specific objects the children were taught to request with the SGD. Moreover, in the former study the vocalizations counted were spontaneous, whereas in the latter they were elicited. In the first study, the children were not taught a communicative function with the SGD, but in the second they were (i.e., requesting). In addition, little was reported about the preexisting vocal imitation skills of the learners in the first study, whereas the second study provided preassessment data to this effect. There are many more differences that could be discussed. The point is that it is premature to draw any implications for practice from only two studies.

Implications for Practice

Based on the appraised evidence concerning the use of treatment packages involving SGDs, it seems imperative that SGDs not be automatically discounted as an AAC option for children with autism. Automatic exclusion is grounded in the generally held believe that children with autism tend to process visual stimuli more readily than auditory stimuli. Although this may be an appropriate statement in general, the evidence suggests that is plausible to explore the use of SGDs with these children. In fact, as some of the studies that used isolated speech output as an independent variable have shown, it may be much more productive to view the processing strengths of children with autism relative to specific task-demands, such as spelling with an SGD (see Schlosser and Blischak 2004), rather than have treatment choices dictated by generalized statements.

Implications for Future Research

Although great strides have been made in researching the effects of SGDs and speech output, there is much more to be done. Given that SGDs and speech output seem to work better for some learners than for others (see the spelling and requesting studies)—an often-observed phenomenon with single-subject adapted alternating treatment designs (Yoder and Compton 2004)—future research should be directed toward identifying participant characteristics that serve as predictors of treatment outcomes. The use of randomized, controlled trials and growth curve analyses, as exemplified by Yoder and Stone's two 2006 studies on the effects of PECS versus RPMT, could provide a viable avenue for future research on SGDs.

The role of SGDs in facilitating speech production is still in its infancy and warrants a concerted effort in the field. Although speech production is not the primary aim of AAC intervention, it remains an important desirable outcome for many AAC stakeholders. Finally, some of the studies that were appraised as inconclusive should be replicated using more appropriate designs and methodologies. The comparison of SGDs versus PECS (Son et al. 2006) is a case in point.

Graphic Symbols

Compared with manual signing, graphic symbols are a relatively newer AAC mode for children with autism, both in practice and in the development of a research base. However, as early as the 1980s, authors drew attention to the potential benefits of graphic symbols based on their nontransient nature (e.g., Schuler and Baldwin 1981). Graphic symbols are part of sets or systems. Sets are collections of symbols that do not have clear rules for their creation and expansion, whereas systems are rule-governed (see Lloyd, Fuller, and Arvidson 1997). Graphic symbols in the studies reviewed here were drawn from the following sets and systems: PCS, line drawings, colored photographs, Premack (all sets); Blissymbols, Orthography, and Rebus (all systems). Studies from Wendt (2006) were included in Table 15.3 if they used graphic symbols as part of a nonelectronic selection-based communication system. Studies that employed graphic symbols as part of the PECS or other exchange-based approaches or as part of an SGD intervention appear in other tables and were not duplicated in Table 15.3. All of the studies located used SSEDs.

Results

Most of the suggestive or better studies focused on the teaching of requesting (Johnston et al. 2003; Kozleski 1991; Sigafoos 1998). Taken together, these studies provide suggestive to conclusive evidence that teaching the use of graphic symbols is effective in promoting the acquisition of requesting behavior in children with autism. Children in these studies were successfully taught to request to play or to gain access to preferred objects and activities. In one of these studies, several graphic symbol sets/systems were compared (Kozleski 1991) to determine whether they varied in effectiveness and efficiency. Each of the graphic symbol sets/systems used produced a perfect PND of 100%, suggesting that they are equally effective. In terms of efficiency, Kozleski (1991) observed that sets/systems associated with a higher degree of iconicity (i.e., bearing a greater visual resemblance between symbol and referent) appear to be acquired more readily. However, because iconicity was not manipulated a priori, this assertion is difficult to sustain; after all, the sets/systems differ in other ways besides associated iconicity (Schlosser and Sigafoos 2002).

Beyond requesting, one study provided suggestive evidence that graphic symbols used as visual supports may be highly effective (PNDs of 100%) in cutting down the latency between an instructional cue and beginning a new activity in children with autism (Dettmer et al. 2000). Transitions are difficult to handle for children with autism. If this evidence were to be substantiated further in future research, it would be a welcome addition to an empirically based repertoire for teaching children with autism the use of graphic symbols, not only for expressive purposes but also for receptive goals. The study by Hetzroni and Shalem (2005) offered preponderant evidence that children with autism may also learn to match orthographic symbols to corresponding logos in an effective manner. However, this matching does not speak to the communicative use of the same orthographic symbols.

Implications for Practice and Future Research

Currently, the use of graphic symbols for the teaching of requesting offers the most solid empirical evidence. That being said, the research has not yet reached a level and critical mass at which it could productively inform choices of one graphic symbol set or system over others. Therefore, it would be prudent to study the type of graphic symbol set/system or even characteristics of

TABLE 15-3

Studies on Graphic Symbol Acquisition and Use: Summary and Appraisal

Study	Purpose	Participants (n, CA, and Preexisting Speech Skills)	Design	Graphic Symbols	Outcomes (DVs)	PND or MBR	Appraisal
Johnston et al. (2003)	To determine whether creating communication opportunities, modeling, prompting, and providing natural consequences are effective in terms of requesting	Three children: Brad (4-3), with autism + cognitive delay + dysmorphic features + 1- to 2-word utterances Alex (5-3), with PDD + cognitive delay + 4- to 6-word utterances Billy (5-1), with autism + multiple disabilities + jargon-speech	MPD across subjects	PCS on a flashcard	Correct requests to play, via graphic symbol or verbal (acquisition, maintenance, generalization)	*Requesting—Acquisition:* Brad (95) Alex (53) Billy (45) *Maintenance:* Brad (100) Alex (100) Billy (100) *Generalization:* No PND— inconclusive	*Conclusive— Acquisition:* Sound design; solid IOA and excellent TI. *Inconclusive— Generalization:* No baseline.
Hetzroni and Shalem (2005)	To evaluate the effectiveness of multilevel software in teaching identification of orthographic symbols	Six children with autism and moderate mental retardation: Max (11), with few 1-word utterances Bob (11), with no speech Gina (13), with no speech Lara (10), with no vocalizations Sara (10), with no functional speech + echolalia Al (10), with no functional speech + echolalia	MPD across subjects	Orthographic symbols on personal computer screen	Number of orthographic symbols correctly matched to corresponding logos	Max (67) Bob (70) Gina (88) Lara (60) Sara (82) Al (50)	*Preponderant:* The design was sound; it was unclear whether the intervention phase reported probe or training data. IOA was good but was collected only during generalization tasks and was not representative of all probes. TI was excellent.

TABLE 15.3 (continued)

Study	Purpose	Participants (n, CA, and Preexisting Speech Skills)	Design	Graphic Symbols	Outcomes (DVs)	PND or MBR	Appraisal
Dettmer et al. (2000)	To evaluate the effectiveness of visual supports (schedules, boxes, timers) in facilitating transitions	Two children: Jeff (7) Josh (5)	A-B-A-B withdrawal design	Visual schedule and album with line drawings	1. Latency to begin new activity 2. Number of physical removals 3. Number of verbal and physical prompts	1. *Latency:* Jeff (100), Josh (100) No PNDs were calculated for outcomes 2 and 3 because there was only one data point.	*Suggestive:* Design was appropriate; IOA was good but was based on only 15% of sessions; TI was not reported.
Sigafoos (1998)	To evaluate the effects of differential reinforcement of reaching and requesting on conditional requesting	One child: Larry (6), with occasional babbling	A-B-A-C (B = request training; C = conditional request training)	Black and white line drawing for "want"	Aided requesting and conditional requests (reaching versus pointing to symbols)	*Requests:* Pointing to symbol, PND 83; reaching, MBR 89 *Conditional requests:* PND and MBR not calculated*	*Suggestive:* Sequence effects were not controlled (minor flaw); the change from "Assessment B" to "Conditional Use" did not demonstrate a functional relation between IV and DV.
Stiebel (1999)	To study the effects of teaching parents the problem-solving strategy of spontaneous picture card use	Three children: Steven (4-2), with lack of spontaneous language Tommy (6-8), with 3- to 5-word vocalizations Jose (4-6), with vocalizations	Non-concurrent MBD	Colored photographs	Spontaneous picture card use (pointing to, handing over, or attempting to hand a card to an interactant for unspecified communicative function)	*Acquisition:* Steven (100) Tommy (57) Jose (78) *Follow-up:* Steven (100) Tommy (80) Jose (40)	*Suggestive:* Non-concurrent MBD is less convincing than MBD. In addition, no TI data are available. IOA was excellent.

Study	Purpose	Participants	Design	Independent variable	Dependent measure	Results (PND)	Outcome
Kozleski (1991)	To compare the effectiveness and efficiency of request training using various graphic sets/systems in terms of requesting	Four children with no speech: Kevin (7-10) Jessica (12-7) Brian (7-7) Malay (13-6)	MBD across subjects with multiple interventions introduced in counterbalanced order across subjects	Premack, colored photographs, Blissymbolics, Orthography, Rebus	Requesting—Premack Requesting—Colored photographs Requesting—Blissymbolics Requesting—Orthography Requesting—Rebus	Kevin (100) Jessica (100) Brian (100) Kevin (100) Malay (100) Kevin (100) Brian (100) Malay (100) Jessica (100) Malay (100) Jessica (100) Brian (100)	*Suggestive:* The comparative design relied on between-subject control of sequence effects; sets were equated through informal means; TI was not reported; IOA was excellent.
Dexter (1998)	To evaluate the effects of aided language stimulation in terms of imitative and spontaneous communicative behaviors	Six children with PDD-NOS and limited verbal output: Andre (8-1) Tony (9-2) Peter (9-3) Carl (9) Sam (7-2) Brad (6-5)	MBD across subjects	PCS in aided language stimulation	1. Spontaneous PCS use during joint book reading (number) 2. Spontaneous spoken output (number) 3. MLU	PNDs were not calculated because of inconclusive evidence.	*Inconclusive:* Baseline data were followed by intervention data rather than probe data, making a comparison tedious.

TABLE 15.3 *(continued)*

Study	Purpose	Participants (n, CA, and Preexisting Speech Skills)	Design	Graphic Symbols	Outcomes (DVs)	PND or MBR	Appraisal
Hamilton and Snell (1993)	To study the effects of milieu teaching on use of a communication book across environments	One child: Carl (15), with no speech	CCD within an MPD	Communication book: PCS + photos	Correct responses using communication book	PND was not calculated because the evidence was inconclusive.	*Inconclusive:* Increases in the untreated baselines and training performance could be just a continuation of a trend. No probe data were reported during training phases. IOA and TI were excellent (based on a small % of observations).
Spencer (2002)	To compare the effectiveness and efficiency of static pictures and video modeling on request behavior	Four children: Tom (7), verbal + echolalia Nathan (7), verbal + echolalia + perseverations Donald (7), minimally verbal + 1- to 2-word utterances Chase (9), vocalization + 1-word utterances	AATD combined with an MPD across subjects	*Static:* digital photographs *Dynamic:* video modeling	Number of requests (spoken, pointing to or touching the symbol of an object)	PNDs were not calculated because of inconclusive evidence.	*Inconclusive:* Although the AATD was appropriate, the procedure of providing only the static photographs as a response option biased the results in favor of this condition. IOA was excellent, but TI was not reported.

*An MBR for reaching could not be calculated because the conditional use phase did not supply reaching data; a PND for pointing to the symbol when the object was out of reach could not be calculated due to a ceiling effect in the preceding baseline ("Assessment B").

AATD, adapted alternating treatments design; CA, chronological age (yr or yr-mo); CCD, changing criterion design; DV, dependent variable; IV, independent variable; MBR, mean symbols their relation to referents (e.g., iconicity) prospectively as independent variables while keeping the instructional method constant. In addition to requesting, the evidence supporting the use of graphic symbols as part of visual schedules is suggestive but is limited to only one study. Children with autism seem to be able to match graphic symbols to orthographic symbols, but it is yet to be examined whether this matching could lead to enhanced communication.

Manual Signs and Gestures

Manual signs and gestures represent unaided forms of communication—communication that does not rely on any aids or devices external to the body and uses only body parts (Lloyd, Fuller, and Arvidson 1997). Manual signing was one of the first forms of AAC applied to nonspeaking individuals with autism. It was introduced in the 1970s and has been used successfully with this population for more than 30 years. The term *manual signs* can refer to a natural sign language (e.g., American Sign Language) or to the production of manual signs as a code for a spoken language (Blischak, Lloyd, and Fuller 1997).

Gestures are body movements or sequences of coordinated body movements that represent an object, idea, action, or relationship without the linguistic features of manual signs. Examples of gestures include pointing and yes/no headshakes. In general, gestural communication is one of the earliest-developing nonlinguistic forms of unaided communication. Before linguistic development starts, young children typically use gestures in symbol formation when communicating and interacting with the environment (Loncke and Bos 1997). Therefore, the use of gestures serves as a precursor to later development of language skills (Morford and Goldin-Meadow 1992). Individuals with autism, however, rarely use gestures as an alternative communication strategy, even if they have difficulty speaking (Loveland et al. 1988).

By the mid-1980s, manual signing was often used in combination with speech. This approach was termed "total" or "simultaneous" communication (SC) (Mirenda and Erickson 2000). SC emphasized use of the most appropriate communication strategy for the individual, and during the 1980s it became the preferred AAC approach for people labeled as "severely handicapped" (including those with autism) in the United States, the United Kingdom, and Australia.

For this chapter, we extracted experimental studies that focused on the acquisition and use of manual signs or gestures from the systematic review by Wendt (2006). A total of 17 studies met the inclusion criteria of that meta-analysis. These studies, which include 16 SSEDs and 1 group design, are summarized in Table 15.4. There were additional manual sign studies that focused on speech production as an outcome; they are summarized in the next section (see Table 15.5). Following the study appraisal format for this chapter, we focus on the evidence that is ranked better than inconclusive, beginning with conclusive evidence and proceeding to suggestive evidence. The group study and two of the SSEDs were ranked as inconclusive; their results can be found at the bottom of Table 15.4 but are not discussed in further detail here. The remaining SSEDs targeted different outcome variables: Ten studies focused on teaching manual signs or gestures and primarily monitored symbol acquisition as an outcome variable, and another two studies compared the effects of SC versus sign alone and/or speech training. Results are reported according to these two major groups.

Results for the Acquisition and Production of Manual Signs and Gestures

These studies varied in terms of the conditions under which signs or gestures were taught and the specific behaviors that were observed to indicate that the symbol was acquired. Among those studies with conclusive evidence, one monitored the acquisition of sign items for six participants as part of an experiment comparing acquisition and use of manual signs versus PECS (Anderson 2001). Although overall the PECS training was superior, all six participants were very successful in acquiring manual signs, with all PNDs equal to 100%. Another study, by Buffington and colleagues (1998), taught gestures in combination with speech (saying "look") for indicating tasks and measured the frequency of correctly produced gestural and verbal responses. This intervention yielded PND scores in the highly effective range for all four participants.

Among the studies with preponderant evidence, Tincani (2004) conducted another experiment comparing manual signing with PECS in terms of their effects on requesting and speech production. For requesting, manual signing was fairly effective for two participants, but not as effective as PECS (see earlier discusion of PECS studies). For speech production, another two participants were highly successful in increasing their vocalizations after manual signing was introduced, as demonstrated by PNDs equal to 100%. In this case, manual signing appeared to be superior to PECS (see earlier discussion).

The majority of studies provided suggestive evidence, including a study by Carr and colleagues (1978), which evaluated the impact of a training procedure that used prompting, fading, and stimulus rotation on a sign production task. The procedure yielded highly effective expressive sign labeling, with PNDs equal to 100 for all four participants. Carr and Kemp (1989) conducted an experiment to determine whether leading could be replaced with a pointing gesture as a means of requesting. Again, the intervention led to highly effective use of pointing for requests in all four participants. A study by Carr and Kologinsky (1983—Experiment 1) evaluated whether a combination of prompting, fading, differential reinforcement, and incidental teaching affects

TABLE 15.4

Studies Involving Manual Signs and Gestures: Summary and Appraisal

Study	Purpose	Participants (n, CA, and Preexisting Speech Skills)	Design	Outcomes	PND or ES	Appraisal
Anderson (2001)	To compare PECS with manual signing in terms of acquisition	Six children: John (2-11), few words Cory (2-3), nfs Alex (2-7), nfs Maya (2-10), nfs Ryan (4-11), few words Sara (1-11), nfs	AATD with MPD	Sign item acquired	John (100) Cory (100) Alex (100) Maya (100) Ryan (100) Sara (100)	*Conclusive:* Strong design. IOA and TI were solid as well.
Buffington et al. (1998)	To demonstrate the effects of modeling, prompting, and reinforcement on the acquisition of gestures	Four children with some spoken language: Anne (6-5) Oscar (6-4) Kevin (4-5) Nick (4-5)	MPD across behaviors	*Acquisition:* Pointing and saying "look" to indicate *Generalization:* Across settings and stimuli	*Acquisition:* Anne (94) Oscar (96) Kevin (96) Nick (95) *Generalization:* Time-series data were not provided.	*Conclusive—Acquisition:* Excellent design, IOA, and TI. *Inconclusive—Generalization:* The generalization was unclear based on the results reported.
Tincani (2004)	To compare manual signing with PECS in terms of requesting and speech production	Two children: Carl (5-10), with no speech but some imitations Jennifer (6-8), imitates words and phrases	AATD	Independent requesting; word vocalizations	*Requesting:* Carl (82) Jennifer (78) *Speech production:* Carl (100) Jennifer (100)	*Preponderant:* The natural speech design and the intervention design involved non-continuous data collection. TI and IOA were strong.

TABLE 15.4 (continued)

Study	Purpose	Participants (*n*, CA, and Preexisting Speech Skills)	Design	Outcomes	PND or ES	Appraisal
Barrera, Lobato-Barrera, and Sulzer-Azaroff (1980)	To compare simultaneous communication, sign-only, and oral communication in terms of expressive sign or spoken labeling	One child: L.S. (4–6), with a history of mutism	AATD	Expressive sign or spoken labeling	*Sign alone:* 56 *Simultaneous:* 89 *Oral:* 67	*Suggestive:* Both sequence and carryover effects were minimized with the design and procedural safeguards. Sets were equated but only through informal means and without considering all known variables contributing to learning difficulty. IOA was good, but TI was lacking (for a more detailed appraisal, see Schlosser 2003).
Carr et al. (1978)	To evaluate whether prompting, fading, and stimulus rotation alone improve expressive signs	Four children with nfs and few sounds: Bob (15) Dan (15) Doug (14) Patrick (10)	MBD	Expressive sign labeling	Bob (100) Dan (100) Doug (100) Patrick (100)	*Suggestive:* Strong design and IOA, but TI was missing.
Carr and Dores (1981)	To evaluate the effects of simultaneous communication training on receptive signing and	Three children with no intelligible speech: Jon (10) Mel (11) Len (11)	MBD	Correct responses on receptive language task (receptive speech or receptive signing)	Jon (100) Mel (100) Len (100)	*Suggestive:* A strong design with solid IOA, but TI was not reported.

Study	Purpose	Participants	Design	Dependent variable	Results	Evaluation
Kemp (1989)	whether leading can be replaced with pointing as a means of requesting	with nfs but vocalizations: Cal (5) Jim (3) Sue (3) Mike (5)	across subjects	requesting (new adults, new settings, new reinforcers) via pointing and via leading	Cal (100) Jim (100) Sue (100) Mike (100) *Leading:* Cal (100) Jim (100) Sue (100) Mike (100)	excellent IOA, but TI was lacking.
Carr and Kologinsky (1983)—Experiment 1	To evaluate whether a combination of prompting, fading, differential reinforcement, and incidental teaching results in the acquisition of spontaneous requesting and generalization across partners	Three children, with nfs and no sounds: John (9) Mike (10) Bob (14)	MBD with a reversal design	Acquisition of spontaneous requests; generalization of requests across partners	*Acquisition:* John (100) Mike (100) Bob (100) *Generalization:* John (100) Mike (100) Bob (100)	*Suggestive—Acquisition and Generalization:* Strong intervention and generalization design, and strong IOA, but no TI.
Carr and Kologinsky (1983)—Experiment 2	To evaluate whether targeted prompting and reinforcement results in greater signed requesting and generalization across adults and settings	Three children with lack of speech: Tom (10) Andy (11) Len (14)	A-B-C-B-C-D (B = only sign 1 treated; C = only sign 2 treated; D = both signs treated)	Acquisition of spontaneous requests; generalization of requests across partners and settings	*Acquisition:* Tom (100) Andy (91) Len (100) *Setting generalization:* Tom (100) Andy (100) Len (100) *Partner generalization:* Andy (100) Len (83)	*Suggestive:* Strong design (order effects are not a problem here because it is the same treatment, just a different sign across phases) and strong IOA, but no TI.

TABLE 15.4 *(continued)*

Study	Purpose	Participants (*n*, CA, and Preexisting Speech Skills)	Design	Outcomes	PND or ES	Appraisal
Carr, Kologinsky, and Leff-Simon (1987)	To examine the effects of prompting, fading, stimulus rotation, and differential reinforcement on descriptive signing of action-object phrases	Three children: Ron (15), nonvocal and babbling Dave (16), nonverbal and babbling Rick (11), nonverbal and babbling	MBD across three actions	Expressively signed novel (i.e., generalized) action-object phrases	Ron (92) Dave (100) Rick (95)	*Suggestive:* Design was strong, IOA was excellent, but TI was lacking.
Keogh et al. (1987)	To evaluate the effects of verbal prompts, modeling, physical guidance, positive reinforcement, fading, and chaining procedures on sign initiations, signed responses, and nonsigning responses	One child: Kirk (14), with occasional vocalizations	MPD across dialogue situations	Acquisition and generalization to client–client interaction (sign initiations, responsive signs, and nonsigning responses)	*Acquisition:* 100 *Generalization:* 40	*Suggestive—Acquisition and Generalization:* Strong intervention and generalization designs; IOA was excellent, but TI was lacking. In addition, all three DVs were added together in the graph, making it difficult to determine specific effects.

Study	Purpose	Participants	Design	Dependent variables	Results	Appraisal
Remington and Clarke (1983)	To compare simultaneous communication training with sign-alone training on expressive sign labeling and comprehension	Two children: Diane (10), with no functional speech and babbling sounds John (15), with some nonfunctional verbal speech	AATD	Expressive sign labeling and speech comprehension	*Expressive signing:* Diane (100) John (100) *Speech comprehension:* Diane (100) John (100)	*Suggestive:* Both sequence and carryover effects were minimized through the design and procedural safeguards. The within-subject replication strengthened the internal validity of findings. Sets were equated using objective methods. IOA was excellent, but TI was lacking (for a more detailed appraisal, see Schlosser 2003).
Schepis et al. (1982)	To evaluate the effects of modified incidental teaching strategies on sign acquisition	Four children: Participant 1 (11), occasional verbalizations Participant 2 (7), no intelligible speech Participant 3 (9), no intelligible speech Participant 4 (11), no intelligible speech	MBD across time of day and subjects	Expressive signing (communicative function unclear); vocalizations	*Expressive signing:* Participant 1 (29) Participant 2 (83) Participant 3 (92) Participant 4 (59) *Vocalizations:* PND was not calculated because there were no time-series data.	*Suggestive—Expressive signing:* The design was strong and so was the IOA, but TI was lacking. *Inconclusive—Vocalizations:* Data were collapsed into means.
Sommer, Whitman, and Keogh (1988)	To examine the effects of a program that teaches severely mentally retarded individuals to sign with one another	One child: Kirk (14), with occasional vocalizations	MPD across subjects	Acquisition and generalization across situations (sign initiations, responsive signs, and nonsigning responses)	*Acquisition:* 67 *Generalization:* 67	*Suggestive:* Strong design, IOA was excellent, but TI was lacking. In addition, all three DVs were added together in the graph, making it difficult to determine specific effects.

TABLE 15.4 *(continued)*

Study	Purpose	Participants (*n*, CA, and Preexisting Speech Skills)	Design	Outcomes	PND or ES	Appraisal
Brady and Smouse (1978)	To compare the effects of simultaneous communication, sign-alone, and oral training in terms of receptive speech	One child: Child 1 (6-4), with spontaneous unintelligible vocalizations	ATD with most effective treatment in third phase	Receptive speech	PNDs were not calculated because the evidence was inconclusive.	*Inconclusive:* The design (using the same words and objects across conditions) did not rule out carryover effects. TI was lacking as well (see also Schlosser 2003).
Hundert (1981)	To compare multiple-stimulus training with single-stimulus training in terms of expressive sign labeling	One child: Graig (10) with vocabulary of about 25 sign-picture associations but cannot generalize to difference trainers or other pictures of same objects	AATD	Expressive sign labeling	PNDs were not calculated due to inconclusive evidence.	*Inconclusive:* Although random assignment was used, no evidence was provided that the sets were truly equated.
Saraydarian (1994)	To evaluate whether the use of simultaneous communication to model object referents enhances referent recognition and production abilities	Experimental group: 10 children (mean CA, 6-2; nonspeaking or severely delayed in oral/gestural language development) Control group: children with other disabilities	RCT	Receptive speech and expressive labeling (using sign, speech, or both)	ES was not calculated because of inconclusive evidence.	*Inconclusive:* The design was fatally flawed because the children in the control group were not all children with autism; no TI.

the acquisition of spontaneous sign requests and generalization of requests across communication partners. All three participants in this study were very successful in acquiring spontaneous requesting and generalizing those requests across partners (PNDs were constantly equal to 100%). In a related study (Carr and Kologinsky 1983—Experiment 2), the authors investigated whether targeted prompting and reinforcement increased signed requesting and its generalization across adults and settings. In terms of acquisition, the procedure was highly effective for three participants. It also proved to be highly effective for all participants when generalization across settings was targeted. Slightly different results were obtained for generalization across partners; the procedure was highly effective for one participant and fairly effective for another.

As a follow-up to their 1983 study, Carr, Kologinsky, and Leff-Simon (1987) examined the effects of prompting, fading, stimulus rotation, and differential reinforcement on descriptive signing of action-object phrases. PND scores revealed this teaching procedure to be highly effective for the three participants in this study. All of them acquired signed action-object phrases and were able to generalize those to new situations. Keogh and associates (1987) evaluated the effects of a treatment package that included verbal prompts, modeling, physical guidance, positive reinforcement, fading, and chaining procedures to teach one participant an interactive signing dialogue within a naturalistic snack time routine. The intervention was highly effective in increasing the participant's sign repertoire but led to a PND representing ineffectiveness when it came to generalizing signed communication to new partners. In a related experiment (Sommer, Whitman, and Keogh 1988), the same participant was taught a behavioral script to sign interactively with other children in a play situation. PND scores indicated questionable effectiveness of this intervention for sign acquisition and also for generalizing signed communication to another play situation. Finally, Schepis and colleagues (1982) investigated the effects of modified incidental teaching strategies on manual sign acquisition in four participants. These students presented with mixed rates of success for learning manual signing. PND scores indicated that the teaching program was highly effective for one participant, fairly effective for another, of questionable effectiveness for the third, and ineffective for the last participant when expressive signing was observed. In the only study in this category looking at receptive speech and receptive signing, Carr and Dores (1981) found that SC was highly effective for three participants.

Results for Studies Comparing Simultaneous Communication,
Sign-Alone Instruction, and Oral Instruction

Studies in this category compared the effects of SC versus sign-alone training and/or oral training. Barrera, Lobato-Barrera, and Sulzer-Azaroff (1980) taught expressive language skills to one participant using three different instructional models: SC, nonverbal sign-alone training, and oral training. Increases in expressive language skills were recorded as the number of words successfully produced through either expressive signing or oral speech. Whereas sign-alone and oral training resulted in PND scores of questionable effectiveness, SC led to a fairly effective PND value. Remington and Clarke (1983) compared SC versus sign-alone training in two participants and monitored the effects on expressive sign labeling and speech comprehension. For both participants, PND scores revealed no difference between the treatment conditions, which were both highly effective in increasing sign production as well as speech comprehension.

Implications for Practice

The available body of research on manual signs and gestures for children with autism reveals strong intervention effectiveness scores for symbol acquisition and production, as well as for related outcomes such as speech comprehension and speech production. These results suggest that use of manual signing and gestures is a very effective communication option for children with autism. Among the various potential reasons for this success, some of the most important are the following. Learning manual signs or gestures has numerous specific advantages over learning speech. It may be an easier option than speech, because many children with autism struggle when asked to echo sounds but can imitate at least a few fine or gross motor movements demonstrated by their communication partners (Sundberg and Partington 1998). Furthermore, if an individual does not possess a strong motor or vocal imitative repertoire, then it might be less difficult to teach him the imitation of motor movements than to teach echoing a word (Sundberg 1993). Motor imitation is an easier behavior to teach because the teacher can make use of physical prompting and fading procedures (Sundberg and Partington 1998). Manual sign training also benefits from the fact that, for many of the signed responses, there is an iconic relation to the object they represent; that is, the signed response strongly resembles the object (Loncke and Bos 1997). This iconic relation between object and response may give sign acquisition an advantage over vocal acquisition.

A major drawback of communicating through manual signs and gestures relates to the demands it places on communication partners. Communication partners who are not skilled in manual signing or gestural communication can have great difficulty understanding the individual with autism who has had that training (Mirenda and Erickson 2000). Untrained communication partners might understand some of the more iconic signs and gestures but struggle with the more abstract signs, requiring an interpreter to act as an intermediary. The learning demands for family members, teachers, classmates, and community members who need to communicate with a child with autism via manual signing or gestures are heavy if independence from an interpreter is desired (Mirenda and Erickson 2000). Nevertheless, manual signs and gestures can play a significant role as one component of a multimodal communication system that works across various communication environments including partners with and without experience in using manual signs and gestures.

Implications for Future Research

Whereas the majority of studies on manual signing and gestures documented the successful acquisition and, in some cases, generalization of these communication modes, only few studies actually compared manual signing or gestures against an aided mode of communication such as graphic symbols. More comparative efficacy studies are needed to clarify whether learners with autism actually do better with, or have a preference for, one communication modality over another. This could provide further clarification on the everlasting debate as to whether aided or unaided communication is a better choice for individuals with autism (Mirenda 2003). Given the high training demands placed on communication partners, it seems plausible that manual signs and gestures might play a bigger role than they do today if they were part of a multimodal communication system consisting also of graphic symbols, communication boards, SGDs, and vocalizations (when available). The idea is that children who seem to learn the use of manual signs well may continue to benefit from this learning advantage while being mindful of the environmental and contextual limitations of manual signs in some settings and with some communication partners. This development, however, would require further research into effective strategies for teaching the conditional use of manual signs. To date, very few studies are available that contrast manual sign or gesture use with other modes of communication. One of the exceptions is the study by Sigafoos (1998) in which a child was taught to use an SGD when it was present and a gesture (i.e., reaching) when the SGD was not available. Sigafoos and Drasgow (2001) contrasted manual sign use with SGD use in one child with developmental disabilities, but the child did not have a confirmed diagnosis of autism. Therefore, it is clear that more research is warranted to study strategies of conditional use of manual signs and gestures.

It is noteworthy that the majority of studies on manual signing and gestures were appraised at the suggestive level. On closer examination, this rating was almost exclusively a result of lack of reporting of treatment integrity data (Schlosser 2002). This is regrettable but can be explained historically, because many of these studies were implemented before the field shifted toward emphasizing the importance of treatment integrity (e.g., Peterson, Homer, and Wonderlich 1982). Therefore, it may be worthwhile to replicate some of these studies, because it is unclear whether the treatments were carried out as intended.

When comparing the number of studies based on manual signs versus those based on gestures, it appears that gestures are underrepresented and not well researched in this population. This is surprising, because gestural communication has been positively correlated with vocal use in typical children and in those with autism; presumably, it precedes speech development (Mundy and Gomes 1998; Mundy, Sigman, and Kasari 1990). More research investigating the effects of gestures is needed to build up the empirical support for this unaided communication mode.

AAC and Speech Production

Families of children with autism are frequently concerned about the impact of the use of AAC on speech production. In his systematic review, Wendt (2006) included studies that isolated the effects of AAC interventions on speech production (i.e., Charlop-Christy 2002; Dexter 1998; Dyches 1998; Jones 2004; Parsons and La Sorte 1993; Sigafoos, Didden, and O'Reilly 2003; Tincani 2004). This systematic review demonstrated that there is considerable variation in how natural speech is measured, ranging from vocalizations to verbalizations to imitative speech to spontaneous speech to changes in MLU. For this body of included studies, statistical analyses revealed that AAC interventions were equally effective in promoting imitative versus spontaneous speech. Further, the presence of speech output yielded statistically higher levels of vocalizations compared with not having speech output.

Schlosser and Wendt (2007 *Effects of AAC*) conducted a systematic review specifically on the effects of AAC intervention on natural speech production in autism. They revised the Wendt (2006) and Millar, Light, and Schlosser (2006) inclusion criteria and searched for more recent evidence. To be included, studies had to meet the following criteria (provided in abridged form here):

1. The intervention was classified as being within the scope of AAC.
2. The intervention did not involve functional communication training with AAC, because speech production was not a target of these interventions.
3. The participants were not functionally speaking.
4. Speech production was monitored as a dependent variable— anecdotal reports of changes in speech production did not qualify; similarly, studies that included speech as only one of several modalities constituting a correct response were excluded; and studies in which the dependent measure required natural speech and an AAC mode (or natural speech and/or an AAC mode) to be counted as correct were excluded as well.
5. Data for speech production from SSEDs lended themselves for the calculation of PND, and data from group designs permitted the calculation of ES.

6. Participants had a diagnosis of autism or pervasive developmental disorder–not otherwise specified (PDD-NOS)—participants with concomitant disabilities, such as intellectual disabilities, also qualified if they had a concurrent diagnosis of autism or PDD-NOS; participants described as "autistic-like" and those with other disabilities did not qualify.

7. Quasi-experimental designs such as selected group designs or SSEDs were used for evaluating an intervention—pre-experimental designs such as A-B designs or group equivalents such as pre-test/post-test designs were excluded.

8. In a group design, all subjects were classified as autistic or PDD-NOS, and more than 90% of the enrolled subjects were entered in statistical analyses.

9. The study was published in a peer-reviewed journal or approved as a dissertation or thesis.

10. The study was dated between 1975 and 2007.

The studies included are summarized in Table 15.5 (i.e., Charlop-Christy et al. 2002; Olive et al. 2006; Parsons and La Sorte 1993; Schlosser et al. 2007; Tincani 2004; Tincani, Crozier, and Alazetta 2006; Travis 2006; Yoder and Layton 1988; Yoder and Stone 2006 *A randomized comparison*). As is evident from Table 15.5, very few studies have addressed this question in a focused manner. Three of the studies examined the effectiveness of either PECS itself (Charlop-Christy et al. 2002; Travis 2006) or PECS in comparison with another treatment approach (Tincani 2004; Yoder and Stone 2006 *A randomized comparison*). Two studies examined the effects of speech output (Parsons and La Sorte 1993; Schlosser et al. 2007), and two studies looked into the effects of manual signing (sign alone) relative to variations of manual sign instruction or other treatment approaches (Tincani 2004; Yoder and Layton 1988). Because of the relatively small number of studies devoted to each treatment approach and the heterogeneity of how speech production was measured across studies, we chose not to aggregate the outcomes statistically.

The studies investigating the effects of speech output were equivocal as well. Even though they had the same two conditions in common (speech output and no speech output), the purposes of the studies varied considerably. Schlosser and colleagues (2007) taught a new AAC modality for requesting, whereas Parsons and La Sorte (1993) did not teach a new AAC modality at all.

Given the heterogeneity across the comparative studies in terms of measurement and purpose of study and the small number of studies tackling any one comparison, the data are equivocal, and evidence-based recommendations to favor one or the other AAC mode in promoting natural speech would be premature. For instance, our calculation of effect sizes (*d* and *g*) based on the original data by Yoder and Layton (1988) revealed no differences in speech production among various methods of sign instruction

TABLE 15.5
Studies on the Effects of AAC Intervention on Natural Speech Production in Autism: Summary and Appraisal

Study	Participants (n, CA, and IVI)	AAC Approach	Design		Speech	PND or ES	Appraisal
			Intervention	Speech			
Yoder and Stone (2006 *A randomized comparison*)	36 preschool children (mean CA, 33.6 mo)	Aided (PECS) versus RPMT	RCT: children were randomly assigned to either group	RCT		PECS was more successful than RPMT in terms of nonimitative spoken communicative acts and number of different nonimitative words	*Conclusive:* Strong design. IOA and TI were strong as well.
Tincani, Crozier, and Alazetta (2006)—Study 2	One child: Carl (9-2)	Aided (PECS)	A-B-A-B	A-B-A-B		*Speech production:* word vocalizations = 0, word approximations = 100; no requesting data reported	*Conclusive:* Strong design. IOA and TI were strong as well.
Schlosser, Luiselli, Augermeier, Schooley, Sigafoos, and Belfiore (2007)	Five children, ages 8, 8, 9, 9, and 10 yr; only one child demonstrated vocal imitation (60%)	Aided (SGD; synthetic speech)	AATD	Multiple pre-treatment, within-treatment, and post-treatment probes (every other session)		Four children remained at baseline in terms of elicited vocalizations (PND = 0). The one child who did improve over baseline was the only child with an initial vocal imitation repertoire.	*Preponderant:* The speech and intervention design were strong and ruled out carryover effects and sequence effects; TI and IOA data were strong; however, instruction did not continue until criterion

Study	Participants	AAC type	Design	Probes	Results	Certainty of evidence
Tincani (2004)	Two children, ages 6 and 7 years	Aided (PECS) versus unaided (manual sign)	AATD	Multiple pre-treatment, within-treatment, and post-treatment probes	Both children improved word vocalizations more with manual signing than with PECS; however, the PND metric was not sensitive to this difference, because it showed 100% in both conditions.	*Preponderant:* The natural speech design and the intervention design involved non-continuous data collection. TI and reliability were strong.
Charlop-Christy et al. (2002)	Three children: Alex (3) Jake (5) Kyle (12) Although not formally assessed, all children were able to imitate	Aided (PECS)	MBD across subjects	Multiple pre-treatment, within-treatment, and post-treatment probes	Elicited vocalizations (Alex 25, Jake 90, Kyle 28), imitation (Alex 25, Jake 50, Kyle 28), and MLU (Alex 25, Jake 50, Kyle 17) increased somewhat even with novel partners, non-training settings, and nontraining stimuli.	*Suggestive:* The speech design ruled out threats to internal validity; strong IOA data; TI data were lacking.
Olive et al. (2007), 3-9	Three children Mickey (?) Rocky (4) Terrence (5-6)	Aided (SGD; digitized)	MPD across subjects	Multiple pre-treatment and within-treatment probes	*Elicited vocalizations:* Mickey (0) Rocky (0) Terrence (83)	*Suggestive:* TI and IOA were strong; minor design flaws because teaching and testing were not separated (however, only unprompted responses were counted).

TABLE 15.5 *(continued)*

Study	Participants (*n*, CA, and IVI)	AAC Approach	Design			PND or ES	Appraisal
			Intervention	Speech			
Parsons and La Sorte (1993)	Six children, ages 4 to 6 years; all were able to produce speech (but not functional)	Aided (SGD; synthetic speech)	A–B–BC–B–BC / A–BC–B–BC (additive and reductive)	Continuous probes		Intervention without speech output produced no change in terms of elicited or child-initiated utterances (PND = 0 in five subjects and PND = 9 in one subject). When speech output was added, vocalizations increased (83, 75, 100, 100, 50, and 92).	*Suggestive:* The speech design was mapped onto the intervention design. Order effects were controlled across subjects with an *n* of only 3 (between-group *n* requirements not satisfied); no TI data.
Tincani, Crozier, and Alazetta (2006)— Study 1	Two children: Damian (10-2) Bob (11-9)	Aided (PECS)	MBD across subjects plus CCD	MBD across subjects plus CCD		*Word vocalizations:* Damian: 0 Bob: 0 *Approximations:* Damian: 11 (phases I–III = 0; phase IV = 100) Bob: 0	*Suggestive:* MBD was across only 2 students, and teaching and testing were confounded. IOA and TI were very good.

| Yoder and Layton (1988) | 60 children (mean CA, 5 yr) | Unaided (manual sign): 1 = speech 2 = sign 3 = alternating 4 = simultaneous | RCT: 15 children were randomly assigned to each of the four groups | RCT | *1 versus 2*: Cohen's d = 0.73; Hedges' g = 0.19, LCI = -0.04; UCI = 1.50; p = .06
 1 versus 3: Cohen's d = 0.43; Hedges' g = 0.11; LCI = -0.33; UCI = 1.18; p = .25
 1 versus 4: Cohen's d = 0.33, Hedges' g = 0.09; LCI = -0.42; UCI = 1.08; p = .37
 2 versus 4: Cohen's d = 0.33, Hedges' g = 0.09; LCI = -1.08; UCI = 0.43; p = .38
 2 versus 3: Cohen's d = 0.30, Hedges' g = 0.08; LCI = -1.05; UCI = 0.35; p = .42 | *Suggestive:* Strong design and IOA. However, there was a lack of TI data. |

TABLE 15-5   (*continued*)

Study	Participants (*n*, CA, and IVI)	AAC Approach	Design: Intervention	Design: Speech	PND or ES	Appraisal
Travis (2006)	Two children: M.M. (9-10) N.N. (9-6)	Aided (PECS)	MBD across subjects	MBD across subjects	PNDs were not calculated because the study was inconclusive.	*Inconclusive:* MBD with only 1 replication (minor design flaw). For N.N., data on unstructured activities showed increasing trends in the treated and untreated baselines (fatal flaw). No TI data were available. IOA was adequate but was based on only 10% of sessions; also, IOA was not separated for each measure. Because of the acknowledged co-intervention in the classroom and at home during nontreatment times, the source of the obtained results was difficult to interpret (fatal design flaw).

AAC, augmentative and alternative communication; AATD, adapted alternating treatments design; CA, chronological age (yr or yr-mo); CCD, changing criterion design; ES, effect size; IVI, initial vocal imitation; LCI, lower confidence interval; MBD, multiple baseline design; MLU, mean length of utterance; MPD, multiple probe design; PECS, Picture Exchange Communication System; PND, percentage of nonoverlapping data; RCT, randomized control trial; RPMT, Responsive Education and Prelinguistic Milieu Teaching; SGD, speech-generating device; UCI, upper confidence interval.

(i.e., sign alone, simultaneous use of sign and speech, and alternating between sign and speech) or between sign-alone instruction and speech-alone instruction. This is in stark contrast to Yoder and Layton's results reporting that speech alone, alternation between sign and speech, and simultaneous use of sign and speech all yielded superior speech production, compared with sign alone. Regardless of treatment condition, they did find that pretreatment vocal imitation ability predicted performance in natural speech production. This appears to be consistent with the findings in the study by Schlosser and colleagues (2007), in which only the participant with vocal imitation ability improved in speech.

Tincani's (2004) study revealed perfect PNDs (100%) for both manual signing and PECS with both children. When there is perfect nonoverlap between baseline and treatment, as is the case here, the PND does not distinguish the magnitude of that nonoverlap (i.e., both render a PND of 100%). Additional visual analysis suggested that manual signing was superior to PECS in yielding speech with both children. The child who had poor hand motor imitation skills seemed to acquire PECS more readily than manual signs. However, there were only two children involved, and the explanatory assertions are provided post hoc.

Therefore, at this time, practitioners may need to let other considerations guide the selection of appropriate AAC modes. For example, if a child has good hand motor skills and his or her daily communication partners understand manual signing, then perhaps manual signing is indicated (regardless of its projected impact on natural speech production [Seal and Bonvillian 1997]). Likewise, if a child seems to enjoy communicating with speech output and his or her communication partners communicate more with the child when speech output is provided, perhaps an SGD is indicated. There are, of course, a myriad of other assessment considerations that go into such a decision, and we realize that we have oversimplified the issue. The point is that the projected impact of various AAC modes on speech production, based on research evidence to date, does not yet have any informative or distinguishing value in guiding the selection of AAC modalities.

The following additional conclusions can be drawn. First, none of the studies registered a decline in natural speech production as a result of AAC intervention. Unless there is an undocumented publication bias at work (such that studies that show a decline are less likely to get published[1]), this finding should put many families of children with autism more at ease when considering AAC for their children. Second, five of the seven studies documented an increase in speech production. In the report of Schlosser and colleagues (2007), only one of five children improved somewhat in terms of speech production, and he was the only participant who had demonstrated vocal imitation skills before the study.

Implications for Future Research

Interestingly, the speech production data appear to be independent of how well a child has acquired the introduced AAC modality per se. That is, even though one child in Tincani's (2004) study acquired PECS more effectively than manual signing and the other child showed little difference between these modalities, both children did better in speech production with manual signing. This finding, however, is based on only two children. Research is urgently needed to better understand the relationship between the effectiveness of acquiring an AAC modality and speech production. Tincani (2004) raised the possibility that perhaps differential pre-treatment hand motor imitation skills led one of the participants to do better with PECS than with manual signing.

■ Summary and Conclusions

Many children with autism are candidates for AAC use due to limited or no functional speech. This chapter provided an evidence-based review of various AAC approaches including PECS, graphic symbols, SGDs, and manual signs. Our primary purpose was to provide the practitioner and other relevant stakeholders with prefiltered evidence so that this information might inform their clinical and educational decision making. Hence, we described numerous implications for practice balanced in light of the evidence. That being said, it is important to acknowledge that evidence itself cannot and should not be the only consideration when making decisions. Practitioners still need to integrate any suggested course of action gleaned from appraised research evidence with their clinical or educational expertise as well as relevant stakeholder perspectives. Therefore, it is imperative that practitioners engage in assessments of the individual child and elucidate the perspectives of relevant stakeholders about the research evidence and assessment findings.

In terms of the research evidence itself, it is becoming more and more clear that generalized characteristics of children with autism cannot and should not dictate the selection of AAC approaches. Children with autism present with varying profiles that, from a population perspective, deserve the label of "heterogeneity." There is growing evidence that it might be more productive to view the selection of AAC approaches in relation to specific task demands and how the characteristics of individual children are apt to meet these specific demands, rather than focusing on generalized characteristics as predictive and prescriptive indicators. The work of Yoder and Stone (2006 *A randomized comparison,* 2006 *Randomized comparison*) is a noteworthy example of such an approach, because they looked at task-specific characteristics such as object exploration or preexisting joint attention skills relative to outcomes.

Clearly, great strides have been made in research. Yet, there is much more to be accomplished. Based on the appraised research evidence, we also projected several suggested directions for future research. Naturally, the recommendations varied by AAC approach depending on the respective status of research in each area. For instance, several recent studies have provided conclusive evidence that PECS works under ideal conditions (Robey 2004 called this "efficacy"; Schlosser 2003 called it "effectiveness under ideal conditions"). Although there are numerous avenues for continuing with such investigations, the existing efficacy studies need to be replicated under more typical conditions in order to establish that PECS works under these conditions as well (Robey 2004 called this "effectiveness;" Schlosser 2003 called it "effectiveness under typical conditions"). With other AAC approaches, we still need to establish that they work under ideal conditions before progressing to typical conditions.

■ References

References marked with an asterisk indicate primary research studies from systematic reviews.

*Anderson, A.E. (2001). *Augmentative communication and autism: A comparison of sign language and the Picture Exchange Communication System.* Unpublished doctoral dissertation, University of California, San Diego.

*Angermeier, K., Schlosser, R.W., Luiselli, J.K., Harrington, C., and Carter, B. (2006). *Effects of iconicity on requesting with the Picture Exchange Communication System in children with autism spectrum disorder.* Available at DOI10.1016/grasd.2007.09.004 (accessed December 2007).

*Barrera, R.D., Lobato-Barrera, D., and Sulzer-Azaroff, B. (1980). A simultaneous treatment comparison of three expressive language training programs with a mute autistic child. *Journal of Autism and Developmental Disorders,* 10, 21–37.

Beck, A.R., Stoner, J.B., Bock, S.J., and Parton, T. (in press). Comparison of PECS and the use of VOCA Application. *Education and Training in Developmental Disabilities.*

Biermann, A. (1999). *Gestützte Kommunikation im Widerstreit.* Berlin: Edition Marhold im Wissenschaftsverlag Volker Spiess GmbH.

Bird, F., Dores, P., Moniz, D., and Robinson, J. (1989). Reducing severe aggression and self-injurious behaviors with functional communication training. *American Journal on Mental Retardation,* 94, 37–48.

Blischak, D.M., Lloyd, L.L., and Fuller, D.R. (1997). In *Augmentative and alternative communication: A handbook of principles and practices* (eds. L.L. Lloyd, D.R. Fuller, and H.H. Arvidson), pp. 38–42. Needham Heights, Mass.: Allyn and Bacon.

Bondy, A., and Frost, L. (1994). The Picture Exchange Communication System. *Focus on Autistic Behavior,* 9 (3), 1–19.

Bopp, K.D., Brown, K.E., and Mirenda, P. (2004). Speech-language pathologists' role in the delivery of positive behavior support for individuals with developmental disabilities. *American Journal of Speech-Language Pathology,* 13, 5–19.

*Brady, D.O., and Smouse, A.D. (1978). A simultaneous comparison of three methods for language training with an autistic child: An experimental single case analysis. *Journal of Autism and Childhood Schizophrenia, 8,* 271–279.

*Buckley, S.D., and Newchok, D.K. (2005). Differential impact of response effort within a response chain on use of mands in a student with autism. *Research in Developmental Disabilities, 26,* 77–85.

*Buffington, D.M., Krantz, P.J., McClannahan, L.E., and Poulson, C.L. (1998). Procedures for teaching appropriate gestural communication skills to children with autism. *Journal of Autism and Developmental Disorders, 28,* 535–545.

Campbell, J.M. (2003). Efficacy of behavioral interventions for reducing problem behavior in persons with autism: A quantitative synthesis of single-subject research. *Research in Developmental Disabilities, 24,* 120–138.

*Carr, E.G., Binkoff, J.A., Kologinsky, E., and Eddy, M. (1978). Acquisition of sign language by autistic children. I: Expressive labeling. *Journal of Applied Behavior Analysis, 11,* 489–501.

*Carr, E.G., and Dores, P. (1981). Patterns of language acquisition following simultaneous communication with autistic children. *Analysis and Intervention in Developmental Disabilities, 1,* 347–361.

*Carr, D., and Felce, J. (2006). Brief report: Increase in production of spoken words in some children with autism after PECS teaching to phase III. *Journal of Autism and Developmental Disorders,* published on-line, DOI 10.1007/ s10803–006–0204–0. Available at http://www.springerlink.com (accessed November 2, 2007).

*Carr, D., and Felce, J. (2006). The effects of PECS teaching to phase III on the communicative interactions between children with autism and their teachers. *Journal of Autism and Developmental Disorders,* published on-line, DOI 10.1007/s10803–006–0203–1. Published on-line. Available at http://www. springerlink.com (accessed November 2, 2007).

*Carr, E.G. and Kemp, D.C. (1989). Functional equivalence of autistic leading and communicative pointing: Analysis and treatment. *Journal of Autism and Developmental Disorders, 19,* 561–578.

*Carr, E.G., and Kologinsky, E. (1983). Acquisition of sign language by autistic children II: Spontaneity and generalization effects. *Journal of Applied Behavior Analysis, 16,* 297–314.

*Carr, E.G., Kologinsky, E., and Leff-Simon, S. (1987). Acquisition of sign language by autistic children. III: Generalized descriptive phrases. *Journal of Autism and Developmental Disorders, 17,* 217–229.

Chambers, M., and Rehfeldt, R.A. (2003). Assessing the acquisition and generalization of two mand forms with adults with severe developmental disabilities. *Research in Developmental Disabilities, 24,* 265–280.

*Charlop-Christy, M., Carpenter, M., Le, L., LeBlanc, L., and Kellet, K. (2002). Using the Picture Exchange Communication System (PECS) with children with autism: Assessment of PECS acquisition, speech, social-communicative behavior, and problem behavior. *Journal of Applied Behavior Analysis*, 35, 213–231.

Cohen, J. (1977). *Statistical power analysis for the behavioral sciences* (Rev. ed.). New York: Academic Press.

Cohen, J. (1988). *Statistical power analysis for the behavioral sciences* (2nd ed.). Hillsdale, N.J.: Erlbaum.

*Dettmer, S., Simpson, R.L., Smith Myles, B., and Ganz, J. (2000). The use of visual supports to facilitate transitions of students with autism. *Focus on Autism and Other Developmental Disabilities*, 15, 163–169.

*Dexter, M.E. (1998). *The effects of aided language stimulation upon verbal output and augmentative communication during storybook reading for children with pervasive developmental disabilities*. Unpublished doctoral dissertation, The Johns Hopkins University, Baltimore.

*Dyches, T.T. (1998). Effects of switch training on the communication of children with autism and severe disabilities. *Focus on Autism and other Developmental Disabilities*, 13, 151–162.

*Frea, W.D., Arnold, C.L., and Wittinberga, G.L. (2001). A demonstration of the effects of augmentative communication on the extreme aggressive behavior of a child with autism within an integrated preschool setting. *Journal of Positive Behavior Interventions*, 3, 194–198.

Frost, L.A., and Bondy, A.S. (2004). *The Picture Exchange Communication System training manual* (2nd ed.). Newark, Del.: Pyramid Educational Consultants.

*Ganz, J.B., and Simpson, R.L. (2004). Effects on communicative requesting and speech development of the Picture Exchange Communication System in children with characteristics of autism. *Journal of Autism and Developmental Disorders*, 34, 395–409.

Granlund, M., and Olsson, C. (1999). Efficacy of communication intervention for presymbolic communicators. *Augmentative and Alternative Communication*, 15, 25–37.

Hamilton, B.L., and Snell, M.E. (1993). Using the milieu approach to increase spontaneous communication book use across environments by an adolescent with autism. *Augmentative and Alternative Communication*, 9, 259–272.

*Hetzroni, O.E., and Shalem, U. (2005). From logos to orthographic symbols: A multilevel fading computer program for teaching nonverbal children with autism. *Focus on Autism and Other Developmental Disabilities*, 20, 201–212.

Horner, R., and Day, H.M. (1991). The effects of response efficiency on functionally equivalent competing behaviors. *Journal of Applied Behavior Analysis*, 24, 719–732.

*Hundert, J. (1981). Stimulus generalization after training an autistic deaf boy in manual signs. *Education and Treatment of Children*, 4, 329–337.

*Johnston, S., Nelson, C., Evans, J., and Palazolo, K. (2003). The use of visual supports in teaching young children with autism spectrum disorder to initiate interactions. *Augmentative and Alternative Communication*, 19, 86–103.

*Jones, C.M. (2004). *Using the Picture Exchange Communication System and time delay to enhance the spontaneous speech of children with autism.* Unpublished doctoral dissertation, Claremont Graduation University, California.

Kahng, S., Iwata, B.A., and Lewin, A.B. (2002). The impact of functional assessment on the treatment of self-injurious behavior. In *Self-injurious behavior: Gene-brain-behavior relationships* (eds. S.R. Schroeder, M.L. Oster-Granite, and T. Thompson), pp. 119–131. Washington, D.C.: American Psychological Association.

*Keogh, D., Whitman, T., Beeman, D., Halligan, K., and Starzynski, T. (1987). Teaching interactive signing in a dialogue situation to mentally retarded individuals. *Research in Developmental Disabilities,* 8, 39–53.

*Kozleski, E. (1991). Visual symbol acquisition by students with autism. *Exceptionality,* 2, 173–194.

*Kravits, T.R., Kamps, D.M., Kemmerer, K., and Potucek, J. (2002). Increasing communication skills for an elementary-aged student with autism using the Picture Exchange Communication System. *Journal of Autism and Developmental Disorders,* 32, 225–230.

Liddle, K. (2001). Implementing the Picture Exchange Communication System (PECS). *International Journal of Language and Communication Disorders,* 36 (Suppl.), 391–395.

Lipsey, M.W., and Wilson, D.B. (2001). *Practical meta-analysis.* Thousand Oaks, Calif.: SAGE.

Lloyd, L.L., Fuller, D.R., and Arvidson, H.H., eds. (1997). *Augmentative and alternative communication: A handbook of principles and practices.* Needham Heights, Mass.: Allyn and Bacon.

Loncke, F., and Bos, H. (1997). Unaided AAC symbols. In *Augmentative and alternative communication: A handbook of principles and practices* (eds. L.L. Lloyd, D.R. Fuller, and H.H. Arvidson), pp. 80–106. Needham Heights, Mass.: Allyn and Bacon.

Lonigan, C., Elber, J., and Johnson, S. (1998). Empirically supported interventions for children: An overview. *Journal of Clinical Child Psychology,* 27, 138–145.

Loveland, K.A., Landry, S.H., Hughes, S.O., Hall, S.K., and McEvoy, R.E. (1988). Speech acts and the pragmatic deficits of autism. *Journal of Speech and Hearing Research,* 31, 593–604.

Magiati, I., and Howlin, P. (2003). A pilot evaluation study of the Picture Exchange Communication System (PECS) for children with autistic spectrum disorders. *Autism,* 7, 297–320.

Mancil, G.R. (2006). Functional communication training: A review of the literature related to children with autism. *Education and Training in Developmental Disabilities,* 41, 213–224.

*Marckel, J.M., Neef, N.A., and Ferreri, S.J. (2006). A preliminary analysis of teaching improvisation with the Picture Exchange Communication System to children with autism. *Journal of Applied Behavior Analysis,* 39, 109–115.

Millar, D., Light, J.C., and Schlosser, R.W. (2006). The impact of augmentative and alternative communication intervention on the speech production of individuals with developmental disabilities: A research review. *Journal of Speech, Language, and Hearing Research*, 49, 248–264.

Mirenda, P. (2001). Autism, augmentative communication, and assistive technology: What do we really know? *Focus on Autism and Other Developmental Disabilities*, 16, 141–151.

Mirenda, P. (2003). Toward functional augmentative and alternative communication for students with autism: Manual signs, graphic symbols, and voice output communication aids. *Language, Speech, and Hearing Services in Schools*, 34, 203–216.

Mirenda, P., and Erickson, K.A. (2000). Augmentative communication and literacy. In *Autism spectrum disorders: A transactional developmental perspective* (eds. A.M. Wetherby and B.M. Prizant), pp. 333–367. Baltimore: Paul H. Brookes.

Mirenda, P., and Schuler, A. (1988). Augmenting communication for persons with autism: Issues and strategies. *Topics in Language Disorders*, 9 (1), 24–43.

Morford, M., and Goldin-Meadow, S. (1992). Comprehension and production of gesture in combination with speech in one-word speakers. *Journal of Child Language*, 19, 559–580.

Mundy, P., and Gomes, A. (1998). Individual differences in joint attention skill development in the second year. *Infant Behavior and Development*, 21, 469–482.

Mundy, P., Sigman, M., and Kasari, C. (1990). A longitudinal study of joint attention and language development in autistic children. *Journal of Autism and Developmental Disorders*, 20, 115–128.

Nußbeck, S. (1999). *Gestützte Kommunikation. Ein Ausdrucksmittel für Menschen mit geistiger Behinderung?* [Facilitated Communication. A means of expression for people with mental retardation?]. Göttingen, Germany: Hogrefe-Verlag.

Olive, M.L., and Smith, B.W. (2005). Effect size calculations and single subject designs. *Educational Psychology*, 25, 313–324.

*Olive, M., de la Cruz, B., Davis, T.N., Chan, J.M., Lang, R.B., O'Reilly, M.F., and Dickson, S.M. (2007). The effects of enhanced milieu teaching and a voice output communication aid on the requesting of three children with autism. *Journal of Autism and Developmental Disorders*, 37, 1505–1513.

*Parsons, C.L., and La Sorte, D. (1993). The effect of computers with synthesized speech and no speech on the spontaneous communication of children with autism. *Australian Journal of Human Communication Disorders*, 21, 12–31.

Peeters, T. and Gillberg, C. (1999). *Autism: Medical and educational aspects.* London: Whurr.

Peterson, L., Homer, A.L., and Wonderlich, S.A. (1982). The integrity of independent variables in behavior analysis. *Journal of Applied Behavior Analysis*, 15, 477–492.

Petticrew, M., and Roberts, H. (2006). *Systematic reviews in the social sciences: A practical guide.* Malden, Mass.: Blackwell.

Probst, P. (2005). "Communication unbound—or unfound"?—Ein integratives Literatur-Review zur Wirksamkeit der "Gestützten Kommunikation" ("Facilitated Communication/FC") bei nichtsprechenden autistischen und intelligenzgeminderten Personen. *Zeitschrift für Klinische Psychologie, Psychiatrie und Psychotherapie,* 53, 93–128.

Reichle, J., and Wacker, D.P. (1993). *Communicative alternatives to challenging behavior: Integrating functional assessment and intervention strategies.* Baltimore: Paul H. Brookes.

*Remington, B., and Clarke, S. (1983). Acquisition of expressive signing by autistic children: An evaluation of the relative effects of simultaneous communication and sign-alone training. *Journal of Applied Behavior Analysis,* 16, 315–328.

Robey, R.R. (2004). A five-phase model for clinical-outcome research. *Journal of Communication Disorders,* 37, 401–411.

Sackett, D.L., Straus, S.E., Richardson, W.S., Rosenberg, W., and Haynes, R.B. (2000). *Evidence-based medicine: How to practice and teach EBM* (2nd ed.). New York: Churchill Livingstone.

*Saraydarian, K.A. (1994). *Simultaneous referent recognition-production training for nonverbal children with autism.* Unpublished doctoral dissertation, Columbia University Teachers College, New York.

*Schepis, M.M., Reid, D.H., Behrmann, M.M., and Sutton, K.A. (1998). Increasing communicative interactions of young children with autism using a voice output communication aid and naturalistic teaching. *Journal of Applied Behavior Analysis,* 31, 561–578.

*Schepis, M.M., Reid, D.H., Fitzgerald, J.R., Faw, G.D., VanDenPol, R.A., Welty, P.A. (1982). A program for increasing manual signing by autistic and profoundly retarded youth within the daily environment. *Journal of Applied Behavior Analysis,* 15, 363–379.

Schlosser, R.W. (2002). On the importance of being earnest about treatment integrity. *Augmentative and Alternative Communication,* 18, 36–44.

Schlosser, R.W. (2003). *The efficacy of augmentative and alternative communication: Toward evidence-based practice.* San Diego, Calif.: Academic Press.

Schlosser, R.W., and Blischak, D.M. (2001). Is there a role for speech output in interventions for persons with autism? A review. *Focus on Autism and Other Developmental Disabilities,* 16, 170–178.

*Schlosser, R.W., and Blischak, D.M. (2004). Effects of speech and print feedback on spelling in children with autism. *Journal of Speech, Language and Hearing Research,* 47, 848–862.

*Schlosser, R.W., Blischak, D.M., Belfiore, P.J., Bartley, C., and Barnett, N. (1998). The effects of synthetic speech output and orthographic feedback on spelling in a student with autism: A preliminary study. *Journal of Autism and Developmental Disorders,* 28, 319–329.

Schlosser, R.W., and Raghavendra, P. (2004). Evidence-based practice in augmentative and alternative communication. *Augmentative and Alternative Communication*, 20, 1–21.

Schlosser, R.W., and Sigafoos, J. (2002). Selecting graphic symbols for an initial request lexicon: Integrative review. *Augmentative and Alternative Communication*, 18, 102–123.

Schlosser, R.W., and Sigafoos, J. (2006). Augmentative and alternative communication interventions for persons with developmental disabilities: Narrative review of comparative single-subject experimental studies. *Research in Developmental Disabilities*, 27, 1–29.

Schlosser, R.W., and Sigafoos, J. (2007). Moving evidence-based practice forward [editorial]. *Evidence-based Communication Assessment and Intervention*.

*Schlosser, R.W., Sigafoos, J., Luiselli, J., Angermeier, K., Schooley, K., Harasymowyz, U., and Belfiore, J. (2007). Effects of synthetic speech output on requesting and natural speech production in children with autism. *Research in Autism Spectrum Disorders*, 1, 139–163.

Schlosser, R.W., and Wendt, O. (in press). Effects of augmentative and alternative communication intervention on speech production in autism: A systematic review. *American Journal of Speech-Language Pathology*.

Schlosser, R.W., Bevetvas, N., and Wendt, O. (2007). *Effects of the Picture Exchange Communication System in individuals with autism spectrum disorders: A systematic review.* Manuscript in preparation.

Schuler, A.L., and Baldwin, M. (1981). Nonspeech communication and childhood autism. *Language, Speech, and Hearing Services in Schools*, 12, 246–257.

Schwartz, I.S., Garfinkle, A.N., and Bauer, J. (1998). The Picture Exchange Communication System: Communicative outcomes for young children with disabilities. *Topics in Early Childhood Special Education*, 18, 144–159.

Scotti, J.R., Evans, I.M., and Meyer, L.H., and Walker, P. (1991). A meta-analysis of intervention research with problem behavior: Treatment validity and standards of practice. *American Journal on Mental Retardation*, 96 (3), 233–256.

Scruggs, T.E., Mastropieri, M.A., and Casto, G. (1987). The quantitative synthesis of single subject research methodology: Methodology and validation. *Remedial and Special Education*, 8, 24–33.

Scruggs, T.E., Mastropieri, M.A., Cook, S.B., and Escobar, C. (1986). Early intervention for children with conduct disorders: A quantitative synthesis of single-subject research. *Behavioral Disorders*, 11, 260–271.

Seal, B., and Bonvillian, J. (1997). Sign language and motor functioning in students with autistic disorder. *Journal of Autism and Developmental Disorders*, 27.

*Sidener, T.M., Shabani, D.B., Carr, J.E., and Roland, J.P. (2005). An evaluation of strategies to maintain mands at practical levels. *Research in Developmental Disabilities*, 27, 632–644.

*Sigafoos, J. (1998). Assessing conditional use of graphic mode requesting in a young boy with autism. *Journal of Developmental and Physical Disabilities,* 10, 133–151.

*Sigafoos, J., Didden, R., and O'Reilly, M. (2003). Effects of speech output on maintenance of requesting and frequency of vocalizations in three children with developmental disabilities. *Augmentative and Alternative Communication,* 19, 37–47.

Sigafoos, J., and Drasgow, E. (2001). Conditional use of aided and unaided AAC: A review and clinical case demonstration. *Focus on Autism and other Developmental Disabilities,* 16, 152–161

*Sigafoos, J., Drasgow, E., Halle, J.W., O'Reilly, M.O., Seely-York, S., Edrisinha, C., and Andrews, A. (2004). Teaching VOCA use as a communicative repair strategy. *Journal of Autism and Developmental Disorders,* 34, 411–422.

Simeonsson, R., and Bailey, D. (1991). Evaluating programme impact: Levels of certainty. In *Early intervention studies for young children with special needs* (eds. D. Mitchell and R. Brown), pp. 280–296. London: Chapman and Hall.

*Sommer, K.S., Whitman, T.L., and Keogh, D.A. (1988). Teaching severely retarded persons to sign interactively through the use of a behavioral script. *Journal in Developmental Disabilities,* 9, 291–304.

*Son, S.H., Sigafoos, J., O'Reilly, M., and Lancioni, G.E. (2006). Comparing two types of augmentative and alternative communication for children with autism. *Pediatric Rehabilitation,* 9, 389–395.

Spencer, L.G. (2002). *Comparing the effectiveness of status pictures vs. video modeling on teaching requesting skills to elementary children with autism.* Unpublished doctoral dissertation, Georgia State University, Atlanta, GA.

Spillane, M.M. (1999). *The effect of instructional method on symbol acquisition by students with severe disabilities.* Unpublished doctoral dissertation, University of Nebraska, Lincoln, NE.

Stiebel, D. (1999). Promoting augmentative communication during daily routines: A parent problem-solving intervention. *Journal of Positive Behavior Interventions,* 1, 159–169.

Sundberg, M.L. (1993). Selecting a response form for nonverbal persons: Facilitated Communication, pointing systems, or sign language? *The Analysis of Verbal Behavior,* 11, 99–116.

Sundberg, M., and Partington, J. (1998). *Teaching language to children with autism or other developmental disabilities* (Version 7.1) [computer manual]. Pleasant Hill, Calif.: Behavior Analysts.

*Tincani, M. (2004). Comparing the Picture Exchange Communication System (PECS) and sign-language training for children with autism. *Focus on Autism and Other Developmental Disabilities,* 19, 152–163.

*Tincani, M., Crozier, S., and Alazetta, L. (2006). The Picture Exchange Communication System: Effects on manding and speech development for school-aged children with autism. *Education and Training in Developmental Disabilities,* 41, 177–184.

*Travis, J. (2006). *The effectiveness of the Picture Exchange Communication System (PECS) as an augmentative communication system for children with autism spectrum disorders (ASD): A South African pilot study.* Unpublished masters thesis, University of Cape Town, South Africa.

Wendt, O. (2006). *The effectiveness of augmentative and alternative communication for individuals with autism spectrum disorders: A systematic review and meta-analysis.* Unpublished doctoral dissertation, Purdue University, West Lafayette, Ind.

Yoder, P.J., and Compton, D. (2004). Identifying predictors of treatment response. *Mental Retardation and Developmental Disabilities Research Reviews,* 10, 162–168.

Yoder, P., and Layton, T. (1988). Speech following sign language training in autistic children with minimal verbal language. *Journal of Autism and Developmental Disorders,* 18, 217–229.

*Yoder, P.J., and Stone, W.L. (2006). A randomized comparison of the effect of two prelinguistic communication interventions on the acquisition of spoken communication in preschoolers with ASD. *Journal of Speech, Language, and Hearing Research,* 49, 698–711.

*Yoder, P., and Stone, W. (2006). Randomized comparison of two communication interventions for preschoolers with autism spectrum disorders. *Journal of Consulting and Clinical Psychology,* 74, 426–435.

*Yokoyama, K., Naoi, N., and Yakamoto, J.-I. (2006). Teaching verbal behavior using the Picture Exchange Communication System (PECS) with children with autism spectrum disorders. *Japanese Journal of Special Education,* 43, 485–503.

Zipoli, R.P., and Kennedy, M. (2005). Evidence-based practice among speech-language pathologists: Attitudes, utilization, and barriers. *American Journal of Speech-Language Pathology,* 14, 208–220.

SECTION 4

BEHAVIOR SUPPORT AND INTERVENTION

16. ANTECEDENT (PREVENTIVE) INTERVENTION

James K. Luiselli

Children with autism frequently demonstrate challenging behaviors such as self-injury, aggression, property destruction, and tantrum outbursts. These and similar problems can be threaten health, cause disruption, and be socially stigmatizing. In addition, challenging behavior interferes with instruction, limiting effective teaching interactions and skill acquisition.

Applied behavior analysis (ABA) is an evidence-based approach to challenging behavior backed by almost four decades of successful intervention research (Baer, Wolf, and Risley 1968). Behavioral intervention has been implemented in specialized educational programs for children with autism and in public schools, homes, and community settings. The defining characteristics of this intervention are objective measurement of clinically relevant target behaviors, application of empirically supported procedures, data-driven decision making, and outcome evaluation. ABA intervention also has focused on implementation by natural care providers. Therefore, teachers, parents, therapists, and peers have been instrumental as change agents.

The extensive research literature concerned with behavioral intervention for children who have autism has been dominated by consequence-control methods (Luiselli 2004). One strategy has been to strengthen responses and establish skills that are incompatible with challenging behavior. An example would be presenting a child with positive consequences (e.g., social approval, access to preferred play, a favorite food) when he or she speaks appropriately instead of screaming. A second strategy has been implementing a negative consequence contingent on challenging behavior. For example, if a child misbehaves, he or she could receive a reprimand, be instructed to correct the effects of the behavior, have voluntary movement restricted, or be contacted with an aversive stimulus. These behavior-contingent methods qualify as punishment (Lerman and Vorndran 2002).

Although consequence-control intervention can be effective, professionals have noted several potential implementation concerns. First, although many children respond well to positive reinforcement procedures, many do not, either because preferences cannot be identified or because reinforcement by itself is not consistently successful. With regard to behavior-contingent consequences, some procedures are physically invasive and subject to mis-application. For example, having a teacher immobilize (restrain) a student's movement after disruptive behavior could result in injury. This procedure could also cause distress, agitation, and resistance, further complicating an already difficult situation. Concerns about physical intervention are ampli-fied further because many practitioners find it unacceptable, favoring a "less aversive" approach that is better suited to natural settings.

Contemporary behavior analysts continue to debate intervention phi-losophy and the types of behavior-reduction procedures that are considered evidence-based (Carr and Sidener 2002; Johnston et al. 2006; Lerman and Vorndran 2002). In particular, there is division about whether challenging be-havior can be effectively treated using "positive" approaches exclusively, whether it is clinically justified to use deprivation procedures, and whether the distinc-tion between positive behavior support (PBS) and ABA is legitimate (Carr et al. 1999; Johnston et al. 2006; Reid et al. 2003). Luiselli (2004) proposed that be-havioral intervention with people who have developmental disabilities has changed over "generations," evolving from consequence-focused (and, largely, punishment-oriented) procedures to an orientation that stresses skill-building and prevention. *Antecedent intervention*, the topic of this chapter, is one of the areas that has received increased clinical and research attention (Luiselli 2006; Luiselli and Cameron 1998; McGill 1999; Smith and Iwata 1997).

■ Overview of Antecedent Intervention

Defined broadly, antecedent intervention has the purpose of preventing the occurrence of challenging behavior. In contrast to consequence procedures, antecedent intervention is implemented before the challenging behavior is demonstrated. Therefore, instead of waiting for a child to display aggression and having someone apply a controlling consequence, an antecedent ap-proach manipulates conditions to eliminate the probability that aggression will be encountered.

Antecedent intervention is particularly advantageous for seriously chal-lenging behavior. It is possible, for example, to use therapeutic restraint (pro-tective holding) as a consequence in a plan that addresses self-injury and other health-threatening behaviors (Harris 1996). However, given the reasons dis-cussed earlier, it would be more desirable if a teacher or parent did not have to apply such a procedure. Also, challenging behavior frequently is situation specific, meaning that it occurs under certain environmental conditions and not others. Often, these conditions can be modified by changing distinct an-tecedent features, the result being permanent elimination of the challenging behavior. And as noted previously, practitioners may judge antecedent intervention as being more acceptable than "reactive" (consequence) methods. However, antecedent procedures are rarely incorporated as a sole component of intervention; typically, they are applied in concert with one or more consequence strategies (Ricciardi 2006).

This chapter is organized in several sections. First, I present a conceptual framework for formulating antecedent intervention. Next, functional assessment and analysis is addressed as a first step in designing an antecedent-focused behavior support plan. The remainder of the chapter describes evidence-based antecedent procedures that have been effective with challenging behavior of children with autism.

■ Conceptual Framework for Antecedent Intervention

Both people and the physical environment can acquire *stimulus control* over behavior. To illustrate, if a teacher is consistently positive during interactions with students, they may be more likely to approach the teacher, follow her instructions, and participate in activities. Conversely, if a teacher is harsh and rarely positive, students may avoid that person and respond less favorably during instruction. Similarly, children may be uncomfortable within, avoid, or seek to escape settings in which they have had negative experiences. Common examples are hospital or dental clinics where physically invasive procedures have been encountered in the past (O'Callaghan et al. 2006).

Stimulus control occurs through the pairing of "antecedents" (people, places, objects) with positive and negative consequences. A *discriminative stimulus*, or S^D, is defined as a stimulus that has been associated with positive reinforcement. Relative to antecedent intervention, the principle of discriminative stimulus control allows for various manipulations to induce behavior change. Consider again the teacher who has positive stimulus control with her students. She could conduct instruction together with less effective staff personnel, with the ultimate objective of "transferring" stimulus control to them. Once control is achieved, the teacher removes herself gradually so that staff eventually are solely responsible for instruction.

A stimulus control approach to intervention also can be applied to environments. In the case of a child who becomes agitated within a medical setting, the intervention might concentrate on teaching the child to tolerate the earliest steps in a graduated "approach" sequence (Ricciardi, Luiselli, and Cammere 2006). Using the dental distress example, this sequence could start by having the child sit calmly and quietly in a dentist's office. The next steps might be having the child interact briefly with the dentist in the reception area, walk into the dental suite, sit in the dentist's chair, and so on, until she is about to receive treatment compliantly. Again, this example illustrates how an emphasis on stimulus control qualifies as antecedent intervention.

Changing a person's *motivation* to respond is another antecedent manipulation. Behavior analysts explain motivation with reference to the concept of an *establishing operation* (EO). As defined by Michael (1993, 192), an EO is "an environmental event, operation, or stimulus condition that affects an organism by momentarily altering *(a)* the reinforcing effectiveness of other events and *(b)* the frequency of occurrence of that part of the organism's repertoire to those events as consequences." So conceived, an EO influences responding, first, by increasing the value (or potency) of consequences that have functioned as positive reinforcement, and second, by evoking behaviors that were previously reinforced. As exemplified by a child who receives food as positive reinforcement for correct learning responses, the motivation to respond accurately should be greater in instructional sessions that are scheduled before instead of after the lunch meal (Zhou, Iwata, and Shore 2002). This effect is predicted because being hungry (a state of deprivation) increases the enjoyment of food consumption and, contemporaneously, the behaviors that produce food.

Food is a primary, or tangible, consequence, but the concept of an EO extends to other events. For a child who experiences long periods without social contact, peer or adult attention may be highly reinforcing. The same result is apparent for a child who enjoys sensory stimulation but has not had access to toys or motor activities. Keep in mind that deprivation states relative to tangible, social, and sensory stimuli strengthen motivation, but the resulting increase in "stimuli-contacting" behavior could be either appropriate or inappropriate. Consider that increasing a child's motivation to consume food may lead to better performance in the classroom where food is used as positive reinforcement but also to an unacceptable behavior such as food-stealing.

The concept of an EO extends to *biological* influences and health conditions as well (Kennedy and Becker 2006). In one study, Kennedy and Meyer (1996) found that the challenging behavior of three students during instruction was most frequent when one student had allergy symptoms and two students had reduced hours of sleep the night before. When the students were allergy-free and had slept more soundly, challenging behavior was less frequent. A similar relationship has been reported with conditions such as constipation (Carr and Smith 1995), otitis media (Luiselli, Cochran, and Huber 2005; O'Reilly 1997), and premenstrual syndrome (Carr et al. 2003). From a clinical perspective, practitioners should consider a range of preventive and ameliorative health-care treatments combined with evidence-based behavior supports.

Michael (1993) also proposed the term "abolishing operation" for events that *reduce* the effectiveness of consequences that were reinforcing and the frequency of behavior that has been reinforced. More recently, Friman and Hawkins (2006) suggested the term "disestablishing operation," or DO, to explain the same concept. Whereas deprivation is the critical element with an EO, satiation is linked to an abolishing/disestablishing operation. So, for a child who demonstrates challenging behavior reinforced by adult attention, giving the child more frequent and noncontingent praise and approval could be therapeutic, because the motivation to behave inappropriately would be lessened. Or, challenging behavior that is maintained by sensory consequences could be reduced by allowing the child scheduled access to acceptable objects that produce the same or similar preferred stimulation (Lerman and Rapp 2006).

In summary, this conceptual framework for antecedent intervention includes discriminative stimulus control and motivational operations (EO and DO). Acknowledging that both an S^D and EO/DO are defined in relation to positive reinforcement, the distinction is that an S^D signals the availability of reinforcement, whereas an EO/DO determines the relative strength (effectiveness) of reinforcement. Each of these concepts is elucidated further in the section describing clinical applications of functionally derived antecedent intervention.

■ Functional Assessment and Analysis

The objective of functional assessment and analysis is to identify variables that "cause" challenging behavior. Put succinctly, function is synonymous with purpose. Functional assessment and analysis methods address both the conditions that provoke and those that maintain challenging behavior. Knowing the conditions that set the occasion for challenging behavior and how they interact with consequence events is integral to the formulation of antecedent intervention. Furthermore, behavior-function must be isolated in order for intervention to be "matched" with one or more sources of control.

Behavior analysts concentrate on three *response-reinforcer* relationships in the context of functional assessment and analysis. *Social-positive reinforcement* refers to challenging behavior that is maintained by various forms of attention. Attention-maintained challenging behavior is seen, for example, in a child who has tantrum outbursts because he enjoys the resulting social reactions of adults who tell him to "stop," show disapproval, or engage him in a preferred interaction. Having the child contact preferred *tangible* items (e.g., toys) contingent on a tantrum outburst also describes a social-positive reinforcement function.

Social-negative reinforcement applies to challenging behavior that is maintained by avoidance or escape from a nonpreferred condition. For many children, receiving instructional demands from a teacher represents an "unpleasant" interaction. If a child hits her teacher and demands are eliminated each time, aggression may increase, because the behavior produces escape and is negatively reinforced. In this example, an avoidance function would operate if the teacher postponed instruction as a consequence for aggression.

The third response-reinforcer relationship is termed *automatic reinforcement.* Included here is challenging behavior that is reinforced by its own sensory consequences. Stereotypy (repetitive motor responses) and some forms of self-injury frequently are maintained by behavior-produced visual (e.g., waving hands in front of eyes), tactile (e.g., scratching skin), or proprioceptive (e.g., rocking body) stimulation. In effect, the challenging behavior occurs independent of social contingencies.

With *functional assessment,* the objective is to identify conditions that are associated with challenging behavior; in contrast, *functional analysis* incorporates direct manipulation of possible controlling conditions (Iwata, Vollmer, and Zarcone 1990). *Indirect* functional assessment relies on the subjective report of caregivers, sometimes gathered through informal review or completion of a written inventory or interview protocol, such as the Motivation Assessment Scale (MAS) (Durand and Crimmins 1988) or the Functional Assessment Interview (FAI) (O'Neill et al. 1997). *Descriptive* functional assessment is a more empirical method, consisting of behavior recording in the form of a scatter-plot (Touchette, MacDonald, and Langer 1985) or an antecedent-behavior-consequence (ABC) data sheet. The information and data obtained with indirect and descriptive assessment helps formulate an hypothesis regarding behavior-function, but the findings are correlational and a conclusive cause-and-effect relationship cannot be inferred.

Functional analysis evolved from the seminal research of Iwata and associates (1982). It involves "the direct observation of problem behavior under at least one test condition in which the effects of a particular consequence for problem behavior are evaluated in the presence of a relevant establishing operation (EO) and one control condition in which the same consequence and establishing operation is absent" (Tiger, Hanley, and Bessette 2006, 107–108). A study published by Luiselli and colleagues (2004) illustrates how a functional analysis is implemented. The student was a 6-year-old boy who had autism and engaged in repetitive saliva-play by placing fingers in his mouth, rubbing together his saliva-coated fingers, and drooling saliva onto his chin. Each day at his school, saliva-play was measured during a 10-minute session with the boy and a therapist under one of the following conditions:

Attention: The therapist sat beside the boy at a table but did not interact with him. When saliva-play occurred, the therapist responded with the verbal directive, "No, don't put your hands in your mouth." This was the test condition for social-positive reinforcement.

Demand: Using learning tasks that had been selected for the boy, the therapist provided instruction during the session. Prompts were given by the therapist if the boy did not respond independently. If the boy engaged in saliva-play, the therapist removed materials and ceased interaction for 30 seconds. This was the test condition for social-negative reinforcement.

Ignore: The therapist sat with the boy as in the attention condition but did not respond when saliva-play occurred. This was the test condition for automatic reinforcement.

Play: The boy sat at a table beside the therapist and had access to several toys. The therapist presented attention to him ("e.g., "I like your shirt") every 30 seconds during the session and ignored saliva-play. This was a control condition.

Figure 16.1 shows the frequency of saliva-play during the four functional analysis conditions. These data indicated that the boy played with saliva during all conditions and that frequency was undifferentiated. The resulting behavior hypothesis was that saliva-play was maintained by automatic reinforcement and not by attention or escape. This formulation (reviewed later in the chapter) produced an intervention evaluation of noncontingent (response-independent) access to alternative oral stimulation.

It is critical to complete a functional assessment and analysis before formulating an intervention plan. A functional analysis is the desired experimental methodology, often is executed under analog (simulated) conditions, but can

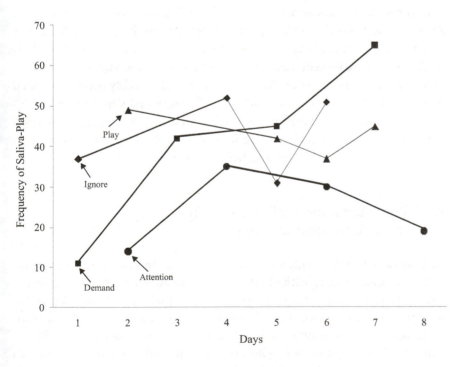

FIGURE 16.1. Frequency of saliva play by a 6-year-old boy with autism during a functional analysis.

be adapted efficiently to natural settings (Hanley, Iwata, and McCord 2003). Many practitioners rely on functional assessments obtained through indirect and descriptive methods, because, when compared to a functional analysis, they are easier to perform. However, data interpretation from descriptive assessments and more controlled functional analyses may be comparable (Hanley, Iwata, and McCord 2003).

Regarding the functional assessment and analysis of antecedent events, several lines of research have evolved. Unique stimulus variables can affect the results of functional analysis, including the physical properties and presence of materials (Carr, Yarbrough, and Langdon 1997), verbal directives (Piazza et al. 1997), and pace of task presentation (Smith et al. 1995). Other studies have demonstrated differential stimulus control exerted by *person-specific* attributes. For example, the outcome from a functional analysis may differ based on the gender of the therapist (LeBlanc et al. 2001) or whether procedures were implemented by a parent versus grandparent (Ringdahl and Sellers 2000), a parent versus direct-care staff (McAdam et al. 2004), or familiar versus novel practitioners (Progar et al. 2001).

Finally, situations that precede a functional analysis can affect results. McComas, Thompson, and Johnson (2003) demonstrated that presession social attention was associated with a reduced level of attention-maintained challenging behavior during the functional analysis. Here, the attention delivered before the session served as an abolishing operation. More recently, Roantree and Kennedy (2006) reported an opposite finding, in which a child's socially reinforced challenging behavior *increased* during functional analysis sessions that were preceded by a period of noncontingent attention. The presession attention in this study functioned as an EO, possibly because it "acted to prime attention as a positive reinforcer" (Roantree and Kennedy 2006, 383). The implication from these findings is that, in order to adequately interpret data from a functional analysis, practitioners should control the presence and absence of motivational operations before and during sessions.

■ Clinical Applications of Functionally Derived Antecedent Intervention

This section samples evidence-based antecedent intervention procedures that have been effective with children who have autism and challenging behavior. Procedures are described for attention-maintained (social-positive reinforcement), escape-motivated (social-negative reinforcement) and automatic reinforcement functions. Some of the procedures have been evaluated with each behavior-function, whereas others are more function specific. To better exemplify certain antecedent intervention procedures, research with clinical populations other than children with autism is also referenced on several occasions.

Social-Positive Reinforcement

Noncontingent reinforcement (NCR) is the response-independent presentation of one or more reinforcers. The term actually is inaccurate, because reinforcement by definition cannot be noncontingent (Skinner 1948), and the procedure typically does not strengthen behavior. Nonetheless, several clinical procedures have been categorized as NCR, and the term remains the contemporary convention (Carr and LeBlanc 2006).

For a child demonstrating attention-maintained challenging behavior, NCR would be implemented by having a caregiver praise the child or show approval on a predetermined schedule unrelated to behavior frequency (Hanley, Piazza, and Fisher 1997). Research suggests that the initial schedule for delivering NCR should be "dense"—that is, near-continuous in the beginning, and gradually increased or "thinned" over time. Usually, a fixed-time (FT) schedule is programmed and, subsequent to fading, is shifted to a variable-time (VT) schedule. Advantages of NCR for attention-maintained challenging behavior are that it is relatively easy to implement, compares well to other intervention methods, and has practical appeal (Carr and LeBlanc 2006).

Choice making is another antecedent intervention procedure that can be effective in reducing challenging behavior that has a social-positive reinforcement function. The initial procedural steps are to verify that a child is able to make choices and, if not, to teach this skill (Cannella, O'Reilly, and Lancioni 2005). Next, caregivers must present the child with suitable choice-making opportunities during situations that occasion challenging behavior.

Carlson and associates (in press) evaluated choice making as an intervention to reduce public disrobing and associated urinary incontinence displayed by a 13-year-old girl with autism and a 5-year old boy diagnosed with pervasive developmental disorder–not otherwise specified (PDD-NOS). Pre-intervention functional assessment suggested that the children removed and urinated on their clothing because the customary consequence was to have them changed into "preferred" apparel. During intervention, each child had scheduled choice opportunities to change into alternative clothes presented by staff at their schools. Figure 16.2 shows that public disrobing and urinary incontinence were eliminated with the choice-making intervention, compared with a baseline phase. This study identified the challenging behaviors as having a tangible-eliciting function; giving the children acceptable choices to change their clothes served as an abolishing operation that lessened the motivation to disrobe.

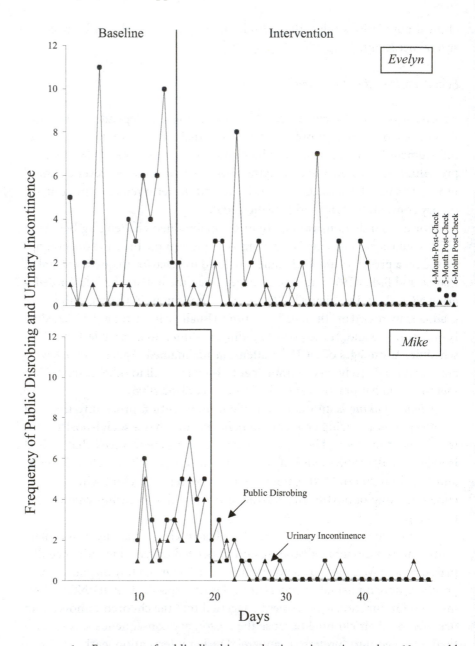

FIGURE 16.2. Frequency of public disrobing and urinary incontinence by a 13-year-old girl with autism and a 5-year-old boy with PDD-NOS during baseline and intervention (choice-making) phases.

Improving the communication abilities of children who have autism is a generally accepted strategy to decrease challenging behavior (O'Reilly et al. 2006). One particular procedure, called functional communication training (FCT), teaches a child to elicit reinforcement through an acceptable language response. In an initial evaluation of FCT, Carr and Durand (1985) identified attention-maintained challenging behavior in children with developmental disabilities and eliminated the behavior by teaching them to make requests such as, "Am I doing good work?" Subsequent research has replicated these findings, both when FCT is the only intervention and when it is combined with other behavior-reduction methods (O'Reilly et al. 2006). Functional communication training can also be adapted to communication modalities other than spoken language, such as with children who use vocal output communication aids (Sigafoos, Arthur, and O'Reilly 2003) and the Picture Exchange Communication System (Charlop-Christy et al. 2002).

Social-Negative Reinforcement

Escape-maintained challenging behavior can occur in a variety of instructional contexts in which a child is requested to perform learning responses. When it is determined that challenging behavior is, in fact, motivated by escape, intervention formulation begins by identifying the "demand" features of instruction. For example, instruction by a teacher could be unpleasant for a child because the response requirement is unclear, confusing, effortful, or difficult to execute. Knowing these influences enables an instructor to make one or more antecedent changes.

Various elements of instruction can be modified to decrease demands that result in escape-motivated challenging behavior. Miltenberger (2006, 104) posited that, "When the frequency or difficulty of the demands is decreased, the aversiveness of the task is decreased, thus eliminating (or minimizing) the EO for the problem behavior maintained by escape from the task." Modifying task difficulty can be accomplished by presenting students with preferred tasks (Foster-Johnson, Ferro, and Dunlap 1994), shorter tasks (Dunlap et al. 1995), or easy tasks interspersed with more difficult tasks (Kennedy, Itkonen, and Lindquist 1995). The pace of instruction also can be altered with good outcome, by either increasing or decreasing the frequency of requests (Dunlap, Dyer, and Koegel 1983; Zarcone et al. 1993). The common characteristic of these and related procedures is delivering instruction at a level that is comfortably tolerated (absence of challenging behavior) and slowly increasing demands to facilitate optimal learning.

Noncontingent escape (NCE) allows a child brief interruption from instruction, independent of challenging behavior, on an FT or VT schedule. Although it does not exclusively address children with autism, there exists an emerging research literature documenting NCE as effective intervention. For example, in a study with students with mental retardation, Vollmer, Marcus, and Ringdahl (1995) began with a "no demand" (continuous break) schedule and progressively increased the time between breaks to 2.5 and 10 minutes. A similar intervention approach was reported by Kodak, Miltenberger, and

Romaniuk (2003) with children with autism. In their study, the children started with a continuous break from instruction, which was increased to a FT-2 minute schedule.

As is often the case, several antecedent intervention procedures can be implemented simultaneously. This was illustrated by Butler and Luiselli (2007) in a study that combined instructional fading with NCE. The participant was a 13-year-old girl who had autism and escape-motivated challenging behavior (self-injury, aggression, tantrum outburst). The NCE component of intervention allowed the girl a brief break from an instructional session commencing at an FT-20 second schedule and advancing in 10- to 30-second increments whenever challenging behavior was recorded during 20% or less of a session. With instructional fading, requests initially were eliminated during sessions and thereafter were increased by two per session when challenging behavior was recorded during 20% or less of a session. This multicomponent intervention plan successfully eliminated challenging behavior; NCE was increased to an FT-5 minute schedule; and, by the final session, the girl was responding correctly to one instructional request approximately every 20 seconds.

The application of *choice making* as intervention for escape-maintained challenging behavior was illustrated nicely in a study by Romaniuk and associates (2002). Through functional analyses, they identified children with challenging behavior that was maintained by attention and escape. During intervention, the students were allowed to choose academic tasks during instructional sessions. For the children with escape-maintained challenging behavior, choice making was an effective intervention. However, choice making was not effective for the children with attention-maintained challenging behavior. Choice making, then, should not be considered a universal intervention for challenging behavior but must be tied to functional influences in order to work successfully

Automatic Reinforcement

Challenging behavior maintained by automatic reinforcement occurs independent of social consequences. Stereotypy is the most common example of behavior that is reinforced by its own sensory consequences. Different types of sensory stimulation can function as reinforcement; as noted previously, these must be identified through functional assessment and analysis before intervention is formulated and implemented. When designing antecedent intervention for automatically reinforced challenging behavior, it is desirable to "match" procedures to the maintaining sensory stimulation (Piazza et al. 2000).

Sensory extinction is a procedure initially reported by Rincover and associates as a way to mask or attenuate behavior-elicited automatic reinforcement (Rincover 1978; Rincover et al. 1979; Rincover, Newsom, and Carr 1979). Rincover (1978) was able to eliminate object-spinning in a child with autism by placing carpet on a table so that auditory feedback (the source of reinforcement) no longer was produced. Rincover and colleagues (1979) effectively reduced finger and arm stereotypies of two children by having them wear a small vibrating device on the back of their hands to mask proprioceptive sensation that was produced by the behaviors. In the area of self-injury, examples of sensory extinction include having children wear a padded helmet for head-banging (Rincover and Devany 1982), rubber gloves for skin scratching (Rincover and Devany 1982), and pliable plastic cuffs for wrist biting (Luiselli 1988). This research, as well as more recent applications (Tang, Patterson, and Kennedy 2003), support sensory extinction as intervention for automatically reinforced stereotypy and self-injury, but the procedure also has several restrictions. One concern is that having a child wear equipment such as a padded helmet or gloves can be socially stigmatizing and, in most cases, interferes with instruction. Furthermore, it may not be possible to successfully block some forms of sensory stimulation. One additional constraint is that the continuous wearing of equipment must eventually be faded, for example, by reducing the amount of time it is worn or reducing its physical dimensions.

Another intervention strategy is allowing a child continuous access to stimuli that are similar to the sensory consequences that maintain the automatically reinforced challenging behavior. The intervention phase of the previously cited study by Luiselli and colleagues (2004) illustrates this approach. Recall that a functional analysis conducted with a 6-year-old boy diagnosed with autism confirmed that his saliva-play was automatically reinforced. The purpose of intervention was to reduce saliva-play by giving the boy noncontingent access to alternative oral stimulation consisting of chewing gum or an hygienic "chew-object." These procedures were evaluated by comparing them with a baseline (nonintervention) phase in a multielement experimental design. The results, displayed in Figure 16.3, were that access to the "chew-object" eliminated saliva-play, which was unaffected when the boy chewed gum. Although these findings are not conclusive, one interpretation is that the "chew-object" provided the boy the same type of sensory reinforcement as saliva-play.

Environmental enrichment is another antecedent intervention that provides continuous access to sensory stimulation. The available stimulation is not matched to the source of automatic reinforcement but, instead, functions as an alternative sensory event or promotes responses that compete with the challenging behavior. Concerning intervention for stereotypy, environmental enrichment usually consists of introducing highly stimulating toys and objects requiring motor manipulation (Hanley et al. 2000; Lindberg, Iwata, and Kahng 1999; Ringdahl et al. 1997). One issue with environmental enrichment and other noncontingent procedures is that a child is able to contact the alternative sensory stimulation and still perform the challenging behavior. Accordingly, intervention may require prompting the child's engagement with the alternative and competing stimuli (e.g., guiding the child to play with toys).

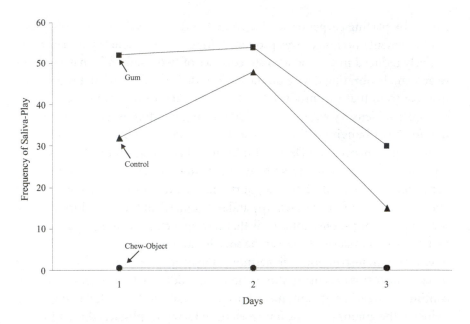

FIGURE 16.3. Frequency of saliva play by a 6-year old boy with autism during an intervention evaluation that included continuous access to alternative sensory (oral) stimulation.

In addition to allowing continuous access, alternative sensory stimulation can be presented noncontingently on an FT schedule. As intervention for a child's hand-mouthing, Simmons, Smith, and Kliethermes (2003) presented food on an FT schedule, and the behavior decreased, possibly because chewing food may offered the same sensory stimulation as hand-mouthing. Lyons and colleagues (2007) evaluated a similar methodology with two children who had postmeal ruminating (repetitive regurgitation and reingestion of consumed food). Using a FT-30 second schedule, rumination was eliminated with both children when they were presented with small portions of specific food and liquid items after meals.

■ Summary and Conclusions

Antecedent intervention is one of several approaches to behavior support for children with autism. The procedures reviewed in this chapter have been re-searched and replicated by many behavioral scientists, producing evidence-based recommendations and practice guidelines. As I have written previously (Luiselli 2006; Luiselli and Cameron 1998), the chief advantage of antecedent intervention is the focus on preventing challenging behavior by assessing and manipulating its provoking conditions. This preventive orientation usually ap-peals to practitioners who are responsible for service delivery with children in school, clinic, home, and community settings. In fact, the further evolution of antecedent intervention rests with persuasive studies that are conducted under the most naturalistic conditions. Future antecedent intervention research likely will identify additional strategies that advance education and treatment services for children with autism.

■ References

Baer, D.M., Wolf, M.M., and Risley, T.R. (1968). Some current dimensions of applied behavior analysis. *Journal of Applied Behavior Analysis*, 1, 91–97.

Butler, L.R., and Luiselli, J.K. (2007). Escape-maintained problem behavior in a child with autism: Antecedent functional analysis and intervention evaluation of noncontingent escape and instructional fading. *Journal of Positive Behavior Interventions*, 9, 195–202.

Cannella, H.I., O'Reilly, M.F., and Lancioni, G. (2005). Choice and preference assessment research with people with severe to profound developmental disabilities: A review of the literature. *Research in Developmental Disabilities*, 26, 1–15.

Carlson, J.I., Luiselli, J.K., Slyman, A., and Markowski, A. (in press). Choice making as an intervention for public disrobing in children with developmental disabilities. Submitted for publication.

Carr, E.G., and Durand, V.M. (1985). Reducing behavior problems through functional communication training. *Journal of Applied Behavior Analysis*, 18, 111–126.

Carr, E.G., Horner, R.H., Turnbull, A.P., Marquis, J.G., Magito-McLaughlin, D., and McAltee, M.L. (1999). *Positive behavior support as an approach for dealing with problem behavior in people with developmental disabilities: A research synthesis*. Washington, D.C.: American Association on Mental Retardation.

Carr, J.E., and LeBlanc, L.A. (2006). Noncontingent reinforcement as antecedent behavior support. In *Antecedent control: Innovative approaches to behavior support* (ed. J.K. Luiselli), pp. 147–164. Baltimore: Paul H. Brookes.

Carr, J.E., and Sidener, T.M. (2002). On the relation between applied behavior analysis and positive behavior support. *The Behavior Analyst*, 25 (2), 245–253.

Carr, E.G., and Smith, C.E. (1995). Biological setting events for self-injury. *Mental Retardation and Developmental Disabilities Research Reviews*, 1, 94–98.

Carr, E.G., Smith, C.E., Giacin, T.A., Whelan, B.M., and Pancari, J. (2003). Menstrual discomfort as a biological setting event for severe problem behavior: Assessment and intervention. *American Journal on Mental Retardation*, 108, 117–133.

Carr, E.G., Yarbrough, S.C., and Langdon, N.A. (1997). Effects of idiosyncratic stimulus variables on functional analysis outcomes. *Journal of Applied Behavior Analysis*, 30, 673–686.

Charlop-Christy, M.H., Carpenter, M., Le, L., LeBlanc, L.A., and Kellet, K. (2002). Using the Picture Exchange Communication System (PECS) with children with autism: Assessment of PECS acquisition, speech, social-communication behavior, and problem behavior. *Journal of Applied Behavior Analysis*, 35, 213–231.

Dunlap, G., Dyer, K., and Koegel, R.L. (1983). Autistic self-stimulation and inter-trial interval duration. *American Journal on Mental Deficiency*, 88, 194–202.

Dunlap, G., Foster-Johnson, L., Clarke, S., Kern, L., and Childs, K.E. (1995). Modifying activities to produce functional outcomes: Effects on the problem behaviors of students with disabilities. *Journal of the Association for Persons with Severe Handicaps*, 20, 248–258.

Durand, V.M., and Crimmins, D.B. (1988). Identifying the variables maintaining self-injurious behavior. *Journal of Autism and Developmental Disorders*, 18, 99–117.

Foster-Johnson, L., Ferro, J., and Dunlap, G. (1994). Preferred curricular activities and reduced problem behaviors in students with intellectual disabilities. *Journal of Applied Behavior Analysis*, 27, 493–504.

Friman, P.C., and Hawkins, R.O. (2006). Contribution of establishing operations to antecedent intervention. In *Antecedent control: Innovative approaches to behavior support* (ed. J.K. Luiselli), pp. 31–52). Baltimore: Paul H. Brookes.

Hanley, G.P., Iwata, B.A., and McCord, B.E. (2003). Functional analysis of problem behavior: A review. *Journal of Applied Behavior Analysis*, 36, 147–185.

Hanley, G.P., Iwata, B.A., Thompson, R.H., and Lindberg, J.S. (2000). A component analysis of "stereotypy as reinforcement" for alternative behavior. *Journal of Applied Behavior Analysis*, 33, 285–296.

Hanley, G.P., Piazza, C.C., and Fisher, W.W. (1997). Noncontingent presentation of attention and alternative stimuli in the treatment of attention-maintained destructive behavior. *Journal of Applied Behavior Analysis*, 30, 229–237.

Harris, J. (1996). Physical restraint procedures for managing challenging behaviors presented by mentally retarded adults and children. *Research in Developmental Disabilities*, 17, 99–134.

Iwata, B.A., Dorsey, M.F., Slifer, K.J., Bauman, K.E., and Richman, G.S. (1982). Toward a functional analysis of self-injury. *Analysis and Intervention in Developmental Disabilities*, 2, 3–20.

Iwata, B.A., Vollmer, T.R., and Zarcone, J.R. (1990). The experimental (functional) analysis of behavior disorders: Methodology, applications, and limitations. In *Perspectives on the use of nonaversive and aversive interventions for persons with developmental disabilities* (eds. A. Repp and N. Singh), pp. 301–330. Sycamore, Ill.: Sycamore Publishing.

Johnston, J.M., Foxx, R.M., Jacobson, J.W., Green, G., and Mulick, J.A. (2006). Positive behavior support and applied behavior analysis. *The Behavior Analyst*, 29 (1), 51–74.

Kennedy, C.H., and Becker, A. (2006). Health conditions in antecedent assessment and intervention of problem behavior. In *Antecedent control: Innovative approaches to behavior support* (ed. J.K. Luiselli), pp. 73–97). Baltimore: Paul H. Brookes.

Kennedy, C.H., Itkonen, T., and Lindquist, K. (1995). Comparing interspersed requests and social comments as antecedents for increasing student compliance. *Journal of Applied Behavior Analysis, 29,* 97–98.

Kennedy, C.H., and Meyer, K.A. (1996). Sleep deprivation, allergy symptoms, and negatively reinforced problem behavior. *Journal of Applied Behavior Analysis, 29,* 133–135.

Kodak, T., Miltenberger, R.G., and Romaniuk, C. (2003). The effects of differential negative reinforcement of other behavior and noncontingent escape on compliance. *Journal of Applied Behavior Analysis, 36,* 379–382.

LeBlanc, L.A., Hagopian, L.P., Marhefka, J.M., and Wilke, A.E. (2001). Effects of therapist gender and type of attention on assessment and treatment of attention maintained destructive behavior. *Behavioral Interventions, 16,* 39–57.

Lerman, D.C., and Rapp, J.T. (2006). Antecedent assessment and intervention for stereotypy. In *Antecedent control: Innovative approaches to behavior support* (ed. J.K. Luiselli), pp. 125–146). Baltimore: Paul H. Brookes.

Lerman, D.C., and Vorndran, C.M. (2002). On the status of knowledge for using punishment: Implications for treating behavior disorders. *Journal of Applied Behavior Analysis, 35,* 431–464.

Lindberg, J.S., Iwata, B.A., and Kahng, S.W. (1999). On the relation between object manipulation and stereotypic self-injurious behavior. *Journal of Applied Behavior Analysis, 32,* 51–62.

Luiselli, J.K. (1988). Comparative analysis of sensory extinction treatments for self-injury. *Education and Treatment of Children, 11,* 149–156.

Luiselli, J.K. (2004). Behavior support and intervention: Current issues and practices in developmental disabilities. In *Behavior modification for persons with developmental disabilities: Treatments and supports* (eds. J.L. Matson, R.B. Laud, and M.L. Matson), pp. 33–54. Kingston, N.Y.: NADD.

Luiselli, J.K., ed. (2006) *Antecedent assessment and intervention: Supporting children and adults with developmental disabilities in community settings.* Baltimore: Paul H. Brookes.

Luiselli, J.K., and Cameron, M.J., eds. (1998) *Antecedent control: Innovative approaches to behavior support.* Baltimore: Paul H. Brookes.

Luiselli, J.K., Cochran, M.L., and Huber, S.A. (2005). Effects of otitis media on a child with autism receiving behavioral intervention for self-injury. *Child and Family Behavior Therapy, 27* (2), 51–56.

Luiselli, J.K., Ricciardi, J.N., Schmidt, S., and Tarr, M. (2004). Brief functional analysis and intervention evaluation for treatment of saliva play. *Child and Family Behavior Therapy, 26* (3), 53–61.

Lyons, E.A., Rue, H.C., Luiselli, J.K., and DiGennaro, F.D. (2007). Brief functional analysis and supplemental feeding intervention for post-meal ruminating in children with developmental disabilities. *Journal of Applied Behavior Analysis, 40*(4), 743–747.

Michael, J. (1993). Establishing operations. *The Behavior Analyst,* 16 (2), 191–206.

McAdam, D.B., DiCesare, A., Murphy, S., and Marshall, B. (2004). The influence of different therapists on functional analysis outcomes. *Behavioral Interventions,* 19, 39–44.

McComas, J.J., Thompson, A., and Johnson, L. (2003). The effects of presession attention on problem behavior maintained by different reinforcers. *Journal of Applied Behavior Analysis,* 36, 297–307.

McGill, P. (1999). Establishing operations: Implications for the assessment, treatment, and prevention of problem behavior. *Journal of Applied Behavior Analysis,* 16, 393–418.

Miltenberger, R.G. (2006). Antecedent interventions for challenging behaviors maintained by escape from instructional activities. In *Antecedent control: Innovative approaches to behavior support* (ed. J.K. Luiselli), pp. 101–124). Baltimore: Paul H. Brookes.

O'Callaghan, P.M., Allen, K.D., Powell, S., and Salama, F. (2006). The efficacy of noncontingent escape for decreasing children's disruptive behavior during restorative dental treatment. *Journal of Applied Behavior Analysis,* 39, 161–171.

O'Neill, R.E., Horner, R.H., Albin, R.W., Sprague, J.R., Storey, K., and Newton, J.S. (1997). *Functional assessment and program development for problem behavior: A practical handbook.* Pacific Grove, Calif.: Brookes/Cole.

O'Reilly, M.F. (1997). Functional analysis of episodic self-injury correlated with recurrent otitis media. *Journal of Applied Behavior Analysis,* 30, 165–167.

O'Reilly, M.F., Cannella, H.I., Sigafoos, J., and Lancioni, G. (2006). Communication and social skills interventions. In *Antecedent control: Innovative approaches to behavior support* (ed. J.K. Luiselli), pp. 187–206). Baltimore: Paul H. Brookes.

Piazza, C.C., Adelinis, J.D., Hanley, G.P., Goh, H.L., and Delia, M.D. (2000). An evaluation of the effects of matched stimuli on behaviors maintained by automatic reinforcement. *Journal of Applied Behavior Analysis,* 33, 13–27.

Piazza, C.C., Contrucci, S.A., Hanley, G.P., and Fisher, W.W. (1997). Nondirective prompting and noncontingent reinforcement in the treatment of destructive behavior during hygiene routines. *Journal of Applied Behavior Analysis,* 31, 705–708.

Progar, P.R., North, S.T., Bruce, S.S., DiNovi, B.J., Nau, P.A., Eberman, E.M., Bailey, J.R., and Nussbaum, C.N. (2001). Putative behavioral history effects and aggression maintained by escape from therapists. *Journal of Applied Behavior Analysis,* 34, 69–72.

Reid, D.H., Rotholz, D.A., Parsons, M.B., Morris, L., Braswell, B.A., Green, C.W., and Schell, R.M. (2003). Training human service supervisors in aspects of PBS: Evaluation of a statewide, performance-based program. *Journal of Positive Behavior Interventions,* 5, 35–46.

Ricciardi, J.N. (2006). Combining antecedent and consequence procedures in multicomponent behavior support plans: A guide to writing plans with functional efficacy. In *Antecedent control: Innovative approaches to behavior support* (ed. J.K. Luiselli), pp. 227–245). Baltimore: Paul H. Brookes.

Ricciardi, J.N., Luiselli, J.K., and Cammare, M. (2006). Shaping approach responses as intervention for specific phobia in a child with autism. *Journal of Applied Behavior Analysis, 39,* 445–448.

Rincover, A. (1978). Sensory extinction: A procedure for eliminating self-stimulatory behavior in developmentally disabled children. *Journal of Abnormal Child Psychology, 6,* 299–310.

Rincover, A., Cook, A.R., Peoples, A., and Packard, D. (1979). Sensory extinction and sensory reinforcement principles for programming multiple adaptive behavior change. *Journal of Applied Behavior Analysis, 12,* 221–233.

Rincover, A., and Devany, J. (1982). The application of sensory extinction to self-injury. *Analysis and Intervention in Developmental Disabilities, 2,* 67–82.

Rincover, A., Newsom, C.D., and Carr, E.G. (1979). Use of sensory extinction procedures in the treatment of compulsive-like behavior of developmentally disabled children. *Journal of Consulting and Clinical Psychology, 47,* 695–701.

Ringdahl, J.E., and Sellers, J. (2000). The effects of different adults as therapists during functional analyses. *Journal of Applied Behavior Analysis, 34,* 247–250.

Ringdahl, J.E., Vollmer, T.R., Marcus, B.A., and Roane, H.S. (1997). An analogue evaluation of environmental enrichment: The role of stimulus preference. *Journal of Applied Behavior Analysis, 30,* 203–216.

Roantree, C.F., and Kennedy, C.H. (2006). A paradoxical effect of presession attention on stereotypy: Antecedent attention as an establishing operation, not an abolishing operation. *Journal of Applied Behavior Analysis, 39,* 381–384.

Romaniuk, C., Miltenberger, R.G., Conyers, C., Jenner, N., Jurgens, M., and Rigenberg, C. (2002). The influence of activity choice on behavior problems maintained by escape versus attention. *Journal of Applied Behavior Analysis, 35,* 349–362.

Sigafoos, J., Arthur, M., and O'Reilly, M.F. (2003). Effects of speech output on maintenance of requesting and frequency of vocalizations in three children with developmental disabilities. *Augmentative and Alternative Communication, 19,* 37–47.

Simmons, J.N., Smith, R.G., and Kliethermes, L. (2003). A multiple-schedule evaluation of immediate and subsequent effects of fixed-time food presentation on automatically maintained mouthing. *Journal of Applied Behavior Analysis, 36,* 541–544.

Skinner, B.F. (1948). "Superstition" in the pigeon. *Journal of Experimental Psychology, 38,* 168–172.

Smith, R.G., and Iwata, B.A. (1997). Antecedent influences on behavior disorders. *Journal of Applied Behavior Analysis, 30,* 343–375.

Smith, R.G., Iwata, B.A., Goh, H.L., and Shore, B.A. (1995). Analysis of establishing operations in self-injury maintained by escape. *Journal of Applied Behavior Analysis, 28,* 515–535.

Tang, J., Patterson, T.G., and Kennedy, C.H. (2003). Identifying specific sensory modalities maintaining the stereotypy of students with multiple profound disabilities. *Research in Developmental Disabilities,* 24, 433–451.

Tiger, J.H., Hanley, G.P., and Bessette, K.K. (2006). Incorporating descriptive assessment results into the design of a functional analysis: A case example involving a preschooler's hand mouthing. *Education and Treatment of Children,* 29, 107–124.

Touchette, P.E., MacDonald, R.F., and Langer, S.N. (1985). A scatter plot for identifying stimulus control of problem behavior. *Journal of Applied Behavior Analysis,* 18, 343–351.

Vollmer, T.R., Marcus, B.A., and Ringdahl, J.E. (1995). Noncontingent escape as treatment for self-injurious behavior maintained by negative reinforcement. *Journal of Applied Behavior Analysis,* 28, 15–26.

Zarcone, J.R., Iwata, B.A., Vollmer, T.A., Jagtiani, S., Smith, R.G., and Mazaleski, J.L. (1993). Extinction of self-injurious escape behavior with and without instructional fading. *Journal of Applied Behavior Analysis,* 26, 353–360

Zhou, L., Iwata, B.A., and Shore, B.A. (2002). Reinforcing efficacy of food on performance during pre- and post-meal sessions. *Journal of Applied Behavior Analysis,* 35, 411–414.

17. Using Positive Reinforcement to Decrease Challenging Behavior

Lee Kern and Anastasia Kokina

The previous chapter illustrated how antecedent and setting events in a child's environment can be arranged to prevent problem behaviors from occurring. In an ideal world, preventative approaches would be sufficient to avoid challenging behaviors altogether. However, because of the difficulties children with autism encounter when learning to communicate, interact socially, and negotiate their environment, challenging behaviors may persist despite well-crafted prevention strategies. This can happen for a number of reasons. Most common is that challenging behaviors have been reinforced in the past by others. That is, in the absence of a repertoire of socially acceptable ways to get what they need or want, children with communication difficulties frequently find that others pay attention and respond to severe forms of behavior, such as self-injury, aggression, and disruption. Challenging behaviors with such a history of reinforcement are likely to re-emerge, even in the context of compelling preventative efforts. A second explanation for the persistence of challenging behaviors is that antecedents and setting events associated with challenging behaviors are sometimes difficult to specify. Even highly skilled practitioners may be unaccustomed to considering atypical or idiosyncratic events that can occasion undesirable behaviors (e.g., Carr, Yarbrough, and Langdon 1997). In the absence of clear information about events that precede challenging behavior, effective preventative interventions are not forthcoming.

In general, best practice with respect to challenging behaviors dictates a comprehensive approach that combines preventative interventions with reinforcement for appropriate behavior, new skill instruction, and consequences for challenging behavior (see Chapters 18 and 19). This collection of interventions arranges the circumstances so that optimal learning will occur. That is, environmental conditions are arranged to reduce the likelihood of challenging behaviors. At the same time, instruction is in place to teach behaviors and skills that replace challenging behavior both immediately and over the long term.

Thus, desirable behavior is reinforced, and challenging behaviors are discouraged. Such a comprehensive approach offers the best likelihood that behavior challenges will be permanently eliminated (Bambara and Kern 2006). This chapter focuses on the use of positive reinforcement as a strategy for addressing behavior problems. We begin with an overview of the purpose and rationale of positive reinforcement approaches in the context of challenging behavior. This is followed by a description of specific strategies that rely on positive reinforcement to promote appropriate behavior and, in turn, decrease challenging behavior.

■ Overview of Positive Reinforcement

As infants and toddlers develop, they begin to learn the words, word sequences, and word combinations that are needed to attain what they want. Initially, rudimentary approximations of words are interpretable to parents, who in turn attend to their child's requests. As language is prompted, shaped, and especially rewarded or reinforced, it grows in complexity and precision. When children have difficulties learning language, however, they must find alternative ways to control their environment and see that their needs are met. It is under these circumstances that forms of challenging behavior frequently emerge. Because such behaviors are extreme in nature, they tend to evoke the attention and actions of others in a way that usual behaviors do not.

To illustrate, consider Johnny, a boy who screams at an ear-piercingly high pitch when struggling to get dressed to go for a walk. Most likely, an adult, taking note of his frustration with the task at hand, will rush to his assistance. Similarly, Maria, a girl who has been ignored by her babysitter, begins to bang her head forcefully against the wall. The babysitter is alarmed, and, to stop Maria before she injures herself, gathers her up, holds her, and attempts to comfort her. As these examples show, Johnny's and Maria's challenging behavior serves their individual interests by helping them to send a communicative message to others in the absence of the skills required to do so in a more appropriate manner. In turn, the challenging behaviors have resulted in positive reinforcement: Johnny received help with a difficult task, and Maria received attention. Regrettably, positive reinforcement has followed undesirable behavior, which will result in the behavior's continuing or even increasing. Although such responses to extreme behaviors are not uncommon, it is critical that positive reinforcement be used in ways that reduce challenging behavior, rather than increase it. In the remainder of this chapter, we delineate specific approaches and procedures that use positive reinforcement to increase appropriate behavior and thereby reduce challenging behaviors.

Before we begin, a few considerations warrant mention. First, although the strategies we describe in this chapter can sometimes be used successfully with limited information about why challenging behavior is occurring, they are typically more effective if the reasons for the behavior's occurrence are taken into account. That is, challenging behavior often serves a particular function, the intent being to communicate a desire to obtain something that is pleasant or to avoid or escape something that is unpleasant. Interventions are usually most effective and efficient when they benefit from knowledge about what it is the child is trying to obtain or escape from—in other words, the particular function of behavior. To obtain this knowledge, a functional assessment is conducted. The assessment requires obtaining information about events that both precede and follow challenging behavior, in order to generate data-based hypotheses about why problem behaviors occur. The emergent information can then be used to facilitate intervention selection.

A second consideration is that interventions built on positive reinforcement strategies are most effective when additional interventions are also in place to ensure that challenging behavior is not reinforced; hence, the need for a comprehensive approach. Specifically, whether challenging behavior will occur is a matter of the probability or rate of reinforcement that follows. That is, the frequency, quality, and/or immediacy of positive reinforcement provided for desirable behavior must supersede that which follows challenging behavior. In essence, a child must learn that engaging in desirable behavior is a more effective and efficient way to obtain reinforcement than engaging in challenging behavior. Such a lesson requires that responses to challenging behavior do not function as reinforcement. Therefore, consequences for problem behavior must be carefully planned, using procedures such as those described in Chapter 19.

A final consideration is that positive reinforcement relies on providing something desirable after the child exhibits the behavior that one wishes to increase. This requires an understanding of exactly what is "desirable" for each individual. Because preferences can be highly idiosyncratic, an indispensable and underlying requisite of reinforcement-based approaches is to accurately identify desirable items, activities, or events. Once again, it is often useful to consider the function of the challenging behavior that is targeted for reduction. For example, if challenging behavior frequently occurs to obtain access to a particular video, it is likely that that item is highly preferred and can function as a reinforcer. Similarly, if problem behavior occurs because a child prefers to be alone, rather than completing instruction with an adult, time alone can be provided after completion of a task. In addition to considering reinforcement in relation to challenging behavior, there are a number of structured approaches to individually identify preferred items. For example, one strategy is to observe the items or activities an individual engages with most frequently. Another approach is to sequentially present pairs of items, ranking those selected most to least frequently (e.g., Hagopian, Long, and Rush 2004).

In the following sections, we describe specific research-based strategies for using reinforcement to increase appropriate behavior, which consequently leads to reductions in inappropriate behavior. The descriptions include when the use of each strategy is recommended, how the strategy is used, and advantages and disadvantages of the strategy. In addition, we provide examples of applications of the strategy, both when the function of challenging behavior is known and when it is not known.

■ Differential Reinforcement Procedures to Reduce Challenging Behavior

One group of procedures that can reduce challenging behaviors through positive reinforcement is differential reinforcement of behavior. *Differential reinforcement procedures* are so termed because reinforcement is differentially provided when a child either engages in a particular type or rate of appropriate behavior or refrains from engaging in inappropriate behavior. The procedure delivers reinforcement after intervals with appropriate behavior or intervals absent of inappropriate behavior. In turn, the child's behavior changes in one of two ways. When reinforcement is delivered after appropriate behaviors, those behaviors increase, replacing inappropriate behaviors. When reinforcement is delivered for the absence of inappropriate behaviors, they decline. Three types of differential reinforcement procedures are described: differential reinforcement of other behavior (DRO), differential reinforcement of alternative behavior (DRA) and the related procedure of differential reinforcement of incompatible behavior (DRI), and differential reinforcement of low rates of behavior (DRL).

Differential Reinforcement of Other Behavior

DRO is a procedure that is effective when the goal is to entirely eliminate a specific problem behavior. Consequently, it is also referred to as differential reinforcement of zero rates of behavior, or differential reinforcement of the omission of behavior. In this procedure, positive reinforcement is provided when targeted challenging behavior is absent during a specified period of time. The designated period can range from successive short intervals that are seconds in duration (e.g., 10 seconds) to a long interval that corresponds to a learning session or activity, such as morning circle time. At the end of the designated time interval, reinforcement is provided only in the case of nonoccurrence of the problem behavior throughout the entire interval.

To illustrate, Mr. Reyes wanted to eliminate Carl's self-picking, which caused tissue damage and bleeding to his hands and arms. To do so, he used a DRO procedure in which he gave Carl a preferred edible (a Skittle, a grape, or a sip of soda) at the end of each 5-minute interval in which Carl refrained from picking. After the rate of behavior stabilized, Mr. Reyes gradually increased the length of the interval during which Carl had to refrain from picking to earn the preferred edible.

Choosing the appropriate initial interval length is crucial, because it influences the effectiveness of a DRO procedure. In the case of behaviors that occur at a high rate, if the interval is too long, the child may never receive reinforcement. On the other hand, if the interval is too short, the child can continue to engage in the challenging behavior while still receiving a significant amount of reinforcement. The optimal starting interval length can be calculated based on the current rates of challenging behavior. This is accomplished by first determining the rate of the behavior during a baseline period, before introducing the intervention. Those data are used to determine the average inter-response time, which is the average interval between each occurrence of the targeted behavior (e.g., skin-picking). Then, an interval slightly shorter than the average inter-response time is designated for the initial interval length. This calculation makes it highly likely that the child will be able to meet the demand requirements and will receive reinforcement.

The length of the interval can be either fixed or variable. In fixed-interval DRO, each interval is of equivalent length. For instance, reinforcement is provided for the nonoccurrence of a targeted aggressive behavior at the end of each 10-minute interval. Conversely, with a variable-interval DRO, the length of each interval varies but remains 10 minutes on average. That is, intervals may range in duration from 7 minutes to 13 minutes, averaging 10 minutes overall. Sometimes variable intervals are more effective because children cannot predict when reinforcement is coming.

In Carl's case, Mr. Reyes determined baseline rates of picking by selecting a half-hour period of time across 3 days for observation. During the observations, Mr. Reyes made a note of each incident of skin-picking. On the first day, Carl picked his skin five times during the 30-minute period. On the second day, Carl picked four times, and on the third day, he picked six times. Thus, on average across the 3 days, Carl picked five times in 30 minutes, for an average inter-response time of 6 minutes between each picking incident. Therefore, Mr. Reyes selected a slightly shorter interval of 5 minutes to begin the DRO procedure and decided to deliver reinforcement on a fixed schedule.

The final step before implementing the DRO procedure is to determine the reinforcer that will be provided when challenging behavior is absent. This must be something that is highly valued by the child. In situations where the function of behavior is known, the effectiveness of DRO may be enhanced by linking it to the behavioral function. For example, if aggression functions to gain attention from others, providing attention as reinforcement for the absence of aggression is likely to make the procedure highly effective.

Returning to Carl, a preference assessment indicated that certain edibles were highly preferred. Therefore, at the end of each 5-minute interval in which Carl refrained from picking, Mr. Reyes approached him, provided verbal praise ("Great, Carl, you didn't pick at all during the last five minutes"), and offered a choice of an edible reinforcer. Mr. Reyes noted a rapid decrease in Carl's picking. When behavior decreased to low levels, Mr. Reyes began to fade the schedule of reinforcement. After each week that Carl earned reinforcement (refrained from skin picking) for at least 90% of the 5-minute intervals, Mr. Reyes gradually increased the interval length by 1 minute. In this way, changes in reinforcement were not abrupt, but eventually reinforcement could occur at an infrequent rate.

Another way that DRO can be programmed is to reinforce the zero rate of challenging behavior only at a specific moment, rather than throughout the entire interval. This is referred to as momentary DRO. A variable interval should be used with momentary DRO, because, otherwise, children may begin to predict when the interval will end and adjust their behavior accordingly. Lindberg and colleagues (1999) demonstrated that the effectiveness of variable-momentary DRO was comparable to that of fixed-interval and variable-interval DRO procedures. Momentary DRO may offer a better contextual fit in situations where staff members have many responsibilities and are unable to observe a child on an ongoing basis to determine whether behavior was absent. For example, classroom teachers who are responsible for instructing multiple students may find this procedure quite feasible.

A few additional issues deserves mention. First, even when DRO procedures are highly effective, challenging behavior is still likely to occur from time to time. If it should occur, it is typically ignored. On occasion, however, the effectiveness of DRO can be enhanced by introducing a consequence for challenging behavior, such as stating "Carl, no picking." Second, as mentioned earlier, it is important to select powerful and highly desirable reinforcers. This may help avoid the need for additional reductive procedures. Finally, it is generally useful to simultaneously encourage appropriate responses as substitutes for the target behavior or to teach alternative responses if they are not yet in the student's repertoire, as described in Chapter 18.

DRO is an effective procedure that has been used successfully with a variety of challenging behaviors, including self-injury (e.g., Lindberg et al. 1999), disruption (Reese, Sherman, and Sheldon 1998), aggression (Britton et al. 2000), and stereotypic behavior (Haring and Kennedy 1990). In addition, it can be used when behavioral function is not readily evident or prior to conducting a functional assessment. It can be immediately applied while a more comprehensive and systematic intervention is being developed. As research indicates, in some cases it results in sufficient decreases in problem behavior when implemented alone.

One limitation of the procedure is that reinforcement is provided only for nonoccurrence of a designated target behavior, regardless of whether the child engages in other inappropriate behaviors. Take, for example, the student who must refrain from talking out in class to obtain reinforcement. According to this contingency, he may wander around the classroom, fail to complete his assignments, and engage in other disruptive behaviors while still meeting the requirement to receive reinforcement. Further, it is not unusual for different topographies of problem behavior to emerge or increase once others are no longer reinforced. For this reason, it is important to carefully monitor the occurrence of challenging behaviors that are not subject to the DRO program. If other problems emerge or increase, the DRO procedure can be modified to include additional problematic behaviors, or alternative interventions can be simultaneously introduced.

A second limitation is that reinforcement is provided on a schedule determined by someone other than the recipient of the reinforcement. Although the schedule may be carefully calculated to match the child's rate of problem behavior and apparent desire for reinforcement, the child is nonetheless left without control over when reinforcement is forthcoming. For this reason, it is important to combine DRO procedures with instructional strategies to teach the child appropriate means for obtaining reinforcement.

To summarize, DRO is a procedure that is used to completely eliminate the undesirable behavior (Table 17.1). It involves providing reinforcement if the behavior in question has not occurred during a preselected period of time. This approach may be particularly appropriate for challenging behaviors that cannot be tolerated, such as self-injury, aggression, and destruction of property. To enhance the effectiveness of the procedure, it is recommended that the function of the challenging behavior be taken into account and that the selected reinforcer match the function that is maintaining the challenging behavior.

Differential Reinforcement of Alternative and Incompatible Behaviors

DRA and DRI also are used when problem behavior needs to be eliminated. In addition, they have the purpose of strengthening a desirable behavior by providing reinforcement contingent on that behavior. In other words, unlike DRO, these procedures reinforce a particular behavior, rather than simply providing reinforcement for the absence of challenging behavior. Although the two procedures essentially are similar, DRA and DRI differ slightly in that the behavior reinforced during DRA is one that is an alternative to the challenging behavior, whereas the behavior reinforced during DRI is not just alternative but also is incompatible with the challenging behavior. An incompatible behavior is one that physically could not occur at the same time as the challenging behavior.

To illustrate, Mr. Ellis wants to decrease Trent's self-injury, which takes the form of slapping his face with his hand. The self-injury happens primarily

TABLE 17.1

Steps and Tips for Implementing DRO

Step	Helpful Tips
Measure baseline occurrences of challenging behavior and calculate the inter-response time	Divide the length of the observation by the average number of behaviors
Establish an interval length for reinforcement	The interval should be slightly shorter than the mean inter-response time
Identify the type of reinforcer that will be used	Choose highly powerful reinforcers and link to function, if known
Decide whether to respond to or ignore inappropriate behavior	If using consequences, make sure that they are effective and as mild as possible
Revise the procedure if other challenging behaviors increase or new ones emerge	Add additional target behaviors to the DRO system; introduce alternative interventions
Gradually increase the length of the interval	Determine a reasonable amount of time for behavior to become stable; change interval length slowly and systematically

DRO, differential reinforcement of other behavior.

when Trent is asked to complete academic tasks that he finds difficult. Applying a DRA procedure, Mr. Ellis might provide Trent with reinforcement each time he raises his hand and asks for assistance with his work. The behavior is an alternative to face-slapping, which Mr. Ellis has concluded occurs in the context of difficult work. Logically, reinforcement would come in the form of assistance with the work, perhaps accompanied with praise for appropriately requesting assistance. The success of this procedure comes about because performance of the alternative behavior decreases the likelihood that the inappropriate behavior will occur.

If Mr. Ellis were to apply a DRI procedure, he might provide reinforcement to Trent when he is writing with one hand on his paper and the other hand on his pencil. Clearly, when Trent is actively engaged in writing with both hands occupied, this behavior is incompatible with face-slapping, in that they cannot simultaneously occur.

One advantage of DRA is that an alternative behavior can be selected that is matched to the function of the challenging behavior. This is referred to as a *functionally equivalent* replacement behavior. In the example given, the DRA procedure ultimately teaches Trent an appropriate behavior for requesting assistance when he is confronted with difficult work, rather than simply encouraging him to engage in a topographically incompatible behavior. Once more, it should be noted that identifying an alternative behavior that serves the same purpose of the challenging behavior requires knowledge of behavioral function. That is, when used in this way, the procedure relies on functional assessment information.

To implement DRA and DRI procedures, an alternative (if possible, one that is functionally equivalent) or an incompatible behavior is selected to be reinforced. The procedure is much easier if the behavior to be reinforced is already in the child's repertoire. If it is not, a plan should be developed to teach the alternative or incompatible behavior. For example, if Trent does not already raise his hand and request assistance, Mr. Ellis can provide him with a verbal prompt to do so.

Next, a schedule of reinforcement is determined. This is done by calculating the average inter-response time, in the same manner as described for DRO. At the same time, the inter-response time for the behavior to be reinforced also is determined. The schedule of reinforcement should consider both the rate of problem behavior and the rate at which the appropriate behavior already occurs. If appropriate behavior rarely occurs, it will need to be taught or prompted in some way. With Trent, face-slapping occurred an average of once every 5 minutes, whereas hand raises and appropriate requests for assistance occurred every 10 minutes on average. Therefore, Mr. Ellis decided to wait for intervals of approximately 4 minutes to see whether Trent raised his hand to request assistance. If he did not, Mr. Ellis approached him and prompted him to raise his hand if he needed help.

As with DRO, it is important to identify reinforcers that are more powerful than those maintaining the inappropriate behavior. It this does not happen, it is improbable that the alternative or incompatible behavior will occur rather than the challenging behavior. As noted by O'Brien and Repp (1990, 155), "the individual must find the effects of emitting the incompatible behavior or omitting the target behavior at least as reinforcing as emitting the target response."

A few additional parameters regarding reinforcement are relevant for DRA procedures to be effective when the alternative behavior is linked to the function of the challenging behavior. First, if the alternative behavior requires a great deal more effort than the challenging behavior, it is not likely to successfully replace the behavior. That is, for a child who is nonverbal and has difficulty with ambulation, throwing an object is a much easier way of obtaining her mother's attention than walking across the room and tapping her politely. In this situation, an easier alternative behavior from the perspective of the child would be to make sure she carries with her a communication device that can be easily activated to issue a request for attention.

A second consideration is that the alternative behavior needs to result in reinforcement that is as rich as or richer than reinforcement for challenging behavior. In other words, it must be of at least equivalent quality and immediacy. For example, if activating a device to solicit attention results in a mother's brief comment along the lines of "Hi, Adrienne. How are you?" whereas throwing an object is met with the mother's approach followed by a lengthy discussion of why she should not throw toys, Adrienne may opt to throw toys because she prefers the proximity and lengthy engagement the behavior has produced.

A final issue, as mentioned earlier, is that many children engage in challenging behaviors because they have no means of communicating. In these situations, it is critical to immediately begin to teach functionally equivalent replacement behaviors in the context of DRA/DRI. This instruction, termed functional communication training (FCT) (e.g., Carr and Durand 1985), is most effective if it is used systematically to initially establish communication. That is, specific schedules of instruction, as well as prompting procedures that effectively elicit communication, should be in place. It may take time to teach and establish a functionally equivalent replacement behavior, and this is another reason that instruction must be systematic. Readers are referred to Chapters 15 and 18 for more specific parameters for developing an FCT program.

When DRA and DRI procedures are first introduced, it is important to reinforce every occurrence of the incompatible or alternative behavior. In this way, the child rapidly learns that reinforcement is consistently forthcoming for appropriate behavior, thereby increasing the likelihood that the reinforced behavior will successfully replace challenging behavior. Once appropriate behavior is well established, it is important to systematically thin the schedule of reinforcement. Ideally, the need to program reinforcement eventually will be obviated, because the appropriate behavior will be maintained by natural contingencies. For instance, in Trent's situation, he will learn that he routinely gets help at school with difficult work when he raises his hand and requests assistance.

As with DRO, when challenging behavior occurs, it can be ignored. In situations where challenging behavior persists or the alternative or incompatible behavior is not well established in the child's repertoire, the challenging behavior can be interrupted by prompting appropriate behavior. For example, at the first sign of face-slapping, Mr. Ellis could remind Trent how to get assistance by stating, "Trent, raise your hand if you need help." For children without Trent's verbal skills, a physical prompt may be more effective, such as physically guiding the child's hand to a communication device programmed to state, "I need help, please" when challenging behavior is observed. Finally, an undesirable consequence can be introduced when instances of the challenging behavior occur. In Trent's case, Mr. Ellis might remove a point from the class-wide incentive system each time Trent engages in face-slapping.

Both DRA and DRI have been used to reduce a number of inappropriate behaviors, such as stereotypic behaviors (Favell 1973), out-of-seat behavior (Friman 1990), self-injurious behaviors (Day et al. 1988), destructive behaviors (Piazza, Moes, and Fisher 1996), and disruptive behaviors (Ayllon and Roberts 1974). Recent applications have favored the use of DRA with replacement behavior that is functionally equivalent to the challenging behavior.

In summary, DRA and DRI are effective procedures that are relatively easy to implement (Table 17.2). Implementation is somewhat more complicated when it is linked to function, requiring a functional behavioral assessment. At the same time, the advantage of teaching functionally equivalent behavior is that, as with DRO, control over the delivery of reinforcement lies with the child. The procedures also are more complex when the alternative or incompatible behavior is not part of the child's repertoire and requires systematic prompting or training.

Differential Reinforcement of Low Rates of Behavior

It is sometimes the case that, although problem behavior is undesirable when it occurs at high rates, it is not beneficial to eliminate it entirely. As an example, Carolina talks almost continually; however, it would not be desirable to eliminate talking entirely. Similarly, Joe is very attached to his toy airplane and wants to carry it with him all the time, even during academic instruction. It is not necessary to remove his toy entirely, only to reduce the amount of time he carries it. In situations such as these, DRL is an appropriate strategy. The procedure involves providing reinforcement only if the child engages in a behavior no more than a predetermined low (or lower) number of times.

There are three ways in which a DRL procedure can be implemented. The first is termed spaced responding. As the label implies, a behavior is reinforced only when a specified interval of time has passed since the prior occurrence of the behavior. If the goal is to achieve delays between occurrences of behavior, so that the behavior is somewhat equally spaced, this form of DRL is appropriate. For example, Connie eats far too fast, often choking on her food. Her parents wish to slow her rate of eating so that she will place a bite of food in her mouth, then fully chew and swallow it, before taking another bite. This takes approximately one full minute. Therefore, the parents design a schedule whereby Connie receives a reinforcer, in the form of a small chocolate or cookie piece that will accumulate for her to have for dessert, each time one full minute passes between bites of food.

A second format is full-session DRL. In this procedure, reinforcement is delivered at the end of a session, such as a 40-minute math period, if the total number of instances of behavior during that session is equal to or less than a preset limit. For instance, during group instruction, Maura almost constantly

TABLE 17.2

Steps and Tips for Implementing DRA/DRI

Step	Helpful Tips
Select behavior that is incompatible or alternative to the target behavior	If possible, select behavior that the child already knows how to perform; preferably, select a functionally equivalent behavior
Record baseline data on occurrence of the challenging behavior and of appropriate behaviors; calculate the inter-response time	Divide the length of observation by the average number of behaviors; incompatible/alternative behavior should occur often enough for reinforcement to be effective
Establish an interval length for reinforcement	The interval should be slightly shorter than the mean inter-response time; at the early stages, reinforcement of each occurrence of appropriate behavior may be necessary
Decide whether alternative skills will be taught	Use effective teaching techniques (e.g., prompting, shaping) to teach the alternative skill; consider teaching functionally equivalent communication responses (FCT)
Identify the type of reinforcer that will be used	Choose highly powerful reinforcers; choose reinforcers that are easy to perform; link to function, if known
Decide whether to respond to or ignore inappropriate behavior	Use effective and least restrictive responses; be consistent
Plan to gradually fade the schedule of reinforcement	After behavior is stable, increase interval length slowly and systematically

DRA, differential reinforcement of alternative behavior; DRI, differential reinforcement of incompatible behavior; FCT, functional communication training.

yells out answers to questions posed to the class. Her teacher has decided to set up a full-session DRL procedure whereby Maura earns a reward if she yells out answers fewer than five times during math class.

The third form is interval DRL. It is similar to full-session DRL, except that the session is divided into smaller time segments, such as eight 5-minute intervals, and reinforcement is provided at the end of each interval when behavior has occurred at or less frequently than the predetermined criterion. Typically, if the behavior exceeds the criterion before the end of the interval, the time is reset. Smaller intervals are most appropriate when the behavior occurs at a high rate and the child needs frequent feedback about the rate of behavior. Also, with full-session DRL, if the child exceeds the threshold for reinforcement, the motivation to decrease the rate of behavior for the remainder of the session is eliminated. In this situation, an interval with a reset procedure is likely to be more successful. Some other factors that might be taken into consideration when choosing between interval and full-session DRL are the child's age and individual level of tolerance for thinner schedules of reinforcement (i.e., self-control). Clearly, with younger children and those who have difficulty waiting for reinforcement, interval DRL is preferable. On the other hand, the full-session procedure may be more feasible in general education classrooms with a higher student-to-teacher ratio. In addition, the full-session DRL procedures can be implemented in a way that is compatible with natural routines and procedures.

To determine the initial criterion, the average baseline frequency of the behavior during each session or interval is determined. This can be accomplished very simply by noting the start time of an observation, making a tally each time challenging behavior occurs, and noting the end time of the observation. The total frequency of behaviors observed is then divided by the observation time (e.g., number of minutes) to produce the rate of behavior (occurrences per minute).

As with the other differential reinforcement procedures, a preferred reinforcer must be identified. After the child consistently meets or surpasses the low criterion number of occurrences in an interval, the procedure can be faded by gradually changing the criterion for reinforcement. This can be accomplished by gradually increasing the duration of time between behaviors (spaced-interval DRL), by gradually increasing the interval length (interval DRL), or by gradually increasing the acceptable number of behaviors for earning reinforcement (interval or full-session DRL).

Some decisions related to DRL are whether to make the child aware of the "rules of the game" or the schedule of reinforcement and whether to provide feedback about occurrences of challenging behavior. The decision as to whether to inform the child must be made in accordance with his or her individual characteristics and abilities and to achieve the best fit to the ecology of a particular classroom. For example, Mrs. Samuel posts the rules of conduct on the blackboard for her group of excessively active 13-year-olds. The rules permit no more than three disruptions (talking-out without raising a hand, being out-of-seat without permission, talking to a classmate) per student throughout the school day. She puts checks on the students' charts to keep track of their behavior. Ten minutes before the end of each day, every student who has three checkmarks or fewer earns an early dismissal. When new rules come in place that permit no more than two disruptions per day, Mrs. Samuel explains the updates to the students and posts them on a blackboard. This works very well with her students, because they are can comprehend the rules and are motivated to follow them. Other teachers may decide not to inform their students about the exact details of the procedure, if they determine that such an explanation would be beyond the students' comprehension. Instead, the students learn to understand the contingencies as they are applied. With respect to feedback regarding occurrences of challenging behavior, it is sometimes helpful to inform children when they have engaged in challenging behavior. One consideration, however, is whether the behavior functions to obtain attention. If this is the case, providing feedback that a behavior has occurred may inadvertently reinforce the behavior by providing attention to the child.

The research reported in the literature illustrates many different applications of DRL. The procedure has been used successfully to decrease stereotypic behavior, such as rocking, mouthing, and finger movements (Singh, Dawson, and Manning 1981); to reduce off-task verbalizations, including changing topic or disputing; and to decrease repetitive speech (Handen, Apolito, and Seltzer 1984). Classroom applications have consisted of reducing out-of-seat behavior (Harris and Sherman 1973) and decreasing talking-out behaviors (Deitz and Repp 1973, 1974).

A limitation of DRL is that it can be time-consuming and labor intensive to implement. Specifically, the number of behaviors that occur during a given period of time or the duration between behaviors must be carefully measured or counted. When behaviors occur at a high rate, full attention is required, and this may render DRL unfeasible in certain situations.

In conclusion, DRL is used in cases when behaviors should not be eliminated altogether (Table 17.3). It is an effective procedure that programs for the progressive reduction of behavior. It is applicable across a wide variety of behaviors and settings.

■ Noncontingent Reinforcement

In situations when application of differential reinforcement procedures is not feasible for logistical reasons (e.g., lack of time, high student-to-staff ratio), noncontingent reinforcement (NCR) may become the intervention of choice due to its ease of implementation. NCR involves delivering of a reinforcer that is known to maintain the inappropriate behavior regardless of whether challenging behavior occurred. That is, reinforcement is not in any way linked to the child's participation in challenging behavior such as engaging in low rates (as in DRL) or refraining therefrom (as in DRO). Instead, it is delivered at preselected intervals of time, usually fixed intervals, independent of behavior. As the definition of NCR implies, some understanding of the function of the challenging behavior is needed. Examples of NCR include periodic breaks from a difficult assignment,

TABLE 17.3

Steps and Tips for Implementing DRL

Step	Helpful Tips
Measure baseline level of target behavior to establish initial criterion	Count the frequency of behavior during a preestablished period of time
Choose full-session or interval format	Consider age of student and rate of behavior
Choose initial length of the intervals	Begin the program at an interval slightly shorter than the average baseline level of behavior occurrence
Decide whether to inform students about the rules of the procedure and whether to provide feedback about occurrence of challenging behavior	Consider whether the student can understand the rules of the DRL procedure; feedback may not be appropriate if the function of behavior is obtaining attention
Decide whether to respond to or ignore inappropriate behavior	Use effective and least restrictive responses; be consistent
Determine what to do if behavior exceeds the criterion before the end of the interval	Typically, time is reset for a new interval
Plan to gradually fade the schedule	After rate of behavior is stable, establish a lower criterion of behavior for reinforcement or increase the interval length

DRL, differential reinforcement of low rates of behavior.

episodic attention from a preferred person, access to a preferred activity spaced throughout the day, or time to engage in sensory activities.

Results of a functional assessment are needed to identify reinforcers to use during the NCR intervention that are directly linked to the function of the problem behavior. To illustrate, consider Manny, who frequently talks out in class; this often leads to adults' reprimanding or redirecting her. After conducting a functional assessment, Manny's teacher, Ms. James, hypothesizes that Manny's challenging behavior serves the function of obtaining the adults' attention. Ms. James then decides to provide Manny with attention on a fixed-interval schedule of once every 2 minutes, regardless of whether she talks out.

To further illustrate, Sam often throws tantrums when he is prompted to continue work that he finds difficult; this challenging behavior serves the function of escaping the assignment. To decrease Sam's tantrums, his teacher decides to let him take a break from work and relax on a couch every 10 minutes for a brief amount of time.

NCR is one of the most frequently reported function-based interventions for challenging behaviors in the recent literature (Carr et al. 2000). The logic behind the success of this intervention is simple: As a reinforcing consequence is delivered independent of the occurrence of challenging behavior, the challenging behavior and the reinforcement become disassociated. In other words, because reinforcement is regularly and noncontingently delivered, the need for challenging behavior to obtain the identical form of reinforcement is obviated. At the same time, challenging behavior declines because it is ignored (not reinforced).

Initially, NCR should be administered on a fairly dense schedule. The schedule can be determined in much the same way as a DRO schedule. That is, the schedule of reinforcement should be derived from current rates of challenging behavior. In the case of disruptive behavior that functions to provide escape from a task and occurs an average of every 10 minutes, brief breaks should be provided on a slightly more dense schedule, perhaps once every 8 minutes. After the challenging behavior has decreased, the schedule is gradually thinned by slowly and systematically lengthening the interval required before reinforcement. The ultimate goal, as with any reinforcement procedure, is to fade the schedule of reinforcement to socially acceptable levels, such as taking breaks together with the entire class once every 40 minutes. A final note about NCR is that it can be combined with reductive procedures, such as blocking or saying "No." This may be desirable in the case of extremely dangerous behaviors.

As mentioned, NCR most often involves a fixed-interval schedule of reinforcement delivery. However, if behavior is maintained by automatic or sensory reinforcement that is available on an ongoing basis, an interval schedule may not be sufficient to compete with the continuous schedule. In situations such as these, it is possible to provide NCR continuously, should the classroom context allow. For example, to decrease Ray's self-injurious behavior, arm rubbing, which was maintained by automatic (sensory) reinforcement, an electronic massager was provided to him on a continuous basis; this led to rapid and significant decreases in the challenging behavior (Roscoe, Iwata, and Goh 1998).

NCR is an effective procedure that has been used to reduce a number of challenging behaviors, such as self-injurious behavior (DeLeon et al. 2000), inappropriate speech (Carr and Britton 1999), tantrums and aggression (Britton et al. 2000), and self-stimulatory behaviors (Luiselli 1994). NCR offers a good contextual fit in many applied settings, because it is simple and easy to implement compared with other procedures. Moreover, research has found it to be comparable in effectiveness to differential reinforcement procedures. This, in part, may be attributed to the fact that, unlike differential reinforcement, NCR necessarily incorporates information about the function of challenging behavior. Another advantage of NCR is that it often results in a higher rate of reinforcer delivery, compared with differential reinforcement procedures in which reinforcement is withheld when challenging behavior occurs.

One caution regarding NCR is the possibility of accidentally strengthening challenging behavior. This can occur when noncontingent reinforcement is delivered after the occurrence of challenging behavior and the child incorrectly associates the two events. If the challenging behavior occurs at a high rate and reinforcement is dense, this possibility is increased. One way to avoid this situation is to withhold the delivery of reinforcement if challenging behavior has occurred just before the end of an interval. Another option is to briefly delay reinforcement if challenging behavior coincides with the end of an interval.

Another potential concern with NCR is that it does not strengthen any particular behavior, nor does it teach any appropriate alternative behavior. For this reason, it is often used in conjunction with another reinforcement procedure, such as DRA or FCT. Such a combined intervention approach may be especially advantageous for students who engage in severe challenging behaviors but do not yet possess appropriate alternative skills that would allow them to access reinforcement. A related limitation is that, although reinforcement is delivered on a schedule that is matched to the rate of challenging behavior, this does not necessarily ensure that it will coincide with occasions when the individual desires reinforcement. For example, although brief breaks from a task may be scheduled every 10 minutes, a child may desire a break from a particularly fatiguing task after 5 minutes. If the child has not been taught an appropriate way to request a break, challenging behavior is likely to re-emerge in order to access reinforcement. This is another example of why it is important to simultaneously teach alternative and functionally equivalent behaviors.

In summary, NCR serves as a feasible option for teachers, parents, and caregivers who are looking for a simple and easily implemented procedure for behavior reduction (Table 17.4). It is an effective intervention that can produce rapid decreases in challenging behavior by taking into consideration the function of that behavior. When combined with procedures for teaching appropriate functionally equivalent responses, such as FCT, it can offer a comprehensive approach to instruction and behavior reduction.

■ Conclusions

Positive reinforcement strategies represent a powerful component among the array of behavior support interventions for children with autism. By

TABLE 17.4

Steps and Tips for Implementing NCR

Step	Helpful Tips
Determine function of challenging behavior	Possible functions include escaping something nonpreferred, obtaining something preferred, or sensory stimulation
Select reinforcer	The reinforcer should serve the same function as the challenging behavior
Establish initial schedule of reinforcement	Continuous or very dense fixed-interval schedules are recommended initially; deliver reinforcer independent of challenging behavior
Teach appropriate alternative skills	Consider teaching functionally equivalent skills; consider using in combination with DRA or FCT
Decide what to do if challenging behavior occurs just before planned delivery of NCR	Refrain from delivery of reinforcer and reset the interval; postpone the delivery of reinforcer
Decide whether to react to or ignore inappropriate behavior	Use effective and least restrictive responses
Gradually thin schedule of reinforcement	After behavior is stable, increase interval length slowly and systematically

FCT, functional communication training; NCR, noncontingent reinforcement.

rewarding children for appropriate behavior, or for the absence of inappropriate behavior, this category of interventions leads to decreases in challenging behavior. When linked to functional assessment information, positive reinforcement approaches are particularly effective, in that they focus on encouraging adaptive responses that will replace the challenging behavior. The many different permutations of positive reinforcement interventions make them adaptable to a range of goals related to challenging behavior. The goals may involve reducing behaviors to appropriate levels (DRL), increasing appropriate alternative or incompatible behaviors (DRA or DRI), eliminating challenging behaviors altogether (DRO), or eliminating the need for challenging behavior by providing the reinforcer that maintains it (NCR). Further, many configurations are feasible to implement even in the context of multiple competing demands, such as a busy classroom. Finally, practitioners and parents alike find it gratifying to focus on and reward the desirable behaviors that children display.

■ References

Ayllon, T., and Roberts, M.D. (1974). Eliminating discipline problems by strengthening academic performance. *Journal of Applied Behavior Analysis*, 7, 71–76.

Bambara, L.M., and Kern, L. (2006). *Individualized supports for students with problem behaviors: Designing positive behavior plans*. New York: Guilford Press.

Britton, L.N., Carr, J. E., Kellum, K.K., Dozier, C.L., and Weil, T.M. (2000). A variation of noncontingent reinforcement in the treatment of aberrant behavior. *Research in Developmental Disabilities*, 21, 425–435.

Carr, J.E., and Britton, L.N. (1999). Idiosyncratic effects of noncontingent reinforcement on problematic speech. *Behavioral Interventions*, 14, 37–43.

Carr, J.E., Coriaty, S., Wilder, D.A., Gaunt, B.T., Dozier, C.L., Britton, L.N., Avina,C., and Reed, C.L. (2000). A review of "noncontingent" reinforcement as treatment for the aberrant behavior of individuals with developmental disabilities. *Research in Developmental Disabilities*, 21, 377–391.

Carr, E.G., and Durand, V.M. (1985). Reducing behavior problems through functional communication training. *Journal of Applied Behavior Analysis*, 18, 111–126.

Carr, E.G., Yarbrough, S.C., and Langdon, N.A. (1997). Effects of idiosyncratic stimuli variables on functional analysis outcomes. *Journal of Applied Behavior Analysis*, 30, 673–686.

Day, R.M., Rea, J.A., Schussler, N.G., Larsen, S.E., and Johnson, W.L. (1988). A functionally based approach to the treatment of self-injurious behavior. *Behavior Modification*, 12, 565–589.

Deitz, S.M., and Repp, A.C. (1973). Decreasing classroom misbehavior through the use of DRL schedules of reinforcement. *Journal of Applied Behavior Analysis*, 6, 457–463.

Deitz, S.M., and Repp, A.C. (1974). Differentially reinforcing low rates of misbehavior with normal elementary school children. *Journal of Applied Behavior Analysis*, 7, 622.

DeLeon, I.G., Anders, B.M., Rodriguez-Catter, V., and Neidert, P.L. (2000). The effects of noncontingent access to single- versus multiple-stimulus sets on self-injurious behavior. *Journal of Applied Behavior Analysis*, 33, 623–626.

Favell, J.E. (1973). Reduction of stereotypies by reinforcement of toy play. *Mental Retardation*, 11 (4), 21–23.

Friman, P.C. (1990). Nonaversive treatment of high-rate disruption: Child and provider effects. *Exceptional Children*, 57, 64–70.

Hagopian, L.P., Long, E.S., and Rush, K.S. (2004). Preference assessment procedures for individuals with developmental disabililties. *Behavior Modification*, 5, 668–677.

Handen, B.L., Apolito, P.M., and Seltzer, G.B. (1984). Use of differential reinforcement of low rates of behavior to decrease repetitive speech in an autistic adolescent. *Journal of Behavior Therapy and Experimental Psychiatry*, 15, 359–364.

Haring, T., and Kennedy, C. (1990). Contextual control of problem behavior in students with severe disabilities. *Journal of Applied Behavior Analysis*, 23, 235–243.

Harris, V.W., and Sherman, J.A. (1973). Use and analysis of the "good behavior game" to reduce disruptive classroom behavior. *Journal of Applied Behavior Analysis*, 6, 405–417.

Lindberg, J.S., Iwata, B.A., Kahng, S.W., and DeLeon, I.G. (1999). DRO contingencies: An analysis of variable-momentary schedules. *Journal of Applied Behavior Analysis*, 32, 123–136.

Luiselli, J.K. (1994). Effects of noncontingent sensory reinforcement on stereotypic behaviors in a child with posttraumatic neurological impairment. *Journal of Behavior Therapy and Experimental Psychiatry*, 25, 325–330.

O'Brien, S.O., and Repp, A.C. (1990). Reinforcement-based reductive procedures: A review of 20 years of their use with persons with severe or profound retardation. *Journal of the Association for Persons with Severe Handicaps*, 15, 148–159.

Piazza, C.C., Moes, D.R., and Fisher, W.W. (1996). Differential reinforcement of alternative behavior and demand fading in the treatment of escape-maintained destructive behavior. *Journal of Applied Behavior Analysis*, 29, 569–572.

Reese, R.M., Sherman, J.A., and Sheldon, J.B. (1998). Reducing disruptive behavior of a group-home resident with autism and mental retardation. *Journal of Autism and Developmental Disorders*, 28, 159–165.

Roscoe, E.M., Iwata, B.A., and Goh, H.L. (1998). A comparison of noncontingent reinforcement and sensory extinction as treatments for self-injurious behavior. *Journal of Applied Behavior Analysis*, 31, 635–646.

Singh, N.N., Dawson, M.J., and Manning, P. (1981). Effects of spaced responding DRL on the stereotyped behavior of profoundly retarded persons. *Journal of Applied Behavior Analysis*, 14, 521–526.

18. BEHAVIOR-CONTINGENT (RESTRICTIVE) INTERVENTION: A FUNCTION-BASED APPROACH

Dorothea C. Lerman

Research conducted over the past several decades has demonstrated the efficacy of treatments derived from functional assessments of problem behavior. As described in previous chapters, function-based interventions that include reinforcement, extinction, and establishing (motivational) operations are highly effective for treating a wide range of behavior disorders. Nonetheless, more intrusive procedures are sometimes needed for individuals with serious behavior problems. These procedures may be the initial treatment of choice if behavior must be suppressed rapidly to prevent physical harm (e.g., Foxx 2003). In other cases, restrictive interventions may be evaluated after reinforcement-based treatments fail to produce acceptable clinical outcomes (e.g., Fisher et al. 1993; Hagopian et al. 1998; Hanley et al. 2005; Wacker et al. 1990).

A variety of more intrusive, or restrictive, interventions based on the process of punishment have been examined for treating problem behaviors exhibited by individuals with autism and other developmental disabilities. This expansive literature has demonstrated the advantages and disadvantages of this approach to treatment, with a primary focus on the development of safe and effective procedures. The objectives of this chapter are to describe commonly used intrusive procedures, to summarize research findings on punishment, and to offer some guidelines for selecting and using punishment effectively. The relevance of behavioral function when developing treatments based on the process of punishment is also discussed. Although punishment is more likely to be needed when the function of behavior is unknown (Kahng, Iwata, and Lewin 2002; Pelios et al. 1999), this approach to treatment should always be guided by information about the antecedents and consequences that may be relevant or irrelevant to occurrences of problem behavior.

■ Types of Punishment Procedures

A particular intervention is classified as a punishment procedure based on its behavioral effect, not on the formal features of the procedure. Thus, a fairly intrusive procedure might function as a punisher for some people but as a reinforcer for others (e.g., water mist; Fisher et al. 1994 *A preliminary evaluation*). An intervention is termed "positive punishment" if the contingent presentation of a stimulus, such as verbal reprimands or brief physical restraint, decreases the future likelihood of the behavior (Cooper, Heron, and Heward 2006). "Negative punishment," the contingent removal of a stimulus, decreases the future likelihood of behavior via the removal of a specific amount of a positive reinforcer (response cost) or the loss of access to reinforcement for a specific period of time (time-out from positive reinforcement). For descriptive purposes, it is helpful to organize the various punishment procedures into these broad categories. However, in practice, many commonly used interventions contain components from multiple categories. For example, time-out is often combined with some type of physical restraint. The following is an overview of procedures that have been found to be safe and effective.

Positive Punishment Procedures

A variety of stimuli, including verbal reprimands, physical contact, noise, water mist, and shock, have been evaluated for the treatment of problem behavior. Verbal reprimands have frequently taken the form of brief statements of disapproval or instruction (e.g., a stern "No" or "Don't do that, you'll hurt yourself") (e.g., Maglieri et al. 2000; Richman et al. 2001; Van Houten et al. 1982). Results of studies suggest that verbal reprimands are more effective when they are *(a)* paired with eye contact and physical contact (e.g., a firm grasp on the shoulder) and *(b)* delivered in close proximity to the behaver (e.g., Richman et al. 2001; Van Houten et al. 1982).

A variety of punishment procedures also involve some type of physical contact between the caregiver and the child. These procedures have been used as the primary intervention or in concert with other punishers (e.g., overcorrection; time-out). Response blocking and response interruption, the least intrusive forms of these procedures, involve the use of brief physical contact to prevent a response from occurring or, once it has initiated, to prevent it from continuing to occur (e.g., Lalli, Livezey, and Kates 1996; Lerman et al. 2003; Reid et al. 1993). In Lerman et al. (2003), for example, a participant with developmental disabilities engaged in high rates of stereotypic behavior in the form of head- and tooth-tapping. The experimenter guided the participant's hand away from her head and face as soon as she began to engage in the behavior.

Physical contact that occurs for the purpose of restricting or limiting an individual's movement for a specific period of time (typically, 30 to 60 seconds) is referred to as physical restraint. Procedural variations of restraint have included "hands down," or holding the individual's hands to the side (Hagopian et al. 1998; Lerman et al. 1997); "baskethold," or crossing the individual's arms across the chest and holding them from behind (Fisher et al. 1994 *Empirically derived consequences*), and "movement suppression time-out," or using the least amount of physical contact necessary to keep the individual motionless while standing in a corner (Rolider and Van Houten 1985). Because the child typically cannot access reinforcing stimuli while restrained, these physical restraint procedures are necessarily combined with time-out from positive reinforcement.

Some interventions require the individual to engage in an effortful response after instances of problem behavior. This type of punisher is commonly called "overcorrection" if the contingent response is topographically similar to the problem behavior, is considered to be an appropriate replacement behavior, or is linked to the problem behavior in some other way (e.g., Cipani et al. 1991; Foxx and Azrin 1972, 1973; Rollings, Baumeister, and Baumeister 1977). For example, an individual whose problem behavior results in damage or disruption to the physical environment might be required to restore the environment to a state that is even better than its original state, a variant called "restitutional overcorrection." In Carey and Bucher (1981), participants who engaged in inappropriate eating (e.g., stuffing food into the mouth, touching food with hands) were required to wipe their hands, face, table, chair, and floor with a wet cloth for 2 minutes after each occurrence of the behavior. In some cases, a child might be required to repeatedly engage in an appropriate alternative behavior. This variant, called "positive practice overcorrection," has been implemented both in conjunction with restitutional overcorrection and as the sole intervention. For example, in Carey and Bucher's (1981) study, participants were required to engage in appropriate eating (e.g., hold fork and knife correctly, cut a small portion of food) 10 times, contingent on each occurrence of inappropriate eating. Other commonly used effort procedures, such as contingent demands (e.g., Fisher et al. 1993; Watson 1993) and contingent exercise (e.g., Kahng, Abt, and Wilder 2001), are not classified as overcorrection because the contingent response is unrelated to the problem behavior.

Other positive punishers that have been found to be safe and effective for severe behavior disorders include the contingent delivery of water mist sprayed to the lower area of the face (e.g., Dorsey et al. 1980; Friman, Cook, and Finney 1984), lemon juice or vinegar squirted into the mouth (e.g., Cipani et al. 1991; Cook et al. 1978; Paisey and Whitney 1989), an aromatic ammonia capsule held under the nose (e.g., Altman, Haavik, and Cook 1978; Singh, Dawson, and Gregory 1980 *Suppression of chronic hyperventilation*), and brief electric shock applied to the arm or leg (Duker and Seys 1996; Linscheid et al. 1990; Foxx 2003). As discussed latter in the chapter, there are many concerns when considering these procedures, including the degree of intrusiveness, potential for misapplication, and acceptance by care providers.

Negative Punishment Procedures

As noted previously, response cost and time-out from positive reinforcement are the two main procedural variations of negative punishment. Time-out involves the contingent loss of access to positive reinforcers for a period of time. For example, the individual might be moved to a less reinforcing environment, such as a barren room, partitioned area, or corner (i.e., "exclusionary" or "seclusionary" time-out) (e.g., Toole et al. 2003). Alternatively, the child might lose access to reinforcement in the current environment ("nonexclusionary time-out"). The latter variant has been accomplished in a variety of ways. For example, a hand, mask, or cloth was placed over the child's eyes (called a "visual screen") (e.g., Singh, Watson, and Winton 1986; Rush, Crockett, and Hagopian 2001); a ribbon worn by the student was removed to coincide with the unavailability of reinforcement (called a "time-out ribbon") (e.g., Foxx and Shapiro 1978; Salend and Gordon 1987); the individual was required to remain in a location that was situated near the reinforcing environment (called "contingent observation") (e.g., Porterfield, Herbert-Jackson, and Risley 1976); and ongoing sources of stimulation (e.g., music, leisure materials) were terminated (e.g., Falcomata et al. 2004; Keeney et al. 2000). When time-out is combined with some type of physical contact or restraint, the reductive effects of this intervention may be partially or solely due to this positive punisher.

Response cost refers to the contingent removal of a specific amount of reinforcement. Typically, the reinforcers lost are those that the individual had previously earned through appropriate behavior (e.g., differential reinforcement of alternative behavior). Although response cost is most commonly used within the context of token economy systems (e.g., LeBlanc, Hagopian, and Maglieri 2000; Truchlicka, McLaughlin, and Swain 1998), a few studies have examined the contingent loss of other forms of reinforcement, such as books and audiotapes (Kahng, Tarbox, and Wilke 2001), money (Epstein and Masek 1978; Long et al. 1999), and participation in tournaments (e.g., Allen 1998).

■ The Effects of Punishment on Behavior

Direct Effects of Punishment

Research findings indicate that punishment usually produces an immediate decrease in problem behavior (see Lerman and Vorndran, 2002, for a review). In fact, results of some applied studies indicate that intrusive interventions may produce more robust treatment effects than those based on behavioral function (e.g., extinction, differential reinforcement) (Grace, Kahng, and Fisher 1994; Hagopian et al. 1998; Wacker et al. 1990). For example, Hagopian and colleagues (1998) found that, for the majority of participants, treatment with functional communication training was ineffective as the schedule of reinforcement was thinned unless punishment was included as part of treatment. Nonetheless, various factors related to the use of these procedures can influence clinical outcomes. Rich schedules of noncontingent reinforcement, for example, may lead to almost complete response suppression at the outset of treatment (e.g., Vollmer et al. 1998), an outcome that is not always associated with punishment (e.g., Vorndran and Lerman 2006). Basic and applied studies have identified a number of variables that may alter the effectiveness of punishment (see Lerman and Vorndran, 2002, for a review). The following is a brief overview of this research.

Procedural Parameters

Several parameters related to the delivery of the punishing consequence may be critical to treatment efficacy. In general, the consequence should be delivered immediately after most instances of the behavior (e.g., Abromowitz and O'Leary 1990; Azrin, Holz, and Hake 1963; Calhoun and Matherne 1975; Lerman et al. 1997; Thomas 1968). That is, the consequence should occur close in time to the behavior and should follow the behavior on a frequent basis. Basic studies with humans and nonhumans suggest that intrusive interventions may not reduce problem behavior if the consequence is delayed by even 20 or 30 seconds (e.g., Banks and Vogel-Sprott 1965; Trenholme and Baron 1975). Nonetheless, a few cases have been reported in which delayed punishment was successful in the absence of strategies designed to compensate for this delay. In the study by Maglieri and associates (2000), for example, verbal reprimands delivered up to 10 minutes after the consumption of prohibited food items decreased this behavior to zero levels in a girl with Prader-Willi syndrome. It should be noted, however, that delayed punishment was used after food stealing had been suppressed with immediate reprimands in a previous phase.

Basic and applied studies also suggest that almost every response must be followed by the punisher to produce acceptable clinical outcomes (e.g., Azrin, Holz, and Hake 1963; Calhoun and Matherne 1975). Nonetheless, moderately dense schedules of intermittent punishment (such as variable ratio [VR] 4) may be effective with some types of punishers (Cipani et al. 1991), particularly if the behavior has already been exposed to a continuous schedule of punishment (e.g., Clark et al. 1973; Luiselli, Suskin, and McPhee 1981; Romanczyk 1977). The generality of these findings is unclear, however, because punishment appeared to be confounded with extinction or other potential punishers (e.g., verbal reprimands) in the majority of studies.

In addition to immediacy and schedule, the intensity or duration of punishment may influence treatment efficacy (e.g., Hobbs, Forehand, Murray 1978; Richman et al. 2001; Stricker et al. 2003; Williams, Kirkpatrick-Sanchez, and Iwata 1993). However, results of studies on this parameter have been somewhat inconsistent. In the study by Richman and colleagues (2001), for example, soft reprimands were much less effective than loud reprimands in treating breath-holding exhibited by a teenager with mental retardation. Nonetheless, increasing the duration of time-out, overcorrection, and restraint has not reliably improved treatment efficacy relative to shorter durations (e.g., Cole et al. 2000; Singh, Dawson, and Manning 1981; White, Nielsen, and Johnson 1972). A clinical strategy that involves enlarging the magnitude of an ineffective punisher does not have strong empirical support and may even promote resistance to punishment (see further discussion later in this chapter). Ideally, a magnitude that is likely to be effective should be selected initially, and an alternative consequence should be evaluated if treatment is unsuccessful.

Availability of Reinforcement

The delivery of reinforcement during treatment may be either beneficial or adverse, depending on the response that is reinforced. Results of basic studies indicate that treatment will be compromised if the punished response also leads to reinforcement (Azrin and Holz 1966). In such cases, the punisher may even acquire discriminative or conditioned reinforcing properties, leading to an increase in the behavior rather than a decrease (e.g., Holz and Azrin 1961). This finding has critical implications for application, because punishment is more likely to be used when the reinforcer maintaining a behavior is unknown or cannot be controlled. Nonetheless, a number of applied studies have shown that punishment can be highly effective in the absence of extinction (e.g., Fisher et al. 1994 *Empirically derived consequences;* Keeney et al. 2000; Lerman et al. 1997; Thompson, et al. 1999).

If extinction is not used, potential problems may be minimized by ensuring that alternative sources of reinforcement are readily available for engaging in other responses (Holz, Azrin, and Ayllon 1963; Rawson and Leitenberg 1973; Thompson et al. 1999). This includes the use of reinforcers that are maintaining the problem behavior (if possible) or reinforcers that are highly substitutable for the maintaining reinforcers. In the investigation by Thompson and colleagues (1999), for example, treatment for self-injury maintained by automatic reinforcement was more effective when punishment was combined with reinforcement of toy play than when either punishment or reinforcement was implemented alone. Punishment may be most effective when reinforcement can be obtained through a variety of sources (e.g., both contingent upon and independent of responding).

History

Basic research suggests that prior exposure to certain procedures and contingencies might alter the effectiveness of a current intervention. In particular, prior exposure to a punishing stimulus could reduce the effectiveness of the stimulus when it is used as a consequence later (e.g., Capaldi et al. 1985; Halevy, Feldon, and Weiner 1987). Resistance to punishment may be particularly problematic if the intensity or magnitude of the punisher is gradually increased over time (Cohen 1968; Terris and Barnes 1969). Habituation or adaptation to the stimulus most likely accounts for these findings. Although these basic findings have tremendous relevance to application, no applied studies have systematically evaluated the role of history on treatment efficacy with punishment. However, some published data suggest that the child's previous experience should be given consideration when designing interventions. For example, in White, Nielsen, and Johnson (1972), the effectiveness of three durations of time-out (1, 15, and 30 minutes) was compared by exposing different groups of participants to all durations but in a varying order. Results suggested that the 1-minute time-out was effective in reducing problem behavior only if it was evaluated before the lengthier time-out durations.

To summarize, basic and applied research suggest that the manner in which punishment is delivered, the availability of alternative sources of reinforcement, and prior exposure to certain procedures and contingencies are important determinants of treatment effects. Direct translation of these findings into an applied technology raises difficulties for those working in service delivery settings. That is, basic and applied research suggests that practitioners should use novel punishers of sufficient magnitude and should deliver consequences immediately after almost every instance of the targeted problem behavior while exposing the problem behavior to extinction and providing reinforcement for alternative behavior. Given the typical constraints of applied settings, close adherence to these guidelines may be the exception rather than the rule. Later in the chapter, potential strategies to increase the practicality of intrusive interventions are discussed.

Indirect Effects of Punishment

When it is initially implemented, punishment may be associated with a variety of desirable and undesirable side effects. However, the probability of obtaining these side effects and the forms that they may take are difficult to predict in individual cases. For example, several studies have reported increases in aggression or crying during treatment with punishment (e.g., Duker and Seys 1996; Hagopian and Adelinis 2001), whereas these same response forms have also been reported to decrease under punishment (e.g., Bitgood et al.1980; Linscheid et al. 1990). Likewise, some studies on punishment have shown collateral increases in positive affect or appropriate behavior, such compliance and toy play (e.g., Koegel et al. 1974; Rolider et al. 1991; Toole et al. 2003), whereas others have reported decreases in these appropriate behaviors (e.g., Lerman et al. 2003; Thompson et al. 1999).

Basic and applied research on punishment suggests that increases in aggression and other undesirable indirect effects may be less likely to occur if exposure to the punishing stimulus is minimized (i.e., by using brief punishers that are highly effective in suppressing behavior), if punishment is combined with rich schedules of reinforcement for alternative behavior, and if practitioners ensure that reinforcement is withheld for functionally equivalent problem behavior (Lerman and Vorndran 2002).

Maintenance and Generalization

Clinically important reductions in behavior have been shown to be maintained from several months to 25 years after the initiation of treatment with punishment (e.g., Altman, Haavik, and Cook 1978; Duker and Seys 1996; Foxx, Bittle, and Faw 1989; McGlynn and Locke 1997; Richman et al. 2001; Rolider et al. 1991; Salvy et al. 2004). In the 2001 study by Richman's group, for example, a verbal reprimand combined with differential reinforcement of other behavior (DRO) continued to suppress breath-holding in a 16-year-old with severe mental retardation up to 7 months after the initial treatment evaluation. Long-term effectiveness of treatment has even been obtained when the original treatment was partially withdrawn or eliminated completely (e.g., Salvy et al. 2004).

Although these findings are encouraging, they must be interpreted with caution, because treatment relapses have been reported in a number of studies on punishment (e.g., Duker and Seys 1996; Foxx and Livesay 1984; Ricketts, Goza, and Matese 1993; Williams, Kirkpatrick-Sanchez, and Iwata 1993). Moreover, the long-term evaluation of any treatment is methodologically challenging. Maintenance of rigorous data collection and evaluation procedures may be cost-prohibitive. It is probably for this reason that many studies have relied on anecdotal information, archival records, indirect measures, and limited observation of participants. In addition, factors that may affect the efficacy of the intervention become increasingly more likely over an extended period of time. These include changes in the individual's medications, daily activities, and treatment integrity. Specific strategies to prevent relapse have not yet been examined in a systematic manner. Nonetheless, research findings suggest that successful maintenance is more likely to occur if (*a*) treatment is implemented correctly and consistently, (*b*) the child receives reinforcement for appropriate behavior, and (*c*) reinforcement is withheld for problem behavior (e.g., Foxx, Bittle, and Faw 1989; Foxx and Livesay 1984; Foxx 2003; Linscheid, Hartel, and Cooley 1993).

Successful transfer of treatment effects to contexts that are not associated with the intervention may prove more challenging. Generalization of punishment has rarely been reported in the basic or applied literatures (e.g., Birnbrauer 1968; Corte, Wolf, and Locke 1971; O'Donnell et al. 2000). These findings are troubling, because caregivers are rarely able to implement treatment across all relevant settings and situations. It should be noted, however, that research in this area is highly limited. Results of a few studies suggest that carefully designed tactics might be successful in promoting generalization. For example, in Corte, Wolf, and Locke (1971), rates of self-injurious behavior decreased to zero levels when a stimulus that was discriminable for punishment (the experimenter) was hidden from view while the consequence continue to be delivered for the response. Although the authors did not report generalization to a setting that was never associated with the punisher, this strategy might be useful for maintaining treatment effects when the treatment will be discontinued or implemented inconsistently. A more practical strategy was evaluated by Maglieri and colleagues (2000). As discussed previously, they decreased food stealing in an individual with Prader-Willi syndrome by delivering a verbal reprimand if the behavior had occurred anytime during the previous 10 minutes. An orange sticker then was established as a discriminative stimulus by punishing the consumption of food from a container bearing the sticker while withholding the consequence if food was consumed from an unlabeled container. Food stealing was subsequently eliminated when the sticker was placed on a refrigerator in the kitchen. Unfortunately, the long-term efficacy of this strategy has not been assessed. Current research findings indicate that problem behavior is likely to emerge wherever the punisher is withheld, especially if the behavior continues to produce reinforcement. In the absence of further studies on successful generalization tactics, implementing the intervention in all settings and contexts constitutes best practice.

■ Selecting Punishment Procedures

Professional and ethical guidelines mandate use of the least restrictive procedure that is clinically effective for the individual (e.g., Behavior Analysis Certification Board 2004; Van Houten et al. 1988). Numerous authors have established guidelines for identifying punishment procedures based on the least restrictive mandate (e.g., Alberto and Troutman 2006; Foxx 1982; Lovaas and Favell 1987; Repp and Deitz 1978). This approach to treatment selection requires a clear definition or measure of "restrictiveness," an arrangement of potential procedures based on this property, and criteria for designating a given treatment as "clinically effective." Procedures are typically hierarchically arranged according to the degree to which the procedure limits individual freedom, intrudes into the child's life or produces discomfort, pain, or distress. For example, nonexclusionary time-out and response cost are commonly considered the least restrictive of the procedures described here, followed by exclusionary time-out, overcorrection, and other physical punishers. In actuality, these arrangements require fairly subjective determinations of restrictiveness.

As noted earlier, the least restrictive mandate also requires a clear criterion for treatment success. Clinicians must evaluate punishment procedures on a trial basis, starting with the least restrictive procedure that may be effective and moving to more restrictive procedures until an effective intervention is identified. For example, caregivers may be taught to use a 5-minute time-out procedure to reduce a child's disruption (e.g., Clark et al. 1973). If this intervention does not reduce disruption to an acceptable level, caregivers may be told to increase the duration of the time-out or to implement a more restrictive procedure (e.g., overcorrection). This process would continue with increasingly more restrictive procedures (e.g., restraint) until a clinically important decrease in behavior is achieved. Relative to nonintrusive treatments, the criterion for treatment success should be stringent when evaluating putative punishers, so that the individual is not exposed to ineffective restrictive procedures for lengthy periods. Decisions about treatment effectiveness could be based on overall levels of behavior (e.g., no more than 0.5 responses per minute) or decreases relative to baseline (e.g., 90% reduction from baseline) (Hagopian et al. 1998). In any case, consideration also should be given to the severity of the behavior, the optimal amount of change that can be expected based on research findings, and the context in which the behavior occurs.

Although this trial-and-error approach to treatment selection is consistent with the least restrictive mandate, it has a number of disadvantages. It could delay the onset of treatment and expose the student to progressively more intrusive interventions. It should not be assumed that a more restrictive procedure (e.g., restraint) has a greater chance of success than a less restrictive procedure (e.g., verbal reprimands). The fact that a fairly intrusive procedure might function as a punisher for one person but as a reinforcer for another (e.g., Fisher et al. 1994 *A preliminary evaluation*) is disregarded when the focus is on the topography of an intervention rather than its function. In fact, the various punishment procedures described earlier could actually worsen the behavior of some individuals. For this reason, knowledge about the function of the problem behavior is particularly important. Certain interventions may be indicated or contraindicated, depending on the reinforcers that maintain the problem behavior. Finally, other factors should be considered when selecting a punishment procedure, including the severity of the behavior, the likelihood of undesirable side effects, and caregivers' willingness to use the procedure (Van Houten et al. 1988; Vollmer and Iwata 1993). As discussed in the following sections, several assessment methodologies have been developed that may permit clinicians to predict which procedures are likely to be effective while avoiding the trial-and-error approach to treatment selection.

Functional Analysis

The comprehensive functional analysis described by Iwata and colleagues (1994/1982), which includes "attention," "demand," "alone," and "play" conditions, is particular useful when punishment is being considered for clinical use. Results may not only identify the reinforcers maintaining problem behavior but reveal sensitivity (or lack thereof) to consequences that could function as punishers for the behavior. The effects of two commonly used punishers (verbal reprimands and time-out) are evaluated in the "attention" and "demand" conditions. The "play" condition serves as a control by which to evaluate the effects of these contingencies on problem behavior. Assessment outcomes may indicate whether a particular procedure is likely to be effective, unlikely to be effective, or contraindicated for the targeted problem behavior.

For example, if levels of problem behavior are lower in the attention condition than in the control condition, contingent verbal reprimands and/or physical contact may serve as an effective intervention. Alternatively, these consequences may have no effect on problem behavior during the functional analysis, providing a basis for excluding them from consideration as punishment. Most importantly, results may show that problem behavior is sensitive to attention as a reinforcer. Punishment procedures that involve verbal or physical interaction (e.g., reprimands, blocking, overcorrection, physical restraint) would probably be contraindicated in such cases, whereas procedures associated with a contingent decrease in attention (e.g., time-out) would be specifically indicated (Hagopian et al. 1998).

Outcomes for the demand condition would produce similar types of information, because the contingent removal of ongoing interaction and instructional materials is directly tested in this condition. Treatment with time-out would be a viable option if levels of problem behavior were lower in the demand condition than in the play condition. If levels of problem behavior in the demand condition were similar to those in the play condition, loss of access to attention or materials (i.e., time-out) might not be particularly effective. Punishment procedures that require the removal or delay of demands, such as time-out, physical restraint, or protective equipment, would be contraindicated if the results indicated that behavior is reinforced by escape from demands (Magee and Ellis 2001). On the other hand, procedures that involve a contingent increase in demands, such as additional work, exercise, and overcorrection, might be especially indicated for behavior maintained by escape (Hagopian et al. 1998).

Stimulus Avoidance Assessment

Fisher and colleagues developed an efficient methodology for evaluating individuals' responses to various potential punishers (Fisher et al. 1994 *Empirically derived consequences;* Fisher et al. 1994 *A preliminary evaluation*). Called a "stimulus avoidance assessment," this approach may be useful for identifying the efficacy of multiple interventions. In one study (Fisher et al. 1994 *A preliminary evaluation*), for example, participants were exposed to water mist, time-out, restraint, and contingent effort independently of responding for 15 to 180 seconds. One procedure was presented on each trial. Results showed that procedures associated with the highest rates of avoidance responses (e.g., dropping to the floor) and negative vocalizations (e.g., crying) were most likely to function as punishers when subsequently applied contingent on problem behavior. Such an assessment appears to be useful for predicting the relatively efficacy of multiple procedures that are being considered for clinical use.

Brief Punisher Assessment

Brief punisher assessments also can provide information about the potential efficacy of multiple interventions in an efficient manner. In several studies, the effects of various interventions on problem behavior were evaluated during short (e.g., 10-minute) sessions (e.g., Fisher et al. 1994 *Empirically derived consequences;* Fisher et al. 1994 *A preliminary evaluation;* Thompson et al. 1999). Results appeared to have good predictive validity when the punisher associated with the lowest levels of problem behavior was evaluated over lengthier periods. In one study, (Fisher et al. 1994 *A preliminary evaluation*), for example, one of three different procedures (e.g., contingent demands, facial screen) was used to treat pica during 10-minute sessions that were alternated in a multielement design. The intervention that produced the lowest levels of pica during the assessment was then successfully used as part of a treatment package for the three participants. These findings suggest that brief punisher assessments are useful for identifying the most effective intervention while minimizing delays to the onset of treatment and exposure to ineffective interventions.

■ Potential Strategies to Increase the Efficacy of Intrusive Interventions As Typically Applied in Community Settings

As noted earlier, factors that have been found to alter the effects of punishment (e.g., delayed or intermittent consequences, prior exposure to the intervention) may commonly undermine treatment in the natural environment.

Procedures designed to compensate for these factors are critically needed. Nonetheless, most research has focused on the direct effects of various intrusive interventions rather than on specific strategies to enhance the efficacy of treatment in applied settings. The following is a brief description of research on strategies that might improve clinical outcomes when the consequence is likely to be delivered in a manner that is less than optimal.

Mediating Delayed Punishment

Delivery of the programmed consequence immediately after occurrences of the targeted behavior may be impractical in schools, homes, and public settings. For this reason, punishment is likely to be delayed. Strategies that may mediate this gap between the behavior and the consequence have been evaluated in several studies on delayed punishment (e.g., Maglieri et al. 2000; Van Houten and Rolider 1988). For example, in Van Houten and Rolder (1988), a participant with developmental delays was prompted to engage in the targeted behavior (theft) and then received the punishing consequence (reprimand combined with movement suppression time-out) three times if stolen items were found in her bedroom during a regularly scheduled check. In another study, the participants' parents played audiotaped recordings of tantrums that had occurred earlier in the day and then delivered the consequence (Rolider and Van Houten 1985). This strategy was highly successful in both studies, although it is possible that the delayed punisher alone would have been effective in these cases.

Decreasing the likelihood of problem behavior via stimulus control may be helpful in maintaining treatment effects when the consequence will be delayed or delivered infrequently. In at least two applied studies, discriminative control over the punished response was first established by pairing the presence of a particular stimulus with punishment for engaging in the behavior (e.g., Maglieri et al. 2000; Piazza, Hanley, and Fisher 1996). The mere presence of this stimulus then effectively suppressed problem behavior, even though no consequences were delivered for responding. Piazza, Hanley, and Fisher (1996), for example, treated cigarette pica in a man with developmental disabilities via a response interruption procedure. Pica was punished in the presence of a purple card but not in the presence of a yellow card. No pica occurred in the presence of the purple card when stimulus control was subsequently evaluated in the absence of the punishment contingency. Presumably, the purple card could be used to bridge the gap between the response and the consequence. As discussed previously, a similar strategy effectively reduced food stealing in the study by Maglieri and colleagues (2000). Despite these promising results, the durability of this strategy should be evaluated before it is routinely recommended as a best practice.

Finally, various antecedent intervention procedures are another strategy to decrease the probability of problem behavior. To illustrate, Luiselli and colleagues (Luiselli et al. 2000; Luiselli, Dun, and Pace 2005) reduced the frequency of physical restraint with children and adolescents who had developmental disabilities through antecedent change methods that decreased the behaviors requiring restraint. Further analysis of antecedent intervention in conjunction with punishment is warranted.

Fading

Gradual modifications to the consequence may result in a more practical intervention that nonetheless remains effective in applied settings. Although research on this strategy is quite limited, some findings suggest that careful fading of certain dimensions of punishment (e.g., schedule, delay, magnitude) might enable caregivers to implement consequences that would otherwise be ineffective. For example, results of several studies suggest that it may be possible to slowly thin the schedule of punishment after obtaining clinically significant reductions in behavior under a continuous schedule (e.g., Barton, Brulle, and Repp 1987; Lerman et al. 1997). Lerman and coworkers. (1997) found that the schedule of contingent time-out or restraint could be successfully thinned from FR 1 to fixed interval (FI) 300 seconds for two of four participants who engaged in self-injury maintained by automatic reinforcement. A systematic approach for fading other dimensions of punishment was described by Foxx and colleagues (see Foxx, 2003, for a review). In Foxx, Bittle, and Faw (1989), for example, an initial treatment package that included contingent electric shock was gradually modified by pairing the more intrusive punisher with a time-out procedure, replacing the shock component with a time-out procedure and then slowly decreasing the duration of the time-out. Concerning physical restraint, Luiselli and colleagues have shown that systematically decreasing the duration of restraint by imposing fixed-time instead of behavior-contingent release can reduce the total time exposed to intervention (Luiselli et al. 2004; Luiselli, Pace, and Dunn 2006). Further research is needed on the efficacy, practicality, and durability of such fading procedures.

Use of Conditioned Punishers

Intermittent, mild, or delayed consequences may be effective if used in combination with conditioned punishers. Basic and applied research findings indicate that this can be accomplished by pairing neutral consequences with punishing stimuli (e.g., Dixon et al. 1989; Dorsey et al. 1980; Hake and Azrin 1965; Lovaas and Simmons 1969; Salvy et al. 2004; Vorndran and Lerman 2006). In Dorsey and colleagues (1980), for example, a verbal reprimand was ineffective in suppressing self-injury exhibited by two individuals. After the word "no" was repeatedly paired with water mist contingent on occurrences of the behavior, the verbal reprimand alone suppressed self-injury in the treatment setting and in a different setting. Such a strategy is useful as long as the conditioned consequence can be readily delivered.

Vorndran and Lerman (2006) evaluated the durability of this approach with two individuals who engaged in problem behavior maintained by automatic reinforcement. For both participants, a less intrusive intervention (calling the participant's name while gently nudging a shoulder) was delivered immediately before a more effective yet intrusive consequence (contingent demands or facial screen combined with brief restraint) after occurrences of the problem behavior. After repeated pairings, the less intrusive intervention alone successfully reduced the behavior for both participants. The conditioned punisher continued to suppress behavior for up to 7 months in the absence of the original punisher for one participant. For the other participant, the effectiveness of the less intrusive procedure depended on periodic pairings between the conditioned and unconditioned punishers.

■ Conclusions

For some individuals with autism, restrictive interventions are a necessary and beneficial component of behavior programs. Research findings on best practices indicate that a variety of punishment procedures can produce durable reductions in problem behavior, even when the function of the behavior cannot be determined. Nonetheless, information about behavioral function combined with some type of pretreatment punisher assessment should guide decisions when selecting the most appropriate intervention. Basic and applied findings also suggest that caregivers should (a) deliver the punishing consequence immediately after each instance of the behavior, (b) ensure that alternative sources of reinforcement are readily available for appropriate behavior, and (c) withhold reinforcement for problem behavior. If these recommended procedures are difficult to carry out in community settings, strategies such as establishing discriminative control over the punished response, fading various dimensions of the consequence, and developing and using conditioned punishers may enhance the efficacy of treatment. Further research is needed on ways to ensure the long-term maintenance of treatment effects and to promote generalization in community settings.

■ References

Abromowitz, A.J., and O'Leary, S.G. (1990). Effectiveness of delayed punishment in an applied setting. *Behavior Therapy,* 21, 231–239.

Alberto, P.A., and Troutman, A.C. (2006). *Applied behavior analysis for teachers* (7th ed). Upper Saddle, N.J.: Pearson Merrill Prentice-Hall.

Allen, K.D. (1998). The use of an enhanced simplified habit reversal procedure to reduce disruptive outbursts during athletic performance. *Journal of Applied Behavior Analysis*, 31, 489–492.

Altman, K., Haavik, S., and Cook, J.W. (1978). Punishment of self-injurious behavior in natural settings using contingent aromatic ammonia. *Behaviour Research and Therapy*, 16, 85–96.

Azrin, N.H., and Holz, W.C. (1966). Punishment. In *Operant behavior: Areas of research and application* (ed. W.K. Honig), pp.380–447. New York: Appleton.

Azrin, N.H., Holz, W.C., and Hake, D.F. (1963). Fixed-ratio punishment. *Journal of the Experimental Analysis of Behavior*, 6, 141–148.

Banks, R.K., and Vogel-Sprott, M. (1965). Effect of delayed punishment on an immediately rewarded response in humans. *Journal of Experimental Psychology*, 70, 357–359.

Barton, L.E., Brulle, A.R., and Repp, A.C. (1987). Effects of differential schedule of time-out to reduce maladaptive responding. *Exceptional Children*, 53, 351–356.

Behavior Analysis Certification Board. (2004). *Guidelines for responsible conduct for behavior analysts*. Available at http://www.bacb.com (accessed November 2, 2007).

Bitgood, S.C., Crowe, M.J., Suarez, Y., and Peters, R. (1980). Immobilization: Effects and side effects on stereotyped behavior in children. *Behavior Modification*, 4, 187–208.

Birnbrauer, J.S. (1968). Generalization of punishment effects. A case study. *Journal of Applied Behavior Analysis*, 1, 201–211.

Calhoun, K.S., and Matherne, P. (1975). The effects of varying schedules of time-out on aggressive behavior of a retarded girl. *Journal of Behavior Therapy and Experimental Psychiatry*, 6, 139–143.

Capaldi, E.D., Sheffer, J.D., Viveiros, D.M., Davidson, T.L., and Campbell, D.H. (1985). Shock preexposure and the reduced effectiveness of shock. *Learning and Motivation*, 16, 357–380.

Carey, R.G., and Bucher, B. (1981). Identifying the educative and suppressive effects of positive practice and restitutional overcorrection. *Journal of Applied Behavior Analysis*, 14, 71–80.

Cipani, E., Brendlinger, J., McDowell, L., and Usher, S. (1991). Continuous vs. intermittent punishment: A case study. *Journal of Developmental and Physical Disabilities*, 3 (2), 147–156.

Clark, H.B., Rowbury, T., Baer, A.M., and Baer, D.M. (1973). Timeout as a punishing stimulus in continuous and intermittent schedules. *Journal of Applied Behavior Analysis*, 6, 443–455.

Cohen, P.S. (1968). Punishment: The interactive effects of delay and intensity of shock. *Journal of the Experimental Analysis of Behavior*, 11, 789–799.

Cole, G.A., Montgomery, R.W., Wilson, K.M., and Milan, M.A. (2000). Parametric analysis of overcorrection duration effects: Is longer really better than shorter? *Behavior Modification*, 24, 359–378.

Cook, J.W., Altman, K., Shaw, J., and Blaylock, M. (1978). Use of contingent lemon juice to eliminate public masturbation by a severely retarded boy. *Behaviour Research and Therapy*, 16, 131–134.

Cooper, J.O., Heron, T.E., and Heward, W.L. (2006). *Applied Behavior Analysis* (2nd ed). Upper Saddle River, N.J.: Merrill/Prentice-Hall.

Corte, H.E., Wolf, M.M., and Locke, B.J. (1971). A comparison of procedures for eliminating self-injurious behavior of retarded adolescents. *Journal of Applied Behavior Analysis*, 4, 201–213.

Dixon, M.J., Helsel, W.J., Rojahn, J., Cipollone, R., and Lubetsky, M.J. (1989). Aversive conditioning of visual screening with aromatic ammonia for treating aggressive and disruptive behavior in a developmentally disabled child. *Behavior Modification*, 13, 91–107.

Dorsey, M.F., Iwata, B.A., Ong, P., and McSween, T.E. (1980). Treatment of self-injurious behavior using a water mist: Initial response suppression and generalization. *Journal of Applied Behavior Analysis*, 13, 343–353.

Duker, P.C., and Seys, D.M. (1996). Long-term use of electrical aversion treatment with self-injurious behavior. *Research in Developmental Disabilities*, 17, 293–301.

Epstein, L.H., and Masek, B.J. (1978). Behavioral control of medicine compliance. *Journal of Applied Behavior Analysis*, 11, 1–9.

Falcomata, T.S., Roane, H.S., Hovanetz, A.N., Kettering, T.L., and Keeney, K.M. (2004). An evaluation of response cost in the treatment of inappropriate vocalizations maintained by automatic reinforcement. *Journal of Applied Behavior Analysis*, 37, 83–87.

Fisher, W.W., Piazza, C.C., Bowman, L.G., Kurtz, P.F., Sherer, M.R., and Lachman, S.R. (1994). A preliminary evaluation of empirically derived consequences for the treatment of pica. *Journal of Applied Behavior Analysis*, 27, 447–457.

Fisher, W.W., Piazza, C.C., Bowman, L.G., Hagopian, L.P., and Langdon, N.A. (1994). Empirically derived consequences: A data-based method for prescribing treatments for destructive behavior. *Research in Developmental Disabilities*, 15, 133–149.

Fisher, W.W., Piazza, C.C., Cataldo, M.F., Harrell, R., Jefferson, G., and Conner, R. (1993). Functional communication with and without extinction and punishment. *Journal of Applied Behavior Analysis*, 26, 23–36.

Foxx, R.M. (1982). *Decreasing behaviors of retarded and autistic persons*. Champaign, Ill.: Research Press.

Foxx, R.M. (2003). The treatment of dangerous behavior. *Behavioral Interventions*, 18, 1–21.

Foxx, R.M., and Azrin, N.H. (1972). Restitution: A method of eliminating aggressive-disruptive behavior of retarded and brain damaged patients. *Behaviour Research and Therapy*, 10, 15–27.

Foxx, R.M., and Azrin, N.H. (1973). The elimination of autistic self-stimulatory behavior by overcorrection. *Journal of Applied Behavior Analysis*, 6, 1–14.

Foxx, R.M., Bittle, R.G., and Faw, G.D. (1989). A maintenance strategy for discontinuing aversive procedures: A 32-month follow-up of the treatment of aggression. *American Journal on Mental Retardation, 94,* 27–36.

Foxx, R.M., and Livesay, J. (1984). Maintenance of response suppression following overcorrection: A 10-year retrospective examination of eight cases. *Analysis and Intervention in Developmental Disabilities, 4,* 65–79.

Foxx, R.M., and Shapiro, S.T. (1978). The timeout ribbon: A nonexclusionary timeout procedure. *Journal of Applied Behavior Analysis, 11,* 125–136.

Friman, P.C., Cook, J.W., and Finney, J.W. (1984). Effects of punishment procedures on the self-stimulatory behavior of an autistic child. *Analysis & Intervention in Developmental Disabilities, 4,* 39–46.

Grace, N.C., Kahng, S.W., and Fisher, W.W. (1994). Balancing social acceptability with treatment effectiveness of an intrusive procedure: A case report. *Journal of Applied Behavior Analysis, 27,* 171–172.

Hagopian, L.P., and Adelinis, J.D. (2001). Response blocking with and without redirection for the treatment of pica. *Journal of Applied Behavior Analysis, 34,* 527–530.

Hagopian, L.P., Fisher, W.W., Thibault-Sullivan, M., Acquisto, J., and LeBlanc, L.A. (1998). Effectiveness of functional communication training with and without extinction and punishment: A summary of 21 inpatient cases. *Journal of Applied Behavior Analysis, 31,* 211–235.

Hake, D.F., and Azrin, N.H. (1965). Conditioned punishment. *Journal of the Experimental Analysis of Behavior, 8,* 279–293.

Halevy, G., Feldon, J., and Weiner, I. (1987). Resistance to extinction and punishment following training with shock and non-reinforcement: Failure to obtain cross-tolerance. *Quarterly Journal of Experimental Psychology B: Comparative and Physiological Psychology, 39* (2-B), 147–160.

Hanley, G.P., Piazza, C.C., Fisher, W.W., and Maglieri, K.A. (2005). On the effectiveness of and preference for punishment and extinction components of function-based interventions. *Journal of Applied Behavior Analysis, 38,* 51–65.

Hobbs, S.A., Forehand, R., and Murray, R.G. (1978). Effects of various durations of timeout on the non-compliant behavior of children. *Behavior Therapy, 9,* 652–656.

Holz, W.C., and Azrin, N.H. (1961). Discriminative properties of punishment. *Journal of the Experimental Analysis of Behavior, 4,* 225–232.

Holz, W.C., Azrin, N.H., and Ayllon, T. (1963). Elimination of behavior of mental patients by response-produced extinction. *Journal of the Experimental Analysis of Behavior, 6,* 407–412.

Iwata, B.A., Dorsey, M.F., Slifer, K.J., Bauman, K.E., and Richman, G.S. (1994). Toward a functional analysis of self-injury. *Journal of Applied Behavior Analysis, 27,* 197–209. (Originally published in *Analysis and Intervention in Developmental Disabilities, 2,* 3–20, 1982).

Kahng, S., Abt, K.A., and Wilder, D. (2001). Treatment of self-injury correlated with mechanical restraints. *Behavioral Interventions, 16,* 105–110.

Kahng, S., Iwata, B.A., and Lewin, A.B. (2002). Behavioral treatment of self-injury, 1964 to 2000. *American Journal on Mental Retardation*, 107, 212–221.

Kahng, S., Tarbox, J., and Wilke, A.E. (2001). Use of a multicomponent treatment for food refusal. *Journal of Applied Behavior Analysis*, 34, 93–96.

Keeney, K.M., Fisher, W.W., Adelinis, J.D., and Wilder, D.A. (2000). The effects of response cost in the treatment of aberrant behavior maintained by negative reinforcement. *Journal of Applied Behavior Analysis*, 33, 255–258.

Koegel, R.L., Firestone, P.B., Kramme, K.W., and Dunlap, G. (1974). Increasing spontaneous play by suppressing self-stimulation in autistic children. *Journal of Applied Behavior Analysis*, 7, 521–528.

Lalli, J.S., Livezey, K., and Kates, K. (1996). Functional analysis and treatment of eye poking with response blocking. *Journal of Applied Behavior Analysis*, 29, 129–132.

LeBlanc, L.A., Hagopian, L.P., and Maglieri, K.A. (2000). Use of a token economy to eliminate excessive inappropriate social behavior in an adult with developmental disabilities. *Behavioral Interventions*, 15, 135–143.

Lerman, D.C., Iwata, B.A., Shore, B.A., and DeLeon, I.G. (1997). Effects of intermittent punishment on self-injurious behavior: An evaluation of schedule thinning. *Journal of Applied Behavior Analysis*, 30, 187–201.

Lerman, D.C., Kelley, M.E., Vorndran, C.M., and Van Camp, C.M. (2003). Collateral effects of response blocking during the treatment of stereotypic behavior. *Journal of Applied Behavior Analysis*, 36, 119–123.

Lerman, D.C., and Vorndran, C.M. (2002). On the status of knowledge for using punishment: Implications for treating behavior disorders. *Journal of Applied Behavior Analysis*, 35, 431–464.

Linscheid, T.R., Hartel, F., and Cooley, N. (1993). Are aversive procedures durable? A five year follow-up of three individuals treated with contingent electric shock. *Child and Adolescent Mental Health Care*, 3 (2), 67–76.

Linscheid, T.R., Iwata, B.A., Ricketts, R.W., Williams, D.E., and Griffin, J.C. (1990). Clinical evaluation of the self-injurious behavior inhibiting system (SIBIS). *Journal of Applied Behavior Analysis*, 23, 53–78.

Long, E.S., Miltenberger, R.G., Ellingson, S.A., and Ott, S.M. (1999). Augmenting simplified habit reversal in the treatment of oral-digital habits exhibited by individuals with mental retardation. *Journal of Applied Behavior Analysis*, 32, 353–365.

Lovaas, O.I., and Favell, J.E. (1987). Protection of clients undergoing aversive/restrictive interventions. *Education and Treatment of Children*, 10, 311–325.

Lovaas, O.I., and Simmons, J.Q. (1969). Manipulation of self-destruction in three retarded children. *Journal of Applied Behavior Analysis*, 2, 143–157.

Luiselli, J.K., Dunn, E.K., and Pace, G.M. (2005). Antecedent assessment and intervention to reduce physical restraint (protective holding) of children and adolescents with acquired brain injury. *Behavioral Interventions*, 20, 51–65.

Luiselli, J.K., Kane, A., Treml, T., and Young, N. (2000). Behavioral intervention to reduce physical restraint of adolescents with developmental disabilities. *Behavioral Interventions,* 15, 317–330.

Luiselli, J.K., Pace, G.M., and Dunn, E.K. (2006). Effects of behavior-contingent and fixed-time release contingencies on frequency and duration of therapeutic restraint. *Behavior Modification,* 30, 442–455.

Luiselli, J.K., Suskin, L. and McPhee, D.F. (1981). Continuous and intermittent application of overcorrection with a self-injurious autistic child: Alternating treatments design analysis. *Journal of Behavior Therapy and Experimental Psychiatry,* 12, 355–358.

Luiselli, J.K., Treml, T., Kane, A., and Young, N. (2004). Physical restraint intervention: Case report of an implementation-reduction strategy and long term outcome. *Mental Health Aspects of Developmental Disabilities,* 7, 91–96.

Magee, S.K., and Ellis, J. (2001). The detrimental effects of physical restraint as a consequence for inappropriate classroom behavior. *Journal of Applied Behavior Analysis,* 34, 501–504.

Maglieri, K.A., DeLeon, I.G., Rodriguez-Catter, V., and Sevin, B.M. (2000). Treatment of covert food stealing in an individual with Prader-Willi syndrome. *Journal of Applied Behavior Analysis,* 33, 615–618.

McGlynn, A.P., and Locke, B.J. (1997). A 25-year follow-up of a punishment program for severe self-injury. *Behavioral Interventions,* 12, 203–207.

O'Donnell, J., Crosbie, J., Williams, D.C., and Saunders, K.J. (2000). Stimulus control and generalization of point-loss punishment with humans. *Journal of the Experimental Analysis of Behavior,* 73, 261–274.

Paisey, T.L., and Whitney, R.B. (1989). A long-term case study of analysis, response suppression, and treatment maintenance involving life-threatening pica. *Behavioral Residential Treatment,* 4, 191–211.

Pelios, L., Morren, J., Tesch, D., and Axelrod, S. (1999). The impact of functional analysis methodology on treatment choice for self-injurious and aggressive behavior. *Journal of Applied Behavior Analysis,* 32, 185–195.

Piazza, C.C., Hanley, G.P., and Fisher, W.W. (1996). Functional analysis and treatment of cigarette pica. *Journal of Applied Behavior Analysis,* 29, 437–450.

Porterfield, J.K., Herbert-Jackson, E., and Risley, T.R. (1976). Contingent observation: An effective and acceptable procedure for reducing disruptive behavior of young children in a group setting. *Journal of Applied Behavior Analysis,* 9, 55–64.

Rawson, R.A., and Leitenberg, H. (1973). Reinforced alternative behavior during punishment and extinction with rats. *Journal of Comparative and Physiological Psychology,* 85, 593–600.

Reid, D.H., Parsons, M.B., Phillips, J.F., and Green, C.W. (1993). Reduction of self-injurious hand mouthing using response blocking. *Journal of Applied Behavior Analysis,* 26, 139–140.

Repp, A.C., and Deitz, D.E.D. (1978). On the selective use of punishment: Suggested guidelines for administrators. *Mental Retardation,* 16, 250–254.

Richman, D.M., Lindauer, S.E., Crosland, K.A., McKerchar, T.L., and Morse, P.S. (2001). Functional analysis and treatment of breath holding maintained by nonsocial reinforcement. *Journal of Applied Behavior Analysis,* 34, 531–534.

Ricketts, R.W., Goza, A.B., and Matese, M. (1993). A 4-year follow-up of treatment of self-injury. *Journal of Behavior Therapy and Experimental Psychiatry,* 24, 57–62.

Rolider, A., and Van Houten, R. (1985). Suppressing tantrum behavior in public places through the use of delayed punishment mediated by audio recordings. *Behavior Therapy,* 16, 181–194.

Rolider, A., Williams, L., Cummings, A., and Van Houten, R. (1991). The use of a brief movement restriction procedure to eliminate severe inappropriate behavior. *Journal of Behavior Therapy and Experimental Psychiatry,* 22, 23–30.

Rollings, J.P., Baumeister, A.A., and Baumeister, A.A. (1977). The use of overcorrection procedures to eliminate the stereotyped behaviors of retarded individuals: An analysis of collateral behaviors and generalization of suppressive effects. *Behavior Modification,* 1, 29–46.

Romanczyk, R.G. (1977). Intermittent punishment of self-stimulation: Effectiveness during application and extinction. *Journal of Consulting and Clinical Psychology,* 45, 53–60.

Rush, K.S., Crockett, J.L., and Hagopian, L.P. (2001). An analysis of the selective effects of NCR with punishment targeting problem behavior associated with positive affect. *Behavioral Interventions,* 16, 127–135.

Salend, S.J., and Gordon, B.D. (1987). A group-oriented timeout ribbon procedure. *Behavioral Disorders,* 12, 131–137.

Salvy, S., Mulick, J.A., Butter, E., Bartlett, R.K., and Linscheid, T.R. (2004). Contingent electric shock (SIBIS) and a conditioned punisher eliminate severe head banging in a preschool child. *Behavioral Interventions,* 19, 2004, 59–72.

Singh, N.N., Dawson, M.J., and Gregory, P.R. (1980). Suppression of chronic hyperventilation using response-contingent aromatic ammonia. *Behavior Therapy,* 11, 561–566.

Singh, N.N., Dawson, M.J., and Manning, P.J. (1981). The effects of physical restraint on self-injurious behavior. *Journal of Mental Deficiency Research,* 25, 207–216.

Singh, N.N., Watson, J.E., and Winton, A.S.W. (1986). Treating self-injury: Water mist spray versus facial screening or forced arm exercise. *Journal of Applied Behavior Analysis,* 19, 403–410.

Stricker, J.M., Miltenberger, R.G., Garlinghouse, M., and Tulloch, H.E. (2003). Augmenting stimulus intensity with an awareness enhancement device in the treatment of finger sucking. *Education and Treatment of Children,* 26, 22–29.

Terris, W., and Barnes, M. (1969). Learned resistance to punishment and subsequent responsiveness to the same and novel punishers. *Psychonomic Science,* 15, 49–50.

Thomas, J.R. (1968). Fixed-ratio punishment by time-out of concurrent variable-interval behavior. *Journal of the Experimental Analysis of Behavior,* 11, 609–616.

Thompson, R.H., Iwata, B.A., Conners, J., and Roscoe, E.M. (1999). Effects of reinforcement for alternative behavior during punishment of self-injury. *Journal of Applied Behavior Analysis, 32*, 317–328.

Toole, L.M., Bowman, L.G., Thomason, J.L., Hagopian, L.P., and Rush, K.S. (2003). Observed increases in positive affect during behavioral treatment. *Behavioral Interventions, 18*, 35–42.

Trenholme, I.A., and Baron, A. (1975). Immediate and delayed punishment of human behavior by loss of reinforcement. *Learning and Motivation, 6*, 62–79.

Truchlicka, M., McLaughlin, T.F., and Swain, J.C. (1998). Effects of token reinforcement and response cost on the accuracy of spelling performance with middle-school special education students with behavior disorders. *Behavioral Interventions, 13*, 1–10.

Van Houten, R., Axelrod, S., Bailey, J.S., Favell, J.E., Foxx, R.M., Iwata, B.A., and Lovaas, O.I. (1988). The right to effective behavioral treatment. *Journal of Applied Behavior Analysis, 21*, 381–384.

Van Houten, R., Nau, P.A., MacKenzie-Keating, S.E., Sameoto, D., and Colavecchia, B. (1982). An analysis of some variables influencing the effectiveness of reprimands. *Journal of Applied Behavior Analysis, 15*, 65–83.

Van Houten, R., and Rolider, A. (1988). Recreating the scene: An effective way to provide delayed punishment for inappropriate motor behavior. *Journal of Applied Behavior Analysis, 21*, 197–192.

Vollmer, T.R., and Iwata, B.A. (1993). Implications of a functional analysis technology for the use of restrictive behavioral interventions. *Child and Adolescent Mental Health Care, 3*, 95–113.

Vollmer, T.R., Progar, P.R., Lalli, J.S., Van Camp, C.M., Sierp, B.J., Wright, C.S., Nastasi, J., and Eisenschink, K.J. (1998). Fixed-time schedules attenuate extinction-induced phenomena in the treatment of severe aberrant behavior. *Journal of Applied Behavior Analysis, 31*, 529–542.

Vorndran, C.M., and Lerman, D.C. (2006). Establishing and maintaining treatment effects with less intrusive consequences via a pairing procedure. *Journal of Applied Behavior Analysis, 39*, 35–48.

Wacker, D.P., Steege, M.W., Northup, J., Sasso, G., Berg, W., Reimers, T., Cooper, L., Cigrand, K., and Donn, L. (1990). A component analysis of functional communication training across three topographies of severe behavior problems. *Journal of Applied Behavior Analysis, 23*, 417–429.

Watson, T.S. (1993). Effectiveness of arousal and arousal plus overcorrection to reduce nocturnal bruxism. *Journal of Behavior Therapy and Experimental Psychiatry, 24*, 181–185.

White, G.D., Nielsen, G., and Johnson, S.M. (1972). Timeout duration and the suppression of deviant behavior in children. *Journal of Applied Behavior Analysis, 5*, 111–120.

Williams, D.E., Kirkpatrick-Sanchez, S., and Iwata, B.A. (1993). A comparison of shock intensity in the treatment of longstanding and severe self-injurious behavior. *Research in Developmental Disabilities, 14*, 207–219.

19. FAMILY SUPPORT AND PARTICIPATION

Jennifer B.G. Symon and Mendy A. Boettcher

Because behaviors serve as the criteria for diagnosing individuals with autism spectrum disorders (ASD), those who are so labeled represent a diverse group who range widely in their social, communicative, and behavioral profiles. Considering the diversity among individuals with ASD, it should not be surprising that there is not one best intervention approach that is suitable for each person. However, one common factor among all children diagnosed with ASD is that each is a member of a family. The importance of the family's role in the child's treatment and well-being cannot be underestimated. Over the last decade, more children have been diagnosed with ASD, with prevalences as high as 1 in 150 reported (Burton 2002; Center for Disease Control 2007; Fombonne 2003, 2006; Gillberg et al. 2006). With many more children receiving this diagnosis, treatment providers face new challenges in providing effective support, not only for these children, but also for their family members. This chapter highlights the importance of valuing and including family members and the family system when developing intervention plans for individuals with autism. Pertinent issues that often arise for families of children with ASD are presented, followed by the identified benefits of including family members in intervention planning. Finally, strategies for success are introduced for those who support individuals with autism and for their families.

In an effort to address the comprehensive needs of individuals with disabilities and those who support them, positive behavior support (PBS) emerged from multiple areas of the field, including applied behavior analysis, social and organizational psychology, and the normalization and inclusion movements (Carr et al. 2002). More than ever before, PBS places a focus on improving overall quality of life for individuals with disabilities and their team members (Albin et al. 1996; Carr et al. 2002).

Social systems theory recognizes the dynamics between individuals and the social environments in which they interact. This framework includes the interactions among individuals, families, and systems (Brofenbrenner 1986). A pivotal component of PBS and family systems theories is the recognition of children within a larger social system or context (Brofenbrenner 1986; Carr et al. 2002; Turnbull and Turnbull 1990)—in this case, the family unit. The PBS intervention approach considers individual, family, and larger system variables that influence behaviors. Further, this intervention approach targets the development of multicomponent, comprehensive support interventions. In addition to focusing on support for each individual with special needs, PBS focuses systems-level support for individuals within family, school, and community systems. From this viewpoint, PBS values family members as essential team members throughout the assessment, planning, intervention, and follow-up phases of support. When working within a PBS framework, families are considered the "experts" with regard to their children (Dunst, Trivette, and Deal 1994; Turnbull and Turnbull 1990). Specifically, family members have rich knowledge of their child's history, past experiences, interests, and motivations. Further, family members will most likely support the child throughout his or her life, whereas professionals may enter and exit over time. Therefore, focusing on the family system is a critical element in the provision and longevity of appropriate support.

■ Individual Differences in Families

It is important to recognize the diversity among families in addition to the diversity among children with disabilities (Kalyanpur and Harry 1999). Many are nuclear families, consisting of two parents and their children. Others represent less traditional, yet equally or more common constellations, such as single parents, blended families, same-gender parents, and families that involve extended family members, sometimes in the primary caregiving role. Although the majority of research with families has focused on parents, one must also consider the importance of including other key members in the target child's life (e.g., siblings, other caregivers).

Aside from the variability in family constellation, practitioners must recognize other factors, such as ethnicity, culture, linguistics, and socioeconomic status, that may affect the family's values, priorities, and needs. Previous parenting experience and knowledge of autism may also influence a family's support needs and their ability to work with their child. These and many other variables affect the type of support family members need and desire. For example, some parents have access to the Internet and enjoy researching and reading literature on autism, whereas other parents find this stressful and overwhelming. Further, some parents who wish to do research of this nature may not understand or have access to terminology, may not have adequate reading ability, or may not speak the language in which the information is presented. In another example, some families surround themselves with strong social networks (e.g., extended family, church group), whereas others are more comfortable with support from a few close friends or relatives. Some families may have been relatively isolated and lacking in adequate social support even before their child received the diagnosis. When a child receives a diagnosis of ASD, the amount and type of support a family already has should be considered in the intervention process. In summary, families present with a variety of issues that must be considered in the intervention process, and treatment plans must be individualized (Moes and Frea 2002).

■ Issues for Families

Receiving a Diagnosis

Becoming a parent has been considered the most significant life-changing event for many people (Gelles and Gelles 1995). With the birth of a baby come significant changes in emotions and responsibilities. Because autism is not diagnosed at birth, this experience is usually similar for parents of children with autism and for those of children without special needs. However, at some point within the child's first few years, parents of children with autism learn that their child is exhibiting behavioral deficits or excesses compared with nondisabled peers. The child then eventually receives an ASD diagnosis.

There is large variability in response when family members first learn that their child has a diagnosis of autism or ASD. Many parents report experiencing negative feelings, such as loss, guilt, devastation, anger, grief, or denial. Although parents never want to learn that their child has a disability, some families report a sense of relief; the diagnosis may validate previous concerns parents had about their child's skills. Receiving a diagnosis also leads to educational support and services for children, often leading to an increased sense of support for the parents as well. Provision of such services may also produce a sense of progress or control, in that one is "taking action" concerning the diagnosis. Some parents may spend time focused on receiving an accurate differential diagnosis along the autism spectrum (e.g., Autism versus Asperger's Disorder; Autism versus pervasive developmental disorder); however, addressing the child's needs is the most important aspect of the process.

For parents who are not comfortable with or who disagree with their child's diagnosis, it may be helpful to focus on the individual child's skills or lack thereof. Rather than focusing on where the child's behaviors fall along the autism spectrum, it is often more productive to concentrate on what skills the child is not displaying that need to be learned for success in home, school, and community settings. Once parents understand these deficits, intervention can focus on teaching these skills, regardless of the differential diagnosis (Koegel and Lazebnik 2004). Parents who spend significant energy and effort trying to obtain the correct differential diagnosis may be allocating precious resources (e.g., financial, emotional, psychological) in an area that will not directly benefit the child. Helping them to refocus their efforts onto treatment can be an important shift for both the child and the family.

Increased Family Stress

Having a child with a disability intensifies the emotions and stress that come with parenthood, and there are specific challenges when a child is diagnosed with autism. Parents and families may react to the stress of having a child with special needs in different ways. Some literature has noted that the experiences of these parents may be similar to those of people who have experienced a traumatic event (Ferguson 2001; Turnbull and Turnbull 1990). A large body of literature has also documented the high levels of stress associated with parenting a child with special needs (e.g., Singer and Powers 1993). In contrast, a small number of articles have mentioned that generalized stress may not differ between parents of children with autism and those of children without disabilities (Koegel et al. 1978). A few articles have even highlighted the positive ways in which families cope and the child's contributions reported by parents of children with special needs (Pakenham, Sofronoff, and Samois 2004; Risdal and Singer 2004; Summers, Behr, and Turnbull 1989; Turnbull and Turnbull 1990). Although the challenges are great, all parents have hope that. with appropriate services and support, their children will live full lives.

In spite of the variation in parent and family reactions, many parents and family members experience feelings of loss or devastation when their child receives a diagnosis of ASD. They are unexpectedly thrown into a nightmare that changes their expectations and crushes their hopes. Compared with children who have other special needs, autism is a severe disability that carries unique challenges for families. Data collected during clinical work with families have demonstrated that parents of children with autism consistently rate themselves at clinically significant stress levels on stress measures (Abidin, Flens, and Austin 2006; Baker-Erikzen, Brookman-Frazee, and Stahmer 2005; Koegel et al. 1992; Moes 1995: Moes et al. 1992). This finding is not surprising, considering the challenges that children with autism can present. However, even when parents are included in the intervention process and their children's skills improve, parents of children with ASD may continue to score in the clinical range on stress measures (Schreibman and Koegel 2005). In fact, some research has demonstrated that parent education and parent involvement may lead to increased stress levels if parents are too overwhelmed when these services are provided. At times, it may be appropriate to use a clinician model when parents are unable to effectively participate in intervention. More research is needed to better understand how families can be assisted in ways that not only improve the skills of parents and children but also make strides toward improved quality of life and decreased stress levels. Promising results suggest that adding a component of social support into the parent education program leads to improved mastery of the techniques and long-term gains, compared with a parent education-only model (Stahmer and Gist 2001).

Challenging Behavior

Social and Communication Deficits

The unique characteristics of individuals with autism, namely social and communication deficits, social avoidance, self-stimulatory behavior, and serious behavior problems, can create specific challenges for families. Even compared with children who have other severe disabilities, the core deficits of autism can be extremely difficult for families to cope with. Communication deficits often result in increased challenging or aggressive behavior. Children with ASD often engage in disruptive behaviors because they do not have more adaptive means of having their needs met (e.g., they cannot verbally communicate). Because social deficits are a central feature of autism, children with this diagnosis may also avoid social interaction. Socially avoidant behavior can be devastating for parents and families to experience. Most young children and children with other disabilities seek attention and initiate social interactions with adults and peers (e.g., Allen et al. 1964; Hall, Lund, and Jackson 1968). In contrast, children with autism make social initiations far less frequently. When they do initiate, it is often for the purpose of making a request, rather seeking social attention, and they may also initiate in socially inappropriate ways that are stigmatizing or embarrassing for parents and families. As a result, parents may decrease their number of attempts at interacting with their children over time, due to their negative experience of failed or negative interactions.

Repetitive Behaviors and Restricted Interests

Children with autism may also have restricted interests and/or self-stimulatory behaviors, which cause them to stand out from others. These behaviors are often stigmatizing and increase the family's stress because they increase the amount of isolation that may occur. For example, if a family is self-conscious about their child's self-stimulatory behaviors, they may attend fewer family or community events, may decrease their social interactions with supportive friends, and may have an increased tendency to keep the child at home, thus limiting normal daily activities. The repetitive nature of these behaviors can also be very anxiety-provoking for families, because parents often become frustrated by repeated unsuccessful attempts at decreasing the behavior. Further, the rigid nature of behaviors often associated with ASD can interfere significantly with daily activities and routines, as parents often make changes in routines to accommodate obsessive and rigid behaviors in order to avoid tantrums that may otherwise occur. Parents frequently report they do not wish to make these accommodations but that the possibility of a tantrum is more stressful than the necessary change in routine.

Social Isolation as a Result of Disruptive Behavior

The behavioral excesses and difficulties associated with ASD can exacerbate the already limited social opportunities for the child as well. When children are disruptive or aggressive, they may become isolated from social experiences, especially because they are rarely then invited to participate in social gatherings (e.g., play dates, birthday parties). As mentioned earlier, families who feel embarrassed or frustrated by their child's behavior may withdraw from social activities. The families may chose not to socialize with friends, go to public events, or take their children to parties, restaurants, or parks. Children who have social deficits need these opportunities more than anyone else, to learn appropriate behaviors for use in social settings, if they are to function adequately as members of a community. For example, they may need experience with social rules and norms, such as standing in line to ride on a rollercoaster, waiting one's turn, speaking quietly in a bookstore or library, remaining silent during a movie, or staying seated in a restaurant. It is extremely unlikely that a child will learn these crucial adaptive skills if opportunities are not provided. To provide these experiences, families need the support to feel comfortable practicing these skills in community settings.

Unknown Prognosis

Years ago, most individuals with autism resided in institutions and did not have access to inclusive settings. Increased technology and empirically based interventions have been widely used to improve skills for children (Carr et al. 2002; Lovaas 1987; Koegel et al. 1999 *Pivotal response intervention I;* National Research Council 2001). A strong movement toward inclusive education and practices has also led to different experiences for those with ASD and their families (Boutot and Bryant 2005). More recently, children receiving the diagnosis of ASD have gained more access to inclusive settings, such as living in homes, attending neighborhood schools, and participating in community activities. Although the results of years of work show promise, prognoses are still unclear for those with ASD. Researchers have identified some skills (i.e., initiations, joint attention, language level, cognitive ability) that suggest favorable outcomes (Bruinsma, Koegel, and Koegel 2004; Koegel et al. 1999 *Pivotal response intervention II;* Lord and Bailey, 2002; Lovaas et al. 1973). That is, studies have shown that children who spontaneously made or were taught to make social initiations had better outcomes than children who were unable to learn this skill (Ingersoll, Schreibman, and Stahmer 2001; Koegel et al. 1999b). Research has also demonstrated that joint attention skills and language level are important prognostic indicators, especially in young children (Bruinsma, Koegel, and Koegel 2004; Koegel, Bruinsma, and Koegel 2005; Whalen, Schreibman and Ingersoll 2006). Finally, children who have at least average cognitive abilities have typically fared better than children with borderline cognitive abilities or mental retardation (e.g., Bartak and Rutter 1976).

The issue of an unknown prognosis probably contributes to families' heightened stress levels. It is important that parents and family members understand that autism is a lifelong disorder; however, educating families about prognostic indicators is often helpful and may be important in increasing parental understanding about individual children's prognoses and needs. For example, some families may benefit from knowing that their child shows some very positive prognostic signs, because this information will give them hope and keep them motivated to maintain intensive levels of intervention. Other families may benefit from knowing that their child's impairment is severe, because they can more accurately predict the child's future and plan for ongoing intensive levels of support. When talking with families about prognosis, it is important to consider the level of understanding and acceptance of the diagnosis so that information can be discussed accordingly. Even for families with severely impaired children, parents have repeatedly stated they need clinicians to help them maintain hope and optimism and to prevent them from becoming overwhelmed or depressed. Therefore, in many cases, helping a family understand prognosis in a realistic way, while still focusing on positive variables, can be as important as the prognostic information itself.

Selecting an Intervention

With more and more individuals being diagnosed with ASD, the stereotypes concerning individuals with autism (e.g., that they isolate themselves from social interactions, that they have savant skills) are changing, and variability among individuals is more broadly recognized. The volume of research studies and information on ASD has ballooned as scientists search to determine etiologies, improve assessment tools, identify prognostic indicators, develop and enhance interventions, and achieve more socially valid, widespread impacts on the lives of children and families coping with ASD. Information on autism has become prevalent in the media, with reports appearing on local and national television shows (e.g., Cable Network News, Supernanny [Powell and Armstrong 2005]) and also in popular health, business, and music magazines (e.g., Time Magazine, Newsweek, Shape, Rolling Stone).

Through the media, families are exposed to anecdotal reports documenting the successes of individuals who overcame autism. It is understandable that parents are eager and willing to try new approaches that tout significant progress within short time frames. Often, however, the interventions presented in such case reports are not evidence-based and do not have empirical support using robust research methodology (i.e., controlled clinical trials with large sample size or robust single-case design methodology) (Lord et al. 2005). Parents may become inundated by the abundance of information presented in the media and in research studies. They may become even more overwhelmed by the fact that the information is often contradictory and frequently makes impressive proclamations of significant progress or full recovery from autism. Similarly, when parents seek help from professionals, they may receive differing opinions, leaving them to make their own decisions about which treatments are best suited for their child and family. It is not surprising that a common challenge for all families of children with ASD involves sifting through information, learning about the treatment options, and selecting appropriate interventions for their children. Although professionals disagree regarding the best approaches for intervention, one issue they agree on is the importance of family members in the rehabilitation process for individuals with ASD (e.g., Siegel 2003).

Broad Framework for Understanding Intervention

In 2001, the National Research Council's Committee on Educational Interventions for Children with Autism reviewed multiple university-based treatment programs and outlined common characteristics of programs considered to be empirically supported. Empirically supported programs generally fell into three categories: developmental, behavioral, and combined or naturalistic. Developmental programs target cognitive, communicative, social, and emotional development and are often based on developmental theories, such as those of Piaget (1966). These interventions take place in developmentally appropriate settings (e.g., preschool) through play and relationship-based activities. Advocates of these models have argued that traditional behavioral treatment approaches are too circumscribed in their discrete target behavior approach to have a fundamental impact on symptoms in children with ASD.

Behavioral programs are based on principles of applied behavior analysis (ABA) and target language, social, cognitive, developmental, academic, and play skills using systematic and measurable teaching methodologies. These programs traditionally occurred in a discrete trial format during one-to-one intervention with the child by a highly trained behavioral clinician. These are known as discrete trial training programs and represent some of the earliest and most systematic forms of autism intervention (e.g., Lovaas 1987). Finally, the naturalistic or modified behavioral programs use the same systematic and measurable ABA-based teaching methodologies; however, the principles are embedded in natural interactions with the child during daily routines and activities (e.g., Koegel et al. 1999a). The programs that fall into each category, as reported by the National Research Council (2001), can be found in Table 19.1.

TABLE 19.1

Empirically Supported University-Based Programs for Children with Autism

Program	Program Type	Empirical Support
Developmental Intervention Model at The George Washington University School of Medicine (Floortime)	Developmentally based model	Greenspan and Wieder 1997
Denver Model at the University of Colorado Health Sciences Center	Developmentally based model	Rogers and DiLalla 1991; Rogers et al. 1986; Rogers and Lewis 1988; Rogers, Lewis, and Reis 1987
Douglas Developmental Center at Rutgers University	Behaviorally based: traditional	Handleman and Harris 2000; Harris et al. 1990, 1991, 2000
University of California, Los Angeles Young Autism Project	Behaviorally based: traditional	Lovaas 1987; McEachin, Smith, and Lovaas 1993; Anderson et al. 1987; Birnbrauer and Leach 1993; Sheinkopf and Siegel 1998; Smith, Donahue, and Davis 2000
Children's Unit at State University of New York, Binghamton	Behaviorally based: traditional	Romanczyk, Lockshin, and Matey 2000; Taylor and Romanczyk 1994)
Learning Experiences, an Alternative Program for Preschoolers and their Parents (LEAP) Preschool at the University of Colorado School of Education	Behaviorally based: naturalistic	Hoyson, Jamieson, and Strain 1984; Strain 1987; Strain and Hoyson 2000
Pivotal Response Model at the University of California, Santa Barbara	Behaviorally based: naturalistic	Koegel et al. 1999 Pivotal response intervention I; Koegel et al. 1999 Pivotal response intervention II

TABLE 19.1   *(continued)*

Program	Program Type	Empirical Support
Walden Early Childhood Programs at the Emory University School of Medicine	Behaviorally based: naturalistic	McGee, Daly, and Jacobs 1994; McGee, Feldman, and Morrier 1997; McGee, Morrier, and Daly 1999
Individualized Support Program at the University of South Florida at Tampa	Behaviorally based: naturalistic	Dunlap and Fox 1996, 1999; and others
Treatment and Education of Autistic and Related Communication Handicapped Children (TEACCH) at the University of North Carolina School of Medicine at Chapel Hill	Structured teaching approach with environmental organization to support the child	Mesibov 1997; Marcus et al. 1978; Schopler, Mesibov, and Baker 1982; Venter, Lord, and Schopler 1992; Ozonoff and Cathcart 1998

From National Research Council. (2001). *Educating young children with autism.* Washington, D.C.: National Academy Press.

Choosing the right intervention can be difficult when parents do not have knowledge of the broader picture of autism research and available services. Understanding the characteristics of the programs endorsed as empirically supported by the National Research Council (2001) can be very helpful when learning about and choosing service agencies in one's area. Even though many families do not have access to one of these 10 programs, many towns have service providers who use these methodologies, and parents who are equipped with the knowledge to understand the services offered in their area will be able to make more educated decisions than those who do not understand this broader intervention framework. It may also be helpful to educate parents about common characteristics of programs and help them to understand which components their child may need. For example, many children with autism receive specific treatments outside of school and ABA programming, such as speech therapy and occupational therapy. Educating parents about these various program components and how they complement one another can help them make educated decisions and feel confident that their child has a comprehensive program in place.

Program Characteristics

In-depth discussion of the important program characteristics of empirically supported programs proposed by the National Research Council is beyond the scope of this chapter; however, a brief overview is provided here to increase the reader's awareness of information that may be helpful to parents and empower them in making informed decisions about their child's services. More detailed information about these program characteristics can be found in the book, *Educating Young Children with Autism* (National Research Council 2001). The program characteristics are as follows:

1. Focus on early intervention
2. Intensity of hours (20 to 45 hours per week of combined services)
3. Active family involvement in intervention
4. Highly trained staff
5. Ongoing assessment using objective assessment measures
6. Use of a systematic and planful teaching curriculum
7. Intervention focused on communication and other developmental areas
8. Intervention that systematically plans for generalization and maintenance of skills
9. Individualized programming, documented in an IEP or IFSP
10. Supported and planned transitions

Increasing parents' awareness of these variables and helping them to evaluate how available programs address these issues will be very helpful in empowering them and developing their skills at choosing and evaluating programs for their child over time.

One particularly important issue to address with parents is the intensity of intervention and number of hours. This issue can be especially confusing for parents, because different programs recommend different amounts of intervention per day or week. The National Research Council (2001, 152) proposed that "Intensity is best thought of in the context of large numbers of functional, developmentally relevant, and high interest opportunities to respond actively". That is, it is important that intervention be intense in nature, but this intensity can be provided by a combination of multiple types of programming. It is not necessarily defined by long hours of discrete trial training, as has been the traditional standard in some programs. For example, a child may attend school, receive speech and occupational therapy, have ABA services, and attend a playgroup. This combination of developmentally appropriate activities may make for an adequately intensive level of intervention depending on the individual child's needs. Another child may be adequately served by a school program and playgroup supplemented by natural social opportunities provided by the parents (e.g., play dates, extra-curricular activities). The issue of adequate number of hours can be especially important to address with parents so that they can develop reasonable and developmentally appropriate expectations about what constitutes adequate programming. Whereas highly specialized, intensive treatment models are appropriate for many children with ASD, they are not necessary for all children with this diagnosis.

Psycho-education

Parents may also benefit from psycho-education about types of services their child may need and how to obtain them. For example, many parents need to be educated about the Individual Family Service Plan (IFSP) or the Individual Education Plan (IEP) process and need assistance in developing adequate goals for their child. Parents are often not aware of their child's educational rights under the Individuals with Individuals with Disabilities Education Act (IDEA) of 1990 (Public Law 101–476), the Individuals with Disabilities Education Act Amendments of 1997 (Public Law 105–17), and the Individuals with Disabilities Education Improvement Act of 2004 (Public Law 108–446). They may need assistance in understanding the law and its implications for their child. Many children with autism have some combination of the following services, which parents may need help understanding and selecting:

1. Special education services (e.g., special day class placement, one-to-one aide support, resource support)
2. ABA-based services (in home or at school, naturalistic or structured)
3. Speech therapy
4. Occupational therapy
5. Social skills interventions
6. PBS plan (based on functional assessment)
7. Pharmacologic interventions
8. Ongoing monitoring and standardized testing at appropriate intervals

Some combination of these services is applicable to most children with autism. Parents often need support in choosing what service combination is appropriate for their child and in evaluating whether the services are resulting in meaningful treatment gains.

Different children respond best to different types of services, settings, and programs. For example, some children benefit from the structure and systematic nature of discrete trial training (e.g., Lovaas 1987). Others children may become frustrated and unmotivated with this structured model and do much better with a more naturalistic model, such as pivotal response training (Koegel et al. 1999a) or incidental teaching (McGee, Morrier, and Daly 1999). Some children have many disruptive behaviors and require intensive behavior modification, whereas others easily function in a variety of settings without behavioral difficulties. Some children do well in unstructured, play-based inclusive settings, and others require the structure, increased adult attention, and highly specialized programming typically available in more restrictive environments, such as special education classrooms. Researchers have developed assessments to identify child characteristics that may make a child more likely to respond to a particular intervention. These findings allow clinicians to predict which treatments are likely to lead to the greatest gains for an individual child (Cohen 2003; Gabriels et al. 2001; Sherer and Scheinmann 2005).

■ Benefits of Including Families in the Intervention

Child Benefits

Decades of research documents the effects of including parents in their children's education (e.g., Lovaas et al. 1973). The child, family and team members all benefit when parents and family members are included as valued educational team members. For the child, family involvement increases the consistency of behavioral expectations across settings from school to home, thereby decreasing confusion and increasing learning. In addition, the child gains many more opportunities for learning throughout the varied settings (e.g., school, home, restaurants, church, parks, parties, sports events) and routines (e.g., mealtime, traveling, nighttime, dressing) in which families typically interact. This increase in learning opportunities accelerates the rate of learning, increases the child's motivation, and provides the child and family with access to inclusive activities. When family members are included, children maintain and more easily generalize their skills to novel settings, activities, and partners.

Family Benefits

For the family, providing input, gaining knowledge, and learning strategies to support their child leads to increased social validity of intervention strategies and goals from the parents' perspective. This increase in social validity affects "buy-in" to the intervention program in general, thereby affording parents the opportunity to gain confidence, empowerment, and more positive interactions with their children (Dunst, Trivette, and Deal 1994). Parents may then enhance their own and their families' lives by engaging in more activities and joining more events. Through such occasions, they can expand their social networks and improve their quality of life (Becker-Cottrill, McFarland, and Anderson 2003; Turnbull and Turnbull 1990).

Team Member Benefits

For team members and professionals, collaborating with parents allows for stakeholder "buy-in," which has been shown to be a critical element in effective intervention programs (Hieneman and Dunlap 2001). Without the inclusion of parents in the assessment, planning, and intervention process, even the most well-designed plan may be unsuccessful, because critical information about the child may not be available to the team. On the other hand, with parent involvement, professionals can increase their competence and the success of the program through combining their expertise about intervention programming and the parents' expertise about the child's history, strengths, weaknesses, needs, and motivations. This parent–professional collaboration ultimately results in a more sustainable program (L.K. Koegel et al. 2005; Brookman-Frazee 2004; Turnbull et al. 1999).

■ Research Findings Regarding Families and Intervention

Several decades of research documents the benefits that accrue when parents and other family members are included in the intervention process for children with ASD. Specifically, parent education is considered a critical and essential component of any intervention program (National Research Council 2001). Special education laws (IDEA) and best practices state the necessity of including family members in the decision-making processes for their children's educational, home, and community programs (e.g., Mahoney et al. 1999; Turnbull et al. 1999). Parents have been included in a variety of roles, as direct interventionists, advocates, mentors, trainers, and policy makers (Turnbull and Turnbull 1990), and a large body of literature supports the positive effects that result.

Parents as Intervention Providers

Social learning theory supports the notion that all children learn by interacting with and observing the behavior of others, making it important that parents model appropriate behavior (Bandura 2000; Dunst et al. 2001; Hart and Risley 1992, 1995). For children with autism, however, even when parents provide rich communicative environments to facilitate development of social language, skills are not acquired in the same way as for nondisabled peers. Instead, parents often must learn specific strategies to teach language, communication, and social skills to their children. These strategies are also frequently necessary to aid in the reduction of challenging behaviors. When parents learn effective techniques to interact with their children, they may provide their children with an increased number of opportunities to learn a variety of skills during natural routines.

In the role of direct interventionists, parents have been taught specific procedures to teach skills and aid in the reduction of problem behaviors. For example, parents have been taught naturalistic teaching strategies and ABA techniques to improve their children's verbal skills (Charlop-Christy and Carpenter 2002; Koegel, Symon, and Koegel 2001; Laski, Charlop, and Schreibman 1988; Siller and Sigman 2002), and augmentative communication skills (Granlund, Bjorck-Akesson, and Olsson 2001; Sigafoos et al. 2004; Stiebel 1999); to reduce maladaptive behavior (Koegel, Bimbela, and Schreibman 1996; Koegel et al. 2006); to increase homework completion (R.L. Koegel et al. 2005); to decrease food overselectivity (Brown, Spencer, and Swift 2002); to teach self-help skills (Katz and Kenig 1985); and to improve social play (Siller and Sigman 2002; Werner et al. 2005). The results from these studies and many others show how successful parents have been when they were included into the intervention to directly teach their children. Specifically, the children in these studies acquired the targeted skills or demonstrated decreases in inappropriate behavior. In addition, the gains maintained over time and generalized to other situations more effectively when parents were involved in the intervention, compared with a clinician model only (e.g., Koegel et al. 1978; Lovaas et al. 1973).

Parents as Mentors for Other Parents

Parents have taken on another role in the special education literature, the role of mentors to other parents. One example of this model is the "Parent-to-Parent" program, whereby one parent who has previous experience supporting a child with special needs volunteers to support another parent who is seeking assistance through the process (Ainbinder et al. 1998). Volunteer parent mentors can be very helpful to less experienced parents, who may need information about resources, services, programs, and intervention strategies. Parent mentors also frequently offer to share their personal experiences, which creates a social support system. In this role, the mentor parents are viewed as knowledgeable experts. Such programs can be extremely helpful for families. In particular, those who have recently received an ASD diagnosis are often presented with a tremendous amount of unfamiliar information and may be feeling socially isolated. Research suggests that it is important to appropriately match families, because participants reported higher levels of satisfaction when their children and experiences were similar to those of their mentors (Ainbinder et al. 1998). These programs acknowledge the expertise that parents gain through personal experience, place experienced parents in a position of empowerment, and provide important assistance to less experienced parents who are attempting to navigate the process of supporting their children.

Parents as Trainers

Most parent education programs include families as observers, intervention-ists, mentors, and collaborators. More recent research has expanded the role of parents into an even more elevated position, as experts and trainers of others in research-based techniques (Symon 2005; Symon, Koegel, and Singer 2005). Before this work, parents had rarely been considered authorities on teaching strategies and were seen only as sources of information about their individual child (Jenkins, Stephens, and Sternberg 1980). In these recent studies, primary caregivers participated in parent education programs in which they mastered the use of specialized interventions, applying ABA procedures and natural language strategies to improve their children's social communication (Symon 2005; Symon, Koegel, and Singer, 2005). The participant parents then taught these skills to other care providers (i.e., other parents, caregivers, therapists) who also spent a significant amount of time with the child. The identified caregivers met criteria on fidelity of implementation measures after being trained by the parents. Further, the children's social communication and behaviors improved during interactions with these other adults.

Parents as Policy Advocates

Parents and family members have played significant roles in the lives of their children with ASD. However, the contributions made by families stretch far beyond the benefits already mentioned. The advantages of including parents and family members has led to stronger advocacy and changes in policy for individuals with autism (Buswell, and Schaffner 2002; Mulick and Butter 2002; Soodak and Erwin 1995). With the development of special education laws, many families have advocated for themselves, their children, and other families. They enter IEP meetings informed of parents' and children's rights; they are knowledgeable about treatment options; and they are familiar with the laws (Block, Weinstein, and Seitz 2005). In cases in which school or educational systems were not adhering to the laws requiring appropriate support and education for children with autism, families have embarked on emotional and financial struggle in entering into the litigation process (Mandlawitz 2002; Mulick and Butter 2002). This litigation has often resulted in positive changes for individual children, while also setting legal precedents that lead to improved services for children being served by those educational systems in the future.

As an extension of family members' personal efforts to improve education and lives for individuals with autism, they have formed collaborative organizations with professionals and scientists to raise awareness and generate funds for research on causes, treatment, prevention, and education in autism; examples include Autism Speaks, Cure Autism Now, Families for Early Autism Treatment (FEAT), and the UC Davis M.I.N.D. Institute. These local and national efforts have generated millions of dollars contributed toward these goals. Although funding and resources remain inadequate, considering the epidemic of autism, family members' efforts have led to significant movement toward their mission.

■ Strategies for Success

Merge Research with Practice

The aim of this section is to provide strategies that have been documented in the literature and successfully implemented through clinical work to improve child outcomes and overall quality of life for the children, their families, and their educational team members. An important concept to consider in providing support to children with autism and their families is the need to merge research with practice.

Social Validity and Functional Skills

When conducting research, it is important to focus on topics and issues that are important to families, so that the research has social validity. The skills that are taught to the children should be functional and should strive to enhance the individuals' social interactions, communication skills, independence, and quality of life. For example, teaching a preschooler to approach peers by saying "Hi, can I play with you?" often results in rejection. This verbal initiation is not how young children typically enter into play with peers. If learning and displaying this behavior leads to social rejection, it could be considered a nonfunctional skill. On the other hand, teaching the child to find a toy that is similar to the toys that peers are playing with and join in the action is a more functional skill and will likely lead to better peer interactions. Often, families have values and priorities that influence what skills are considered functional for a specific child. Taking into account the family's perspective in goal setting becomes very important in deciding what skills to teach.

Ecocultural Validity

In addition, research should be conducted in settings in which skills will need to be demonstrated. For instance, school, home, and community settings are all environments where children will need to apply social communication skills and demonstrate appropriate behavior. Therefore, these settings should be included in research studies to increase generalization, maintenance, functional use of skills, and social validity. Researchers who take family dynamics into consideration and value individual family priorities are able to design studies to address these important areas. If the child with autism is viewed as an isolated individual independent of the larger family unit, the research may demonstrate how to teach skills, but the findings may not generalize to situations in which the child will need to display them. As a result, although the research findings may support an intervention, the child may not have actually acquired a functional skill.

Use of Evidence-Based Practices

In addition to participating in research, many children receive services from direct service providers who are not associated with research. Those working directly with the children (e.g., teachers; parent educators; behavior, speech, occupational, and physical therapists) must be familiar with evidence-based practices to design and deliver the most effective treatment. As discussed earlier, many interventions are available for children with autism; however, only some of them have strong empirical support. Although professionals may disagree about the best interventions, they agree on the need for intensive and early interventions (National Research Council 2001; Siegel 2003). Therefore, is critical that those providing services be aware of the most current research findings, whether they support the interventions or not. Valuable intervention hours are better spent using approaches that have been repeatedly shown to be effective, rather than those that have not been shown to effectively improve social communication and behavioral difficulties. Further, clinicians who develop what they believe to be highly effective strategies should collaborate with researchers to support their work. One cost-effective way to merge research with practice is for school districts and family members to collaborate with local universities, hospitals, and research institutes that specialize in treatment for autism. These partnerships can often provide children and their team members with intervention support as they are investigating new areas of research and developing best practices.

Collaboration: Critical for Success

Like any athletic team or business partnership, the educational team members supporting a child with autism are required to work together and need to share visions and goals. Collaboration between team members is possibly the most essential element for success. Even with the best intervention plans in place, poor collaboration or lack of "buy-in" among team members (e.g., co-teachers, caregivers, administrators, specialists) can lead to inconsistency in programming, frustration for the team members and, ultimately, confusion for the child (Hieneman and Dunlap 2001). Successful collaboration is a complex process that requires commitment (Soodak and Erwin 2000). When deciding on types of support, placement, interventions, or goals, all team members must be included in the process and have opportunities to express their knowledge, ideas, and opinions, beginning with family members. Consistent with the values of PBS and social systems theory, a child with autism is viewed in the context of a larger system, namely that of a family, classroom, school, or community (Brofenbrenner 1986; Carr et al. 2002; Gallimore et al. 1993). Therefore, successful interventions need to include individuals who support the child across these different contexts. Several examples from different settings highlight how the lack of collaboration can lead to inconsistency, increased stress among team members, and lack of skills gained by the child.

Family System Examples

In a family system, one parent may provide clear opportunities for the child to make verbal requests during mealtime, such as by saying "chicken" before providing the child with a meal. If the other caregiver responds to the child's inappropriate behavior (e.g., crying, screaming) and then provides the meal after these behaviors, the child is intermittently reinforced for the inappropriate behaviors and is therefore less likely to learn appropriate communication. In another example, one caregiver may expect a child to remain seated for mealtimes, using rewards and systematically increasing the demands, while the other allows the child to get out of his seat or walk around while eating. This lack of collaboration can easily cause tension between the already stressed parents and can also lead to confusion for the child.

Teaching Team Examples

In a classroom example, the teaching team, including teachers, assistants, instructional aides, and classroom aides, must work together in determining the classroom rules, the roles of each team member, and how to respond to and teach each child. Without good collaboration, a team member may feel frustrated by his or her lack of support or lack of training in how to best support the child with autism. Many students with ASD spend time in classrooms with support from instructional aides. These aides often do not receive adequate training to learn effective strategies to support the children with autism. Their role in the classroom is often not clearly defined, and they are frequently left to develop their own strategies through trial and error. Classroom teachers (in general or special education) often are overwhelmed with their caseloads and do not have time allotted to collaborate with their other teaching team members. To combat this problem, educational teams are encouraged to include in the child's IEP specific planning and collaboration times. With teachers' and professionals' heavy workloads, excessive meetings scheduled, and in-service trainings, it is unlikely they will have time to meet without prioritizing prescheduled collaboration times.

Individual Service Provider Examples

In addition to the classroom team, there are support providers and specialists such as resource teachers; speech, occupational, and physical therapists; and behavioral service providers. These individuals often work directly with children in one-to-one settings; increasingly, they providing services directly in the children's educational classrooms. These team members provide expertise in particular techniques and make significant gains with the child. Their collaboration is essential to the long-term gains and generalization of skills for the child. When services are provided in a segregated setting, the specialists prioritize teaching the other professionals how the target goals can be met in the absence of the specialist. For example, if a child receives speech therapy in individual sessions weekly outside of the classroom, the teaching team often does not learn about the strategies used to facilitate the therapy goals (e.g., speech/communication, motor skills, social skills). Considering the limited amount of time the child spends in therapy compared to the many hours spent in the classroom, the child could greatly benefit from coordination of these services. Specifically, the teaching team can learn how to implement the strategies and embed communication opportunities throughout the classroom routines.

In a different situation, when services are provided for behavior intervention through an independent agency, the therapists working directly with the child often do not have enough time to coordinate services with the other involved professionals. Discussions in monthly meetings are one important form of collaboration; however, occasionally overlapping schedules to observe one another's sessions can lead to better program consistency.

Parent-Professional Partnerships: Everybody's Responsibility

In addition to the necessary collaboration among those working within each setting, the relationship between parents and professionals is important. Parents have been included in the team process as recipients of information and learners of strategies, yet resent research suggests that the benefits of creating a partnership between parents and professionals are significant for all involved entities (parents, children, and professionals) (Brookman-Frazee 2004; Soodak and Erwin 2000; Turnbull et al. 1999). Further, parents are increasingly being considered "experts" in their own right, because they can provide a wealth of information about the child that professionals may not have. All team members can assume responsibility for creating a positive working relationship and establishing a partnership. Allowing family and team members to share in the decision-making processes and having each play a role in developing programs can only benefit the child and lead to faster rates of skill acquisition. Sharing information, such that parents are learning new strategies and team members are gaining information about the child, furthers the progress of the child as well.

Although it can be taxing to support children with ASD or behavioral challenges (e.g., self-stimulation, nonresponsiveness, disruptiveness) in the classroom setting, it is important to provide appropriate support for these children and to allow them to access the appropriate educational curriculum regardless of the setting. Family members and school team members often disagree on the best placement or appropriate services for a child with ASD, and many cases have led to due process and court decisions (e.g., Mulick and Butter 2002). These situations do not benefit the child or the team members. Although it is sometimes difficult to agree on strategies, goals, services, or placement, maintaining a positive relationship is critical to the success of the program. Collaboration can be achieved through the distribution of responsibility of each team member. It is also important to note that building a strong collaboration takes time and ongoing effort. If team members feel unsure at the outset about whether the team will be collaborative, it can be important to give the team members time to become comfortable working together and build faith in one another as positive, supportive contributors. Over time, the collaboration improves, especially if team members can maintain a willingness to learn and embrace the challenges each student presents. Some suggestions are provided here to enhance the efforts of all team members, including administrators, teachers, and family members.

Suggestions for Administrators and School Personnel

A first impression makes a lasting impression and sets the stage for future interactions. As a child begins a new school or enters a new classroom, the administrators, teachers, and other school personnel must openly welcome all students into their schools and into their classrooms. Through recognizing, understanding, or empathizing with the challenges and elevated levels of stress that most families of children with autism experience, school personnel may be more willing to accept having children with autism placed in their schools and classrooms and to take on the challenges of supporting these students (Jordan 2005). Families are likely to feel welcomed if school personnel maintain positive attitudes and remain optimistic that they can successfully support children with autism in their classrooms.

Building rapport with families and students, opening the communication lines, being willing to attend team meetings, and proactively putting necessary supports in place for the child are responsibilities of the administrators and school members. Viewing family members as team partners can assist in this process. For instance, not only should educational goals include functional skills, but these skills should also be ones that are valued by the parents, so that the goals have social validity and ecocultural importance. Although it can be difficult for all team members to agree on goals, it is important that the team be open minded about addressing goals and implementing strategies that have good contextual fit with family values.

An essential responsibility on the part of the school administration is providing specialized and ongoing staff training for those supporting students with autism. Without ongoing training and support for the team members, staff may burn out and have difficulty maintaining their roles in the child's program and as positive, contributing members of the educational teams. Individuals who support children with autism often do not have adequate specialized training in autism, familiarity with new research, or knowledge of evidence-based practices sufficient to support the particular needs of children with autism (e.g., reducing ritualistic or perseverative behavior, improving social communication) (Giangreco et al. 2001; Marks, Schrader, and Levine 1999; Riggs and Mueller 2001). Along with ongoing training, administrators should allow scheduled time for teaching teams, including paraprofessionals, to meet for ongoing collaboration, evaluation, and coordination of support.

Within a classroom, the teaching team can begin the collaborative process through building rapport with their students, including students with ASD. One of the greatest benefits when working with children with ASD is the variability and endearing qualities they possess. Teachers, assistants, and paraprofessionals can maintain an open attitude toward individualizing techniques, modifying the curriculum, or learning new strategies for a specific student with ASD. They may need to be flexible and not defensive when consultants, specialists, and family members offer suggestions. On the other hand, they need to be respected as the team members who spend a great deal of time providing direct support and have the large responsibility of instruction, meeting goals, and evaluating progress for every student in their class. Providing their insight as front-line supporters to other professionals, and also listening to suggestions that might assist them in their classrooms, can help teachers to feel equipped and supported in their work.

Suggestions for Family Members

As was suggested for school personnel, it is equally important that family members be open-minded about working within the "culture" of the school (e.g., observing school rules and traditions) and that the goals for their child fit with educators' priorities, routines, and experience. It is especially important for parents to be flexible about such issues when teachers are working within educational guidelines that are legislatively mandated, because these guidelines place pressure on teachers from another angle besides that of the individual child. Parents can facilitate the collaborative process by attending team meetings, providing school personnel with as much information as possible about their child's needs, and keeping an optimistic, open mind throughout the academic year.

There are many specific strategies that family members can use to help establish a positive relationship with school personnel. First, it is very helpful to provide the teachers and assistants with as much positive feedback as possible. Many general and special education teachers and paraprofessionals do not receive enough specialized training to adequately support children with ASD in their classrooms (Giangreco and Broer 2005). Therefore, they may feel anxious about their abilities and overwhelmed due to the amount of support that is required to meet the child's individual needs. To enhance their competence, it is very helpful to provide them with compliments and re assurance regarding the skills they are using that are effective. Recognizing such positive attributes can help maintain a positive relationship among the child, teachers, family, and other team members. This positive feedback is especially important when it comes from parents, who know their children well and can often quickly recognize what strategies will be successful. It is also helpful to encourage openness in team members, which can result in increased willingness to learn new strategies. Advocating for team member training can also be very important. Team members may feel a sense of relief when family members provide possible solutions to skills areas that are weak, rather than just focusing on the weakness.

Individual Educational Planning meetings are sometimes extremely stressful, and some attendees may not be familiar with the student. To foster the relationship between the child and the team members, families can provide pictures of their child and a list of the child's strengths and highly preferred interests to personalize the meeting and provide important information in a collaborative manner. Family members can also bring snacks and can encourage their child to draw a picture, write a story, or create a gift to give their teacher or assistant to show appreciation for their support. These small gestures can be greatly valued by staff working with the child, and they can help to strengthen the partnership between home and school.

It is also often helpful for families to form alliances with other families who have similar needs, to strengthen the role of special education families in the school. If approaching school personnel about difficult issues seems to be the best avenue for change, a team of families who are working together may increase their influence in making positive changes in the education of children with special needs. Family members can also become actively involved in the school climate by serving on committees, volunteering at the school, and playing other roles that a parent of any child might play (e.g., donate time in classrooms or office, supervise the play yard, support school fundraisers). These gestures of involvement can be important in building rapport with school personnel and demonstrate a commitment to the school overall, rather than just to their individual child's needs.

Maintaining Home–School Communication and Coordination

After rapport is established, parents and teachers can maintain good communication through a simple daily checklist or feedback form that is specific to the child's goals and behaviors. Many students with autism have difficulty communicating with their parents about the events of their school day. Therefore, keeping in contact with the teaching team is important so that parents can know how their son or daughter is doing in school. Daily writing in a journal or log can be time-consuming and may not provide specific critical information for families; however, creating an individualized and simple communication tool can provide family members with the information that is most important to them without taking away valuable instruction and support time from the staff. The teaching team and parents can provide input and create a form based on the information about the child that is of highest importance to them.

In addition to informing family members about the child's behavior and daily participation, this communication tool can also be used to help coordinate goals across environments. Priming or preteaching is a method of presenting information to students, in an informal way and with low demands, before it is introduced in class. Studies indicate that when students with autism are familiar with the information before it is presented in class, they demonstrate a reduction in problem behavior and an increase in academic responding (Koegel et al. 2003). A section on the communication form can be provided for general themes (e.g., presidents), concepts (e.g., habitats, rhyming) or specific page numbers of assignments for upcoming lessons. In this way, parents can be made aware of the upcoming lessons and can work with their children at home by discussing the themes or concepts or practicing the lessons at home before they are presented in class. A sample communication form is provided in Table 19.2 to demonstrate how this communication tool can be individualized and used efficiently.

Set High Expectations

A suggestion for families and all team members is to set and maintain high expectations for children with ASD. Although ASD is categorized as a severe and pervasive disability, the outcomes for many individuals with these diagnoses are positive. It is likely that children will meet our expectations of them, and it is important for family members to set goals that are essential for their family functioning. For instance, if eating dinner at restaurants and seeing movies are activities that a family enjoys, then goals for the child with ASD should include learning appropriate behaviors to participate in these activities with the family. In this case, the child would need to learn to wait in line, remain seated at the table, order food, purchase theater tickets, and remain quiet throughout

TABLE 19.2
Sample Checklist for Home–School Collaboration

Child's Name: Date:

☐   Followed classroom routines independently
☐   Required minimal prompts to follow the classroom routines
☐   Required frequent prompts to follow the classroom routines
S/he
☐   Actively participated in class lessons throughout the day and across activities
☐   Some participation in class lessons and during some activities
☐   Little participation in class lessons and across activities
During free play and unstructured activities, s/he
☐   Interacted appropriately with peer(s)
        Peer(s):   _____
        Activity: _____
☐   Played appropriately with toys
☐   Engaged in repetitive or self-stimulatory play
Regarding her/his behavior, s/he
☐   Was well behaved throughout the day
☐   Engaged in minimal challenging behavior at times during the day
☐   Engaged in frequent challenging behavior throughout the day.

Strategies/Suggestions:

Priming:
Regarding coordination with home support, we are working on the following
themes and skills this week:
        1.
        2.

---

the show. If full-inclusion education is a priority for an educational team, then intervention should include teaching behaviors that are appropriate in the classroom environment, such as remaining on-task, imitating peers, appropriately requesting assistance, transitioning between lessons, and so forth. In a final example, if a family strives to have their son or daughter act appropriately at social gatherings, then the family should work on skills to familiarize the child with parties and social functions. Targeting these goals will improve the quality of life, not only for the child with ASD, but also for the family (Lucyshyn et al. 2002).

Embedded into the idea of setting high expectations is the value of teaching skills to foster independence. Family members (or teachers) may feel a need to provide extra assistance when a child has a disability; however, encouraging the child to become as independent as possible provides long-term benefit. Teaching self-help skills such as dressing, bathing, and toilet training and teaching skills in the classroom through self-management procedures all serve to increase independence and autonomy (Callahan and Rademacher 1999; Harrower and Dunlap 2001).

Parents: Take Care of Yourselves

The responsibilities of parenting a child with special needs can include spending a great deal of time learning about special education, attending meetings, and providing intervention. Parents often experience heightened levels of stress and worry about how to best support their child. These issues lead many families to modify numerous aspects of their daily activities and events, which can ultimately change their intended lifestyle. In an attempt to provide their child with ASD the best support and resources possible, family members may sacrifice activities and aspects of their life that they truly enjoyed for themselves, such as exercising, spending time with other children, reading a book, vacationing, or going out with a spouse. A recommendation for family members is to find balance in their lives without isolating themselves and without sacrificing all the things that provide them with enjoyment, fulfillment, accomplishment, and confidence. Building social support networks, exposing their children to activities that are valued by the family, and spending time in activities that are enjoyable for themselves are all suggestions for creating a better quality of life for the family as well as for the child with ASD.

■ Conclusion

This chapter described some challenges for family members of individuals with ASD, research that has included families in the rehabilitation process, and strategies for success. Family systems are complex, and individualization is necessary to provide interventions and support that have that good contextual fit with family values. For school personnel, a central message is to maintain an optimistic attitude, invite and encourage parents and other family members into the educational process, and maintain the goal of empowering families. A vital message for family members is to build positive partnerships with those who work with their child. Families should also strive to set goals that are consistent with individual family values and priorities that will allow their child to function in educational, family, and community-based settings and activities. With high expectations and successful collaboration, the lives of individuals with ASD have progressed from institutionalization to educational, community, and family inclusion. Supporting individuals with ASD in the contexts in which they live is essential, and family support is a critical part of this process.

■ References

Abidin, R., Flens, J.R., and Austin, W.G. (2006). The Parenting Stress Index. In *Forensic uses of clinical assessment instruments* (ed. R.P. Archer), pp. 297–328. Mahwah, N.J.: Lawrence Erlbaum Associates.

Ainbinder, J.G., Blanchard, L.., Singer, G.H.S., Sullivan, M.E., Powers, L., Marquis, J., and Santelli, B. (1998). A qualitative study of parent-to-parent support for parents of children with special needs. *Journal of Pediatric Psychology,* 23 (2), 99–109.

Albin, R.W., Lucyshyn, J.M., Horner, R.H., and Flannery, K.B. (1996). Contextual fit for behavioral support plans: A model for "goodness of fit." In *Positive behavioral support: Including people with difficult behavior in the community* (eds. L.K. Koegel, R.L. Koegel, and G. Dunlap), pp. 81–98. Baltimore: Paul H. Brookes.

Allen, K.E., Hart, B., Buell, J.S., Harris, F.R., and Wolf, M.M. (1964). Effects of social reinforcement on isolate behavior of a nursery school child. *Child Development,* 35, 511–518.

Anderson, S.R., Avery, D.L., DiPietro, E.K., Edwards, G.L., and Christian, W.P. (1987). Intensive home-based early intervention for autistic children. *Education and Treatment of Children,* 10, 352–366.

Autism Speaks. Available at http://www.autismspeaks.org (accessed November 2, 2007).

Baker-Erikzen, M., Brookman-Frazee, L., and Stahmer, A. (2005). Stress levels and adaptability in parents of toddlers with and without autism spectrum disorders. *Research and Practice for Persons with Severe Disabilities,* 30 (4), 194–204.

Bandura, A. (2000). Social-cognitive theory. In *Encyclopedia of psychology* (Vol. 7) (ed. A.E. Kazdin), pp. 329–332. Washington D.C.: American Psychological Association.

Bartak, L., and Rutter, M. (1976). Differences between mentally retarded and normal intelligence autistic children. *Journal of Autism and Childhood Schizophrenia,* 6 (2), 109–120.

Becker-Cottrill, B., McFarland, J., and Anderson, V. (2003). A model of positive behavioral support for individuals with autism and their families: The family focus process. *Focus on Autism and Other Developmental Disabilities,* 18 (2), 110–120.

Birnbrauer, J.S., and Leach, D.J. (1993). The Murdock Early Intervention Program after two years. *Behavior Change,* 10, 63–74.

Block, J., and Weinstein, J., and Seitz, M. (2005). School and parents partnerships in the preschool years. In *Autism spectrum disorders: Identification, education, and treatment* (3rd ed). (ed. D. Zader), pp. 229–265. Mahwah, N.J.: Lawrence Erlbaum Associates.

Boutot, E.A., and Bryant, D.P. (2005). Social integration of student with autism in inclusive settings. *Education and Training in Developmental Disabilities,* 40 (1), 14–23.

Brofenbrenner, U. (1986). Ecology of the family as a context for human development: Research perspectives. *Developmental Psychology,* 22 (6), 723–742.

Brookman-Frazee, L. (2004). Using parent/clinician partnerships in parent education programs for children with autism. *Journal of Positive Behavior Interventions,* 6 (4), 195–213.

Brown, J.F., Spencer, K., and Swift, S. (2002). A parent training programme for chronic food refusal: A case study. *British Journal of Learning Disabilities,* 30 (3), 118–121.

Bruinsma, Y., Koegel, R.L., and Koegel, L.K. (2004). Joint attention and children with autism: A review of the literature. *Mental Retardation ad Developmental Disabilities,* 10 (3), 169–175.

Burton, D, Chairman. (2002). *The autism epidemic: Is the NIH and CDC response adequate?* [Opening statement.] Hearing of the Committee on Government Reform, U.S. House of Representatives, Washington, D.C. April 18.

Buswell, B.E., and Schaffner, C. (2002). Families as creative and resourceful collaborators in inclusive schooling. In *Creativity and collaborative learning: The practical guide to empowering students, teachers, and families* (2nd ed). (eds. J. Thousand, R. Villa, and A. Nevlin), pp. 13–20. Baltimore, MD: Paul H. Brookes.

Callahan, K., and Rademacher, J.A. (1999). Using self-management strategies to increase the on-task behavior of students with autism. *Journal of Positive Behavior Interventions,* 1 (2), 117–122.

Carr, E.G., Dunlap, G., Horner, R.H., Koegel, R.K., Turnbull, A.P., Sailor, W., Anderson, J., Albin, R.W., Koegel, L.K., and Fox, L. (2002). Positive behavior support: Evolution of an applied science. *Journal of Positive Behavior Support,* 4 (1), 4–16.

Center for Disease Control. (2007). Available at http://cdc.gov/autism (accessed December 13, 2007).

Charlop-Christy, M.H., and Carpenter, M.H. (2002). Modified incidental teaching sessions: A procedure for parents to increase spontaneous speech in their children with autism. *Journal of Positive Behavior Interventions,* 2 (2), 98–112.

Cohen, I. (2003). Criterion-related validity of the PDD Behavior Inventory. *Journal of Autism and Developmental Disorders,* 33 (1), 47–53.

Cure Autism Now. Available at http://www.autismspeaks.org (accessed November 2, 2007).

Dunlap, G., and Fox, L. (1996). Early intervention and serious problem behaviors: A comprehensive approach. In *Positive behavioral support: Including people with difficult behavior in the community* (eds. L.K. Koegel, R.L. Koegel, and G. Dunlap), pp. 31–50). Baltimore: Paul H. Brookes.

Dunlap, G., and Fox, L. (1999). A demonstration of behavioral support for young children with autism. *Journal of Positive Behavior Interventions,* 2, 77–87.

Dunst, C.J., Bruder, M.B., Trivette, C.M., Hamby, D., Raab, M., McLean, M. (2001). Characteristics and consequences of everyday natural learning opportunities. *Topics in Early Childhood Special Education,* 21 (2), 68–92.

Dunst, C.J., Trivette, C.M., and Deal, A. (1994). Enabling and empowering families. In *Supporting and strengthening families. Vol. 1: Methods, strategies, and practices* (eds. C.J. Dunst and C.M. Trivette), pp. 2–11. Cambridge, Mass.: Brookline Books.

Families for Early Autism Treatment (FEAT). Available at http://www.feat.org (accessed November 2, 2007).

Ferguson, P. (2001). Mapping the family: Disability studies and the exploration of parental response to disabilities. In *Handbook of disability studies* (eds. G. Albrecht, K. Seelman, and M. Bury), pp. 373–395. Thousand Oaks, Calif.: Sage.

Fombonne, E. (2003). The prevalence of autism. *Journal of the American Medical Association,* 289 (1), 87–89.

Fombonne, E. (2006). Past and future perspective on autism epidemiology. In *Understanding autism: From basic neuroscience to treatment* (eds. S.O. Moldin and J.L. Rubenstein), pp. 25–48. Boca Raton, Fla.: CRC Press.

Gabriels, R.L., Hill, D.E., Pierce, R.A., Rogers, S.J., and Wehner, B. (2001). Predictors of treatment outcome in young children with autism. [Special issue: Autism.] *Early Interventions,* 5 (4), 407–429.

Gallimore, R., Weisner, T.S., Bernheimer, L.P., and Guthrie, D., and Nihira, K. (1993). Family responses to young children with developmental delays: Accommodation activity in ecological and cultural context. *American Journal on Mental Retardation,* 98 (2), 185–206.

Gelles, R.J., and Gelles, J.S. (1995). *Contemporary families: A sociological view.* Thousand Oaks, Calif.: Sage.

Giangreco, M.F., and Broer, S.M. (2005). Questionable utilization of paraprofessionals in inclusive schools: Are we addressing symptoms or causes? *Focus on Autism and Other Developmental Disabilities,* 20 (1), 10–26.

Giangreco, M.F., Edelman, S., Broer, S.M., and Doyle, M.B. (2001). Paraprofessional support of students with disabilities: Literature from the past decade. *Exceptional Children,* 68 (1), 45–64.

Gillberg, C., Cederlund, M., Lamberg, K., and Zeijlon, L. (2006). Brief report. "The autism epidemic": The registered prevalence of autism in a Swedish urban area. *Journal of Autism and Developmental Disorders,* 36 (3), 429–435.

Granlund, M. Bjorck-Akesson, E. Olsson, C. (2001). Working with families to introduce augmentative and alternative communication systems. In *Communicating without Speech: Practical augmentative and alternative communication* (eds. H. Cockerill and L. Carroll-Few), pp. 88–102. New York: Cambridge University Press.

Greenspan, S.I., and Wieder, S. (1997). Developmental patterns and outcomes in infants and children with disorders in relating and communicating: A chart review of 200 cases of children with autistic spectrum diagnoses. *The Journal of Developmental and Learning Disorders,* 1, 87–141.

Hall, R.V., Lund, D., and Jackson, D. (1968). Effects of teacher attention on study behavior. *Journal of Applied Behavior Analysis,* 1 (1), 1–12.

Handleman, J.S., and Harris, S.L. (2000). *Preschool education programs for children with autism* (2nd ed). Austin, Tex.: PRO-ED.

Harris, S.L., Handleman, J.S., Arnold, M.S., and Gordon, R.F. (2000). The Douglass Developmental Disabilities Center: Two models of service delivery. In *Preschool education programs for children with autism* (2nd ed) (eds. J.S. Handleman and S.L. Harris), pp. 233–260. Austin, Tex.: PRO-ED.

Harris, S.L., Handleman, J.S., Kristoff, B., Bass, L., and Gordon, R. (1990). Changes in language development among autistic and peer children in segregated and integrated preschool settings. *Journal of Autism and Developmental Disorders,* 20, 23–31.

Harris, S.L., Handleman, J.S., Gordon, R., Kristoff, B., and Fuentes, F. (1991). Changes in cognitive and language functioning of preschool children with autism. *Journal of Autism and Developmental Disabilities,* 21, 281–290.

Harrower, J.K., and Dunlap, G. (2001). Including children with autism in general education classrooms: A review of effective strategies. [Special issue: Autism]. *Behavior Modification,* 25 (5), 762–784.

Hart, B., and Risley, T.R. (1992). American parenting of language-learning children: Persisting differences in family child interactions observed in natural home environments. *Developmental Psychology,* 28 (6), 1096–1105.

Hart, B. and Risley, T.R. (1995). *Meaningful differences in the everyday experience of young American children.* Baltimore: Paul H. Brookes.

Hieneman, M., and Dunlap, G. (2001). Factors affecting the outcomes of community-based behavioral support. II: Factory category importance. *Journal of Positive Behavior Interventions,* 3 (2), 67–74.

Hoyson, M., Jamieson, B., and Strain, P.S. (1984). Individualized group instruction of normally developing and autistic-like children: A description and evaluation of the LEAP curriculum model. *Journal of the Division of Early Childhood,* 8, 157–181.

Individuals with Disabilities Education Act of 1990, 20, U.S.C. 1400 et seq.

Individuals with Disabilities Education Act Amendments of 1997, 20 U.S.C. 1400 et seq.

Individuals with Disabilities Education Improvement Act of 2004, 20 U.S.C., et seq.

Ingersoll, B., Schreibman, L., and Stahmer, A. (2001). Brief report: Differential treatment outcomes for children with autistic spectrum disorder based on level of peer social avoidance. *Journal of Autism and Developmental Disabilities,* 31 (3), 343–349.

Jenkins, S., Stephens, B., and Sternberg, L. (1980). The use of parents as parent trainers of handicapped children. *Education and Training of the Mentally Retarded,* 15 (4), 256–263.

Jordan, R. (2005). Managing autism and Asperger's syndrome in current educational provision. [Special issue: Education as Pediatric Rehabilitation]. *Pediatric Rehabilitation*, 8 (2), 104–112.

Kalyanpur, M., and Harry, B. (1999). *Culture in special education: Building reciprocal family professional relationships.* Baltimore: Paul H. Brookes.

Katz, S., and Kenig, D. (1985). A group individual method of training parents for teaching self-help skills to their mentally handicapped children. *British Journal of Mental Subnormality*, 31 (61), 80–87.

Koegel, L.K., Koegel, R.L., Boettcher, M.A., and Brookman, L. (2005). Extending behavior support in home and community settings. In *Individualized supports for students with problem behaviors: Designing positive behavior plans* (eds. L.M. Bambara and L. Kern), pp. 334–358. New York: Guilford.

Koegel, L.K., Koegel, R.L., Frea, W., and Green-Hopkins, I. (2003). Priming as a method of coordinating educational services for children with autism. *Language, Speech, and Hearing Services in Schools*, 34 (3), 228–235.

Koegel, L.K., Koegel, R.L., Harrower, J.K., and Carter, C.M. (1999a). Pivotal response intervention I: Overview of approach. *Journal of the Association for Persons with Severe Handicaps*, 24, 174–185.

Koegel, L.K., Koegel, R.L., Shoshan, Y., and McNerney, E. (1999b). Pivotal response intervention II: Preliminary long-term outcome data. *Journal of the Association for Persons with Severe Handicaps*, 24, 186–198.

Koegel, L.K., and Lezebnik, C. (2004). *Overcoming autism: Finding the answers, strategies and hope that can transform a child's life.* New York: Viking Press.

Koegel, R.L., Bimbela, A., and Schreibman, L. (1996). Collateral effects of parent training on family interactions. *Journal of Autism and Developmental Disorders*, 26 (3), 347–359.

Koegel, R.L., Bruinsma, Y., and Koegel, L.K. (2005). Developmental trajectories with early intervention. In *Pivotal response treatments for autism: Communication, social, and academic development* (eds. R.L. Koegel and L.K. Koegel), pp. 131–140. Baltimore: Paul H. Brookes.

Koegel, R.L., Koegel, L.K., Boettcher, M.A., Harrower, J., and Openden, D. (2006). Combining functional assessment and self-management procedures to rapidly reduce disruptive behaviors. In *Pivotal response treatments for autism: Communication, social, and academic development* (eds. R.L. Koegel and L.K. Koegel), pp. 245–258). Baltimore: Paul H. Brookes.

Koegel, R.L., Schreibman, L., Loos, L.M., and Dirlich-Wilhelm, H. (1992). Consistent stress profiles in mothers of children with autism. *Journal of Autism and Developmental Disorders*, 22 (2), 205–216.

Koegel, R.L., Schreibman, L., O'Neill, R.E., and Burke, J.C. (1983). The personality and family-interaction characteristics of parents of autistic children. *Journal of Consulting and Clinical Psychology*, 51 (5), 683–692.

Koegel, R.L., Symon, J.B., and Koegel, L.K. (2001). Parent education for families of children with autism living in geographically distant areas. *Journal of Positive Behavior Interventions*, 3 (3), 160–174.

Koegel, R.L., Tran, Q.H., Mossman, A., and Koegel, L.K. (2005). Incorporating motivational procedures to improve homework performance. In *Pivotal response treatments for autism: Communication, social, and academic development* (eds. R.L. Koegel and L.K. Koegel), pp. 81–92). Baltimore: Paul H. Brookes.

Laski, K.E., Charlop, M.H, Schreibman, L. (1988). Training parents to use the Natural Language Paradigm to increase their autistic children's speech. *Journal of Applied Behavior Analysis*, 21 (4), 391–400.

Lord, C., and Bailey, A. (2002). Autism spectrum disorders. In *Child and adolescent psychiatry* (4th ed) (eds. M. Rutter and E. Taylor), pp. 664–681. Oxford: Blackwell Scientific.

Lord, C., Wagner, A., Rogers, S., Szatmari, P., Aman M., and Charman, T., Dawson,G., Durand, M., Grossman, L., Guthrie, D., Harris, S., Kasari, C., Marcus, L., Murphy, K., Odom, S., Picklets, A., Scahill, L., Shaw, K., Siegel, B., Sigman, M., Stone, W., Smith, T., Yoder, P. (2005). Challenges in evaluating psychosocial interventions for autistic spectrum disorders. *Journal of Autism and Developmental Disorders*, 35 (6), 695–708.

Lovaas, O.I. (1987). Behavioral treatment and normal educational and intellectual functioning in young autistic children. *Journal of Consulting and Clinical Psychology*, 55, 3–9.

Lovaas, O.I., Koegel, R.L., Simmons, J.Q., and Long, J. (1973). Some generalization and follow-up measures on autistic children in behavior therapy. *Journal of Applied Behavior Analysis*, 6 (1), 131–164.

Lucyshyn, J.M., Horner, R.H., Dunlap, G., Albin, R.W., and Ben, K.R. (2002). Characteristics and context of positive behavior support. In *Families and positive behavior support: Addressing problem behaviors in family contexts* (eds. J.M. Lucyshyn, G. Dunlap, and R.W. Albin), pp. 3–43. Baltimore: Paul H. Brookes.

Mahoney, G., Kaiser, A., Girolametto, L., MacDonald, J., Robinson, C., Safford, P., and Spiker, D. (1999). Parent education in early intervention. *Topics in Early Childhood Special Education*, 19 (3), 131–140.

Mandlawitz, M. (2002). The impact of the legal system on educational programming for young children with autism spectrum disorders. *Journal of Autism and Developmental Disabilities*, 32 (5), 495–508.

Marcus, L.M., Lansing, M., Andrews, C.E., and Schopler, E. (1978). Improvement of teaching effectiveness in parents of autistic children. *Journal of the American Academy of Child Psychiatry*, 17, 625–639.

Marks, S.U., Schrader, C., and Levine, M. (1999). Paraeducator experiences in inclusive settings: Helping, hovering, or holding their own? *Exceptional Children*, 65 (3), 315–328.

McEachin, J.J., Smith, T., and Lovaas, O.I. (1993). Long-term outcomes for children with autism who received early intensive behavioral treatment. *American Journal on Mental Retardation*, 4, 359–372.

McGee, G.G., Daly, T., and Jacobs, H.A. (1994). The Walden Preschool. In *Preschool education programs for children with autism* (2nd ed) (eds. J.S. Handleman and S.L. Harris), pp. 127–162), Austin: PRO-ED.

McGee, G.G., Feldman, R.S., and Morrier, M.J. (1997). Benchmarks of social treatment for children with autism. *Journal of Autism and Developmental Disorders*, 27, 353–364.

McGee, G.G., Morrier, M.J., and Daly, T. (1999). An incidental teaching approach to early intervention for toddlers with autism. *Journal of the Association for Persons with Severe Handicaps*, 24, 133–146.

Mesibov, G.B. (1997). Formal and informal measures on the effectiveness of the TEACCH program. *Autism*, 1 (1), 25–35.

Moes, D. (1995). Parent education and parenting stress. In *Teaching children with autism: Strategies for initiating positive interactions and improving learning opportunities* (eds. R.L. Koegel and L.K. Koegel), pp. 79–94. Baltimore: Paul H. Brookes.

Moes, D.R., and Frea, W.D. (2002). Contextualized behavioral support in early intervention for children with autism and their families. *Journal of Autism and Developmental Disorders*, 32 (6), 519–533.

Moes, D.R., Koegel, R.L., Schreibman, L., and Loos, L.M. (1992). Stress profiles for mothers and fathers of children with autism. *Psychological Reports*, 71, 1272–1274.

Mulick, J.A., and Butter, E.M. (2002). Educational advocacy for children with autism. *Behavioral Interventions*, 17 (2), 57–74.

National Research Council. (2001). *Educating young children with autism*. Washington, D.C.: National Academy Press.

Ozonoff, S., and Cathcart, K. (1998). Effectiveness of a home intervention program for young children with autism. *Journal of Autism and Developmental Disorders*, 28 (1), 25–32.

Pakenham, K.I., Sofronoff, K., Samois, C. (2004). Finding meaning in parenting a child with Asperger syndeome: Correlates of sense making and benefit finding. *Research in Developmental Disabilities* 25 (3), 245–264.

Piaget, J. (1966). *Psychology and intelligence*. Totowa, N.J.: Littlefield, Adams.

Powell, N., and Armstrong, C., executive producers. (2005). November 4. *Supernanny* [Television broadcast]. ABC Network. November 4.

Riggs, C.G., and Mueller, P.H. (2001). Employment and utilization of para-educators in inclusive Settings. *Journal of Special Education*, 35 (1), 54–62.

Risdal, D., and Singer, G.H.S. (2004). Marital adjustment in parents of children with disabilities: A historical view and meta-analysis. *Research and Practice for Persons with Severe Disabilities*, 29 (2), 95–103.

Rogers, S.J., and DiLalla, D.L. (1991). A comparative study of the effects of a developmentally based instructional model on young children with autism and young children with other disorders of behavior and development. *Topics in Early Childhood Special Education*, 11, 29–47.

Rogers, S.J., Herbison, J.M., Lewis, H.C., Pantone, J., and Reis, K. (1986). An approach for enhancing the symbolic, communicative, and interpersonal functioning of young children with autism or severe emotional handicaps. *Journal of the Division for Early Childhood*, 10, 135–148.

Rogers, S.J., and Lewis, H. (1988). An effective day treatment model for young children with pervasive developmental disorders. *Journal of the Academy of Child and Adolescent Psychiatry,* 28, 207–214.

Rogers, S.J., Lewis, H.C., and Reis, K. (1987). An effective procedure for training early special education teams to implement a model program. *Journal of the Division for Early Childhood,* 11, 180–188.

Romanczyk, R.G., Lockshin, S.B., and Matey, L. (2000). The children's unit for treatment and evaluation. In *Preschool education programs for children with autism* (2nd ed) (eds. J.S. Handleman and S.L. Harris), pp. 49–94), Austin: PRO-ED.

Schopler, E., Mesibov, G.B., and Baker, A. (1982). Evaluation of treatment for autistic children and their parents. *Journal of the American Academy of Child Psychiatry,* 21, 262–267.

Schreibman, L., and Koegel, R.L. (2005). Training for parents of children with autism: Pivotal responses, generalization, and individualization of interventions. In *Psychosocial treatments for child and adolescent disorders: Empirically based strategies for clinical practice* (2nd ed) (eds. E.D. Hibbs and P.S. Jensen), pp. 605–631. Washington, D.C.: American Psychological Association.

Sheinkopf, S.J., and Siegel, B. (1998). Home-based behavioral treatment of young children with autism. *Journal of Autism and Developmental Disabilities,* 28, 15–23.

Sherer, M., and Schreibman, L. (2005). Individual behavioral profiles and predictors of treatment effectiveness for children with autism. *Journal of Consulting and Clinical Psychology,* 73 (3), 525–538.

Siegel, B. (2003). *Helping children with autism learn: Treatment approaches for parents and professionals.* New York: Oxford.

Sigafoos, J., O'Reilly, M.F., Seely-York, S., Weru, J., Son, S.H., Green, V.A., Lancioni, G.E. (2004). Transferring AAC intervention into the home. *Disability and Rehabilitation: An International Multidisciplinary Journal,* 26 (21–22), 1330–1334.

Siller, M., and Sigman, M. (2002). The behavior of parents of children with autism predict the subsequent development of their children's communication. *Journal of Autism and Developmental Disorders,* 32 (2), 77–89.

Singer, G.H.S, and Powers, L.E., eds. (1993). *Families, disability, and empowerment: Active coping skills and strategies for family interventions.* Baltimore: Paul H. Brookes.

Smith, T., Donahue, P.A., and Davis, B.J. (2000). The UCLA Young Autism Project. In *Preschool education programs for children with autism* (2nd ed) (eds. J.S. Handleman and S.L. Harris), pp. 29–48), Austin: PRO-ED.

Soodak, L.C., and Erwin, E.J. (1995). Parents, professionals, and inclusive education: A call for collaboration. *Journal of Educational and Psychological Consultation,* 6 (3), 257–276.

Soodak, L.C., and Erwin, E.J. (2000). Valued member of tolerated participant: Parents' experiences in inclusive early childhood settings. *Journal of the Association for Persons with Severe Handicaps,* 25 (1), 29–41.

Stahmer, A.C., and Gist, K. (2001). The effects of an accelerated parent education program on technique master and child outcome. *Journal of Positive Behavior Interventions,* 3 (2), 75–82.

Stiebel, D. (1999). Promoting augmentative communication during daily routines: A parent problem-solving intervention. *Journal of Positive Behavior Interventions,* 1 (3), 159–169.

Strain, P.S. (1987). Comprehensive evaluation of young autistic children. *Topics in Early Childhood Special Education,* 7, 97–110.

Strain, P.S., and Hoyson, M. (2000). On the need for longitudinal, intensive, social skill intervention: LEAP follow-up outcomes for children with autism as a case-in-point. *Topics in Early Childhood Special Education,* 20 (2), 116–122.

Summers, J.A., Behr, S.K., and Turnbul, A.P. (1989). Positive adaptations and coping strengths of families who have children with disabilities. In *Support for caregiving families: Enabling positive adaptation to disability* (eds. G.H.S. Singer and L.K. Irvin). pp. 27–40. Baltimore: Paul H. Brookes.

Symon, J.B. (2005). Expanding interventions for children with autism: Parents as trainers. *Journal of Positive Behavior Interventions,* 7 (3), 159–173.

Symon, J.B., Koegel, R.L., and Singer, G.H.S. (2005). Parent perspectives of parent education programs. In *Pivotal response treatments for autism: Communication, social, and academic development* (eds. R.L. Koegel and L.K. Koegel), pp. 93–115. Baltimore: Paul H. Brookes.

Taylor, J., and Romanczyk, R. (1994). Generating hypotheses about the function of student problem behavior by observing teacher behavior. *Journal of Applied Behavior Analysis,* 27, 251–265.

Tonge, B., Brereton, A., and Kiomall, M. (2006). Effects on parental mental health of an education and skills training program for parents of young children with autism: A randomized controlled trial. *Journal of the American Academy of Child and Adolescent Psychiatry,* 45 (5), 561–569.

Turnbull, A.P., Blue-Banning, M., Turbiville, V., and Park, J. (1999). From parent education to partnership education: A call for a transformed focus. *Topics in Early Childhood Special Education,* 19 (3), 164–172.

Turnbull, A.P., and Turnbull, R. (1990). *Families, professionals, and exceptionality: A special partnership* (2nd ed.). Columbus, Ohio: Merrill.

UC Davis M.I.N.D. Institute (University of California, Davis Medical Institute of Neurodevelopmental Disorders). Available at http://www.ucdmc.ucdavis.edu/mindinstitute (accessed November 2, 2007).

Venter, A., Lord, C., and Schopler, E. (1992). A follow-up study of high-functioning autistic children. *Journal of Child Psychology and Psychiatry,* 33, 489–507.

Werner, G.A., Vismara, L.A., Koegel, R.L., and Koegel, L.K. (2005). Play dates, social interactions, and friendships. In *Pivotal response treatments for autism: Communication, social, and academic development* (eds. R.L. Koegel and L.K. Koegel), pp. 197–213. Baltimore: Paul H. Brookes.

Whalen, C., Schreibman, L., and Ingersoll, B., (2006). The collateral effects of joint attention training on social initiations, positive affect, imitation, and spontaneous speech for young children with autism. *Journal of Autism and Developmental Disorders,* 36 (5), 655–664.

Yell, M.L., and Drasgow, E. (2000). Litigating a free appropriate public education: The Lovaas hearings and cases. *Journal of Special Education,* 30, 205–214.

INDEX